THE FASCIST CHALLENGE AND THE POLICY OF APPEASEMENT

The Fascist Challenge and the Policy of Appeasement

Edited by
Wolfgang J. Mommsen and
Lothar Kettenacker

London
GEORGE ALLEN & UNWIN
Boston   Sydney

George Allen & Unwin (Publishers) Ltd,
40 Museum Street, London WC1A 1LU, UK

George Allen & Unwin (Publishers) Ltd,
Park Lane, Hemel Hempstead, Herts HP2 4TE, UK

Allen & Unwin, Inc.,
9 Winchester Terrace, Winchester, Mass. 01890, USA

George Allen & Unwin Australia Pty Ltd,
8 Napier Street, North Sydney, NSW 2060, Australia

First published in 1983

The editorial work on this volume was undertaken by
The German Historical Institute, 17 Bloomsbury Square,
London WC1A 2LP.

British Library Cataloguing in Publication Data

The Fascist challenge and the policy of appeasement.
1. Europe – Foreign relations – 1918–1945
I. Kettenacker, Lothar   II. Mommsen, Wolfgang J.
327′.094   D727
ISBN 0-04-940068-1

Library of Congress Cataloging in Publication Data

Main entry under title:
The Fascist challenge and the policy of appeasement.
Includes index.
1. World War, 1939–1945 – Causes – Addresses, essays,
lectures.   2. Europe – Foreign relations – 1918–1945 –
Addresses, essays, lectures.   3. Europe – Politics
and government – 1918–1945 – Addresses, essays,
lectures.   4. Fascism – Addresses, essays, lectures.
5. World politics – 1933–1945 – Addresses, essays,
lectures.   I. Kettenacker, Lothar.   II. Mommsen,
Wolfgang J., 1930–
D741.F37   1983   940.53′1   83-3759
ISBN 0-04-940068-1

Set in 10 on 11 Times by Rowland Phototypesetting Ltd.
Bury St Edmunds, Suffolk
and printed in Great Britain by
Mackays of Chatham

Contents

Foreword

Even in the 1930s contemporaries were already bitterly divided about why the Western democracies did not put an early stop to National Socialist aggression while it might still have been possible to prevent a second World War. None other than Winston Churchill in his *History of the Second World War* vehemently denounced the ill-fated policies of Neville Chamberlain and, his Cabinet during the years leading up to Munich. In the Federal Republic of Germany it was fashionable for many years to point out that the West let Hitler get away with his policies for such a long time that the boost given to his political prestige at home by his successes in foreign policies made it virtually impossible to get rid of him again. It is obvious that such arguments tend to be motivated at times by an apologetic desire. None the less, it is only fair to pose the question as to whether the Western powers did indeed have any chance of averting the disaster at an early stage by a strong and determined policy of keeping Hitler at bay, instead of appeasing him again and again until it was too late.

However, after twenty years of detailed research into the policies of appeasement it has become abundantly clear that the inability of Britain and France to stop Hitler in time was not simply, or even primarily, due to misjudgement of the aggressive dynamics of National Socialist Germany and fascist Italy and the grandiose designs of the dictators, or *naïveté* as regards the trustworthiness of Hitler or Mussolini, even though such errors of judgement certainly played a role. It gradually became apparent that an assessment of the motives, misconceptions, or failures of those statesmen primarily responsible for the great decisions at that time did not tell the whole story. The interaction of international policies and internal developments in the various countries has long since been recognised, and consequently a whole range of parliamentary, financial, economic and social policy issues which influenced the decisions on foreign policy has been introduced into the debate.

The quandaries in which the democratic statesmen of the West found themselves, in particular those in London and Paris, have been researched to a remarkable degree. Maurice Cowling recently analysed in painstaking detail the policies of the main actors on the British scene, interpreting them as being largely conditioned by party-political considerations and parliamentary constellations, the natural priorities of politicians who are dependent upon parliamentary majorities and the votes of the people. He was able to temper the lofty moralist tone in which the debate had been conducted during the first two decades after 1945. German research, on the other hand, tended to emphasise those domestic factors which narrowed down the British government's room for manoeuvre. In particular Bernd-Jürgen Wendt and, more recently, Gustav Schmidt have pointed to the fact that Great Britain was in the midst of a transitional crisis which negatively affected both social stability and economic recovery; consequently, she could not afford any early and swift military steps against the fascist challenge.

Closer scrutiny of the international scene in the 1930s tends to lend further support to this line of interpretation. However, there is little point in singling out Great Britain or, for that matter, France in this respect. It is obvious that most, if not all, of the Western powers, the dominions included, were by and large in favour of a policy that would avert a major conflict with the fascist powers, if at all possible, even though this would mean partially abandoning the political system in Europe set up by the Paris Peace Conference in 1919–20. For diverse reasons they all favoured, at least for the time being, a policy of appeasing the dictators, rather than attempting to fight tooth and nail for a political order which in any case seemed to have become untenable. Political, military, economic and party-political motives of various sorts all suggested that the only sensible line to pursue was a policy of peace, even at considerable cost, rather than a policy of firmness which involved the risk of an early war under unfavourable international conditions. It was not only Chamberlain who felt 'that we were in no position to justify waging a war today in order to prevent a war hereafter'.* Hence, British appeasement policies must not be seen in isolation, but in their international context. Indeed the momentous events which eventually culminated in the catastrophe of the Second World War should no longer be discussed within the framework of national policies alone. As Professor Donald C. Watt points out in the introductory essay to this volume, the interwar period must be seen, at least to some degree, as a 'European civil war' in which the divisions between the antagonist groupings often ran right across the nations involved. The conflict was one not only between states, but between rivalling ideologies, rivalling cultures and, to some degree, also antagonistic social groupings throughout Europe.

Furthermore, the developments on the periphery of Europe, in particular the emergence of Japan as a major power, had far-reaching repercussions upon European politics. The Japanese invasion of Manchuria posed a serious threat to the existing balance of power in the Far East. Henceforth, Japan had to be reckoned with as a severe menace to the British Commonwealth in the Far East, a fact which put an additional burden upon the already overstretched commitments of British strategy. Apart from that the opinions of the dominions could no longer be discarded as being of secondary importance in British decision-making on matters of grand strategy. They were, however, very reluctant to be drawn into a major confrontation between Britain and France on the one hand, and the fascist powers on the other, since they tended to see this as an exclusively European matter.

Last but not least, the role of the United States was of the greatest importance, even though neither the British nor the French wanted any direct interference by the United States in the European theatre. In London the feeling prevailed that in such an event the latent differences between British and American policies regarding the future of the British Commonwealth would surface at once, confronting British policy-makers with rather unpleasant options. On the other hand, the apparent reluctance of the

---

* cf. Maurice Cowling, *The Impact of Hitler. British Politics and British Policy 1933–1940* (Cambridge, 1978), p. 198.

United States to play an active part in European politics or, at any rate, to participate directly in defending the existing political system on the European continent against blatant infringements by the dictators, played into the hands of the fascist powers. Hitler, and indeed his conservative partners, got the impression that the United States could be discounted as a major obstacle to German expansionism at least for the time being, even though this was bound to upset the fragile balance of power in Europe which the Americans had helped to stabilise by economic means in the later 1920s.

Finally, the USSR had to be considered as an unknown factor, even though she had consolidated into a major power since the October Revolution. Her military might still seemed doubtful and her domestic troubles were believed to be far from over, even though the Soviets were now firmly in control. Neither did the Russians themselves know how best to cope with the fascist threat that had emerged almost overnight. The official Marxist-Leninist doctrine lent support to the idea that a period of intensified strife amongst the capitalist nations was imminent and that it would be futile to prevent them from embarking upon internecine warfare. They might as well embark upon a policy of appeasement too, as Lord Beloff points out with justification in his contribution published here. Nor had the Western powers any clear notion as to whether Soviet Russia should be incorporated into a defensive alliance against National Socialist Germany and fascist Italy, despite Poland's intransigent attitude in this matter, or whether this would merely constitute yet another liability of unknown proportions.

One further aspect should be mentioned. British and French policies in the years preceding the Second World War cannot be adequately assessed without taking into consideration the forms in which the fascist threat to the international system was perceived by contemporaries. With hindsight it seems clear beyond doubt that Hitler was bound to unleash a world war as he had already indicated fairly bluntly in *Mein Kampf*. But at the time it was by no means clear that there were no chances of talking him into some sort of compromise by a combination of concessions and firmness. Also, the possibility of separating Hitler from the German people, once things began to get tough economically and politically, could not be ruled out. It seemed that the most sensible course of action would be to help a moderate regime to come to power in Germany, if at all possible, thus averting a disaster of unknown but surely terrible proportions. For this reason the foreign policies of National Socialist Germany, and to some extent fascist Italy, are analysed in the first section of this book, paying particular attention to the various rival groupings which took part in their formation. Recent research has made it fairly clear that the National Socialist drive for world power could neither have been stopped by a skilful combination of firmness and concessions, nor tamed by a network of international treaty agreements. Nor could the attempts by the opposition groupings be trusted to oppose Hitler and prevent him from precipitating a world war. Mussolini, on the other hand, was too dependent upon Hitler, ideologically and morally, ever to be used as an effective instrument to block his grandiose designs.

The essays assembled in this volume collectively reassess the policies of appeasement in the light of all the issues just enumerated. Of course, it is impossible to give full coverage to all of them here. None the less, an attempt has been made to throw new light upon the 1930s which may, in a way, be considered the swan-song of Europe as an independent entity in international politics. Particular consideration has been given to the nature of the fascist threat and the contemporary perception of it, and to the manifold factors, whether political, financial, economic, or strategic, which determined the evolution of the Western powers' policy, both in the domestic and in the international arena. Though the authors look at the issues in question from very different angles, and approach them with different methods, their analyses converge in many ways. They demonstrate, above all, that any alternative course of action would have had to overcome almost insurmountable obstacles of various sorts. Perhaps this is shown most strikingly by Robert Shay in a piece of counterfactual history which tries to put together an alternative, albeit fictitious scenario of British policies 1930 to 1938.

Taken together the essays present a fascinating picture of the magnitude of the problems confronting the statesmen of the West. They widen our knowledge not only with regard to the various domestic factors which conditioned the decision-making process, in particular in Downing Street and at the Quai d'Orsay; they also show how closely the issues in the European theatre were intertwined with global problems caused by the secular decline of imperial rule, reflected in particular by the gradual, silent emancipation of the dominions from their mother country, and the decline of British imperial power, both in political and in military terms.

The contributions to this volume originate from papers given at a conference on 'The Threat to the International System by the Fascist Powers and the Policies of Appeasement', which was held at Cumberland Lodge, Windsor Great Park from 23 to 25 May 1980 under the auspices of the German Historical Institute, London. They have, however, been extensively revised for publication, although the results of research which have subsequently become accessible have not, of course, been taken into account. The German contributions have been translated by Mr Stephen Conn and Mrs Janet Sondheimer. We are very grateful for the editorial assistance of Dr Alan Sked of the London School of Economics.

London, May 1981   WOLFGANG J. MOMMSEN

Part One

Fascist Aggression and the West

I

THE CRISIS OF THE EUROPEAN
POLITICAL ORDER

1 The European Civil War

DONALD C. WATT

The proposition which this paper[1] puts forward is that the events of the 1920s and 1930s in Europe, the first two years of the Second World War and the European aspects of the three years that followed can be seen in three, apparently mutually exclusive, ways. They can be seen as a 'struggle for mastery in Europe', to use A. J. P. Taylor's phrase,[2] between the leading nation states of the European continent, a struggle which moved from the pre-violent to the violent stages of war or from a 'cold' to a 'hot' war, into which the two Super Powers of the post-1945 war were reluctantly drawn in 1941. They can be seen as a Manichaean struggle between competing ideologies, between Nazism and fascism on the one hand, arrayed behind the banner of anti-Bolshevism, and the forces of the peoples of Europe on the other, allied together after 1942 into the United Nations. Some American historians, especially those of the New Deal school, tend to see events very much in this light; and despite the label of the 'Great Patriotic War' applied by Soviet historians to the war on the eastern front,[3] as soon as they move into the European aspects of the Second World War, Soviet historians begin to employ the same approach and to use the same rhetoric. The third way is to see events in Europe in this period as a European civil war into which the two great non-European powers, who had spent much of the 1930s trying to preserve or enhance their isolation from European politics, were drawn to intervene in the way Spain and Sweden, for example, were drawn to intervene in the Thirty Years' War in Germany.

I have called these interpretations, these perceptions of the development of international politics in Europe in the 1930s '*apparently* mutually exclusive' for a twofold reason: first, they only *appear* to be mutually exclusive; and secondly, they are themselves concerned with *appearances*, that is, with perceptions, both contemporary and historical, and with interpretations. We are not, in fact, talking about the formal description of those events which led up to the issue of an ultimatum by the governments of Britain and France to that of Germany in the morning of 3 September, 1939, and their subsequent declaration, consequent upon the failure of the German government to respond to that ultimatum, that a state of war existed between their states and the German Reich. We are talking about how those events were perceived, construed and interpreted by those responsible for the policy decisions on which the said course of events was dependent and by those to whom they in turn were responsible, as well as by those who regarded themselves as neutral bystanders, non-participants, not involved, not aligned with any of the participants in the conflict.

That these three alternative interpretations appear mutually exclusive is equally *un faux problème*: they would only be mutually exclusive if they were advanced or entertained by the same people at the same time and were taken as covering the same aspects of the events perceived. In fact, in so far as we are discussing the perceptions of events which were entertained by observers of those events contemporary with or immediately following their occurrence, in so far as these three interpretations differ from one another, they were entertained by differing sets of observers at differing times. It is also true that so far as the third of these possible alternatives is concerned, that is, what for the sake of brevity may be called the 'European civil war' perception, it was adopted subconsciously by a considerable body of persons who, at first sight, would appear to share in the first of the three alternatives, that which might be called the 'clash between national states' perception. To elucidate this paradox we need to consider the nature of this set of perceptions and of the concomitant and accompanying perceptions entertained by those who held them. If such an examination is conducted, we are immediately faced with a paradox: that some of those who held the 'war between nation states' group of perceptions, held them as an ideology and would appear therefore to belong to the second group of observers, those who held the 'clash of ideologies' set of perceptions. Yet others who appear to hold the 'war between nation states' set of perceptions accompany this with a set of perceptions about the nature of relations between selective groups of nation states, more particularly between those which they define as 'European', so that they are in fact perceiving those relations as taking place within the confines of a set of shared assumptions, rules, conventions, and so on, larger than those which see the nation state as the highest form of political organisation *per se*. Hitler, to judge from *Mein Kampf*, the second, so-called 'secret book' and the secret speeches, made the conflict between nation states into an ideology, National Socialism in fact. Chamberlain seems to have had a vision of a self-regulating European system of states which excluded the United States and the Soviet Union on the grounds that neither was a European state, while reluctantly recognising that if his efforts to keep the European system functioning were to break down it might be necessary to call in one or, still worse, both of the future Super Powers to redress the balance.

What differentiates both these sub-sets of perceptions, the 'nation state of ideology' and the 'nation state as part of a system', from the strict 'war between nation states' set of perceptions with which at first sight both appear to be identical, is that the 'war between nation states' set of perceptions is in its purest sense non-moral, or at the least morally relativist, in that there is nothing very much that the outsider can say about the moral issues involved in such a struggle. Whether one particular nation state is right or wrong in its decision to engage in or stand aloof from a particular conflict is essentially a matter of viewpoint. To say this does not imply that a historian who adopts as his own this particular bundle of perceptions is a moral relativist. No one who is the least familiar with Mr Taylor's work could accuse him of being a moral relativist. He is a man of very strong moral convictions; they do not however seem to relate to determining between the conduct of the governments of nation states which he regards with generally jaundiced condemnation.[4]

With this introduction, let us return to the question of the European civil war, with which this paper is concerned. It is my contention, first, that during the 1930s the view that a European civil war was in progress was one which was widely held at all levels of British and continental opinion and was reflected in the perceptions of European politics served to the American public by the influential corps of international foreign correspondents;[5] further, that via the much more widely held sub-set of perceptions to which I earlier gave the label of the 'nation state as part of a system' approach, this 'European civil war' came to embrace a very much larger section of what might loosely be stigmatised as 'European opinion'; and that the existence of this set of perceptions has been almost entirely neglected in the development of European historiography of the origins and course of the Second World War with perhaps two significant exceptions. The first of these is in the field of what might loosely be called 'resistance studies'; the second is in the work of those, such as Professor Walter Lipgens of Saarbrücken[6] or Dr Peter Ludlow of London University, on the wartime origins of the post-1945 movement for European unity.

The 'European civil war' group of perceptions is to be distinguished from the 'clash of rival ideologies' group by one simple test. The 'clash of rival ideologies' group assumes a world divided into separate parts, as it were Christendom and the *partes infidèles* of the Crusades, the *dar-ul-Islam* and the *dar-ul-harb* of classical Islamic international law,[8] the socialist and capitalist systems of Stalinist orthodoxy and of the Brezhnev doctrine,[9] parts between which conflict is inevitable and peace at best the outcome of a set of highly short-term tactical agreements. So bitter can civil war become that it can easily develop into such a state and become *une guerre à l'outrance*, the mutually destructive *stásis* which Toynbee identifies in his monumental *Study of History*[10] from the examples provided by Thucydides.[11] But it need not end that way and by definition it cannot begin that way. A civil war is a war which develops within a *civitas*, a polity, a political society. If we are to speak of a European civil war, we are by the use of that word European assuming that such a polity, which would be 'transnational'[12] as much as, if not more than, it would be international, was perceived to exist, indeed in so far that the assumption of its existence was an important factor underlying the debates and decisions on policy of national governments that it did, in fact, exist. Like the unicorn in the virgin's mirror in Rainer Maria Rilke's sonnets to Orpheus,[13] this transnational polity existed *in* and *through* its incorporation into the structure of thought and attitudes of the makers of national policy and of those to whom they were responsible.

What then was the nature of the European polity of the interwar years? The short answer must be that like the 'European civil war' it existed on both the subjective and the objective planes. Subjectively, it existed in the minds and perceptions of those who entertained a range of perceptions of 'Europe' as something more than a geographical term. Objectively, it can be defined as a set of political, social, economic and cultural relationships the strength of which differed from one social group to another within the various elements which made up the politically active elements within each of the European states which can be identified as members of the system.

Political science analysts have concentrated so far on the second set of considerations, elements which have variously been identified as 'transnational'.[14] Several sets of elements can be isolated: the political rules and conventions, amounting in practice to customary law, which it was accepted governed relations between states, and breaches of which were recognised as such; institutions of co-operation such as the conferences which ended the First World War and governed the peace settlement which followed, the ambassadors' conferences and the League of Nations itself which, in its political concerns, was very largely a European organisation; institutions, both formal and informal, of economic co-operation, of which the Bank of International Settlements, established in 1928, was the most recent; the organisations of technical co-operation from the International Postal Union onwards to the International Labour Office and the other agencies founded in the wake of the League of Nations. Military arrangements, alliances, conventions, pacts, and so on, tied states into regional security arrangements within the general orbit of the security arrangements involved in articles 10 and 16 of the Charter of the League of Nations. Outside the League, at least until 1934 when the Soviet Union joined it, there were the security arrangements which linked Britain in with the states of the Commonwealth, and with the United States and Japan in the Pacific system set up by the 1922 Washington Treaties on the one hand and, on the other hand, the states on the Soviet Union's western borders in the system of non-aggression pacts with the Soviet Union set up in the period 1921–5 and periodically revised thereafter.[15]

But these institutional links only existed by virtue of the attitudes and perceptions of those who operated and inhabited them. It is to this, the subjective element, that the historian must turn to discover how far the politically active elements in the various European nations recognised the existence of a European polity in the years between the two world wars.

The subjective element in this examination can itself be seen as involving the answers to the separate questions: who were the groups who thought of themselves as 'Europeans' and what did they imply or think of as constituting the qualities of being 'European'? This analysis can be pursued further by considering the groups who constituted the politically active elements in the various European nations in the light of these alternative degrees of classification; by their membership of the various generational groups into which their society was divided by their membership or approximation to membership of the dominant ruling groups and systems in the various nations; and by their membership of the various broad socio-economic classifications into which their respective social systems believed themselves to be divided, such as nobility, *haute bourgeoisie*, professional classes, *petit bourgeois*, working class, peasants, and so on.[16]

To take these in order: contemporary observers were apt to take the generational divisions extremely seriously. The governments of Britain and France in the 1930s were headed by men in their sixties or more, men who in many cases had already been too old to fight in the 1914–18 war. To talk of the 'lost' generation of the 1914–18 war and to regret their absence from the political lists in the 1930s was a common theme of contemporary political commentary. The annual ceremonies of 'Armistice Day', the ubiquitous war memorials of village and town, school and railway station, business community and social lodge, combined to lay upon the consciences of those who had escaped the ordeal of the trenches a burden of guilt which was itself a common theme of contemporary literature. Some younger political figures, most notably perhaps Anthony Eden, Captain Eden as he was normally referred to, at least until he attained Cabinet rank, benefited notably in their careers from their status as representatives of the generation of the trenches.

Of the generation which was in its sixties in the 1930s, it is well to remember that their formative years and more besides had been spent in the spacious years of the late Victorian era, years redolent of national-imperial competition, justified by various versions of Social Darwinism and backed by the very far-reaching changes in economic growth, in technological change and in philosophical certainty that had been the distinguishing marks of the last ante-bellum decade and a half. Even before the guns of August 1914 had sounded, they had seen the advent of the internal combustion engine and the aeroplane, of mass suffrage and of demands for female suffrage, of trades union and syndicalist organisation, of political terrorism on the left and street violence on the right. They had seen their belief in the immutability of scientific laws shaken by the physicists' revolution, in the immutability of personality by Freud, and in the values of academic art by the successive waves of innovation from *Jugendstil* and the *Sezession* through post-Impressionism, Cubism, Vorticism and Expressionism. Christian certainties had yielded already to Darwin and Huxley. Scientific certainties were now threatened by Einstein. Economic certainties were swept away by the effects of the war of 1914–18 and the hyper-inflation which followed in so many of the defeated nations. Even the pound was no longer based on gold; promissory notes bearing the signature of Sir Joseph Bradbury replaced the sovereign. The proud vainglorious run-away competitive imperialism of the 1890s and the 1900s had been replaced, not surprisingly, by a desperate search for stability almost at all costs.

Nowhere was this stronger than among those who had enjoyed power, wealth and influence before 1914. In this era there was certainly a European system and a consciousness of being European. The ruling élites of Britain, France, Germany and Austro-Hungary were linked by marriage, social custom and travel, wealth and investment patterns and a common artistic, educational, literary and musical culture, in which English and Scottish literature, painting and design mingled with and enriched the great artistic and literary traditions of Paris, Vienna and the German courts, with the music and opera of Vienna, Paris and Milan, with the philosophy of Hegel and the German idealists, and with the exotic importations of Moroccan, Chinese and Japanese decorative painting and ceramics and with the Diaghilevian revolution in ballet which swept the European capitals in the decade before 1914.

These ruling élites were drawn very largely from an admixture of land-owning nobility and wealth-owning *haute bourgeoisie*, the basis of whose wealth was constantly enlarging itself with fortunes made out of banking and industry and with the new fortunes made out of mass selling, mass distribution and mass communication. Moreover, they set the pattern for the professional classes who not only aspired to the landed status that their 'betters' enjoyed (something by no means unthinkable in the more open societies of Britain and France), but who found in the international scientific, academic and professional associations whose development was so noticeable a feature of the period before 1914, the linkages which for their 'betters' were provided by letters of introduction, by the grand tour, by intermarriage, and so on.

These linkages were themselves copied by the representatives of the political working class in Europe via the second international and, as with the bourgeois revolutionaries of the 1830s and 1840s before them, by the common experience of asylum in London, Vienna, Paris, or Zurich, shared by their revolutionary extremist wings who formed their own networks of transnational linkages. That these linkages were too frail to survive the shock of arms in 1914 is a cliché. But they none the less existed before 1914 – and were to express themselves much to the Soviets' benefit in 1917–18 and thereafter.

One element these so socially differentiated elements of the pre-1914 generation shared in common was a deep-rooted belief in progress. Before 1914 they would have agreed that progress was inevitable. The experience of 1914–18 destroyed the belief in its inevitability but not in its desirability. Its chances were now recognised as precarious, at least in the short run, even by those revolutionaries who embraced the Soviet model in 1917–19 and gave it their undivided loyalties thereafter. Civilisation and progress came to be seen to be like a great rock perched on a cliff, overhanging an abyss, threatened, in peril, precarious in balance, but none the less real for all of this.

Much has been made of the generation of the wartime years. In the 1930s much play was made, from the Prince of Wales's address in 1935 to the British legionaries visiting Germany, to the pronouncements of the German propagandists who welcomed them, with the concept of *Grabenkameradschaft*, the brotherhood of the trenches.[17] This followed on the anti-war movement of the late 1920s which was itself a product of the emotions recollected in tranquillity of those overpowered by the senselessness of trench warfare as a mode of combat, a revulsion already expressed in the wartime poems of the British war poets and in the novels of Henri Barbusse, whose *Le Feu*[18] with its unforgettable evocation of Verdun appeared as early as 1916. But it was to take a decade or more before the public was ready to make Sassoon and Remarque into middle-brow best-sellers.[19] These pacifists were to be severely attacked by Italian Fascists and by Nazi writers alike for their work in rotting the 'moral fibre' of the nation. Fascism and Nazism were themselves products of much the same experience with an added factor mixed in.

Sassoon's poems, and his trilogy, *Memoirs of a Fox-Hunting Man*, *Memoirs of an Infantry Officer* and *Sherston's Progress*, were essentially an attack on the bourgeois patriotism of the home front which gave power and authority so blindly to the military élites who could find no way out of the war of attrition which was waged on the western front from 1915 onwards. But the terms of the attack borrowed from an aristocratic revulsion against bourgeois values one can already find expressed in the writing of the Sitwells and the Vorticist manifestos of Wyndham Lewis well before the events of 1914, let alone of the Somme and Passchendaele. The *Fasci combattimenti* and the *Freikorps* movement in Germany, of which the first Nazi *Sturmabteilungen* who took part in the 1923 Putsch were so small a part, were drawn from rather different milieux.[20] Their recruits were from the middle bourgeoisie, the sons of the professional men of the much less socially mobile and more rigidly hierarchical societies of the pre-1914 Germany and Austro-Hungary. By virtue of the destruction of much of the aristocratic officer corps of 1914 in the encounter battles of 1914–15, and the insatiable need created by the process of attrition for junior officers, they had found themselves, if not ennobled, at least made gentlemen officers. The end of the war in Italy, defeat in Germany, changed all that. Von Seeckt's army was led by a largely 'rearistocratised' officer class.[21] In any case the abdication of the emperors had destroyed the hierarchies of status of their youthful ambitions. For such a chance of advancement, the brief expectation of life which was all a young officer cadet could count on was perhaps worthwhile. Its total abolition when coupled with the defeat of Germany, the disappointment of the ambitions fed by imperial propaganda to counter the increasing social strains of war and blockade was a psychological trauma of the first order. On none was the impact greater than on those age-groups which had been cheated by the events of October and November 1918 of their baptism of fire.

Even in the victorious countries the effects of this reprieve from death were deeply unsettling, as the memoirs of André Malraux[22] or the university diaries of Evelyn Waugh[23] bear abundant witness. But the effects of these events on their German and Italian equivalents, for whom eleven battles of the Isonzo and the postdated victory of Vittorio Veneto were hardly adequate compensation either for the shame of the Caporetto panic or the defeat of Italian imperial ambitions in Africa and Ottoman Turkey at the Paris Peace Conference, can be seen in the career of d'Annunzio[24] or the novels of Ernst von Salomon.[25]

Thus it was that the years 1918–23 saw the first upsurge of anti-parliamentary nationalist and extremist street violence in central Europe. In Budapest, Munich, Berlin and Hamburg, as in Milan and Rome, it could be said to have been influenced by the fear or even the momentary threat of revolution from the left on the Soviet model. But while there were blood-baths on the left in Hungary, the same could hardly be said of the largely pacifist Italian socialist organisations and the disorganised and doctrinaire few who tried to seize power in Germany. The violence of the right in Germany and Italy was that of those who felt that they had been openly robbed of status not of those desperate through oppression. Moreover, it was the violence of those trained in the expectation of modern industrialised war to believe in the good of the nation (or of that image of the nation with which they identified their own good) and in nothing whatever beyond it. If their enemy could be identified as cosmopolitan or with links with trans-national movements outside the national corpus, then this made it the tool of foreign threats to national well-being. The Red menace, the Jewish menace, Moscow gold, the 'Jewish–Bolshevik world hydra'[26] became the Satanic embodiment of all forces inimical and threatening to the well-being of the nation, the culture, the race in a Manichaean world in which the forces of darkness could always triumph and lay always in ambush and the price of national survival was the suppression of liberty as well as eternal vigilance.

The first phase of the European civil war was ended essentially by the détente of 1924–5 in Franco-German relations. By that date, however, Italy, whose parliamentarianism had been poised on an electoral system which gave only a small minority of Italians any stake in its survival, had succumbed to extremist nationalism, a nationalism which was eventually to make a peace of convenience with the Vatican, then obsessed by the threat of Bolshevik atheism. It was not until the breakdown not of the Franco-German détente but of the economic revival which had made it possible that extremist anti-parliamentary nationalism was to stage its second great surge towards power in Germany. I mention this because although the leadership of the Nazi Party in the years 1929–33 was drawn from the same displaced desperadoes of the trenches as those who had made up the *Freikorps*, the *Einwohnerwehren*, the *Black Reichswehr*, the SA and the other paramilitary units of 1918–23 Germany, the rank and file were not, any more than was the case with the rank and file membership of the patriotic leagues who rioted in Paris in February 1934, or of Mosley's Blackshirts, of Degrelle's Rexistes, or of the Dutch and Norwegian Nazi movements. Like the Greenshirts in Egypt[27] or the pathetic White Russian Fascists in exile,[28] these were essentially phenomena of mimesis, attempts to ape the models set by fascism and Nazism in very different socio-political contexts from those which had carried Mussolini or Hitler to power, even if the economic conditions which surrounded them seemed to be the same.

Even in Germany this second wave of xenophobic, anti-European, anti-internationalist, anti-parliamentarian integral nationalism could not achieve power of its own. It came to power essentially as a result of a personal intrigue, and a blindness among the parliamentary forces as to the strengths of the anti-parliamentary right and the consequences of financing it. It is true that the security forces of the state lost their nerve and declined to take the initiative in suppressing. But it may be doubted whether, apart from Hitler, any other of the possible leaders of the anti-parliamentary right in Germany at this time would have possessed either the vision or the dominance over his fellows which could outface Röhm with the SA and the Strassers in Berlin and restrain his hotheads from challenging the *Reichswehr* head on. Had Hitler persisted with the Nazi 'martyrs' to whom *Mein Kampf* was dedicated, it is difficult to see any other figure who possessed both the charisma and the sense of caution, let alone the irrevocable *petit bourgeois* element which made so many think that he could be, or was being, manipulated.[29]

What distinguished Britain and France from Germany was that the political leadership never faltered in their grasp in Britain and that no effective unified challenge to the politicians emerged in France. Where the 'leagues' could not unite, the left and centre had no such difficulty, even once the February 1934 riots were over, behind the implausible figure of Gaston Doumergue. With the Popular Front of 1936 Léon Blum was a far more credible leader; and though the right grew progressively less patriotic, if more anti-Semitic, they were no closer to producing a real alternative to him.[30] The crumbling of the Popular Front, as power moved back to the Radical Socialist centre, from Blum via Chautemps to Daladier, followed the same pattern as had overtaken the *Cartel des Gauches* in the 1920s. What killed the Third Republic was defeat in war, not revolution from the right, as the serio-comic episode of the *Cagoulard* conspiracy of 1937 more than adequately proved. The *Reichswehr* of von Manstein and Guderian, the products of von Seeckt's aristocratic but professionalised officer corps of the 100,000 men army, defeated France; not Hitler, or the SS, or Nazism. They came afterwards. The fall of France was a phenomenon of the war between nations, not of the European civil war. The French reaction to defeat was, however, very much a product of the civil war mentality.

Indeed, this mentality had already manifested itself very strongly in the reaction of French internal security forces to the outbreak of war when they took advantage of their emergency powers to intern as much of the European anti-Fascist emigration in Paris as possible.[31] It continued to express itself in the extraordinary efforts made by the French General Staff in the winter of 1939–40 to carry on war against the Soviet Union.[32] The ideology of the Vichy army, with its doctrines of national regeneration, of reliance on *la France seule*, represented a total abandonment of the idea of their being anything outside the nation. Laval and others might pay lip-service to the pan-Europeanism of the SS, the anti-Bolshevik crusade, and so on. But for the officers of the Vichy army the nation was itself the highest ideal,[33] and the Maquis suspect because of its English, American and Russian, in a word its internationalist, linkages.

It is to the internationalism of the left that we now must turn. Before 1914 the principal institution by which the international solidarity of the working class was expressed was the Second International. The failure of its component parties to honour their international commitments in July–August 1914 has led a generation of historians to write it off as an essentially fraudulent and hypocritical organisation. So to dismiss its members is not only to ignore the very genuine links of doctrine and fraternity which linked them together simply because the tug of patriotism proved the stronger in the emotional circumstances of 1914; it is equally to pass over the psychological factors which made it easy for the members of a movement which was fundamentally opposed to the ruling élites of all governments to fasten that hostility on those ruling élites which ruled and directed the governments of their enemies. For Bebel and the German socialist rank and file the enemies were the Tsar and the Tsarist repression, or British imperialism and the British colonial class. For the British their German enemy was personified in the Kaiser and the Prussian militarist–aristocratic system. When the forces of their own governments appeared to be directed against what they believed to be a genuine working class government as in 1918–19, their working-class solidarity was apt to express itself in transport and dock strikes on the home front and a distinct unwillingness to take decisive action while at the front in Murmansk or in the Baltic states. Inspired leadership and the dawning realisation that the appearance and behaviour of the Bolshevik forces could only with considerable difficulty be squared with their self-image of British working-class virtues kept the British forces largely immune to Bolshevik attempts to subvert them. But the French forces in southern Russia were not so fortunate.

It was at this point, however, that the unholy influence of Lenin, determined to wreak doctrinal vengeance for what he saw as the intellectual, political, ideological and moral weakness both of social patriots and of social pacifists alike, made itself felt. His determination to expel the moderates and the backsliders outrivalled that of Calvin or John Knox. The Third International divided and destroyed the European working-class movement and the trades union movement with them, in France, in Germany, in Italy, in Scandinavia, in Bulgaria, in Hungary. Its influence delivered the Italians into the hands of the Fascists, left the leadership of the Spartacists to die at the hands of the *Freikorps*, reinforced the links between the German majority socialists and the army leadership and split the French left, destroying for ever the last of that healing and unifying influence that had once been personified in Jaurès.

In the place of the Second International there sprang two or as it was to prove three internationals: the reborn links between the democratic socialist parties of Western Europe centring on The Hague; the increasingly Stalinised leaderships of the parties represented in the Comintern; and the cosmopolitan literary cultural front organisations built up by Willi Münzenberg on the basis of the *Internationale Arbeiter-Hilfe* organisation which Lenin left to his erstwhile Zurich companion as a consolation for giving the Comintern to Zinoviev.[34] The conflicts and confrontations which Stalinist leaders forced on their followers were to create a new class of political and social *déracinés* and *déclamés*, 'dead souls on furlough' in Arthur Koestler's phrase, the 'scum of the earth' of his 1941 book on the remnants of the international brigades of the Spanish Civil War, interned in southern France in 1940.[35]

This concept 'dead souls on furlough' has very little Russian about it but very much of the romanticism with which the literary refugees from bourgeois Europe regarded the Russia of Tolstoy and Gogol. 'Dead souls on furlough', for all that their fate at the hands of the NKVD was already threatening, is not the phrase that occurs to anyone contemplating Radek, Litvinov, Borodin, Tomsky, Rykov, or Bukharin. The Russian leadership in the post-Leninist era was more and more Russian and less and less the Russian wing of the European revolutionary movement that it had represented in the years of Lenin's exile in London, Vienna and Zurich.

The socialist and communist exiles began to pile up in Paris, Prague, Madrid and Amsterdam from 1922 onwards. To the Italian refugees from Fascism were added the refugees from Alexander's Yugoslavia, those from Pilsudski's Poland, left-wing Jewish refugees from the Baltic states, illegal communists and socialists from Dolfuss's Austria, refugees from Hitler's Germany, from Danzig, the Saar, Hungary, Romania and Greece. They became the international European resistance to Nazism and fascism, their activities, their facts and their propaganda dramatising the conflict between the extremist nationalism of Hitler, Mussolini and their imitators and the internationalism, or more strictly the transnationalism of the European democratic working class movement. Their perception of their own role was particularly influential on American opinion through the network of British, American and French foreign correspondents who did most, some innocently, some by design, to perpetuate the image of a European civil war in the years from 1933–9, particularly after the Comintern embraced the strategy of the Popular Front from 1935 onwards.[36]

It should be noted that the internationalist revolutionary opposition to fascism and Nazism in terms of age and upbringing belonged as much to the pre-1914 world as did the members of the parliamentary governments of the European democracies or the leaders of the integral nationalist ideologies of Nazism and fascism. They shared one common attitude, a view of the European political system which made it largely coterminous with the world political system. Their view of the world, if translated into geographical projections in atlas form, would hardly have changed very much from the projections of Ptolemy or the medieval or Renaissance map-makers. Certainty and certain knowledge was focused on Europe. The system of political power relationships which concerned the politicians and statesmen, the forms of economic organisation or integral nationalism backed by large-scale capital which concerned the internationalist left was European. Their images of America had hardly changed from the utopias of sixteenth-century writers. Rumours, images, textual constructions for political sermons, the dream images of the cinematograph, the exaggerated letters and pictures of an earlier generation of immigrants and of returnees made rich – at least by the standards of the societies to which they were returning – combined together to remove the power of the United States, the realities of its social organisation, the outlook of its citizens, the disparate and fragmented nature of its political processes from any calculations of immediate reference. To the leaders of France in 1938–40, as witness Paul Reynaud's despairing appeal of 1940, the United States was a *dea ex machina*, who would descend from the heavens to rescue *la belle France* in her hour of extremity.[37] It was to prove one of the ironies of history that she was later to figure in French political mythology not as France's salvation but as one of the most continuous opponents of France's self-induced resurrection.

Equally to Hitler, America was an alien, a somewhat incredible land. In the 1920s when he listened to Harvard's unworthy alumnus, Putzi Hanfstaengl,[38] and may have been sustained by Ford's money,[39] he appears to have been struck by the racialist element in the American immigration laws[40] and to have grasped to some degree the economic strength which was growing across the Atlantic.[41] But the Wall Street crash and the consequent retreat into isolationism of the first Roosevelt administration seems to have convinced him that America did not matter; and from 1938 onwards he was to reject the advice of those who sought to convince him otherwise.[42] Beyond that of course America still remained the ultimate challenge to German world hegemony; and the basis of his various 'offers' to 'guarantee' the British Empire lay in his perception (correct as to fact but wrong as to time-scale, like so many of his insights) of America's challenge to and succession to Britain's extra-European position. His military advisers on the other hand remained convinced that America would, sooner or later, support Britain in the event of an Anglo-German conflict, and that to risk war with Britain would be criminal folly and lead to Germany's destruction.[43] To this extent, and in this dimension alone, Hitler may at first sight seem to have abandoned his nationalist solipsist approach to international politics, in that he and his generals agreed in seeing the United States as part of a geopolitical state system of which Germany was a member. But their disagreement in fact centred on the proposition as to whether such a system existed in the sense that its internal structure would make British opposition to Germany and American support of Britain inevitable. Hitler appears to have believed that the moment for conflict with Britain or the United States was something he was entirely free to choose, that there were no systemic compulsions or inhibitions on the free exercise of his volition. His America was therefore a fantasy, a projection of his own imagination, uncorrected by any evidence uncongenial to that faculty. To some extent General Ludwig Beck's America was equally an intellectual construct; Beck's sources of first-hand information on the United States were not impressive. But the construct was grounded on precedent, and involved a recognition of Anglo-American linkages to which Hitler with no first-hand contacts with Britain or British visitors at any time before 1933[44] remained entirely blind.

When one turns to the British situation in the 1930s one enters into a much more complicated scene. Britain's ruling élites exhibit an extraordinary degree of fragmentation in their attitudes to Europe in the 1930s. At the Cabinet level, especially at that of successive Prime Ministers (though they would not have expressed themselves in these terms), the image they entertained of Britain was one of a power uniquely balanced between and a member of at least three political state systems, two of which, the European and Far Eastern, were seen as constructed essentially of economic, political and strategic elements while lacking any very considerable degree of social linkages, and one, the commonwealth and imperial, consisted of economic, political and social linkages, but, except where Britain, the hub of the commonwealth, was concerned, had no common strategic interests. In the Far Eastern system the obligation on Britain to defend Australia and New Zealand, and the very considerable British financial and trading stake in China and South-East Asia, made Britain constantly apprehensive about the balance of power and the level of international security. But from 1921 onwards such plans and commitments as Britain had towards the stability of that system rested on the hypothetical improbability of threats developing simultaneously to the stability of the European and of the Far Eastern state systems. From 1933 onwards that hypothesis became ever increasingly untenable, and British policy, willy-nilly, was forced to concentrate on persuading the United States to take the main burden of maintaining that stability.

Where the European system was concerned Britain passed from a phase of attempting to restrain France, through a period of guarantees, towards the increasingly interventionist role she occupied from 1936 onwards. But the idea of engaging the United States or the Soviet Union into the maintenance of the European balance seems to have been excluded from serious consideration at Cabinet level by a conviction that the price of

American intervention would prove so high that it should be postponed as long as possible (certainly long beyond the point of conviction, not reached by Chamberlain until the winter of 1938, that any American goodies were genuinely on offer); so far as the Soviet Union was concerned, the suspicion that she was actively interested in fomenting a war, in which geographical distance and military weakness would combine to debar her from serious participation (though not from profiting very markedly from its outcome), appears to have been the major factor in deafening British ears to Maiski and Litvinov's (and Churchill's) pleas for a Grand Alliance. Chamberlain's perception of Europe was attained at the Munich Conference: a system settling its crises without external intervention. Unfortunately for him, the events of the next three months, still more of the period after his January 1939 visit to Mussolini, were to provide him with abundant evidence, which he accepted, albeit reluctantly, that two of his four partners in no way accepted his version of a European comity. The dictators were nationalist solipsists; and nothing was going to alter this.

The degree to which the bureaucratic and military elements of the British ruling élites accepted this multiple membership was conditioned by two factors: their own training, background and experience, and their common conviction that Britain could not bear the costs of belonging to so many systems and ought to pull out of one or more of them. Their perceptions of Britain's position in the world, of the threats to that position and of Europe, the United States and the Soviet Union have been analysed in considerable detail in much recent work by British and other historians.[45]

Three observations can, however, be made. The defence establishment by background were very rarely committed to the European option by anything except what might loosely be described as *une déformation profes-sionelle*. Senior army staff officers and military planners were conceptually committed to war in Europe since in such a war the army would, as in 1914–18, play the major role. By background and experience, however, they were considered to be imperialist in their outlook. The emotional commitment of the CID since its inception had been towards the develop-ment of commonwealth and imperial unity by functional means. The absence of a common commonwealth strategic interest save in Britain's survival against European threat enabled them to avoid the logical choice between continent and commonwealth: but until that threat became immediate, the military opposed any continental commitment from the proposed draft Treaty of Mutual Guarantee in 1923 to the proposed Anglo-French staff talks in April 1936 and April 1938.

The Admiralty and senior naval officers were professionally committed to war in the Far East from 1921 onwards, since only in such a war would the fleet be involved in a major role. But from 1930 onwards they were equally certain that Britain lacked the necessary margin of power to make any major role possible.[46] They were opposed to involvement against Italy in the Mediterranean[47] and until March 1939 equally ill disposed towards any European commitment which might lead to a denunciation by Germany of the Anglo-German Naval Agreement.[48]

The Air Staff were equally ill disposed towards commitments in Europe as they were unable to envisage the possible nature of warfare in the Pacific. They were committed to the maintenance of British isolationism through strategic deterrence. Such details as to who was to be deterred were not discussed; but then the Air Ministry was not allowed an Air intelligence staff on regional lines as opposed to a general repository of clandestine reports until 1936, and when one was set up its views were ignored.[49] When the Air Planning Staff found themselves committed to war in Europe with aircraft that could not hit German targets from British bases, then the Air Staff became committed to an Air component to a British Expeditionary Force at a time when it was not at all clear that a BEF would be sent to the European mainland.[50] Emotionally and by background, however, the Air Staff, veterans of the air war in 1917–18, were imperialist to a man, the sole role that they had been allowed to play in the 1920s being that of imperial policemen in the Middle East, in Iraq, Somalia and the Aden protectorate. The larger the part the defence component of the CID played in the general formulation of British foreign policy, the less weight would be given to considerations of alliances and commitments to co-operation in Europe, until the ultimate emergency of 1939 appeared.

The Treasury component in the foreign policy-making powers were equally unlikely to be committed to co-operation either in Europe or with the United States, concerned as they were to recover the central position that London had occupied before 1914 in world finance. Montague Norman's over-commitment to Europe and to the Bank of International Settlements was irretrievably connected in their minds with the disaster of 1931. The United States had destroyed all hopes of currency stabilisation in 1933 and wilfully upset the Chinese silver-backed currency in 1935. It is hardly surprising therefore to find little love for either France or the United States in the breasts of senior Treasury officials from Sir Warren Fisher downwards.[51]

The combined weight of the bureaucratic and professional advice on foreign policy issues to confront the Cabinet tended inherently to strengthen the tendency towards isolationism towards Europe and settlement in the Far East. But common to most was the assumption that Britain's national interests could only be conceived of or protected within an international system of rules, conventions and customary law. Instinctively they were drawn towards conciliation and the avoidance of conflict within the system. But between their outlook, their perception of Britain's role and the national solipsism of Hitler and Mussolini there could be no reconciliation in the long run. There was thus no way in the long run of avoiding conflict with Germany or Italy under such leadership. National solipsism, among the British professional advisers, is only encountered among the more simple-minded British military who rejected German opponents of Hitler on the grounds that they were traitors to their own country and therefore morally reprehensible.[52] After 1940 attitudes to the German opposition to Hitler were to be governed less by this kind of attitude than by the conviction that self-styled opponents of Nazism needed to distance themselves much more clearly from Hitler's formulation of Germany's national aims than any of those who made contact with British representatives felt able to do for

Britain to be able to recognise their claims. Seen from London, such claims only impressed a minority of the politically active; few if any were in a position to influence Cabinet policy.[53]

Outside the active members of the British foreign policy-making élite, there is a plethora of influences: interest groups and social networks plugged in various ways and for various purposes into each other, whose activities and relationships still lack serious historical examination.[54] The quality press,[55] the international connections of the labour[56] and trades union movements, the connections of the leading British multinationals,[57] of the Federation of British Industry, of the merchant banking houses of the City of London, the private newsletters which provided alternative channels of information to those plugged up by those who controlled the quality press, the League of Nations Union,[58] the Friends of Europe, the Gentile Zionist network,[59] the Churches,[60] the Pilgrim Trust/English Speaking Union Anglo-American network, the Left Book Club management and readership,[61] all of these require examination before anything more than the crudest pronouncements can be made as to how they perceived Britain in relation to Europe. Such preliminary study as has been made [62] supports that while most had in common a perception of British power which grossly overestimated the range of choice open to the British government, all shared the common belief that Britain was part of a Christo-European system of law, social relationships, culture and convention which was being challenged by a new barbarism, an atavistic 'throw-back' to the tribal chaos of the Dark Ages and the break-up of Roman civilisation.

These attitudes were essentially confined to the politically active elements from the urban bourgeois and professional classes and from the industrial working classes, numerically only a small minority of the British electorate as a whole, whose reactions to the onrush of events in the 1930s still need detailed year by year and issue by issue analysis. The reactions of mass opinion are much more difficult to chart. Opinion sampling only began in the late 1930s and the data on the unstructured attitudes and opinions of the British people as a whole accumulated by Mass Observation only covers the period from early 1938 to the outbreak of war in September 1939. Such indicators as are available (beyond the purely anecdotal) suggest that public opinion *en masse* changed as government leadership changed, and may have changed even faster than the government realised in the last five months of peace.[63] It is this that suggests that those who argue that stronger leadership on Churchillian lines from 1935 onwards would have produced a more rapid change in mass attitudes towards war and peace, are assuming a more direct relationship than either experience of parallel situations or the available evidence warrants.

To conclude: examination of the European political scene in the interwar years produces a picture of rival concepts and perceptions which have been loosely classified under three headings: the struggle between nations, the dualist Manichaean struggle between competing ideologies, and the European civil war in which widely different factions were confronted with alternatives of participation on one side or other or of a retreat into neutralism. Further examination of these labels shows that the first label covers two very different kinds of perception, one which accepts that relations between the nation states originated within a 'transnational' system, defined in various contemporaneously recognised and subsequently recognisable ways, and the other of which, referred to here as national solipsism, does not recognise any claims that such a 'transnational' system existed as anything more than window-dressing at least. It emerges further that the most prominent contemporaneous representatives of the solipsist view were those states and their leaders who had raised nationalism to the status of an ideology ('integral nationalism', it has been called), of which Nazism, Italian fascism, Falangism and some varieties of French fascism, that of the Croix de Feu for example, which remained anti-German throughout the 1940–5 period, are most characteristic. These make up by far the largest group of parallel ideologies which employers of the 'competing ideologies' system of classification would put on the right-hand side of their Manichaean scale of opposites. The thrust of this demonstration that the first category disintegrates into variants of the second or third categories is to argue that it is the third which most corresponds to and casts most light on the complicated realities of the national and international politics of the principal European states in the interwar period. It has been further argued that the 'European' element in this classification can be justified by demonstrating that calculations of American or Soviet involvement in this process of continuous interaction between the various factions and traditions which made up the main streams of European political activity in this period partook of a degree of fantasy: and that direct experience or examination of the costs and benefits of American or Soviet entry into the system produced in those responsible for the conduct of governmental policy the conviction that such entry should only be sought as an alternative to defeat, it being assumed that victory for the forces of integral nationalism would mean the destruction of the European system as such, and that given the alternative of Europe under Nazism or under American influence and indebtedness the second was demonstrably superior and preferable to the first. It would follow from this that very much of the work that remains to be done on the history of the interwar years in Europe, especially as the emphasis moves from the level at which government policy is formulated to that of the groups of whose interests and opinions policy-makers were cognisant and the political environment in which and against which they acted, should concentrate not only on the national but on the 'European' aspects of their attitudes, perceptions and actions, and on the affinities as well as the conflicts which existed between them.

Notes: Chapter 1

1   This paper to some degree rehearses the arguments originally advanced in the first of my 1973 Lees-Knowles lectures, later published as *Too Serious a Business. European Armed Forces and the Approach to the Second World War* (London and Los Angeles, 1975). See also D. C. Watt, 'European military leadership and the breakdown of Europe 1919–1939', in Adrian Preston (ed.), *General Staffs and Diplomacy before the Second World War* (London and Ottawa, NJ, 1978).

2   A. J. P. Taylor, *The Struggle for Mastery in Europe, 1868–1918* (Oxford, 1954).
3   Institute of Marxism Leninism of the Central Committee of the Communist Party of the Soviet Union, *History of the Great Patriotic War of the Soviet Union* (Moscow, 1960).
4   On A. J. P. Taylor's moral approach to the history of European international relations see for example D. C. Watt, 'Some aspects of A. J. P. Taylor's work as diplomatic historian', *Journal of Modern History*, vol. 47 (1977), pp. 19–33.
5   J. Hohenberg, *Foreign Correspondents. The Great Reporters and Their Times* (New York, 1964).
6   W. Lipgens (ed.), *Europa-Föderationspläne der Widerstandsbewegungen, 1940–1945* (Munich, 1968); *Die Anfänge der Europäischen Einigungspolitik, 1945–1950, I. Teil, 1945–47* (Stuttgart, 1977).
7   P. W. Ludlow, 'The unwinding of appeasement', in L. Kettenacker (ed.), *The 'Other Germany' in the Second World War* (Stuttgart, 1977), pp. 9–48; id., 'Scandinavia between the Great Powers', *Historik Tidskrift* (Sweden), 1974, pp. 1–58.
8   On the difference between the *dar-ul-Islam* (the abode of peace) and the *dar-ul-Harb* (the abode of chaos) and the impossibility of any legal relationship between the two under classic Islamic law see M. Khadduri, 'International law', in M. Khadduri and H. J. Liebesney (eds), *Law in the Middle East*, Vol. I: *The Origins and Development of Islamic Law* (Washington, DC, 1955), pp. 349–72.
9   On the Brezhnev doctrine see the entries in *Encyclopaedia Britannica* (1974 edition *Micropaedia*) and the references there cited.
10 A. J. Toynbee, *A Study of History*, Vol. IV (London, 1939), pp. 201–6.
11 Thucydides, *The Peloponnesian War*, bk III, chs 70–85, IV, chs 46–8 on the case of Corcyra.
12 R. Aron, *Paix et guerre entre les nations* (Paris, 1962).
13 R. M. Rilke, *Die Sonette an Orpheus* (Leipzig, 1923), pt 2, no. IV:

> O dieses ist das Tier, das es nicht gibt . . .
> Zwar war es nicht. Doch weil sie's liebten, ward
> ein reines Tier . . .
>   Sie nährten es mit keinem Korn,
> nur immer mit der Möglichkeit, es sei . . .
> Zu einer Jungfrau kam es weiss herbei –
> und war im Silber-Spiegel und in ihr.

14 See R. O. Keohane and T. S. Nye (eds), *Transnational Relations and World Politics* (Cambridge, Mass., 1972).
15 D. C. Watt, 'The breakdown of the European security system 1930–1938', paper presented to the XIV International Congress of the Historical Sciences (San Francisco, Calif., 1975).
16 This note was written before the appearance of R. Wohl, *The Generation of 1914* (London, 1980), with its detailed documentation of the problem of generations.
17 G. Wootton, *The Official History of the British Legion* (London, 1956). See also 'Influence from without: German influence on British opinion, 1933–38', in D. C. Watt, *Personalities and Policies. Studies in the Formulation of British Foreign Policy in the Twentieth Century* (London and South Bend, Ind., 1956), pp. 117–35.
18 H. Barbusse, *Le Feu. Journal d'une escouade* (Paris, 1916).
19 S. Sassoon, *Memoirs of a Fox-Hunting Man* (London, 1928); *Memoirs of an Infantry Officer* (London, 1930); *Sherston's Progress* (London, 1932); E. M. Remarque, *Im Western nichts Neues* (Berlin, 1930).
20 See R. G. L. Waite, *Vanguard of Nazism* (Cambridge, Mass., 1952); H. Schulze, *Freikorps und Republik, 1918–1920* (Boppard am Rhein, 1969).
21 See the statistics cited in Karl Demeter, *The German Officer Corps in Society and State 1650–1945*, trans. A. Malcolm (London, 1965), p. 54.
22 A. Malraux, *L'Espoir* (Paris, 1937).
23 M. Davie (ed.), *The Diaries of Evelyn Waugh* (London, 1977).
24 A. Rhodes, *D'Annunzio: The Poet as Superman* (London, 1960).
25 See especially *Die Geächteten* (Berlin, 1931); *Die Kadetten* (Berlin, 1933); *Der Fragebogen* (Hamburg, 1951).
26 The phrase is Hitler's. See W. W. Pese, 'Hitler und Italien 1920–1926', *Vierteljahreshefte für Zeitgeschichte*, vol. 3, (1955), pp. 113–26.

27   P. T. Vatikiotis, *The Modern History of Egypt* (London, 1969), pp. 288–9, 318.
28   See E. Oberländer, 'The all-Russian fascist party', *Journal of Contemporary History*, vol. I, no. 1 (1966), pp. 158–73.
29   See for example R. Olden, *Hitler the Pawn* (London, 1934).
30   On the French right at this period see C. Micaud, *The French Right and Nazi Germany* (Toronto, 1944); H. Tint, *The Decline of French Patriotism, 1870–1940* (London, 1964).
31   For accounts of this see A. Koestler, *The Scum of the Earth* (London, 1941).
32   On which see for example *Die Geheimakten des französischen Generalstabs* (Berlin, 1940). See also C. O. Richardson, 'French plans for Allied attack on the Caucasian oil fields, January–April 1940', *French Historical Studies*, vol. III (1973), pp. 130–56.
33   R. O. Paxton, *Parades and Politics at Vichy. The French Officer Class under Marshal Pétain* (Princeton, NJ, 1966), pp. 51–4.
34   On Münzenberg see B. Gross, *Willi Münzenberg. Eine politische Biographie* (Stuttgart, 1967); H. Gruber, 'Willi Münzenberg. Propagandist for and against the Comintern', *International Review of Social History*, vol. X (1965), pp. 188–210.
35   Koestler, *The Scum of the Earth.*
36   See J. Haslam, 'The Comintern and the origins of the Popular Front, 1934–1935', *Historical Journal*, vol. 22 (1979), pp. 673–91.
37   Georges Bonnet's claims to the Foreign Ministry of France in the Daladier government of 1938–9 lay in his alleged knowledge of the United States acquired during his tenure of the Washington Embassy. His actual knowledge of or contacts with the Roosevelt administration would appear to have been tenuous in the extreme.
38   Ernst Hanfstaengl, *Hitler, The Missing Years* (London, 1957).
39   The evidence is inconclusive. See J. and S. Pool, *Who Paid Hitler?* (London, 1978), pp. 85–130.
40   D. C. Watt (ed.), *Hitler's Mein Kampf* (London, 1969), pt II, ch. III, p. 400.
41   See *Hitlers Zweites Buch*, ed. G. L. Weinberg (Stuttgart, 1961).
42   See the very careful examination of the information sources in the United States to which Hitler was prepared to give a hearing in J. V. Compton, *The Swastika and the Eagle* (Boston, Mass., 1967).
43   See the account in K. J. Müller, *Das Heer und Hitler. Armee und nationalsozialistisches Regime, 1933–1940* (Stuttgart, 1969), pp. 301–39.
44   Recent speculation concerning Hitler's alleged Liverpudlian experience as contained in B. Bainbridge, *Young Adolf* (London, 1978) is entertaining but entirely implausible.
45   On the general picture see D. C. Watt, 'The nature of the British foreign-policy-making élite', in *Personalities and Policies*, pp. 1–18; on the attitudes of members of the British diplomatic service and Foreign Office staff see, *inter aliis*, N. Rose, *Vansittart. Study of a Diplomat* (London, 1978); on the attitudes of the military élite see N. Gibbs, *Grand Strategy*, Vol. I (London, 1976); M. Howard, *The Continental Commitment* (London, 1972); P. Dennis, *Decision by Default. Peace-Time Conscription and British Defence 1919–1927* (London, 1972); B. Bond, *British Military Policy between the Wars* (Oxford, 1980); R. Meyers, *Britische Sicherheitspolitik, 1934–1938* (Düsseldorf, 1976); on the attitude of Lord Hankey and the Committee of Imperial Defence see S. Roskill, *Hankey. Man of Secrets*, Vols II and III (London, 1972, 1974); Lord Ismay, *The Memoirs of Lord Ismay* (London, 1960); B. Bond (ed.), *Chief of Staff, the Diaries of Lieutenant-General Sir Henry Pownall* (London, 1972); on the attitude of senior naval officers, Lord Chatfield, *It Might Happen Again* (London, 1947); L. W. Pratt, *East of Malta, West of Suez* (Cambridge, 1975); R. Pritchard, 'Far Eastern influences upon British strategy towards the Great Powers, 1937–1939', unpublished Ph.D thesis, University of London, 1979; on the attitude of the Air Ministry and senior Air Staff see U. Bialer, *The Shadow of the Bomber. The Fear of Air Attack and British Politics, 1932–1939* (London, 1980); H. Montgomery Hyde, *British Air Policy between the Wars* (London, 1976); Sir J. Slessor, *The Central Blue* (London, 1956); on the attitude of the Treasury see R. P. Shay, Jr, *British Rearmament in the 1930s. Politics and Profits* (Princeton, NJ, 1977); G. C. Peden, *British Rearmament and the Treasury, 1932–1939* (Edinburgh, 1979); on the general direction of British trading interests see A. Teichova, '40 years after. An economic reassessment', inaugural lecture, Norwich, 1978; id., *An Economic Background to Munich. International Business and Czechoslovakia 1918–1938* (Cambridge, 1974); B. J. Wendt, *Economic Appeasement. Handel und Finanzen in der britischen Deutschland-Politik, 1933–1939* (Düsseldorf, 1971);

C. A. Macdonald, 'Economic appeasement and the German "moderates"', 1937–1939', *Past and Present*, vol. 56 (1972), pp. 105–35. G. van Kessel, 'The British reaction to German economic penetration in south east Europe, 1938–1939', unpublished Ph.D thesis, University of London, 1972.

46 Pritchard, thesis.

47 Pratt, *East of Malta, West of Suez*.

48 See D. C. Watt, 'Anglo-German naval negotiations on the eve of the Second World War', *Journal of the Royal United Services Institute For Defence Studies*, vol. 103 (1958), pp. 201–7, 384–91.

49 See the draft memoirs of its chief, Air Marshal Sir Victor Goddard, Liddell Hart Centre for Military Archives, King's College, London. See also F. H. Hinsley *et al.*, *British Intelligence in the Second World War* (London, 1980).

50 Gibbs, *Grand Strategy*, vol. I, pp. 625–33; Patrick Friedenson and Jean Lacuir, *La France et la Grande Bretagne face aux problèmes aériens* (1935–Mai 1940) (Vincennes, 1976).

51 D. C. Watt, 'Sir Warren Fisher and British rearmament against Germany' in *Personalities and Policies*, pp. 100–16; G. R. Peden, 'Sir Warren Fisher and British rearmament against Germany', *English Historical Review*, vol. XCIV (1979), pp. 29–47.

52 See David Astor, 'Why the revolt against Hitler was ignored', *Encounter*, June 1969, pp. 3–13. See also the references in Vol. IV of the draft memoirs of Admiral Sir John Godfrey, Churchill College, Cambridge.

53 Cf. Kettenacker, *The 'Other Germany'*; D. C. Watt, 'Les Allies et la résistance allemande, 1939–44', *Revue d'histoire de la deuxième guerre mondiale*, 1959, p. 65.

54 A lot of new material but no analysis of any value may be found in D. Aigner's *Das Ringen um England. Das deutsch-britische Verhältnis. Die öffentliche Meinung 1933–1939, Tragödie zweier Völker* (Munich, 1969); and *On Producing 'Chaff'. Materials for an Enquiry* (Mannheim, 1979).

55 F. R. Gannon, *The British Press and Nazi Germany, 1936–1939* (Oxford, 1971).

56 J. F. Naylor, *Labour's International Policy. The Labour Party in the 1930s* (London, 1969).

57 On the oil companies see P. Marguerat, *Le III Reich et le pétrol roumain 1939–1940* (Leiden, 1977, and bibliography); M. Pearton, *Oil and the Roumanian State* (Oxford, 1971). On other British multinationals see Teichova, *Economic Background to Munich*; Wendt. *Economic Appeasement*; W. J. Reeder, *Imperial Chemical Industries. A History* (Oxford, 1975).

58 D. Waley, *British Public Opinion and the Abyssinian War 1935–1936* (London, 1975); S. A. Thompson, 'The League of Nations Union and the promotion of the League idea in Britain', *Australian Journal of Politics and History* (1972), no. 1, pp. 52–61.

59 N. A. Rose, *The Gentile Zionists* (London, 1973); N. A. Rose (ed.), *Baffy. The Diaries of Blanche Dugdale 1936–1947* (London, 1973).

60 See D. C. Watt, 'Christian essay on appeasement', *Wiener Library Bulletin*, vol. XIV, no. 2 (1960), pp. 30–1, and 'German influence on British opinion 1933–38', in *Personalities and Policies*, esp. pp. 124–9 and sources there cited.

61 S. Samuels, 'The Left Book Club', *Journal of Contemporary History*, vol. I, no. 2 (1966), pp. 65–86.

62 A. Marwick, 'Middle opinion in the 1930s. Planning, progress and political agreement', *English Historical Review*, vol. LXXIX (1964), pp. 285–98.

63 D. C. Watt, 'British domestic politics and the onset of war. Notes for a discussion, in C.R.N.S.', *Les Relations France-Britanniques de 1935 à 1938, Communications présentées aux colloques France-Britanniques* (Paris, 1975), pp. 243–61; C. E. Madge and T. Harrisson, *Britain by Mass Observation* (London, 1939).

2 The Failure of Collective Security in British Appeasement

R. A. C. PARKER

It would be incorrect to think of a 'failure of collective security' as something independent of the policies and wishes of British governments. Their policies were as much a cause as a consequence of any such 'failure'. Except in two of the several senses of the phrase, 'collective security' was not the first choice of British governments as a means of facing the German problem. In this paper I shall consider four distinct meanings of 'collective security' and discuss the British attitude to the workings of each of them. I hope to show that the object most sought in international affairs by the British government – conciliation – was thought easier to secure outside the League, while the coercive functions of collective security were thought to make peaceful settlements more remote. One sense of 'collective security' was reliance on the influence of world opinion to prevent a resort to force, or the threat of force, in pursuit of national ambitions. British governments would, of course, have been relieved of all their problems in foreign policy if this had been practicable. In the years 1933–9 its futility was clear: the Japanese, Italian and German governments more or less openly insisted on the merits of armed strength as a means of forcing change. Lord Cecil made the point in May 1936: 'I put aside, personally, all hope of maintaining peace by objurgation or appeals or even the unassisted influence of world opinion. These influences . . . have never yet succeeded in preventing a war which has been determined upon by any powerful country.'[1] The other sense in which 'collective security' might have been fully acceptable to British governments was as a means of pacifying international trouble-makers by the use of the League of Nations to negotiate the redress of their grievances. Sir Eric Phipps wrote from Berlin in April 1935 to suggest that the British government should

> take things quietly and see if something can be done to strengthen the League and convert it from a purely passive into a really active instrument, not for the preservation of obsolete treaties but for their revision. Somewhere in that direction lies the only hope of progress. It may sound a platitude but unless there is some machinery for dealing promptly and effectively with European problems they will be solved ultimately by the sword.[2]

By that time, however, the British had experienced the failure of the Disarmament Conference to work out an agreed revision of the military clauses of the Treaty of Versailles which would win German consent. Two linked conclusions were drawn: that the failure of disarmament had been principally the fault of the French and that the multilateral negotiation implied by League procedures facilitated obstructiveness and made mutual bargaining more difficult. By contrast, the British were delighted with their Naval Agreement with Germany – an unexpected by-product of direct discussions with Ribbentrop with no League |involvement.[3] Scepticism about the League as an instrument for negotiating concessions, that is, for advancing 'European appeasement', therefore grew and at the same time made it less likely that the League would be used in what now seems to have been its most important capacity – as a deterrent to armed aggression.

That third sense of 'collective security' was defined by Lord Cecil in May 1936 in the memorandum already quoted:

> I am one of those who believe that Germany is preparing for war . . . I do, however, believe that if Germany were assured that any particular hostile action would be met by a combination of all the forces of the members of the League she would probably refrain from it. That seems to me the only solid hope for world peace.[4]

Again, in leading a deputation from the League of Nations Union to see Eden in February 1937 he declared: 'On the continent there was a conviction that war was inevitable. It would be avoided if we made it clear that any aggression would be met with overwhelming force.'[5] One difficulty that concerned the makers of British policy was the idea of resistance to *any* aggressor. Far from strengthening a British defence of international law and order, this seemed an unlimited extension of British commitments which in practice would bring no compensating accretion of strength. Both the Manchurian and Ethiopian crises confirmed this view.

The problem that the League presented to the British government was that it compelled at least a clarification of attitudes to threats to peace. The British, and therefore the League, were powerless to resist the Japanese conquest of Manchuria. France took little interest, the United States government was ready to denounce Japan but not to join in any action. British naval strength was circumscribed by the absence of any fleet base east of Malta. The effect of British support for 'collective security' was to make it more difficult either to do nothing or to attempt to work out a bargain with Japan by negotiating spheres of interest. Critics of 'collective security' (amongst whom were to be found those who regretted dependence on the unpredictable United States and the loss of the Anglo-Japanese alliance) were able to argue that the absence of the USA foredoomed the League to failure.

The Ethiopian crisis produced a still clearer demonstration of the way in which collective security could cause Britain to risk war in a conflict in which British interests were not directly involved. The League could succeed in curbing Italian designs on Ethiopia only if Britain were prepared to risk war but the government was prevented by French manoeuvres from doing so.

Once again, therefore, the League 'failed'. It failed to stop Italy and frustrated any possibility (if it ever existed) of an Anglo-Italian entente.[6]

The inconvenience of the League – that it might compel Britain into war in defence of something other than specifically British interests – was vigorously set out in 1935, the year in which effective preparations for war began to be considered. The Defence Requirements Sub-Committee of the Committee of Imperial Defence, which included Vansittart from the Foreign Office as well as the service chiefs, reported on the League in November 1935 that

> we feel bound to bring to notice the very serious effect of the system, in its present stage, on our own defence requirements as illustrated by the Manchurian and Abyssinian episodes . . . In 1932–33, and again in 1935, owing to our obligations under the Covenant and the position we occupy as the one great sea-power remaining in the League, we had no alternative but to play our part – inevitably a leading part – in disputes in which our national interest was at most quite secondary . . . On each occasion we have come within sight of war and aroused the bitterness of old friends and allies, including, in the recent past, not only Italy, but even France, hitherto our closest but not always reliable friend.

The committee did not believe that collective security would bring a compensating addition of strength:

> It is almost impossible to forecast the nations with which we might be brought into conflict owing to a breach of the Covenant and still more impossible to forecast those on whose material support we could count. If the Covenant breaker were Germany, that support would be even less reliable than in the present case [i.e. Italy].[7]

After sanctions against Italy were ended the British Cabinet came near to deciding on a public repudiation of British obligations under the Covenant in Eastern Europe and it was in effect agreed that those obligations would not be carried out in practice.[8]

The government's views had parted from those of League supporters. To the most important of the government's advisers collective security through the League might compel Britain to risk war without adequate help in defence of parts of the *status quo* she did not wish to defend. At the same time, the League seemed an ineffective mechanism for peaceful change. The views expressed, for instance, by Churchill on 5 November 1936 were in sharp contrast, when he urged 'the plan of standing by the Covenant of the League of Nations, and trying to gather together, under the authority of the Covenant, the largest possible number of well-armed, peace-seeking Powers in order to overawe, and if necessary to restrain, a potential aggressor, whoever he may be'. In the same speech he felt obliged, however, to

> make it clear that those who are devoted and sincere supporters of the Covenant of the League of Nations do not confine their position to an armed and combined defence of the *status quo*. We contemplate machin-

ery for the redress of legitimate grievances between nations, and we must contemplate that if a grievance is shown to be justified it shall be corrected even against the wishes of nations who would be unwilling to make the sacrifice.[9]

The most effective and clear-headed advocates of the League argued that it was the fault of British policy if it were true that British loyalty to the Covenant would not bring an increase in strength to balance the dangers it would involve. Lord Cecil argued that the British government should make clear its readiness to apply the Covenant to the fullest extent whenever it was possible to do so and, when it was not possible, should clearly and openly explain why. Thus, he believed, the British would be able to maintain the future support for League action of powers which might otherwise be discouraged by the shifty evasiveness which inaction without reasonable explanation would produce. Over Manchuria, Cecil suggested that the British government if

they think it desirable to make a real effort to save China . . . must make it perfectly clear that that is their intention to the Japanese, and take economic action, with all its consequences, to coerce the Japanese. I am quite aware that that cannot be done effectively without the support of the United States, and if this policy is adopted, the United States ought to be asked quite plainly what their policy is and whether they would support action such as I have suggested. If not, it is for consideration whether we should not make it clear that it is the want of American support which has prevented us from doing anything effective.[10]

Over Ethiopia the League of Nations Union executive committee proposed to Eden in November 1935 that 'as soon as ever the British government think it possible to do so, and in any case not later than two months hence, we should definitely propose to the French the severing of communications between Italy and Abyssinia and, if necessary, tell them that if they are unable to accept that view, we shall have to make it quite plain to our own people that we have made the proposal and that it has been turned down by them'.[11]

This approach could have convinced smaller powers that Britain would lead the League into serious action whenever possible and make them feel that such a lead would be safe to follow. The snag was that it would make it much more difficult to pacify the possible opponents – in these cases, Japan and Italy. The threat to Laval that Cecil proposed during the Ethiopian crisis would make far more difficult the attainment of the main aim of British policy towards France – persuading the French to moderate their refusal to make concessions to German demands. Unless ardent support for the League were to put at Britain's disposal strength sufficient simultaneously to intimidate Germany, Italy and Japan, British support for the League was bound to be hesitant and ambiguous. The League 'failed' because the British thought it was more dangerous to British security to use it than not to do so: the 'failure' of the League was a consequence rather than a cause of British policy. The idea of some autonomous 'failure of the League' was, however, convenient for British ministers; it made it much easier to defend British refusal to use it. From the British government's point of view what, in fact, made 'collective security' through the League unacceptable was not its weakness as an agent of coercion of aggressors but its ineffectiveness as a means for forcing concessions on their potential victims. Pursuit of 'appeasement' was itself a cause not a consequence of the 'failure' of the League. Vansittart saw the point in his memorandum of February 1936 when he advocated further attempts to make a 'general settlement' with Germany and urged that it was at Geneva that 'the real settlement must be threshed out and concluded, provided that the members of the League face the fact that no durable peace with Germany is possible unless they are liberal enough to deprive her of at least part of her grievance mongering as well as strong enough to make her realise that a settlement will be better for her than aggression'.[12]

The same argument applies to the fourth form of 'collective security' – the construction of alliances. Alliances would make it hard to reach settlements with Germany. Until 1939 alliance with France was thought likely dangerously to encourage French resistance to compromises with Germany and to make Germany even less tractable. Thus, early in 1938, the Chiefs of Staff opposed staff talks with the French:

> We feel certain that the opportunity of turning such conversations to their own political advantage would be seized on by the French with avidity. The temptation to arrange a leakage of the information that such collaboration was taking, or had taken, place, would, in our opinion, prove irresistible to them in order to flaunt an Anglo-French accord in the face of Germany . . . We consider, therefore, that the military advantages of closer collaboration with the French regarding concerted measures against Germany . . . would be outweighed by the grave risk of precipitating the very situation we wish to avoid, namely the irreconcilable suspicion and hostility of Germany.[13]

During the spring and summer of 1938, when 'appeasement' reached its climax, British policy was to compel Czechoslovakia into making concessions to Germany by a refusal to pledge British assistance to Czechoslovakia if Germany attacked or to France if France assisted Czechoslovakia. The French would be encouraged to make Beneš conciliatory by the absence of British participation in automatic collective security against aggression.[14]

The same argument applied to alliance with the Soviet Union: such an alliance, it was thought, would be a signal to Germany that no concessions were available and that war was the only alternative to the renunciation of German aspirations. The Chiefs of Staff inserted in their Cabinet paper of September 1936 the unasked-for comment that 'it is fully realised that, if Germany is given a free hand in Central and Eastern Europe, there is a danger of the result recoiling ultimately on our heads. On the other hand, it would be disastrous if an appeasement in Western Europe were rendered impossible by over-consideration of Russian interests.'[15] In December 1936 when Paul Reynaud talked to him about his plan for strengthening the Franco-Russian alliance, Vansittart warned him that 'if the French Government proceeded at this moment to supplement the Franco-Soviet pact by a military treaty on staff conversations, the Germans would immediately say that this had rendered all further progress impossible, and would allege that they would otherwise have been perfectly ready to come to a satisfactory agreement. They would in fact cause the entire blame for failure to be laid, with some plausibility, on French shoulders.' Eden applauded Vansittart's 'excellent advice'. In 1938, after the *Anschluss*, when Litvinov declared that 'the Soviet Government is . . . prepared to participate in collective actions . . . which should have as its aim the stopping of the further developments of aggression', the British made it clear that they gave priority to conciliation: 'A conference only attended by some of the European Powers, and designed less to secure the settlement of outstanding problems than to organise concerted resistance against aggression, would not necessarily . . . have such a favourable effect upon the prospects of European peace.'[16] Even after March 1939 when the British government tried to get the Soviet Union to provide whatever help against aggression might be asked of it, the same fear that an effective alliance might destroy hopes of conciliation continued to dominate the minds of Chamberlain and Halifax. On 5 April Chamberlain told the Cabinet that an 'arrangement with Russia . . . would certainly provoke an explosion' and that 'if an arrangement which included Russia would be likely to cause an explosion, the question of making any arrangement with Russia was obviously one which required a great deal of further consideration'.[17] On 28 May he told his sister that 'the Alliance would definitely be a lining up of opposing blocs and an association which would make any negotiation or discussion with the totalitarians difficult if not impossible'.[18]

In November 1935 Orme Sargent and Ralph Wigram of the Central Department of the Foreign Office wrote a long paper in which they urged that the British had a choice of three policies – doing nothing, encircling Germany, or coming to terms with Germany. They referred both to encirclement and conciliation as 'collective security'. Britain 'might become the central force in a great anti-revisionist block dressed in the cloak of collective security' or, on the other hand, 'not merely Great Britain, but Europe as a whole, must needs benefit from the success of a policy which aims at securing collective security and international co-operation through the reconciliation of Europe with a Germany, which is at present re-armed, proud, powerful and yet aggrieved'.[19]

For successive makers of British policy, collective security as conciliation of Germany was preferred to collective security as resistance to Germany. Conciliation was more difficult to pursue through the League than resistance would have been. British governments, however, felt politically inhibited from open abandonment of the League as an unhelpful nuisance. The League had too wide a body of support. Once Russia was in the League (from September 1934) it stretched from Churchill to the communists, moving by way of progressive conservatives, high-minded liberals and pacifist socialists through trade union leaders and fellow travellers. In criticising the suggestion made by Wigram and Sargent that Britain should encourage France to abandon Eastern Europe, Vansittart pointed out, on 13 October 1935, that they did 'not seem to have allowed enough for the inevitable play of home politics. Our national unity – it comes rather surprisingly near to that at present [when Hoare and Eden seemed to be leading the League in successful action against Italy] – is due to the fact that we carry so much of the left centre and left with our foreign policy. That is largely due to the fact that we are on better terms with Russia, that Russia is in the League, and that Russia stands to gain by collective security.'[20]

Indeed, when the League ceased to be prominent in the government's policy national unity was broken and the most coherent line of attack on the Baldwin and Chamberlain governments came to be their neglect of 'collective security' in its coercive form. One result was to elevate Churchill into a symbol of national unity. Another was to provide a justification for resistance to British rearmament on the grounds either that the need for it resulted from neglect of collective security or because that neglect implied that the government was in truth anti-Russian and pro-fascist, and that therefore resistance to Germany required its overthrow. These attitudes provided a pretext and a defence (if not an explanation) of the most serious resistance to rearmament – that of trade unionists to increased labour productivity.[21] If resistance to German threats and aggression rather than the pacification of Germany had been what the government had most wanted then 'collective security through the League of Nations' would have been the best way of getting support for it. The British government, however, did not wish to try; nor is it certain that it would have got enough support if it had done so. Hence the 'failure' of collective security.[22]

Notes: Chapter 2

1   Copy memorandum by Cecil sent to Eden and Halifax, British Library (BL), Add. MSS. 51083, fo. 109.
2   W. N. Medlicott and D. Dakin (eds), *Documents on British Foreign Policy*, second series (DBFP/ii), Vol. XII, no. 694.
3   See, for instance, Phipps to Wigram, 18 June 1935, Public Record Office (PRO), FO 371/18847/C 5004, and minute by Eden, 27 July 1935, on C 5280 in FO 371/18848.
4   BL, Add. MSS. 51083, Fo. 108.
5   ibid., fo. 125.
6   On this possibility see W. N. Medlicott's introduction to DBFP/ii, Vol. XV, pp. ix–x.
7   PRO, CAB 4/24, DRC 37, pp. 6–7, 9.
8   PRO, CAB 23/85, fo. 61, 6 July 1936.
9   W. S. Churchill, *Arms and the Covenant* (London, 1938), pp. 361–3.
10   DBFP/ii, Vol. IX, p. 368.
11   Copy Cecil to Eden, 14 November 1935, BL, Add. MSS. 51083, fo. 94.
12   PRO, CAB 27/599, fo. 116v.
13   PRO, CAB 4/27, fo. 115v (4 February 1938).
14   For the formal execution of this policy see DBFP/iii, Vol. I, nos 106, 135, 138.
15   DBFP/ii, Vol. XVII, p. 208.
16   DBFP/iii, Vol. I, nos 90, 116.
17   PRO, CAB 23/98, fos 212–13.
18   Birmingham University Library, NC 18/1/1101.
19   DBFP/ii, Vol. XV, App. I, paras 3, 4, 5, 32.

20   PRO, FO 371/18810, minute on C 6952.
21   R. A. C. Parker, 'British rearmament 1936–9: Treasury, trade unions and skilled labour', *English Historical Review*, vol. 96 (1981), pp. 306–43.
22   Halifax made the point to Cecil on 8 March 1938, BL, Add. MSS. 51084, fo. 138.

II

FOREIGN POLICY MAKING IN
NATIONAL SOCIALIST GERMANY

3 Nazi Dynamics, German Foreign Policy and Appeasement

RONALD M. SMELSER

One of the crucial questions in assessing the policy of appeasement during the late 1930s is whether that policy ever had a reasonable chance of success under the prevailing circumstances. To address that question one must develop as complete an understanding as possible of the nature of the threat posed to the international system at the time, an understanding which entails centrally a grasp of Germany's foreign policy during these years, for Germany, although not the only, was the most dangerous of the challengers to the international *status quo*.

Here a whole cluster of issues appear from the outset to complicate the problem: to what extent did Hitler's foreign policy represent elements of continuity and discontinuity? What was the relationship, if any, between foreign and domestic policy in Nazi Germany? How crucial was Hitler's role, including his plans and decision-making process, *vis-à-vis* other factors in determining foreign policy? These and other questions must be addressed – and indeed have been in a number of recent publications on German foreign policy.[1] But the work so far has been of necessity tentative and exploratory; many questions still await an answer, many trains of events their interpretive framework. The whole issue of appeasement gives us the opportunity to continue to address the complex question of the threat posed by Nazi Germany.[2]

In this paper I will assert a close connection between domestic and foreign policy.[3] I propose that the Nazi regime, arising as it did out of a society in disintegration, posed by its very nature, apart from any concrete goals in the mind of the dictator, a revolutionary threat to the stability of the international order during the 1930s. Moreover, I would suggest that this threat did not represent a challenge to Hitler as chief foreign policy formulator, but rather dovetailed closely with his own long-range goals, gave impetus to his own eagerness to radically alter the face of Europe and, in fact, provided a momentum on all fronts that his own day-to-day style of leadership failed to do. Finally, I would suggest that what amounted then to a dual threat to the system – Hitler himself and, in a nearly autonomous way, the regime over which he presided – operated in such a way as to very nearly preclude success on the part of the appeasement policy especially as it was timed and practised.

By now it has been firmly established and generally accepted by most scholars that the Nazi regime was hardly the efficient monolith its propagandists made it out to be.[4] Rather, it was a competitive bureaucratic jungle, characterised by confused and overlapping jurisdictions, personalised power, duplication of function and administrative chaos. This bureaucratic 'state of nature', this war of all against all, unarguably redounded to Hitler's benefit, for it enhanced his power by putting him in the position of ultimate arbiter. And perhaps for that very reason he encouraged the rivalries and exacerbated the confusion in his decisions – or lack of them. But the chaotic Führer-State was far more than simply a function of Hitler's erratic leadership techniques: it was a reflection of and a response to what had happened to German society in the years preceding the Nazi *Machtergreifung* and was a phenomenon which was not only revolutionising German society, but which also had ominous implications for the international *status quo*, for it provided the dynamic which propelled the Nazi revolution far beyond the borders of the German Reich.

The well-known and often observed dynamic of the Nazi system derived in large measure from the general disintegration of German society which took place during the 1920s and 1930s in the wake of national defeat and economic catastrophe. That societal disintegration produced in turn a radical disjuncture among the variables of class, status and wealth and destroyed any national consensus which might have existed.[5] Politically, this was reflected in the total breakdown of the Weimar Republic and its liberal parliamentary form of government.

National Socialism arose as a concrete response to this situation of political fragmentation and social disintegration and achieved much of its success by promising (1) to restore national consensus, in part by redefining what the nation was, who belonged to it and who did not, and (2) to create a world of equal opportunity to all in the process of creating a utopian society freed of caste and class strife. One of the ways in which the Nazis tried to realise these rather nebulous if noble sounding goals once they were in power was, paradoxically, to desociologise politics (that is, to pretend that the class struggle had been terminated) and simultaneously to politicise society. This second step was particularly important, because it enabled the Nazi leaders to direct Germans towards what already during the Weimar period had been the most open path of upward mobility – politics.[6]

Indeed, it has been observed that the Nazis had no parallel in Germany in introducing a sense of public spiritedness on a widespread grass roots level among people who traditionally had been 'apolitical'.[7] By creating, then, through the party a mechanism by which to involve ordinary people in an expanded arena of politics the Nazis could address simultaneously their dual problem of restoring national consensus and opening opportunity, by creating in the minds of Germans a close link between the fate of the nation and their own career advancement. If one could aid in building the *Volksgemeinschaft* and build a career at the same time, so much the better. In this context, of course, it was desirable to make the world of politics as broad as possible, hence the emergence of what Fraenkel has called the 'dual state', one in which, as he says, 'the "political" sphere is not one sphere of the state separated from the others by law; it is an omnicompetent sphere independent of all legal regulation'.[8] It is this combination of factors – the confluence of career opportunity, a sense of redefining the nation and an expanded realm of politics – that created the arena for dynamic political entrepreneurship which characterised Nazi Germany from the outset. It was a world which seemed to offer no limitations beyond the parameters set by the often vaguely expressed will of the Führer: no limitation on the accumulation of power, for it was almost a caricature of the open-ended liberalism of the nineteenth century; no limits on jurisdiction, for the individual was not just filling an office or a post, he was creating a totally new society. Hence, the multiplicity of plans in the minds of Nazi big-wigs which betrayed their own sense of omnicompetence: the SA-State of Roehm, the Labour-State of Ley, the Stahlhelm-State of Hierl, the HJ-State of Schirach, and ultimately the most successful in its multi-jurisdictional reach – the SS-State of Himmler.[9]

This world of political free enterprise was made even more competitive by the additional factor of chaos. The striking thing about the Nazi political structure was its lack of rules. This absence of norms, of course, redounded to the benefit of Hitler himself, for it made him the ultimate and only arbiter, and so he encouraged it. But the chaos existed for other reasons as well, reflecting again the fragmentation of German society. In all modern societies, there is a tendency to replace traditional organic associations (kinship, village, guild) with functional ones (trade and manufacturing associations, unions, and so on). Indeed, this development seems to be an accompanying phenomenon of modernisation.[10] In liberal societies, that is, those which have a broad societal consensus, this process goes on within a generally accepted political and constitutional framework which provides a set of impersonal rules by which these functional associations may be created and interrelate with one another. In the absence of a broad societal consensus, however, no normative framework exists, and chaos is liable to result from the process. This is precisely what happened in Germany. Even before the Nazis came to power, German society, basically illiberal in its development,[11] socially only part way into modernisation, lacked the social consensus which would have supported the orderly change from organic to functional association. After the Nazis came to power the situation became worse. Faking the existence of a social consensus, the Nazis proceeded quite consciously to enormously accelerate the process by destroying wholesale traditional, organic, autonomous organisations and replacing them with their own politicised 'functional' ones within the sphere of the regime. For them it was a necessary task and an integral part of the *Gleichschaltung* policy by which they established their control over the German people. But the very lack of consensus which lay behind the lie of *Volksgemeinschaft*, the same lack of social consensus which had been a hallmark of German society before the *Machtergreifung*, continued to prohibit the formulation of any set of rules by which the new associations would function or relate to each other. The result was that the new 'functional' associations, that is, the personal bureaucratic empires of Nazi big-wigs like Ley, Goebbels and Himmler, would be operating, not in a normative structure, but in a competitive jungle.[12]

No wonder then that from the outset these Nazi competitive structures spilled over the normally prescribed boundaries by which functional groups operate and relate to one another in modern society. This was true with respect to the means by which they operated, which came to include treachery, intrigue and even murder, and in terms of their range of activities, which exhibited the pronounced tendency to collect a series of otherwise unrelated jurisdictions as part of a bureaucratic empire. In what 'liberal' country, for example, could a Hermann Goering have managed to be head of the air force, economic tsar, chief forester, foreign policy meddler and much else besides?[13] Important to our considerations here, however, is that the lack of rules also enabled the Nazi functional organisations to spill over the boundary which separated domestic politics from foreign policy.

This already existing tendency to allow a dynamic progression from the arena of domestic policy to that of foreign policy was exacerbated by yet another feature of German society at the time – the continued existence of the former ruling classes and the necessity to reach an accommodation with them.[14] It is well known that Hitler frustrated the desires on the part of millions of his middle- and lower-middle-class followers to create a new society in their image in that he came to terms with the traditional forces he needed to make Germany powerful and to realise his dreams of conquest – the army, the civil service and big business. Because this accommodation was necessary, the regime, whether consciously or not, took the sting out of its failure to completely restructure the country by recreating society in a parallel Nazi world. The component parts of this Nazi world (DAF, KdF, Nährstand, SS) were the 'functional' associations to which I have alluded. The hallmark of this parallel society was that one could rise faster and have a better chance to realise one's utopian dreams in it than in the real society. It was, after all, easier to become an SS general than a regular army general, to run an SS office than to be a *Staatssekretär*, because in the parallel society the roadblocks posed by the old society were absent. The criteria of birth, established wealth, status and membership in an 'old boy' network were replaced by the more accessible ones of political loyalty and racial purity. The problem was – as the continued presence of titled conservatives and wealthy *Generaldirektoren* gave witness – that both societies continued to exist side by side, and any ambitious Nazi had to go on living in both. Therefore, every political aspirant lived in a kind of force field of tension created by the fact that the status and rewards of the one society did not often translate into the currency of the other. Indeed, despite the fact that many upwardly mobile Nazis hated the older class society and those who stood at its apex, at the same time they often could not escape its symbols, rewards and sanctions. It was as if they realised the bogus nature of the shadow Nazi world and tried to square the circle either by trying to become part of the other world, or to translate the successes in the Nazi world into its own rewards, or – most ominously – when these devices did not succeed, to lash out beyond the old society in a manner which would ultimately destroy it. We have much evidence for this perceived tension at virtually every level of the Nazi system.[15] Within the context of the appeasement issue, for example, it is interesting to note that Ribbentrop's first attempt to venture into the world of foreign policy was to submit an essay in application for the post of

Staatssekretär in the Auswärtiges Amt in 1933. And while, of course, creating his own functional organisation in the shadow world, the *Büro Ribbentrop*, never ceased trying to translate his activities into the coinage of the traditional realm. Twice more, in 1935, he requested that Hitler make him *Staatssekretär*. Ultimately, of course, he was appointed Foreign Minister and, characteristically, largely abandoned his 'functional' *Büro* in the shadow world.[16]

It is this very tension, and the inability to overcome it, that will help cause the dynamic of the Nazi system, not only with respect to the tendency of Nazi formations to spill beyond the realm of traditional jurisdictions, but more importantly, for them all as a group to overreach the borders of German society itself – into the social *tabula rasa* of Eastern Europe. For only there could Nazi dreamers and power-seekers create a world in which only their symbols, sanctions, power and status would have exclusive validity.[17] This obviously has enormous consequences for German foreign policy, for it means that the very mechanism by which Nazi political society functioned practically predisposed that system to challenge the international social and political order, completely apart from any concrete plans that Hitler might have formulated. As we shall see, it was the misapprehension of this fact that allowed the appeasers to go on as long as they did in pursuing a policy which, given the nature of the Nazi system, was probably futile from the start. As far as the dictator himself was concerned, this interpretation of the dynamics of Nazi society and the tendency for the organisations that made up the regime to spill over into a foreign policy of expansion suggests that there was no real tension between Hitler and the system. Rather it is more likely that the two, Hitler, with his *Stufenplan* for achieving German hegemony over Europe and then the status of a world power, and the dynamic, if frustrated, group of Nazi political entrepreneurs, were operating in tandem. Hitler was well aware of the dynamic which propelled his regime. He was animated by some of the same drives which characterised his followers. His task was to formulate, more carefully, the *Endziele* and alternately to restrain, or unleash, the dynamic as thought useful. In light of this fact one would suggest that views of German foreign policy which are too Hitler-centric miss one important source of the pressure behind the expansionist policy of Nazi Germany.[18]

It is necessary at this point to demonstrate that the Hobbesian state of nature that characterised the Nazi system domestically also obtained, if to a more limited extent, in the foreign policy area as well. Contemporary observers certainly noted the fact. Already in July of 1933 Mussolini complained:[19]

> There seemed to be six if not seven members of the German government who acted from time to time as foreign minister. Hitler . . . Neurath . . . Goering . . . Papen, Goebbels and Rosenberg, not to mention General Blomberg who was brought into all discussions of foreign affairs. This rendered dealing with the German government a matter of considerable difficulty.

Over four years later, the Italians were still complaining. Mussolini's son-in-law, Italian Foreign Minister Count Ciano, said on the occasion of Lord Halifax's visit to Berlin in November 1937:[20]

> Zuviel Hähne im Hühnerstall. Es gibt mindestens vier Aussenpolitiken: die von Hitler, die von Goering, die von Neurath, die von Ribbentrop. Von den kleineren ganz abgesehen. Es ist schwierig, vollkommen auf dem laufenden zu bleiben.

Not only Germany's friends noticed this tendency; representatives of her potential enemies did so as well. French Ambassador André François-Poncet observed with respect to foreign policy:[21]

> There is not merely one minister, nor is there only one foreign office. There are a half-dozen. When it is a question of Austria, Habicht is heard. When it is a question of Hungary or Rumania, one perceives that Rosenberg and his office still retain a particle of authority. When it is necessary to take up the Saar, or the Vatican, or France, one addresses Papen. When there is a reason to send a message to Mussolini, it is Goering who leaps into his airplane. Even the influence of the whimsical Dr Hanfstaengl comes into play when America is under discussion.

Even the man ostensibly in charge of carrying out German foreign policy, Neurath, told a visitor in the summer of 1937: 'Don't take Goering too seriously. In Germany, everyone concerns himself with foreign policy.'[22] What contemporary observers noted has been largely confirmed by scholarship during the past decade or so. I do not propose here to discuss in detail the various organisations involved in the formulation of Nazi foreign policy, but rather to make several generalisations about them germane to the theme of appeasement.[23]

(1) Competing Nazis ventured into the foreign policy arena for a variety of reasons, most of which arose from that same combination of utopian vision, careerist opportunism and inadvertent spill-over produced by the very dynamic of the system as we have described it. Ernst Bohle, founder of the *Auslandsorganisation* of the party, dreamed of harnessing ethnic Germans all over the world as tools for National Socialism. His goal was to help bring Germany into the first rank of world powers. 'I was absolutely fascinated and dominated by the conception of a German Reich which, in spite of a completely different structure, would, in every respect, enjoy absolute equality with England in the concert of world powers.'[24] Himmler dreamed of a great racial empire to the East, where he could realise his visions of resettlement.[25] Rosenberg cherished visions of a break-up of the Great Russian state and an accompanying *nordisch-deutsch* racial renewal.[26] None of these men thought small. On the contrary, their vision is to a great extent millennial, reflecting perhaps a combination of frustration and aspiration.

Occasionally, forays into foreign policy would be a result of simple expansion of a domestic power structure: as when Propaganda Minister, Goebbels, tried to get control of Nazi propaganda abroad;[27] or when the SS extended its intelligence activities beyond Germany's borders in search of exiles and ideological enemies. Sometimes foreign policy involvement would arise from a dilettantism with a particular geographic predisposition: Goering's fascination for Italian or Polish relations,[28] Rosenberg's interests in Hungary and Romania,[29] Ribbentrop's mercurial relationship with the English,[30] to name only the most important. But more often than not, in any given case, a multiplicity of motives was involved. The best example for this was the SS, whose involvement in foreign policy was a gradual affair arising from intelligence activities, ideological dreaming, solid business interest, police work and its own troubles generally in defining a mission for itself.[31]

In all cases, though, the ultimate effect of this activity was aimed in one way or another at changing the *status quo* in Europe and the world. What all these dreams and ambitions have in common was a disruption, a radical one, even a millennial one, of the international system.

(2) The same tensions and conflicts created by the existence of two parallel societies in the domestic arena were reproduced as well in the foreign policy sphere. Indeed they are, if anything, more clearly delineated here, because the two conservative strongholds which were vital in Germany's foreign relations – the army and the Foreign Office – were involved. It was here that the Nazi rulers had to make the most far-reaching accommodations in terms of personnel, and here where conservatives seemed to preserve their traditional power and perquisites. No wonder, then, that the field of foreign policy became one of the main fields of struggle between radical Nazis and conservative traditionalists.

We know now that conservative strength was not what it seemed at the time. But optically it must have seemed so. After all, Hitler's short-range policies dovetailed neatly with the long-range goals of the conservatives, so that there appeared a community of interest which did not really exist. Moreover, Hitler found it necessary to rein in the more competitive foreign policy aspirants from time to time, which made him look perhaps more moderate than we know him to have been.[32] And, finally, even with respect to personnel, aspiring Nazis may be forgiven for having thought that German society had not changed as much as they had hoped it would with the coming of the Nazi regime. Everywhere they looked, the old masters still seemed to be around. The diplomatic corps had a higher percentage of titled aristocrats than during the Weimar period and even the SS itself had a disproportionate number of nobles in its upper ranks.[33] All this was fuel for the fierce fire of jurisdictional conflict.

(3) This rivalry in the foreign policy arena did not represent a steady state, a static situation where each side held its own. Rather it was a dynamic conflict in which over the years between 1933 and 1937 the radicals gradually got the upper hand. Though Neurath and the Foreign Service were more powerful and effective initially than hitherto supposed, as Heineman's new biography of Neurath suggests, it is nevertheless true that by 1936 the conservatives had their backs to the wall through personnel attrition, fierce competition from a variety of Nazis, and Hitler's increasing use of foreign policy agencies other than the traditional apparatus. By the end of 1937 the

battle had been won, with serious consequences for the policy of appeasement.

(4) The transfer of the competitive structure of the Nazi state to the arena of foreign policy worked almost entirely to the benefit of Hitler as he began the pursuit of his long-range vision. It allowed him to explore options and probe weaknesses without bearing any of the consequences as head of state. This was most dramatically demonstrated in the case of Austria in July 1934.[34] It gave a set of ideas and tools which helped to counterbalance his own lack of previous experience in foreign affairs. It created situations which he could exploit when he believed the situation to be ripe. This represented a real advantage to the dictator who hated day-to-day governance and preferred to let situations drift until they became critical.[35] Other statesmen did not have this advantage. And finally, of course, the endless rivalry and competition grew out of a dynamic which Hitler knew full well, whatever the varieties of dreams and aspirations might have been, would coincide with his own desire to radically restructure Europe. In this sense, he could be sure that the long-term evolution of Nazi society would coincide with his long-term goals.

Having said this, it is necessary to note that despite the enormous centrifugal force that the dynamic Nazi system generated, there were practical limits in its day-to-day functioning in foreign policy, even though its long-term prospects promised international upheaval. Hitler, careful not to upset the international system before German strength was commensurate with the task, imposed sharper restrictions on the competition in foreign policy than he did with domestic affairs. Here it is very important in the assessment of German foreign policy to strike a proper balance between Hitler's own initiative and control and the spontaneous activities of his underlings.[36]

(5) Finally, it is of great importance to our theme here to note that the culmination of the struggle in foreign policy between radicals and traditionalists in victory for the radicals coincided almost exactly with an increase in German economic and military strength to a point where Hitler believed that he could proceed beyond his short-term goals (and the long-range ones of the conservatives) towards his long-range ones (which coincided with the dreams of many radicals).[37] It is a tragedy that the conjuncture for these two developments coincides in turn with a third – the evolution of British policy from passive to active appeasement. And it is to that problem and its relationship to the structure and formulation of German foreign policy that we must now turn.

It is one of the more tragic conjunctures of the period, that the transition from a policy of passive appeasement to one of active appeasement occurred simultaneously with two other developments which boded ill for the success of that strategy: the gradual realisation on Hitler's part that Britain would not be an ally of Germany, but more likely an enemy; and the victory of the radicals in Germany over the traditionalists.

If we can establish the inauguration of active appeasement with the visit of Lord Halifax to Berlin on 18 November 1937, then this conjuncture becomes clear. Halifax in his discussions with Hitler, Goering and other German leaders himself opened the question of concessions to Germany in Central Europe; that is, he practically established an agenda by means of which the Austrian and Czechoslovak problems could be addressed on an international level. Under more normal, traditional circumstances this would have been a completely rational step: to address problems concerning the powers so that they could be settled peacefully before they reached a stage of crisis where lack of resolution might threaten the peace.[38] But Halifax and the other British statesmen were not operating under traditional circumstances. In Germany, they were dealing with a power whose leader had radical goals far beyond those tolerable within any framework the British envisioned; and whose political system possessed a dynamic which also posed a direct threat to the *status quo*. A succession of events just before and shortly after Halifax's visit dramatically illustrate the point. On 5 November, just two weeks before Halifax's arrival, Hitler, in his secret speech to Neurath and the army commanders, had already put Austria and Czechoslovakia on an agenda – not one of negotiation but rather of military conquest. Moreover, it also emerged in the speech that he anticipated Britain no longer as an ally, but rather as one potential enemy.[39]

It was also during these last several months in 1937 that the fierce struggle on several fronts within Germany between radical Nazis and more traditional conservatives was approaching an end with the general collapse of the conservatives and victory by the radicals. The resignation of Schacht on 26 November, just one week after Halifax's visit to Berlin, represented more than simply the loss of one prominent conservative. It reflected the break-up of a political united front on the part of big business, and, as one scholar suggests, a further stage in the general disintegration of German society. The result was to give still more impetus, opportunity and *Spielraum* to the competitive Nazi formations.[40] The subsequent scandals surrounding War Minister von Blomberg and Commander-in-Chief of the army, von Fritsch, resulting in Hitler's direct take-over of the military as well as his replacement of Neurath with Ribbentrop as Foreign Minister, represented the collapse of the conservative position in two other former bastions – the army and the Foreign Office.[41] Accompanying these dénouements, virtually unnoticed at the time, but no less ominous, was the victory of the SS in the area of the *Volkstum* struggle, with the dismissal of Hans Steinacher as head of the VDA and the establishment of the *Volksdeutsche Mittelstelle* as a command post for manipulation of German communities abroad.[42] In fact, the capitulation of Konrad Henlein, leader of the Sudeten Germans, to Hitler's will *on the same day* as Halifax's arrival, signalled that even as the British were giving the dictator a legitimate excuse to raise the question of Czechoslovakia's future in the international forum, the leader of the German minority in that country was giving him the tool to deal with Czechoslovakia in a manner not envisioned in British councils.[43] The British knew of most of these developments – at least the changes in personnel, but either underestimated their impact or misunderstood them entirely. Henderson wrote to the king from Berlin that these changes 'left the German army with a say in Foreign affairs' and 'had strengthened the hand of the peace party in Germany'.[44]

Thus, the policy of active appeasement, of taking the initiative in raising issues germane to the peace of Europe instead of passively awaiting moves on the part of the dictator, a policy which might have weighed measurably in the scales if undertaken earlier in the year, was begun under the most inauspicious circumstances towards the end of 1937, and at the beginning of 1938, at a time when Hitler's views of what he might venture without disproportionate risk had expanded to the point where he was willing to see Britain as the enemy, and when the dynamic of the Nazi revolution had cleared the decks for action by eliminating any restraining competition.[45]

Beyond this unfortunate conjuncture of developments, there was another factor which cast a grave shadow over the possibilities offered by the policy of appeasement as it emerged in late 1937. If we look at the goals being pursued by the British government, at the language in which these goals were formulated and at the framework in which the British leadership viewed international relations, it becomes clear that Chamberlain and his associates were operating on a very different plane from that of the Nazi leadership. This fact may be so glaringly obvious that it scarcely needs to be asserted, but I do feel it is important to explore it briefly in one of its aspects, for the extremely divergent views of the world which separated the German from the British leadership themselves are evidence of a disintegration of the international system and suggest, in retrospect, a gloomy prognosis for the policy of appeasement.[46] Where the two groups differed perhaps most greatly was on the subject of empire-building.

The radical differences in goals, language, spirit and concepts which separated the British leadership from the Nazi German in terms of imperial expansion have their origins partly in the very different stages of development in which the two countries found themselves. By the 1930s, Great Britain had reached a stage of development where she was a mature, satiated imperial power. Her leaders for the most part had recognised the aspirations to which both the Wilsonian and Lenin revolutions had given expression and, though the British government was moving at a glacial pace in direction of devolution, it at least had progressed beyond the nineteenth century in its attitudes towards imperialism and empire-building.[47] This is not to deny that there were plenty of Englishmen who still nostalgically harboured Kipling-esque dreams of empire, but the point is that public opinion and that of most responsible leaders had passed them by. Illustrative in this context is the book *The Lost Dominion*, published in 1924 by B. C. H. Calcraft-Kennedy, a high-ranking official in the Indian administration, under the alias Al. Carthill.[48] The book is a passionate plea for Britain's right to rule India and in the traditional manner. But although the author thought that the Raj could continue to control India, by 'administrative massacre' if necessary, he also realised and admitted that it was utopian to try to do so, for public sentiment, shaped by the left-wingers and humanitarians whom the author loathed so much, would never permit such a thing.

Germany, by contrast, having come late to nationhood and only briefly enjoyed the fruits of colonial empire, had not evolved as far as Britain with respect to imperial attitudes. Even Germany's respectable leaders still talked during the 1920s very much in terms of retrieving lost colonies abroad. It was the Nazi political entrepreneurs, though, who really represented a kind of nineteenth-century anachronism in their imperial attitudes. There were several reasons for this. First, Nazi ideology had borrowed heavily on the racial thought of the late nineteenth century and made the racial imperative the core of their dreams of empire. Secondly, the enormous tensions and compulsions which lay at the heart of the competitive Nazi political system generated aspirations and dreams on a Cecil Rhodesian scale. This factor, in turn, was exacerbated by the social backgrounds of many of the Nazi dreamers. A goodly number of them had their origins in the middle and lower-middle class. Only now, with the advent of the Nazi equal opportunity revolution, itself a product of a social upheaval which English society had escaped, could they aspire to imperial careers which a generation or two earlier had been reserved for their social betters. They represented then, as far as foreign policy was concerned, 'petit bourgeois Bismarckians'.[49] But the tardy arrival of their chance for empire could still not disguise the fact that in the fourth decade of the twentieth century they were historical anachronisms. A Carl Peters might say with equanimity in the 1880s that he 'was fed up with being counted among the pariahs and wanted to belong to a master race,' and not attract undue attention, because there were plenty of Frenchmen and Englishmen who shared his racial view of empire.[50] That kind of language used nearly half a century later, however, failed to recognise all the changes that had occurred in the interim. It is ironic in this context to realise that Joseph Chamberlain might have understood the Nazis far better than his son, Neville. For this ardent imperialist, ambitious, vain, combative, inexperienced in foreign affairs yet with an eye for power, a man described variously as 'a Sicilian bandit' and 'almost the greatest jingo' in the Cabinet, would have been much more in tune with the Faustian scope of the Nazi thrust forward and vision of empire.[51] What neither Chamberlain would have understood, however – and this was the second factor which put the British and Nazi German leaders during the 1930s on two different planes – was the 'leap' by which the Nazis transferred their imperial vision from the classically recognised field for empire of Africa and Asia to the vast reaches of Eastern Europe.[52] It was Russia and not Tanganyika which was to provide the experimentation ground for Himmler's resettlement schemes, the political battleground for the establishment of Rosenberg's 'Nordische Schicksalsgemeinschaft', the apocalyptic battleground for the destruction of the 'Drahtzieher des Judentums' projected by Goebbels and the geopolitical foundation for Hitler's dreams of Germany's coming role as *Weltmacht*.[53]

There was to be sure a certain terrible logic in this turning to the east for empire. The 'leap' from seeing foreign continents as areas for imperial expansion to seeing the eastern regions of Europe in the same fashion came easy to a people who traditionally over the centuries had expanded in that direction rather than overseas; and the leap must have been all the easier when the rationale of racial superiority came into play. The Nazi goal was a second *Drang nach Osten* with racial and apocalyptic overtones. And indeed the Nazis were not the first Germans to see Eastern Europe in this fashion. Already at the turn of the century Ernst Hasse, head of the Pan-German League, proposed treating certain nationalities such as Poles, Czechs, Jews and others 'in the same way as overseas imperialism treated natives in non-European continents'.[54] The attitude of the generals during the period of military dictatorship which followed Bethmann's dismissal was not much different.[55] And even far more respectable figures than Hasse or the generals had developed from time to time grandiose schemes for the reconstitution of Eastern Europe.[56] Moreover, given Germany's geographic position, constricted as she was in the heart of Central Europe, an eastward move was the only way in which Germany could gain the requisite continental hinterland to join Britain, with her overseas realm, and America, with its continental base, as world powers.[57] Finally, and perhaps most importantly, the very dynamics of the chaotic Führer-State itself dictated eastward expansion, for only here could the aspiring Nazi imperialist find the social *tabula rasa* which would enable them to escape the tensions which they experienced living in the dual society of Germany. In this sense, the Nazi entrepreneurs may have sensed the same thing that many nineteenth-century statesmen, concerned about the impact of overseas adventure on the established national state at home, had instinctively been aware of – that a new expansion movement 'could only destroy the body politic of the nation state'.[58] For many a National Socialist visionary, steeped in the millenarian vision of a racial empire and disgusted with the flaws in traditional German national life, the image of destruction might well have been an attractive one.

But whatever the compulsions of logic might have been, they represented Nazi logic, not that of the British leaders. Hitler might draw all the admiring parallels he wanted between the British Empire in India and the coming German Empire in Russia, the British would never have been ready (even had they been aware of the exact nature of Hitler's vision) to accept the 'leap' which the Germans had taken. On the contrary, British leaders, with very few exceptions,[59] insisted on placing German aspirations within the strictures both of the traditional European continental balance of power system, and within the system of national self-determination for all peoples established by Wilson in 1918 (although eventually the British by and large backed down on the second, as the Munich Agreement attests).

There was, thus, a stability to British society and in the backgrounds of her leaders over the decades which permitted an evolutionary change in viewing the international relations that was by and large lacking in the much more unstable German society, where a new political élite emerged, armed with apocalyptic visions, animated by a sense of radical mobility and equipped with a set of nineteenth-century imperial ideas.

The disintegration of German society produced a dynamic and radical movement which spilled over into foreign expansion and threatened to overturn established international relationships. The Nazis were abetted in their challenge to the *status quo* by the fact that the traditional international Great Power system itself was in disintegration. The British statesmen, who were confronting the Nazi challenge, were hindered in doing so by the fact that they had one foot in the old system (that of European balance of power and imperial preservation) and one in the new (national self-determination and collective security). As a result, they fell between the stools. Neither approach worked in dealing with the Nazis, because their challenge was too radical to be kept within either system. When the British tried to deal in postwar terms, calling, for example, for the integrity of Austria and Czechoslovakia, they encountered refusal by Nazis who were thinking at the very least of German domination of Central Europe. When they tried to deal in prewar terms, resorting to the Congress system, as they did at Munich, then their success was only temporary, for Nazi ambitions were great enough to make the balance of power concept itself anachronistic. Indeed, the very fact that the Munich Conference, probably the last example of the European Congress system at work, appears to us today as such a shabby betrayal and disgraceful interlude indicates the extent to which both the ideas of Wilson and Lenin as well as the challenge of Nazism had made it outmoded in 1938.

Notes: Chapter 3

1 The list includes the following publications, but does not exhaust the field by any means: K. Hildebrand, *Deutsche Aussenpolitik 1933–1945 Kalkül oder Dogma?* (Stuttgart, 1973); and *Vom Reich zum Weltreich. Hitler, NSDAP und koloniale Frage 1919–1945* (Munich, 1969); A. Hillgruber, *Deutsche Grossmacht- und Weltmachtpolitik im 19. und 20. Jahrhundert* (Düsseldorf, 1977); E. Jaeckel, *Hitlers Weltanschauung. Entwurf einer Herrschaft* (Tübingen, 1969); G. Weinberg, *The Foreign Policy of Hitler's Germany* (Chicago, Ill., 1979); also three excellent compendiums: M. Funke (ed.), *Hitler, Deutschland und die Mächte* (Düsseldorf, 1976); W. Michalka (ed.), *Nationalsozialistische Aussenpolitik* (Darmstadt, 1978); and G. Ziebura (ed.), *Grundfragen der deutschen Aussenpolitik seit 1871* (Darmstadt, 1975).
2 One impetus for this study was a series of questions posed by Hillgruber in his essay 'Kontinuität und Diskontinuität in der deutschen Aussenpolitik von Bismark bis Hitler', in Ziebura, *Aussenpolitik*, p. 19.
3 Several recent essays have addressed themselves to this question, including K. Hildebrand, 'Innenpolitische Antriebskräfte der nationalsozialistischen Aussenpolitik', in Michalka, *Nationalsozialistische Aussenpolitik*, pp. 175–200; T. Mason, 'Zur Funktion des Angriffskrieges 1939', in Ziebura, *Aussenpolitik*, pp. 376–416; and, examining an earlier period, E. Kehr, 'Englandhass und Weltpolitik. Eine Studie über die innenpolitischen- und sozialen Grundlagen der deutschen Aussenpolitik um die Jahrhundertwende', in ibid., pp. 132–62.
4 See, among many other studies, W. Pedwaidic, *Die authoritäre Anarchie. Streiflichter des deutschen Zusammenbruchs* (Hamburg, 1946); or more recently, R. Bollmus, *Das Amt Rosenberg und seine Gegner. Zum Machtkampf im nationalsozialistischen Herrschaftssystem* (Stuttgart, 1970).
5 On the theme of the disintegration of German society, see T. Mason's essay 'Der Primat der Politik – Politik und Wirtschaft im Nationalsozialismus', *Das Argument*, vol. 8 (1966), pp. 473–94; also M. Broszat, 'Soziale Motivation und Führer-Bindung des Nationalsozialismus', *Vierteljahrshefte für Zeitgeschichte*, vol. 18 (1970), pp. 392–409; R. Dahrendorf, *Society and Democracy in Germany* (New York, 1979), pp. 381–96; D. Schoenbaum, *Hitler's Social Revolution* (New York, 1967), esp. pp. 234–88; T. Parsons, 'Democracy and social structure in pre-Nazi Germany', in *Essays in Sociological Theory*, rev. edn (Glencoe, Ill., 1954), pp. 104–24, in which the author concentrates on malintegration, tension and strain in the social structure. Most recently, see J. Rhodes, *The Hitler Movement, a Modern Millenarian Movement* (Stanford, Calif., 1980), which views the disintegration of German society as so far-reaching in terms of loss of material comfort, loss of predictability and loss of permanence, that the Nazi response to it took on the dimensions of a modern millenarian movement. Though Rhodes is unwarranted in his rather monistic approach, he is right in singling out the utopian and apocalyptic tendencies which are internalised in Nazis at all levels. They play an important part in the dynamic of the regime.
6 Dahrendorf notes with respect to Weimar, 'the political elite, in the sense of the leadership

of parties and parliaments, has been one of the few upwardly mobile groups in the German upper classes' (*Society and Democracy*, p. 249).

7 ibid., p. 296.
8 E. Fraenkel, *The Dual State. A Contribution to the Theory of Dictatorship* (New York, 1941), pp. 68–9.
9 This sense of omnicompetence seems to have permeated very deeply into society. R. Heberle, *From Democracy to Nazism* (Baton Rouge, La, 1945), p. 120, quotes a peasant who said: 'We believe that in the Third Reich, we, the farmers, will be so strong a power that we can shape it as we desire.'
10 See S. Wolin, *Politics and Vision. Continuity and Vision in Western Political Thought* (Boston, Mass., 1960), ch. 10; G. Mosca, *The Ruling Class* (New York, 1939); K. Mannheim, *Freedom, Power and Democratic Planning* (New York, 1950), ch. 3; and T. Lowi, *The End of Liberalism. Ideology, Policy and the Crisis of Public Authority* (New York, 1969). One of Lowi's observations applies particularly well to the Nazi regime: 'Government that is unlimited in scope but formless in action is government that cannot plan. Government that is formless in action and immoral in intention (i.e. ad hoc) is government that can neither plan nor achieve justice' (p. x).
11 See F. Stern, *The Failure of Illiberalism* (Chicago, Ill., 1955).
12 It is important to note the depth of this phenomenon. It did not occur solely at higher levels, but permeated the entire system. H. Mommsen, *Beamtentum im Dritten Reich* (Stuttgart, 1966), p. 22, notes that the Ämtereroberung on the part of the Nazis after January 1933, 'vor allem in der kommunalen Selbstverwaltung und den Landkreisen vollzog sich spontan und entbehrte eines einheitlichen Konzepts'.
13 It is interesting to note that one British observer, Lord Halifax, took notice of this variety of activities, but in his curious, dispassionate way both missed its significance and trivialised the violence which permitted Goering his range of jurisdictions. 'I was immensely entertained at meeting the man. One remembered all the time that he had been concerned with the "clean-up" in Berlin on June 30, 1934 and I wondered how many people he had been responsible for getting killed . . . A modern Robin Hood: producing on me a complete impression of film-star, gangster, great landowner, interested in his property, Prime Minister, Party manager, head gamekeeper at Chatsworth.' Quoted in K. Middlemas, *The Strategy of Appeasement* (Chicago, Ill., 1972), p. 61.
14 Long ago, D. Lerner, *The Nazi Elite* (Stanford, Calif., 1951), pp. 14, 34–6, noted the combination of marginal petit bourgeois plebeians, who had risen with the regime, and the sizeable number of survivors from the old regime who populated the officer corps, civil service and other institutions.
15 This contention needs to be demonstrated by further prosopographical studies of Nazi organisations. In the meantime, a number of peaks attest to the existence of an iceberg. Himmler's continuing wonder at the frantic ambition of his deputy head of the Volksdeutsche Mittelstelle, Hermann Behrends, and his telling observation that had Behrends been in the other world he would have been a *Staatssekretär* is one example. See H. Heiber (ed.), *Reichsführer! Briefe an und von Himmler* (Stuttgart, 1968), p. 172. But it was not only at the higher levels that such tensions were in evidence. As one of the countless trustees put in charge of confiscated estates in the east remarked to the former aristocratic owner, he (the trustee) was in charge even if his name was Kleinschmidt and not *von* Kleinschmidt. Letter from Fritz von Hertzberg to RKFDV Staff Main Office, 14 February 1940, National Archives Microcopy T-74, Roll 6, Frames 37693–65. This mixture of old class system and new Nazi system can be seen in microcosm in the *Freundeskreis Himmler* and the resulting tension in the career of its presiding director, Fritz Kranefuss. See R. Vogelsang, *Der Freundeskreis Himmler* (Göttingen, 1972), pp. 78, 138.
16 See J. Heineman, *Hitler's First Foreign Minister* (Berkeley, Calif., 1979), pp. 126, 131; also H.-A. Jacobsen, *Nationalsozialistische Aussenpolitik* (Frankfurt/M., 1968), pp. 252–318. Büro Ribbentrop became Dienststelle Ribbentrop in 1935.
17 H. Arendt has sensed this same need to displace domestic tensions abroad in nineteenth-century imperialists. 'The truth was that only far from home could a citizen of England, Germany or France be nothing but an Englishman or German or Frenchman. In his own country he was so entangled in economic interests or social loyalties that he felt closer to a member of his class in a foreign country than to a man of another class in his own.' *Origins of Totalitarianism*, new edn (New York, 1966), p. 154. One should also note that tension in

Nazi society can also have arisen from the paradoxical fact that for all the competition there was a great deal of stagnation in the upper levels of the Nazi élite (Dahrendorf, *Society and Democracy*, p. 216).

18 For a summary of Hitler's 'programme' see Hildebrand, 'Hitlers *Programm* und seine Realisierung 1939–1942', in Funke, *Hitler, Deutschland und die Mächte*, pp. 63–93.

19 Quoted in Heineman, *Hitler's First Foreign Minister*, p. 117.

20 Quoted in W. Michalka, 'Die nationalsozialistische Aussenpolitik im Zeichen eines *Konzeptionen-Pluralismus* – Fragestellungen und Forschungsaufgaben', in Funke, *Hitler, Deutschland und die Mächte*, pp. 46–62.

21 Quoted in Heineman, *Hitler's First Foreign Minister*, p. 117.

22 Quoted in J. G. Leithäuser, *Diplomatie auf schiefer Bahn* (Berlin, 1953), p. 19.

23 Jacobsen (*Nationalsozialistische Aussenpolitik*) gives an excellent analysis of the structure of Nazi foreign policy.

24 See D. McKale, *The Swastika outside Germany* (Akron, Ohio, 1977), p. 46. McKale also notes the tension which existed between Nazi party people and German diplomats abroad arising out of the two worlds in which they lived (p. 60).

25 For Himmler's vision of the future society that would be created by a Nazi policy of conquest in the East see J. Ackermann, *Heinrich Himmler als Ideologe* (Göttingen, 1970), pp. 195–231.

26 On Rosenberg's aspirations see Jacobsen, *Nationalsozialistische Aussenpolitik*, pp. 449–52, 483–95.

27 For a report projecting the possibilities for the Propaganda Ministry to exert influence abroad see Hasenörhl, 10 January 1939, in Politisches Archiv des Auswärtigen Amtes, Bonn, Dienststelle Ribbentrop, 14/1. Generally on Goebbels' role in foreign policy see Jacobsen, *Nationalsozialistische Aussenpolitik*, pp. 360, 377, 380, 393, 436, 452, 456, 460.

28 On Goering see ibid., pp. 358, 361, 398, 410, 423, 429, 433–40.

29 On Rosenberg's interests in Hungary and Romania see ibid., pp. 79–84.

30 For an overview of Ribbentrop's English role see Weinberg, *Foreign Policy*, pp. 202–15, 271–93. Jacobsen gives a detailed analysis of Ribbentrop's apparatus, pp. 252–318.

31 For a discussion of the various paths which led the SS-SD into foreign policy see R. Smelser, *The Sudeten Problem 1933–1938* (Middletown, Conn., 1975), ch. VIII; also H. Höhne, *The Order of the Death's Head* (New York, 1971), ch. XI.

32 This was especially true in the world of *Volkstumspolitik* (see Smelser, *The Sudeten Problem*).

33 I. J. Edinger, 'Continuity and change in the background of German decision-makers', in *The Western Political Quarterly*, vol. XIV (1961), p. 28, asserts that the number of German diplomats who were aristocrats had dropped from 89 per cent in 1906 to 42 per cent in 1926, but had risen again to 61 per cent in 1936. The higher ranks of the SS also had a disproportionate number of titled aristocrats (Höhne, *The Order of the Death's Head*, p. 153); Schoenbaum (*Hitler's Social Revolution*, p. 279), in fact, sees the SS as a bridge for the old élite into the Third Reich.

34 See Weinberg, *Foreign Policy*, pp. 87–106; for an overview see J. Gehl, *Austria, Germany and the Anschluss 1931–1938* (London, 1963).

35 For an extended discussion of Hitler's leadership style, see Jacobsen, *Nationalsozialistische Aussenpolitik*, pp. 319–80.

36 My emphasis on the dynamic structure of the system and its benefits to Hitler is somewhat at odds, for example, with that of J. Dülffer, who chooses to emphasise Hitler's initiative and minimise the impact of competing Nazi organisations. See 'Zum *decision-making process* in der deutschen Aussenpolitik', in Funke, *Hitler, Deutschland und die Mächte*, pp. 186–204.

37 Hildebrand notes that up to a point there is a dovetailing between Hitler's initial plans and the long-term ones of his conservative opponents. Then, however, 'the Program which had originally served both Hitler and his conservative helpers now moved toward its fulfillment with an almost automatic momentum'. See *The Foreign Policy of the Third Reich*, trans. A. Fothergill (Berkeley, Calif., 1973), pp. 97–8. I am suggesting that the pressure created by the dynamic nature of the Nazi system engendered in part that 'almost automatic momentum' that Hildebrand mentions.

38 On Halifax's proposals as noted by the Germans see Schmidt Aufzeichnung, 19 November

1937, in *Akten zur Deutschen Auswärtigen Politik*, series D, vol. 1, no. 31 (Baden-Baden, 1949); also Middlemas, *The Strategy of Appeasement*, pp. 133–6.

39 See Niederschrift über die Besprechung in der Reichskanzlei am 5. November 1937 vom 16:15 bis 20:30, ibid., no. 19.

40 Broszat ('Soziale Motivation', p. 100) sees the resignation of Schacht as marking the end of the political *Mitbestimmung* of big business; Mason ('Der Primat der Politik', p. 145) sees the period 1929–33 as the disintegration of German bourgeois society, while the period 1936–9 marks the disintegration of German capitalism.

41 For an overview of the Fritsch–Blomberg crisis see A. Bullock, *Hitler, A Study in Tyranny*, rev. edn (New York, 1961), pp. 361–7; and A. J. P. Taylor, *The Origins of the Second World War* (New York, 1963), pp. 128–30, who provides the most iconoclastic interpretation.

42 Smelser, *The Sudeten Problem*, pp. 201–2.

43 ibid., p. 205.

44 See I. Colvin, *The Chamberlain Cabinet* (New York, 1971), p. 91.

45 It is interesting to note that precisely at the point where Chamberlain was concocting grandiose plans for territorial adjustments in Africa during the first weeks of January 1938 (Middlemas, *The Strategy of Appeasement*, pp. 141–3), Ribbentrop, sensing his master's intentions, was submitting a memorandum advocating violent expansion to the East and a possible war with France and Britain (Notiz für den Führer, 7 January 1938, ADAP, D, I, no. 93).

46 For an enlightening discussion of the political/philosophical background of appeasement see M. Gilbert, *The Roots of Appeasement* (New York, 1966), esp. ch. I.

47 On the changes in British attitude and practice with regard to the empire see R. von Albertini, 'The impact of two world wars on the decline of colonialism', *Journal of Contemporary History*, vol. 4, no. 1 (1969), pp. 17–36; D. McIntyre, *The Commonwealth of Nations. Origins and Impact 1869–1971* (Minneapolis, Minn., 1977), pp. 181–243; N. Mansergh, *The Commonwealth Experience* (London, 1969), chs 9 and 10; and J. Morris, *Farewell the Trumpets. An Imperial Retreat* (London, 1978), V and XIII.

48 On the meaning of this book see B. Parry, *Delusions and Discoveries. Studies on India in the British Imagination* (Berkeley, Calif., 1972), pp. 26–7; Arendt, *Origins of Totalitarianism*, p. 216.

49 We see here an ideological survival made possible by a social lag. One is reminded of a similar phenomenon within the otherwise very different context of America's proselytising abroad. Baptists and other evangelical denominations, which by and large are representative of the middle and lower-middle strata, are still sending missionaries abroad with many nineteenth-century attitudes out of place in an age of national liberation. The Episcopalians and Unitarians, which typically represent the upper strata, were, by contrast, very active in missionary work during the nineteenth century, but have now largely abandoned the 'white man's burden' for more cosmopolitan, secular forms of aiding their fellow man.

50 Quoted in Arendt, *Origins of Totalitarianism*, p. 189.

51 It was Salisbury who described Chamberlain as a 'Sicilian bandit' and Granville as the greatest jingo. See R. Rhodes James, *The British Revolution: 1880–1939* (New York, 1977), pp. 167, 64.

52 Hillgruber hints at this sort of *Sprung* in the area of *Vernichtungspolitik*, a leap made by the Germans but not others with a similar colonial/political background (*Deutsche Grossmachtund Weltmachtpolitik*, p. 42).

53 That these plans and visions were not just envisioned by those at the top in Berlin is attested to by the fact that in early 1938 Gauleiter Röver of Oldenburg confided in a German diplomat that within ten years the East as far as the Baltic states and the Caucasus would become new settlement territory for the Germans (Jacobsen, *Nationalsozialistische Aussenpolitik*, p. 356).

54 Taken from his *Deutsche Politik*, vol. 1: *Das Deutsche Reich als Nationalstaat, 1905*, p. 62 (cited in Arendt, *Origins of Totalitarianism*, p. 223, n. 8).

55 D. Calleo in his recent study *The German Problem Reconsidered* (Cambridge, 1978), p. 48, notes that 'increasingly absent from German calculations [during World War One] was any conception of a general balance, or of the necessity of leaving other countries some acceptable role and situation in the interests of long-range peace. Europe was to be treated

by the Germans as India or Africa had been by the British.' This suggests an element of continuity in German policy.

56 Friedrich Meinecke, himself no supporter of the more radical annexationists could nevertheless write to W. Goetz on 6 May 1915: 'Bez. unserer östlichen Wünsche kommt mehr und mehr ein Gedanke auf, der in dieser oder jener Gestalt vielleicht fruchtbar ist: Russland soll uns da oder dort Land abtreten ohne Menschen. Die Menschen nimmt es in sein Inneres und gibt uns dafür die Wolgadeutschen. Vor allem aber brauchen wir mehr Raum für innere Kolonisation. Meine Idee war schon längst: einen Teil des polnischen Grossgrundbesitzes nach dem uns als autonomen Staat anzugliedernden Kongresspolen zu verpflanzen und dadurch den deutschen Charakter Posens und Westpreussens fest-zulegen. Aber kann nicht auch Kurland, einem autonomen Polen vorgelagert, für uns brauchbar werden als bäuerliches Kolonisationsland, wenn wir die Letten nach Russland abschieben?' See L. Dehio and P. Claasen (eds), *Friedrich Meinecke, Werke*, Vol. VI: *Ausgewählter Briefwechsel* (Stuttgart, 1962), pp. 58–9.

57 Calleo, *The German Problem Reconsidered*, ch. X, explores precisely this logic.

58 Arendt, *Origins of Totalitarianism*, p. 125.

59 One of them was the 'super appeaser', Neville Henderson. In a memorandum composed shortly before his appointment as Ambassador in Berlin he wrote: '[Eastern Europe] emphatically is neither settled for all time nor is it a vital British interest, and the German is certainly more civilised than the Slav, and in the end, if properly handled, also potentially less dangerous to British interests – one might even go so far as to assert that it is not even just to endeavour to prevent Germany from completing her unity or from being prepared for war against the Slav, provided her preparations are such as to reassure the British Empire that they are not simultaneously designed against it.' But then, as Eden's private secretary, Oliver Harvey, said of Henderson: 'I hope we are not sending another Ribbentrop to Berlin.' (Quoted in Middlemas, *The Strategy of Appeasement*, pp. 73–4.)

4 Conflicts within the German Leadership on the Objectives and Tactics of German Foreign Policy, 1933–9

WOLFGANG MICHALKA

'Halifax's visit to Germany is a new proof of the anomalies in the Reich's foreign policy. Too many cocks in the henhouse. There are at least four foreign policies – Hitler's, Goering's, Neurath's, Ribbentrop's. Without counting the minor ones. It is difficult to co-ordinate them all properly.'[1] This is how the generally well-informed Italian Foreign Minister, Count Ciano, described the foreign policy of National Socialist Germany towards the end of 1937. Ciano's comments, by no means the only example of such an opinion,[2] are in contradiction to Hitler's own image of himself, since in his opinion he, and he alone, was responsible for foreign affairs; for example, even Joachim von Ribbentrop, Foreign Minister from 1938, had to confess frankly to the French Ambassador in Berlin, Robert Coulondre: 'The policy I follow is not mine but the Führer's.'[3] This has largely been confirmed by historical research as there is general consensus of opinion that German foreign policy between 1933 and 1945 was determined and directed in all essentials by Adolf Hitler.[4]

In examining possible dissent within the German leadership about the objectives and tactics of German foreign policy, the following consideration must be borne in mind: reference has been made to Ciano's views on German foreign policy in order to point out the difficulties one faces in assessing this policy. And this is true not only of Ciano's time; for the contemporary observers did not necessarily see Hitler as the sole, uncontested decision-maker of German policy. On the contrary, Hitler appeared to be sandwiched between rival groups who advocated divergent lines of (foreign) policy, so much so that it was not always clear who was actually determining and controlling German foreign policy.[5] This heterogeneous aspect of National Socialist foreign policy, characterised by conflict within the leadership, left its mark on information reaching the outside world and influenced other states' policy *vis-à-vis* the Reich. Consequently, an attempt to differentiate and analyse the various foreign policy concepts of the Third Reich's ruling élite promises to shed some light on the external image of National Socialist Germany at that time, the political strategies developed on the basis of this image and, finally, on the foreign policy of those states confronted and threatened by Hitler's Germany. This provides an appropriate basis for assessing whether British appeasement policy can be considered realistic and effective. With this in mind the following questions are to be examined:

(1) Which objectives and tactics were developed and put into practice by which groups in the leadership?
(2) How and to what extent could these alternative policies exert influence and so determine the course of National Socialist foreign policy?
(3) To what extent did the leading conservatives co-operate with National Socialist decision-makers?; and finally
(4) To which traditions in German policy did these alternative policies appeal?

When Hitler was appointed Chancellor of a Cabinet of 'national unity' on 30 January 1933, Germany was pursuing with greater energy than before a policy of revisionism. The effects of the world depression in the Danubian Basin and the Balkans provided new prospects, both economically and politically.[6] Whereas problems in the West had previously been given absolute priority, from now on Eastern and south-eastern Europe also emerged on the landscape of German politicians. After the Rhineland had been evacuated of Allied occupation troops, it now seemed as if revisionist objectives could also be achieved in the east. Traditional German plans for Central Europe were revived; now, however, they were to be implemented primarily in their relation to economic and commercial aspects. The appropriate panacea for solving the economic crisis from now on seemed to be a large economic unit controlled and dominated by the German Reich with the aim of regaining the Great Power status enjoyed by Germany before the First World War.

Parallel to these economic strategies which were being developed and partly initiated by them in the wake of the slump, the successors of Gustav Stresemann tried to solve the reparations issue in Germany's favour by means of a calculated policy of energetic revisionism. Heinrich Brüning hoped 'within one-and-a-half to two years' to use reparations as a means of 'making the whole Treaty of Versailles rock to its foundations without even talking about it'.[7] Brüning's successors were to reap what he had sown: a final regulation of the reparations question and the formal recognition of Germany's 'equality of status'. This newly gained freedom of action in foreign affairs was particularly apparent in the field of disarmament. Berlin's ultimatum and withdrawal from the Geneva Disarmament Conference at the end of 1932 was part of a political tactic which subsequently led to the withdrawal of the German Reich from both the League of Nations and the Disarmament Conference in October 1933. For since 1930 at the latest there had been agreement both in the Wilhelmstrasse and the Bendlerstrasse that the League of Nations was more obstructive than beneficial to Germany's aims of revising the Treaty of Versailles. In view of this new style in German revisionism, 30 January 1933 – the day of the so-called 'seizure of power by the National Socialists' – did not initially represent a break with German foreign policy in previous years. The 'Führer' of the National Socialist mass movement had his 'hands tied' as Chancellor of the German Reich by the majority of conservative ministers in his Cabinet, and it was therefore considered that he had been 'tamed'.[8] This attempt at 'taming' Hitler seemed to be particularly effective in the sphere of foreign affairs. Baron Constantin von Neurath, Foreign Minister in the Papen and Schleicher Cabinets, remained in office and indeed the staff of the Foreign Ministry remained virtually unchanged until 1938.[9] At this time there was consensus between the National Socialists and the representatives of nearly all political, economic and military decision-makers so far as the objectives and methods of Germany's revisionist foreign policy were concerned.

After the *de facto* solution of the financial and economic problem of reparations, the next step towards the definitive revision of the Treaty of Versailles was to be intensive military rearmament. 'In the lee of a conservative revisionist policy'[10] Hitler endeavoured to lay the necessary domestic foundations for the realisation of his foreign policy 'programme', while at the same time allaying the fears of foreign powers about Germany's intentions. In doing so he had a surprising degree of success – not least because his foreign and rearmament policies[11] served to stabilise the system, by integrating the various interest groups[12] – the Foreign Ministry, economic circles, the *Reichswehr* and also the NSDAP institutions on foreign affairs (set up particularly in the early years of his Chancellorship) – into his 'programme', thereby assuring for himself the support of these groups.

In view of this apparent agreement on objectives in foreign policy, which was no doubt reinforced by Hitler's initial reserve in this field, the opening years of the Third Reich were characterised by a series of in part contradictory strategies on policy. This debate about the nature of future German policy was typical of the initial phase of Hitler's rule.

The declaration of principle by Reich Foreign Minister, von Neurath, in Cabinet on 7 April 1933[13] can be seen as the first binding statement on the course German foreign policy should pursue since the Nazi take-over. It corresponded with the views on foreign policy advocated by a majority of the staff of the Foreign Office, economic interest groups, the *Reichswehr* and conservative political parties and also reflected the views on foreign affairs put forward by the right wing of the NSDAP. This guideline on foreign policy originated with Bernhard von Bülow, Under-Secretary of State at the Foreign Office since 1930 and without doubt the most important decision-maker in German foreign policy throughout this period of transition.[14]

This analysis was based on the common conviction that, despite the diplomatic isolation and political weakness of the German Reich at the beginning of 1933, a revival of Germany's fortunes was nevertheless on its way.[15] It can clearly be seen that the staff of the Foreign Office were endeavouring to develop an independent line of foreign policy for the coming years, in contrast – indeed quite contrary – to the 'programme' of their new Chancellor which had been received with such suspicion, especially abroad.[16] By means of a cautious but resolutely conducted foreign policy they wanted, on the one hand, to shield from the outside world ('abschirmen') what was happening inside Germany in the name of *Gleichschaltung*;[17] on the other hand, they aimed to revive the Foreign Office as the decisive instrument of foreign policy – a trend which is to be interpreted as a reaction to the less ambitious outlook of the *Wilhelmstrasse* under Stresemann, Brüning and Papen.[18]

As far as Weimar's revisionist policy was concerned the Treaty of Versailles provided the frame of reference which both restricted and defined German foreign policy. The most vital task therefore had to be its definitive revision.[19] Given the military weakness of the Reich this involved above all taking advantage of the opportunity to 'instrumentalise' by means of economic action the crisis facing the world economic order: 'Above all the central position of Germany, the interest of the creditor nations in a sound German economy and the skilfull deployment of Germany's economic potential in specific spheres of foreign trade should be used to our advantage to ensure the rapid rise of Germany to a leading position scarcely conceivable before the World Depression set in.'[20] Such a view was very reminiscent of the political calculating of Stresemann and Brüning; unlike them, however, Bülow and Neurath used the economy only as a means of paving the way for future German policy. Accordingly they left no doubt about the fact that the territorial revision of the Treaty of Versailles was the cornerstone of their objective in foreign policy. Of central importance was the 'revision of the eastern borders, aiming at the recovery of all the Polish territories in question and rejecting all forms of partial or transitional solutions'.[21] The following statement plainly illustrates the clear-cut distinction between Stresemann's views on the one hand and those of Bülow and Neurath on the other: 'There shall only be one more partition of Poland.'[22] A policy which envisaged a fourth partition of Poland can by no means be regarded as a mere revision of the Treaty of Versailles and re-establishment of the frontiers of 1914; it was much more closely related to the war aims and the territorial expansion of the victorious German Reich in the east in 1917–18 under the terms of the Treaty of Brest-Litovsk.

However, Bülow and Neurath's 'revisionist' objectives were not just restricted to the German borders in the east; they were also aimed at a revision of the boundary of Schleswig and Denmark, the recovery of Malmedy and in the longer term a settlement of the Alsace-Lorraine question. Thereafter the recovery of previous German colonies was also to be tackled. And ultimately attention was to be turned towards the *Anschluss* of Austria with the Reich. Alongside these 'traditional' objectives new perspectives were indicated ranging much further than the aims of a revisionist policy, and pointing to the next phase in German foreign policy. Neurath said that 'the strengthening of Germany was to be encouraged in all directions'. We can only speculate as to what he meant by this but he expressly called for the opening up of new markets, while hoping to prevent the industrialisation of agrarian countries.[23] In this context the *Auslandsdeutschtum* – German culture and Germans living outside the Reich – were to play a major role.[24]

The above-mentioned foreign policy strategies associated with leading figures in the Foreign Office are linked to the traditional schemes for *Mitteleuropa*[25] which despite defeat and the Reich's greatly reduced position as a Great Power had never been completely written off. These objectives partially overlapped those of Hitler.

However, at this stage there was already evidence of a qualitative disagreement between conservative politicians and the National Socialist Führer, namely, on the assessment and appraisal of the Soviet Union and of Poland. Bülow and Neurath, whose arguments were in line with traditional Weimar foreign policy, Rudolf Nadolny,[26] at this time head of the German delegation at the Geneva Disarmament Conference, and the then German Ambassador in Moscow, Herbert von Dirksen,[27] all considered Soviet backing indispensable for their policy *vis-à-vis* Poland. Political, economic and military relations between both partners were so good that they tried to persuade Hitler that 'as the Italian example shows an out-and-out struggle against communists and "cultural Bolshevism" need not necessarily impair German-Russian relations for ever'.[28] This plea for close German-Soviet co-operation was in stark contrast to Hitler's views on Russia which were inspired by racial ideology and ultimately aimed at the extermination of the Russian population and the colonisation of the vast territory of the Soviet Union. Hitler saw the enemy, not in Poland, but in 'Jewish, Bolshevist Russia'.

These conflicting ideas clashed during discussion with the Führer on 26 September 1933 and as a result Rudolf Nadolny felt obliged to resign the following year as German Ambassador in Moscow.[29] This dissension clearly illustrated that the initial agreement between Hitler and conservative leaders on foreign policy was only partial and of short-term duration.[30] In the initial phase of National Socialist rule, however, a revisionist policy, pursued at least since the time of Brüning with greater vigour, and a revival of Wilhelmine foreign policy provided a common platform on which both conservative decision-makers and the National Socialists could develop and apply their foreign policy.

At this time the Foreign Ministry, the Army Command, the Admiralty, industrialists and economic circles as well as National Socialist politicians were all anxious to secure British assistance in implementing their apparently common aims. London appeared to be much more favourably inclined than Paris towards Berlin's revisionist demands. The disarmament negotiations in the years 1932–4 were proof of this. Hitler's countless declarations of goodwill towards Britain,[31] Rosenberg's efforts towards an Anglo-German understanding (albeit somewhat dampened by his débâcle in London in May 1933),[32] Ribbentrop's 'private diplomacy' at the end of 1933 and the beginning of 1934[33] – all were evidence of Berlin's wish to stay on good terms with London. However, this wooing of Great Britain, which for Hitler was of central importance for future German policy, was viewed by conservative politicians with much more sceptical and dubious eyes[34] than Hitler and his closest advisers cared to admit. The Admiralty in particular, which in the Weimar Republic had already followed the British example in its attempts to expand naval strength in the lee of Great Britain,[35] warned of exaggerated and unrealistic hopes and of having to pay too high a price for an Anglo-German alliance however desirable it might be. As with the case of Poland and Russia, so also *vis-à-vis* Britain, a divergence of opinion in the objectives and tactics to be followed soon became evident. However, Hitler and his ideas finally won the day; the signing of the Anglo-German Naval

Agreement on 18 June 1935 marked his first widely acclaimed triumph in foreign affairs. Hitler now considered Ribbentrop, head of the German delegation in London negotiating this agreement, an expert on British affairs.[36]

Nevertheless, despite this success in diplomacy, conservative circles, and in particular those representing economic interests, had other ideas. Hjalmar Schacht, for example, who described himself as a 'fervent champion of the course of colonial policy'[37] and an advocate of a 'governmental–liberal course of policy',[38] was of the opinion that the stimulation of foreign trade would be particularly effective for the aggrandisement of the German Reich.[39] In his view in order to promote foreign trade the acquisition of colonies remained a central factor since there was no simpler solution to the problem of 'old states bursting at the seams'.[40] It was therefore only logical that Schacht had been aiming at good Anglo-German relations since 1933 – for without the consent of Great Britain it seemed impossible for the German economy to 'move freely into the former German overseas territories and begin economic operations'.[41] Schacht's numerous demands regarding colonies[42] reflect his chief aim which was ultimately[43] to achieve colonial revision with the peaceful consent of Britain.[44]

His ideas brought Schacht close to the Foreign Office[45] and, given the revisionist theories of Neurath and Bülow, they did not fall on deaf ears. Therefore the common interests of the 'politically nationalist, economically free enterprise orientated grande bourgeoisie', for which Schacht was, so to speak, spokesman,[46] and the conservative groups in the Wilhelmstrasse, found expression not only in their congruent political philosophy, but also in their mutual opposition to Hitler's policy. Indeed, although the Führer, the Foreign Office and financial and economic circles around Schacht were all aiming at an understanding with Britain, there was nevertheless a wide gulf between Hitler and the conservatives on the tactics, line of approach and long-term objectives of such a policy: Hitler wanted to secure an entente with the British by renouncing colonial interests, in order to gain a free hand in Europe, whereas the conservatives wanted to pursue colonial interests while refraining from action in Europe.[47] Thus the wide-ranging differences between Hitler and his traditional-minded economic advisers specifically came to light over the colonial issue; in this disagreement we can see the first signs of later conflict. The same discrepancy between objectives and tactics was also to arise in Ribbentrop's policy in the years 1937–8. Meanwhile, however, Hitler could hope that 'Schacht's economic approach to German aggrandisement would be of considerable advantage as a preparation for his own aims'.[48] For Schacht's policy was anchored in the so-called 'New Plan', based on the bilateralisation of trade, which was to provide a new framework for the reorganisation of German foreign trade from September 1934.[49]

The 'New Plan' was accepted by Great Britain shortly after its announcement. London showed its readiness to negotiate and in an Anglo-German payment agreement on 1 November 1934[50] declared itself willing to recognise the bilateral principle of the 'New Plan' in an international treaty.[51] This payment agreement can be seen as an economic 'peace treaty'[52] and marks the end of a period of conflict since 1933 in the trading and financial relations of both countries.[53] Moreover, British willingness to compromise seemed to nourish the well-founded hope that the economic agreement could 'also provide the basis for lasting relations in the political sphere'.[54] To a certain extent the 'New Plan' ran parallel to Hitler's attempts to extend the scope of German action in the diplomatic field on the same basis of bilateral agreements. So, alongside the Anglo-German Naval Agreement, Germany had also succeeded in reaching a bilateral entente with Britain on foreign trade.

It seemed as if even Hitler was gradually becoming converted to this policy. Whereas in the years up to 1935 the colonial demands of leading economic circles were diametrically opposed to Hitler's willingness to compromise in this field, in 1936 the Führer for the first time publicly demanded the return of former German colonies. To all appearances – and presumably this is how contemporary observers interpreted these developments – Hitler had let himself be influenced by economic interests, above all by Ribbentrop's theories on colonial policy,[55] and had himself now fallen into line with traditional colonial revisionist demands.[56] It could hardly have been clear to contemporary observers[57] that Hitler had launched his colonial campaign solely for tactical reasons, and not in anticipation of the achievement of his 'ultimate aims'.[58] It cannot therefore be said that his 'new' approach to the colonial issue was due to pressure from industrialists interested in overseas trade.[59] This tactical deployment of colonial demands was based on his experience with Britain and this is what was essentially influencing his thoughts on colonial policy. Nevertheless Hitler's demands for territories overseas were also of considerable relevance for domestic politics. For it was precisely by putting forward these claims that the Führer articulated the demands and wishes of political and economic groups in Germany which since 1935 had been increasingly joining in the clamour for colonies,[60] and in this way skilfully integrated these groups into his 'programme'.[61]

In Britain such unanimous German claims for overseas territories did not go unheeded. Schacht, seen in Britain as 'an opponent of an uneconomical pace of rearmament and therefore indirectly acclaimed as an upholder of the peace',[62] helped, by proposing the return of Togoland and the Cameroons to Germany in the summer of 1936, to lead the British to cherish hopes that, if Britain gave in on the colonial issue, the Reich would be bound by international commitments[63] and could as a result be contained in Europe.[64]

However, only a few members of the British government had recognised the real intentions of the German dictator, and realised that 'in reality all Hitler wanted was a free hand on the continent'.[65] This can be seen particularly in the talks between Lord Halifax and Hitler at the end of 1937. It is striking to note that in Halifax's attempt to reach a general settlement with the Reich via a colonial settlement, the proposals put forward by the British politician corresponded exactly to the principle of peaceful revision of the Treaty of Versailles, both in Europe and overseas, long advocated by the staff of the Foreign Ministry and leading economic circles.[66] The fact, however, that the Halifax mission was nevertheless a failure shows exactly who was responsible for German foreign policy at this time and whose ideas were decisive in steering its course. Against the wishes of the Foreign Office and in opposition to the well-known views of economic interests, Hitler declined the British offer.

The dominant position held meanwhile by Hitler in respect of decisions on foreign policy, which made it possible for him to turn down Halifax's offer without regard for political and economic interest groups, becomes even more evident when we bear in mind that the competing theories on foreign policy put forward by national-conservative circles and by the National Socialists – for example, Goering – were in fact much more realistic and more likely to be achieved than the aims of Hitler's 'programme'.[67] Moreover, they corresponded not only to ideas in Great Britain, but also to widely held views in the Reich. The fact that Neurath and Schacht, or the interest groups they represented, were, nevertheless, not successful in enforcing their policy must be taken as proof of the steady decline in influence on the formulation of foreign policy of both economic circles and the Foreign Ministry since 1935.

Schacht's fate is particularly indicative of the decline in influence of economic circles on National Socialist foreign policy – which in any case had been minimal at the best of times. Schacht had previously safeguarded the right of the industrialists to manage the economy and guaranteed their links with policy-making, for his position was 'practically identical with that of heavy industry'.[68] He objected not only to the Four Year Plan's principle of autarky, which ran completely counter to his New Plan, but above all to the objective of belligerent expansion explicitly stipulated in this memorandum.[69] As long as Hitler kept up the appearance of following a revisionist policy – as economic circles must have assumed he was since the Führer left them in the dark on his expansionist ambitions[70] – and as long as his aim of regaining Great Power status for Germany corresponded to the interests of society as a whole, he could count on a national consensus for his policy. The Four Year Plan, however, especially in view of its belligerent implications, was in contradiction to Schacht's traditionally orientated economic policy and 'his so to speak "normal-imperialist" concept of the pre-eminence of the economic factor, as opposed to military expansion, as a vehicle for aggrandisement'.[71] The Economics Minister, therefore, began to head more and more for a collision course with Hitler. Schacht's resignation, or to be more precise, the Chancellor's 'estrangement' from his minister, illustrates that the Führer only tolerated rival concepts to his 'programme' if they posed no threat to his own far-reaching ambitions. Until 1936 the economic lobby around Schacht, which had opted for an Anglo-German entente and peaceful revisionism, had not prevented Hitler from following his own foreign policy – on the contrary. Now, however, the tables were turned. Until then revisionistic aims, allegedly identical, had served as a cloak for entirely different foreign policy concepts. Since Hitler had accelerated the realisation of his expansionist policy and was obviously no longer prepared to exclude the risk of war, the underlying divergence of opinions about the course of German foreign policy came to light. It turned out that Hitler's aim of westward expansion was out of the question for both the Foreign Ministry and the General Staff – at least at this stage – since such a policy would involve the risk of having to face Great Britain as an enemy. The same probably applied to the 'liberal economic expansionist' lobby around Schacht, even if we can assume that a limited degree of expansion to the east, such as the economic penetration of South-eastern Europe, could be reconciled with the interests of industrialists, constantly aiming at expansion.[72]

Throughout 1938, especially during the Sudeten crisis, the Führer found himself confronted by two conflicting camps, both trying to channel his decisions in their respective direction. On the one hand an '*ad hoc* action group'[73] had been formed around the under-secretary in the Foreign Office, Ernst von Weizsäcker, which included both Neurath and Goering and which enjoyed the sympathies of Schact and the army.[74] The common aim of these 'moderates'[75] was to avoid armed conflict with the Western powers at all costs and to solve the Sudetenland problem by a peaceful revision of frontiers in accordance with British appeasement policy. On the other hand, Ribbentrop, whose importance in the determination of foreign policy had increasingly gained ground since 1937 and particularly since he had taken over the Foreign Ministry from Neurath at the beginning of 1938, was prominent in the 'extremist' camp.

Originally convinced of the possibility of an Anglo-German alliance, Ribbentrop began to realise the futility of such a policy, in particular during his spell as German Ambassador at the court of St James's, when he gradually adopted an anti-British line. Accordingly he wanted to persuade Hitler to agree to a reorientation of his previous 'programmatic' British policy. The National Socialist 'British expert' argued that since London was not ready to accept the 'possibility that the previous balance of power in Europe might be upset', Germany was considered by Great Britain to be 'the most dangerous of all possible enemies'. For this reason Britain would always oppose German plans of eastward expansion. Even the 'territorial revision of Czechoslovakia', Ribbentrop warned, would inevitably mean war. An understanding 'on our terms' was, therefore, out of the question. Moreover, the British government, working towards the 'systematic encirclement of Germany', were 'only trying to stave us off'. 'But if the odds are ever on Britain's side, they'll fight.' On this basis German policy had to prepare itself from the outset for armed conflict with the British Empire and forge a powerful anti-British network of alliances.[76] These recommendations corresponded exactly to what Ribbentrop had in mind and what he was stubbornly trying to convince Hitler of: officially the wooing of Britain was to be continued, but at the same time a counter-alliance was to be built up in all secrecy and with dogged determination, powerful enough either to prevent the outbreak of a war between National Socialist Germany and the British Empire, deemed as inevitable, or to decide its outcome in the Reich's favour. It is not surprising that Ribbentrop advocated the 'Anti-Comintern Pact' between Berlin and Tokyo; for, despite its anti-Communist appearances, it was to all intents and purposes anti-British, especially after the accession of Rome to the Pact in November 1937; all three powers were impeded in their expansionism, not by the Soviet Union, but by Great Britain.

Ribbentrop's analysis of British policy *vis-à-vis* the Reich and the concept of power politics he derived from it did not fail to influence Hitler. Increasingly, too, the Führer began to have doubts about the feasibility of his idea of an alliance with Britain, with the result that a gradual transformation of his position *vis-à-vis* London can be observed throughout 1937. On 5 November the Führer – he had no doubt been influenced by Ribbentrop – spoke for the first time of the 'two arch-enemies, Britain and France', with whom German policy would have to reckon in the future, since 'a strong German giant' in central Europe is a 'thorn in the flesh to both of them'.[77] Henceforth – but especially in 1938 – an 'ambivalent course'[78] characterised German relations with Britain. From now on Hitler intended to realise the aims of his programme, 'no longer *with* Britain according to the "Mein Kampf" theory, but simply *without* Britain, though, if at all possible, not *against* Britain'.[79] During the Sudetenland crisis, Ribbentrop, hoping to prevent a peaceful settlement to the conflict, advised the Führer to 'hold out to the bitter end'.[80] Hitler, however, was evidently not yet prepared to steer an anti-British course; instead he followed the solutions put forward by the moderates around Weizsäcker and Goering who were advocating a peaceful settlement of outstanding grievances in line with British appeasement policy.

Although the terms of the Munich Agreement marked the failure of Ribbentrop's 'anti-British' line, some days later he was to receive the assurance that Hitler would henceforth abandon his 'without Britain' course and fall in line with Ribbentrop's anti-British concept. On 21 October 1938 the Führer announced his intention to recover the ground he had lost in Munich by marching on Prague as soon as possible and 'smashing the Czech remnants'.[81] After that an 'interlude war' against Western powers was to be 'fitted in' to secure Germany's rear for the 'march on the east'.[82]

Hitler had deliberately opted for the collision course advocated by his Foreign Minister. For by comparison with the views of the traditional ruling élite, economic circles and also Hermann Goering, Ribbentrop's foreign policy concept seemed to be the most far-reaching and, for the Führer's objectives, the most effective. While Hitler re-thought the tactics for the implementation of his 'programme', Ribbentrop, now confirmed in his anti-British policy, went on to develop this policy in ways which left their mark on the foreign policy of the Third Reich, above all in the years 1938–40. Anglo-German antagonism became more and more evident, at the latest by 1938. Ribbentrop realised that, apart from Japan and Italy, the only remaining major ally for a Germany bent on becoming a truly Great or World Power was the Soviet Union. Since Britain refused to accept German hegemony in Europe and come to terms with Hitler, and also because of the impending entry of the USA into the war on the side of Great Britain, the establishment of a four-power pact, based on Europe and Asia, became indispensable for Ribbentrop's anti-British policy. With the aid of a mighty, if not invincible, continental block extending from Gibraltar to Yokohoma, he would put Britain, a traditional sea power, in her place and lead the Reich out of its narrow confines in Central Europe. Only in this way could, in his opinion, Germany blossom into a world power on equal footing with the

British Empire and the United States of America. Ribbentrop's foreign policy concept, based on power politics and clearly owing much to the imperialism of Wilhelm II – though adjusted to the changed international situation for reasons of practical politics – was nevertheless quite incompatible with Hitler's 'programme'. Hitler, who was always flexible in power politics but rigid in terms of his racial ideology, fell in line with the course steered by his Foreign Minister for a brief period (that is, 1939–40) as a result of the 'unprogrammatic' behaviour of Great Britain. That did not prevent him launching an ideological war of annihilation against the Soviet Union in 1941.

Notes: Chapter 4

1   *Ciano Diary 1937–1938*, trans. A. Mayor (London, 1952), p. 35.
2   See W. Michalka, *Ribbentrop und die deutsche Weltpolitik 1933–1940. Aussenpolitische Konzeptionen und Entscheidungsprozesse im Dritten Reich* (Munich, 1980), pp. 214 ff. and *passim*.
3   R. Coulondre, *Von Moskau nach Berlin, 1936–1939. Erinnerungen des französischen Botschafters* (Bonn, 1950), p. 367.
4   See for example N. Rich, *Hitler's War Aims. Ideology, the Nazi State and the Course of Expansion* (New York, 1973), p. 11. Research resumed in K. Hildebrand, *Das Dritte Reich* (Munich/Vienna, 1979), pp. 168–80.
5   See for example Leeper to Vansittart, 14 April 1937 (Public Record Office, London: FO 371/20710).
6   See H. Sundhausen, 'Die Weltwirtschaftskrise im Donau-Balkan-Raum und ihre Bedeutung für den Wandel der deutschen Aussenpolitik unter Brüning', in W. Benz and H. Graml (eds), *Aspekte deutscher Aussenpolitik im 20 Jahrhundert* (Stuttgart, 1976), pp. 121–64; R. Berndt, 'Wirtschaftliche Mitteleuropapläne des deutschen Imperialismus (1926–1931)', in G. Ziebura (ed.), *Grundfragen der deutschen Aussenpolitik seit 1871* (Darmstadt, 1975), pp. 305–34; H.-J. Schröder, 'Deutsche Südosteuropapolitik 1929 –1936. Zur Kontinuität deutscher Aussenpolitik in der Weltwirtschaftskrise', in W. Schieder (ed.), *Geschichte und Gesellschaft*, vol. 2 (1976), pp. 5–32.
7   H. Brüning, *Memoiren, 1918–1934*, Vol. 1 (Munich, 1972), p. 203.
8   On the 'taming illusion' see, among others, K. D. Bracher, *Die Auflösung der Weimarer Republik*, 4th edn (Stuttgart/Düsseldorf, 1964), p. 423.
9   See in general H.-A. Jacobsen, *Nationalsozialistische Aussenpolitik 1933–1938* (Frankfurt/M., 1968), pp. 20 ff.
10   K. Hildebrand, *Deutsche Aussenpolitik 1933–1945. Kalkül oder Dogma?*, 3rd edn (Stuttgart, 1976), p. 34.
11   H.-A. Jacobsen, 'Zur Kontinuität und Diskontinuität in der deutschen Aussenpolitik im 20. Jahrhundert', in id. (ed.), *Von der Strategie der Gewalt zur Politik der Friedenssicherung. Beiträge zur deutschen Geschichte im 20. Jahrhundert* (Düsseldorf, 1977), p. 21.
12   See Jacobsen, *Aussenpolitik*, *passim*.
13   ADAP, C, I, 1, no. 142.
14   See G. Wollstein, 'Eine Denkschrift des Staatssekretärs Bernhard von Bülow vom März 1933. Wilhelminische Konzeption der Aussenpolitik zu Beginn der nationalsozialistischen Herrschaft', *Militärgeschichtliche Mitteilungen*, vol. 1/73, pp. 77 ff.
15   cf. ibid., p. 78.
16   cf. ibid., p. 78.
17   P. Krüger and E. J. Hahn, 'Der Loyalitätskonflikt des Staatssekretärs von Bülow im Frühjahr 1933', *VjhZG*, vol. 20 (1972), p. 387.
18   cf. W. Weidenfeld, *Die Englandpolitik Gustav Stresemanns. Theoretische und praktische Aspekte der Aussenpolitik* (Mainz, 1972), pp. 144–5.
19   cf. Wollstein, 'Denkschrift', p. 82.

20 ibid., p. 79.
21 ibid., p. 80.
22 ibid.
23 ibid.
24 cf. in particular R. Jaworski, *Vorposten oder Minderheit? Der Sudetendeutsche Vokstums-kampf in den Beziehungen zwischen der Weimarer Republik und der ČSR* (Stuttgart, 1977), and R. M. Smelser, *Das Sudetenproblem und das Dritte Reich 1933–1938. Von der Volkstumspolitik zur nationalsozialistischen Aussenpolitik* (Munich/Vienna, 1980).
25 See H. C. Meyer, *Mitteleuropa in German Thought and Action 1815–1945* (The Hague, 1955), and, of more recent date, the documentation by R. Opitz (ed.), *Europastrategien des deutschen Kapitals 1900–1945* (Cologne, 1977).
26 cf. G. Wollstein, 'Rudolf Nadolny – Aussenminister ohne Verwendung', *VjhZG*, vol. 28 (1980), pp. 47–93.
27 cf. Michalka, *Ribbentrop*, pp. 187 ff.
28 Wollstein, 'Denkschrift', p. 91.
29 cf. Wollstein, 'Nadolny', p. 60.
30 cf. Michalka, *Ribbentrop*, pp. 172 ff.
31 cf. in particular J. Henke, *England in Hitlers politischem Kalkül 1935–1939* (Boppard/Rhine, 1973), pp. 32–4.
32 cf. Michalka, *Ribbentrop*, pp. 47 ff.
33 See ibid., pp. 69 ff.
34 See ibid., pp. 190–1.
35 cf. J. Dülffer, *Weimar, Hitler und die Marine. Reichspolitik und Flottenbau 1920–1939* (Düsseldorf, 1973), and G. Schreiber, 'Zur Kontinuität des Gross- und Weltmachtstrebens der deutschen Marineführung', *Militärgeschichtliche Mitteilungen*, vol. 2/79, pp. 101–71.
36 See Michalka, *Ribbentrop*, pp. 94 ff.
37 H. Schacht, *Abrechnung mit Hitler* (Hamburg, 1948), p. 63.
38 K. Hildebrand, *Vom Reich zum Weltreich. Hitler, NSDAP und koloniale Frage 1919–1945* (Munich, 1969), p. 204.
39 See G. Wollstein, *Vom Weimarer Revisionismus zu Hitler. Das Deutsche Reich und die Grossmächte in der Anfangsphase der nationalsozialistischen Herrschaft in Deutschland* (Bonn/Bad Godesberg, 1973), p. 161.
40 Quoted from Hildebrand, *Weltreich*, p. 208.
41 H. Schacht, *76 Jahre meines Lebens* (Bad Wörrishofen, 1953), p. 477.
42 cf. for example Schacht's speech on colonial issues in ADAP, C, III, no. 544.
43 cf. Schacht, *Abrechnung*, p. 63: 'I have never demanded lebensraum but in the colonies.' Also in: DDP, IV, no. 50, p. 299: A solution to the 'lack of lebensraum can only be found in colonial territories' (Schacht's speech on 9 December 1936). For Schacht's views on foreign policy in general, see Michalka, *Ribbentrop*, pp. 192–7.
44 cf. Schacht, *76 Jahre*, pp. 475–83; Hildebrand, *Weltreich*, pp. 209 ff.
45 cf. Michalka, *Ribbentrop*, p. 194.
46 W. Treue, 'Die Einstellung einiger deutscher Grossindustrieller zu Hitlers Aussenpolitik', *GWU*, vol. 17 (1966), p. 498.
47 cf. Hildebrand, *Weltreich*, p. 465.
48 Wollstein, *Revisionismus*, p. 162.
49 On the 'New Plan' cf. H.-J. Schröder, *Deutschland und die Vereinigten Staaten 1933–1939. Wirtschaft und Politik in der Entwicklung des deutsch-amerikanischen Gegensatzes* (Wiesbaden, 1970), pp. 127–35; H. Pentzlin, *Hjalmar Schacht. Leben und Wirken einer umstrittenen Persönlichkeit* (Berlin/Frankfurt/M./Vienna, 1980), pp. 202–23.
50 On the Anglo-German payment agreement cf. in particular F. C. Child, *The Theory and Practice of Exchange Control in Germany. A Study of Monopolistic Exploitation in International Markets* (The Hague, 1958); B.-J. Wendt, *Economic Appeasement. Handel und Finanz in der britischen Deutschland-Politik 1933–1939* (Düsseldorf, 1971), pp. 260–87.
51 See ibid., p. 286.
52 ibid., p. 260.
53 ibid., p. 269.
54 ibid., p. 286.

55   cf. Michalka, *Ribbentrop*, pp. 138–49.
56   cf. M. Gilbert and R. Gott, *The Appeasers* (London, 1963), pp. 90–1.
57   cf. Hildebrand, *Weltreich*, p. 478.
58   ibid., passim.
59   cf. W. Schumann and L. Nestler (eds), *Weltherrschaft im Visier. Dokumente zu den Europa- und Weltherrschaftsplänen des deutschen Imperialismus von der Jahrhundertwende bis Mai 1945* (Berlin, 1975), pp. 22–3.
60   ibid., nos 92, 95.
61   cf. Hildebrand, *Deutsche Aussenpolitik*, pp. 44–5.
62   Wendt, *Economic Appeasement*, p. 312.
63   cf. R. A. C. Parker, 'Grossbritannien und Deutschland 1936–1937', in O. Hauser (ed.), *Weltpolitik 1933–1939* (Göttingen, 1973), pp. 66–7.
64   cf. Hildebrand, *Weltreich*, pp. 477–8.
65   E. Kordt, *Nicht aus den Akten . . . Die Wilhelmstrasse in Frieden und Krieg. Erlebnisse, Begegnungen und Eindrücke 1928–1945* (Stuttgart, 1950), p. 95.
66   cf. Gilbert and Gott, *The Appeasers*, pp. 95 ff.
67   cf. W. Michalka, 'Die nationalsozialistische Aussenpolitik im Zeichen eines "Konzeptionen-Pluralismus. Fragestellungen und Forschungsaufgaben"', in M. Funke (ed.), *Hitler, Deutschland und die Mächte. Materialien zur Aussenpolitik des Dritten Reiches* (Düsseldorf, 1976), p. 60.
68   D. Schoenbaum, *Hitler's Social Revolution* (New York, 1967), p. 134.
69   cf. T. Vogelsang, *Die nationalsozialistische Zeit, Deutschland 1933–1939*, 2nd edn (Berlin/ Frankfurt/M., 1974), p. 73.
70   cf. H. Kaiser, 'Probleme und Verlauf der nationalsozialistischen Aussenpolitik', *Politische Bildung*, vol. 5 (1972), p. 59.
71   A. Hillgruber, 'Die weltpolitische Lage 1936–1939', in Hauser (ed.), *Weltpolitik*, p. 278.
72   cf. D. Eichholtz and W. Schumann (eds), *Anatomie des Krieges. Neue Dokumente über die Rolle des deutschen Monopol-kapitals bei der Vorbereitung und Durchführung des 2. Weltkrieges* (Berlin, 1969), pp. 214–15; W. Schumann (ed.), *Griff nach Südosteuropa. Neue Dokumente über die Politik des deutschen Imperialismus und Militarismus gegenüber Südosteuropa im zweiten Weltkrieg* (Berlin, 1973), passim.
73   See Henke, *England*, p. 180.
74   cf. K. J. Müller, *Das Heer und Hitler. Armee und nationalsozialistisches Regime 1933–1940* (Stuttgart, 1969), pp. 345 ff., and now in particular by the same author, *General Ludwig Beck. Studien und Dokumente zur politisch-militärischen Vorstellungswelt und Tätigkeit des Generalstabschefs des deutschen Heeres 1933–1938* (Boppard/Rh., 1980), pp. 272 ff.
75   cf. B.-J. Wendt, *München 1938. England zwischen Hitler und Preussen* (Frankfurt/M., 1965), pp. 46 ff.
76   cf. Michalka, *Ribbentrop*, pp. 249 ff. and passim.
77   ADAP, D, I, no. 19 (Hossbach-Niederschrift).
78   cf. Hildebrand, *Aussenpolitik*, p. 56; A. Hillgruber, *Deutschlands Rolle in der Vorgeschichte der beiden Weltkriege* (Göttingen, 1967), p. 87.
79   Henke, *England*, p. 101.
80   ibid., p. 180.
81   ADAP, D, Vol. IV, no. 81.
82   cf. Henke, *England*, pp. 154–5; Hildebrand, *Aussenpolitik*, p. 72, and now in particular, Müller, *Beck*, pp. 288 ff. and résumé of documentation, pp. 512 ff.

5 The German Military Opposition before the Second World War

KLAUS-JÜRGEN MÜLLER

How well organised was German opposition to Hitler in the 1930s and to what extent could British governments have taken it into consideration as an aspect of their foreign policies? These are the questions to be discussed below. In practice, however, given the nature of the regime one will be focusing attention on the upper echelons of the military leadership and the various centres of opposition to which they are linked.[1]

Our investigation of the problem falls into two parts. We shall start by sketching out a frame of reference, with the help of which the phenomenon usually referred to in blanket terms as 'the' German opposition or 'the' military resistance can be more precisely defined.[2] The second part of the discussion, which concentrates on the years 1938 and 1939, will then examine the structure of the so-called 'military opposition' in terms of its personnel, political composition and capacity for action.

Let us begin with the historical frame of reference. The 'military opposition' is to be understood, first, as a special category of quite distinct opposition from the so-called 'national conservative elements' which term relates specifically to the traditional power élites and their adjustment to the National Socialist regime. The coalition of 30 January 1933 can in fact be interpreted as an 'entente' between influential sections of these élites and the leaders of the National Socialist mass movement. As a consequence any investigation of the national conservative opposition must begin here.

Within this entente the army saw itself as holding a privileged position, an idea which received endorsement from Hitler's formula of the 'twin pillars' – the army and the party – on which the regime rested. This proved to be a skilful tactical play on the expectations of the military. The latter saw the entente as guaranteeing the successful realisation of their two essential goals:[3] in internal politics, the re-establishment of the military élite in positions of power within the state and society, positions which since 1918, if not earlier, had seemed increasingly insecure; in external politics, the restoration of the Reich to the position of a Great Power defined in a militaristic, power-political sense. This twofold objective was to play a decisive part in the development of relations between the National Socialist regime and the military élite. To put it more concretely, relations between the military and the regime developed (1) in the *internal sphere* in accordance with the realisation or frustration of the army's claim to a position of equal power in the state, and (2) in the *external sphere* in accordance with the progress of Germany's great-power aspirations in the sense already defined.

With the help of these co-ordinates we can hope to trace the phenomenon of the 'military opposition' with some historical precision, the military opposition being defined as a phenomenon complementary to those traditional élites operating an entente with Hitler.

Within the framework of that entente, military opposition thus presents itself as a conflict-phenomenon of a special kind.[4] In order to show the full scale of the phenomenon, which covers alternative positions running all the way from acquiescence to resistance, and to be able to understand the divergent reactions of individual members of the military élite to the challenges presented by the regime – responses which differed in content as well as intensity – we need to make some further distinctions.

First, it should be asked in relation to the military, which of its two essential goals appeared to be endangered: the concept of the regime as a partnership or the concept of a great power foreign policy or both? If the question is posed in this way it is easier to find plausible explanations for the fact that, whereas certain immoral aspects of the regime provoked merely disapproval in military circles, considerable opposition was provoked by Hitler's risky foreign policy, Roehm's ambitions to meddle in military politics and the intrigue against Fritsch.

Secondly, it should be asked how the military conceived of the source and nature of the threat to their objectives. The answers which emerge should then make it possible to comprehend the whole range of possible reactions to conflict-situations: defensive measures to safeguard existing positions; active measures to restore the equilibrium (for example, by 'cleansing the regime of "radical elements"'); subversive measures to destabilise the system. Differing assessments of the danger or the adversary determined to a large extent the character of the military's reaction. The dissimilarities in the reaction to the Roehm affair of June 1934, to the disputes, at times very heated, between party organs and the army during 1934–7 and, finally, to the Fritsch–Blomberg crisis, show that the intensity and character of the reaction by the military élite was almost exclusively a function of the threat to their policies and the source from which it came.

A third question concerns priorities. Within the military élite there were divergent views about the relative importance of particular goals, and this in turn gave rise to divergent strategies for their implementation. Such differences were also important in determining attitudes to the regime and types of reaction in conflict-situations. In the Sudeten crisis, for example, differences regarding the order of priority were a serious impediment to concerted action:[5] some sections of the opposition advocated a political purge designed to overthrow the regime, while others sought to avert the war which Hitler's policies were threatening, a war which would have placed all German aspirations to great power status in jeopardy. Similar differences can be observed in the reaction to particular events.[6] Divergences as regards the ordering of priorities, together with divergences in the strategies adopted for their implementation, had thus an appreciable effect on the nature of any action by the opposition.

Analysis on the foregoing lines has already yielded results relevant to our theme: first, that it is not possible to form a qualitative judgement of the opposition in the years 1938–9 if it is viewed as a coherent and monolithic phenomenon; and second, that its prospects of success and opportunities for effective action should not be regarded as depending solely on Britain's readiness and determination to fight. A more discriminating analysis is clearly called for. What may also have become apparent is that, *in substance*, the 'opposition' at present under consideration was related to an internal power struggle, concerning the political role of the traditional élites.

Using the basis established above we shall attempt to analyse the so-called military 'opposition', both with reference to the years 1938 and 1939 and with regard to its structural aspects: personnel, political character-istics and capacity for action.

Up to the time of the Fritsch–Blomberg crisis[7] activity occurred on two levels. Literature exclusively concerned with resistance, however, is apt to see everything in terms of absolute resistance. Closer inspection, on the other hand, shows that it was nothing of the sort. Take *first* the activities of the internal information and intelligence service built up within the *Abwehr* (Military Intelligence Agency) by *Oberstleutnant* (Lieutenant-Colonel) Os-ter, which service Canaris knew of and helped to promote: its chief targets were the party organs hostile to the army (SS and SD) and their criminal machinations.[8] It constituted 'no weaving together and enlargement of the conspiracy beginning to take shape in the second half of the thirties';[9] rather, it was more like a very loose integrated 'old boy network' composed of former members of the *Free Corps* and right-wing conservatives, along with a few discontented individuals brought in by chance contact or social connection. Secondly, there was the concern of Fritsch and Beck to gather, so far as they were able, unfiltered and comprehensive information on internal and external affairs. For this they turned to military attachés who had their personal confidence (Geyr von Schweppenburg, for example) and who sent information on a variety of topics through unofficial channels. They also exploited private individuals among their wider circle of personal and official acquaintances.[10] Here special mention should be made of Karl Goerdeler who, in the course of numerous visits abroad, starting in the summer of 1937, established contact with the Foreign Office. Goerdeler, however, in his talks with foreign contacts could only have put forward his own opinions, whatever he may have said to suggest otherwise; he had behind him no group resembling an organised opposition; at best he reflected the mood prevailing in certain national conservative *milieux*.[11] Thus, although in Goerdeler the army leadership had an informant of high calibre, he in no sense represented them.

These two activities – inside the Military Intelligence Agency and in the army's High Command – neither of which was wholly contained within its narrowly official sphere, were far from being preparations for an opposition conspiracy; they were purely and simply initiatives on the part of high officials to compensate for the dearth of information symptomatic of a totalitarian society. That these initiatives also yielded results in terms of the domestic power struggle, which in any case revolved around the army, was only to be expected.

The Fritsch–Blomberg crisis represents a milestone in the history of the later military opposition.[12] To the many national conservatives who were already to a greater or lesser degree critical of certain aspects of the regime, and of particular tendencies they saw developing, the affair became a turning-point, the beginning of their progressive disillusionment with the regime as a whole. In addition, the crisis acted so to say as a catalyst: individuals, and groups of individuals, between whom there had previously been little contact, were now brought for the first time into direct relations with one another. But just as the motives for forming such connections varied, so did the nature of the opposition.[13]

First these are the efforts of *Generaloberst* von Fritsch's lawyer, von der Goltz, with assistance from one or two members of the Justice Department within the War Ministry, not merely to clear his client but to cast light on the background to the affair. Oster and his network lent valuable support to these endeavours, which to begin with were in essence non-political. Next came more or less unco-ordinated attempts by a few people outside the armed forces to make senior military personnel aware of the background to the case, in the hope of persuading them to intervene: moves of this nature, however, were doomed to disappointment, the moral impetus behind them being in inverse proportion to their realism.

Oster, in company with a few sympathisers and friends from the *Abwehr* (Liedig, Heinz) and the old *Freikorps* days (Nebe), and with vigorous encouragement from Dr Dohnany, private secretary to the Minister of Justice, set going intensive activities of a conspiratorial type, the aim of which was twofold: to expose the SS, the SD and the Gestapo as the authors of the malicious intrigue against the top military leadership; and to pave the way for action by the army of an unorthodox, coercive type, as a means of self-help against those organisations. This was calculated both to remove the greatest threat to the position of the army in the state *and* to bring about a reform of the internal political situation in the sense of restoring to the regime its character of an entente.

In the context of settling the Fritsch case at the highest military level, the Chief of the General Staff, the head of the *Abwehr* and the Adjutant-General of the *Wehrmacht*, himself just discharged, took the initiative with Hitler, in order to stabilise the position of the armed forces in the state and to restore the regime to what they thought was its original character.[14] Beck was working at this time for a reorganisation of the top military command structure, which would have brought the army's High Command into a key role. Canaris and Hossbach tried to induce the Chief of the General Staff and some other generals to present Hitler with a kind of ultimatum, with the aim of stripping the SS and Gestapo leadership of its power and in this way to bring about the 'liberation of the army from the nightmare of a Tscheka'.[15] Whereas what Oster and his circle had in view was a forcible purge as a means of effecting change in the internal political situation, what these senior military men had in mind was something akin to an officially sanctioned reallocation of responsibilities which would strip certain members of the SS and the Gestapo of their powers and hence consolidate the army's position within the regime. Thus although the Fritsch crisis brought the domestic power struggle to a climax, no kind of conspiracy emerged which was aimed, even in its original intention, at the overthrow of the regime. It was a time of activity by groups of individuals who differed widely in motivation, outlook, method and opportunity. On some points there was co-operation between them, but were far from being a singleminded force of opposition.

Further decisive shifts occurred only with the Sudeten crisis of 1938.[16] During this crisis there emerged for the first time a loose combination of forces which merits the description 'anti-war party' and which lent fresh impetus to the two tendencies discussed above: the one aimed at *reforming the regime*, and the other at *purging it by force*. Having these three components, the phenomenon all too often referred to without differentiation as *the* opposition or *the* resistance becomes a very complex body, which forbids the use of labels suggestive in any way of a closely knit, organised conspiracy.[17]

The three most prominent members of the 'anti-war party' during the crisis period of 1938 were General Beck, his successor General Halder and the chief of the *Abwehr*, Admiral Canaris.[18] To illustrate the way in which efforts to prevent war merged to some degree with manifestations of an internal power struggle, but, more important, to demonstrate the political priorities of the anti-war party as well as the limitations these imposed on its willingness to act, we can cite the thinking and behaviour of Ludwig Beck, Chief of the General Staff.[9] Put briefly, Beck's notion of the way to implement the goals of foreign policy comprised two elements in combination: a display of military strength and a system of military-political alliances. War was not a necessary part of this conception, but neither was it ruled out on principle. Limited wars, kept under political control, had a place in Beck's thinking.

As a possessor of such views, and in particular as the successful instigator of a programme of military reorganisation and rearmament, Beck eventually found himself in a blind alley. In his famous harangue of 5 November 1937 Hitler included among the justifications for his policy of planned militarist expansion the time pressure imposed by the arms race. In a very few years Germany's potential rivals would be stronger than the Reich. That Hitler could argue in this way was due not least to the success of Beck's military and rearmament policies. Beck was therefore not disposed to criticise even these directly expansionist aims, with which in principle he agreed: as he put it, the existence of the Republic of Czechoslovakia 'in its present form' was 'intolerable' to Germany.[20]

He may have disagreed with Hitler in foreign policy over matters of timing and tactics. Yet there was no fundamental conflict of views over 'whether', merely a disagreement over 'how' and 'when'. What should have given Beck's dissent a keener edge was his conviction that a war fought at the wrong time and in unfavourable conditions would be a catastrophe for the Reich.

But Hitler's reaction at the time of the famous weekend crisis of May 1938[21] made it clear to Beck – and the revelation was little short of a bombshell – that Hitler was not merely aiming at a military conflict with Czechoslovakia timed for as early as 1938 but that he was speaking – and this, for Beck, was incomprehensible – of the possibility of a conflict with the Western powers. In face of this, the basic assumptions of Beck's military policy stood virtually in ruins. Hence it followed that the developments at the end of May 1938 became for him a crucial turning-point. From the end of that month, as he later confided to a friend, he had only one thought in mind: 'How can I prevent a war?'[22] The reaction of Canaris and Halder to the May crisis was similar. Anxiety that conflict with Czechoslovakia at the wrong time, that is, before Germany was fully armed and externally secure, would plunge Europe into a major war – a risk which Hitler not only accepted but even allowed for – was enough to turn all three men into confirmed opponents of a risk-running policy, no matter what they had done in the past to create the conditions in which such a policy was feasible. In the persons of its prominent representatives, what might at this date be termed the German opposition was thus offering neither an alternative to the system nor an alternative foreign policy but had simply come into being as an 'anti-war party' born of disagreements about timing and methods.

The ensuing conflict between Beck and Hitler, in which Canaris and Halder sided with Beck, has been described many times. However, to represent it as a first attempt at a coup[23] gets it wrong; to label it 'struggle against war',[24] and ignore its character of an internal political power struggle, not to mention the profundity of its military–political dimension, would be cutting it too short. The methods Beck employed in his exertions during the summer of 1938 show two distinct stages. (1) At first he tried to achieve his aim, the prevention of war, by use of the accepted, official means of persuasion (memoranda, reports, and so on). (2) Later, by which time the influence of Canaris on the Chief of the General Staff was clearly consider-able, Beck sought to attain his goal by less orthodox means, for example the collective resignation of the commanding generals. Lastly, returning to the plan worked out by Canaris and Hossbach at the time of the Fritsch crisis, he contemplated bringing overwhelming pressure to bear on Hitler, that is, by coupling the threat of resignation with action by the military to clear the political decks: this would strip of their power those 'radical elements' who appeared to share responsibility for the gambles in foreign policy and who in internal politics had long since identified themselves as rivals to the army. Beck's plans thus illustrate the convergence, as it were, of the struggle against war with the long-standing internal power struggle to uphold, or as the case might be to restore, the twin-pillar character of the regime.

To sum up what has so far been established: during the Sudeten crisis, when the danger of war seemed acute, some kind of 'anti-war party' emerged.[25] It owed its existence to a handful of senior military men who were anxious, for tactical reasons, to avoid a conflict which, according to their judgement at the time, it would be impossible to contain. Generally speaking they were by no means opposed to the establishment of a hegem-onial position for the Reich in Central Europe, and they had no fundamental objection to the use of military force (Beck) and measures of political and military subversion (Canaris)[26] as the means of achieving this goal.[27]

What prospects did this 'anti-war party' have? What political weight did it carry? In attempting to answer these questions the following factors have to be taken into consideration. Beck and Canaris were not contemplating a military putsch carried out by lower-ranking officers or a few detached units. Since they themselves were in subordinate positions, they could do nothing effective without the holder of the supreme command. This meant that the leadership of the army, that is to say the Commander-in-Chief and the top-ranking generals, had to lend their support to the efforts to prevent war. Yet it was precisely these key figures that Beck and Canaris failed to win over to the anti-war policy. No doubt this had something to do with the personalities occupying the top rungs of the hierarchy. But for the real reasons we must look elsewhere. First, it was clearly not possible to make the Commanders-in-Chief of the navy and the air force chief participants in the common action. Goering, profoundly suspect in the eyes of the army leadership since the Fritsch crisis, had so far shown no sign of swinging over to an anti-war policy; and the High Command of the navy, with no interest in the Czechoslovak conflict, was fully occupied with long-term plans and strategies which fitted the context of a world power philosophy with a plainly anti-British slant.[28] Secondly – and this was still more conclusive – Beck and Canaris did not manage to convince even the Commander-in-Chief and other high-ranking generals of the army that the Western powers would not fail to intervene in the military conflict on which Hitler was bent. Since from a purely professional standpoint Beck could offer no convincing proof of the correctness of his prognosis, neither could he offer any such proof for the correctness of the premises on which the proposed course of action was based.

It is in this connection that the various secret missions, so often described, acquire their functional importance as flanking moves in the anti-war policy of Beck and Canaris. The prime purpose of these missions, whether launched by Canaris, by the Oster circle, or by von Weizsäcker, not always by mutual agreement, was to establish the correctness of the premisses for an anti-war policy, namely, that in the event of a German attack on Czechoslovakia the Western powers would intervene. This was the task assigned to, amongst others, Kleist-Schmenzin (18 August 1938 onwards), the Kordt brothers (Erich, through working on Brauchitsch, Theo Kordt in London, between 23 August and 7 September) and Carl Jacob Burckhardt (late August – early September). However, as everyone knows, the endeavours in Berlin were fruitless and the hoped for signals from London, providing convincing proof that the prognoses of the anti-war party were correct, were not forthcoming. Beck thus saw the anti-war policy doomed to frustration by the lack of evidence as to foreign intervention as well as by the consequences of his own policies of military reorganisation and rearmament. His resignation is therefore to be interpreted more as a sign of surrender than as a symbol of revolt.[29]

Further pointers to the prospects and importance of the 'anti-war party' emerge from an analysis of its structure. As its essential core it had the two senior military men, Beck and Canaris. With them can be counted, in the diplomatic corps, Permanent Under-Secretary of State von Weizsäcker, who initiated parallel activities which – as it appears – were also in part co-ordinated with those of Beck and Canaris. At a level below this small inner group of senior government officials was the Oster–Gisevius circle. Here, in contrast with the Beck–Canaris–Weizsäcker group, the anti-war campaign quickly became a vehicle for organising a coup against the regime. For as far as this group was concerned overthrow of the regime was the prime objective, in relation to which the prevention of war assumed a secondary, instrumental function. As an opposition, they were more radical in their intentions, but as an effective influence they were seriously restricted by their position in the power structure. There was finally a third tier, composed of personalities brought into play by the two other groups and whose functions were of an auxiliary character. These were drawn from the milieu of discontented national conservatives and their criticism of the regime was of varying character. Several – von Kleist, for example – held idiosyncratic political views which they voiced in their missions abroad; it was largely for this reason that their foreign contacts were left with a picture of the German opposition scene which was certainly no clearer, and if anything more confused.[30] Even though they undoubtedly played a useful part as auxiliary agents of the 'anti-war party' or of the more radical group, as an opposition force in their own right they carried no weight.

The auxiliary activities so far described belong within the framework of the policy to prevent war which was being pursued by a group of high officials. To be clearly distinguished from these are the activities of a handful of national conservatives with opposition leanings who were acting on their own initiative: as examples may be cited von Koerber's approach to the British military attaché or the contacts made by Goerdeler on his round of foreign visits. These people made frequent reference to their high-up military connections, but they had no mandate from that quarter; they represented themselves as spokesmen for an opposition, but did no more than reflect the mood prevailing in certain national conservative circles; they were in no way involved in the anti-war policy pursued by Beck and Canaris, nor were they supporters of the coup entertained by the Oster–Gisevius group. An equally clear distinction is to be made between the activities in this field of the 'anti-war party' and the consultations, often attributed all-embracingly to *the* opposition, which were merely part of the official or semi-official German–British dialogue then in progress;[31] this applies, for example, to the activities of Wiedemann and Hewel, and to some of von Weizsäcker's, in which it is very hard to draw a line, so to speak, between consultations in an official capacity and private political initiatives. It seems necessary to subject the concept 'opposition' to analysis of this somewhat schematic kind in order to counter ideas that ascribe to it an underlying coherence and unity which did not in fact exist.

We have seen that in the summer of 1938 the position was as follows. A number of high-ranking officials in military, diplomatic and secret service circles were struggling to avert a war in face of a situation which they themselves had helped to create. Since they started with the supposition that what they chiefly had to contend with was the warmongering of certain 'radical forces' in the National Socialist movement, and since they regarded these same forces as a threat to the 'twin pillar' theory of the regime, their policy of preventing war became merged with political engagements in an already long-established internal power struggle. Working from a base inside this constellation, a small and more radically inclined group tried hard to widen the aims of the policy of war prevention to include a coup d'état, or at least a purge forceful enough to modify the regime. However, because they carried no weight they did not succeed.

There was a decisive change in this state of affairs in the next phase, which opened with Halder's assumption of office (1 September).[32] The Oster–Gisevius group took advantage of the changeover to obtain from Halder and Canaris some sort of authorisation to make preparations for a coup and conversely to place the services of their own potential opposition at the disposal of the anti-war group. The policy to avert war thereby took on a new dimension, since from now on it could operate at two different levels. The distinguishing mark of this phase, therefore, was that conspiratorial activity in preparation for a coup, and activity through political and secret diplomatic channels to prevent war, from now on ran alongside each other as alternatives, even though at times there was little co-ordination between the two.

The secret consultations abroad, begun in Beck's time, were thus continued, principally by von Weizäcker and Canaris but with Halder also taking a hand (Boehm–Tettelbach mission), just as pressure continued to be brought to bear on top-ranking officials, Keitel and Brauchitsch for example, to exercise the appropriate influence on Hitler; but at the same time, on instructions from Halder, the Oster–Gisevius circle embarked on practical preparations for a coup d'état.

In contrast with what had happened in Beck's time, there was now in being an active link between highly placed representatives of the anti-war policy and the activist elements in subordinate positions who were plotting subversion. This had the further effect of adding to the strength a number of people whose contribution, in practical, as well as political terms, was not insignificant.[33] For the first time it is possible to speak of an opposition mounted against the leadership of the regime from within the ranks of the military, and indeed extending at some points well beyond the military sphere. It was nevertheless an opposition characterised by fundamental divergences in both motives and aims. In the calculations of Halder and Canaris, the coup d'état figured only as a last, despairing resort to prevent the outbreak of war, something to be prepared for only as an emergency; in the eyes of the Oster–Gisevius circle it was the real objective, most likely to be attained if an outbreak of war appeared imminent.[34]

Divergence in motives and goals also explain why it was that, after Halder had allowed direct preparations for a coup to continue unchecked throughout the critical days of the Godesberg negotiations,[35] once the news of the impending Munich Conference was known, the link between these different and very variously motivated groupings rapidly disintegrated, with the result that during the decisive months to come they were virtually paralysed. After the Munich Conference the 'anti-war party' no longer had any reason to resort to destabilising measures, since with the danger of war so obviously averted the chief aim of its policy had been achieved. Conversely, the other group, aiming at the overthrow of the regime, considered themselves robbed by the Munich Conference of the essential prerequisites for their action (a spectacular diplomatic defeat for Hitler or alternatively the direct imminence of war) and went so far as to blame this on the Western powers ('Chamberlain has saved Hitler!').[36] For London, however, as for Halder, Canaris and von Weizsäcker, the major concern was to prevent an armed conflict, rather than to create on behalf of a small and politically insignificant group of conspirators, whose preparations had at no time advanced beyond the stage of improvisation,[37] the right political and psychological conditions for a coup d'état.

An analysis of this so-called September Plot yields therefore the following results. The nub of it was the continuation of an anti-war policy, but this now had two sides to it, activities through political and secret diplomatic channels being complemented by plans initiated by Canaris and Halder for the eventuality of a coup d'état. But the latter was not the main objective, which continued to be the prevention of war. Running through the contingency planning, however, was an undercurrent which threatened to develop into an independent plot the aims of which went beyond the mere prevention of war to encompass full-scale subversion and assassination, not just to elimin-ate the germs of war present in the regime but as a prelude to the introduction of a new political and social order. The radical character of these goals stood, it is true, in inverse proportion to the official and political weight of those who plotted to implement them. The 'anti-war party', after all, was composed of people high up in the official power structure; the group of conspirators, by contrast, was not on its own a political force to be reckoned with. At the time composition of what is commonly called 'the German opposition' was thoroughly heterogeneous and encompassed a wide diversity of objectives and methods.

Characteristic of the period between the Munich Conference and the outbreak of war was the loosening of the connection between the various personalities and groups with opposition leanings, which had become closer during the phase between the Fritsch crisis and Munich; also apparent was the complete divergence of the two tendencies, the one seeking to prevent war and the second working principally towards the overthrow of the regime.[38]

Among the forces hostile to the regime as such internal tensions pre-dominated: former contacts were severed; discussions among critics of the regime now out of office (von Hassell, Goerdeler, Planck, and so on) produced nothing positive; they criticised events as they happened, but had nothing to offer beyond cloudy deliberations over the long term (von Witzleben, von Sodenstern) or *ad hoc* plans that were totally unrealistic (Gisevius, Schacht). Munich had left these forces completely stranded; they were no longer in touch with what was happening.[39]

For the exponents of an anti-war policy, by contrast, the period which terminated with the outbreak of war was one of intensified, if ultimately fruitless, activity. In personnel the structure of this group remained more or less unchanged, aside from the fact that in the fateful phase immediately preceding the outbreak of war Goering's efforts and the efforts of this group converged. The plan of action embraced a number of activities and operated at several levels. The prime objective in all cases was to bring about a situation in which Hitler would be forced or frightened into dropping war from his agenda. For this to happen evidence must be produced that the Western powers would oppose with armed force any further German expansion; that if war came, Germany's allies would not rally to the side of the Reich; that the German economy was not prepared for war; and finally that the desired aim could be achieved without resort to armed force.

The activities of the anti-war forces were therefore deployed at several levels. At home efforts were made to influence the decision-making process at the very highest level. This endeavour admittedly did not yet constitute resistance in the sense of undermining the system, but in the circumstances of a totalitarian dictatorship it can certainly qualify as opposition in the widest sense of the term. Abroad, the anti-war forces pursued their goal by way of consultations and démarches. In the period up to the outbreak of war there was no cessation in the stream of envoys and intermediaries, most of them bound for London. In Germany, too, ways were found of passing information on a variety of topics to the representatives of foreign powers. The undeviating purpose of this 'counter-diplomacy' was (1) to convey to the Western powers warnings of Hitler's warlike intentions, and (2) to provoke the British into vigorous counter-measures.

That these endeavours ultimately proved fruitless can be explained in a number of ways. London, for all its growing disillusionment over Hitler's policies, found it very hard to extract from the welter of information coming out of Germany, much of it contradictory, elements decisive enough to influence the conduct of Britain's foreign policy: all the more so when conversation with German contacts left the British with a picture of the anti-war forces in Germany that was far from uniform.[40] Among the reasons for failure at a deeper level was the lack of unanimity within the 'anti-war party' about the reaction it was hoped to elicit from the British. Some wanted threatening gestures on a spectacular scale, of a kind which made plain to the German public the bankruptcy of Hitler's foreign policy and exposed him as a warmonger. Hopes of this nature surely underestimated the opportunities for manipulation of the news media at the disposal of a totalitarian regime, and furthermore reduced British policy to the function of subserving the internal struggle in Germany. But there were also some like Canaris and von Weizsäcker who, while wanting Great Britain's determination to fight to be made explicit and unambiguous, were also insistent that it be made known as discreetly as possible, so as not to provoke the 'Führer' into aggressive counter-measures and push him into the arms of party extremists whose thinking on foreign policy followed a radical line.[41] The interventions of the 'anti-war party' were therefore sometimes at cross purposes.[42] It was a further and profound handicap to the 'anti-war party' that Hitler's policy, from the moment he embarked on his confrontation course with Poland, converged so completely with their own Prussian-German revisionist goals in regard to that country; what added to the handicap was that they themselves had prepared the way for Hitler's Polish policy (Canaris by his nationalist and anti-Polish policy in respect of the Ukraine, von Weizsäcker by his efforts, late in 1938, to divert Ribbentrop's and Hitler's attention from the remnant of Czechoslovakia to Poland)[43] and had hence contributed to its fateful activation. Once again, therefore – as previously with Beck – subscription to a revisionist great power policy, with all that it entailed in terms of objectives, underlying principles and even, in some respects, of tactics, had come to play an essential part in dooming the policy of the anti-war party to failure.

To sum up the activities characteristic of the anti-war party between Munich and the outbreak of war: they consisted, on the one hand, of attempts to frustrate Hitler's war plans by a counter diplomacy which operated in part through secret diplomatic channels and in part within the framework of ordinary official contacts; on the other, it consisted of attempts to influence the internal decision-making process in Berlin by means of information (or misinformation) planted with the help of other high officials. During this phase there were no thoughts, or at any rate no preparations, to overthrow the system as a means of preventing war.[44]

Analysis of the composition, aims and methods of the forces which emerged during the crisis of 1938–9 in the guise of 'opposition' suggests that only *after* a successful coup d'état could they have become a factor seriously to be taken into account in British policy. Yet the opposition believed that their policy, the prime object of which (save in the case of the small fraction aiming directly at a coup, whose chances were nil) was to prevent a war, depended heavily, even if, in the last resort, attempting a coup d'état, on British support. There was thus a paradox at work: it was not the case that the opposition was a decisive factor in British policy but that a particular kind of British policy had become the prerequisite of action by the opposition. London, however, still had other options to choose from, options less doubtful and less nebulous than the prospects offered by this peculiar opposition. The fact of the latter's close involvement with German hegemonial thinking of a strongly militaristic tendency further reduced its attractiveness to the British as a political alternative. Its origins therefore in a domestic power struggle were an important factor in inhibiting its decision in favour of a coup, especially since the principal goal, at any rate so far as the essential nucleus was concerned, was the prevention of war. It therefore did not develop into a major alternative in German politics.

Notes: Chapter 5

1   This means that the 'resistance of the left' and the action of groups whose main concern was with espionage and sabotage remain outside the scope of this study. For them in general consult the specialised bibliographies compiled by U. Hochmuth, *Fascismus und Widerstand. Ein Verzeichnis deutschsprachiger Literatur* (Frankfurt/M., 1973), and R. Büchel, *Der deutsche Widerstand im Spiegel von Fachliteratur und Publizistik seit 1945* (Munich, 1975); and see further the review articles by K. O. Frhr v. Aretin, *Geschichte in Wissenschaft und Unterricht*, vol. 15 (1974), pp. 507 ff. and 565 ff., and R. Mann, 'Widerstand gegen den Nationalsozialismus', *Neue politische Literatur*, vol. 22 (1977), pp. 425–42.

2   For amplification see 'Die deutsche Militäropposition gegen Hitler. Zum Problem ihrer Interpretation und Analyse', in K.-J. Müller, *Armee, Politik und Gesellschaft in Deutschland 1933–1945* (Paderborn, 1979), pp. 101–23. On resistance as a concept see Mann,

'Widerstand', pp. 425–42 and – at a fundamental level – P. Hüttenberger, 'Vorüberlegungen zum "Widerstandsbegriff"', *Theorien in der Praxis des Historikers*, ed. J. Kocka (*Geschichte und Gesellschaft*, Sonderheft 3/1977).

3   It is not intended here to unravel a third strand in the military's aspirations, namely, its perception of the total mobilisation of society as an indispensable prerequisite to becoming a Great Power. Also passed over is the problem of exactly how far the aspirations of the conservative resistance were identical with those of Hitler – that is, wholly, in part, or not at all.

4   This enables us to draw a distinction between opposition from the military as compared with resistance from opponents to the regime who, in view of their *a priori* position *vis-à-vis* National Socialism, were left with no option between antagonism and co-operation.

5   On this see K.-J. Müller, *Das Heer und Hitler* (Stuttgart, 1969), chs VIII and IX, and P. Hoffmann, *Widerstand, Staatsstreich, Attentat. Der Kampf der Opposition gegen Hitler* (Munich, 1979), ch. IV.

6   Thus the Hitler–Stalin pact of 1939 was seen by some as definitive proof of the revolutionary and destructive character of the regime and of its 'Führer', whereas for others it appeared to banish the spectre of a war on two fronts.

7   On this see Müller. *Heer und Hitler*, chs IV and V, and Hoffmann, chs II and III.

8   For this see in particular H. Höhne, *Canaris. Patriot im Zwielicht* (Munich, 1976), ch. VIII.

9   Hoffmann, ch. II, is very informative on the subject of these personal interconnections; for the passage quoted see the same work, p. 52.

10   See Müller, *Heer und Hitler*, pp. 232 ff.

11   British reactions to Goerdeler's information and the value placed on his reports is described in detail by S. Aster, *1939. The Making of the Second World War* (London, 1973); see in particular pp. 43 ff., 45–9, 57, 230 ff., 345, 362.

12   On this and what follows see H. C. Deutsch, *Das Komplott oder die Entmachtung der Generale. Blomberg- und Fritsch-Krise, Hitlers Weg zum Krieg* (Eichstätt, 1974), Hoffmann, ch. III, and Müller, *Heer und Hitler*, ch. VI. For Canaris see Höhne, *Canaris*, pp. 244 ff.

13   The background to these developments was the increasingly critical attitude prevailing in sectors of the national conservation milieu where there was disillusionment at the way the regime was evolving. But discontent emanating from circles which in 1933 had joined wholeheartedly in the 'national rising' can in no way be classed as 'opposition'. It was at best the seed-bed in which opposition properly so called might start to germinate. It is however true that many disillusioned national conservatives, misunderstanding the power set-up, tended when abroad to speak of this discontent as an opposition (cf. for example Koerber's statements to Mason MacFarlane, *DBFP*, 3rd series, Vol. II, no. 595). Beck, Canaris and Hossbach were entirely free of such illusions.

14   On Canaris: Höhne, *Canaris*, VIII; on Hossbach cf. Deutsch, *Das Komplott*, and for Beck see Müller, *Heer und Hitler*, pp. 262, 267 ff. and 281–98, and by the same author, *Ludwig Beck. Studien und Dokumente zur politischen Vorstellungswelt und dienstlichen Tätigkeit des Generalstabschefs 1933–1938* (Boppard, 1980), ch. III.

15   Müller, *Heer und Hitler*, doc. no. 34. The exact wording sheds interesting light on the power struggle aspect: 'Liberation of the *Wehrmacht*' (not of the nation!).

16   On this and what follows see H. K. G. Roennefarth, *Die Sudetenkrise in der internationalen Politik 1938* (Wiesbaden, 1961), and Müller, *Ludwig Beck*, chs V and VI.

17   As is suggested in particular by Hoffmann.

18   One could add to the list Staatssekretär v. Weizsäcker: cf. W. Michalka's contribution in this volume.

19   This and what follows is treated fully in Müller, *Ludwig Beck*; for a more summary account see the same, *Armee, Politik und Gesellschaft*, pp. 51–100.

20   Memorandum dated 29.5.1938, ibid., doc. no. 46.

21   On this see in particular J. Henke, *England in Hitlers Kalkül, 1935–1939* (Boppard, 1973), ch. III, pp. 150–62.

22   Müller, *Ludwig Beck*, doc. no. 55.

23   Thus Hoffmann, *Widerstand*, pp. 104 ff. and pp. 685 f., going against the majority of research on the subject.

24   As described by the great majority of historians on the subject, adopting the phrase from W. Foerster, *Generaloberst Ludwig Beck. Sein Kampf gegen den Krieg* (Munich, 1953).

25   Often cited in this connection are notes and memoranda by senior naval officers (Guse, Heye), dated around July 1938. H. Krausnick, in his 'Vorgeschichte und Beginn des militarischen Widerstandes gegen Hitler', in *Vollmacht des Gewissens*, Vol. I (Frankfurt/M., 1960), pp. 315 f., overestimated their importance by 'mistaking them for a resistance plot' (thus M. Salewski, *Die deutsche Seekriegsleitung, 1935–1945*, Vol. 1 Frankfurt/M., 1970, p. 45).

26   See Höhne, *Canaris*, pp. 277 ff., and Helmut Groscurth, *Tagebücher eines Abwehroffiziers, 1938–1940*, ed. H. Krausnick and H. C. Deutsch (Stuttgart, 1970), pp. 120 ff.

27   cf. Beck's memorandum of 16.7.1938 (in Müller, *Ludwig Beck*, doc. no. 49/50): 'to defer the idea of solving the Czechoslovak problem by force until there has been fundamental alteration in the state of military preparedness. At present I see no prospect of this . . .'

28   See G. Schreiber, *Marine und Weltmachtstreben* (Stuttgart, 1978), ch. III, and the same author's 'Zur Kontinuität des Gross- und Weltmachtstrebens der deutschen Marineführung', *Militärgeschichtliche Mitteilungen*, vol. 2/79 (1979), pp. 101–72.

29   cf. *Die Weizsäcker-Papiere, 1933–1950*, ed. L. E. Hill (Berlin, 1974), p. 169: 'Definitely opposed to war was Beck, Chief of the General Staff. He told me early in August that he was resigning, not wanting to share responsibility for the coming calamity. I tried to dissuade him, but his answer was that since as a soldier one could not resign in a crisis, it would have to be done beforehand. As to my case his opinion was different,for the reason that a politician, unlike a soldier, has opportunities to deflect events right up to the last' (note written mid-October 1939).

30   See Aster, *1939*, and B.-J. Wendt, *München 1938, England zwischen Hitler und Preussen* (Frankfurt/M., 1965).

31   For this see the works by Aster, Henke and Michalka already mentioned, and *Weizsäcker-Papiere*.

32   For a detailed account of the events see Hoffmann, *Widerstand*, ch. IV/4; and cf. the analysis in Müller, *Heer und Hitler*, ch. VIII.

33   Politically important: the contact between Halder and Schacht and the loose contact, by way of Gisevius, with Goerdeler. Useful from a practical viewpoint were the connections established with the Chief of Police, Helldorff, and his deputy, Schulenburg; the group round F. W. Heinz had tenuous connections with a few former trade unionists (Leuschner).

34   For details about Oster's plans see Hoffmann, *Widerstand*, pp. 118 ff., and Müller, *Heer und Hitler*, p. 369.

35   It is clear that at the crisis point of Anglo-German negotiations, 26–29 September, Halder and Witzleben drew Brauchitsch into their anti-war activities; what remains uncertain is whether he was informed of the coup being planned.

36   cf. Goerdeler's comments in his letter of 11 October 1938, reproduced in G. Ritter, *Carl Goerdeler und die deutsche Widerstandsbewegung* (Stuttgart, 1954), p. 198, and the diary entry in U. v. Hassell, *Vom anderen Deutschland* (Zürich–Freiburg, 1946), p. 18; likewise Weizsäcker's remark to Canaris: 'Action from within is impossible, there's no Führer there and the people have become used to living in a Napoleonic age' (Groscurth, *Tagebücher*, p. 159).

37   A ground plan of the *Reichskanzlei*, essential to the operations of the shock troops, was not obtained until 24 September (E. Kordt, *Nicht aus den Akten* (Stuttgart, 1950), p. 263). Halder criticised Witzleben for having given too little attention to detailed planning (Ritter, *Carl Goerdeler*, p. 479, n. 61).

38   For a summary of these developments see Hoffmann, *Widerstand*, ch. IV, and, offering a different evaluation, Müller, *Heer und Hitler*, ch. IX.

39   For critical comments by someone involved see H. Gisevius, *Bis zum bitteren Ende* (special edition in one volume, Hamburg, n.d.), pp. 403 f. Even the occupation of the remnant of Czechoslovakia did not – as Beck observed – stir up any excitement (Gisevius, ibid., p. 389).

40   Convincing evidence for this is to be found in the material used by Aster. Besides, the British had also to cope with official envoys from Hitler like Wiedemann, Reichenau and the rest, whose visits to London were not part of the diplomatic routine.

41   cf. Höhne, *Canaris*, pp. 325 f., and *Weizsäcker–Papiere*, pp. 155 ff. and pp. 175–80.

42   For instance, Schwerin proposed to the British that they send a naval formation to the Baltic as a demonstrative gesture just at the time when Weizsäcker, in an effort to relieve

the tension, was trying to restrain Hitler from sending à German naval formation to Danzig. (For Schwerin's mission see Aster, *1939*, pp. 235, 237 f.).

43   For Canaris see Höhne, *Canaris*, pp. 302 f. and 320 ff., and Groscurth, *Tagebücher*, pp. 171 and 173 ('The Führer's great speech to the *Reichstag* clears the way for the task in respect of Poland. That is good, and it was not before time') and pp. 175 f. For Halder see evidence in Müller, *Heer und Hitler*, pp. 545 f. and p. 567 in illustration of his anglophobia and his assent to an 'adjustment' of the problem of the eastern frontier. In a letter, dated 15 October 1965, Halder wrote to the present author as follows: 'I have never doubted that England was the real driving force in the conflict of the Western Powers with Germany.'

44   When in May 1939 Goerdeler reported to the British that the German army was at that very moment prepared to mount a coup against the regime, 'but the decision is a question of timing', that he himself was in favour of striking now, but that 'the leader of the whole movement . . . considered it still too early', the information was totally erroneous, born no doubt from wishful thinking (quoted in Aster, *1939*, pp. 230 f.).

Part Two

Appeasement Policies in Great Britain

I

THE POLICY-MAKERS

6 Chamberlain and Appeasement

ROY DOUGLAS

When Neville Chamberlain became Prime Minister on 28 May 1937, there was already a very clear danger that the world would soon drift into war.

Since the League of Nations was incapable of preserving peace, the only chance of doing so lay in either individual or collective action by powers who did not wish to see the settlement of Versailles disrupted by force. In the middle of 1936, the British Chiefs of Staff recognised Germany, Italy and Japan as countries which were 'by their systems of government and by economic need, potential aggressors'.[1] Britain – the argument ran – could hope to deal successfully with any one of those three countries; but she could not possibly deal with all of them together. As one of the Chiefs of Staff wrote some time afterwards: 'We all agree – we want peace; not only because we are a satisfied and therefore naturally a peaceful people; but because it is in our imperial interests, having an exceedingly vulnerable Empire, not to go to war.'[2]

There was little doubt that major changes, perhaps involving frontier alterations, would soon take place, whatever Britain might do. The operative question which faced Chamberlain was whether those changes could be brought about without war. The foreign policy always linked with Chamberlain's name is labelled 'appeasement'. Like many political words, it was of uncertain significance. As Anthony Eden, then the Foreign Secretary, would later have cause to point out, the dictionary offers a range of meanings, extending from the idea of making peace by inducing agreement to the idea of making peace by offering concessions.

The Prime Minister certainly conceived 'appeasement' in the first sense. Granted the general analysis made by the Chiefs of Staff – and nobody seems to have confuted that analysis – it was manifestly not possible to meet the problem by merely making concessions to the various threatening powers. 'Appeasement', as Chamberlain understood it, required a settlement, or a series of settlements, with the three powers: contracts involving concessions on both sides, which would thereafter be honoured. This approach was natural for a man with Chamberlain's commercial background; but the principle involved was widely accepted. The Anglo-German Naval Agreement, reached a couple of years earlier, was perhaps a fair example of that kind of 'appeasement'.

Of the three countries perceived by the Chiefs of Staff as potential threats, Japan presented the least immediate danger during Chamberlain's premiership. Japan was a long way off; she was deeply involved in conflict with China; and any hostile action which she might take against British interests was likely to bring her simultaneously into conflict with other European powers, and with the United States. Thus Japan did not play a large part in major discussions of the period. The Chiefs of Staff in 1936 had recognised Germany as the most dangerous single threat to the British Empire 'because, geographically, she is already in a position to strike a severe blow at the heart, or, by occupying the Low Countries, to get into a position where the blow would be even more serious'.[3] 'If only we could get on terms with the Germans I would not care a rap for Musso',[4] wrote the Prime Minister in a private letter. Yet Germany was not at that moment making insistent demands against other countries, though many people guessed that she was proposing soon to do so. Italy was the immediate subject of concern. When Abyssinia was attacked in 1935, Britain and France adopted a very hostile attitude towards Italy, and sought through the League of Nations to impose economic sanctions. These visibly failed in their primary object. The Italians were not convinced that Britain's concern over Abyssinia was altruistic, suspecting that it was motivated by anxiety over her own imperial interests in East Africa. At times they wondered whether Britain was merely trying to gain time until her rearmament was complete, and she could effectively coerce Italy. Yet Britain and France did not make the best of a bad job, cut their losses and restore relations with Italy. They refused to recognise the Italian conquest – which antagonised Italy and faced her with certain financial difficulties, without helping the unfortunate Abyssinians. The Abyssinian difficulty had been compounded by the engagement of Italian and French sympathies on opposite sides in the Spanish Civil War: a situation partly ideological in origin, but exacerbated by the widespread (though erroneous) suspicion that Italy sought to acquire the strategically important Balearic Islands in event of a Franco victory.

Behind such immediate issues lay an even deeper, more fundamental consideration: for there was a profound ambiguity about Italian interests. While Mussolini was undeniably a 'revisionist' in the Mediterranean and Africa, he also had an interest in preserving stability in Central Europe against any attempt which Hitler might make to disrupt it. 'Italy lives in dread of a German menace through Austria and the Tyrol, to say nothing of Yugoslavia', wrote the Secretary of the British Chiefs of Staff in 1936.[5] This fact had been brought out dramatically by Mussolini's vigorous and effective action to prevent a Nazi take-over in Austria in 1934, and was re-emphasised when the Stresa Front was established early in the following year. Surely it was possible to do a deal with Mussolini by which – in return for some concessions to his 'revisionist' interests in the south – he could be brought to co-operate again with Britain and France against the far more dangerous 'revisionism' of Germany in central Europe? Thus might Italy be turned from a battering-ram into a buttress.

Not long before Chamberlain took office, the British government had received warning from their Ambassador, Sir Eric Drummond, to the effect that Italy's whole future orientation would depend on the willingness, or otherwise, of Britain to take action through the League of Nations which would lead to the general recognition *de jure* of her conquest of Abyssinia. If that was conceded 'then Italy will resume, perhaps not wholeheartedly at first, her collaboration with the League'. If not, then 'Italy will definitely leave the League, and will finally align completely with Germany, perhaps by a formal pact'.[6]

In the summer of 1937, considerable discussions took place between ministers and their advisers about a new approach to Italy. Count Grandi, the Italian Ambassador, had an interview with the new Premier on 27 July, at which Chamberlain took the occasion for one of his dramatic gestures. In the presence of the Ambassador, he wrote a personal letter to Mussolini, urging a *rapprochement*. Conversations should be inaugurated as soon as the Duce wished. Mussolini, who was surely entitled to believe that the British government really meant business, sent an equally warm reply, and Drummond was instructed by the Foreign Office 'that we hope to see discussions start towards the end of August or beginning of September'.[7]

Eden was never convinced of the value of Chamberlain's approach, although he had not made a clear stand against it when he was entitled to do so. During August, the Prime Minister and Viscount Halifax, Lord President of the Council, gradually perceived the width of the gulf. The appropriate action, surely, was to take the whole matter to the Cabinet, and force the issue one way or the other. None of the three men seemed anxious for this to happen, and much delay followed. The conversations which both Chamberlain and Mussolini were so anxious to hold were delayed further and further by the Foreign Office. The critical moment for any action preparatory to recognition of Italy's position in Abyssinia would be the meeting of the League. On 13 September the League met, without any British initiative having been prepared; on the 25th of the same month Mussolini arrived in Munich on a visit to Hitler. Italy had been more or less forced to take her choice.

Chamberlain was conscious that the Foreign Office had been making difficulties for his policy. 'But really that F.O.!', he wrote on 24 October. 'I am only waiting for my opportunity to stir it up with a long pole.'[8] This judgement was wholly valid; but the Prime Minister mistook the particular location in the Foreign Office whence his main trouble came. Not long before, the leading permanent officials had begun to wake up to the dangers of the Italian situation.[9] Perhaps it was already too late; but in any event Office correspondence makes it clear that Eden was still unconverted, and – led by his second-in-command, Viscount Cranborne – became increasingly hostile to the proposed deal with Mussolini.[10] 'The more I look into it the more I dislike the idea of this bargain',[11] he wrote to Chamberlain on the first day of the new year. Yet he did not take an equally implacable view about the possibility of appeasing Hitler. 'I entirely agree that we must make every effort to come to terms with Germany',[12] he wrote a few weeks later.

Early in February 1938 everything suddenly began to move at once. By an extraordinary piece of 'personal diplomacy', Mussolini was able to satisfy himself that Chamberlain still wanted Anglo-Italian conversations to take place. A few days later, the Austrian Chancellor was browbeaten by Hitler and compelled to incorporate a couple of Nazis in his government. The Italians pressed urgently for conversations with Britain, with overtones of real panic in their communications. Then, on 18 February, Grandi met Chamberlain. The Ambassador hinted strongly that failure to improve

Anglo-Italian relations had already made it impossible to save Austria from the *Anschluss*, and that more developments there could be expected soon. Furthermore: 'If it was impossible to improve relations with Great Britain, then it would be necessary for Italy to draw still closer to Germany. The decision would then be final. It was not final yet, but there was very little time left.'[13]

In the next couple of days, emergency meetings of the Cabinet were held. At last the issue was squarely faced. Chamberlain insisted on the inauguration of conversations; Eden opposed it. The debate was confused and acrimonious. At the end Eden resigned, and was soon replaced as Foreign Secretary by Viscount Halifax. Chamberlain had certainly been obtuse about Eden – perhaps because he relied upon personal loyalty. 'I had no idea until the 18th that it would come to a break',[14] he wrote a few days later.

On 11 March troops of the German Reich crossed the frontier into Austria; and a few days later the *Anschluss* was complete. For the first time since the early 1920s, a frontier in Europe was changed without general endorsement from the powers. These sudden events in Austria admitted of two interpretations. Many people believed, and some still do believe, that Hitler took the departure of Eden as a green light. But, as we have already noted, Eden's implacable opposition was not to Hitler but to Mussolini. Surely a likelier explanation is that Hitler perceived that Britain and Italy were in the process of resolving their differences, that a new Stresa Front was in the process of being erected and that it was now or never.

It is impossible to overstate the importance of the *Anschluss* in the rush to war of the late 1930s. Without Austria, Hitler's road to the east was blocked. From both a military and a moral point of view, it is difficult to conceive of any major move against Czechoslovakia before Austria had fallen. Chamberlain's attempt to appease Italy was far more hopeful than his later efforts to appease Germany; and the failure of that policy is not attributable to any foreign statesman but to Anthony Eden and the British Foreign Office. 'It is tragic to think', wrote Chamberlain not long after the *Anschluss*, 'that very possibly this might have been prevented if I had had Halifax at the FO instead of Anthony at the time I wrote my letter to Mussolini.'[15]

It is arguable that Hitler could have gone into Austria, with or without Mussolini's consent. In one sense that is true, for it is difficult to see how Italy could have resisted him by force of arms. Yet such action would certainly have incurred Mussolini's enduring ill-will, which Hitler was very anxious to avoid. If Mussolini had felt sure of the friendship of Britain and France, it appears unlikely that the *Anschluss* would have taken place.

I have spoken of the 'failure' of Chamberlain's Italian appeasement. Yet perhaps that word should be qualified by the adjective 'relative'. It was too late to save Austria, too late to avert war: but the temporary improvement in relations with Italy which followed Eden's departure did enable Mussolini to take a line of his own with Hitler later in 1938; and this may possibly have deflected Hitler from going to war over Czechoslovakia in September. Britain and France were even less prepared for war then than they were a year later; and it is arguable that the year of delay thus secured was of crucial importance in determining the outcome of the war.

In the immediate aftermath of the *Anschluss*, Britain apparently had a choice between several policies towards Germany. At that moment, these did not include 'appeasement' at all, for Britain was neither seeking nor offering concessions.

Simplest of these policies was to do nothing; and on the face there was much to be said for this. Britain had no subsisting military treaties with countries in Central and Eastern Europe; for her traditional policy had been to incur no obligations to countries which she could not reach by sea. This was a not unreasonable policy, for the British navy was enormous and the army microscopic. The fate of Central and Eastern Europe – save for the Mediterranean seaboard – was scarcely vital either to Britain's economic prosperity or to her strategic interests. Yet the apparently attractive course of continued disinterest was scarcely considered. The overriding reason appears to have been France. The French had a mutual defence treaty with Britain, and also one with Czechoslovakia: a treaty, incidentally, which Britain had not liked from the start. If Germany attacked Czechoslovakia and (as appeared likely) the Czechs resisted, this would activate the French treaty. If France went to war, then by common consent Britain would probably be involved sooner or later on France's side.

What were the prospects of helping Czechoslovakia in such a situation? As Chamberlain wrote on 20 March:

> You have only to look at the map to see that nothing that France or we could do could possibly save Czechoslovakia from being overrun by the Germans if they wanted to do it . . . Czechoslovakia . . . would simply be a pretext for going to war with Germany. That we could not think of unless we had a reasonable prospect of being able to beat her to her knees in a reasonable time and of that I see no sign.[16]

The Chiefs of Staff provided a much fuller analysis, which was considered by the Cabinet. Even if Germany fought alone, she would rapidly destroy Czechoslovakia and the Western Allies would face the prospect of a long war. If Italy and Japan fought as Germany's allies, then Britain and France would probably be defeated. Chamberlain and Halifax admitted that they had both originally contemplated some kind of guarantee to Czechoslovakia; but in light of this 'exceedingly melancholy document' – Halifax's words – such action was out of the question.[17]

Thus the two most obvious policies were both excluded. There remained a third possibility, which commended itself generally to the Cabinet. Any trouble over Czechoslovakia was likely to be related closely to the real or imaginary grievances of the $3\frac{1}{4}$ or $3\frac{1}{2}$ million Sudetendeutsche who lived in the country's western fringes. Neither the Sudetendeutsche nor the Reich government had yet declared what they actually wanted for those people. If some kind of 'internal solution' could be achieved satisfactory both to the Sudetendeutsche and to the Czechoslovak government, then presumably the whole situation could be defused, for Hitler would have neither excuse nor occasion to intervene. Accordingly the British government decided to bend its efforts to achieve mediation.

It is useful to look at what the government's critics were saying at the time. Down to the middle of 1938, such Labour and Liberal documents as I have seen appear more concerned with Spain than with Central Europe. In so far as an 'opposition' policy was being proposed for the Czechoslovak situation, that policy was 'collective security', relying on the League of Nations and particularly on Russia. The possibility of countries in Central and Eastern Europe participating in a conflict over Czechoslovakia had been examined by the British Chiefs of Staff; but the general view seemed to be that they would become involved on different sides if so, and thus more or less neutralise each other.

Russia's position, however, is particularly interesting, for Russia had a treaty with Czechoslovakia. If Czechoslovakia was attacked and fought back, and France then went to her aid – in these circumstances Russia was obliged also to go to war on Czechoslovakia's side. However, a glance at the map shows that Russia did not have a common frontier with either Czechoslovakia or Germany. Perhaps she could fly in a few aeroplanes without too much trouble; but large Russian land forces could only reach Czechoslovakia if they crossed Romania or – much more likely – Poland. There was not the faintest doubt that the Poles would resist any such move by Russia. Furthermore, Stalin had recently liquidated two-thirds of the Red Army High Command and was perpetrating an unprecedented reign of terror throughout the country. It was impossible for outsiders to form any reliable assessment of how valuable or otherwise such a country would be if it became involved in war. Thus any 'collective security' against Hitler could be little more than bluff, and would be immediately perceived as such. It was not easy for Chamberlain to make such points in public debate.

The story of Britain's attempt to secure mediation between the Czech government and the Sudetendeutsche is familiar, and so also is the very evident unwillingness of both parties to make any concessions to the other. It is arguable that Viscount Runciman's Mission got them to the very edge of agreement on 6 September, and that this prospect was finally destroyed by the unbelievably irresponsible *Times* editorial on the following day. Be that as it may, by mid-September there was no remaining doubt that mediation had become impossible; that the Sudeten Germans were now insisting on incorporation in the Reich; and the Reich Germans were poising themselves to invade Czechoslovakia. On 10 September hints began to appear that the French were not over-keen on fulfilling their treaty with Czechoslovakia, should need arise; and three days later the Foreign Minister Georges Bonnet, 'in a state of collapse', unburdened his mind to the British Ambassador: 'We cannot sacrifice ten million men in order to prevent 3½ million Sudetens joining the Reich.'[18] For some time there was considerable doubt whether Premier Edouard Daladier was of the same mind; but whether he was or not, this uncertainty about French foreign policy was an exceedingly important new factor.

Chamberlain's thinking at the time is well indicated by his interview with a delegation from the Labour Party on 17 September. The visitors declared themselves 'hostile to severing territory from Czechoslovakia and handing it over to Germany'[19] and indicated the view that a 'joint ultimatum by Great

Britain, France and Russia . . . would deter Hitler'. The Prime Minister rejoined with the view that unless a solution could be worked out 'which commended itself to the Sudeten Germans and to Germany herself, there was every reason to believe that within a very short time we should be faced with a movement into Czechoslovakia'. In answer to a question, Chamberlain 'replied that he thought Hitler *does* realise that if France comes in we should, sooner or later, come in too, but Hitler does not believe that France will come in. The Prime Minister added that he himself did not think France would come in either.' He gave the most appalling picture of France's unpreparedness: 'The French have only 21 aeroplanes equal to German aeroplanes and they have only 500 altogether.' As for Russia, Chamberlain referred to a recent conversation between Beneš and the Soviet Foreign Minister 'from which it was clear that, though they might raise the matter at Geneva, Russia was not likely to do anything that was effective'. The Labour delegation was obviously much shaken by the news about both France and Russia. With some understatement, the Prime Minister concluded that 'this is not the moment to accept a challenge if we can possibly avoid it'.

What obsessed Chamberlain at this stage of the crisis was the sheer confusion of the situation, with the danger that war might arise, not out of some deep and fundamental clash of vital interests between the powers, but out of bluff, and uncertainty as to each other's purpose. Nobody yet knew what Hitler immediately wanted. At one extreme, he might propose to incorporate the whole of Czechoslovakia in the German Reich, or to divide the country up with Hungary and Poland. At the other extreme, he might desire no more than to annex the Sudetenland. As the British Ambassador to Berlin, Sir Nevile Henderson, had pointed out, there was an argument – even on Nazi premises – that Hitler only wished to rule over Germans, and was content to leave other peoples to their own devices. If that was the case, then a peaceful agreement might be possible.

So Chamberlain decided to cut all intermediaries, and go himself to see Hitler. This was very much the Prime Minister's own idea, and based on a plan which he had been considering for some weeks; but it received well-nigh unanimous approval of the British Press – opposition as well as pro-government newspapers. Chamberlain departed to meet Hitler at Berchtesgaden, where the Führer explained that he only required the Sudetenland. The Prime Minister returned home, and thereupon exerted successful pressure on the Czechoslovak government to make the concession, and on the French to agree to the transaction. The Prime Minister now had another meeting with Hitler, at Bad Godesberg. Here the Führer attempted to step up his demands, but Chamberlain was obdurate and returned home. A few days of mounting tension followed, which was suddenly eased by the announcement that Hitler had invited Chamberlain, Daladier and Mussolini to meet him at Munich. At that meeting, there was no hard bargaining. Virtually, Hitler retreated to his Berchtesgaden position, which was accepted by all concerned. Chamberlain and Daladier were greeted by wildly cheering crowds when they returned to their respective countries. In the view of many people, appeasement had triumphed and achieved a

durable peace which Hitler and Mussolini were both prepared to underwrite.

It is useful to ask at this point what result Chamberlain and his colleagues
expected to flow from the Munich Agreement. There is evidence to suggest
that the Prime Minister thought that he had made an enduring deal with
Hitler; that peace had been saved for the foreseeable future. He probably
vacillated in his own mind on the matter; for a relative of Chamberlain has
recollection of a private letter – unfortunately not preserved – which
expressed the gravest doubts.[20] The Prime Minister was certainly anxious to
determine whether his policy would also be justified if Hitler broke his word.
During the September discussions, advice was sought from the Committee
of Imperial Defence, whose reply was unambiguous: 'From a military point
of view, time is in our favour, and . . . if war with Germany has to come it
would be better to fight her in say 6–12 months' time than to accept the
present challenge.'[21] Chamberlain's colleagues appear on the whole to have
felt less confidence than the Prime Minister himself about the durability of
the agreement; but with the not-too-clear exception of Duff Cooper they
concurred in the wisdom of the substantive decision.

Doubts about the French could not be expressed in public debate. Still less
could the government point out that a great deal of Dominion opinion was
lukewarm on the matter – a consideration which appears to have impressed
the Cabinet considerably. There were other considerations equally important. No British government could have led a united country into the conflict
at the time of Munich. The doubts which we have already noted in France
were paralleled – though for somewhat different reasons – in Britain.
Certain elements of the Press and some public figures – not all of them on the
'right' in politics – had grave doubts about the wisdom or even morality of a
policy which might lead to war in defence of Czechoslovakia. The Sudeten
issue was a very bad one, morally, on which to fight: for to all appearances
the great majority of the Sudeten Germans wished to be incorporated in the
Reich. Furthermore, it was still not conclusively proved that Hitler's international word was wholly unreliable. It was all very well to say that he had
often violated treaties before. There was an argument, however, for the
view that those treaties had been imposed on a weak, defeated Germany;
that Hitler never acknowledged their validity. It is noteworthy that Eden
had written earlier in the year that an agreement with Germany 'might have
a chance of a reasonable life, especially if Hitler's own position were
engaged'.[22] We are driven inescapably to the conclusion that – granted the
situation existing in September 1938 – Chamberlain did about as well as
anybody could have done, and the criticisms levelled against him were only
credible because the government was unable to make its own best case in
reply.

Indeed, there was something unreal about many of the criticisms which
Chamberlain encountered. When news of the impending visit to Munich was
announced in the House of Commons – at a time when it was already clear
beyond doubt that the Sudetenland would be ceded to Germany if any
settlement was reached – the Labour and Liberal leaders expressed their
warm approval of the Prime Minister's decision to go, while future Con-

servative critics like Churchill and Eden were silent. In fact nobody, with the exception of the sole Communist MP, protested. The criticism which exploded soon after Munich was not endorsed by a number of important men on the 'left', including Lansbury, Maxton and Tillett. Viscount Samuel – former Liberal Leader and perhaps the most distinguished living British Jew – strongly supported Chamberlain. Nor did the British criticism have much parallel in other Western countries. In France, a motion in support of Daladier was carried by an overwhelming majority of the Chamber, only the Communists and two other Deputies voting against. The Governor-General of Canada declared himself 'amazed' at the criticisms in the British Press; by comparison the Press of Canada had been 'wonderful'.[23]

On the *Kristallnacht*, the early morning of 10 November 1938, the Munich euphoria disappeared. A few days later Halifax concluded that 'no useful purpose' would be served by resuming Anglo-German negotiations, while Chamberlain declared himself 'horrified' at the event.[24] What completely destroyed appeasement, however, was the annihilation of Czechoslovakia on 15 March 1939. Within a few days enough facts were known to make it plain that further appeasement of Germany was out of the question. 'As soon as I had time to think I saw that it was impossible to deal with Hitler after he had thrown all his own assurances to the wind',[25] wrote the Prime Minister in a private letter on 19 March. With dramatic suddenness, Chamberlain and his Cabinet swung to the utterly different policy of attempting to engineer alliances which would threaten Hitler with war. Whether that policy was wise or unwise is outside the present field of discussion; but it certainly was not appeasement.

Some people have suggested that attempts to appease Germany did not die in March 1939. There were, for example, the contacts maintained with Goering during the summer, and even after war began, through the Swedes Wenner-Gren and Dahlerus. There were the belated efforts of Italy to secure a peace conference – which briefly interrupted plans in the afternoon of 2 September 1939. Yet it seems wrong to link these activities with appeasement. At no point was there any suggestion that the British government might use its influence to induce other countries to make concessions to Germany. The climate of British opinion would have set this beyond the bounds of possibility even if Chamberlain had wanted it – and he certainly did not want it. The importance of such contacts was to make British attitudes absolutely clear, and to remove any remaining danger of war through misunderstanding.

There is another even less convincing candidate for post-Prague appeasement: the extraordinary, and still puzzling, story of a possible loan to Germany. Chamberlain was as mystified as anybody about the 'rumour that we were offering Germany a loan which in three different papers I worked out yesterday was of £100, £500 and £1000 million respectively'.[26] Apparently the story arose out of a conversation between R. S. Hudson, a junior minister at the Board of Trade, and Wohlthat, a close associate of Goering. 'In [Hudson's] account to me there was no mention of a loan but I am not sure that he told me the whole truth', noted the Prime Minister.

We may now stand back and look at the record of Chamberlain's appeasement policy. Appeasement of Italy, so far as it was practised, justified itself to the hilt; the appalling tragedy is that this policy was not worked out to the full as Chamberlain wished it. Appeasement of Germany is much more vulnerable to criticism, but not from the angle from which that criticism is usually launched. A policy of backing up French bluff over Czechoslovakia would almost certainly have resulted in that bluff being called. Perhaps Germany would have fought a very brief war against the Czechs; almost certainly both France and Russia would have avoided taking effective action in the matter. Thus would clear notice have been served on all the smaller European nations that resistance to Germany was futile.

There remains a possible criticism of appeasement from the opposite angle: that Britain was wrong to press her mediation on the Czechs; that she should have kept out of any involvement with countries which she was not in a position to assist directly in event of trouble. This is a much more powerful criticism of Chamberlain's policy, but it is not one which is often advanced. One day, perhaps, it should be examined closely.

Notes: Chapter 6

1   Hankey: Foreign Policy and Imperial Defence, 8 June 1936, Public Record Office (PRO): FO 954/7B, fo. 437.
2   Notes on Vansittart's memo, 5 January 1937, Chatfield Papers, National Maritime Museum (Greenwich): CHT/3/1, fo. 190.
3   Hankey, above.
4   Neville to Ida Chamberlain, 4 July 1937, Neville Chamberlain Papers, University of Birmingham: NC18/1/1010.
5   Hankey, above.
6   Drummond to Eden, 5 March 1937, FO 954/13A, fo. 59.
7   FO to Drummond, 4 August 1937, PRO: PREM 1/276.
8   Neville to Hilda Chamberlain, 24 October 1937, NC 18/1/1025.
9   Vansittart's note, 1 October 1937, FO memo, 2 October, FO371/21162.
10   Cranborne and Eden minutes, 16 November 1937, FO 371/21162.
11   Eden to Chamberlain, 1 January 1938, PREM 1/276.
12   Eden to Chamberlain, 31 January 1938, PREM 1/276.
13   Ingram (draft for Eden to Perth), 21 February 1938, PREM 1/276.
14   Neville to Hilda Chamberlain, 27 February 1938, NC 18/1/1040.
15   Neville to Hilda Chamberlain, 13 March 1938, NC 18/1/1041.
16   Neville to Ida Chamberlain, 20 March 1938, NC 18/1/1042.
17   COS 697 (JP), PRO: CAB 53/37; Cabinet 15(38), 22 March, CAB/23/93.
18   Phipps to Halifax, 14 September 1938, Documents on British Foreign Policy, 3rd series 2, nos 872, 874.
19   Meeting of 17 September 1938 (written 19 September), PREM 1/264 fo. 14.
20   Arthur Chamberlain to Kenneth Humphreys, 2 January 1973, NC7/6/44.
21   Note on whether to fight Germany now (Ismay), 20 September 1938, CAB 21/544.
22   Eden to Chamberlain, 9 January 1938, PREM 1/276.
23   Tweedsmuir to Chamberlain, 27 October 1938, PREM 1/242.
24   FP (36) 32nd meeting, 14 November 1938, FO 800/311; Neville to Ida Chamberlain, 13 November 1938, NC 18/1/1076.
25   Neville to Hilda Chamberlain, 19 March 1939, NC 18/1/1090.
26   Neville to Ida Chamberlain, 23 July 1939, NC 18/1/1108.

7 Had Baldwin Resigned in 1936: A Speculative Essay

ROBERT P. SHAY, JR

It is 16 February 1936. Stanley Baldwin has resigned as Prime Minister two days after his government had been subjected to devastating parliamentary criticism of its handling of Britain's rearmament programme. Leading that criticism had been Austin Chamberlain, the Conservative Party's elder statesman.

He had reminded the House of Baldwin's admission of error the previous May concerning German air strength, stating: 'I recall no comparable pronouncement by the head of a Government on a fundamental issue of defence in the forty odd years of my Parliamentary experience.' Continuing, he noted that Baldwin had

> startled the House and the country by use of language such as none of us had heard in our experience from a Minister of the Crown. He said, on the 19th December, 1935: 'I have seldom spoken with greater regret, for my lips are not yet unsealed.' He was defending the policy of the Hoare–Laval proposals . . . Well, Sir, why do I recite these things? They are not pleasant; they are not reassuring. It is because those things could not have happened if the thinking machine of the Government was working properly, if their defence organisation was really efficient.[1]

Although Austin Chamberlain led the parliamentary attack on Baldwin's leadership, his half-brother, Neville, the Chancellor of the Exchequer, sealed Baldwin's fate. Baldwin's acknowledged successor as leader of the Conservative Party, Neville Chamberlain was the only man with the power to force Baldwin from office. He chose to do so with great personal regret after it had become apparent that Baldwin could not provide the leadership to unify the nation behind a massive rearmament effort; an effort made necessary by the rapidly growing threats to Britain's security posed by Germany, Japan and Italy.

In his first speech as Prime Minister, Neville Chamberlain called upon the nation to set aside issues of class and party, and to join in an effort to prepare Britain to defend herself against her enemies. He announced his intention to meet with the leaders of industry and organised labour to develop plans to expedite the rearmament programme. Industry was asked to give armaments-related contracts strict priority. Parliament was to give that request the force of law. Organised labour was asked to work with the government and industry to help eliminate production bottlenecks resulting from the shortage of skilled men in trades critical to the rearmament effort.

Although the defence budget for the coming fiscal year had already been written, Chamberlain announced that a special minister would be appointed to evaluate the recently completed Ideal Scheme for defence written by the Defence Requirements Sub-Committee of the Committee of Imperial Defence. Operating under the title of Minister for the Co-ordination of Defence, this minister would work with the Treasury and the armed services to develop a coherent plan for rearmament that would not undermine Britain's economy. All supplementary budget requests for defence expenditures would have to be deferred until the rearmament plan was in place.

The German occupation of the Rhineland the following month prompted Chamberlain to request that Parliament authorise the establishment of a Ministry of Supply. This ministry was to have no statutory power to compel industry or labour. At its head would be Thomas Inskip, recently appointed Minister for the Co-ordination of Defence, whose title and function it would absorb. In addition, it would take over the functions of the Principal Supply Officer's sub-committee of the CID and the Board of Trade's Supply Board which were jointly responsible for formulating plans for the mobilisation of Britain's resources in the event of war.

The foregoing rearrangement of reality has, you may be relieved to know, been performed wittingly. The intention of this essay is to try to gain a better understanding of the forces that shaped British rearmament by exploring what might have occurred had a few events happened differently.

While this approach is commonly used by economists, most historians, including myself, have been sceptical, to put it kindly, of its utility in their own endeavours. I have come to the view that this approach may have some use in analysing the rearmament effort only after considering at some length what may and may not be learned from it. In order to discuss that question it is necessary to describe briefly what I intend to do.

Economists using this approach construct models with multiple variables to describe an aspect of reality. They then test the model against reality by altering specific combinations of variables to determine whether the outcomes they know should result actually occur. Models that prove viable then are used to test hypotheses about outcomes involving the alteration of combinations of variables, the effects of which are now known with certainty.

In this case the model is the development as we understand it of British rearmament between February 1936 and September 1939. By altering three variables, then logically considering how those alterations might have affected what happened in reality, it may prove possible to refine our understanding of the forces that shaped British rearmament in the late 1930s.

The three variables that are being altered are (*a*) the timing of Chamberlain's ascent to the premiership, (*b*) Chamberlain's and his party's firmly held opposition to government compulsion of industry, and his consequent opposition to the creation of a Ministry of Supply, and (*c*) his and his party's mistrust of organised labour. The hypothesis that is being tested by altering these variables is that British rearmament would have been more advanced in September 1939 had the nation been led by a Prime Minister of Chamberlain's ability and stature who viewed the strengthening of Britain's defences as the nation's highest priority.

The foregoing being said, I hasten to return to my earlier allusion to what may or may not be learned from this approach. First and foremost, while conclusions will be reached as to the validity of the hypothesis, they will obviously be tentative and open to debate. What I trust will be of value are the questions raised and insights gained as a result of considering what went on during this period from a different factual perspective. My hope is that this discussion will lead to a better understanding of the operation of the political and economic forces that affected British rearmament policy.

Returning to the hypothetical situation sketched in the opening pages, this paper will discuss the rationale for and the possible ramifications of the events described. The rationale for Baldwin's ouster is easy to understand. His leadership during the Hoare–Laval affair and the debates on rearmament that followed had, as Austin Chamberlain noted, left much to be desired, even in the minds of his own backbenchers.[2] There is little question that Neville Chamberlain could have forced him to resign. In reality he remained loyal. In this case, the Chamberlain being hypothesised decided that Baldwin's weakness posed unacceptable dangers to Britain's security.

The primary ramification of Baldwin's hypothetical resignation in 1936 is obvious. It would have given Chamberlain an additional year to organise the rearmament programme.

It is suggested that one of Chamberlain's first steps after replacing Baldwin and calling for national support for the rearmament effort would have been to consult with industry and organised labour. Although the government had in reality consulted closely with industry throughout 1936, the tenor of the discussions in the hypothetical case would have been different from those that actually transpired.

The actual terms under which industry co-operated with the government in assisting with rearmament called for industry to organise itself. These terms had been laid down by the leaders of the Federation of British Industry in a meeting with Baldwin and Chamberlain on 17 October 1935.[3] Baldwin made several speeches pledging co-operation on those terms, and in February the Cabinet confirmed those assurances by pledging not to interfere with trade in the conduct of the rearmament programme.[4]

In the situation being described in this paper, Chamberlain would have taken a much firmer line with industry, insisting that industry co-operate within the organisational framework for rearmament being developed by his government. While this would have run directly counter to industry's insistence that it be permitted to organise itself to co-operate in the rearmament effort, the hypothetical Chamberlain being described here would have insisted on the government's prerogative in being the guiding force. In doing so he would have referred to his government's electoral mandate and his party's support for his programme.

The rationale for this position would have been that the interests of the nation rather than the convenience of industry should have been the principle guiding the organisation of industry in the rearmament programme. The ramifications of such a position taken by a Conservative Prime Minister are fascinating to contemplate.

Whether or not Chamberlain could have succeeded in pursuing this line would have depended upon the amount of influence industry had within the Conservative Party. While most observers, including myself, have concluded that industry's influence was considerable, no systematic work has been done to test that hypothesis.[5] It would be interesting to know how organised and unified industry was, and precisely what its ties to the Conservative Party were. How important was the role of industry in financing and organising political campaigns? Did membership on boards of directors or ownership of equity correlate with voting patterns on issues of interest to industry?

My belief is that business, and industry in particular, had enormous influence, but that is a point that remains to be proven or disproven. However, I believe also that industry was not particularly unified, and that, the implications of the industrialists' October 1935 meeting with Baldwin and Chamberlain to the contrary, had Chamberlain taken a firm line with them they would have grumbled but gone along. The key question is how much influence industry had over Conservative MPs. If Chamberlain had been able to gain the support of his MPs for such a programme, industry would have had little choice but to support it.

An important indicator of how much support Chamberlain might have had for his proposed programme, and of how much influence industry did have, would have been his ability to persuade British industry to give defence contracts priority over civilian production. If industry were to have sought a political confrontation over greater government direction of rearmament, it would have taken its first stand on this issue.

The expedition of defence work would have been Chamberlain's rationale for proposing priority for defence contracts in 1936. In the aircraft industry especially, inability to obtain machinery from the machine tool industry held up the completion of assembly lines for modern types of aircraft.[6] Similar problems also apparently affected the Admiralty's construction programme.

The primary argument against such a measure would have been its adverse effect on the trade balance since it would have shifted production in the exporting industries. George Peden has noted that this was a particular concern of the Treasury and the Economic Advisory Council's Committee on Economic Information. Because it was estimated that as much as 25 to 30 per cent of the cost of British rearmament represented the price of imported raw materials, it would have been argued that anything that would jeopardise exports would jeopardise the rearmament effort.[7]

While this argument is compelling, it would be interesting to know what percentage of exports would actually have been affected by a shift of priorities to defence contracts. A good starting-point for such an analysis would be a study of the effect on exports of the actual declaration of priority for defence contracts passed in March 1938 (if it could be disaggregated from the effects on trade of that year's recession, not an easy trick).

It is my suspicion that such a measure's effect on exports would have been insignificant, that the number of firms whose production would have been affected would have been small and the percentage of contracts they had with firms manufacturing for export smaller still. None the less, it is a supposition that could usefully be tested.

An essential element of Chamberlain's hypothetical programme would have been to consult with organised labour. Shortages of skilled labour in key industries had already begun to slow rearmament by early 1936.[8] If Chamberlain was to have been serious about a unified national effort to rearm he would have had to have called for and actively sought out co-operation with labour as well as industry.

The rationale for securing labour's co-operation would have been to bring organised labour together with industry to work out programmes for shifting skilled labour to defence industries and for breaking down jobs so they could be carried out by less skilled labour. Co-operation along these lines actually was worked out in 1938 when the government was forced by the shortage of labour to consult with Walter Citrine and the Trades Union Congress, and it materially assisted the production of armaments, particularly aircraft.[9]

In 1936, however, the government avoided any contact with labour, fearing, in Thomas Inskip's words, that '[d]irect action by the Government . . . might well lead to very serious labour unrest and concessions to labour apt to damage the position of the export trade'.[10] The government acted as though the Parliamentary Labour Party's continuing opposition to rearmament in 1936 and 1937 reflected the position of labour in general. In fact, as they should have well known, this was anything but the case. John Naylor has noted that as early as February 1936 the General Council of the Trades Union Congress had let it be known that it was concerned about rearmament, and was anxious to assist in expediting the rearmament process.[11]

An initiative such as the one suggested would have tested Citrine's control over the TUC, and certainly worsened the division between organised labour and large segments of the Parliamentary Labour Party. Of these two concerns, the former would have clearly been the more serious. The TUC was already at odds with the majority of the Labour Party over the issue of whether to support rearmament. Moreover, the TUC's support was more important to the parliamentary party than the parliamentary party's was to the TUC.

The larger question, Citrine's ability to win TUC backing for co-operation with the government and industry in rearmament, is more open to doubt. Two years later Citrine did succeed in such an effort, but the menace of the German threat was more considerable at that time and Citrine's hold over the TUC presumably that much stronger. Even in 1938 several of the unions most directly affected rebelled. The resistance of craft unions like the engineers especially comes to mind.[12]

What can be said with some certainty is that in 1936 an initiative on the government's part would have found a positive response on the part of the TUC leadership. The degree to which that could have been translated into increased armaments production is open to greater question. It is my belief that resistance would have been encountered from some skilled crafts unions, but that in the course of 1936 and 1937 the TUC could have assisted materially in easing some of the bottlenecks that developed due to the shortage of skilled labour.[13]

The most striking hypothetical move that would have been made by Chamberlain would have been the establishment in peacetime of a Ministry of Supply without compulsory powers. This new organisation would have taken over the role of overseeing and co-ordinating the rearmament effort from the Minister for the Co-ordination of Defence. At the same time it would have taken over planning for the mobilisation of industry in the event of war. This task was then being undertaken by the Principal Supply Officer's subcommittee of the CID and the Board of Trade's Supply Board headed by Walter Robinson.

There would have been in 1936 several rationales for establishing such an organisation. It would have given the Minister for the Co-ordination of Defence, Inskip, who in this case was to have become the head of the new ministry, a larger staff to oversee and co-ordinate the rearmament effort. This would have made him less reliant on Treasury assistance, hence more independent. It also would have moved forward by one year the process of developing a defence plan, the role played a year later by Inskip's review of defence expenditures in future years. Although this review would not have had any effect on the 1935–6 budget, it would have given the rearmament effort some direction during the fiscal year 1936–7. In terms of planning that year was, as Churchill so strikingly termed it, the year that the locusts ate.[14]

Equally important, it would have greatly expedited the planning for the mobilisation of industry in war. The very establishment of a Ministry of Supply would have created an organisational framework around which planning for the mobilisation of industry could have been carried out. In actuality no decision was made until 1938 as to whether a Ministry of Supply would be created in the event of war. Even that decision remained tentative into 1939.[15]

Establishment of such a ministry would have enabled the planners to organise and staff supply committees that could have worked with industrial trade associations and firms to let them know what would be expected of them in the event of war; what resources they would be allocated, what they would produce, to whom it would be delivered, and so on. It would have enabled the planners to identify and recruit people from industry during the prewar period to join the ministry when hostilities broke out to act as controls or managers for the industries from which they came. The lack of such planning in 1939 was a source of considerable concern to Chamberlain's panel of industrialists.[16] Had it not been for the hiatus of the 'phoney war', this planning failure would have had serious ramifications for the defence effort.

While the rationale for creating such a Ministry of Supply without powers is compelling, the obstacles against its implementation in 1936, even with Chamberlain's firm backing, would have been, to say the very least, formidable. There is a very clear record of where the various parties at interest stood on the subject, for perhaps no other issue pertaining to rearmament in the 1930s was so long or fruitlessly debated.

For Chamberlain to have actively supported such a measure in 1936 would have entailed such a reversal of his actual position that it strains credulity even as a hypothesis. He firmly believed that the creation of such a ministry would be of no avail without powers of compulsion over industry, and to those he was firmly opposed. So strongly held were his views on the subject that I have argued that he requested Inskip's resignation in January 1939 in large part because Chamberlain had learned that Inskip was about to propose to the Committee of Imperial Defence the creation of a Ministry of Supply not unlike the one being suggested here.

Even had Chamberlain mounted a white charger to lead a campaign to create such an organisation, he would have encountered opposition from nearly every quarter. Industry adamantly opposed the idea, believing that it would result sooner than later in compulsion.[17] So strongly held was this view that even in March 1939 Chamberlain's panel of industrialists, made up of the best-informed, most responsible leaders of the industrial community, opposed the creation of a Ministry of Supply until after the outbreak of war.[18] They took this position despite their belief that the government's plans for the mobilisation of industry in wartime were woefully insufficient.

Within government, opposition was also widespread. Maurice Hankey, the father of the existing defence organisation, argued that it would simply hamper rearmament by interposing another layer of bureaucracy. Warren Fisher opposed it on the grounds that it would diminish the Treasury's control over expenditures, and the Admiralty and the Air Ministry opposed it because it would diminish their influence under the existing organisation.[19] Although there was a cadre in Parliament that managed to have the issue brought up for debate on at least three different occasions between 1936 and 1939, nothing was done until circumstances forced the government to create a Ministry of Supply in May 1939.

Returning to the hypothesis, had Chamberlain in 1936 succeeded in having a Ministry of Supply established, the rearmament effort would have benefited on two accounts. Overall defence planning along the lines provided by Inskip's review in 1937 would have been implemented a year earlier. Even considering the time that would have been required to make such an organisation functional, it is arguable that, by moving forward the dates on which key decisions concerning the roles of the different armed services were made, the allocation of resources and consequently arms production would have been expedited.

The second benefit to the rearmament effort would have been that arms production after the onset of war would have been accelerated. Had the organisation for mobilisation of industry been in place before war was declared in 1939, in my view the dislocations that plagued the effort to turn the economy over to full-scale war production during the ensuing nine months would have been materially diminished. Whether this view, which is based on a preliminary survey of the documents for the period, is supportable can only be determined by further study of the forces that shaped industrial mobilisation after the declaration of war. It is a subject that would richly reward anyone who took it up.

Conclusion

Had Chamberlain replaced Baldwin in 1936 and succeeded in implementing the programme outlined in this essay, it is likely that British rearmament would have been considerably more advanced than it actually was in 1939. Presuming that the government had secured the active co-operation of labour as well as industry, and that priority had been mandated for defence-related contracts, it is doubtful whether the shortfalls in aircraft production in the spring of 1938 that so plagued the government would have occurred. The navy's building programme would also have benefited.

It is perhaps appropriate to note here that George Peden and Donald Watt, in comments on this paper, argue that the expansion of productive capacity in the aircraft industry in 1936 and 1937 would not have made much difference to the effective strength of Britain's air force in 1939. The basis for their argument is that the prototypes of the Hurricanes and Spitfires were not completed until late 1937, and production of these aircraft, based as it was on new technologies, could not have begun until 1938. Moreover, because the engineering techniques and production procedures involved in building the new fighters were so revolutionary, productive capacity developed prior to 1938 was essentially useless.

While the facts above are certainly true, the conclusion does not necessarily follow. The stressed steel engineering techniques that were the basis of the Hurricane and Spitfire airframes were revolutionary, requiring new machine tools and different combinations of labour skills to produce. None the less, it required less time to retool existing factories and retrain existing labour forces than to build everything from scratch. Also, the engines for the new aircraft, while new types, were not so radically different from earlier engines as to entail entirely new production procedures. Therefore increased productive capacity for aircraft engines prior to 1938 would have been directly translatable into the increased output of Hurricane and Spitfire engines after that date. While the existence of increased productive capacity prior to 1938 would not have prevented the initial dislocations stemming from the introduction of a new technology, it would have accelerated the rate of increase in production once the new technology had been assimilated.

Returning to this paper's conclusions, earlier ordering of defence priorities and closer oversight of the defence programmes resulting from the establishment in 1936 of a Ministry of Supply would have further benefited the rearmament programmes of the Air Ministry and Admiralty. The army, however, would have been less well served by these measures, as its role in the defence plans would probably have been kept to a minimum. It would have been little consolation that that minimum would have been more clearly defined.

The accelerated rate of armaments production, particularly in 1937, that would have resulted from this programme would have had especially significant financial implications. The armed services would have been able to spend at levels exceeding their 1937 estimates. (Limitations in manufacturing capacity in reality had prevented them from doing this.)[20] In all likelihood this would have advanced by a year the debates about borrowing for defence and perhaps compelled the government to take a firmer stand on the National Defence Contribution.

To the degree that increased arms production reduced manufacturing of goods for export and increased demand for imports, this programme would have affected Britain's foreign exchange situation. Unfortunately space does not permit the unravelling of the many financial implications of the suggested programme. Suffice it to say that the proposed measures would have complicated considerably the Treasury's task of controlling expenditures.

Had earlier government co-operation with labour and industry advanced the rate of manufacturing for defence, it is likely that this would have given rise to intransigence in a few key industrial and labour sectors. This would have resulted in the government being pressured at a much earlier date to take powers to compel industry and labour.

Reference has already been made to the opposition of the engineers' union to the TUC's agreement in 1938 to co-operate with the government. During that same period the machine tool industry had become involved in a running dispute with the government over the industry's refusal to open its books to allow the government to audit defence contracts. The upshot of that dispute was that in May 1939 the government had no choice but to include powers to inspect the books of defence contractors in the legislation it introduced to create a Ministry of Supply. Earlier co-operation with labour and industry resulting in more rapid advances in defence production and earlier exposure of those refusing to co-operate could conceivably have resulted in the government being forced to assume limited compulsory powers early in 1938.

Interesting as these speculations may be, it is important to remember that they are ultimately based on one highly questionable premiss: that a Conservative Prime Minister in the 1930s would have sought to move his government in a direction so inimical to the fundamental beliefs of his own party. In 1936 the great majority of Conservatives believed that industry should be permitted to take the lead in organising its side of the rearmament programme with a minimum of government interference. The great majority of Conservatives saw little distinction between the Parliamentary Labour Party and organised labour, believing that either, if given the opportunity, would seek to take advantage of any government initiative to obtain co-operation in hastening rearmament.

These beliefs were held by most Conservative members of Parliament not because the industrial community was threatening to withdraw its support if they failed to reflect industry's views in their voting. These beliefs were held primarily because most Conservative MPs had the same view of the world and the way it worked as the leaders of commerce and industry. They had attended the same schools, worshipped in the same churches and belonged to the same clubs. While a few of their number like Churchill held to the traditional Conservative precepts of king and country, most had a more worldly view of the nation's interests.

It is significant that no member of the Cabinet suggested seriously that controls be imposed until after the fall of Austria in 1938. Soon after Viscount Swinton broached that possibility, Chamberlain requested his resignation. Only in December 1938 and January 1939 did other Cabinet ministers, invariably those whose ministries had responsibility for defence, begin to entertain the notion that a Ministry of Supply and perhaps some measure of compulsion might be necessary. The leader of this group, Thomas Inskip, the Minister for the Co-ordination of Defence, was asked to resign in January 1939 after suggesting such measures.

Consequently it is difficult to argue that prior to 1939 interest groups such as industry were involved in seeking to alter proposed defence policy. (The defeat of the National Defence Contribution is in some regards an exception to this generalisation.) There was little need to. Between January and early April 1939, however, it could be argued that Chamberlain's opposition to the creation of a Ministry of Supply was attributable in part to his concern about industry's often stated repugnance to it.

Be this as it may, what can be said with some assurance is that there is scant evidence as late as autumn 1937 of support within the Cabinet or the Conservative Party at large for the hypothetical measures set forth at the outset of this essay. Therefore it is difficult to imagine a Conservative who espoused such policies becoming Prime Minister or unifying his party behind them. None the less, the process of considering what the ramifications of such policies might have been has, I hope, provided some perspective on how and why British defence policy after 1936 developed as it did.

Notes: Chapter 7

1   Parliamentary Debates (House of Commons), vol. 308, 14 February 1936, cols 1360–2.
2   R. P. Shay, Jr, *British Rearmament in the Thirties: Politics and Profits* (Princeton, NJ, 1977), pp. 67, 86 ff.
3   Public Record Office, London: CAB 16/112, DRC 38, 17 October 1935, minutes of a meeting between Baldwin, Chamberlain and a delegation from the FBI.
4   Shay, *British Rearmament*, pp. 98 f.
5   ibid., pp. 17 f., 149 ff., 94 ff., 292 ff.
6   ibid., p. 128.
7   G. C. Peden, *British Rearmament and the Treasury: 1932–1939* (Edinburgh, 1979), pp. 62 ff., 96 ff., and passim.
8   CAB 24/260, CP 57 (36), 21 February 1936.
9   Shay, *British Rearmament*, pp. 207 ff.
10 CAB 24/265, CP 297(36), 30 October 1936.
11 J. F. Naylor, *Labour's International Policy. The Labour Party in the 1930s* (Boston, Mass., 1969), p. 152.
12 'The engineers and the government', *New Statesman*, 14 May 1938, pp. 820 f.
13 R. A. C. Parker, in his article 'British rearmament 1936–9: Treasury, trade unions and skilled labour', *English Historical Review*, vol. 96 (1981), pp. 306–43, argues that craft unions materially obstructed efforts to ease bottlenecks in skilled jobs, and therefore constituted the primary obstacle to rearming at a faster rate. The persuasiveness of his argument is seriously undermined by the lack of any supporting quantitative data.
14 Parliamentary Debates (House of Commons), vol. 317, 12 November 1936, col. 1107.
15 R. Shay, Jr, 'Britain's preparations for the mobilisation of industry before the Second World War', working paper, February 1978, p. 13 and passim.

16 CAB 16/222, IP 17th meeting, 6 February 1939.
17 PREM 1/336, 21 October 1938, a letter from Horace Wilson to Chamberlain describing industry's opposition to a Ministry of Supply.
18 CAB 16/228, IP no. 59, 1 March 1939.
19 Shay, *British Rearmament*, pp. 71 f.
20 Peden, *Rearmament and the Treasury*, pp. 105, 165, 172; Shay, *British Rearmament*, p. 194.

II

THE DOMESTIC DIMENSION

8 The Domestic Background to British Appeasement Policy

GUSTAV SCHMIDT

Any attempt to investigate what Great Britain and France could have done to prevent the European civil war provoked by the Hitler regime or at least stop it before it was too late – a controversial issue among contemporaries just as in research – must analyse the extent to which the acceptance of breaches of international law and acts of violence were due to interference in the military-strategic and political power systems. It must also consider the make-up of the political society, assessing the structural advantages and weaknesses of Western democracies confronted with external intimidation and the shifting balance of power. In contrast to the period before the First World War when thanks to its relations with the Great Powers London was to some extent in a position to get round the pressure on domestic politics resulting from the arms race with Germany, in the 1930s the conjuncture of international politics impeded such manoeuvres. Whereas before 1914 the City, in the centre of the world economic system, could defend its network of economic relations as a relatively autonomous one, in the 1930s the increasing politicisation of financial and economic affairs made it more difficult to ensure that by cultivating finance and trade the path would be cleared for successful negotiations and political rapprochement. Furthermore, in reaction to the acute problems facing Britain in August – September 1931 leading politicians opted for a strategy of crisis avoidance. British governments preferred not to overemphasise the external security dilemma; therefore they did not attempt to use the 'German peril' as an excuse for neglecting socio-economic considerations and interests which in the British system tend to spill over from domestic to foreign and security policy; nor did they try to pass the buck on to the Allies. The economy of the country was not to be stimulated and reshaped to suit the needs of rearmament. To what extent, however, did the strategy of crisis avoidance at domestic level and appeasement (that is, preventive diplomacy) mutually interact? Could the British model be interpreted as a counterpart to the militant strategy of totalitarian regimes? For the British, security policy not only involved providing for national and imperial defence but also implied the safeguarding of internal self-determination. The principle behind British security policy was to ward off internal crises, thus assuming only limited commitments in foreign policy.

I

British democracy was confronted with the dilemma of how to face a shift in basic principles and values towards the extreme right or radical left.[1] The distinction between the negotiable and the non-negotiable became acute in a clash of ideologies and systems as a result of the collapse of the world economic order and the Versailles and Washington Treaty systems. Any bona fide endeavours towards genuine *apaisement* by means of revisionism, bargaining, or delimitation of spheres of influence had to be made with reference to the values of the parties concerned and the constraints thereby imposed. However, in order to come to terms with the effective and long-term coexistence of all systems[2] emphasis had to be focused on the non-negotiable. Since political conflict with its ideological, and social under-currents in the era of violence, of 'hot' and 'cold' civil wars was not contained by national frontiers Britain, for both external and domestic reasons, ran the risk of becoming entangled in situations in which questions of foreign policy became first and foremost issues of domestic politics.[3] The threat of a national split along ideological lines originating from abroad (the slogan 'Rather Hitler than Blum' in French politics) seemed by far the most ominous danger,[4] at least to leading members of the British Cabinet (Baldwin, Simon, MacDonald, Halifax), particularly since in view of developments in international relations from the early 1930s (that is, before Hitler seized power) British policy could not get round the question of defence policy.[5] The offensive turn in Japanese and German foreign policy imposed an issue on British society which for social and economic reasons Whitehall would willingly have avoided. In awareness of the relative decline in Britain's position in world trade as a result of the First World War and the Depression, Britain was loath to re-enter the arena of power politics, a fact demonstrated to the outside world by her voluntary arms limitation during the period of the Ten Years' Rule (from 1919–22 in fact until 1934).[6]

As a result of the crisis in the world economic order and the altered system of international relations (following the collapse of the set-up of Versailles and the Washington system in the Near East) London was faced with the question whether and how it could manage to direct German policy towards greater concern for domestic welfare. This was no doubt a priority owing to her political culture and not least her chronic unemployment. London's objective was to appeal to the German people's desire for peace, thus feeding its own preferences and options into the German political debate. Just as the German rulers played on the susceptibility of British public opinion to revisionist arguments, exploiting it as a means of redrafting the map of Europe, British policy aimed at mobilising the latent desire of the German people for peace, security, economic stability and an improvement in living standards against the 'radicals' within the Hitler regime.[7] In signalling its willingness to deal with Germany's legitimate grievances (on military sovereignty in 1933–6 or, for example, on raw materials) the British government had two aims in mind:

(1)   It was assumed that if justified demands for revision were complied

with it would then be difficult for the Hitler regime to incite the German people to launch into action over and above pure revisionism or to make sacrifices in fresh attempts at rearmament[8] (the application of this strategy by Chamberlain in 1938, for example, failed, among other reasons, due to National Socialist propaganda which ridiculed Chamberlain's attempts to secure agreement).[9]

(2) Any progress in the application of peaceful change would remove pressure on Whitehall to accelerate the rearmament process. (In governmental and economic circles differences were drawn between diplomatic crises triggered off by justified demands for revision – which could indeed be conceded within the terms of a general settlement – and military provocation to which London should not react with indulgence; thus preventive diplomacy attempted to shield economic recovery from the interference of external pressure.)[10]

Appeasement can therefore be seen as a form of preventive diplomacy which was to ensure that economic recovery should be absorbed neither primarily nor totally by preoccupation with rearmament, but should benefit the social services.[11] When the four-year armament plan was presented in March 1936, the government reinforced its election campaign pledge that arms expenditure justified by steps taken by other states would not lead to a turnabout in policy at the expense of economic and social policy.[12] 'If only it wasn't for Germany we would be having such a wonderful time just now . . . What a frightful bill do we owe to Master Hitler, damn him!'[13] These comments were made by Chamberlain at a time when as Chancellor of the Exchequer he was preparing the Defence Loans Bill, borrowing for the four-year defence programme; he had put forward the National Defence Contribution as a means of appeasing Labour, something which caused him considerable trouble in business circles. Chamberlain tried to justify his policy in a letter to his sister:

All the elements of danger are here . . . I can see that we might easily run, in no time, into a series of crippling strikes and finally the defeat of the Government and the advent of an ignorant, unprepared and heavily pledged opposition to handle a crisis as severe as that of 1931 . . . I do not say that NDC will prevent all this but I feel sure that it enormously diminishes the danger. It will make the workmen feel that this Government is not in league with their employers to soak them while running off with enormous profits themselves . . . Industrial unrest is only just round the corner – but [NDC] may help and keep it there.[14]

The British government hoped that the widespread rejection of the arms race among the British people as madness would spill over into Germany – London in fact worked towards this end with the result that Hitler would finally be faced with pressure in the opposite direction to that being put on the British political and social system by politicians such as Churchill who were calling for the mobilisation of all resources to keep pace with German armament.[15] Thus Chamberlain cherished the hope 'that the precarious internal situation of Germany is impressing a certain restraining influence on Hitler';[16] and thought that by taking up the thread of the Schacht–Blum talks such restraining influence could be nourished. In assuming that the financial problems of the Third Reich were bound to curb its warmongering policy and pave the way for normal dealings with the powers-that-be in Berlin, the appeasers were projecting the motivation behind their own action and policy on to Germany.[17]

After Hitler seized power and the programme to combat unemployment was enforced, it was assumed in London[18] that 'Such commitments must, for social and political reasons, form a first charge on Germany's available revenue; and so long as this does not increase too rapidly, she will have not much to spare for rearmament or other forms of external adventures.'[19] The scope of London's policy *vis-à-vis* Germany was now defined in terms of the question: 'How far Hitler's foreign policy [is] (and is likely to be) influenced by the absence of an economic recovery in Germany.'[20] Of course the socio-imperialistic techniques of domination were clearly understood – from reports of a slump in Germany it could almost automatically be concluded that trouble was to be expected in foreign affairs.[21] This did not, however, affect the discussion on whether other states (Britain in particular) should for as long as possible run the risk of bolstering the influence of the 'moderates' in the German internal decision-making process by showing willingness to negotiate.[22] For Britain it was clear that sooner or later rearmament in Germany would begin; the question was, would it be within reasonable limits, not posing a security risk to Western democracies, or would it be introduced as a means of reviving the economy, leading to its reorientation (autarky) based on rearmament and liable to explode in the foreseeable future?[23] In the latter case Britain would also as a result be obliged to mobilise her resources for an embryonic war economy.[24] To ward off the loss of substance this would entail for the peacetime economy, the British laid all their hopes on statements made by Hitler to British visitors that higher standards of living were of mutual interest; in the opinion of a number of ministers it was imperative, even if the assurances of peace made by German leaders could not be taken seriously, to 'assume it [i.e. German interest in peace] for our own sake'.[25]

This 'as if' diplomacy which assumed that German policy was guided by a wish for peace and a higher standard of living, might possibly prevent trends in domestic developments in Britain being dictated by the German counterpart. With the efforts towards arms limitation, Whitehall attempted to exploit the (supposed) mutual interest in relieving the problems faced by both governments from an economic angle. Analyses from the British Embassy in Berlin stressed the importance of this aspect, reporting that 'financial stringency will cool even Hitler's heated head'; should London demonstrate with steps towards rearmament that it was not 'decadent' (that is, pacifist), it could always interest the Third Reich in negotiations on arms limitation (the Air pact, and so on).[26]

In the subsequent phase, the transition to armament expansion and borrowing for defence, it was expected that the phenomena accompanying an arms boom (bottlenecks in armament production, the inflationary spiral) would be such that German leaders could no longer ignore the 'German people' factor. Well-informed reports on the extent of these difficulties had been gained in contacts between the Air Ministry and Milch and it seemed that as a result the Hitler regime would possibly be forced to slow down a bit. Without entirely focusing policy on such expectations London was nevertheless loath prematurely to abandon all hope of achieving some form of arms limitation – if only an obligation to disclose defence programmes and commitments over a number of years – and thereby relax international tension.[27] The result was the dual policy which aimed on the one hand at a higher level of peacetime strength by a flexible management of resources, and on the other reinforcing and justifying this policy by a willingness to negotiate; diplomacy was to take advantage of every glimmer of hope so that the government would not constantly be forced to accelerate its programme. Diplomacy should at least reduce the number of potential enemies, so that any increase in defence expenditure could be kept within certain limits, and the economy not totally geared towards this end.

The assumption that the number of potential enemies, and thereby strategic and defence commitments, could be circumscribed by means of diplomacy was closely linked to the expectation that in time as a result of new developments – above all politico-strategical or tactical errors on the part of Britain's opponents – peace could always be saved anew. It was calculated that the aggressive powers would not only waste their energy in political adventuring (for example, Japan in China, 1937) but would also forfeit the chance – by synchronised timing – of taking advantage of the vulnerability of the West. A study group at All Souls, Oxford, expressed the hope that 'If war could be postponed, some new development might occur postponing it still further and it was believed that Japan, by attacking in the Far East this year, while Germany was still unready in Europe, had weakened the German-Italian-Japanese bloc.'[28] The attempt to gain time[29] was not only to let Britain catch up in the arms race, but also reflected interest in using time for negotiating solutions. British generals assessed the views of their political superiors quite correctly: politicians' belief in peace had been too strong to let them now cash in politically on the argument that rearmament could help combat unemployment;[30] they had wanted to keep the defence services out of pocket so as not to bring the dynamics of rearmament into full swing and commit themselves to a war economy.[31]

Did the expectation that in the case of accelerated rearmament certain repercussions would automatically follow affect the political system to the extent that the government became fearful of losing its – by no means purely formal – decision-making monopoly? By 'steering towards rearmament with the hand-brake on' the government could avoid becoming dependent on employers and the unions – the effect of the pressure to show quick results on the government's political position was to become clear, especially to the Exchequer, in view of the difficulties in finding a politically acceptable settlement for the question of profits in the aircraft industry. On the other hand the strategy of limited rearmament – the organisation of production along the lines of voluntary co-operation – met with distinct grass-root suspicions of Whitehall on the part of industry and the unions. Spokesmen for both sides of industry stressed 'that a democratic society could only develop its full resources if it drew on the capacity of its members for self-government and did not take the easier, but . . . less efficient course of concentrating power in the hands of an overworked Civil Service'.[32]

Government, TUC and the employers' associations (FBI, NCEO) were admittedly guided by the ideal that the organisation of industrial mobilisation should only be carried out on the basis of voluntary agreements. However, in view of the demand from in particular the FBI and the NCEO for regular consultation with the government, the question of how the latter could preserve its relative autonomy *vis-à-vis* industry and labour became relevant.[33] The more armament was forced the more necessary it became to develop a concept for the steering of industry. For all those concerned it was clear that in such a situation not only the employers but also the unions had to benefit in some way; control would not only have to be offset by wage increases – however limited they might be – and profit margins; such interference in the economy also implied the delegation of authority to committees in which these organised pressure groups would implement policy. The procedure to date of the selective appointment of individuals to advisory positions (Weir, Balfour, among others) and occasional consultation with the upper echelons of the FBI, NCEO and the TUC would then have to be abandoned and the organisations' claim to participation conceded. The more quickly and the more permanently the economy was geared towards armament production, the more true this became.[34] In the course of various reorganisational projects it had however become obvious that the umbrella organisations were not even in a position to conclude and implement binding agreements on behalf of their members. Thus the disparity between the demands and the competence of these organisations reduced the pressure on the government to give in to the demands of interest group politics. The government was eager to avoid being forced by prior consultation with experts' committees (Import Duties Advisory Committee, Unemployment Assistance Board) into a position where it would have the main responsibility for detailing the economic resources. On the other hand it did its best to avoid fostering the main grievances of the two sides of industry – control on the part of the employers, and dilution and conscription on the part of labour. This 'negative voluntarism'[35] spared the government from having to enter political negotiations with these organisations. With the assurance that it would venture into neither collective bargaining nor individual management, if and for as long as the organisations produced the results guaranteed in voluntary schemes (transfer of skilled labour, expansion of armament industry capacities), the government renounced control but managed to evade any obligation either to collaborate with one side (capital)[36] or having to share or partly cede its sovereignty in decision-making.

II

The role of domestic factors in British foreign policy has been examined on repeated occasions, albeit more within general terms of reference to the 'no more war' atmosphere or the financial difficulties involved in introducing accelerated armament in time.[37] Partly in view of its own negative historical experience, German research takes the British model of civil democracy as a premiss for the theory that sound domestic policy is the most important prerequisite for the successful conduct of foreign affairs; accordingly pluralist systems – compared to dictatorships – are by no means fighting a losing battle. British research, however, seems to be wary of seeing things in such euphemistic terms. In any case to underestimate domestic policy as a determining factor of foreign policy is to close one's eyes to important issues,[38] for example, that the arms question had to be tackled *vis-à-vis* not only allies and enemies but also with regard to British public opinion. After all, expectations abroad diverged considerably from those of British interest groups. It is generally assumed on the basis of the French example that as 'a direct impact of British domestic politics upon the foreign policy, the working of the democratic process' (in Great Britain and France)[39] prejudiced adequate factual decision-making and was therefore a point of weakness. In view of the undisputed predominance of the Conservatives, corresponding in some respects to one-party rule in the 1930s, and the dominant position of Chamberlain in particular as Prime Minister and party leader in an 'oligarchy of consensus', Donald Watt for example has reached the conclusion that 'there was in Britain, in the formal sense, no direct interaction between British politics and British foreign policy in the years 1938/39'.[40] In application of this interpretation, the undeniable indulgence of British foreign policy towards the fascist powers must either be attributed to individuals and their weakness or the buck must be passed on to third parties – France, the opposition, the negligence of previous governments, and so on.

This conventional wisdom has recently been called into question in Britain by Cowling who illustrates that in its calculations British policy weighed up the danger in foreign policy just as much as the threat of socialism; for Cowling it is a question of how in an age of democracy the Conservatives could remain the dominant force in mass politics. Cowling has admittedly not drawn any conclusions from his views on the theme of 'transformation of the class struggle by the challenge from Hitler';[41] his theory that Chamberlain's foreign policy and successful Conservative rule were interdependent remains an interesting topic for further research. It has therefore still to be explained how Chamberlain's confidence in the rationality of England's deterrent force as an element of appeasement could outlive the outbreak of war in 1939[42] despite the fact that the government was not determining the pace and extent of rearmament primarily by the dictates of foreign policy. In any case Britain had not sought arrangements with her allies, such as staff talks with France, but pointed out that since Britain's defence programmes represented a vital insurance premium for her allies, it was her right to determine autonomously the extent and form of these security measures and to conduct exploratory talks with potential aggressors; by making use of contacts with Japan, Italy and Germany it had been hoped that arms limitation could be achieved in certain sectors at least (naval, air force parity)[43] and that the strain on British resources would thus be relieved. 'The real hope for Europe', said Foreign Secretary Simon in 1935, is that 'while the United Kingdom should make preparations as were necessary to defend herself, she should still pursue a policy of a settlement in which Germany could take an equal share'.[44]

Defence policy was to provide England with greater room to manoeuvre in foreign policy. As a result of the various domestic issues involved in the armament question, the importance of moments of crisis in foreign policy tended however to be played down within the continuous rearmament debate. Rearmament was not only considered from the point of view of whether and how one or other of the would-be partners could be assisted in the case of conflict[45] but also with respect to how the external security dilemma would affect the development of the rearmament debate, demands on industry and the position of social groups.[46] At the time of the crisis in March 1936, for example, the French Ambassador in London, Corbin, observed quite correctly that the debate on the Defence White Paper – which was in fact the British 'Four-Year Plan' – was being carried on as if the Rhineland had never been remilitarised.[47] The defence debate was conducted primarily with regard to Britain's (narrowly defined) security interests; measures required were assessed with respect to their likely repercussions on the political stability and the industrial and financial 'effective strength' of British society.[48]

The government, however, hoped that the RAF – given priority[49] – would act as a deterrent, in that it could lead to an encounter with the enemy around the negotiating table as opposed to on the battlefield. 'I am pretty satisfied', wrote Chamberlain in 1936, 'that, if only we can keep out of war a few years, we shall have an Air Force of such striking power that no one will care to run risks with it'.[50] This strategy was based on the assumption that Germany, although not necessarily Hitler himself, would gradually realise that it was not in a position to win the war since it had little with which to resist Britain's power of endurance (a united internal front, lines of communication with the USA and the dominions), its political strength.

My interpretation of British policy between the Depression and the Second World War is based on one particular overall impression: that the National Government, which over lengthy periods until just before the outbreak of war neither wanted, nor was in a position, to risk strategically stabilising measures of a military or economic nature at the trouble-spots in world politics,[51] relied on the political strength of Great Britain as a justification and a safeguard for preventive diplomacy. Aware of both the deficiencies in defence accumulated during the Ten Years' Rule and changes in the world economic order which had restricted Britain's room for manoeuvre, the British government tended to regard political strength as a bastion from which it could demand a say in European affairs. The view that England contributed above all its economic and social stability to the balance of power implied that security policy was as anxious to preserve this source of strength as it was to account for the power shifts in the international scene by rearmament.[52] Due to considerations relating to domestic politics, the USA was inconsistent in security policy; France's role as guardian of the Paris peace settlement of 1919–20 had been weakened by governmental crises and oscillations in economic policy. It therefore became all the more evident that a balance of inner stability had to be maintained: 'Nothing operates more strongly', argued the Minister for the Co-ordination of Defence, Inskip, 'to deter a potential aggressor from attacking this country than our stability . . . but were other countries to detect in us signs of strain, this deterrence would at once be lost.'[53]

Efforts to preserve political strength implied two prerequisites:

(1)   The safeguarding of relative autonomy in the government's political decision-making. This however meant that domestic decision-making processes had to be guarded against foreign interference wherever possible.[54] Then and only then would it be possible to react with flexibility in the case of crises provoked by Japan, Italy, or Germany.

(2)   If at all possible, those internal compromise settlements and agreements should be preserved which upheld Britain's position as an island of stability and common sense, free from the social unrest, civil war and changes of regime on the Continent.

The first point implied guarding the existing social and economic order against revolutionary upheaval and excessive strain, the second 'steering the course of modernisation and rejuvenation – the need for which in a period of rapid change and world-wide upheaval is also recognised by the conservative élite – along the path of evolution and under Conservative leadership'.[55]

British interest in safeguarding limited rearmament by means of a peaceful strategy was based on the assumption that if Britain were forced to rearm, setting off an inflationary spiral by excessive borrowing and a scramble for skilled labour and other scarce resources,[56] the result would be a crisis similar to that of 1931. The policy of limited liabilities followed the principle of remaining for as long as possible below the threshold of the inflationary spiral which could be disastrous for the political and social system. The mobilisation of resources on behalf of security policy had to bear in mind that labour difficulties were probable as soon as defence measures developed their own dynamics in production. Despite growing concern about the 'German peril' the perception of domestic dangers and risks determined the decision-making process in foreign and security policy and led the government alongside the application of the defence programme, considered as indispensable, to look for platforms for diplomatic action to keep the defence spiral in check and remove latent trouble-spots wherever possible. Appeasement policy was determined not so much by illusions on the Third Reich's willingness for negotiation and rapprochement but rather by fears of running into a domestic crisis triggered off by a rearmament race.[57]

The overriding concern, repeatedly mentioned in the source materials, to avoid a recurrence of the crisis of 1931 does not define such a crisis as a revolutionary situation in itself but as the fear of being forced into a situation in which the existing political leadership[58] might have to forfeit its democratic opportunity of being re-elected. The stabilisation of the system therefore required more than a mere Conservative class policy. It had to be made clear that the effects of security policy would not be one-sided and detrimental to the working class. By measures aimed at social appeasement and a continuing search for a European settlement the government tried to prevent losing face among its floating voters which could have resulted in the Conservatives being banished into political exile over a period of years.[59] Following electoral defeat in 1929 Chamberlain, Baldwin and other party leaders had reckoned with a long spell on the opposition benches. It was only the fall of the MacDonald minority government which had been tolerated by the Liberals that gave Baldwin, Chamberlain and Co. another opportunity of taking over the reins of government.[60]

In view of the fact that Britain nevertheless finally declared war on the Third Reich in 1939 and in the decisive field of defence – the air force – caught up with and overtook Germany from 1939,[61] it can be proved beyond doubt that the restraints of domestic policy produced no fatalism or resignation; limited rearmament was based on a careful weighing up of motives posed by both foreign and domestic policy,[62] guided by British interests – the protection of national stability and the preservation of political strength, on the one hand, and on the other precautions for a buffer zone along the Rhine and in the Near East, disregarding *Mitteleuropa*.

III

Any interpretation of British appeasement must examine the criticism (put forward by Churchill in particular) that a government guided by a different 'spirit' and led by 'heroes' other than Baldwin, MacDonald and Chamberlain could have stood up to the challenge from the Hitler regime and even prevented the outbreak of the Second World War.[63] However, the persistence of appeasement policy in offering its services of mediation before and directly after Hitler's successful breakthroughs was backed up by the 'no war' atmosphere within the country which expected policy to be aimed at preserving the peace rather than leading to mere 'bloc formation and an arms race' as before 1914.[64]

To protect Britain from further loss of substance the possibility of a working agreement had to be sounded out for as long as at all possible; this appeared necessary not only due to the weakness of France but in particular to the view that the onus of any action in resisting Germany's 'Griff nach der Weltmacht' would be on Britain, just as in the First World War. Since Britain would therefore be dependent on her own resources it seemed justifiable for London to examine – if necessary single-handedly – the possibilities of containing the damage threatened or already caused by Germany. British foreign policy claimed a leading role in correcting the course of events since 1919 to clear the atmosphere, but (up to 1938) declined, because of 'over-commitments',[65] the responsibility implied by great power status, for example, to make gestures or grant economic assistance to smaller nations, encouraging them to stand up to the dictatorships. The problem was who would bear the burden of adjustment between 'satisfied' nations and 'have-nots'; as the question had arisen time and time again since 1918–19, government departments in the 1930s concluded from their search for an agreement that there was only one way out: the inevitable sacrifices implied in a general European settlement would have to be made by third powers.[66] The Foreign Office put forward – but to no avail – that Britain should be prepared to pay for concessions out of her own pocket by experimenting with colonial appeasement;[67] this, however, came up against the brick wall of a lobby largely opposed to changing the measures implemented in 1931–2, but in favour of political appeasement (that is, conceding Central Europe as a zone of German influence).

Confident of its political strength – also respected by Germany – and of its own negotiating skill, British diplomacy ran the risk of Germany questioning the *status quo* in exploratory talks; still, it was hoped that the essentials of the Western powers could be discussed in a way that change in the *status quo* and German concessions could be tied together as part and parcel of a comprehensive settlement.[68] However, attempts to transform crises into a comprehensive settlement by means of preventive diplomacy – that is, appeasement offensives – were condemned by German policy as 'diplomacy of illusion'.

The economic departments – the Treasury, the Board of Trade, the Ministry of Agriculture, the Ministry of Labour – contested the leading role of the Foreign Office in decision-making on foreign policy. They claimed their due share of responsibility in the light of the economic, financial and social burdens occasioned by the security policy *vis-à-vis* the dictators now that the other pillars of international society, that is, France and the United States,[69] had withdrawn their support. It was not in fact the department formally in charge of foreign relations that determined action necessary to safeguard Britain's security interests at international trouble-spots, but the Treasury, insisting that Britain's commitments be defined in terms of her economic possibilities. The Treasury enforced the principle that the Cabinet should ensure that foreign policy priorities remained in harmony with defence burdens;[70] it argued that the supplies required for a continental commitment would not only overtax the economy but, compared to what the air force and the navy could offer by way of defence for Britain, would constitute misguided investment;[71] the Foreign Office was thus deprived of its pledge of a 'common fate' with France which, in collaboration with French politicians, it tried to impose on British policy. The requirements of the army, the Cinderella of the defence forces, were repeatedly disregarded: to meet them could have led to a dislocation of industries without providing a sufficient safeguard for British security. Chamberlain and Runciman applied the principle that demands on industry and not demands advocated by the service departments and the Foreign Office should be taken as a yardstick for the armament process which actually only began in 1936.[72] For to decide that the production capacities required in the event of a war should be prepared and utilised even before the potential conflict, would be to

subject trade and industry to damage from which it could only expect to
recover after generations – if at all. The economic departments, industrial
advisers and leading economic circles[73] gained acceptance for their opinion
that accelerated rearmament would destroy the confidence which guaranteed the basis for economic revival and an increase of national revenue.[74]

Those in Cabinet responsible for economic policy were unwilling to undo
the package of measures introduced (1931–3) to guard the British economy
from the adverse effects of international economic events for the sake of
Britain's alliance policy. The more difficult it became to conduct 'business as
usual', while at the same time building up peacetime strength to the required
level of the programmes, the more rigorously they defended their point of
view.[75]

Interest in avoiding a deterioration of relations with labour also spoke for
caution in security policy. The government was convinced that Britain could
put up with risks in foreign policy more easily than a conflict with labour.
Therefore the argument that defence programmes could only be implemented if labour co-operated played a prominent role in discussion at
Cabinet level. The government's assurances that rearmament should for as
long as possible be organised on the basis of the willing co-operation of
industry and the unions ran along the same lines.[76] Accordingly it would
have been appropriate to have conducted top-level talks, not only with the
FBI[77] but also with the unions – and before the spring of 1938.[78] In the
first talks in the autumn of 1935, however, it had become clear that as a result
of the close organisational links between the trade union movement and the
Labour Party, the relations between the government and the TUC were of a
different nature to those between the government and industrial umbrella
organisations. The government – emphatically advised by the unions
(Bevin) that it should address its efforts to the Labour Party – was neither
willing nor in a position to play off the unions against the party; neither did
it yield – after Munich – to the temptation of depriving the Labour Party of
the fruits of its publicity campaign (to an even greater extent than by the
November 1935 elections) – for this would only result in bitterness and
jeopardise industrial co-operation in the foreseeable future. However, these
considerations did not go so far as to lead the government to consult either
labour or the Labour Party. A number of arguments were raised in Cabinet
against such consultations: such an invitation would signal an emergency
situation and in view of the international situation would put public opinion
into a state of alarm; the majority tended to repudiate any threat of war. If it
were to come to official negotiations on support for economic and industrial
mobilisation, that is, labour's consent to dilution, and so on, then it would
have to be expected that labour would make demands in return – not only on
foreign policy (the incorporation of the Soviet Union into active peace
policy, consultation with the League of Nations on the Sudetenland question), but also on economic and social policy (conscription of wealth, paid
holidays, compensatory wage increases, and so on). It is not improbable[79]
that the government wanted to wait for events in Europe to teach labour a
lesson – in other words, it was hoped that faced with external pressure the
'sectional prejudices' against intervention into so-called union practices

would gradually subside, so that the government would neither have to make political compromises nor be forced to demand sacrifices from the employers (excess duty with regard to profiteering, wealth tax) similar to the sacrifices expected from labour (transfer of labour forces into the armament industry). The National Defence Contribution, the only large-scale attempt to impose a substantial and symbolic burden on business, had been a disaster for Chamberlain. Although Chamberlain was aware of the need not only to distribute sacrifices evenly but also to consult labour representatives on arrangements in the event of a war, governmental policy was not in a position to create such a balance.

This can be partly explained by the Cabinet's inability to pursue a clear-cut line in security and defence policy:[80] agreement on the guidelines of defence policy was, however, a prerequisite for consultation with the opposition – otherwise their leaders would outline their own terms of reference, thus prejudicing governmental policy.

The need for a foreign and defence policy[81] *geared towards public opinion*[82] – conjuring up images of prewar diplomacy and the crisis of July 1914 as a deterrent – could be used by Britain in critical phases of negotiation as a standard argument[83] – in particular *vis-à-vis* France – for excluding 'irrevocable decisions at this stage' and remaining open instead to possible developments in the German camp; moreover, for concrete reasons (by-elections, the peace ballot campaign, the Hoare–Laval débâcle, opposition to the Unemployment Assistance Board Act) it was even more imperative to take the domestic background to decision-making into consideration.[84] Furthermore, it became obvious that the scope of Britain's partner, France, was also subject to such constraints. British preventive diplomacy, aware of the symptoms of crisis in French politics, in particular the disparity between Paris and the French people (the provincial press), was confirmed in its own claim to leadership *vis-à-vis* its wavering ally; given the discredited French line it demanded the support of *public* opinion in both countries for the British strategy. British politicians moreover had the impression 'that the country will not allow us to take drastic action in what they regard as a pure French interest'.[85] The response to German action on 16 March 1935 for instance, without prior consultation with France and Italy was justified by Foreign Secretary Simon who said that the government would have had to put forward and carry out a 'British policy'; had London delayed the announcement until an allied memorandum of protest had been drawn up, 'British opinion would have gone against France'.[86]

This regard for public opinion finally meant that the decision-making process was partly blocked; the government and public opinion convinced themselves that basically Germany's demands for revision were justified and that both the means of enforcement and the moral justification for even limited measures of retaliation were lacking.[87] Influenced by feelings of guilt about Britain's share of responsibility for Versailles and convinced that an Anglo-German conflict had to be avoided, flexibility was called for in British policy on questions which were classified as 'local' German demands – the range of which was extended from equality of status (in armament) via the Rhineland to the annexation of Austria. Since even the anti-appeasers approved overtures to Germany – 'The approach would have been worth taking (even if Germany declined the terms offered) as putting us right with our own public opinion'[88] – the real problem was practically ignored, that is, the extent to which England's desire for peace and corresponding willingness to negotiate would tip the balance of power in favour of the Third Reich. Potentially dangerous developments which both the government and public opinion had played down (internally) could not suddenly be put forward as a matter of life and death in the event of a critical turn of the tide in Europe. This situation was exacerbated by the fact that the government, in order to keep domestic repercussions at a minimum, tried to dissociate debates on defence programmes from discussions on concrete commitments in foreign policy;[89] moreover, the March crises provoked by the Third Reich just happened to take place while government and opposition were busy defining their positions for the budgetary debates on defence estimates and at a time when at the annual meetings of the constituency parties[90] they could sound reaction at grass-root level. Reports on the general atmosphere reinforced the view that the government would only find support for defence policy if the dip into the taxpayer's pocket were accompanied by an announcement of continued endeavours to strike a balance with Germany and in particular an agreement on arms limitation. 'The policy . . . seemed rather to be that some diplomatic approach to Germany would greatly assist in the preparation of the Defence Programme next month.'[91]

Decision-makers were in agreement on their assessment of public opinion as crises came to a head. The steps taken by Germany were to have been expected and understandable in substance if not in form. The crises should not be used as justification for even more specific defence programmes.[92] Since it had been stressed that it was necessary to replace the obsolete provisions of the Treaty of Versailles by realistic regulations with the aid of legalised German rearmament, British rearmament could not solely be justified as a reaction to the German peril, at least not without associating German armament with the dangers emanating from a dictatorship. If however a tactic were adopted whereby the threat of an attack from Germany was dangled in front of the public's eyes without events actually justifying such a warning (this did not happen until Prague), then all motives and interests aimed at limited armament would have to be thrown overboard. To summarise: it can be said that appeasement as a strategy of crisis avoidance was largely coloured not only by the traditions of British political culture but by domestic circumstances.

Simon, Chancellor of the Exchequer (and former Foreign Secretary), for example, argued against out and out adjustment to National Socialist Germany's rearmament policy; in his opinion to implement such programmes would transform British society and politics beyond all recognition; unlike the German rulers Britain neither wanted nor was in a position to neglect the social security system or write off the foreign debt with the mere stroke of a pen.[93] In a similar vein, Eden, in a statement to foreign press correspondents, justified persistent efforts towards appeasement with the argument that Britain should not seek confrontation in foreign policy – the government's entire domestic policy was aimed at avoiding confrontation;

bloc formation and the doctrine of class struggle were a threat to peace at home and abroad alike.[94] Reflecting the basic conviction of British Conservatives, Premier Baldwin and Foreign Secretary Eden declared that it was preferable to repair a leaking dam – that is, to reconstruct it on a line of retreat – rather than to charge against the floods on an advance front.[95] Instead of sabre-rattling and manoeuvring into a situation where swords would have to be drawn, it was necessary, precisely in times of crisis, to show willingness to negotiate and at the same time to make it clear which operative ideals would under no circumstances be called into question. By acting in a businesslike manner and showing or feigning indifference to positions based on different forms of ideology, a working agreement was to be induced giving no special advantage to either side. Until the opposite had been proved – that is, dictatorial/Bonapartist action in foreign policy[96] – there seemed to be no reason why a political culture in which peaceful change was seen as the essence of a class society (in the guise of the deferrent system) and of the empire/commonwealth should not also try out this domestic approach in the field of foreign affairs.[97] As regards the question of whether normal relations with the Third Reich were possible (a peaceful revision of the *status quo*), confidence was placed in the soothing effect of the strategy of crisis tried out in domestic policy: by making concessions on demands for a change of the *status quo* considered as legitimate grievances, the integrity of the overall system was to be upheld. The ventures into the fields of economic and political appeasement had this aim in mind. Aware of the fact that the German war economy was bound to accelerate German withdrawal from the world economic order (a trend begun with barter trade and foreign exchange control) and threaten the very existence of that system, British policy aimed at reinforcing the position of the 'moderates' and keeping Germany within the Western capitalist system.[98] Nevertheless, in the course of the 1930s British policy had less and less success in drawing the line between adjustment to shifts in the balance of power and interests which would maintain the system on the one hand, and on the other endangering the whole system by giving up objectives which in the past had served as evidence of solidarity and common security interests.

Whereas, British domestic policy, precisely on account of its limited approach to the armament question, signalled its interest in a stabilisation of the system, foreign policy took a critical turn, since one of the parties involved – Hitler – used British reticence to revolutionise the balance of power, while the scope of the other protagonist – France – remained limited.[99] The fact that appeasement as moulded by British domestic politics was conceived as a counter-offensive to the *Machtpolitik* of the National Socialist system (and to the – previous – *status quo* diplomacy of France) faced totally different circumstances and adversaries in the domestic and foreign fields, explains the discrepancy between the relative success of the internal immunisation strategy and the fatal consequences of the 'as if' policy in foreign affairs.

Notes: Chapter 8

For detailed references see my study, *England in der Krise. Grundlagen und Grundzüge der britischen Appeasement-Politik (1930–1937)*, Schriften des Zentralinstituts für sozialwissenschaftliche Forschung der FU Berlin, vol. 34 (Wiesbaden: West-deutscher Verlag, 1981).

1   J. Herz, 'Sinn und Sinnlosigkeit der Beschwichtigungspolitik. Zur Problematik des Appeasement-Begriffs', *Politische Vierteljahresschrift*, vol. V (1964), pp. 370–89; W. J. Hanrieder, 'Dissolving international politics. Reflections on the nation state', *American Political Science Review*, vol. LXXII (1978), pp. 1276–87.
2   Apart from the name 'peaceful coexistence' this has nothing to do with the Soviet term.
3   M. Cowling interprets events rather one-sidedly focusing on manoeuvres in party strategy and tactics. He appropriately describes the context as a 'spectrum of conflict which had been established when Baldwin and MacDonald stabilised the class struggle ten years before' (*The Impact of Hitler. British Politics and British Policies 1933–1940* (Cambridge, 1975), p. 5.) However, since he defines the 'impact of Labour' (*The Impact of Labour, 1920–1924*, Cambridge, 1971) and the 'impact of Hitler' as stages of the transformation of the class struggle he does not stress the differences due to the defence issue (see G. Schmidt, 'Politisches System und Appeasement-Politik. Zur Scharnierfunktion der Rüstungspolitik für die britische Innen- und Aussenpolitik', *Militärgeschichtliche Mitteilungen* 1979/2, pp. 37–53). More appropriate are his comments on the manoeuvres of the government trying to prevent the Labour Party's return to office; they feared that the Labour Party could regain the 'credit' it lost during the 1931 financial crises by exposing itself as the main British (ideological) opponent to Hitler, that is, act according to the device: Whoever is against Hitler and thus on the right side, has a right to determine British politics of the future (pp. 2, 292, 387 ff.). In contrast to Cowling's analysis which concentrates on party manoeuvres, K. Middlemas correctly emphasises the increasing importance of the triangle of relations between government, employers' associations and the unions (*Politics in Industrial Society. The Experience of the British System since 1911*, London, 1980).
4   cf. F. S. Northedge, *The Troubled Giant. Britain among the Great Powers 1916–1939* (London, 1966), pp. 385–6; for further details see Chapter IV of my own study. The circumstances leading to the fall of the second Labour government and the formation of the National Government provided the background to ideological bloc formation. The fact that these remained limited to fringe groups was not only thanks to governmental policy but equally so to Labour and union leadership; if little is mentioned on the latter this is only because attention has of necessity been focused on politicians in charge of governing the country. As regards 'ideological' confrontations, it should merely be pointed out that N. Chamberlain saw 'fascism' (that is, the Croix-de-feu League, among others) as France's point of 'decay': Chamberlain's Diary, 19 February 1938, Chamberlain's Papers, Birmingham University, NC2–23.
5   For a summary of the main points in Chapter IV of my study see the article quoted in note 3 above. Defence policy reflected both changes in attitudes towards other powers affecting Britain's security interests in one way or another as well as social and economic considerations and constraints which in turn determined priorities in domestic and foreign policy.
6   cf. Stanley Baldwin, 9 March 1936, *Hansard, House of Commons*, 5th ser., vol. 309, col. 1832: 'In the post-war years we had to choose between . . . a policy of disarmament, social reform and latterly financial rehabilitation, and . . . a heavy expenditure on armaments. Under a powerful impulse for development, every government of every party elected for the former.'
7   The 'economic appeasers' in particular advised Eden to raise the question of living standards in international politics as a means of mobilising the German people's desire for peace; see Chapter III of my study, 'Economic Appeasement', section A7.
8   Hoare was the first to express this point of view at Cabinet level (9 March 1934): Public Record Office: CAB 23/78, p. 286.
9   W. R. Rock, *British Appeasement in the 1930s* (London, 1977), p. 97.
10   Neville Chamberlain to Hilda, 21 March 1936, Chamberlain Papers, Birmingham: NC 18/1/952. The *Times* leader (9 March 1936), entitled 'A chance to rebuild', exemplifies the

approach predominant in governmental and economic circles; see also Schmidt, *Militär-geschichtliche Mitteilungen* 1979/2, p. 49.

11   cf. K. Feiling, *Life of Neville Chamberlain* (London, 1946), pp. 314 ff.; I. Mcleod, *Neville Chamberlain* (London, 1961), pp. 47, 192, 208; J. Barnes and K. Middlemas, *Baldwin* (London, 1969), pp. 902 ff. For further details see Chapter IV, sections 4, 5, 6.

12   cf. P. Dennis, *Decision by Default* (London, 1972), pp. 81–2; G. Peden, *British Rearmament and the Treasury 1932–1939* (Edinburgh, 1979), pp. 72 ff.

13   Neville Chamberlain to Ida, 7 March 1937, NC 18/1/997 (on the Air Estimates).

14   Chamberlain to Hilda, 25 April 1937, NC 18/1/1003. On the National Defence Contribution see Middlemas, *Industrial Society*, p. 255; Peden, *Treasury*, pp. 87–8; R. P. Shay, *British Rearmament in the Thirties. Politics and Profits* (Princeton, NJ, 1977).

15   The basic position can be illustrated by the slogan 'Watch on the Tyne' – that is, the symbol of the unemployment problem – which was to be taken more seriously than 'Watch on the Rhine' – that is, the borders of the security zone fixed by the victorious Allies in 1919 to contain German militarism. In the debate on the budget (1937) the Labour Party was still arguing that for every pound (£) spent on armament, £1 should be earmarked 'for improving the conditions of the people'. Considering this and other motives, appeasement could be described as a 'conservative blend of pacifism' (W. McElwee, *Britain's Locust Years* (London, 1962), p. 228); see also *The History of the Times*, IV/2, p. 484.

16   N. Chamberlain to Ida, 18 January 1937, NC 18/1/991. On contacts between Schacht and Blum, Schacht and Leith-Ross, see Chapter III; cf. R. Girault, 'Léon Blum: La Dévaluation de 1936 et la conduite de la politique extérieure de la France', in *Relations internationales*, 1978/13, pp. 91–109; C. A. MacDonald, 'Economic appeasement and the German "moderates", 1937/39', *Past and Present*, no. 56 (1972), pp. 105–35; R. A. C. Parker, 'Grossbritannien und Deutschland 1936/37', in O. Hauser (ed.), *Weltpolitik 1933–39* (Göttingen, 1973), p. 73.

17   Feiling, *Neville Chamberlain*, p. 301; Mcleod, *Neville Chamberlain*, pp. 47, 196, 208. To mention briefly other aspects: the legend of the 'stab in the back' spread by the Hitler movement was seen as an indication that before provoking a war the powers-that-be would weigh up the risks involved – that is, whether the home front could stand the strain which perhaps several war-winters would entail.

18   This was partially based on the view in Germany (von Bülow, von Neurath) that for financial and social reasons Berlin just as London would be forced to water down armament projects. For details on the period 1932/3 see E. W. Bennett, *German Rearmament and the West, 1932/33* (Princeton, NJ, 1979).

19   Vansittart, 'A prosperous Germany', 15 June 1933, C 5456/62/18, FO 371–16696, pp. 239 ff.

20   Sargent to Phipps, 28 March 1933, C 9489/319/18, FO 371–16728, p. 295; cf. B.-J. Wendt, *München 1938, England zwischen Hitler und Preussen* (Frankfurt, 1965). British changes in emphasis are worthy of note. At the beginning of 1930, for example, Sargent had estimated: 'The more the Germans get involved in internal wrangles the less danger there is of their adopting a forward foreign policy'; later (to a certain extent as early as after the elections of September 1930) the diversion theory was to predominate. In the former case it was argued that democracies were disunited, too weak in the field of foreign affairs to take adequate decisions; in the latter it is assumed that autocratic regimes prefer to 'take the bull by the horns' and cover up their internal weakness by prestigious success abroad.

21   The Earl of Avon, *The Eden Memoirs,* Vol. I: *Facing the Dictators* (London, 1962), pp. 323–4; in August 1935 (28 August 1935) Sargent had expressed the opinion that the Germans would make 'a diversion in foreign affairs' rather than repeat a bloodbath (the Roehm putsch), faced with a deterioration in the economic situation: see FO 371/18858, p. 392.

22   B.-J. Wendt, *Economic Appeasement. Handel und Finanz in der britischen Deutschland-politik 1933–1939* (Düsseldorf, 1971), and MacDonald, 'Economic appeasement'; see Chapter III of my study with critical comments on the significance of this concept.

23   The politico-economic premises closely correlated to the strategy of 'economic appeasement' have been dealt with collectively under the term 'Stufentheorie'. See Chapter III, section A4.

24   N. Chamberlain postulated: 'The economy of the country could not and must not be stimulated and reshaped to suit the needs of rearmament' (M. M. Postan, *British War*

Production (London, 1952), p. 11); he thereby rejected Churchill's view that Britain had to keep up with their German opponent, channelling some 30 per cent of production capacity into the armament industry to do so.

25　Kingsley Wood and R. MacDonald to Eden, 22 May 1936, FO 371/19906. See in general K. Middlemas, *Diplomacy of Illusion. The British Government and Germany 1937–39* (London, 1972).

26　Breen's comments (the Berlin Embassy) on the Wigram–Sargent–Ashton–Gwatkin memorandum 'Britain, France and Germany', December 1935, in Phipps MSS., Churchill College, Cambridge, vol. 5/6, p. 45. In British diplomatic circles, in the case of Hankey and among right-wing Conservatives, the precarious term 'pacifist/decadent' is identified with opposition to rearmament. The term is however more closely linked to disputes before and during the First World War and in fact does not represent 'adaptation' to National Socialist propaganda.

27　The question became particularly acute in the winter of 1937/8 within the context of Halifax's visit and the efforts to maintain the principle of rationing despite pressure from the service ministers; see Middlemas, *Diplomacy*, pp. 120 ff.; N. Gibbs, 'Rearmament policy', *History of the Second World War*, Vol. 1: *Grand Strategy* (London, 1976), pp. 279 ff., 294 ff., 622 ff.; D. Dilks (ed.), *The Diaries of Sir Alexander Cadogan, 1938–1945* (London, 1971).

28　Meeting of a study group, All Souls College, 2nd day, 19 December 1937, H. Nicolson MSS. Balfour had practised this aphorism during the crises of the First World War; Hankey's 'sitting on the hedges' slogan follows on from Balfour.

29　See Schmidt, *Militärgeschichtliche Mitteilungen* 1979/2, p. 50 on the significance of the time factor.

30　Chamberlain wanted to work on the slogan 'Rearmament – a guarantee for peace and employment' to play the 'two bogeys' (Hitler and Stafford Cripps) off against each other; however, even after the passing of the Four Year Plan in March 1936 the government continued to play this card with considerable restraint.

31　Impressions gained from my interviews (in the 1960s) with generals, diplomats and Rt Hon. Members of the 1930s and 1940s have meanwhile been substantiated by 'direct' access to the papers of Chamberlain, Inskip, Simon and others.

32　A. Bullock, *The Life and Times of Ernest Bevin*, Vol. I, *Trade Union Leader 1881–1940* (London, 1960), p. 636.

33　It would be worth looking into the question whether and to what degree German developments were viewed in the British debate of the 1920s and 1930s in the light of theories on monopoly capitalism, that is, 'organised capitalism', and also the extent to which the development of the British political system was considered as having been influenced by such phenomena. This relates to the genesis of 'collectivist politics' (Finer, Kavanagh).

34　In disputes on whether and to what degree labour forces had to be diverted into specific sectors and enterprises (begun by Swinton in favour of the expansion of the RAF) (see Barnes and Middlemas, *Baldwin*, pp. 1025 ff.; M. Howard, *The Continental Commitment* (London, 1972), pp. 114–15) it also had to be considered with whom and at what level possible negotiations were to be conducted: the higher the level the more far-reaching and drastic the government's concessions would have to be. If, however, action were limited to voluntary contracts, that is, respect for the associations' (TUC and FBI/NCEO) doctrine of self-government, there would be less pressure to compensate for intervention in industrial relations by conceding delegates of those associations administrative competence or a right to participate in the administration.

35　W. R. Garside, 'Management and men. Aspects of British industrial relations in the inter-war period', in B. Barry and B. Supple (eds), *Essays in British Business History* (London, 1977). The government's formula was twofold: (1) it was made clear to industrialists that the government did not want to find itself in a position 'of solving the employer's difficulties by buying off the Trade Unions', and (2) the delegates (FBI deputation, 7 October 1935: NCEO/FBI, 13 May 1937) were warned that their industries would have to accept the 'social sops' planned by the government; otherwise things would get out of hand with the consequence that government and industry would be forced to make further concessions to 'labour' to the great detriment of the common interests of government and industry. 13 May 1937, T 172–1856.

36 The government – and precisely Chamberlain – feared the reproach of a 'capitalist conspiracy' – an unholy alliance between government and armament interests. Other terms of reference are necessary to explain the excesses of profiteering, particularly in aircraft manufacture; see Middlemas, *Industrial Society*, pp. 252 ff.; Shay, *British Rearmament*, pp. 249 ff.; Peden, *Treasury*, pp. 50 ff., 95–6.

37 Gibbs's and Peden's recently published research illustrate that in the phase 1932–4 – in which the military superiority of the Third Reich's neighbours seemed to be established – the Cabinet followed the Chancellor of the Exchequer who, in balancing 'one set of risks . . . against the other, submits that at the present time financial risks are greater than any other that we can estimate' (N. Chamberlain, 17 March 1932, CP 105(32), CAB 24/229). In the phase 1935–8 financial constraints were, however, not the main obstacle to full-scale rearmament. The debate on the postponement of borrowing for defence in 1934–6 was conditioned by political and social considerations, but was also based on an assessment of the international situation which saw no security threat (in the West!); see Chapters I and II of my book.

38 Any interpretation of foreign policy referring to the domestic background is always in danger of being taken for the thesis that the hands of diplomacy were tied by 'difficulties' and that foreign policy was blocked since the actors were caught in the trap of domestic affairs. It is thereby forgotten – among other elements – that any analysis of foreign policy must assume that in a pluralist democracy politicians in office have already been 'socialised' in business and social life.

39 D. C. Watt, 'British domestic politics and the onset of war', in CNRS, *Relations Franco-Britanniques* (1935–9) (1975), pp. 243–61, in particular pp. 243, 249. The assessment is based on questions such as whether opinions and decision-making were influenced by election dates or the atmosphere of election campaigns, the dependence of the government on struggles between the right and left wing and how the informal network of social contacts influences (as a background atmosphere) the framing and the scope of foreign relations.

40 Watt, 'British domestic politics', p. 243.

41 Cowling links criticism of Churchill's party leadership (in the Second World War) with a more of less subtle justification of Chamberlain's strategy: Churchill's leadership was a 'false' form of Conservatism and could not expect to survive in times of peace. From the methodological point of view Cowling has been reproached for overemphasising 'insider' opinions – similar to a parliamentary correspondent – and not aligning his conclusions from these sources on governmental debates and decision-making. My own criticism also concerns his overestimation of party politics to the detriment of the field of interaction: 'politics-economics' (leading economic circles/trade unions) and in particular that Cowling is not aware of the domestic circumstances confining the government's scope in foreign affairs and the extent to which matters of foreign policy encumbered the handling of domestic affairs as a process of continuous interaction.

42 Cowling, *Hitler*, pp. 355 ff.; R. A. C. Parker, 'Britain, France and Scandinavia 1939/40', *History*, vol. 61 (1976), pp. 370 ff.; see also Dirksen to Weizsäcker, 16 December 1938, *Akten zur Deutschen Auswärtigen Politik*, vol. IV, no. 281, p. 306; J. Grenville, 'Contemporary trends in the study of the British "appeasement" policies of the 1930s', *Internationales Jahrbuch für Geschichte und Geographie-Unterricht*, vol. XVII (1976), pp. 236–47.

43 The chances of success were to be improved by offering Japan and Germany an armament level higher than the other parties concerned (France and USA) were willing to offer as an acceptable ceiling. It cannot however be said that the standards considered by Britain would have endangered French security. Whether an agreement on the basis of the 'data' tolerated by Britain would have bound either Japan or Germany in the long run is another question.

44 Simon, 30 April 1935, PM (35) 1, CAB 32/125.

45 This even applies to the guarantee to Poland which was primarily to illustrate a readiness to resist a German attempt to seize world power; Chamberlain, 20 March 1939, CAB 23/98; cf. Gibbs, 'Rearmament Policy', pp. 592–3, 689 ff., 803 ff.; G. Niedhardt, 'Die britisch-französische Garantieerklärung für Polen vom 31.3.1939', *Francia*, vol. II (1974), p. 608.

46 This 'situation' was linked to the fact that both government and opposition (the Labour Party, the Liberals, League of Nations Union *et al.*) preferred to express the problem in

abstract terms – they referred to 'dictators' who were not members of the League of Nations. Whereas the opposition demanded that 'Britain should take the lead', the government rejected the role of the world's policeman on grounds already established by Bonar Law (1922). However, in its publicity work the government could not focus on the main reason, that is, the fear of commitments *vis-à-vis* France and Russia leading to reinvolvement in a European conflict over the 'balance of power' and 'security' and then having to bear the cost of war once the conflict were transformed into an Anglo-German war. By renaming the 'British Expeditionary Force' (a term which seemed rather offensive in the light of the Peace Ballot campaign) the 'Field Force' the government was taking account of the mood of British public opinion against 'bloc formation and an arms race' – see Dennis, *Decision by Default*, p. 35.

47   Ambassador Corbin, 12 March 1936, Documents Diplomatiques Français, 2nd series, vol. I, no. 409, p. 529.

48   Sargent memorandum, 5 December 1934, para. 16, CAB 21/417 (Committee on German Rearmament); cf. Inskip, quoted in note 53.

49   cf. Schmidt, *Militärgeschichtliche Mitteilungen* 1979/2, pp. 44–5. I do not go into the question of working at cross-purposes in defence planning since other contributors to this volume deal with this subject.

50   N. Chamberlain, 9 February 1936: see Feiling, *Neville Chamberlain*, pp. 313–14; cf. Chamberlain, 23 July 1939, also quoted in D. Dilks, '"The unnecessary war". Military advice and foreign policy in Great Britain, 1931–1939', in A. Preston (ed.), *General Staffs and Diplomacy before the Second World War* (London, 1978), pp. 127–8.

51   'We cannot take political initiative in the shape of further commitments. All the more need therefore for economic initiative. Surely this will go a long way to meet criticism of His Majesty's Government at home' (Leeper-Minute, 26 June 1936, FO 371/19933); Eden agreed with this view. From such positions Wendt and MacDonald conclude the importance of economic appeasement in British policy in Europe; in my opinion – see Chapter III – they underestimate that the economic appeasers themselves were aware of the domestic constraints on a foreign policy aimed at achieving international détente by economic means.

52   On factors conditioning Britain's willingness and feasibilities to co-operate see G. Schmidt, 'Interdependenzprobleme und Restrukturierung der internationalen Politik. Das Zusammenspiel sicherheitspolitischer, politischer und ideologischer Faktoren in der britischen Weltpolitik', in K. Rohe (ed.), *Die Westmächte und das Dritte Reich 1933–1939. Klassische Grossmachtrivalität oder Kampf zwischen Demokratie und Diktatur?* (Paderborn, 1982). See also note 6 above.

53   Inskip, 15 December 1937, CP 316 (37), CAB 24/273. Mention should simply be made of the second aspect, that is, that Great Britain's economic and financial strength would be an advantage over Germany in the event of a 'long' war; the momentous studies of Peden; Gibbs; Barnet, *The Collapse of British Power* (London, 1972); R. M. Meyers, *Britische Sicherheitspolitik 1934–38* (Bonn, 1976) deal with this element in full detail.

54   This guarding from foreign interference was first introduced in economic and financial policy (by measures taken in 1931/2) and then in defence policy (see Schmidt, *Militärgeschichtliche Mitteilungen* 1979/2).

55   B. J. Wendt, 'Grossbritannien – "Demokratie auf dem Prüfstand, Appeasement als Strategie des Status Quo"', in E. Forndran *et al.* (eds), *Innen- und Aussenpolitik unter nationalsozialistischer Bedrohung* (Opladen, 1977), pp. 29–30; K. Hildebrand, 'Der Hitler-Stalin-Pakt als ideologisches Problem', in A. Hillgruber and K. Hildebrand, *Kalkül zwischen Macht und Ideologie. Der Hitler-Stalin-Pakt: Parallelen bis heute?* (Zurich, 1980), p. 57.

56   On the inflationary spiral, see Schmidt, *Militärgeschichtliche Mitteilungen* 1979/2, p. 47. Fears were based on experience from the First World War, partly on information on bottlenecks in German rearmament, and partly on the first signs in Britain of competition among arms-manufacturing companies for skilled labour. On the latter see Peden, *Treasury*, pp. 85–6; Shay, *British Rearmament*, pp. 244 ff.; Middlemas, *Industrial Society*, pp. 254 ff.

57   See Chamberlain to Hilda, note 14 above.

58   G. Ziebura (*Bestimmungsfaktoren der Aussenpolitik in der zweiten Hälfte des 20. Jahrhunderts* (Berlin 1974), p. 39) describes the ties between the ruling élite and its supporting

groups with the term 'Herrschaftssynthese' (synthesis of domination); a number of his ideas are obviously influenced by the writings of A. Gramsci. Cowling's 'centrality' theory appropriately reflects the viewpoint of the British political actors of the time; however, it should be noted that this argument was advocated not only by party strategists but also by spokesmen from industry (see Schmidt, *Militärgeschichtliche Mitteilungen* 1979/2, p. 49).

59 The Conservatives feared that by tipping the balance between military and social expenditure in favour of commitments in foreign affairs the government would lose credibility among its wide range of supporters since such interference would accelerate the change of the conditions of living – a process that they were precisely trying to restrain with their policy.

60 The reproach 'confesses putting party before country' (Churchill's famous index to *The Gathering Storm*) – that Baldwin had neglected rearmament because of party interests – has a companion in the dispute between the followers of MacDonald on the one hand and of Henderson/Bevin on the other – particularly after the 1931 crisis – that the latter had shirked their responsibility and were thus not fit to govern the country.

61 On the arms race – with regard to the air force – see R. J. Overy, 'The German pre-war aircraft production plans', *English Historical Review*, vol. 90 (1975), pp. 778–97; idem, *William Morris, Viscount Nuffield* (London, 1976); on the development of the British aircraft industry, see P. Fearon, 'The British airframe industry and the state 1918–1935', *Economic History Review*, vol. XXVII (1974), pp. 236–51 and *Economic History Review*, vol. XXVIII (1975), pp. 658–62; P. Fearon, 'Aircraft manufacturing', in N. K. Buxton and D. H. Aldcroft (eds), *British Industry between the Wars. Instability and Industrial Development 1919–1939* (London, 1979), pp. 216–39.

62 See pp. 107 ff. of this article.

63 Although Churchill welcomes Baldwin's and MacDonald's qualities of leadership and attitudes, he is nevertheless of the opinion that both politicians carried their positions of influence and power over into a period when other standards and criteria should have come to the fore. Cowling, N. Thompson (*The Anti-Appeasers*, Oxford, 1971) and S. Davis ('The British Labour Party and British foreign policy 1935–39', Ph.D thesis, London School of Economics, 1950) give an analysis of why there was no alternative to the National Government before 'Munich'.

64 'Our Foreign Policy is quite clear. We must keep out of troubles in Central Europe at all costs. July 20 years ago stands out as an awful warning': Simon to MacDonald, 27 July 1934 (after the murder of Dollfuss), FO 800/291. The warning not only covered prewar diplomacy but also the improvised defence economy; see Schmidt, *Militärgeschichtliche Mitteilungen* 1979/2, pp. 48–9. Linked to this was the confidence in governmental circles: 'I wonder if we could have kept out of the German war had a Government such as this been in power. I think definitely at any rate that much of the loathsome slaughter and material waste would have been saved': Runciman to Simon, 13 July 1934, Simon MSS. Simon had resigned in 1916 because of the introduction of conscription; Runciman and McKenna had opposed Lloyd George's 'Knock out' war policy.

65 On the 'over-commitment' theory in economic relations see D. Aldcroft and H. W. Richardson, *The British Economy 1870–1939* (London, 1969), pp. 190 ff.; on security policy, P. M. Kennedy, 'Appeasement and British defence policy in the inter-war years', *British Journal of International Studies*, vol. IV (1978), pp. 161–77; G. Schmidt, 'Britische Strategie und Aussenpolitik', *Militärgeschichtliche Mitteilungen*, vol. IX, no. 1 (1971), pp. 197–218.

66 The British government was either wary of or simply refused to define or extend existing commitments and arrange counter measures with other guarantor powers or 'potential' victims of a German breach of international law. While London evaded talks on the endangered *status quo* with the injured parties, it gave signals to Berlin that it was prepared to open negotiations on 'legitimate' grievances. London considered a revision of the *status quo* but wanted no discussion (for example, with France) on any possible alternative solution in the case of Germany offering nothing adequate in exchange.

67 Vansittart, 3 February 1936: 'Our first object . . . [is] to prove to our own people that we have made every effort to secure peace, but not at the expense of other people. That will be highly important, if it comes to a show-down': FO 371/19884; cf. B. Bond, (ed.), *Chief of Staff. The Diaries of Lieutenant-General Sir Henry Pownall*, Vol. I (London, 1972), p. 103.

68   J. T. Emmerson, *The Rhineland Crisis, 7th March 1936. A Study in Multilateral Diplomacy* (London, 1977); Chapter I.2 and Chapter IV.4 of my book.
69   Note 52 above and *Militärgeschichtliche Mitteilungen* 1979/2, pp. 38–9.
70   In foreign economic policy the Treasury, Board of Trade, Ministry of Agriculture *et al.* also ensured that the interests of their 'constituencies' – that is, domestic factors – were brought to bear alongside the 'sacrifices' deemed as necessary by the Foreign Office. The background to this was mistrust in the predominance of internationalistic points of view: in other words, the change of climate in the 1930s compared to the preferences of the 1920s.
71   N. Chamberlain, 25 October 1936, Diary, NC2–23A (record of a conversation with Inskip, 19 October 1936); on the relations between the three defence departments, the problems of co-ordination and the dangers of inflation, see Schmidt, *Militärgeschichtliche Mitteilungen* 1979/2, pp. 47–8.
72   The assessment of capacities of the armament industry had an important role to play in the setting of the target date in July 1935 along with the relaxation of financial restrictions. Chamberlain and Runciman appointed Weir as 'contact man' with industry to the central Cabinet committee on armament to help bolster their argument *vis-à-vis* the services and the Foreign Office. The inclusion of the businessman in the decision-making process (and not only at the stage of the application of already established programmes) was unpopular among heads of staff who wanted to exclude such 'defeatist' influence from deliberations on the British 'Four Year Plan'.
73   On mutual support between the government and industry (FBI), see Schmidt, *Militärgeschichtliche Mitteilungen* 1979/2, pp. 49–50.
74   Inskip, 30 October 1936, CP 297 (36), CAB 24/265; 14 March 1938, CAB 23/92; cf. Middlemas, *Diplomacy*, ch. 6; Gibbs, 'Rearmament policy', pp. 303 ff.; Shay, *British Rearmament*, pp. 197 ff.; Dennis, *Decision by Default*, pp. 63 ff., 79 ff.
75   Chamberlain to the French Financial Attaché, Le Norcy, 19 February 1937: 'At the same time restrictions on foreign issues [embargo on foreign loans] have been in force in this country for a number of years and the present is specially a time at which our savings should be safeguarded in view of the large impending demands for rearmament' (T. 177/34). On 17 February Le Norcy had transmitted an appeal from Blum/Auriol that the scheduled internal measures should coincide with a statement in support of French monetary policy.
76   Baldwin, 26 February 1936, CAB 23–83, pp. 179 ff. cf. Middlemas, *Industrial Society*, p. 256. The employers wanted to forego competitive bidding for skilled labour; the government to avoid taking 'coercive' measures. The principles of willing co-operation were laid down in the 1936 Defence Statement.
77   On the meeting requested by the FBI in October 1935 see Schmidt, *Militärgeschichtliche Mitteilungen* 1979/2, p. 49; Middlemas, *Industrial Society*, pp. 245 ff.; Peden, *Treasury*, pp. 46–7.
78   On the background, form and substance of contacts between government and unions in 1935, 1937, 1938 and 1939 see Middlemas, *Industrial Society*, pp. 225–6, 255 ff.; Shay, *British Rearmament*, pp. 92–133; Gibbs, 'Rearmament policy', pp. 301 ff.
79   This is how Middlemas (*Industrial Society*, p. 262) interprets Chamberlain's statements, CAB 22 (39) 3. See also note 35 above.
80   In discussions with the Defence Deputation of the 'opposition from the right' in July and November 1936 it became apparent that A. Chamberlain, Grigg, Churchill, Amery and others were only in agreement on the fact that Britain had to intensify and accelerate rearmament; it was expected of Baldwin to win over public opinion. In questions of foreign policy and on priorities among the forces, divergence of opinion was similar to that among governmental circles.
81   Chamberlain (26 May 1935) was, for example, of the opinion that RAF expansion could soothe British public opinion and act as a deterrent to Germany (cf. Gibbs, 'Rearmament policy', p. 175); reasons of cost efficiency, strategic arguments and reference to the massive reserve among the 'people' were put forward as grounds for disregarding the demands of the War Office and General Staff.
82   The problems of government propaganda are not to be discussed here. Analysis would have to include an examination of Baldwin's statement – *vis-à-vis* the Defence Deputation – that the platform of Germany as the 'bogeyman' was out of the question; instead

reference would have to be made to democracy as opposed to dictatorship 'which . . . is the one line whereby you can get people to sit up in this country if they think dictators are likely to attack them . . . but I have never seen the clear line by which you can approach people to scare them but not scare them into fits': quoted in M. Gilbert, *Winston S. Churchill*, Vol. V (London, 1976), p. 776. By making the expansion of room to manoeuvre dependent on progress in rearmament the Foreign Office and the service departments put themselves into the hands of those politicians who were said to be able to feel the pulse-rate of public opinion. These politicians (Baldwin, Halifax and to some extent K. Wood) gained a degree of influence in foreign affairs which exceeded their interest and knowledge of these matters.

83 Consideration of parliamentary sovereignty and public opinion meant that British foreign policy always had an argument up its sleeve in defence of its policy, a reason for declining guarantees, and so on. Whereas in the period of imperialism and prewar diplomacy the Conservatives and generals called for a forward policy, their successors in the 1930s had a defensive attitude and could advocate that their foreign policy, aimed at normalisation, reflected the 'no more war' atmosphere at home; they accused the Labour Party and the unions of warmongering. However, we cannot conclude from the reversal of the roles that labour had declared an ideological and economic 'war' (calls for boycotting) on fascism while the right wing either sympathised with the German powers-that-be or turned a blind eye. See D. C. Watt, *Too Serious a Business. European Armed Forces and the Approach to the Second World War* (London, 1975).

84 In the spring of 1936 (29 April and 11 May 1936) a majority in Cabinet, for example, rejected the demand of the service ministers to withdraw forces from the Mediterranean in the interest of concentrating striking power and unimpeded rearmament; the danger of a 'rebellion' of public opinion was considered greater than the dangers of dislocation possibly linked to further stationing of forces in that area.

85 Nicolson Diary, 11 March 1936; N. Nicolson (ed.), *Harold Nicolson, Diaries and Letters in 1930–39* (Fontana Books, 1969), p. 242.

86 J. Simon, 21 March 1935, Diary, Simon MSS.

87 Lord Eustace Percy, *Some Memories* (London, 1958), p. 184: 'The Government had sapped its moral for some months past in its tentative thinking about a future settlement with Hitler. Ministers both in London and Paris had got into the habit of treating [the neutralisation of the Rhineland] as expandable for such a purpose.'

88 H. Nicolson, 19 December 1937, All Souls Meeting, Nicolson Papers.

89 cf. Schmidt, *Militärgeschichtliche Mitteilungen* 1979/2, pp. 40 ff.

90 A search into the local press (1935/7) showed that in February–April a considerable number of MPs attended the general assemblies of constituency parties, kindling debate on rearmament policy. Members of the right wing of course advocated a 'policy of strength' with rearmament as an end in itself (empire isolationism).

91 Eden to Phipps, 24 February 1936 (on the first meeting of the committee on Germany), FO 371/19884 C. 750. cf. T. Jones, *A Diary with Letters 1931–1950* (Oxford, 1954), pp. 175 ff.; Nicolson, *Diary and Letters*, p. 236 (13 February 1936). Thus the centre left movements declared their willingness to support limited rearmament.

92 This is the result of an analysis of the British reaction to 16 March 1935, 7 March 1936 and the *Anschluss* of 1938.

93 M. M. Postan, *British War Production* (London, 1952), p. 17.

94 Eden, 12 January 1937, quoted in A. W. Baldwin, *My Father. The True Story* (London, 1955), p. 265.

95 With reference to similar examples Taylor described the National Government as a club of well-meaning elderly gentlemen, shy of any conflict for as long as withdrawal was possible. It went totally against their grain to turn down compromise in foreign policy which was to a great extent the basis of domestic policy (A. J. P. Taylor, *The Origins of the Second World War*, London/Penguin, 1974), p. 155).

96 See note 82 above on Baldwin's 'democracy v. dictatorship' interpretation; and cf. Lothian's statements in J. R. M. Butler, *Lord Lothian (Philip Kerr), 1882–1940* (London, 1960), p. 229; Barnes and Middlemas, *Baldwin*, p. 857; Gibbs, 'Rearmament policy', p. 647.

97 Reference has already been made to the role of the 'sense of confidence' slogan in both domestic and foreign policy; on this cf. Northedge, *The Troubled Giant*, pp. 618 ff.

98   This is the theme of Wendt's article in this volume.
99   On French policy see the contributions by G. Ziebura and R. Hoehne in Rohe (ed.), *Die nationalsozialistische Herausforderung* (note 52).

9   The British Left and Appeasement: Political Tactics or Alternative Policies?

SABINE WICHERT

The historiography of Britain in the 1930s has only recently begun to change our picture of this period[1] which hitherto had shown the country preoccupied with issues of foreign policy, war and peace, fascism, communism and the Spanish Civil War. No doubt this impression was created because the very people who were concerned about these external issues, external that is to British politics and the interests of the majority of her population, were also the first authors and historians of the period. In other words, intellectuals in the wider sense who had seen their worst fears come true in the war now wrote and thought about the 1930s in terms of explaining the war and the rise and success of Hitler's Germany. Understandable and natural as this may be it has distorted our picture of the 1930s. For it was domestic issues that preoccupied the people as much as the politicians, and even the intellectuals were at the very least as concerned about housing and unemployment as they were about Hitler and Spain. Even the Left Book Club which was founded primarily in order to promote a Popular Front against fascism published and dealt increasingly more with domestic rather than foreign policy matters and topics.[2] With this in mind, the left (by definition at least more concerned with the majority of people) not only had to see foreign policy and appeasement in the context of domestic issues but had also to keep the domestic scene in the forefront of their minds. This divided the political sheep from the theoretical goats, or as Michael Foot put it, 'British capitalism, not German fascism, was the enemy on the doorstep, as ancient as the industrial revolution itself, as modern as the latest Means Test infamy.'[3] The meaning one gave to capitalism would determine one's theoretical stand on the left and what one proposed to do about it was likely to show one's position in the political power game. In other words, only intellectuals and small party groups with not much hope of electoral success could afford to think or act against what had by now emerged as a consensus of the British electorate about the nature and aims of British political life. In some respects the 1930s can be seen as the last time in which a substantial number of intellectuals tried to think against the grain and apply more or less orthodox Marxist concepts to an essentially liberal political culture. The later years of the 1930s saw most of them readjust their thinking to the tradition of radical liberalism which now increasingly incorporated a social democratic end.

In dealing with the left and appeasement, then, one has to set foot on that rather fragile and insecure bridge between intellectual and political history. But it is perhaps only by doing so that one can understand what left-wing attitudes towards Chamberlain's foreign policy imply and mean in the context of their own history as well as the political circumstances of the time.

Who and what then was the left in the Britain of the 1930s? I propose to use the term here in a wide but historical sense, that is, what would have been considered left at the time. In theoretical terms this would have implied groups or individuals who rejected capitalism, or at least some of its forms, that is the labour movement (justified in theory at least by Clause Four) with the addition of communists – party members as well as non-card-carrying intellectuals – and the few intellectuals who sympathised with various groups without becoming members. In more specific terms: the Labour Party incorporating the trade unions, as well as left-wing groups like the Socialist League on the one hand, and on the other what one might roughly call the Marxist orthodoxy, that is, the Communist Party, the Independent Labour Party and the Left Book Club.

The only politically relevant group in this period is, of course, the Labour Party whose attitude towards the appeasement policy of the National Government will have to be explored and explained. To get a complete picture of the whole left spectrum, however, and also in order to understand why the Labour Party rejected a real alternative policy, it will be necessary to investigate the more theoretical left which offered different interpretations and advice for different political action.

The farthest removed both from Labour Party policies as well as from the general British political consensus was the Communist Party.[4] Its dependence on Moscow and the Comintern's changing policies had always left it an alien body on the political scene. When it refused co-operation with the Labour Party in 1932 this was considered strange and politically unwise by its less doctrinaire supporters. Yet the party was insignificant enough for this not to matter. It is ironic that it should be Spain and fascism in the later 1930s and Moscow's need to co-operate with whoever was willing to do so against the threat of Nazi Germany that effected a great boost in membership at a time when a general political success in Britain for communism was much less likely than it ever had been.

The two leading figures in the party at this time were Harry Pollitt, its secretary-general, and Raju Palme Dutt. Dutt was the editor of the *Labour Monthly*, a theoretical communist journal, and the leading communist intellectual at the time with a number of impressive books to his name. As so much of communist writing then, his also suffered from the frequently changing official line. For instance, his *Fascism and Social Revolution*[5] which still followed the Moscow line of 1928–9, that is, that fascism was aided by social democratic parties and that they were therefore an even greater enemy than capitalism, was outdated soon after its appearance. It was, however, his writing which attracted a number of radical politicians and intellectuals to Marxist thinking, foremost among them perhaps being John Strachey who while never joining the party was to become the most important Marxist-communist influence in the Left Book Club.

The official communist answer to appeasement after 1935 was the combined policy of a Popular Front at home and collective security abroad, that is, in line with the French example of coalition government by all anti-fascist parties supported by anti-fascist treaties between Britain, France and the Soviet Union. The greatest obstacle to this policy proved to be the Labour Party which refused even to consider communist proposals. The CPGB thus spent a great deal of its time and energy wooing the Labour Party into some sort of co-operation. But while they were quite successful in attracting public support in the wake of the Spanish Civil War, the Labour Party was not to be won. 'Unfortunately the Labour Movement is led by a handful of reactionary leaders who, consciously or unconsciously, pursue policies which only help the National Government – the Government which is the main obstacle to real collective action on the part of all democratic powers and people against reaction, Fascism and war',[6] complained Pollitt in 1937. But a year later it had to be admitted that 'the Communist Party of Great Britain while it has been able to achieve certain successes in acting as the driving force and organiser of the most active elements within the Labour movement and amongst other sections of the people in the fight against the National Government, has not yet been able to break through the opposition of the dominant Right-Wing Labour leaders that prevents working-class unity being established'.[7]

Every year after the 7th Congress of the Comintern the CPGB applied for affiliation to the Labour Party and was turned down regularly. The *Daily Worker* noticed the growing hostility from the trade unions to any encroachment from communists and featured hunger marches and the exploitation of the working class as the beginning of fascism at home. The Spanish Civil War proved the ideal fighting ground for emotional and ideological battles decided on the pages of this communist daily which doubled its circulation during these years. The non-intervention policy of the National Council of Labour was seen as direct support for the government's policy in giving a free hand to Hitler: 'It must never be forgotten that it is this National Government that has made it possible for Hitler's Fascism to become a menace to the peace of the world. It was the Baldwin Government which encouraged Hitler's war plans against the Soviet Union.'[8]

Whatever their motives, and quite clearly peace for and on behalf of the Soviet Union was their prime motivation, the policy of collective security as understood by the communists did offer a viable political alternative to appeasement. Viable, however, only in theoretical terms, or with hindsight perhaps. British interests (and both the National Government as well as the Labour Party would have conceived of them in these terms) were worldwide and involvement in Europe was given low priority. In other words, for the CPGB British foreign policy did not centre on the indigenous interests of Britain's economic and therefore political needs, as those were understood to be capitalist, but on the Soviet Union as the safeguard of a world revolution which would then also guarantee an eventual communist Britain. Translated into British politics this could read like Pollitt's response to the *Anschluss*:

The German invasion of Austria is the first fruit of the infamous Chamberlain policy which both parties have opposed. There is no need to tell your executive that it is only a first step. Tomorrow it will be Czechoslovakia and then France. The prospect of a Fascist Europe menaces the British people. Only one thing can prevent this – the action of the British people, and the only means of rousing every man and woman in Britain to demand this drastic change of policy, is the co-operation of all the Labour, Communist and democratic forces in Great Britain.[9]

It is perhaps not surprising that this sort of appeal should have struck a chord in so many left-wing intellectuals as well as those, previously vaguely related to the British radical tradition or the Labour movement, who joined the Left Book Club. It did make sense and guaranteed an unusual amount of support until Britain entered the war and the CP had to declare that this was a capitalist war, not in the interest of the Soviet Union or the working classes. Then membership figures started to drop and British radicals remembered their own tradition and reconsidered what they were willing to fight for; ultimately that almost invariably turned out to be British liberal democracy rather than the Soviet Union or a vague future model of a communist Britain.

The part the Communist Party played in the anti-appeasement arena of the left is therefore a small one: influencing public opinion, or a small section thereof, to some slight extent helping to exaggerate the threat from Mosley and his British fascists, perhaps also, by their never-ending attempts to get official co-operation from the Labour Party, turning the Labour Party anti-communist even faster than it would otherwise have become. Communism remained an alien organisation, too undemocratic in its bureaucracy and dealings with its membership, too theoretical in its doctrine, too foreign in its political thinking and tactics to appeal in the end even to the intellectuals for any length of time, and its very success in the mid-1930s made it appear strong enough to invigorate Labour's anti-communism. One cannot see how this vicious circle could have been broken.

In many respects it is rewarding to follow the development of some Marxist or at least Marxist-inclined intellectuals in their reaction to appeasement to see how it was ultimately the British radical tradition that attracted them to Marxism in the first place and also led them to leave these ideas behind when they found their real values were being threatened. The best way to do this is by looking at the Left Book Club which, having once been described as 'the greatest single force in England for the dissemination of left-wing thought',[10] undertook to promote Marxist ideas and policies as well as to create a people's movement and thus enforce a Popular Front; yet both these undertakings were based on a political understanding that owed more to English nineteenth-century liberalism than to Marx's thought.

The Left Book Club was the brainchild of John Strachey and Victor Gollancz who together with Harold Laski constituted the Club's selection committee. It was formed in direct response to the desire for some regular publication to promote a Popular Front. The aims of the Club already gave an indication of the political tradition it sprang from: 'The aim of the Club is a simple one, it is to help in the terrible, urgent struggle for world peace, and for a better social and economic order, and against Fascism, by giving (to all who are determined to play their part in this struggle) such knowledge as will increase their efficiency.'[11] As Stuart Samuels has pointed out, its 'exaggerated faith in the efficacy of reason, the power of public opinion, and the magic of rational argument'[12] was not a new thing in British political life: Corresponding Societies, political clubs and the Anti Corn Law League had been radical forerunners. The only new element was its predominant reliance on the printed word although it very soon branched out into organisational developments beyond the reading of books. Even those, however, were primarily concerned with discussing them. Had it been a communist device – and one can easily see why it was supposed to have become one by many at the time and later – it would have been a very clever design to use and exploit British political traditions for different ends. But as its history shows it worked almost the other way round: communist ideas were used to serve the British radical tradition and were dropped as soon as they began to contradict what was understood to be British liberal democratic interest. In other words, what was lacking even here – except perhaps for a period in Harold Laski's thinking – was the integration of this tradition with Marxist thinking.

At its height, in 1939, the Club served a membership of almost 60,000, not counting the beginning of an international organisation that amounted to an additional 6,000 or so members. This membership was largely middle and lower-middle class and not only bought, and one presumes largely read, the books published by the Club, but was also organised into local and regional discussion groups as well as all kinds of vocational groups. No doubt some of the increase in CP membership was due to its activities and success.

Its promoters believed in the force of knowledge and education, in progress towards an ultimately socialist society and (perhaps the last time in which this was possible) the positive and beneficial power of science and scientific thinking. This almost 'liberal socialism' can also be seen in its policy of publication and propaganda: while clearly biased towards Marxism the Club was open to everyone who was willing to prescribe to its basic and non-committal aims. It published liberal and labour voices as well as communist and independent Marxist ones and its more well-known supporters could be found not only on the left but right into the conservative ranks. This policy, pursued conscientiously, if not always successfully, by Gollancz, became particularly apparent at the big Club rallies which always tried to incorporate all political factions that professed some form of anti-fascism on its public platforms.

Victor Gollancz introduced the selection committee which chose the books to be published each month in the first issue of the *Left Book News* with the following words: 'Professor Laski is a member of the Labour Party: Mr Strachey is in broad sympathy with the aims of the Communist Party: and I am interested in the spreading of all such knowledge and all such ideas as may safeguard peace, combat Fascism, and bring nearer the establishment of real Socialism.'[13] As far as appeasement was concerned, the message the Left Book Club tried to drum home to its members right up to the Soviet–German pact was the aim of collective security and a Popular Front. This was why the Club has mainly been seen in conjunction with the CP and why it came to be hated by the Labour Party.

The driving force behind the Club was Victor Gollancz who made it a success in organisational as well as eventually in financial terms. He believed in a new political education through the written word. 'The Club is a body of men and women united by a passion to fight evil and achieve good, and by an indestructible optimism that they can do it',[14] he wrote; and as Hitler gained in importance he saw the growing need for information and knowledge. Just before Munich he beseeched his membership: 'I now plead with you on this September day of 1938, as I have never pleaded before, to work with all your heart and soul to forge the Left Book Club into an instrument of enlighten- ment which will help – if I may use words which, however worn they may be, carry with them a desperate appeal – to save civilization.'[15] Gollancz was perhaps the most straightforward radical liberal in the trio, not a powerful theoretical thinker, liable to contradict himself in consecutive issues of the *Left News* and to change his opinion on smaller matters, but a steadfast and passionate believer in the good that could come out of education and knowledge.

Intellectually (as opposed to emotionally, in this context) more forceful and persuasive and the Club's directing voice was John Strachey[16] who had been a supporter of Mosley in the second Labour government, followed him into his New Party and turned left as Mosley marched off to the right, taking Palme Dutt as his new political and intellectual mentor. With Gollancz he shared the radical liberal tradition but tried to leave it behind; he thought he had found a more satisfactory answer to the problems of the time in Marxism. It wasn't for want of trying that he never joined the Communist Party. Dutt and Pollitt realised that they wouldn't capture a faithful follower but a troublesome intellectual who would never give up reasoning for the good of the cause even though Strachey proved himself a good enough pupil when he justified the Moscow trials publicly even after he had started to have doubts about Marxism as a creed.[17] It was his books and even more his articles in *Left News*, corrected and straightened out by Palme Dutt who always refused to be publicly credited for this, which shaped what appeared as the official policy of the Left Book Club. It was Strachey and his writing which made the Club into such a useful tool for the CP, to an extent indeed that sometimes even worried Gollancz.[18] Strachey's interpretation of Nazi Germany was the Marxist-communist one: 'Nazi Germany is coming to stand for the absolute rule of the present governing class, the rule of the great industrialist feudalists, the barons of iron and steel, the lords of armour, the magnificos of finance',[19] and so was the conclusion he drew from the German experience for Britain: 'It has proved that the one thing which makes the victory of fascism possible is the passivity of the working class. The one thing which it is utterly and absolutely fatal to do is to do nothing.'[20] Hence the need for the co-operation of socialists and communists, and beyond, to combat fascism. Spain and France were always quoted as examples of Popular Front policies, and treaties were urged with France and the Soviet Union in order to curtail Hitler and Mussolini. This argument was subtly adjusted as the domestic and international situation changed but was maintained in essence up to the beginning of the Soviet–German pact and the war. For want of a strong fascist movement at home the National

Government could be seen as co-operating with and strengthening Hitler, even if it fell only very short of being fascist itself. It was in no position to ban the fascist threat either at home or abroad as fascism and imperialism were bound to work hand in hand. So in 1936: 'Let us resolve now that the fall of Mr Baldwin, which will take place in any event, will not lead to his replacement by a leader of some other school of thought of British Imperialism. For such a one would certainly lead us to war even if he led us by another road';[21] and in 1937: 'Mr Chamberlain wants to do a deal with Italy and Germany because he wishes to make it possible for him to unite with them in hostility to, and ultimately aggression against, on the one hand, the Soviet Union, and on the other, the popular forces all over the world.'[22] This was always combined with accusations of collaboration against the leaders of the Labour Party who were in a position to do something but let things go on as they were. His interpretations were only finally put to the test when the war came and he parted company with the CP arguing that it was more important for Britain to defeat Hitler than to pursue a defeatist policy which according to the CPGB would lead to a communist Britain; but by now Strachey was convinced that this policy would open the door for a fascist Britain. In other words, it was the touch of practical politics that brought Strachey down from his high theoretical horse and united him again with that liberal tradition which he thought he had left behind.[23]

The third man in the selection committee of the Club, Harold Laski,[24] said of himself that he had come 'slowly, even painfully, to Marxism from the Fabian tradition'.[25] Linked with the Labour left at least since 1931, he had repeatedly refused to become a politician[26] preferring to remain the 'eminence grise to those in the seats of political power'.[27] He became an influential member of the Socialist League upon its foundation and quarrelled continuously with the party leadership. He was, however, sufficiently popular with the delegates of the rank and file to sit on the Labour executive from 1937 to 1949. Laski was the only intellectual at the time who tried to adjust Marxism to the British condition. He found finally that capitalism and democracy were incompatible but his emphasis always remained as much on democracy as on socialism. The dictatorship of the proletariat had to be replaced by the 'revolution by consent'[28] which would maintain individual freedom and the rule of democracy. While therefore sympathetic to communist analyses and aims he condemned their technique and was against a permanent alliance between the Labour and the Communist Parties. In Britain socialism could only be achieved within the framework of the existing Labour movement. He thus co-operated with communist views inside the LBC and its journal without ever dropping his critical voice. His aim, after all, had to be education, too, to prepare the consent that would make the revolution possible. But he was realistic about what could be achieved as he showed in reviewing Palme Dutt's *World Politics* with whose conclusions he agreed:

> We alike hold that the ruin of war is rushing upon us; we agree that it can only be prevented by our own action. Most important of all, we agree that such action must come, first, from the whole working class, and second,

from all men and women, of what-ever class, who are prepared to co-operate against the drive to fascism and war. Mr Dutt has shown decisively that fascism needs war; he has more belief than I can share in the power of the workers to prevent fascism from making the attempt.[29]

But this did not prevent him from at least attempting the necessary education: 'I want from our movement [the LBC] to come the inspiration that makes knowledge, that makes organised intelligence, that makes scientific understanding the hall-marks of whatever is significant in the Labour and Socialist movements of this country.'[30] He also had no illusions about the state of the Labour Party, the allegiance the rank and file felt for the leadership, and how therefore education had to concentrate equally on the leaders and officials as on the working people themselves. He fully endorsed the 'official' policy of the LBC towards appeasement and Chamberlain, and provided the *Left News* with perhaps the clearest political analysis of the Labour movement, as well as of Chamberlain's policies. If Gollancz's pleas for socialism, knowledge and understanding represent passion in the LBC,[31] Laski stands for reason. Yet while together they reached thousands of people they did not convince the Labour Party which would have been the only real means through which their policy could have been achieved. The harder they tried the more hostile official Labour grew, then as now afraid of infiltration by communism but equally, however reluctantly, willing to allow Marxist sympathisers to remain inside its ranks as long as they ultimately obeyed party discipline, bowing to the liberal tradition of the culture of which they were and are part.

Finally, the LBC might have influenced a generation, but it did not influence foreign policy (and perhaps one might even argue whether the Beveridge Report would not have been received with the same enthusiasm had it never existed). It certainly helped to boost the CP and perhaps also to consolidate Labour in its control of its rank and file but its overall influence remained at best intellectual. Its policy ultimately differed from that of the CP in that it firmly believed that Marxism and socialism had to be accommodated within the existing Labour movement, not apart from it or against it. That is also why it ultimately failed: the task of injecting Marxism into that essentially liberal tradition proved to be too formidable.

The Marxists inside the Labour Party, including Laski, had after all a better starting position, yet achieved no more. The need for a re-formation of left-wing groups inside the party occurred when the Independent Labour Party disaffiliated in 1932. This event showed how the vast majority of left-wingers inside the Labour movement considered it more promising to stay within the party and hope for some political achievement rather than to insist on principle and choose the political wilderness. The wisdom of their decision was born out by the fact that the membership figures of the ILP dwindled rapidly after 1932, from 16,773 in 1933 to 4,392 in 1935.[32] This is paralleled by a foreign policy that was perhaps furthest removed from any political reality and entirely ideologically motivated. Where the CP was at least committed to Soviet foreign policy the ILP orientated itself solely by the theoretical achievement of socialism which, it believed, could only be reached peacefully by the co-operation of all working classes which had to destroy capitalism (and fascism was seen as a stage of capitalism) inside their own countries without any help from outside. This insistent pacifism plus their refusal to endorse a Moscow-dictated policy led to a great deal of friction with the communists who had been trying to persuade the ILP if not to join them then at least to 'sympathetically affiliate'.[33] Yet they occasionally co-operated on specific issues which in turn lost them more members to the Labour Party.

The ILP's attitude towards appeasement can be gauged from its limited willingness to participate in a Popular Front. 'The ILP is . . . opposed to the tactic of the Popular Front, which aims at combining the working class with the "democratic" elements within the Capitalist parties in opposition to Fascism and Reaction. This tactic ignores the fact that Fascism and Reaction are inseparable from Capitalism and can only be defeated by the overthrow of Capitalism.'[34] It proposed instead a 'Workers Front including all sections of the working class. It proposes in this country that the four working class parties – the Labour Party, the Co-operative Party, the Independent Labour Party, and the Communist Party – should prepare a common programme and mobilise the united forces behind this programme.'[35]

One can see how this got them into the bad books of both the CP and the Labour Party. But the ILP went further by accusing the Labour Party of co-operation with capitalism, and the Communists, while recognising that theirs was the only other revolutionary party in Britain, of pursuing 'tactics which hinder the development of an effective revolutionary Movement. It is sectarian in its attitude and actions; this prejudices its work in the Trade Unions and among the reformist workers and often makes united action difficult. Its organisational basis prevents freedom of discussion and decision within the Party.'[36] Yet at the same time they collaborated with the CP and the Socialist League in issuing a Unity Manifesto confusing not only their own membership but also potential supporters.

Throughout the 1930s they identified Western democracy with capitalism and were not willing in any way to co-operate with it. Yet they were not revolutionary in an activist sense, but followed the rules and participated in the political system they lived in. Fenner Brockway, one of its leaders, wrote with hindsight: 'I was ready to work for a socialist revolution which would sweep away both German Nazism and British imperialism. But I was not prepared to appease Hitlerism as some pacifists did.'[37] The war had to come and it would be an imperialist one, and no support would be given to its participants (including Chamberlain's government of imperialism), but one might set one's hope on a socialist revolution emerging from it: 'The idea of a socialist revolution to inherit the war was not fanciful. Had not the First World War ended with the Soviet revolution?'[38] Theoretical purity was maintained as much towards the Soviet Union as towards the National Government: the USSR was blamed for identifying herself for the duration of the war with 'the policies of its imperialist Allies'.[39]

The small ILP parliamentary group that remained in the Commons consequently voted against all Bills concerning armaments and war including the declaration of war. On the latter occasion the ILP spokesman said: 'I look for a world of peace wherein Hitlerism can be eliminated, but the people who can pull Hitler down are the people of Germany, and Hitler is not confined to the frontiers of Germany. Hitlerism is to be found in every country of the world.'[40] The ideologically consistent stand the ILP took both towards fascism and the National Government throughout these years is best exemplified from a resolution of its 1937 conference, headed 'The Fight against Fascism': 'The ILP recognises that Fascism is Capitalism in its extreme form and that, so long as Capitalism continues the possessing and privileged class will increasingly resort to the methods of Fascism in order to destroy the opportunity of the working class to use democratic liberties in the struggle against Capitalism.'[41] It then continues with examples of how the National Government was moving in that direction.

It is remarkable how consistently the whole left, if in varying degrees, identified the National Government with fascism. But while for the Labour Party and the CP this was primarily a tactical move, for the ILP and all shades of the Marxist left it was a more or less correct deduction from their interpretation of history and politics. While most of the latter individuals and groups, however, tried to influence politics from within by staying inside the broad Labour movement, the ILP removed itself from any effective influence by putting principle above pragmatic possibilities. Probably they were the only group left that had not become disillusioned by the history of failure of international socialism in its pure form, and as a result perhaps they were even further removed from the realities of (British) politics than the Communist Party.

After the ILP had disaffiliated, the left wing of the Labour Party organised itself, in 1932, into the Socialist League. The Labour Party after the débâcle of 1931 with its political 'change of mood' appeared to be a fruitful ground for new intellectual radicalism; a rethinking of socialism not only seemed to be necessary but the chances of it being accepted by the movement as a whole appeared promising. That this was not a change of mind but only an emotional reaction to the MacDonald 'betrayal' became soon enough apparent, but it deceived 'some of the most talented figures in the movement'[42] into attempts of turning the party more left wing. Even without the growing hostility of the trade unions it is doubtful whether the party at any stage in the 1930s (except perhaps very much later in the decade) would have dared to accept more socialist policies. In some respects the Socialist League provided a safety valve in which intellectuals could theorise without disturbing the movement as a whole.

Membership figures in the League seem to have moved between 2,000 and 3,000;[43] largely middle class and led by a group that 'would have done credit to a Labour Cabinet of the sixties'[44] (as far as its educational and social background was concerned), the Socialist League carried on the tradition of a radical wing inside the movement without achieving any more direct results in changing policies than the ILP had done before them. In the long run it might have helped to educate a new generation inside the movement but during the 1930s, and especially as far as Labour's attitude towards appeasement was concerned, it remained isolated and of little importance.

It was encouraged in its more radical stand on domestic policies after successes at the 1932 and 1933 party conferences, but these remained the only ones in its brief existence. Perhaps Pimlott is right in suggesting that it misjudged or was even naïve about the nature of power within the Labour Party. It never seems to have had really important links with the trade unions, after the initial alienation of Bevin, and it underestimated the importance of loyalty in the movement as the whole to the leaders of the day. Its social composition made it difficult to claim a direct link with 'the people'. After originally setting itself up as a research and propaganda body it changed its position into one of 'policy making and policy propaganda'. Born out of a response to domestic circumstances – and despite clashes with the leadership on some issues, overall not unwelcome to the party – the League really only entered the foreign policy debate (like most other left-wing groups) after the Spanish Civil War started. Its general foreign policy line before then had been pacifist and Marxist (for example, seeing the League of Nations as a 'tool of satiated imperialist powers').[45] The National Government was seen as almost fascist itself and certainly as co-operative with imperialism and fascism. Perhaps Gordon's distinction between the 'class-pacifism' of Cripps and the 'ethical pacifism' of Lansbury[46] is useful here, as the arming of the working classes was desirable but not the rearming of the ruling class and its government. The class issue was one of the crucial points of misunderstanding between the Labour movement as a whole and its Marxist left wing. Very few intellectuals, with Laski perhaps constituting a noticeable exception, seem to have realised that at the time. When the British working classes thought of 'Them' and 'Us' they were not entering a train of thought that would lead to revolution, violently or peacefully, but following a long-established pattern of social distinction that would and could find its only political expression in participation in the existing liberal democratic system which, if they looked after their interests, would ultimately benefit them. This seems to be the main reason why no left-wing group ever achieved substantial mass support. The vast majority of the Labour movement was not interested in changing the system, and the Labour Party, being aware of this, could not have adopted more left-wing policies. This is not to say that the movement as a whole did not, albeit on an emotional level, pursue some utopian idea of socialism as a classless society.

The first inkling of how the Socialist League's foreign policy might fare in the future came at the 1935 party conference which saw Lansbury defeated by Bevin, who also defeated Cripps as both used pacifist arguments against the League of Nations involvement in Ethiopia.[47] But even before the SL had shown its willingness to co-operate with the CPGB in a United Front it had got its answer in 'Democracy versus Dictatorship',[48] the 1933 policy resolution of the National Joint Council. The Labour Party would never accept that communist proposals could be beneficial to the working classes of Britain. But the Socialist League went on to propose just such a co-operation, albeit primarily to defeat the class enemy of the National Government within, rather than Nazi Germany at Moscow's doors.

While it rejected the League of Nations, it embraced collective security between peace-loving nations which could stem both imperialism and fascism. A socialist Britain could then help to develop a new socialist international order – the old dream of all the internationals. With this kind of theorising it is not surprising that it drew the increasing scorn of the TUC leadership that had to deal with political and social conditions as they then were and not as they might on some utopian day turn out to be. That this response applied to the movement as a whole can be seen from the poor response which the Socialist League got to its domestic policy proposals even when its foreign policy at first commanded some enthusiasm.

The real difficulties, of course, arose over the Popular Front Campaign, when Cripps and the Socialist League deliberately took on the Labour Party Executive.[49] After enforced disaffiliation it wisely dissolved itself in order not to share the fate of the ILP, but not without announcing that its members would pursue its foreign policy as individuals, and indeed a new group was soon formed, the 'Committee of Party Members sympathetic to Unity' which in turn was banned. The determined stand of Labour's National Executive not only ended all hopes there might have been for a success of the Unity Campaign but also put a definite stop to any substantial organised dissent from official foreign policy. The Socialist League's attempts, originally primarily domestic, to radicalise the movement had ultimately failed over its theoretical stand on foreign policy.

The weakness of the Socialist League within the Labour Party must also be seen in terms of organisation and power distribution, both closely linked to the fate of the party in parliament. After 1931 Bevin had succeeded in reorganising the National Joint Council which had now a majority of TUC General Council members and became the authoritative body in the formulation of Labour's foreign policy. While the links of the Socialist League to the parliamentary party had initially been good, they weakened as that body started to gain numbers and restore a normal political balance through by-elections. Connections with the unions remained weak throughout. Such support as they could find, therefore, could only operate through individuals, which made success unlikely.

What then, finally, was the attitude of the official Labour Party towards appeasement and how were its policies arrived at? As I hope I have shown, the left wing of the party not only failed to impose its interpretation but hardly seems to have been able to influence policies.

When dealing with the power structure of the Labour Party Robert McKenzie talks about the 'bond of mutual confidence between the parliamentary leaders and a preponderant part of the trade union leadership which is an essential key to the understanding of the functioning of the Labour Party'.[50] The vast majority of Labour Party membership has always been trade union membership, and the TUC leadership was therefore of at least equal importance in policy decisions as the leaders of the party in the House of Commons and in Transport House. Their position would be even stronger when the PLP was small and/or weak which was particularly the case after 1931. In order to understand their foreign policy it is therefore important to concern oneself with the influence of Ernest Bevin and Walter Citrine, the two most important trade union figures of the time, as against the party's leaders, Lansbury and Attlee.[51]

The shock of the 1931 election and MacDonald's 'betrayal' had left the movement shaken and distrustful of political leaders. In many respects Lansbury fitted the bill of a new leader: someone who would not impose his policies and personality upon the party. Lansbury was a consistent 'ethical' pacifist whose attitude and pronouncements on foreign policy suited the movement's generally idealistic notions about peaceful international relations. The party as a whole, however, was by no means pacifist, and one can follow the drifting apart of their policy and that of their leader from as early as the sanction debate on Japan.[52]

Hitler's rise to power caught the party in a dilemma between its desire for disarmament and justice for Germany, and the potential threat of German fascism. It was hoped, however, that Hitler could be peacefully contained by removing some of the injustices imposed at Versailles (the Labour Party's version of appeasement). Here already one can see a subtle clash between Lansbury, who idealistically suggested 'the best method of dealing with the position [Germany's desire to rearm] is for this country to carry out in the letter and the spirit all the implications of the treaty of peace and to challenge the German Government to adopt the same policy',[53] and his deputy leader, Attlee, who said earlier in the year: 'I think that this House and this country ought to say that we will not countenance for a moment the yielding to Hitler and force what was denied to Stresemann and reason.'[54] How much the gap between the leader's attitude and his party's towards collective security as a means to stand against fascism had widened can be seen when it came to its head during the debate about the League of Nations sanctions in the Abyssinian affair. It led to an internal crisis in which Lord Ponsonby, the leader of the party in the House of Lords, and Cripps, a member of the Executive, resigned their official positions while Lansbury propagated policies in direct contradiction to the official line. The Brighton Conference of September 1935 has often been seen as a watershed in Labour's foreign policy. But it was perhaps less a change of policy than an assertion of rationality over emotional allegiances. Foreign policy along idealistic lines appealed to the delegates, but it weakened the position of the Executive which had to pursue a rational course in order to provide His Majesty's Opposition with a practicable policy. As on other occasions, before and after, the Conference was allowed an emotional outlet in cheering Lansbury and his faith and conscience, but in the end it was brought to heel by Bevin in his now well-known speech which was considered brutal and cruel at the time. 'Lansbury has been going around dressed in saint's clothes for years waiting for martyrdom. I set fire to the faggots',[55] he commented afterwards. He did secure, however, a fairly rational foreign policy for Labour: collective security backed by sanctions if necessary.

But this position led to what became the vicious circle of Labour's attitude towards appeasement: as Margaret Cole put it with hindsight, 'We were willing to accept the arming of our country, if it meant saving Europe and ourselves from Fascism; but we were not willing to give those armaments into the control of Baldwin or Chamberlain and their friends, lest when zero hour arrived the guns should be found to be pointing the wrong way.'[56] This problem became more relevant over Spain which again excited the emotions of the movement. The new leader, Attlee, considered that an alternative policy could be pursued if Labour came to power. An economic and political alliance between Britain, France and the USSR could stop fascism, both on the Continent and at home. It is not surprising that he was one of the few non-Marxist Labour figures to write for the Left Book Club. The moderate wing of the party, on the other hand, was pragmatically aware that this was a utopian policy as Labour was not in power, and Hitler began to move faster. Dalton fought for rearmament behind the scenes while publicly maintaining a policy of no armament for the National Government.[57] Thus the dividing line ran through the middle of the decision-making body in the party, Attlee acting as the compromise between the Marxist left whose ideology he rejected but whose policy he supported as a real alternative to appeasement and the pragmatic moderates of the TUC and Dalton. Citrine and Bevin had increasingly used their position against the 'intellectual' left and had come to dominate all policy decisions. By presenting a largely unified TUC line at Conference backed up by reasoned argument and making the necessary allowances for emotional responses towards the victims of fascism, they succeeded in steering Labour's foreign policy out of the dangerous waters of theory into a position that stayed nearer to the political realities and possibilities of British foreign policy.[58]

Two aspects of the background to Labour's concepts of foreign policy may help to explain this division further. As Naylor has shown Labour believed in appeasement, but meant something quite different than Chamberlain. Appeasement before Hitler had meant economic concessions in international relations to ease imperial pressures and prepare the ground for socialism to grow. Hitler meant war to many in the movement from the beginning[59] and appeasing him would not end imperialism or capitalism (except for a very few pacifists) but only lead to a worse war. Hence the conflict both with the government and with the Marxist faction inside the movement: as the party increasingly realised that fascism would have to be resisted by force it found itself in the impossible position of not being able to support a government that stood for capitalism and the ruling classes and might use these arms in aid of imperialism not socialism. Equally it could not endorse its left-wing intellectuals as this would weaken the forces that stood inside Britain for socialism by splitting the movement and ultimately working for a non-democratic socialism. The only way out of this could come from the outside and by force.

Dominated in its thinking by domestic issues, the Labour movement was earlier and more aware of what fascism meant in practice, what it had done domestically to the working classes and to democratic values. It was therefore more aware of its implications, expressing this by fighting to maintain strength against internal dissent and fascism at home, as well as realising the dangers of an expansionist fascist power on the Continent.

An alternative began to offer itself in the debates between the *Anschluss* and Munich when Conservative dissenters like Churchill began to talk of a Franco-Anglo-Russian alliance against Chamberlain's unilateral policy. Although both the Russian invitation to talks and the Labour Party's suggestion to take the matter to the League were turned down by Chamberlain, and perhaps also because of it, the conviction began to grow in the party that force would have to be used and that one would have to come to terms with arming the government if absolutely necessary; so Labour finally started to take a constructive interest in defence policies and measures. With its internal dissent firmly under control the party could now face up to the real possibility of war. While not welcome in its own ranks, the Popular Front agitation might have helped Labour's unity in the end in that it made its members more aware of the actual threat of Nazi Germany. The only obstacle that remained – partly for reasons of personal animosity – was Chamberlain. Once he was out of the way Labour was willing to co-operate with the existing government to preserve the existing political system from the external onslaught of fascism. But by then appeasement had proved itself to be an unworkable policy.

If one surveys the whole left and its attitude towards appeasement it appears that the dividing line is an ideological as much as a practical political one. Apart from a brief period of misunderstanding about the meaning of the term between Labour's own traditional appeasement policy in international relations and Chamberlain's usage, it can safely be said that all of the left was anti-appeasement, if for different reasons.[60] This does not, however, imply that alternative policies were always on offer. Only the ideologically committed groups, either for political reasons of their own, like the Communist Party, or from purely theoretical motives, like the Independent Labour Party, or through a combination of the two, consistently suggested collective security based on an alliance with Russia and France. Official Labour, the only politically viable group, though hampered by their parliamentary weakness, might in fact inadvertently have aided Chamberlain's policy by refusing to support rearmament, and might furthermore have pursued a different type of appeasement policy with not dissimilar results had they been in power. On the other hand they did recognise the nature of national socialism and its practical implications in domestic as well as foreign policy long before Chamberlain and might therefore have admitted the need to get fully involved on the Continent much earlier. Whether early enough, though, to prevent a second world war, has to remain an unanswerable question.

Notes: Chapter 9

1 N. Branson and M. Heinemann, *Britain in the Nineteen Thirties* (London, 1971); J. Stevenson, *Social Conditions in Britain Between the Wars* (Harmondsworth, 1977).
2 J. Lewis, *The Left Book Club. An Historical Record* (London, 1970), incorporates an appendix listing the books published by the Club.
3 M. Foot, *Aneurin Bevan. A Biography, Vol. One: 1897–1945* (London, 1962), p. 196.
4 L. J. MacFarlane, *The British Communist Party. Its Origin and Development until 1929* (London, 1966); H. Pelling, *The British Communist Party. An Historical Profile* (London, 1958).
5 R. Palme Dutt, *Fascism and Social Revolution* (London, 1934).
6 H. Pollitt, *Discussion* [a CP monthly], vol. II, no. 5 (October 1937), p. 1.
7 Quoted from the *Daily Worker* in W. Rust, *The Story of the Daily Worker* (London, 1949), p. 47.

8   *Party Organiser*, vol. I, no. 3 (September 1939), p. 9.
9   Quoted in Rust, p. 54.
10 S. Samuels, 'The Left Book Club', *Journal of Contemporary History*, vol. I, no. 2 (1966), p. 84.
11 V. Gollancz, Editorial, *Left News*, no. 24 (April 1938), p. 752.
12 Samuels, p. 86.
13 V. Gollancz, Editorial, *Left News*, no. 1 (May 1936), p. 3.
14 id., Editorial, *Left News*, no. 12 (April 1937), p. 304.
15 id., Editorial I, *Left News*, no. 30 (October 1938), p. 998.
16 H. Thomas, *John Strachey* (London, 1973).
17 ibid., p. 176.
18 ibid., p. 156.
19 J. Strachey, 'Topic of the month: France', *Left News*, no. 1 (May 1936), p. 4.
20 ibid., p. 6.
21 J. Strachey, 'Topic of the month: Mr Baldwin', *Left News*, no. 3 (July 1936), p. 40.
22 J. Strachey, 'Topic of the month: the British government's world policy', *Left News*, no. 17 (September 1937), p. 507.
23 He subsequently joined the Labour Party and after the 1945 election became MP for Dundee; see Thomas, pp. 222 ff.
24 The latest biography, G. Eastwood, *Harold Laski* (London and Oxford, 1977), does not supersede K. Martin, *Harold Laski (1893–1950). A Biographical Memoir* (London, 1953); where the latter is personal, but quite substantial, the former is almost hagiographical and hardly adds anything to our understanding.
25 See also his contribution in *I Believe* (1939), quoted in Eastwood, pp. 109 ff.
26 See Eastwood, pp. 45 ff.
27 ibid., p. 45.
28 Martin, pp. 138–67, where a whole chapter is devoted to the implications of this concept.
29 H. Laski, *Left News*, no. 3 (July 1936), p. 42 (*Review of World Politics, 1918–1936* by R. Palme Dutt, the Chosen Book for July).
30 H. Laski, *Left News*, no. 11 (March 1937), p. 294 (verbatim report of Albert Hall Rally, 7 February 1937).
31 M. Muggeridge, *The Thirties* (London, 1940), p. 273, with his usual acerbity described him thus: 'His oratory, if not lively, was forceful and earnest; the acclamation which greeted his appearance and permeated his discourse, suggested rather a Führer than a publisher.'
32 Pelling, p. 77; R. E. Dowse, *Left in the Centre. The Independent Labour Party 1893–1940* (London, 1966), p. 185.
33 F. Brockway, *Inside the Left* (London, 1942), gives a very good impression of the moral and political scruples operating in the party.
34 ILP pamphlet, *Through the Class Struggle to Socialism*, p. 2 (resolutions adopted at 37th Annual Conference, Easter 1937).
35 ibid., p. 4.
36 ILP pamphlet, *A Socialist Policy for Britain* (London, n.d.), p. 5 (statement to be submitted by the National Administrative Council of the ILP to the Annual Conference of the party, 1935).
37 Brockway, p. 18.
38 ibid.
39 J. McNair, *What the Independent Labour Party Stands for*, ILP pamphlet (London, n.d., post-1945).
40 Quoted in F. Johnson, *The ILP in War and Peace* (London, 1940).
41 Resolution for 45th Conference, 1937.
42 B. Pimlott, 'The Socialist League: intellectuals and the Labour left in the 1930s', *Journal of Contemporary History*, vol. VI, no. 3, p. 12.
43 ibid., p. 27.
44 ibid., p. 23.
45 Quoted in M. R. Gordon, *Conflict and Consensus in Labour's Foreign Policy 1914–1965* (Stanford, Calif., 1969), p. 25.
46 ibid., p. 26.
47 Labour Party Conference Report, 1935, pp. 153–242.
48 Labour Party Conference Report, 1933, p. 277.

49 B. Pimlott, *Labour and the Left in the 1930s* (Cambridge, 1977), pp. 170–82.
50 R. McKenzie, *British Political Parties* (London, 1970), p. 505.
51 Not sufficient work has been done about the TUC in this period to arrive at a satisfactory answer. It seems certain, however, that the trade unions' prime concern in this period centred on industrial and domestic rather than foreign policy matters. For the importance of extra-parliamentary forces in the leadership of the party, see L. Minkin, *The Labour Party Conference. A Study in the Politics of Intra-Party Democracy* (London, 1978), p. 18.
52 For instance, J. F. Naylor, *Labour's International Policy* (London, 1969), pp. 27 ff.
53 HC Debs, vol. 280, 5 July 1933, col. 347.
54 HC Debs, vol. 276, 23 March 1933, cols 608–10.
55 F. Williams, *Ernest Bevin* (London, 1952), p. 186.
56 M. Cole, *Growing Up Into Revolution* (London, 1949), p. 173.
57 K. Martin, *Editor* (London, 1968); H. Dalton, *The Fateful Years* (London, 1957), *passim*; in particular pp. 131–46.
58 The Bournemouth Conference of 1937 was the decisive one where Bevin and Dalton succeeded in having their policy of rearmament adopted.
59 See for instance J. Compton, *Hitlerism* (London, 1933), pp. 14 f.
60 For an assessment of dissent in this period compare also A. J. P. Taylor, *The Trouble Makers* (London, 1957), pp. 152–82.

10 Keynes, the Economics of Rearmament and Appeasement

G. C. PEDEN

This essay has its origin in a remark by Brian Bond that in my book, *British Rearmament and the Treasury*, I had allowed myself little space to explore the applicability of the alternative policies propounded by John Maynard Keynes.[1] It would, of course, be of significance to military and diplomatic history if it could be shown that British governments, by failing to adopt the advice of the most brilliant economist of the age, had economised unnecessarily on defence expenditure. Indeed, an assumption that Keynes did offer alternative policies applicable to rearmament is apparent in the work of a number of historians, who have either mentioned his name[2] or who have criticised the Treasury's 'penchant for balanced budgets'.[3] However, the assumption that Keynes offered alternative policies with regard to rearmament begs the important question of whether Keynes's advice on the economics of rearmament differed significantly, for practical purposes, from advice being given to ministers from within Whitehall. What follows is a comparison of the economic advice of Keynes with official views in Whitehall, set in the context of appeasement, with a view to discovering whether a greater readiness on the part of government to take Keynes's advice would have made a significant difference to the course of events.

By the time the government had worked out its rearmament programme, at the beginning of 1936, Keynes had completed his great work, *The General Theory of Employment, Interest and Money*, but changing economic circumstances in the later 1930s meant that the problems of public finance were more complex than they had been in the years when Keynes had been writing that book. Whereas domestic prices had been stable, and there had been no pressing balance of payments problems between 1933 and 1936, from 1936 the Board of Trade wholesale price index rose rapidly (except in 1938), and an adverse balance of payments became a matter of increasing concern. Thus whereas Keynes had ignored the external balance in his *General Theory*, he was unable to do so after 1936. Moreover, while unemployment continued to be high, by 1936 recovery from the Depression had reached a point when cyclical unemployment, which had been the major problem while the *General Theory* was being written, was nearly at an end; what remained was frictional, structural, or regional.[4]

Keynes first entered public debate on rearmament in July 1936, four months after Baldwin had announced the rearmament programme to Parliament. In a letter to the *New Statesman and Nation* Keynes lent support to the Prime Minister against left-wing opposition to rearmament, arguing that 'a state of inadequate armament on our part can only encourage the brigand Powers' (by which he meant Germany, Italy and Japan).[5] He did not, however, enter public debate on borrowing for defence until February 1937, at a time when the government was seeking parliamentary authority to borrow up to £400 million over five years for rearmament. The Labour opposition attacked the Defence Loans Bill as inflationary, and the City seemed to have agreed, since there was a sharp fall in gilt-edged stocks. On the day before the Chancellor of the Exchequer, Chamberlain, was due to defend the Defence Loans Bill in Parliament, Keynes gave his annual address to members of the National Mutual Life Association, and he took the opportunity to tell them, and through them the City, that he had no doubt that the sum which the Chancellor proposed to borrow was well within the nation's capacity. Chamberlain took the opportunity to quote Keynes, whose speech had been printed in *The Times*, as evidence against the charge that the proposed borrowing would be inflationary – an example of the Treasury making use of the reputation of a man more usually thought of as its critic.[6]

The following month Keynes developed his arguments on the financing of rearmament in an article entitled 'Borrowing for defence: is it inflation?'. This article is best read in conjunction with three others which he had published two months earlier on how to avoid a slump.[7] Keynes believed that 'by painful degrees we have climbed out of the slump', and that demand in the home market was 'temporarily inflated' with non-recurrent investment. Using the concept of the multiplier, he concluded that the additional investment represented by loan expenditure on rearmament '*need* not be inflationary', inflation being defined not merely as rising prices and wages but that point in the economy 'when increased demand is no longer capable of materially raising output and employment and mainly spends itself in raising prices'. Keynes did warn, however, that the proposed loan expenditure might be 'rather near the limit. This is particularly so in the near future. It is in the next year or eighteen months that congestion is most likely to occur . . . In two years time, or less, rearmament loans may be positively helpful in warding off a depression.' Just as it would have been advisable for the government to incur debt during the slump, so it was now advisable that it should incline to the opposite policy. 'In view of the high cost of the armaments, which we cannot postpone, it would put too much strain on our fiscal system actually to discharge debt, but the Chancellor of the Exchequer should . . . meet the main part of the cost of armaments out of taxation, raising taxes and withholding all reliefs for the present as something in hand for 1938 or 1939.' Public works should be delayed where possible, and Keynes even suggested 'procrastination at the Ministry of Health', presumably to hold up local authority housing. The Treasury was already thinking along similar lines and, following Keynes's articles on how to avoid a slump, Sir Frederick Phillips, the under-secretary dealing with finance, wrote to Sir Richard Hopkins, the Permanent Secretary's deputy for finance, that to try to run civil and military capital expenditure at full blast simultaneously would be to create conditions which would produce a great industrial slump, since then there would be great excess capacity once the rearmament programme was complete. Phillips suggested that there were some roads and housing schemes which could be done away with, and that the Treasury could 'tell the Ministry of Health to obstruct local authorities' programmes'.[8] Competition from housing meant that the Air Ministry, for example, was having difficulty in obtaining building labour, especially for aerodromes, which were often in the south-east of England, but far from main population centres, and in March 1937 the Under Secretary of State for Air admitted in the Commons to 'a certain amount of embarrassment' over the consequential delays.[9] Ministers, however, feared the political consequences of what Keynes and Phillips were suggesting, and one finds Sir Thomas Inskip, Minister for Co-ordination of Defence, writing to Ernest Brown, the Minister of Labour, in June 1937: 'With regard to the slowing down of the housing programme, I am very averse, as no doubt you are, to coming to any decision that this is necessary.' Instead the government preferred to find what cuts it could make in its other demands on building labour – postponement of direct government works outside the defence programme amounting to £300,000 in the financial year 1937–8 and £1 million in 1938–9 being described by Inskip as 'a step in the right direction'.[10]

Despite the pressures in the economy, Keynes advised in January 1937 against raising interest rates. He held that a low, stable long-term rate of interest was essential to eliminate uncertainty from financial markets. He argued: 'If we allow the rate of interest to [rise], we cannot easily reverse the trend. A low enough long-term rate of interest cannot be achieved if we allow it to be believed that better terms will be obtained from time to time by those who keep their resources liquid.' He believed that if the Stock Exchange became unduly excited in a boom, investors would be insensitive to interest rates, unless confidence were affected, which might have excessive reactions, and, therefore, that it would be better to control investment through informal methods, such as a hint to the Committee of the Stock Exchange to exercise discrimination in granting permissions to deal.[11] The Treasury official reviewing Keynes's articles, Ralph Hawtrey, disagreed with Keynes about the efficacy of interest rates, but, for his own reasons, agreed that interest rates for the time being should remain low. Hawtrey noted:

> There is a tendency (from which Mr. Keynes himself is not free) to overestimate the extent of the revival already accomplished . . . In all directions activity is being held back by a scarcity of skilled labour, or of raw materials, or of transport facilities. So long as these obstacles are being overcome it is important that expansion of general demand should continue to give an adequate spur to traders to overcome them.[12]

Phillips, Hawtrey's superior, wrote to the Chancellor that 'we should . . . be glad to keep interest rates down . . . but we doubt the possibility'.[13] The monetary authorities wished to keep a tight control on the expansion of credit, and, although Bank Rate remained at 2 per cent, there was a slight hardening of interest rates in 1937 and 1938. The monetary authorities may thus have been responsible for raising somewhat the cost of borrowing for defence, but, on the other hand, their policy probably helped to discourage new civil investment from competing with rearmament work.

Hypothetically, physical controls over scarce factors of production could have been a more effective method of ensuring priority for rearmament. However, while Keynes was willing to contemplate informal guidance to capitalists through the Committee of the Stock Exchange, he held to the market economy as the best method of allocating resources. Although believing that rearmament would strain the economy, he argued in March 1937 that it was 'most important that we should avoid [quasi-] war-time controls, rationing and the like'. He apparently approved the government's decision a year earlier that rearmament should not interfere with ordinary business, and, as an alternative to government controls, he pointed to the unemployed labour in depressed regions away from the south-east of England, and suggested that these regions represented 'our main reserve of resources available for rearmament without undue interference with the normal course of trade'.[14] This regional approach to economic problems was a new one for Keynes, in that regional policy has no place in the *General Theory*. The government did not, however, need Keynes to point out the advantage of unemployed labour in depressed areas from the point of view of keeping down wage costs. As early as February 1936 the Ministry of Labour had pointed to the reserves of skilled labour in areas of high unemployment, and since December 1936 the Treasury had been urging defence departments to place contracts in such areas.[15]

Keynes, however, looked to the depressed regions not merely because there were reserves there of labour for work on rearmament contracts, but also because he saw the depressed export trades of these areas – coal, cotton and shipbuilding – as playing a vital role in dampening down inflation. He argued that the multiplier effect of loan expenditure on rearmament might tend to increase national income by more than domestic output could be increased, but that the balance of the increased demand could be met by increased imports. This he welcomed as an alternative to the higher domestic prices which would otherwise result from increased domestic demand, and he advised that the worsening trade balance likely to result from armament expenditure, from associated industrial activity and from higher prices for raw materials should be viewed with equanimity, even although there might be a temporary strain on the Exchange Equalisation Fund. The response to the worsening trade balance should be steps to increase exports, not steps to reduce imports. He went on: 'It remains particularly advisable to do anything to stimulate our staple exports. For it is there that our reserves of surplus labour are chiefly to be found. It is no paradox to say that the best way of avoiding inflationary results from the Chancellor's loan is to increase both imports and exports.'[16]

Within the government the prospective worsening of the trade balance was not always viewed with equanimity. By late 1936 it was apparent that economic recovery was tending to suck in imports, while many British manufacturers were so busy with domestic orders that they were making little effort to win export orders. This, the Economic Advisory Council's

Committee on Economic Information reported, was particularly true of the iron and steel and engineering industries, which, in the years immediately preceding 1936, had made a rapidly expanding contribution to the credit of Britain's balance of payments.[17] Rearmament contracts undoubtedly contributed to this tendency, and in December 1936 the President of the Board of Trade, Walter Runciman, took the opportunity of speaking at the London Iron and Steel Exchange dinner to warn that 'the time will certainly come when the rearmament programme is completed . . . Let our industries see to it that when that time comes they have not lost their export connections.' Runciman asked Sir Frederick Leith-Ross, the chief economic adviser, to prepare a Cabinet paper on trade trends. Like Keynes, although without benefit of his macroeconomic analysis, Leith-Ross said it was inadvisable to restrict imports, and saw the remedy to a worsening trade balance in an expansion of exports, although Leith-Ross seems to have looked to the 'newer light industries to develop the export side of their business', rather than expect substantial recovery in coal or cotton exports.[18]

It was easier for Keynes and the Board of Trade to prescribe the remedy of an increase in exports than it was to bring this about. British exports had gained a competitive advantage on world markets when sterling had depreciated after the departure from the gold standard in 1931, but this advantage had been lost as other countries had devalued, and in the later 1930s it was American policy to prevent competitive devaluations. In September 1936, on the initiative of the Secretary of the US Treasury, Henry Morgenthau, the treasuries of America, Britain and France had accompanied French devaluation with a tripartite agreement 'to maintain the greatest possible equilibrium in the system of international exchanges',[19] and when, in 1938, Keynes and fellow economists on the Economic Advisory Council's Committee on Economic Information examined currency depreciation as a means of making British exports more competitive, they reported: 'We are somewhat sceptical of the possible results of such a degree of currency depreciation, as under the Tripartite agreement and the Anglo-American trade agreement [of 1938] is open to us.'[20] A deliberate repetition of the 1931–2 depreciation of sterling was not an option compatible with good Anglo-American relations in the later 1930s, and indeed the US Treasury kept a close watch on the dollar-sterling exchange rate to make sure that the British did not gain any marked competitive advantage.[21]

However, the recession in 1938 banished for the time being fears of inflation caused by loan expenditure on rearmament. Keynes now saw such expenditure as helping to solve the problem of unemployment,[22] and even in the Treasury Hopkins's view by the end of the year was that

> Not many months ago when unemployment had come down low and was still sinking and when industry was humming throughout the land I used . . . to point to the dangers of inflation as one of the principal dangers facing us if the cost of armaments got out of hand. Today the conditions are very different . . . and generally apart from armament expenditure the country is in a bad way . . . One can agree that with unemployment reaching two million and likely shortly to exceed that figure and with the

cost of living still moderate the danger of inflation seems as remote as it seemed insistent in 1937 before the renewed collapse of the U.S.A. [i.e. the recession of 1937–8] began.[23]

In the light of increased unemployment, then, the focus of official concern was no longer the budgetary balance: rather, the focus had moved to the balance of payments. In 1937 and 1938 Britain was running a current balance of payments deficit, excluding gold movements, of rather more than £50 million. On the other hand, whereas in 1937 Britain had been gaining gold and convertible currency reserves (as she had been doing since 1934) since foreigners looked on London as a safe haven for their funds, from the spring of 1938 there was a steady efflux of gold from London. At the end of 1938 Keynes helped draw up a report which identified the balance of payments as 'the key to the whole position' regarding the economic problems raised by accelerating rearmament expenditure.[24] Keynes drew attention to the fact that the adverse balance of payments as a result of the imbalance between imports and exports would not be unduly disturbing were it not for the risk that on that drain there might be superimposed a large outward movement on capital account.[25] He and his fellow members of the Committee on Economic Information formed the view that the position at the end of 1938 was potentially no less dangerous than that of 1931, when a crisis in confidence had led to a run on sterling and the abandonment of the gold standard. If there were to be another run on sterling, then 'not only might we have to consider protecting the sterling exchange, by the most stringent and unsatisfactory forms of exchange control, that is to say exchange control which applied to foreign as well as British capital, but also it would be necessary to confine British purchases abroad strictly within the limits set by our current receipts.'[26]

This, the committee pointed out, would be a serious handicap to the rearmament programme, for British industry was still undergoing an adjustment process necessary before it could cope with the demands of the programme, and in so far as armament goods could be imported, then some of the most difficult problems of industrial adjustment could be avoided. Industrial bottlenecks, for example shortages of machine tools or steel, could best be overcome by increasing imports, and any move which reduced the possibility of such imports was to be avoided.

Keynes argued that repayment of loans by foreigners would enable Britain to maintain 'for a considerable period' an adverse balance of payments of £50 million a year, 'without any strain on our exchange', if measures could be taken to prevent incoming funds being lent abroad again. He put forward a number of suggestions how this might be done, but the Treasury and Bank of England thought that the measures he proposed would have little effect. For example, Keynes suggested that borrowing by the dominions and by India in London should be limited, and that these countries should be urged to raise loans in America. The monetary authorities believed that this might be taken as a sign of weakness, and that such a measure, by reducing confidence in sterling, might defeat its own end. On the other hand, Keynes's suggestion that British investors be invited not to increase their American investments for the time being was not rejected by the monetary authorities – although it may be noted in passing that Keynes thought that informal requests to the banks, Stock Exchange and chief institutional investors would be more effective than direct prohibitions. Keynes and the monetary authorities were agreed that Britain might be better off without the large sums of liquid resources held by nervous foreigners, and that withdrawals of such money could not justify exchange controls, but the monetary authorities felt that Keynes underestimated the volume of bear speculation against sterling.[27] It is impossible to say whether the optimistic view of Keynes or the pessimistic view of the monetary authorities was correct in the circumstances, which, in any case, were changing rapidly. What one can point to is the tremendous outflow of gold and convertible currency which in fact occurred. In the year to March 1939 the reserves fell by £225 million to £600 million, and the rate of the outflow increased as anxiety on money markets increased following the German seizure of Czechoslovakia and the British guarantee to Poland. In the twenty weeks to the end of July 1939 the reserves fell by £96 million, with a further £92 million being lost between 1 and 22 August.[28] On the other hand, even in August 1939 only one-tenth of the outflow was British capital seeking refuge abroad,[29] so that the monetary authorities preferred to let sterling depreciate rather than impose formal exchange controls.

The monetary authorities also seem to have been less optimistic than Keynes about domestic borrowing for rearmament in 1939. One recent historian of rearmament, indeed, believes that 'had the Treasury heeded Keynes, it would have been spared much of its concern about the size of the rearmament programme', and attributes Treasury officials' failure to heed Keynes to their alleged adherence to the doctrines of classical economics.[30] However, it is unwise to lay much stress on the Treasury's adherence to classical economics by 1939. As Susan Howson has shown, the leading Treasury officials dealing with finance in the 1930s were prepared to consider Keynes's views seriously, and advocated policy innovations which, although tentative, were to provide a basis upon which economic management on Keynesian principles could be developed.[31] Keynes predicted in April 1939 that increased loan expenditure on rearmament in the financial year 1939–40 would so stimulate demand that the problem of abnormal unemployment would cease, with the Exchequer benefiting from reduced unemployment relief as well as increased revenue. He estimated that the national income would increase by £400 million, or about 8 per cent, over the year, and that the savings necessary to meet the government's loan expenditure would 'come into existence *pari passu* with the expenditure', although there might have to be 'some postponement of full maintenance' and some reduction of stocks by industry.[32] Hawtrey, examining Keynes's arguments, agreed that this was 'a *possible* calculation', but he also pointed out that increased loan expenditure on rearmament in 1938 had been accompanied by an increase in unemployment, owing to a world recession, and that, 'if the existing hesitation in the United States turned into a renewed recession', increased loan expenditure in 1939 might not be accompanied by an increase in employment or national income.[33] Hawtrey's superiors seem to have shared his uncertainty, and in its advice to the Cabinet about the extent of national savings out of which borrowing for defence should come, the Treasury, while admitting that there was 'an element of truth' in Keynes's theory of expenditure creating savings, also stated that 'there was no action which the Government could take which would increase the total volume of savings of the country as a whole'.[34]

However, despite this divergence of views with regard to national income and savings, the Treasury did not believe, any more than did Keynes, that loan expenditure on rearmament would cause inflation while there was unemployed capacity in the economy. Hawtrey noted in April 1939 that 'the strain in the near future will be greater, but there is every reason to believe that it will be within the country's power to provide the necessary resources without any undesirable inflation. That there should be such a "reflation" as will permit of full employment everyone will regard as desirable.' Hawtrey also reported that the Ministry of Labour thought that rearmament work was more likely to be helpful in reducing unemployment than ordinary public works had been, for armament work gave additional employment not only to navvying, and building and steel trades – the only kinds of employment to gain much direct help from ordinary public works – but also to almost the whole range of engineering, chemical and shipbuilding industries, and a host of ancillary trades.[35]

The trouble was that no one knew how many of the unemployed were able to take up the jobs on offer in 1939, or, therefore, when the economy would reach full employment in the sense that further increases in demand would raise prices rather than employment. Keynes himself stressed that he was not competent to express an opinion on the number of the unemployed who were for practical purposes unemployable, but in April 1939 he believed that the Treasury's programme of borrowing for the year 1939–40, which was then given as £350 million, could create jobs for upwards of a million men, and that 750,000 additional workers would be required as a minimum. Far from expecting that absorbing that number of men into the appropriate jobs would be easy, he observed that it would require very good organisation by government and industry, and goodwill on the part of trade unions, to overcome the problems raised by an acute shortage of skilled labour, restrictive practices, the task of moving workers to districts where demand was greatest, and competition between government and civil orders.[36] Although 1,234,000 insured workers were registered as unemployed in May 1939, Keynes noted then that 'even optimists' would not put the proportion capable of being employed higher than two-fifths or perhaps three-fifths.[37] If even an optimistic estimate of the supply of employable labour in May was less than 750,000, and given that Keynes had estimated the previous month that loan expenditure of £350 million in 1939–40 would need a minimum of 750,000 men, it can safely be assumed that he shared the Treasury's view that the further expenditure of £120 million which was added to the rearmament programme between April and July would place very severe pressure on the economy, and, if met out of borrowing, would tend to be inflationary.[38]

The Treasury in June 1939 did not expect loan expenditure on rearmament to begin to create inflation until some time in the autumn of 1939, since the number of Treasury bills held by the market was below normal, and the normal level of short-term borrowing would not be reached before the end of September. Thereafter whatever had to be borrowed would have to be borrowed on medium or long term.[39] Keynes had early seen that such a situation might lead the market to expect a rise in interest rates on government stock, and in April 1939 he had suggested that the Chancellor should announce 'that in no circumstances' will he offer loans carrying a rate of interest in excess of 2½ per cent. He criticised the Treasury for having reduced the floating debt in 1938–9, and within the Treasury Hawtrey conceded that Treasury funding operations might well have resulted in loan expenditure on rearmament being less reflationary than might otherwise have been the case over the past two years. Keynes's alternative to higher interest rates was government control of the Stock Exchange, with government finance being given priority over new issues.[40] Whether or not because of Keynes's arguments, the Treasury warned the Cabinet at the beginning of July that, to avoid inflation, it would shortly be necessary for the government to take powers to prohibit new issues on the Stock Exchange, to control companies' dividends and investment of their reserves, and to control building society loans and bank advances – the timing of these measures being whenever the economy reached full employment, probably in the late autumn.[41] While there were thus some differences of opinion between Keynes and the Treasury as to the likely extent of non-inflationary borrowing, there was agreement that inflation would follow full employment at some stage in 1939–40, were the government not to mobilise private capital and savings for rearmament.

What the foregoing comparative analysis of Keynes's and official economic views on rearmament shows is that, despite differences about economic theory, the extent of practical agreement between Keynes and Whitehall was far more significant than the extent of disagreement. Indeed, the extent of disagreement was no more than one would expect between, on the one hand, a Cambridge don who could produce clear argument uncluttered by compromise, and, on the other, men dealing with the political world where uncertainty and compromise were the essence of decision-making. It is hard to believe that the scope of the rearmament programme would have been any greater even had Keynes been in charge of the Treasury. At the beginning of 1937 Keynes believed that the proposed level of £400 million for loan expenditure on defence over five years was as high as the economy could cope with for the time being, and that the main means of financing armaments should be taxation, and he still seems to have held these views at the end of the year, when he wrote that public expenditure should not be pushed 'at present'.[42] Thus Keynes was substantially in agreement with the Treasury's view in 1937 that defence expenditure should be kept within the cash limits set by the anticipated revenue over five years from the existing level of taxation – £1,100 million – plus the £400 million under the Defence Loans Act, a total of £1,500 million, unless the Cabinet felt that the international situation warranted an increase in taxation. The Cabinet decided in December 1937 to set out priorities in defence policy in the light of the £1,500 million cash limit, and it was then that the notorious decision was made not to prepare an expeditionary force to serve on the European continent until such time as Britain's air and sea defences were secure.[43]

Both Keynes and the Treasury agreed that a recession in 1938 meant that acceleration of the rearmament programme in that year would not be likely to be inflationary, and, indeed, the £400 million spent on defence in the financial year 1938–9 was well in excess both of the £265 million spent in 1937 and of the level implied by the £1,500 million cash limit set for the quinquennium 1937–42. However, since British aircraft production was still lagging behind Germany's, there was no change in policy regarding the army until February 1939. Meanwhile the *rate* of defence expenditure was dictated by the pace with which manufacturers could keep up with their contracts, and Treasury control was exercised from the point of view of securing an orderly flow of production. Treasury resistance in 1938 and 1939 to proposals for increases in the *scope* of the rearmament programme arose out of a belief that industry could not cope, and that the balance of payments deficit threatened another crisis of confidence on the scale of 1931. Keynes agreed that such a crisis was possible, and his suggestions in 1938 for informal measures to control capital outflows were superseded by the expansion of the rearmament programme in 1939. Forecasts of defence expenditure for the financial year 1939–40 steadily increased from £580 million in February 1939 to £750 million in July – far above the £400 million spent in 1938–9 (£400 million represented about 8 per cent of national income in 1938–9, and £750 million would have represented over 13 per cent of national income in 1939–40). Since the expenditure of £400 million had been associated with a current balance of payments deficit of over £50 million, it was unlikely that Keynes's proposals of 1938 to cover a deficit of £50 million would have been adequate in 1939–40 anyway, and the likelihood of full employment being reached in 1939–40 added the threat of domestic inflation as a reason for general government control of private capital. As in 1937, so in 1939, Keynes and the Treasury could agree that greater armaments production could only be achieved at the expense of civil demand for scarce resources.

This in turn suggests that historical inquiry at the macroeconomic level as to whether greater rearmament would have been possible between 1936 and 1939 should be directed to the political possibilities of the state securing a greater share of national resources, through greater taxation, controls over capital, or physical controls over producer goods. However, as noted above, Keynes himself was opposed, at least in 1937, to '[quasi] war-time controls, rationing and the like'. A more fruitful area of inquiry for historians is likely to be the microeconomic problems of introducing new technology – both new weapons and new techniques of production – and of making better use of scarce resources, especially labour. Significantly, Keynes admitted that his economic competence did not extend to such problems as labour mobility or relaxation of restrictive practices. Another important area of historical inquiry is likely to be management of, and productivity in, industry. For example, Air Ministry surveys of nine leading aircraft manufacturers in 1936 and 1937 found that, from the point of view of production, three were incompetent and two were disappointing, and the Air Ministry insisted on management changes. In the case of shipbuilding, output per man towards the end of the 1930s was very little, if at all, greater than before the First World War.[44]

Of course, it can be argued that the industrial problems of rearmament were as great as they were in 1936–9 largely because of earlier retrenchment, and had 'Keynesian' rather than 'orthodox' policies been pursued earlier there would have been less leeway to make up after 1936. Budget deficits for most of the interwar period would have been 'Keynesian', but, so far as one can tell, it would not have been the intention of Keynes himself that production of armaments should have been greater than it was before 1936. The Liberal Party's 'Yellow Book' of 1928, of which Keynes was part author, advocated not only more public works to cure unemployment but also economy on armaments so as to ease the burden of national taxation. The 'Yellow Book''s calculations of the cost of defence as a percentage of national income seem to bear the mark of Keynes, and it is significant that the 'Yellow Book' advocated a reduction from about 3 per cent of national income – the level estimated for 1928 – to at least 2 per cent – the level of 1875.[45] A concern about reducing defence expenditure may seem to be pre-Keynesian to anyone who supposes that Keynes was concerned simply to advocate budget deficits to cure unemployment, but, in reality, Keynes was no less aware than the Treasury that 'sound' financial policies were in order when there was a real risk of financial collapse. For example, in March 1931 he wrote to the Prime Minister warning that a crisis of confidence was 'very near' and that the budget must be balanced.[46] Had Keynes been Chancellor rather than Snowden in 1931 he would, like the Labour Chancellor, have sought to reduce defence expenditure, and there is no reason to suppose that the defence estimates for 1932 – the nadir of interwar defence expenditure – would have been any higher than they were. Indeed, although from 1933 Keynes was urging a policy of 'doing all in our power to stimulate loan-expenditure',[47] and although Keynes was aware from the time the Nazis took power that Britain faced 'the hideous dilemma' of allowing Germany to rearm or 'the horror of a preventive war',[48] he does not seem to have advocated expenditure on armaments before 1936. Presumably his own Liberal prejudices inhibited him from doing so, and, in any case, it is likely that what as late as September 1936 he called the 'overwhelming success of pacifist propaganda in this country'[49] would have made armaments politically unacceptable as a form of unemployment relief.

When one moves to the period 1936–9, one finds that Keynes and the government's official economic advisers shared an assumption that war with the fascist powers could be avoided, and this uncertainty about whether, or when, war would come made decisions as to how Britain should allocate her economic resources for defence very difficult. It would be wrong to identify Keynes too closely with the government's ideas about foreign policy. He wrote in August 1936 of 'the discreditable failure of our foreign policy during the Abyssinian War and on many other occasions', and, while supporting the government's attempt at achieving a general ban on intervention in Spain, he wished 'that there had been some clearer declaration of where this country's sympathies stand'.[50] However, at the same time he opposed a suggestion by the editor of the *New Statesman* that the government should align itself definitely against the dictatorships:

> Mr Baldwin may be wiser than you are [Keynes wrote]. He may be hesitating because he knows that *nothing* is certain. It may conceivably prove to have been right on our part not to clinch the position; not to crystallise the fatal alignment of forces. The best, the only, hope of peace lies in a policy which does not regard war as certain; which breaks down no bridges and makes no final commitments. Herr Hitler, however disagreeable a creature, is a queer one. National hysterias do not last for ever. Something totally unexpected may suddenly change.[51]

The Treasury held similar views as to the necessity of avoiding an open breach with Germany. An internal Treasury memorandum of 1937 argued that it was possible that Germany was a 'beast of prey waiting for an opportunity to pounce', but it was also possible that the Nazi struggle was primarily one for self-respect, and that Germany was 'appealing to the least unfriendly boy in the school to release him from the Coventry to which he was sent after the war'. The memorandum went on: 'Even if it were thought that the former view is nearer the truth, our dealings with Germany should . . . be based on the second . . . since if the former hypothesis be true, war is inevitable.'[52] Sir Warren Fisher, the Permanent Secretary of the Treasury, warmly approved this memorandum, and sent it to the Chancellor, but there is no reason to suppose, on the basis of shared hope that war might be avoided, that either Fisher or Keynes wished Britain to be inadequately defended. Fisher had been an advocate of greater armed preparedness since 1933, and Keynes in 1936 saw an 'enormously superior' navy as a suitable reply to the fascist powers.[53]

However, the economic consequences of a policy of not regarding war as inevitable was uncertainty as to the correct balance between expenditure on armaments (some of which might rapidly become obsolete) and retention of financial strength – the 'fourth arm of defence', to use the Treasury's phrase – which was necessary to maintain armed forces in war. If Britain attempted to rearm too quickly the government might exhaust its ability to raise credit, the economy might become destabilised and the gold and convertible currency reserves might be exhausted, thus making it impossible to conduct the long war which, in 1937, the Chiefs of Staff believed Britain and France would find necessary to defeat Germany.[54] No wonder Fisher noted in 1937; 'I am as anxious as my military colleagues to make this country safe against foreign gangsters, but we are running a danger of smashing ourselves.'[55] From 1937 the Treasury feared 'another 1931' and, by the end of 1938 at least, Keynes felt that the financial position had potential dangers not less than those of 1931.

Even at the time of Munich, however, Keynes lacked that perfect knowledge so often assumed in economics textbooks. Indeed, while passing adverse moral judgements on Chamberlain, Keynes could think of no alternative to what Chamberlain took responsibility for. Certainly Keynes thought that the collaboration of the USA and Russia ought to be invited in securing a settlement, but we know now that Roosevelt had no intention of becoming involved directly, and Keynes himself observed at the time 'there has never been any convincing evidence of Russia's reliability'. The Keynes wrote in August 1938 that over Czechoslovakia Britain 'should bluff to the hilt: and if the bluff is called, back out . . . What we ought to work for is a maintenance of Cz[echo]-Slo[vakia]'s integrity apart from frontier revisions.' After Munich he deplored the 'terrific reverse' which 'honourable international policy' had suffered, but went on to say: 'It is *not certain* that the present settlement may not be a good thing in the long term. Viewed quite drily, there is a great deal to be said for it. Hitler's next move is not very obvious or easy . . . [The government] may, by historical luck, have carried through a necessary thing which decent men could not have accomplished.'[56] That passage illustrates perfectly how the Cambridge don, while free to indulge in criticism without responsibility, was no more blessed with foresight in political matters than the men he criticised.

Political uncertainty, then, begat economic uncertainty, and it was only gradually that the scope of the rearmament programme was increased as fears of impending war overcame fears of a financial crash. Keynes's macroeconomic analysis of the situation leads one to the view that greater rearmament would have involved reduction of civilian demand in 1937, and government controls over private capital whenever the external balance or inflation demanded it. He himself was not disposed to urge upon Britain the 'authoritarian state systems [which] seem to solve the problem of unemployment at the expense of efficiency and freedom', and wanted somehow to combine the enlargement of the functions of government necessary for sustained full employment with 'the advantages of decentralisation and the play of self-interest'.[57] The problem of political understanding and political will necessary to achieve conditions suitable for Keynes's economics are beyond the scope of this paper, but it is by no means clear that they are easily achieved. At all events the evidence presented here of Keynes's views on the economics of rearmament, and on appeasement, may be sufficient to persuade historians not to call upon Keynes as a *deus ex machina* providing an easy solution to the dilemmas of defence and foreign policy in the 1930s.

Notes: Chapter 10

The author wishes to thank Professor William Ashworth, Kathleen Burk and Roger Middleton for comments on this paper, and the Social Sciences Research Council for financing some of the research.

1   B. Bond, *Journal of Strategic Studies*, vol. 2 (1979), p. 363, reviewing G. C. Peden, *British Rearmament and the Treasury: 1932–1939* (Edinburgh, 1979).
2   For example, M. Howard, *The Continental Commitment* (London, 1972), pp. 98 f.; S. Roskill, *Hankey, Man of Secrets*, Vol. 3 (London, 1974), p. 251; and R. Shay, Jr, *British Rearmament in the Thirties* (Princeton, NJ, 1977), p. 278.
3   F. Coghlan, 'Armaments, economic policy and appeasement. Background to British foreign policy, 1931–7', *History*, vol. 57 (1972), p. 213.
4   For economic trends see B. Mitchell, *Abstract of British Historical Statistics* (Cambridge, 1962), p. 477, for prices; R. Sayers, *The Bank of England 1891–1944*, Appendices (Cambridge, 1976), pp. 307–34, for balance of payments; and C. Feinstein, *National*

Income, Expenditure and Output of the United Kingdom 1855–1965 (Cambridge, 1972), T 128, for unemployment. For discussion of the nature of unemployment in the 1930s see A. Booth and S. Glynn, 'Unemployment in the interwar period: a multiple problem', *Journal of Contemporary History*, vol. 10 (1975), pp. 611–36.

5   *New Statesman and Nation*, vol. 12 (1936), pp. 82 f.

6   House of Commons Debates, 5th series, 1936–7, vol. 320, col. 2226; *The Times*, 25 February 1937, p. 22. Keynes's speech was filed in the Chancellor of the Exchequer's Office, Treasury Papers, T. 172/1853, in Public Record Office, London.

7   What follows is based on J. M. Keynes, 'How to avoid a slump', *The Times*, 12–14 January 1937, all pp. 13 f., and 'Borrowing for defence', ibid., 11 March 1937, pp. 17 f. Keynes's advice is also incorporated in the Twenty-second Report of the Economic Advisory Council's Committee on Economic Information, 19 February 1937, printed in S. Howson and D. Winch, *The Economic Advisory Council 1930–1939* (Cambridge, 1977), pp. 343–53.

8   Phillips to Hopkins, 19 January 1937, Treasury Papers, T. 161/783/S.48431/02/1. Earlier discussion of these matters can be found in Phillips to Hopkins, 31 December 1936, T. 175/96 (part 2).

9   House of Commons Debates, 5th series, 1936–7, vol. 321, cols 1670 f.

10 Inskip to Brown, 14 June 1937, T. 177/37 (part 2).

11 'How to avoid a slump: II Dear money', *The Times*, 13 January 1937, p. 13.

12 Hawtrey, 13 February 1937, T. 208/196.

13 Phillips, 25 February 1937, T. 172/1853.

14 *The Times*, 11 March 1937, pp. 17 f.

15 G. C. Peden, 'Keynes, the Treasury and unemployment in the later nineteen-thirties', *Oxford Economic Papers*, vol. 32 (1980), pp. 16 f.

16 *The Times*, 13 January 1937, pp. 13 f. and 11 March 1937, pp. 17 f.

17 Twenty-first Report of the Committee on Economic Information, 18 December 1936, Cabinet Papers, CAB 58/21, in Public Record Office, London.

18 Memorandum by Chief Economic Adviser, 18 December 1936, CAB 24/265.

19 For origins of this agreement see S. V. O. Clarke, *Exchange-Rate Stabilization in the Mid-1930s: Negotiating the Tripartite Agreement* (Princeton, NJ, 1977).

20 Twenty-sixth Report, 16 December 1938, CAB 58/23.

21 The American attitude was explained by Harry White, one of Morgenthau's economic advisers, as follows: 'Any significant decline in sterling below the traditional parity at this time may create monetary disturbances throughout the world . . . Our own business situation is such that any significant worsening of our trade position, such as would be caused by a substantially lower sterling rate and by the adverse effects of instability on foreign currencies, might seriously jeopardize our recovery to the detriment of the whole world as well as of the United States' – The Sterling Situation, by White for Secretary Morgenthau, 31 August 1938, Reading Files of Harry Dexter White, General Records of the Department of the Treasury, Record Group 56, National Archives, Washington.

22 *Economic Journal*, vol. 48 (1938), p. 454.

23 Hopkins to Chancellor of the Exchequer, 23 December 1938, T. 175/104 (part 1) and Hopkins, 3 January 1939, T. 175/104 (part 2).

24 Twenty-sixth Report of the Committee on Economic Information, 16 December 1938, CAB 58/23.

25 Paragraphs of the draft twenty-sixth report prepared by Mr Keynes, 28 November 1938, ibid.

26 Twenty-sixth Report, 16 December 1938, ibid.

27 ibid., para. 23; Views of the Treasury and Bank of England on suggestions made in paragraph 23 of Economic Advisory Committee Report of 16 December 1938, T. 175/104 (part 1).

28 Sir Ralph Hawtrey's unpublished history of the Treasury in the Second World War, p. 1, Hawtrey Papers 2/1, Churchill College, Cambridge.

29 Telegram for the Acting Secretary of the Treasury, from US Embassy in London, 24 August 1939, Henry Morgenthau Diaries, vol. 206, fo. 290-H, Franklin D. Roosevelt Library, Hyde Park, New York State.

30 Shay, pp. 277 f., 286. Shay cites a memorandum by Keynes, 28 May 1939, in T. 175/47, but the author was unable to find any memorandum by Keynes in that file. Keynes's views had

been published earlier, however, in two articles on 'Crisis finance', *The Times*, 17–18 April 1939, and in a letter to *The Times*, 4 May 1939, all of which were noted in T. 208/201.

31   S. Howson, *Domestic Monetary Management in Britain 1919–38* (Cambridge, 1975), p. 143.

32   'Crisis finance', *The Times*, 17 April 1939, p. 13 and 18 April 1939, p. 15.

33   Hawtrey, Mr Keynes on crisis finance, 20 April 1939, T. 208/201. Emphasis in original.

34   Cabinet minutes, 23 May 1939, CAB 23/99, p. 234.

35   Hawtrey, 29 April 1939, T. 208/201.

36   'Crisis finance', *The Times*, 17 April 1939, p. 13; letter to *The Times*, 4 May 1939, p. 12.

37   Keynes, 'Will rearmament cure unemployment?', *The Listener*, 1 June 1939, p. 1143.

38   In July the Chancellor thought that the revision of the estimated cost of defence for 1939–40 from £630 million (April estimate) to £750 million probably underestimated the increase – Cabinet minutes, 5 July 1939, CAB 23/100, p. 114.

39   Financial situation. Further memorandum by the Treasury, 13 June 1939, T. 175/115.

40   Keynes, 'Crisis finance', *The Times*, 18 April 1939, pp. 15 f.; Hawtrey, Mr Keynes on crisis finance, T. 208/201.

41   Cabinet minutes, 5 July 1939, CAB 23/100, pp. 110 ff., and Note on the Financial Situation, ibid., p. 138.

42   Letter to *The Times*, 28 December 1937, p. 13.

43   Peden, *British Rearmament and the Treasury*, pp. 41 f., 71–81 and 134–9.

44   P. Fearon, 'Aircraft manufacturing', and J. R. Parkinson, 'Shipbuilding', in N. Buxton and D. Aldcroft (eds), *British Industry Between the Wars* (London, 1979), pp. 87 and 235 f. For trade unions' resistance to relaxation of restrictive practices, see R. A. C. Parker, 'British rearmament 1936–1939: Treasury, trade unions and skilled labour', *English Historical Review*, vol. 9 (1981), pp. 306–43.

45   Liberal Industrial Inquiry, *Britain's Industrial Future* (London, 1928), p. 428. Keynes also seems to have advocated of reduction of defence expenditure in 1929: see Keynes, *Collected Writings*, Vol. 9 (London, 1972), pp. 111 f.

46   R. Middleton, 'The Treasury in the 1930s: political and administrative constraints to acceptance of the "new" economics', *Oxford Economic Papers*, new series, vol. 104 (1982), p. 56.

47   Keynes, *Collected Writings*, Vol. 9, p. 366.

48   Keynes to Kingsley Martin, 15 November 1933, Keynes, *Collected Writings*, Vol. 28.

49   *New Statesman and Nation*, vol. 12 (1936), p. 348.

50   ibid., pp. 219 and 284.

51   ibid., p. 188.

52   E. Hale for Chancellor, 10 August 1937, T. 172/1801.

53   For Fisher's role in rearmament see G. C. Peden, 'Sir Warren Fisher and British rearmament against Germany', *English Historical Review*, vol. 94 (1979), pp. 29–47. For Keynes and navy, see *New Statesman and Nation*, vol. 12 (1936), p. 284.

54   For a Cabinet paper setting out this argument, see N. Gibbs, *Grand Strategy*, Vol. 1, *History of the Second World War, UK Military Series* (London, 1976), pp. 283–5.

55   Fisher, 14 October 1937, T. 161/783/S. 48431/2.

56   Keynes to Kingsley Martin, 26 and 27 August 1938 and 1 October 1938, Keynes, *Collected Writings*, Vol. 28.

57   Keynes, *The General Theory of Employment, Interest and Money* (London, 1936), pp. 380 f.

11 'Economic Appeasement' – A Crisis Strategy

BERND-JÜRGEN WENDT

Before analysing the economic factors involved in British appeasement policy *vis-à-vis* the dictatorships of the 1930s three fundamental points must be made: in the first place we cannot assign merely secondary importance to factors of politics and diplomacy, security, or military strategy, giving total pre-eminence to the economic sphere; neither can we adopt a type of 'pan-economic' point of view discovering economic causes behind each and every political event. The term 'appeasement' rather should be released from a purely political application and be restored to its full significance of settling political, economic and financial conflicts at the international nego-tiating table. *Political* appeasement – and this was undisputed by British leaders, especially Chamberlain, could only be achieved if accompanied by détente in the field of international trade and finance and vice-versa. The concept of *economic* appeasement entailed both the dismantling of trade barriers and the liberalisation of world trade as well as the reconstruction of the international loan and credit system following its partial collapse in the wake of the First World War and the Great Depression. 'Political' and 'economic' appeasement, therefore, were seen as two inseparable aspects of the one political-economic concept which aimed at securing world peace by means of compromise and negotiation. Accordingly the settlement of political conflict was to provide the necessary impulse for the reduction of economic tension and the revival of the international flow of goods and capital; or, conversely, a relaxation of economic tension was to pave the way for a political settlement. Thus at the beginning of March 1938 the British Foreign Secretary, Halifax, stressed to his Ambassador in Washington, Lindsay, the necessity of establishing not merely *political* but also *economic* co-operation in Europe. If the British government were successful in its *political* appeasement, then complementary economic and financial meas-ures would most certainly have to be drawn up. For if Germany and Italy should decide to renounce their plans for autarky in return for a satisfactory political equilibrium, they would find themselves as a result in a very difficult position, both commercially and financially. In the interests of peace Great Britain and the other powers would then have to ask themselves how, individually, they might assist in re-establishing normal commercial and financial relations.[1] For Chamberlain it was undisputed that political conflict was usually caused by economic factors and, conversely, that crises in international trade were often the result of political mistrust.

Given this process of permanent interaction of political and economic objectives, planning and decision-making, a clear line of demarcation cannot realistically be drawn between the two spheres. It can be ascertained

that the rather pro-French and anti-German wing of the Foreign Office
under Vansittart as well as politicians such as Eden saw a political understanding, a 'general settlement' in Europe and prior disarmament or arms
limitation, as absolute prerequisites for economic and financial concessions
from the Western powers in the form of credit expansion or further loans. In
contrast the pro-German lobby in the Foreign Office, represented by the
Economic Director, Ashton-Gwatkin, and by Chamberlain in particular, up
to the spring of 1939, thought it possible to follow a dual strategy tackling
both political and economic détente without any prior political concessions
from Berlin.

After Prague Chamberlain, too, clearly began to change his mind. This
explains his sharp rejection of the Wohlthat mission (expressed in confidence to his sister Ida at the end of July 1939) and what seemed to him the
disloyal line of compromise which the British negotiator Hudson had
apparently adopted with respect to German economic demands. 'The ideas
which he [i.e. Hudson] put to Wohlthat for instance, as his own personal
suggestions, on an economic appeasement (not including a loan) are just
those which we have been discussing in the Departments for 12 months.'[2] By
the summer of 1939 it was in any case too late for Chamberlain to grant
economic or financial concessions to Germany without any reciprocal signs
of a political will to negotiate. Every basis for confidence had been destroyed
and such confidence would have to be re-established before Germany could
be reintegrated into a European monetary and economic block with Britain's assistance. The importance of economic appeasement in the course of
Anglo-German relations within the general context of the British policy of
rapprochement would, therefore, have to be examined from the perspective
of what the individual politician tried to achieve.

A second preliminary remark: any analysis of the factors involved must be
conducted over the long term, and not so much based on individual political
events and concrete decision-making. Such an analysis need not call into
question the drama of the often very short-term and expedient nature of
events, but its aim in principle must be to unveil certain structures with a
relatively high rate of constancy and to outline the complex framework of
the various driving-forces within which short-term and often *ad hoc* decisions were taken by the upper echelons of leadership. For this procedure to
be historically valid it must continually be substantiated by contemporary
evidence. The multidimensional nature of individual decisions in foreign
policy can only be seen against the background, not merely of abstract
economic and financial data, but also of the fundamental influence these
most definitely had on the political and economic debates of the 1930s
among political leaders, on relations between the executive and private
enterprise, on private enterprise itself (in so far as it was an interested
supporter of economic appeasement), on the various sectors of the economy
and on the banking world of the City.

And finally a third preliminary comment: a strategy of crisis such as
appeasement had origins and objectives both in domestic and foreign
affairs. Here again both dimensions – domestic and foreign policy – are so
closely related that it would be misleading and erroneous to give precedence

to either. Economic appeasement was determined first by the crisis of British economic decline which had been gradually fermenting since the late nineteenth century and which came temporarily to a head in the wake of the First World War and the Great Depression of 1929–32; secondly, economic appeasement was the result of the desolate situation of the world trading and financial system of the 1930s; thirdly – and this was not only traditionally German but specifically National Socialist! – it was the response to the challenge from a regime which itself was largely the product of the World Depression and this, it was felt, could master autarkic isolation and belligerent expansionism for *Lebensraum*. Appeasement, therefore, was the response to a whole series of national and international, political, economic and strategic problems with which Britain found herself confronted between the two World Wars, not only bilaterally in her relations with the three dictatorships – Germany, Italy and Japan – but also multilaterally in view of her central position within the world economic order and the great power network. These three closely connected dimensions and levels of analysis of our given subject all merge in the spheres of domestic and foreign policy, economics, finance and diplomacy, armaments and security, state and private enterprise, domestic and foreign trade. These dimensions can merely be touched upon within the context of this essay. Moreover, the levels of analysis have been divided, not to reflect the complexity of the actual subject-matter, but for the sake of more expedient and lucid analysis.

Domestic considerations: economic appeasement as a policy of détente in the field of foreign trade, a policy aimed at the normalisation of both bilateral and multilateral trading and financial relations. This can only be understood with reference to the socio-economic structure of Britain from the nineteenth century. Twice within three decades, directly before the First, and then prior to the Second World War, Britain had been challenged both by the German claim to hegemony on the Continent and by an ever-accelerating international arms race at a time when she herself was undergoing a very difficult and critical stage in her socio-economic development. Before 1914 a temporary boom in armaments concealed the weaknesses and distortions of Britain's industrial and foreign trade structure. For reasons not to be entered into here, the necessary transformation, modernisation and adaptation of her means of production to the new demands of the twentieth century had, in comparison with those of her new rivals on the world market – the USA, Germany and Japan – got off the ground rather belatedly. The shift in emphasis in the leading sectors of the economy away from the 'old and declining industries' dependent on exports (coal, wool, cotton, iron and steel, shipbuilding) towards the 'new and growing industries', largely directed towards the domestic economy (chemicals, the electrical and car industries, plastics, and so on) and the tertiary sector, had just begun: compared to other nations Britain had wasted valuable time in adjusting to this new situation. Between the world wars, however, important steps were taken towards modernising, rationalising and mechanising Britain's economy. But an equilibrium still had to be found for Britain's distorted structure of production as it had emerged from the armament boom of the First World War and even earlier. A further equilibrium had also to be found for those sectors dependent on the domestic economy and those geared towards the export trade, while, finally, the considerable social problems linked with structural changes in the British economy had also to be tackled. Alongside all these tasks it was necessary to redefine the function and role of the state and to take decisive steps in the direction of interventionism. It was vital for Britain, therefore, that this process of structural adaptation and reorganisation should neither upset the balance of payments nor be itself called into question by a renewed threat of war. The latter could trigger off a revived international arms race and generally jeopardise the country's foreign relations both economically and politically.

The vulnerability of Britain's trade balance had become evident as a result of extensive imports of raw materials and foodstuffs and heavy losses in foreign loan capital following the First World War. British interests were naturally linked to an expansion of economic relations with partners such as Germany, which continued after 1933 to guarantee a relatively stable market, above all for the products of the old staple industries such as coal, which although badly shaken by the Depression continued to play a vital role in British foreign trade. The maintenance of foreign trade, international service transactions and income from overseas capital was a prerequisite at the domestic level for the modernisation of the British economy; a smooth flow of trade and the preservation of world peace were guarantees for British security and independence. It was not only a problem of bilateral relations with Germany. The complexity of world trade and the network of London's international financial relations, finely woven over the centuries, made peace seem indispensable for Britain; armed conflict in Europe would inevitably jeopardise the country's economic chances of survival and would be a threat to her vital foreign relations. To lose Germany as a trading partner was not only detrimental to Britain's direct economic interests, but beyond that threatened the triangle of transit trade between Britain, the empire and Germany, thus undermining the economic position of the dominions and the colonies. This was made drastically clear in the summer and autumn of 1934 when German buyers temporarily boycotted the commodity markets causing the prices of wool and cotton, for example, to plummet and eroding the purchasing power and solvency of the producers. The gradual worldwide recovery from the depths of the World Depression then suddenly appeared to have been halted once again by the German transfer crisis. If one may recapitulate at this point, therefore, the economic problems involved in reshaping the British economy and the dependence of British foreign trade on the German market had among other things far-reaching social repercussions on the British labour market.

The question of armaments constituted the decisive link between the various components of appeasement, domestic and foreign trade, politics and economics. Rearmament as dictated by Germany not only meant a new shift towards the armament industries, it also meant that British industrial production would no longer be competitive under normal world market conditions. This in turn entailed a deceleration, if not a halt in the process of modernisation leading to a deterioration in the balance of trade and a weaker pound which would bring with it the danger of inflation. The channelling of potential export capacity into arms production was bound to result in the loss of foreign markets. Moreover, the prospect that Britain might regain her former markets as a result of political tension or an artificial boom in the domestic war industry at a later date were not rosy, even in the event of victory. The debate on appeasement and rearmament from the mid-1930s onwards was influenced throughout, therefore, by alarming reports of diminishing visible and invisible foreign returns, swelling deficits in the balance of payments (1936: £18 million; 1937: £52 million) and a gradual process of dis-investment overseas ('Are we living on capital?'). Foreign trade ranked as the 'fourth branch of service' alongside the three branches of the forces, and a general call for exports to be 'looked after' steadily gained momentum. Rearmament, the arms race and international political tension – given the danger of further distortions in production – were a threat to trade, not only within Britain herself at a very critical stage of her development, but also to her markets overseas. Chamberlain's orthodox programme of 'healthy finances' was liable to fail if international conflict and the international arms race came to a head. The strategy of appeasement was designed to save Britain from setting an inflationary spiral into motion as a result of the forced subsidising of armament production and deficit spending, and from all the negative effects this would have on the economic and social structures of the country. Even during the World Depression of 1938 the Treasury still had severe doubts about using rearmament – on the basis of foreign policy – to inject some life into the domestic economy. The aim of keeping armament expenditure constantly below the inflationary threshold by means of the twofold strategy of détente and moderate rearmament, thus forced the British to fix defensive priorities in armament expenditure and military strategy, for example, with regard to the navy, anti-aircraft defence and fighter planes. Such defensive concepts of military strategy, armaments expenditure and security policy therefore fitted perfectly into the overall strategy of political and economic appeasement.

External factors: Britain's vital interest in re-establishing the international trade and finance system which had collapsed in 1929–32 will now be considered in the light of the National Socialist challenge as it was perceived in Britain. Consideration will also be given to the consequences of that perception and how these were expressed in foreign policy. Once again one can only present the broad outlines of the subject rather than the detailed evidence.

From the British point of view National Socialism was essentially a product of the impoverishment of the German masses and the collapse of the German economic system in the wake of the First World War and the World Depression. Political aggression, demands for *Lebensraum* and militaristic one-upmanship in foreign affairs, radicalism, intolerance and dictatorship in domestic policy, were essentially attributed to economic causes. The declared aim of national isolation and autarky seemed to have been forced on the Germans by the disintegration of the world trading system on the one hand and the egoistic attitude of the victorious powers of the First World War – above all France, Britain and the USA – towards the 'have-nots' of

1918 on the other. This general trend towards autarky was intensified between 1931 and 1933 as a result of Britain's transition to a protective tariff system, the devaluation of the pound, the expansion of the imperial market following the Ottowa Conference of 1932 and, in the USA, by the fall in the dollar and the beginnings of the New Deal, a policy also primarily geared towards national demand. British leaders were fully aware of their basic dilemma: any strategy which drew the logical economic consequences from the above picture of Germany and which as a result worked towards economic and financial concessions in line with a policy of economic appeasement, designed to liberalise Germany by removing the causes of her economic and political grievances (and thereby depriving the radicals of their *raison d'être*), immediately came up against the protective limits of Britain's own markets, clearly defined since 1931/2. Any opening of the British market to German commodities would revive the passionate debate of 1931/2 on the protective tariff, shaking the flimsy consensus between free-traders and protectionists. Here, as in the debate over rearmament, it can be seen time and time again how National Socialist Germany was forcing issues on the British against their will – such as rearmament or foreign trade concessions – issues which, thanks to the consensus in domestic politics, they wanted to avoid as best they could. The lengthy debates in the House of Commons on the Coal Agreement with Berlin of 13 April 1933,[3] as well as the second and third readings of the 'Clearing Office Bill' (concerning unilaterally enforced clearing of German debts) on 25–26 June 1934[4] are examples which illustrate the extent to which the problem of Germany and the related dilemma of concessions or sanctions *vis-à-vis* National Socialism was entangled throughout the 1930s with Britain's internal problem of protecting the economy from German competition.

Yet given her own isolationist measures in the early 1930s Britain had herself doubtless considerably confined her room for manoeuvre with respect to commercial or financial concessions to Berlin. Thus at the beginning of 1938 F. T. Ashton-Gwatkin, Economic Director in the Foreign Office and one of the most ardent advocates of economic appeasement, looked back with considerable self-criticism at the rise of Hitler and the growing threat from National Socialist Germany. As he saw it, Britain herself in 1931/2 had slammed the door in Germany's face and was largely responsible for the collapse of the international trading system which had constituted her grandeur in the nineteenth century. She had rejected every step towards economic appeasement under the slogan 'Home industries and agriculture first, Dominions second, foreigners last'. Her protective tariff legislation had compelled Germany, Italy and Japan to build up their own markets in the Balkans, the Mediterranean and the Far East in order to compensate for trade lost with the dominions.[5]

Regardless of the dilemma between what was recognised as necessary and appropriate from the point of view of foreign affairs and foreign trade on the one hand, and the problem of reconciling this with the narrow confines of the domestic political consensus on the other – a dilemma which Britain always confronted in terms of appeasement – we cannot simply dismiss as whitewash the wide-ranging debate on whether trade and financial relations with the Reich should be expanded in the hope of liberalising the regime or curtailed in retaliation against the growing political aggressiveness of the Brownshirts. On the contrary, this debate reflected intense domestic disagreement over a concept of appeasement in which both political and economic factors and elements of domestic and foreign trade were inextricably intertwined; it was conducted at all levels of the civil service, in Parliament, in the media and in society. According to contemporary sources the dilemma was 'to keep Germany lean or to fatten Germany'. However, 'to fatten Germany' – with credit, loans and trade concessions such as the guarantee of a given share of the British market, export earnings in sterling for German exports, the reduction of certain tariffs of particular importance to Germany, or the keeping open of credit lines – always involved the risk that if not offset by treaty agreements on general disarmament, the National Socialist leadership would use all available resources, including hard currency earned in Britain and the credit provided by British banking companies, to finance German foreign trade, to boost her military capacity and to supply her war industry with raw materials from abroad. Schacht for example in 1936 expressed his concern to Messersmith, the US envoy to Vienna, that since Germany continued to be closely integrated in the world market, a cut in Anglo-US credit would prevent the Reich from pursuing both its industrial and rearmament programmes.[6] This concern, that British concessions would merely be used by Germany to expand her potential for aggression – a concern particularly harboured by the anti-German lobby around Vansittart – was offset by the fear – repeatedly expressed in governmental circles and indeed nourished by reports from the Embassy in Berlin – that a 'lean Germany', cut off from foreign supplies and faced with a foreign trade and credit embargo, would rush headlong into military aggression. Furthermore, any hardening of the British line would only result in the German people flocking behind their Führer in fear of the old 'nightmare of encirclement'. Foreign Office advice against economic sanctions was, therefore, based on careful calculations, reassessed in accordance with developments on a number of occasions from which it can clearly be seen how far Britain's own foreign trade, as well as financial and above all imperial interests, would have been impaired by such sanctions.[7] In any case, since all economic concessions were highly ambivalent and caught up in the domestic controversy over the British protective tariff of 1931, it is hardly surprising that *economic* appeasement was subjected much earlier to more severe criticism than its *political* counterpart.

From the British point of view – and here the ambivalent interpretation of the German threat represented a constant handicap to formulating policy regarding Germany – the German scene was dominated to the end by a permanent conflict between 'moderates' and 'extremists'. The party 'extremists' around Goebbels, Himmler and Ribbentrop could, in Britain's view, only survive politically so long as they succeeded in chaining the impoverished German masses to the Nazi regime. They did this on the one hand by threatening them with the prospect of even greater need if hostile foreign powers should ever get near them, while on the other they dangled before them the carrot of *Lebensraum* in the east to be achieved on the basis of Germany's own might. Opposed to them, as Schacht repeatedly asserted, were the 'moderates' around himself, Goering and the leading trading and economic circles, who were open to political and economic reason. Any economic concession tended, therefore, to bolster them politically within the inner-German power struggle and eroded every justification for a path towards national economic autarky. Hitler, for many, seemed to mediate between the two fronts. Encouraged by success in foreign policy, he always seemed disposed to swing into line with the moderate flank and seek détente, at least in Western Europe.

Finally, in spite of growing commercial and financial restrictions, due above all to the New Plan of September 1934, Germany still ranked third in world trade behind Britain and the USA until the outbreak of war. She was considered as an integral part of the Western capitalist system, particularly when contrasted to 'half-asiatic' Russia. In the summer of 1933 after Hitler had officially declared the end of the 'national revolution' against the left-wing opposition within his party, the liberal *Economist*[8] pointed out with some satisfaction and relief that Germany was a capitalist state and was likely to remain so. Four years later, at the Imperial Conference in May 1937, the then Foreign Secretary, Eden, made the following statement, indicative of the continuity of the policy of economic appeasement:

> But there are many who say that economic appeasement provides the key to our difficulties, and it is certain that with most of our political problems there is an economic problem inextricably intertwined . . . For reasons which in Germany are ascribed to the vindictive policy of the Allies, but elsewhere largely to the blunders of successive German Governments, that great country, which should be the axis of European trade and is still the third most important mercantile nation, has become internationally bankrupt . . . But what is a serious danger is the extent to which she is moving away from the economic system of Western Europe into an idiosyncrasy of attitude not unlike that of Soviet Russia. To those countries who can supply her needs and will take her goods, such as the countries of the Danubian area, the Balkan States and Turkey, she acts as a strong attraction; and this is not without political danger. If this attraction were developed in the direction of Russia, who can supply so many German needs, the danger might become greater, and a division might establish itself between two economic systems in Western and Eastern Europe. It is, therefore, of urgent importance to restore Germany to her normal place in the Western European system.[9]

Here we can find the traditional British 'Rapallo complex' of renewed German dependence on Russia, this time with an economic perspective!

These comments illustrate the essence of economic appeasement and its objective which remained invariable until the outbreak of war: there was a natural identity between the commercial and financial interests of the trading and banking circles of both nations alongside an old tradition of personal business relations; both parties, Germany and Britain, did all they could to the very end to protect their own interests and keep these bilateral trading and financial relations intact and as free as possible from political friction, despite the political tension which mounted from early 1938. In so doing the British also cherished hopes of reserving a basis for détente within the sphere of power politics, of some kind of common ground with the 'powers of reason' in Berlin, of relieving their own economic structure, badly shaken by the crisis, in foreign trade, and of immunising it against external danger. The Germans were clearly concerned with supplying their war economy with raw materials bought with free exchange on the world market, raw materials which would be unobtainable without the foreign exchange obtained through their own markets in south-eastern Europe. Many Britons – including those in the highest echelons of government – were prepared to turn a blind eye to the clearly criminal aspects of the Third Reich and Germany's internal affairs so long as Germany, in the heart of Europe, avoided socialist experiments, guaranteed reliability in business, inspired a certain degree of confidence in British business partners in exports, in the City, in shipping and insurance, and assured prospects of profit for private enterprise.

Economic appeasement as part of Britain's overall policy of appeasement primarily reflected Britain's own interests. It would be absolutely unhistorical to try today, with the benefit of hindsight, to construct alternative concepts to appeasement and to apply a yardstick oblivious to the needs of the 1930s. For internal British reasons and in the light of the obscure power balance in Berlin (at least to British eyes) it was on the one hand out of the question to apply a policy of sanctions against Germany; whilst on the other, a total liberalisation and opening of the British market as a concession to the Third Reich was bound to come up against opposition from the protectionist lobby and was, therefore, doomed to failure. Between these two extremes of sanctions and a policy of liberalisation there still remained in the British view a wide range of measures of co-operation in foreign trade and finance which could be appropriately deployed to keep a foot in the door in Central Europe, to check the general drift towards autarky, to relieve international political tension and thus preserve a basis for the re-establishment in the future of the world economic order, with the inclusion of Germany.

Periodisation: given the 'threat from Germany' which had existed from at least the late nineteenth century, appeasement in the general sense – defined as the attempt to reduce international tension at the negotiating table – cannot be said to have begun with either the so-called 'Machtergreifung' (seizure of power) of the National Socialists on 30 January 1933, or with Chamberlain's entry into office in May 1937. It is necessary, therefore, to reappraise the policy – especially in its economic aspects – at least from the beginning of the 1930s. The collapse of the political order set up by the Treaty of Versailles, the disintegration of the world trading and financial system, the general trend towards more or less autarkic large-scale economic markets, the combatting of economic crises at national level and a certain trend towards political and economic isolationism produced a radical change in the basis, scope and prospects of an economically oriented crisis-management at international level. This applied to bilateral relations between Britain and Germany and equally to political and economic developments within every nation from 1932–3 onwards. In this respect 30 January 1933 in Germany was, at least from the economic point of view, less of a turning-point than a step along a path which had already been marked out under Brüning in 1931 with the introduction of foreign exchange controls. At the latest the collapse of the London World Economic Conference in the summer of 1933 caused largely by the intransigent line of the USA and the German transfer moratorium on medium and long-term liabilities, displayed the incapacity – or perhaps the unwillingness – of the Great Powers to find a common basis for combating the worldwide depression. Henceforth every nation, including Britain, tried to find its own way out of the crisis, even at the price of cutting off all possibilities of international, economic and political co-operation and concessions, as was to be illustrated by Britain's relations with the Balkan states from the mid-1930s. Economic nationalism was the general response from the industrial nations to the international crisis in capitalism.

For the British Empire any move towards isolationism was only partially feasible in view of its great dependence on external trade and Britain's traditional international role in finance, shipping and insurance. The result was that economic appeasement, apart from retaining its political function of reducing tension, was also to a certain extent a corrective of the path towards protectionism embarked upon in 1931/2. As has already been pointed out, the debate on economic appeasement included a certain degree of self-criticism regarding any responsibility the victorious powers of Versailles may have had in encouraging political radicalism in Germany. Economic appeasement, therefore, aimed at stabilising world trade, at least at its reduced level of 1932/3, thus making it immune from political friction and, if possible, increasing and expanding it, so long as this proved compatible with those protectionist interests which were backed by private enterprise and the state. As has already been mentioned more than once, this is where the line was drawn by Britain. This aim of stabilising, cultivating and if possible even expanding foreign trade was a matter of life and death for a trading nation such as Britain, even if it proved a delicate task at the domestic level. It was made even more delicate when in 1933 a regime emerged in Central Europe and on the very 'axis of European trade', for which autarky and *Lebensraum*, whatever that meant, were not merely temporary expedients, but constituted the very essence of a 'Herrschaftsanspruch' (claim to power) based on ideology and race. The National Socialist 'Machtergreifung', moreover, took place during an already extremely critical phase in Anglo-German economic relations, caused by the drastic reduction of German coal imports from England in the spring of 1932 in retaliation to the closure of the British market. Unlike previous German governments, however, the new leadership in Berlin appeared surprisingly conciliatory and co-operative. It not only signed the Coal Agreement of 13 April 1933, but let it be known that, for the time being at least, it was not interested in a further cut-back in the deflated flow of Anglo-German trade. On the contrary, the Coal Agreement of 13 April 1933 – extremely controversial in England – and the extension of the Standstill Agreement on short-term German liabilities which had been signed on 17 February, seemed to provide a certain guarantee that the new regime in Berlin did not wish to heighten international tension, at least not economically, and was thoroughly accessible to reasonable economic arguments. Moreover, its signs of co-operation towards the West shrewdly coincided with similar gestures towards the East – for example, its ratification of the extension of the 1926 Berlin Agreement with Moscow – and indicated that the traditional forces within the Foreign Ministry were still at work.

The *Westminster Bank Review*'s comments on the German 'Four Year Plan' of 1936 and the programme of autarky are indicative of British apprehension from 1933: 'Such a revolutionary change in the economic structure of an important industrial nation cannot come about without grave and far-reaching effects upon every other country with which she wants to do business.' Through the channels of international trade every nation had been affected 'to a greater or lesser degree' by the turn of the tide in Germany. Were Germany to withdraw or cut its demand on the contracted world market the effects on its foreign trade and economic equilibrium of other nations would be far from positive. 'They must either find new markets for their surplus production – and this is not always possible – or curtail their own purchases from other countries. It is evident, that the policy at present being pursued by Germany . . . cannot be regarded with equanimity by other nations – even those which may not appear to be directly affected.'[10]

Britain as one of the leading trading partners of the Third Reich (and vice-versa) was quite definitely 'directly affected' by the changes in the economic structure of National Socialist Germany and not in a position to follow the course of events in Germany 'with equanimity'. The increasing politicisation of German foreign trade and debt-servicing as state intervention grew faced British trading circles, Board of Trade officials and the City with the difficult task of dealing both effectively and flexibly with the commercial practices of a dictatorship, especially with its export offensives and moratoria on transfers, without altering the British system which remained strongly committed to the liberal-capitalist and pluralistic ideal of comparatively 'private and unfettered enterprise'. Trade and finance were too closely integrated into the entire political structure of the state for the confrontation between democracy and dictatorship to take place with no repercussions on the democratic systems themselves. So with the aim of forced export incentives, imposed by the German challenge on continental and world markets from 1935/6, Great Britain could hardly 'take a leaf out of the German book', as was the general slogan in Britain at that time, nor 'beat the Germans at their own game' without a fundamental review of her whole political and economic system. The challenge from three dictatorships simultaneously had a catalysing effect on Britain in that it gave considerable momentum to the debate dating back to the First World War on a new definition of the role of the state within the political and economic system; priority was finally accorded, however, to Britain's survival as a great and world power.

An analysis of British policy *vis-à-vis* Germany focusing on economic factors will necessarily lay different emphasis on the chronological development of bilateral relations than a purely political view. Here the period of gestation of these relations – 1933/4 – gains particular significance as a phase of 'conflict and adjustment'. For in this period the economic and financial guidelines were laid down which steered the course of Anglo-German relations through the years of political crisis – 1935/6/8/9 – to the outbreak of the war. In 1933/4 British foreign traders, the banking world and political leaders, whose intervention in bilateral trade relations to protect British private enterprise was particularly active in these years, were above all concerned to prepare for the arduous and difficult path of adjustment to the growing restrictions and regulations of Germany's trading and debt policy as laid down in a number of unilateral transfer moratoria from Berlin and in Schacht's 'New Plan' of September 1934. The British endeavoured to keep the German market open to their goods, to secure standstill credits and to enforce the medium and long-term outstanding claims of British nationals and City banks. After the threat of an open trade war in the summer of 1934, when the Germans blocked payments and the British took measures of retaliation (the transfer crisis), both parties displaying an equally keen interest in this process of adjustment, British policy finally encountered surprising success. The mutual agreements remained valid in substance until the outbreak of war: the Anglo-German Trade and Payments Agreement of 1 November 1934, with minor amendments on 1 July 1938 following the annexation of Austria, along with the Coal Agreement of 13 April 1933, formed the basis for bilateral economic and financial relations. In this Trade and Payments Agreement[11] the Reichsbank, among others, committed itself to earmarking monthly only 55 per cent (increased to 60 per cent in 1938) of German export earnings in England for the purchase of British commodities. Thus Germany was left with considerable scope to purchase with the aid of British foreign exchange (45 per cent – 40 per cent after 1938 – of returns) those raw materials she needed for her war economy, either via English transit trade or directly on the world market. Without going into the details of this very complicated agreement of the autumn of 1934 and how it functioned in practice in the following years at this point, let us none the less emphasise its generally accepted stabilising effect on bilateral relations, an effect which even the political crises of the subsequent years could not impair. Thus in July 1938 with the Sudeten crisis heading towards its climax, von Dirksen, the German Ambassador to London, explicitly referred to the 1934 Economic Agreement and the 1935 Naval Convention as the 'two main supports which had hitherto carried the swaying structure of foreign relations [i.e. between Britain and Germany] even in critical periods'.[12]

Both agreements were also held in high estimation by the British. 'The recent Payment Agreement', said Ashton-Gwatkin at the beginning of 1936 in a memorandum regarding 'Germany's economic position', 'is in the economic world what the Naval Agreement has been in the political sphere – a sign of moderation, almost friendship'.[13] In fact, the Anglo-German import–export ratio between the crisis year 1934 and 1938 (henceforth including Austria) increased from 100:45·7 to 100:68·3 in Britain's favour on the basis of the Trade and Payment Agreement. If in 1938 in British foreign trade overall the ratio was considerably less favourable (100:51·2), and following the 1934 slump Germany quickly recovered its leading position among continental markets in British exports and re-exports, these facts merely emphasise both the effectiveness of the 1933/4 bilateral agreements and the unimpaired importance of foreign trade in the relations between the two nations, relations from which both Britain and Germany drew advantage.

Finally, in the two years immediately prior to the outbreak of war the Chamberlain government under the impact of a new world economic crisis made five attempts to reach a general settlement with National Socialist Germany; in the background lay the endeavours of the British leadership to bring about economic détente together with political détente and, vice-versa, to use economic arrangements as a basis for political détente: first there was the visit to Berlin in November 1937 by Lord Halifax, Lord President of the Privy Council and later Foreign Secretary; secondly, the Dual Agreement on Transfer and Trading Questions of 1 July 1938, and in an accompanying exchange of letters, the prospect of a subsequent general co-ordination of bilateral trading objectives for the purpose of an expansion and improvement of trading relations; thirdly, there was the Munich Agreement – and the hope that it would act as a pacesetter for close economic co-operation in Europe among the Big Four; fourthly, the so-called 'Düsseldorf deal' of 16 March 1939 between the leading industrial associations of both nations, to be followed by state-sponsored cartels between the individual industrial sectors of both countries with the aim of closer co-operation in dividing world markets; while finally there was the Wohlthat mission in July 1939, the importance of which has admittedly remained controversial ever since.

Until the spring of 1939 Whitehall was in full agreement with leading trading, shipping and financial circles that the policy of economic détente and normalisation should not be jeopardised by sudden conflict in a region such as Czechoslovakia which did not affect the vital interests of Great Britain and the dominions. Even as late as the winter of 1938/9 the British government's chief economic adviser, Sir F. Leith-Ross, drew up a plan for informal talks with German partners according to which the 'spirit of Munich' was to provide the basis for closer European co-operation which in turn would constitute a certain counterbalance in Europe to US influence. Whereas London followed a strategy of bilateral appeasement aimed at keeping the German and Central European Market open even in direct co-operation with the Brownshirts, Washington's Open Door policy followed a concept of multilateral appeasement. This American concept of appeasement was indeed coloured by a considerable degree of mistrust of the British, if not actually levelled against London: the American charge against the British was that they had allowed Berlin to enforce bilateral trade relations – the Düsseldorf deal having given momentum to fears of an Anglo-German financial and commercial conspiracy against third parties. Finally, the American concept of appeasement aimed at opening the imperial preference of Ottawa to the US export trade. Since the British were fully aware of the background to American appeasement policy, it was natural that they should try to strike a certain balance within Europe to the US 'embrace'. However, in so doing London was constantly aware of its financial dependence on the USA in the case of conflict. So here again appeasement policy *vis-à-vis* Germany was to be a form of relief, a means of easing pressure from problematic co-operation with the USA and a way out of a certain dilemma Britain was facing in power politics. This resulted from the fact that Britain herself no longer disposed of the resources necessary to pursue great power policy, especially in the case of war, and was dependent as a result on co-operation with Washington. To fail in appeasement would be to sign the death warrant of Britain as a Great Power.

This on the whole positive appraisal of the economic dimension of British appeasement and bilateral relations between London and Berlin was only corrected by the British government when German troops entered Prague in the spring of 1939. From then on economic and financial concessions were strictly out of the question if not accompanied by political and military détente. Thus economic appeasement quite clearly took second place to political appeasement. Nevertheless, despite lengthy and very heated debates, no one in Whitehall seriously thought of using economic sanctions as a means of retaliation against the German march on Prague. According to contemporary sources the same opinion was voiced in 1939 as in 1933. The British leadership felt it more pragmatic not to force Germany into a corner economically through commercial and financial policy – and thus to risk further aggression.

The final question remains: why was economic appeasement a failure? Why could economic relations and identical economic interests not provide a stable basis for a settlement in European power politics?

The theory has been put forward that the British themselves tied their hands so firmly by the transition to protectionism in 1931–2 that any step towards substantial economic concessions to National Socialist Germany in line with real economic appeasement was immediately blocked by the strong protectionist front at home. This interpretation fails to account for the broad spectrum of British commercial policy, exhaustively discussed in Whitehall, with possibilities ranging on the one extreme from a trade embargo, dictated by political motives, to a general opening of the British market with colonial and imperial concessions, on the other. Within this spectrum the British did steer an economic course, admittedly within somewhat restricted parameters, from the time of the Great Depression onwards, a course which was aimed at the normalisation and expansion of trade and credit with a Third Reich which would be depoliticised, stabilised and immune from political crises.

However, further economic concessions to Germany, even if theoretically conceivable, could not hide the fact that economic appeasement, like appeasement as a whole, was based in the final analysis on a total misinterpretation of the National Socialist regime and its objectives. In return for every agreement, Berlin demanded prior unconditional recognition of its political hegemony on the Continent. Britain could not grant these concessions without sacrificing her own security and risking another continental blockade. Again and again she laid her hopes on the 'moderates' among German politicians and businessmen, but they never really stood a chance against the party extremists led by Hitler. According to the aggressive ideology of *Lebensraum* the German economy as a war economy had the sole function of preparing for autarky and war. Such a policy which from 1938 manoeuvred constantly on the brink of war, and which fully accepted the risk of war, was incompatible with a concept based on 'economic reason' for which the preservation of peace was the basis for combatting national difficulties. That liberalisation of the German economic system which the 'appeasers' were striving towards by keeping open the channels of trade and credit, and which was repeatedly pledged by Schacht, presupposed a fundamental transformation of the National Socialist regime and was as such illusory.

Any attempt to dismiss appeasement, including economic appeasement, as illusionary and dilettantist overlooks three factors of fundamental importance:

(1) The British interpretation of the German political scene and Britain's perception of the challenge from the Reich were based on often very contradictory information from Berlin. Until 1939 Britain had no clear picture of the dictatorship in Germany. It would be ahistoric, therefore, to project back our present-day knowledge of the Third Reich as something which should have been clearly recognised in the 1930s. Precisely because the British government was counting on the 'moderates' and 'economic reason' to the very end, it maintained a certain room for manoeuvre in foreign policy which did not from the very outset lead to the impasse of armed conflict.

(2) The 'anti-appeasers' within the ranks of both the Conservative and Labour Parties had in fact no real alternative to official foreign policy, especially since Labour and the unions had for some time been pledged to a platform of pacifism and disarmament.

(3) *Economic* appeasement as an important aspect of appeasement in general was first and foremost a response to an extremely precarious economic and social situation in Britain herself. In a critical phase of Britain's economic development Whitehall wanted to safeguard a process of internal transformation, adjustment and modernisation against all sources of danger and intimidation from outside, above all against the risks of a distorted domestic boom, triggered off by a revived arms mania. For the Conservative élite peace in foreign affairs meant that the process of modernisation could be steered along a course which would neither revolutionise British society nor allow the social struggle to flare up even more ferociously than during and after the First World War – for example, by a debate on rearmament or a call for 'conscription of wealth'. In the interests of the whole nation British governments saw economic and financial stability as vital for national independence. The First World War had provided an instructive example of war bringing not only enormous dangers and difficulties for the economy and society of the vanquished, but also for those of the victors. Even in the case of victory over Hitler's Germany, it was feared that the political independence of Great Britain and the very existence of her empire would be put at stake.

Notes: Chapter 11

This chapter is a resumé of my theories on British appeasement policy as outlined first in my book, *Economic Appeasement. Handel und Finanz in der britischen Deutschland-Politik 1933–1939*, and later from a different angle in my essay 'Grossbritannien-Demokratie auf dem Prüfstand: Appeasement als Strategie des Status Quo', in E. Forndran, F. Golczewski and D. Riesenberger (eds), *Innen- und Aussenpolitik unter nationalsozialistischer Bedrohung* (Opladen, 1977), pp. 11–31. I have however included many of the suggestions received after publication of my book from constructive criticism from colleagues and the development of the debate on appeasement in both Britain and Germany. In most cases I have therefore not quoted any sources.

1   Foreign Relations of the United States (FRUS) 1938, vol. I, pp. 126 ff. Memorandum of conversation by the Under Secretary of State, 8 March 1938.
2   Chamberlain to his sister Ida, 23 July 1939, in Chamberlain Papers, University of Birmingham, NC 18/1/1108.
3   cf. Wendt, *Economic Appeasement*, pp. 104 ff.
4   cf. Wendt, *Economic Appeasement*, pp. 193 ff.
5   Public Record Office, London, FO 371/21701 / C 1828.
6   FRUS 1936, vol. I, pp. 493 ff.
7   cf. Wendt, *Economic Appeasement*, pp. 316 ff.
8   *The Economist*, vol. 116, 10 June 1933, p. 1237.
9   Imperial Conference 1937, The Economist Aspect of Foreign Policy, Memorandum by the Secretary of State for Foreign Affairs, CAB 32/129 E (37)28.
10   *Westminster Bank Review*, no. 273, November 1936, p. 3.
11   For further details on the Anglo-German Trade and Payment Agreement of 1 November 1934, see Wendt, *Economic Appeasement*, pp. 277 ff.
12   Documents on German Foreign Policy 1918–1945, series D (1937–45), vol. I, no. 793, p. 1156.
13   FO 371/19931/C400.

III

THE STRATEGIC DIMENSION

12 The British Military Establishment and the Policy of Appeasement

JOHN DUNBABIN

The term 'establishment' is taken by the *Supplement to the Oxford English Dictionary* to include not only 'the centres of official power' but also 'the whole matrix of official and social relations within which power is exercised'. And a full account of the evolution of British defence policy would certainly adopt this perspective. Thus, one view has it that 'what counted most was not any assessment of future war conditions, but "dining-out power"', admirals having 'a decisive superiority over the air marshals and generals at the dinner-tables of the ruling circles'.[1] Even if Liddell Hart exaggerates, policy clearly did not evolve from official channels alone, but also from a more fluid group of defence-oriented politicians (like Churchill), publicists (like Liddell Hart himself), former military men (like Trenchard) and scientists (like Tizard and Watson-Watt). Such people could be extremely influential, as was Liddell Hart during his 1937–8 'partnership' with the Secretary for War, Hore-Belisha, or, like Churchill, successful in certain areas (the 1937 transfer to the navy of the Fleet Air Arm), though no more than a general gadfly in others. But they were very far from united. And to get anything done they had to have access to, and retain the confidence of, those formally in office. For the broad lines of policy were set by ministers, in the last resort by the Cabinet collectively. So a second way of approaching defence policy, one that gives a sharp though narrow focus, is to examine decisions at the very top, treating the government and the 'military establishment' as identical. But this has been done elsewhere. Instead, I shall try to adopt an intermediate position, concentrating primarily on the service officers responsible for the suggestion of policy and its processing through the Whitehall machine.

Unlike the wider group of advisers or would-be advisers that we began with, these men enjoyed the advantage of regular and inescapable contact with the service ministers, with all of whom (save Hore-Belisha) they were on fairly easy personal terms. They were also given *collective* voices, as the three service staffs, and more importantly as the Chiefs of Staff Sub-committee of the Committee of Imperial Defence (which was itself serviced by military men, first Hankey, then Ismay). Admittedly the military bureaucrats did not always agree. But they generally sought at least to paper over the cracks, and to avoid the recurrent inter-service warfare of the 1920s and early 1930s[2] by adding individual service positions together rather than choosing between them, or by deferring either to the views of the service most directly involved or to those of their own strongest personality (generally the First Sea Lord, Chatfield). Politicians sometimes realised that the resultant unity might be only superficial. But the collective formulation of the advice of the Chiefs of Staff sounded impressive and was not lightly disregarded by strategic amateurs.

The format in which it was cast was imperial – thus:

Committee of Imperial Defence
Imperial Defence Policy
Annual Review by the Chiefs of Staff Sub-Committee, 1935
(Prepared in connection with discussions with Dominion Prime Ministers)

[begins] At the time of the Imperial Conference of 1930 the centre of gravity of the Defence Problems of the Empire lay in the Far East . . .[3]

To an extent this imperial style and language must have filtered military views and perceptions of events. And Chatfield certainly believed that 'it is our Imperial position which gives this country its great voice in the world. Unless we are willing to maintain that Imperial position we shall become once more nothing but an insignificant island in the North Sea . . . and should carry as much weight in the councils of the world as Italy or Spain.'[4]

Such empire-mindedness probably had two effects on the policy recommendations of the Chiefs of Staff. One was to enhance the importance they attached to imperial communications and interests: 'The broad principles on which our Empire strategy has always been based should not be forgotten, nor should the lessons of history be overlooked. The greater our commitments to Europe, the less will be our ability to secure our Empire and its communications.'[5] This outlook must also have reinforced the inclination towards caution (even pessimism) that was in any case natural to soldiers of the period; for, as Chatfield put it, 'We are in the remarkable position of not wanting to quarrel with anybody because we have got most of the world already . . . and we only want to keep what we have got and prevent others from taking it away from us' – no easy task, given that the empire was 'disjointed, disconnected and highly vulnerable. It is even open to debate whether it is in reality strategically defensible.'[6]

Interesting as such speculations are, one should not overstress them. For the services' own strategic interests seem to have done more than imperial sentiment to determine their attitudes. To meet the Kaiser's fleet the navy had, after all, cut its strength elsewhere and concentrated in home waters; after victory it was bound to look east, since the most likely threat now came from the capital ships of Japan. Most interwar RAF experience was colonial; but considerations of aircraft range meant that its strategic concern had to lie with its neighbours, first France, then Germany. Only the army had a choice – between colonial commitments and the dispatch of another Expeditionary Force to northern France – and it is probably no accident that soldiers were far more vocally divided as to their service's role than were sailors or airmen. As for forebodings of the empire's fragility, Whitehall never advocated the only response that Hitler believed logical, positive alignment *with* Germany to secure her help in maintaining it. Should the worst come to the worst, deliverance was rather looked for (though none too confidently) from the United States, which, while generally friendly to Britain herself, was hostile both to colonial rule and to its economic counterpart, imperial preference.

Appeasement, then, did not mean entering the German camp. But like 'establishment' it is an elusive concept. Hopefully the meanings I attach to it will become clear as I proceed. But one should note in passing that it was applied also to non-fascist countries – thus the Treaty Ports were handed over to the Irish Free State (despite some apprehensions from the navy, but with the enthusiastic support of an army which might otherwise have had to defend them); and (with strong naval endorsement) Britain cultivated Turkey, permitting the re-militarisation of the Dardanelles in 1936 and facilitating the transfer of Hatay from French Syria in 1937–9. Neither Eire nor Turkey could, in isolation, have been much of a threat to British interests. But their goodwill was important in a situation in which Britain was not alone equal to all the challenges to which she might be exposed.

On a larger scale, exactly the same rationale applied to attempts to appease Italy:

> We consider it to be a cardinal requirement of our national and imperial security that our foreign policy should be so conducted as to avoid . . . a situation in which we might be confronted simultaneously with the hostility, open or veiled, of Japan in the Far East, Germany in the West, and any power on the main line of communication between the two.[7]

> Even today we could face without apprehension an emergency either in the Far East or in the Mediterranean, provided that we were free . . . to concentrate sufficient strength in one or other of these areas . . . But the outstanding feature of the present situation is the increasing probability that a war started in any one of these three areas [the third being Western Europe] may extend to one or both of the other two . . . we cannot foresee the time when our defence forces will be strong enough to safeguard our territory, trade and vital interests against Germany, Italy and Japan simultaneously. We cannot, therefore, exaggerate the importance, from the point of view of Imperial defence, of any political or international action that can be taken to reduce the numbers of our potential enemies or to gain the support of potential allies.[8]

These two much-quoted passages sum up the naval case for appeasement. And, in most of what follows, I shall concentrate (as the Chiefs of Staff generally did) on the linked challenges to British interests in the Far East, Western Europe and the Mediterranean.

But to understand the reactions of the Chiefs of Staff one must begin (as they often did) with an assessment of the legacy of the 1920s. 'Except in so far as the country has in the years since the war allowed its defences to deteriorate progressively, the situation is none of our making', remarked the Third DRC Report somewhat smugly.[9] But it had been exacerbated by the vast expansion of British defence commitments implicit in the principle of collective security: 'It is almost impossible to forecast the nations with which we might be brought into conflict owing to a breach of the Covenant and still more impossible to forecast those on whose material support we could count.'[10] Formally the Third DRC Report (written at the height of the Abyssinian crisis) stopped just short of denouncing the League and all its works. But only just – the committee referred, as it had a year earlier, to 'the state of *moral disarmament* of the population' and recommended a 'campaign for the enlightenment of public opinion': 'In particular . . . the importance of defence should be emphasised in our educational system at least to the same extent as, and indeed as an integral element in, the propaganda for peace and the League of Nations that is carried on today in our schools.'[11] The opening shots of such a campaign had, indeed, already been fired in the form of the 1935 Defence White Paper:

> Hitherto . . . public opinion in this country has tended to assume that nothing is required for the maintenance of peace except the existing international political machinery, and that the older methods of defence – navies, armies and air forces – . . . are no longer required. The force of world events, however, has shown that this assumption is premature.[12]

By accident the White Paper went out over the initials of the Prime Minister, James Ramsay MacDonald, who seemed thereby to be renouncing the convictions of a lifetime devoted to appeasement in the sense in which it was then generally understood.[13]

More privately leading military men were anxious to ensure that the League never again led them into trouble. In May 1936 Colonel Pownall (of the CID) noted in his diary:

> It is no good thinking that Articles 10 and 16 of the Covenant can remain. People who rely on them for safety will be let down . . . This the smaller nations are particularly alive to . . . If France wants to keep the articles, we know now, also, that it is purely to make a party to defend her N.E. frontier. And we know *our* public opinion would not allow us to go to war, or even run the risk of it, for Austria or Czechoslovakia, or Memel or the Polish Corridor. So . . . we know now pretty well where we stand, the Experiment has been made and failed. How lucky that it *has* been tried out in this minor test case, lucky for all except Abyssinia.[14]

Accordingly, it is not surprising that when the Naval Staff was consulted in August about the revision of the Covenant, it produced some fairly isolationist replies. Admiral James recommended:

> Firstly – to be *honest*, and cease to enter into a maze of collective security pacts which we have no intention of honouring if the security of *our own people* is simultaneously threatened [by several powers]. Secondly – to be *sanely selfish*, by subduing the modern day passion to intrude into every two-halfpenny quarrel from the Vosges to the Great Wall, be always sure that we can safeguard that quarter of the globe painted Red on our maps (another colour presumably on Russian maps!).[15]

The Admiralty's formal reply was more restrained, but still unenthusiastic about Article 16. Discussions continued until the advent of war, with the Chiefs of Staff anxious for release from automatic obligations to apply sanctions and the government reluctant to take the lead in reforming (or dismantling) the League.

The League and disarmament were the aspects of the legacy of the 1920s to which the Chiefs of Staff drew attention. But equally important were the strategic concepts that had then crystallised. Bureaucratic infighting apart, the services went their separate ways. The army's plans to repel a Russian invasion of Afghanistan had no long-term results. The chief challenge envisaged by the navy was that of the Japanese fleet; and, since cost precluded the permanent stationing of British forces in the Far East, strategy hinged on the dispatch of a large battlefleet to Singapore to hold the Malay barrier. The security of the Dominions of Australia and New Zealand depended on the ability of the mother country to do this; and as late as March–April 1939 they were still being reassured as to the UK's 'firm intention . . . to defend Singapore as one of the two keystones on which the survival of the British Empire depended'.[16] Britain's ability to honour this pledge depended on a number of factors, of which we can note only those relevant to appeasement. The Washington treaties allowed her a 30 per cent naval superiority over Japan, and the Royal Navy rated Japanese efficiency at only 80 per cent of its own. Still this did not leave much of a margin, given that the Japanese could presumably choose their own time for a conflict. In the 1920s the scenario still looked plausible since the only other significant power in British home waters was France (which the navy did not perceive as an enemy). But in the 1930s this position was eroded by:

(1)   the rise of a potentially hostile German fleet;
(2)   the near-collision with Italy in 1935; even a successful war would have brought losses and endangered the navy's ability to contain Japan;
(3)   the longer-term alienation of an Italy that might temporarily be able to close the Mediterranean and force the British fleet to take the slower Cape route to Singapore, and that could certainly threaten British interests in the Middle East if the fleet had to be transferred eastwards.

There were three possible solutions to these dilemmas. One was to change the strategy. In 1934 Neville Chamberlain attempted to 'postpone the idea of sending out . . . a fleet . . . capable of containing the Japanese fleet or meeting it in battle'. His move was highly unpopular with the services; and Hankey induced Baldwin to scotch it by invoking Australasian susceptibilities.[17] In 1937 doubts again surfaced as to the feasibility of the policy, but the commitment was formally reaffirmed. In 1939, though, there was a sudden swing to the idea of first destroying Italy (the weakest opponent) in the Mediterranean, thus liberating British forces for subsequent dispatch elsewhere. But the realisation that such a quick success was militarily unlikely led the Chiefs of Staff that summer to abandon the plan in favour of the cultivation of Italian neutrality.[18] An alternative course, if British naval forces were inadequate for their commitments, was to seek help – from either France or the United States. Unfortunately naval discussions with France during the Abyssinian crisis had proved highly unsatisfactory; and this, together with the fear of the Chiefs of Staff that military conversations would build commitments as they had before 1914, inhibited their resumption until 1939. The new First Sea Lord, Backhouse, then set considerable store on French assistance; but it had the effect of diverting attention to the Mediterranean, the French area of concern, not of resolving the British Far Eastern dilemma. More could be hoped, in this context, from America. And from 1937 onwards, when President Roosevelt floated the idea of a joint cruiser blockade of Japan, the enticing prospect arose of a US commitment to Singapore. Discussions continued sporadically to this end. But, hints apart, Roosevelt would go no further than to return his fleet (at Britain's request in March 1939) to Honolulu to serve as a potential deterrent to Japan. Nor was it clear how much the President could deliver, even if he wished; and the British were perhaps ultra-cautious about being left in the lurch.[19] The third possible solution, if naval strategy could neither be changed nor implemented by proxy, was appeasement – of Japan and/or Germany and/or Italy; and (as we shall see later) all these courses had their advocates.

The less glamorous half of naval war was blockade. Hankey had been a believer in 'seapower and blockade' rather than the western front in the 1914–18 war, and, with Chiefs of Staff support, had held it at the forefront of strategic thinking in the 1920s[20] – it underlay a number of the British naval difficulties with the USA. Planning was taken up in 1933 *pari passu* with other aspects of rearmament, with fairly comforting results. 'In 1938 it was suggested that, if favoured by fortune . . . [Germany] might be able to maintain her industrial resistance, on the basis of stocks [supplemented from adjacent neutral countries] . . . for a year. In August 1939 this estimate was extended to "as much as eighteen months".'[21] Too much emphasis should not be attached to these precise (under-)estimates of German economic capacity. But the belief was general that Britain was bound to win a long war, and it underlay Chamberlain's confidence in late 1939 that 'Hitler had missed the bus'.

Of course, as someone remarked, when Hitler missed the bus he had a habit of turning up by taxi. He was thought to have two possible ways of doing this. One was to overrun France at the outset – a contingency that was laid before the Cabinet in 1937 but not regarded as feasible. The other was to knock out Britain from the air. 'No one can say with absolute certainty', wrote the Chief of Air Staff in April 1938, 'that a nation can be knocked out from the air, because no one has yet attempted it. There can be no doubt, however, that Germany and Italy believe it possible, as there can be no other explanation for their piling up armaments to a level which they could not hope to sustain in a long war.'[22]

This was to attribute to its opponents the RAF's own strategy, which had been thus defined by Trenchard in 1928:

It is not . . . necessary for an air force [unlike the older services], in order to defeat the enemy nation, to defeat its armed forces first. Air power can dispense with that intermediate step, can pass over the enemy navies and armies, . . . and attack the centres of production transportation and communication from which the enemy war effort is maintained. . . . We ourselves are especially vulnerable to this form of attack . . .[23]

The bomber would always get through. So the only adequate defence was deterrence, the possession of 'a number of machines equal to the independent striking force of the strongest air force within striking distance of this country'.[24] When these principles were formulated in 1923 that force had been French; and the preparation of a fifty-two-squadron RAF by way of insurance was soon allowed to slide. But with the failure of the Disarmament Conference in 1933, these precepts were dusted off and applied to Germany. And the early stages of rearmament consisted chiefly of successive air expansions to retain 'parity' with Germany, especially in bombers. In the course of 1935 parity was lost, and subsequent schemes represented attempts to *recover* it – thus in January 1937 it was submitted that Scheme H, though only 'a temporary expedient', 'taking all factors into account . . . should provide an adequate deterrent against the risk of air attack by Germany in 1939', while the following October Scheme J was put forward as 'a reasonably effective deterrent' which would 'enable us to meet Germany as nearly as possible on equal terms' by 1941 (or, at best, 1940). It was a truism that the years of appeasement took place against this background of at least temporary air inferiority, combined with a gross exaggeration of the likely effects of strategic bombing. And the Air Staff would not let anyone forget it: they

> would be failing in their duty were they not to express their considered opinion that the Metropolitan Air Force in general, and the Bomber Command in particular, are at present almost totally unfitted for war; that, unless the production of new and up-to-date aircraft can be expedited, they will not be fully fit for war for at least two and a half years; and that even [then they might well not be equal to Germany].[25]

In November–December 1937, however, the civilian ministers forced through (against strong air force and Foreign Office[26] opposition) a change of emphasis from bombers to fighters, and secured 'a revised programme based on the conception that at the outset of war our first task is to repulse a knock-out blow within the first few weeks, trusting thereafter to defeat the enemy by a process of exhaustion, resulting from our command of the sea'.[27] In keeping with this change 1938–9 saw a greatly increased emphasis on anti-aircraft guns, civil defence and the deployment of radar (which had, indeed, been energetically developed since 1935, but which was only now coming on stream). All this promised a rapid improvement in at least the subjective defence posture. But it still left the country alarmingly exposed in 1938 itself. And this exposure constituted the central feature of Ismay's *Note on . . . whether it would be to our military advantage to fight Germany now, or to postpone the issue*: any enhancement of Germany's war potential or her position on land (made by swallowing Czechoslovakia, fortifications, and so on) would be more than offset by improvements in British defences against air attack:

> We shall have heavily insured ourselves against the greatest danger to which we are at present exposed; indeed by substantially reducing Germany's only chance of a rapid decision, we shall have provided a strong deterrent against her making the attempt.
>
> It follows, therefore, that, from the military point of view, time is in our favour, and that, if war with Germany has to come, it would be better to fight her in say 6–12 months' time than to accept the present challenge.[28]

Munich was not just an attempt to buy time. But that element entered into it. And, since the military were more pessimistic than Chamberlain about the prospect of avoiding an ultimate clash with Germany, it probably figured even more strongly in their support for his policy than it did in the Prime Minister's own mind.[29]

Within these broad lines of military thinking there was naturally room for disputes – as to what role (if any) the army should play, as to the control of the Fleet Air Arm, and as to the relative importance of the fighting services and that fourth arm, finance, that alone could enable Britain to conduct a long war. But the basic principles were accepted throughout Whitehall, and were drawn on, together with the other arguments for appeasement, by non-military as well as military figures. Thus Vansittart (Permanent Under-Secretary for Foreign Affairs, but also a former member of the Defence Requirements Committee) contended, in a memorandum endorsed and circulated to the Cabinet by Eden in February 1936, that

> If neither the devastations of experience, nor strength nor justice nor generosity in others . . . can avail to deter Germany from attempting once more to wrench the world to suit her book – and her book is still *Mein Kampf* unpurged – if the clouds must indeed return after the rain, then our civilisation is doomed. Its only chance of survival is to avoid a fresh and final test . . . I would say definitely that the present rulers of Germany are bent on eventual adventures which will be almost certain to unleash a European war. What we *can* do is to gain time, hoping against hope that there may be some change of heart or system in Germany, or – with better ground – that we and our League associates may within a respite of x years . . . grow to a position where defence can make attack too hopeless to be worth while. But no member of the League has embarked on this course in time, and Germany will be ready before the League . . . That gap in time has somehow to be bridged. Would not a colonial restitution [or – pp. 9, 13 – the agreed re-militarisation of the Rhineland], as part of a reasonable and comprehensive settlement, . . . justifiable in any case, be doubly so if no other bridging material can be devised?[30]

My main thesis, then, is that the chief military contribution to our theme was the establishment (in the 1920s as much as the 1930s) of strategic parameters within which appeasement was a very natural reaction. In the second half of my paper I shall look briefly at some specific policies of appeasement, and finally turn to the role of the military in the shift in 1939 towards a policy of containment.

First, then, the appeasement of Japan. The idea that co-operation with Japan 'may well entail fewer further military commitments than thwarting her' surfaced in the wake of the Manchurian crisis, and commended itself to the Chiefs of Staff in view of the then indefensibility of the British position in the Far East.[31] Unsurprisingly, work on the Singapore defences was resumed in 1932, and further measures were recommended by the Defence Requirements Sub-Committee in 1934. But the DRC set its sights firmly on Germany as 'the ultimate potential enemy', and stressed the necessity of returning 'at least to our old terms of cordiality and mutual respect with Japan'.[32] This represented a toning down of the strong views of Sir Warren Fisher (Permanent Under-Secretary to the Treasury) that only 'if we can emancipate ourselves from thraldom to the United States and thus free ourselves to establish durable relations with Japan [can we] concentrate on the paramount danger at our very threshold'.[33] Fisher's hope was that reconciliation with Japan would make it possible to reduce naval rearmament expenditure, thus leaving more money for the army.[34] And though pro-Japanese sentiment was by no means confined to the Treasury, it was always a Treasury speciality. The chief opponent of thus risking American friendship was the Foreign Office; and its opposition always prevailed, aided admittedly by the real difficulties of using either the 1934–5 Naval Disarmament talks or the 1935–6 Leith-Ross mission to woo Japan. The Admiralty straddled the fence, anxious, as Roskill puts it, 'to reduce their commitments by reaching an agreement with Japan . . . [but] certainly not prepared to do so at the price of alienating the USA'.[35] All this precluded any serious attempt at appeasement – but also at resistance, since (as the Chiefs of Staff put it during the 1939 Tientsin crisis) 'without the active co-operation of the United States . . . it would not be justifiable, from the military point of view . . . to take any avoidable action which might lead to hostilities with Japan'.[36] The dilemma did not in fact become serious till 1939 when Japan forced a British climb-down over the principle of Chinese sanctuary in their concessions, followed next year by the temporary closure of the Burma Road.

To return to Europe, Germany's withdrawal from the League and determination to rearm posed the problem of what (if anything) should be done about it. Early in 1935 the French proposed, as a prerequisite for a relaxation of the Versailles Treaty, a mutual Franco-Anglo-German guarantee against air bombardment; and, with Foreign Office help, they bounced the British Cabinet into agreeing it in principle. The Chiefs of Staff, however, saw the proposal as either unworkable or simply an open-ended commitment to France, and (with Hankey's over-enthusiastic assistance) they torpedoed it.[37] Another alternative was a joint Anglo-Franco-Italian approach to the negotiation with Germany of a general settlement including a measure of agreed rearmament. This was implicit in the Stresa Conference of April 1935. But the following June a bilateral Anglo-German Naval Treaty was concluded, conceding to Germany a fleet 35 per cent the size of the British (more in respect of submarines, but technical developments were believed to have reduced their importance). The treaty was, as Eden admitted, not easy to square with Stresa. But both the Admiralty and the Foreign Office viewed it rather in the context of the Second London Naval Conference discussions. As early as July 1934 the Admiralty had envisaged a significant German navy,[38] nor was Britain put off by subsequent German hints that they would claim a fleet 35 per cent of its own. When in March 1935 Hitler formally demanded this ratio, Simon's chief concern was that it might provoke French and Italian building and so unsettle the whole naval pyramid.[39] As against this, the Admiralty clearly wished to settle while it still could, and also hoped to use agreement with Germany to strengthen its hand in the current international negotiations. Accordingly Britain decided, before Stresa, to proceed on its own. Talks opened in June. And Germany secured British acceptance of the 35 per cent ratio by combining insistence on this as a prerequisite with reassurance elsewhere – the ratio would be a 'final' one irrespective of naval building by third parties, and Germany also accepted the British position on the technical modalities of warship limitation. France was rather sore at this outcome; but America and Japan (the principal naval powers besides the UK) were quite agreeable. At home even Vansittart and Fisher approved, while the Admiralty long remained enthusiastic: as late as April 1938 the Chiefs of Staff were still opposing naval conversations with France on the grounds that, if leaked, they might imperil the 1935 Treaty 'to the maintenance of which the Admiralty attach great importance'.

But if the 1935 Treaty with Germany reassured the Admiralty, it was fully offset by events elsewhere. Consciousness of their overall strategic position may have inhibited the politicians from initiating military action against Italy (and the Chiefs of Staff were certainly anxious that it should), but it did not stop them adopting a policy that would inevitably estrange her. 'It is a disaster', wrote Chatfield privately, 'that our statesmen have got us into this quarrel with Italy, who ought to be our best friend because her position in the Mediterranean was a dominant one'; but as a result of the 'miserable business of collective security' he was 'preparing for war . . . which we have always been told could never happen', to prevent an Italian conquest of Abyssinia to which he personally had 'no objection' as it would prove 'a weakness rather than a strength'.[40] The more the navy prepared for such a war, the colder their feet got (especially as it became clear how little assistance could be anticipated from France). All this underlay the Hoare–Laval pact; but equally it did not prevent Eden from announcing British support for oil sanctions in March 1936. The military had, of course, acquiesced (though the First Lord of the Admiralty had formally recorded his dissent at the relevant Cabinet meeting).[41] However, with Hitler's sudden remilitarisation of the Rhineland on 7 March 1936, the Chiefs of Staff panicked and produced a series of gloomy appreciations of the defencelessness of the country

so long as a large proportion of our naval, military and air forces is locked up in the Mediterranean . . . The naval position, for instance, is such that

> if we became involved in war at the present time with Germany, even if we at once mobilised, the defence of our coasts and of our trade would mainly fall upon French naval forces . . .

> We realise that the main object of the Government's policy is to avoid any risk of war with Germany . . .
> [However] . . . if there is the smallest danger of being drawn into commitments which might lead to war with Germany, we ought at once to disengage ourselves from our present responsibilities in the Mediterranean, which have exhausted practically the whole of our meagre forces.[42]

The government had never had any intention of stopping Jerry going into his own back-garden. But it took seriously these admonitions about cutting British forces in the Mediterranean, and implemented them gradually over the following months.

When the dust settled, the military mood was one adverse to commitments and anxious for the negotiation of a détente with any or all of Britain's major opponents. Thus Pownall's diaries:

> Meanwhile the F.O., and Van[sittart] in particular, keep on saying there's going to be a European war in not more than two years. So there will be, as I've frequently said, if we continue tied to the French and don't come to an arrangement with Germany.[43]

> . . . Why should we make a unilateral pledge [as Eden wished, to the defence of the ex-sanctionist powers, Greece, Turkey and Yugoslavia] . . . We want *peace* in the Mediterranean and as quickly as possible, and freedom to withdraw our forces untrammelled and undelayed by any more assurances.[44]

Similarly in January 1937 Chatfield regarded France as 'an unreliable ally' and saw Britain standing 'more or less alone and unsupported in both hemispheres'. A simultaneous war in both would be fatal, so it was essential 'to make an agreement in one area or the other', aiming for 'an understanding with Japan' and eschewing a continental war with Germany, which should be given 'reasonable satisfaction . . . as part of a general settlement'.[45] Such attitudes fortified the services in refusing to incur major new commitments – Eden would have liked to blockade Spain to prevent the arrival of 'volunteers', and later in 1937 he suggested sinking the Nationalist cruiser *Canarias*.[46] But they did not, in 1936–7, lead to any very positive initiatives.

In the autumn of 1937, however, pressure became more positive. Already in early November Washington learned that the British services 'had represented to their government their wish to compose their differences with Italy' to leave themselves free 'to deal with the Far East menace'.[47] Later in the month, in response to an invitation from the Minister for Co-ordination of Defence, the Chiefs of Staff submitted a *Comparison of the Strength of Great Britain with that of certain other Nations*. I have already cited its essential conclusion that it was impossible to 'exaggerate the importance . . . of any political or international action that can be taken to reduce the numbers of our potential enemies and to gain the support of potential allies'. Of the two, the reduction of the number of potential enemies apparently appealed the more strongly, judging by the Chiefs' cool response to Foreign Office commendation of the resumption of staff talks with France and Belgium – 'it is most important from the military stand-point, that at the present time we should not appear to have both feet in the French camp'.[48] Such military pressure was not, in itself, decisive: Eden had been sniping at the Chiefs of Staff since December, and he induced the Cabinet to overrule their paper on staff conversations.[49] But fundamentally the Prime Minister agreed with the military. Accordingly when Eden could not accept the policy of an immediate approach to Italy, Chamberlain (with full Cabinet support) proceeded without him. The services were no doubt pleased with Eden's supercession,[50] but they had not, in any direct way, brought it about.

Rather clearer is the Chiefs of Staff involvement in the question of Czechoslovakia. Immediately after the *Anschluss* Chamberlain asked them to report on the military implications of a British guarantee. The result was, in the words of the new Foreign Secretary, Lord Halifax, 'an extremely melancholy document'. The *Anschluss* enabled Germany to exert enormous 'peaceful' economic pressure on Czechoslovakia. It had also so turned Czech border defences that nothing

> can prevent Germany either from invading and overrunning Bohemia or inflicting a decisive defeat on the Czechoslovakian Army. If politically it is deemed necessary to restore Czechoslovakia's lost integrity, this aim will entail war with Germany, and her defeat may mean a prolonged struggle . . . by a slow process of attrition and starvation.

It was 'more than probable' that both Italy and Japan would take advantage of such a struggle, converting it into a world war. The Chiefs of Staff cited their earlier warning that British forces would not be equal to such a contingency, and felt that, in German eyes, it would reduce the deterrent effect of the hostility of the British Empire; this would be further discounted if Berlin believed it 'could obtain a knock-out blow against this country by the ruthless use of the German air-striking force'.[51] 'In view of this Report', Halifax continued, 'he felt he was not in a position to recommend a policy involving a risk of war. Consequently he had to consider the alternatives'. Not all the Cabinet accepted this analysis,[52] but most did; and 'several Members . . . including the Prime Minister and the Foreign Secretary, admitted that they had approached the question with a bias in favour of some kind of guarantee to Czecho-Slovakia, but that the investigation . . . had changed their views'.[53] If this is to be taken at face value, it would seem that the Chiefs of Staff had at the least prevented the hardening of British policy after the *Anschluss*. Their advice continued unchanged throughout the Czech crisis – we have already noted Ismay's views on the desirability of postponing hostilities until British air defences had improved, and there is ample evidence that they weighed heavily with Chamberlain. It should also be noted that the judgements of the British military as to the indefensibility of Czechoslovakia (or at least Bohemia) were constantly reinforced by their French counterparts; and British fears of a knock-out blow from the air were restrained in comparison with those emanating from General Vuillemin of the French Air Staff.

If the military softened British policy in 1938, in 1939 they tended to harden it *vis-à-vis* Germany (though *not* Italy and Japan). The shift is striking, and can perhaps be ascribed to four interconnected factors:

(i)   a growing confidence in British strength in the air, and (to a lesser extent) on land;
(ii) changes in the balance of power within the Cabinet and Whitehall, which reduced the power of the Treasury and (to some extent) the Prime Minister and enhanced that of Lord Halifax, the services and, in particular, the army;
(iii) the army's success in securing a commitment to the dispatch of an Expeditionary Force to France;
(iv) a general shift in national sentiment reflected in (as much as caused by) changes in the views of the defence establishment.

Space permits only the most summary treatment of these themes. But it is clear that, rightly or wrongly, Chamberlain felt the Munich respite had been well used. In February 1939 he wrote that 'they could not make nearly such a mess of us now as they could have done then, while we could make much more of a mess of them'. This and other factors had enabled him to take that firmer tone 'which some of my critics have applauded, without apparently understanding the connection between diplomatic and strategic strength'. In April (after Albania) he referred to 'the improvement of the military position of ourselves and France'.[54] And in December he noted 'that Hitler missed the bus in September 1938. He could have dealt France and ourselves a terrible blow, perhaps a mortal blow, then. The opportunity will not recur.'[55] Undeniably a great deal of progress *had* been made in the re-equipment of the RAF with modern fighters, the deployment of the radar screen and the improvement of air raid precautions (both active and passive). Also, though the army was in the throes of crash expansion, at least precise arrangements had been made for the dispatch of the Expeditionary Force to France. Had war come in 1938 it would have gone, but very much worse prepared. But it must be noted that most of these gains had materialised in the second half of 1938–9, and Chamberlain's confidence of February is somewhat curious.

The first signs of the shift in the balance of power in the Cabinet had come in September 1938. Chamberlain had wished to accept Hitler's Godesberg proposals. The Cabinet was not sure. And when discussion resumed the next day, Halifax (who had been subjected to much Foreign Office lobbying) urged rejection. The Cabinet did not accept the proposals, and thus incurred a substantial risk of war. Halifax never broke with Chamberlain; but it is possible to see him as the pivotal member of the Cabinet on a number of key issues in 1938–9. Thus he successfully supported the army in pressing for the abandonment of Chamberlain's 'limited liability' strategy[56] and its replacement by a commitment to the dispatch of troops to France, and (later in 1939) for the introduction of conscription. Also, though (like Chamberlain) Halifax was temperamentally averse to the idea of a Russian alliance, he recognised the force of the French and Chiefs of Staff case for it rather before the Prime Minister, and his conversion appears to have been decisive. In departmental terms the three bodies most closely involved with the formulation of strategic/foreign policy were the Foreign Office, the Chiefs of Staff (who might have to implement it) and the Treasury (which would have to pay for it). Chamberlain had always been closest to the Treasury, but he paid close attention to the Chiefs of Staff, and more particularly the First Sea Lord and the Chief of Air Staff. The losers had been the army (purged in 1937 by Chamberlain's 'new broom' Hore-Belisha and officially reduced to planning for a purely colonial role), and, as was spectacularly demonstrated by Eden's resignation over Italian apppeasement, the Foreign Office. But in 1939 the army escaped from its subordination to the other two services, while politically Halifax proved a far more effective Foreign Office head than had Eden. So it was the Treasury that was reduced to fighting an isolated rearguard action. The RAF had been conceded temporary *carte blance* in November 1938. And in expanding the army the following February the Cabinet accepted that it was incurring financial commitments that could not be sustained in the long run. It did so believing (in Halifax's words) 'that the present state of tension could not last indefinitely and must result either in war or in the destruction of the Nazi regime'.[57] Psychologically such a situation must have been conducive to a show-down.

This army expansion was the result of the definitive decision to commit troops to France. The issue had been in contention ever since 1934. Mindful probably of recent violent inter-service disputes the then Chiefs of Staff had submitted to the Defence Requirements Sub-Committee a 'balanced' programme of something for each service. But (as became clear at the last minute) the RAF had botched its contribution.[58] Common sense as well as constitutional propriety therefore impelled a re-examination by the Cabinet, in which Chamberlain was well to the fore. Considerations of finance, public opinion and strategy[59] led to the expansion of the RAF and the curtailment of army proposals. And the process continued at subsequent defence reviews until in 1937 it was decided that the army should be equipped only for hostilities in an extra-European theatre. This decision the army never accepted, not (as Pownall's diary makes clear) from any special closeness to France, but out of a mixture of resentment that the army should be so overshadowed, conviction that the idea of a 'limited liability' war was a mirage, and concern for the fate of troops sent (as they undoubtedly would be if deterrence failed) unprepared into Europe:

> Haining then argued that we must be prepared to go all out with the resources of the nation in another war. The Army could not be confined to a limited role, leaving the main effort to the other Services . . . From examination they had found that there would be five million men over,

when all industrial needs and all those of the other Services had been fully met. 'It is unthinkable that we should not use them for the Army'. Deverell [then CIGS] endorsed this.

Similarly, Pownall describes as his 'Credo' that 'if we got embroiled in a major European war sooner or later, and I believe *sooner*, British troops would go to France. If that was not recognised . . . in peace then the troops would go untrained and ill-equipped . . . – with dire results.'[60]

Until Munich the army did not go beyond bureaucratic foot-dragging. Afterwards the War Office embarked on a remarkable campaign of persuasion at all levels. Pownall even asked the British military attaché in Paris to solicit French intervention and subsequently grumbled at the weakness of Daladier's response.[61] Daladier might have been initially disappointing, but French pressure for a British *effort du sang* undoubtedly came through in the course of the winter. And, together with the Franco-German Declaration and discussions, it convinced Halifax that only a British continental commitment could preserve the French alliance. He accordingly helped the army in its attempts to convert the Cabinet. Meanwhile the navy's position was transformed by the new First Sea Lord, Admiral Backhouse. Pownall attributed his support to the simple view 'that it's no good having an Army if it is not ready for war . . . And he is very strong too that campaigns will not be won by Air Forces but by the occupation of territory.'[62] Captain Roskill thinks the chief factor was a desire for the help of France's two heavy battle-cruisers in dealing with German commerce-raiders in the Atlantic.[63] In any case Backhouse's support had worn down the RAF's opposition by the end of January 1939.[64] The final factor was the crisis occasioned by (false) intelligence that Germany was on the point of overrunning the Netherlands.[65] Not everybody was entirely convinced. But it led to a decision that this must be resisted, if need be in isolation, and inspired the government to accept the continental commitment, solicit staff talks with France and promise immediate co-operation against any threat to her 'vital interests, from whatever quarter it came'.

The direct effect of these moves was to open the British strategic policy-making process to French influence. In fact the two countries were in surprising agreement. So this had only limited results. France reinforced the British 1939 trend we have already noticed towards a hard line against Italy in the Mediterranean (even at the expense of the Far East), but could not offer sufficient assistance to make it a viable policy in the short run. The French were also, in Halifax's words, 'insistent that negotiations with Russia should not be allowed to break down'.[66] This powerfully reinforced the urgings of the Chiefs of Staff, and brought first Halifax and then Chamberlain reluctantly to accept the necessity of negotiating with the USSR on the latter's terms: but negotiations still broke down. So the direct diplomatic consequences of the British continental commitment of 1939 were surprisingly small. More interesting, though quite imponderable, is the question of what results such a firm commitment *on land* would have had if made in 1934 or 1936. There is the view that it would have produced an altogether more confident and effective Western response to the challenge of the fascist powers. And certainly one of the internal British arguments against staff talks was that they might encourage France to rashness. My own view, for what it is worth, is that such a commitment before mid-1935 could well have led to a more co-operative French stance over Abyssinia and thus to more effective League sanctions. But the effect of such a commitment after March 1936 might have been limited: French foreign and military policy were not co-ordinated; there was little joint planning with her Czech and Soviet allies; the British military contribution before 1939 would still have been small; and before Munich France did not in fact look for a large one, though she would (wisely) have welcomed the aid of mechanised divisions.

Space remains only for one final question, the extent to which the defence establishment merely reflected a much wider shift in British sentiment. This began with Godesberg. The Chiefs of Staff view that 'to take offensive against Germany now would be like "a man attacking a tiger before he has loaded his gun"'[67] can be challenged, but was not then very seriously contested. Nevertheless the Cabinet declined to accept the Godesberg proposals, thus making war more likely than not. In many ways the Chiefs of Staff paper of 25 January 1939 on *German Aggression against Holland* was a re-run of that on the *Military Implications of German Aggression against Czechoslovakia*: Holland could not be defended, and her restoration 'would depend on the later course of the war'. British intervention would almost inevitably trigger that of Italy and 'possibly' also that of Japan; even with France as an ally, this would produce 'a position more serious than the Empire has ever faced before. The ultimate outcome . . . might well depend upon the intervention of other Powers, in particular of the United States'. But the paper's recommendations were quite different from those of the previous year:

> failure to intervene would have such moral and other repercussions as would seriously undermine our position in the eyes of the Dominions and the world in general. We might thus be deprived of support in a sub-sequent struggle between Germany and the British Empire . . . Therefore we have, as we see it, no choice but to regard a German invasion of Holland as a direct challenge to our security.[68]

Both morally and strategically, of course, the Netherlands was in a position very different from that of Czechoslovakia; and the Chiefs of Staff were probably right in their reading of Dominion and US sentiment. But this reading appears to have been founded on instinct rather than inquiry. And its function was arguably to rationalise their disregard of the doubts that (as they admitted) arose 'from the present strength of our defensive preparations'.

The final evolution of British foreign policy, that towards a proliferation of trip-wire guarantees and an attempt at alliance with Russia, is controversial. My present view is that the government, under a compulsion to do *something*, slithered incrementally from one expedient to another, finishing up in a position it would certainly not have chosen *ab initio*. This was chiefly the work of Halifax and the Foreign Office.[69] And the Chiefs of Staff played at first a minor role, being consulted only sporadically and even then sometimes under restrictive terms of reference. Also it has been claimed that their views were misrepresented to ministers in late March by Chatfield, now the new Minister for Co-ordination of Defence. At the same time much of their advice was hedged or hesitant. On occasion, too, they changed their minds. The RAF was distinctly cooler than the army towards commitments to both Poland and Russia.[70] And I have encountered no evidence of any strong feeling in military quarters that the government was acting unwisely in setting their views aside, though (for example) Pownall's diaries abound in such complaints in other connections.

On 18 March 1939, during the Romanian scare that followed the German occupation of Prague, the Chiefs of Staff were distinctly gloomy: if Germany gained control of Romania she would be able to circumvent the blockade that was to be the decisive British weapon in a long war. An ultimatum from Britain, France, Poland *and* Russia might deter her, and the two latter countries should therefore be approached diplomatically. Russia was perhaps more important than Poland, but unless *both* were prepared to assist it would not be well to challenge Germany, for the November 1937 warning against simultaneous war with Japan, Germany and Italy 'still holds good today'.[71] Later in the month Chatfield told his colleagues that, from the military point of view, Poland was probably the best potential ally; and it was only after a guarantee of Poland and Romania had been agreed that the (Deputy) Chiefs of Staff were again formally consulted on the military implications. They were still depressed: such a guarantee might encourage its recipients in intransigence and so 'tend to precipitate a European war before our forces are in any way prepared'; on the other hand, if Britain had to fight Germany, it would be better to do so with Poland as an ally rather than allowing her to be absorbed. For her conquest and garrisoning 'against possible attack from Russia' would tie down German troops that would otherwise suffice for the overrunning of the Netherlands.[72] This was rather ambiguous: Chamberlain is said to have taken it as criticism and prevented its circulation to the full Cabinet.[73] But at that Cabinet Chatfield used it to press (successfully) for a public guarantee to Poland. There remained the question of the desirability and practicability of associating Russia with this guarantee. On this the Chiefs of Staff appear to have shared the general view that too open an association with Russia would be a diplomatic liability: on 10 May (admittedly at short notice) they still preferred to retain Spanish neutrality rather than to seek a Russian alliance, largely on the assumption that, at worst, Russia would be neutral. However, on 16 May, faced with the prospect of a possible breakdown of talks with Russia, they reversed themselves and plumped for an alliance: Chatfield then put their views to his colleagues with considerable vigour; and, as the French were similarly 'insistent', first Halifax and then Chamberlain were brought round.[74]

Ultimately, then, the views of the Chiefs of Staff were crucial. Their military rationale was the need to tie up Germany's troops in the east and to reinforce the blockade by denying her raw materials. The USSR could have performed both these tasks without crossing its own borders – indeed as a sympathetic neutral. Stalin chose not to. But though his defection may have destroyed much of the strategic logic of the containment policy Britain had embarked on that spring, it does not seem greatly to have affected British military confidence. 'If the Nazi regime can be so discredited that it disappears from Germany by German action, i.e. without war, so much the better. If that doesn't happen we must have a war. We can't lose it. Last September we might have lost a *short* war. Now we shouldn't, nor a long war either.'[75] So the military establishment stood by the Polish guarantee, pressing for mobilisation and, in Gort's words, doing 'all we can to keep' the politicians 'up to scratch'.[76]

To this end the military felt able to invoke parliamentary and public opinion. Thus, while urging Hore-Belisha on 27 August to stiffen a draft note to Hitler, Gort, Grigg and Pownall 'got him to see the weakness of' the proposed 'line. I told him the Government would not last a day if such a thing were published.'[77] The contrast with the pre-1939 military invocation of public opinion to head off continental commitments is striking. In both cases the services' assessment of the public's wishes may well have been right. But (in the pre-opinion poll age) it must have been largely instinctive. Nor were such service assessments devoid of institutional self-interest, as emerges clearly from the rival RAF and army views of the desirability of fitting out an Expeditionary Force for France.[78] In the circumstances it is remarkable how closely the evolution of the strategic judgements of the military establishment came to parallel that of public opinion at large. There may have been a divergence at the start of our period, when rearmament (both material and mental) seemed self-evidently desirable to the services, whereas a very sizeable body of the public still adhered to disarmament and the League. But even here the emphasis placed, within the rearmament programme, on the RAF undoubtedly reflected public preferences. And after 1935 military and public opinion probably only got out of step, and then not greatly so, over Abyssinia and Godesberg – in both of which crises the services urged fervently and unitedly that war should be avoided whereas the public (though bitterly divided) was slightly readier to advocate it.

My general conclusion, then, is that both psychologically and constitutionally the military establishment was well integrated into the British political system.[79] (Only the army's lobbying, after Munich, for the revival of a continental expeditionary force went clearly beyond constitutional propriety.) Accordingly the armed forces could be overruled. But their opinions were highly valued and frequently solicited by a somewhat bureaucratically minded government. The Chiefs of Staff were thus often important contributors to the detailed formulation of British policy. They also had a much wider influence in that their strategic concepts entered into the received wisdom of the day, and so did much to set the parameters within which policy was made.

Unhappily many of these concepts seem, with hindsight, to have been distinctly questionable. No doubt one lesson is that defective military strategies are self-imposed handicaps. The Maginot line disastrously limited French military options. And neither 'main fleet to Singapore' nor the British deterrent bomber force of 1934–7 were really viable. But as long as there were no apparent alternatives, the former invited Italian blackmail;

and the latter led the government to chase unavailingly after 'parity' in an arm less important than it believed, and so to conduct foreign affairs from an unnecessarily weak position.[80] Britain ultimately extricated itself from an exclusive dependence on bombers, but never resolved the problems inherent in the naval defence of Singapore, indeed persisted with the policy despite increasing doubts after 1937 as to its feasibility. The moral may seem obvious; but this perspective is perhaps deceptively simple. For there can be no certainty in war; only the event in 1940 could demonstrate the fallacy of another premiss underlying British thinking about hostilities with Germany, namely, that France could withstand any land attack. It is in any case doubtful how far military policy can derive from strategic considerations alone – and regrettably current troop dispositions in West Germany owe more to history, finance and politics than they do to purely military desiderata.

More generally, while Western behaviour in the 1930s can easily be understood, it is a paradigm case of how not to run an alliance. From 1934 France was recognised as vital to British security and vice-versa; and in 1936 the remilitarisation of the Rhineland converted the contingent British responsibility, under Locarno, for France's eastern borders into a definite guarantee. But both countries took an essentially narrow and short-term view of their national interests; so, when these apparently clashed, both preferred to maintain complete freedom of action, a policy enthusiastically endorsed (at least until Munich) by the British Chiefs of Staff – 'the very term "staff conversations" has a sinister purport and gives an impression . . . of mutually assumed military collaboration'.[81] Usually it was France, as the *demandeur*, who suffered most from this; but during the Abyssinian crisis the relationship was reversed, and (as the British military did not forget)[82] French foot-dragging undercut the British position. Much the same can be said in a wider context. Warsaw, for instance, viewed Paris much as Paris viewed London. And there are some similarities, too, in the Anglo-American relationship – Roosevelt's hints of joint action, whether naval or economic, started in 1937, but only after Pearl Harbor were we, as he put it on the phone to Churchill, 'all in the same boat now'. In short all countries in the 1930s exploited the advantages of an 'insular' position *vis-à-vis* their more exposed associates. And, as a result, the collective weight of the countries opposed to the Axis powers was much less than the sum of their parts.

Responsibility for such a state of affairs obviously goes far beyond the British military establishment; and indeed, as Brian Bond shows elsewhere in this volume,[83] one of the arguments Hankey invoked on behalf of a continental Expeditionary Force was that of its *psychological* effect on 'our potential allies'. But the 1930s Chiefs of Staff were very much creatures of their time, doubting the military value of possible associates, reluctant to be drawn into trouble through a repetition of the rigid alliance system of 1914, and, in Sir John Slessor's words, 'never willing to take into account the forces of any potential ally in deciding the strength of the home defences of this country against what might well be a vital blow'. Though a good case can be made out for all these attitudes individually, their cumulative effect was probably unfortunate, and certainly did not succeed in deterring Hitler. So they became less fashionable. And when, after the war, a new challenge was identified from Stalin, it was met (admittedly under strategically more secure American leadership) in a much more collective fashion. In time this approach, too, has come under attack. But it is interesting to note that it appealed to a number of the survivors from the British military establishment of the 1930s: Ismay, for instance, became the first Secretary-General of NATO; while Slessor, Director of the Air Staff Plans branch from 1937, re-ran his earlier rearmament experiences as Chief of Air Staff, and (rightly or wrongly) was convinced that 'if we had seized the several opportunities that were open to us in 1937 and 1938 to cement an Anglo-French-Soviet defensive Alliance, and had seriously got down to building the Air Force that we felt our own strategic requirements justified [instead of pursuing 'parity'] – if in fact we had treated the German menace of 1937 as we did the Soviet menace of 1950 – there would have been no war'.[84]

Notes: Chapter 12

1   B. Liddell Hart, *The Memoirs of Captain Liddell Hart*, 2 vols (London, 1965), Vol. I, p. 326.
2   In the 1920s the other two services had often doubted the need for an air force, and vice-versa. Bones of contention remained throughout the rearmament period – 'bombers versus battleships', the Fleet Air Arm and the feasibility of conveying an Expeditionary Force safely to France; but in an atmosphere of expansion disputes were somewhat less bitter.
3   Public Record Office, London, CAB 4/23/5887.
4   P. Haggie, *Britannia at Bay. The Defence of the British Empire against Japan 1931–1941* (Oxford, 1981), p. 73.
5   1936. Quoted by M. Howard, *The Continental Commitment* (London, 1972), p. 102.
6   L. R. Pratt, *East of Malta, West of Suez. Britain's Mediterranean Crisis, 1936–1939* (London, 1975), p. 3 – the first passage dates from 1934, the second from 1936. Another very similar note of Chatfield's is quoted by Roy Douglas elsewhere in this volume, p. 79.
7   Third Report of the Defence Requirements Sub-Committee, 21 November 1935, p. 7, CAB 4/24/5887.
8   Chiefs of Staff, *Comparison of the Strength of Great Britain with that of certain other Nations as at January 1938*, 12 November 1937, p. 11, CAB 4/26/5887.
9   Third Report of the Defence Requirements Sub-Committee, p. 37.
10 ibid., p. 9.
11 ibid., p. 36.
12 *Parliamentary Papers* (1934–5), Vol. XIII, pp. 805–6. Further public relations work – by which Hankey set considerable store – took the form of his long-prepared evidence given in 1936 to the Royal Commission on the Private Manufacture of Arms to the effect that 'prohibition of private manufacture would be disastrous to Imperial Defence' (S. Roskill, *Hankey, Man of Secrets*, Vol. III, *1931–1963* (London, 1974), pp. 165–7 and 246–9).
13 For which see the *Supplement to the Oxford English Dictionary* (Oxford, 1972).
14 B. Bond (ed.), *Chief of Staff. The Diaries of Lieutenant-General Sir Henry Pownall*, Vol. 1 (London, 1972), p. 112.
15 S. Roskill, *Naval Policy between the Wars*, Vol. II: *The Period of Reluctant Rearmament 1930–1939* (London, 1976), pp. 276–7.
16 ibid., p. 435.
17 See Roskill, *Hankey*, Vol. III, pp. 111, 114–15 and Bond (ed.), *Chief of Staff*, p. 46.
18 Pratt, *East of Malta, West of Suez*, pp. 169–97.
19 Also in January 1938 Chatfield and Chamberlain were reluctant to denude the Mediterra-

nean to mount an Anglo-American naval demonstration in the Pacific as this might weaken the British hand 'just at the time we are trying to come to terms with Mussolini' (Pratt, *East of Malta, West of Suez*, p. 59). For Anglo-American naval relations in general during this period, see J. R. Leutze, *Bargaining for Supremacy. Anglo-American Naval Collaboration, 1937–41* (Chapel Hill, NC, 1977), and Pratt, *East of Malta, West of Suez*, esp. pp. 57–60, 176–9, 189–91.

20   Roskill, *Hankey*, Vol. II: *1919–31* (London, 1972), pp. 463–4.
21   W. N. Medlicott, *The Economic Blockade*, Vol. I (London, 1952), p. 27.
22   Sir J. Slessor, *The Central Blue* (London, 1956), p. 152.
23   H. Montgomery Hyde, *British Air Policy between the Wars* (London, 1976), pp. 224–5.
24   ibid., pp. 110, 134–5, 137.
25   September 1937; quoted by Slessor, *The Central Blue*, p. 158.
26   Eden attached great importance to the deterrent aspect of the RAF, and wished to implement the Air Staff's proposed bomber scheme, if necessary at the expense of army aid to France.
27   Montgomery Hyde, *British Air Policy*, pp. 409–13.
28   20 September 1938, CAB 21/544/5887.
29   cf. Pownall's appreciation of 27 September 1938 (written after discussion with Gort, Adam and others): 'From the military point of view the balance of advantage is definitely in favour of postponement. This is probably an exception to the rule that 'no war is inevitable', for it will almost certainly come later . . . This is not our selected moment, it is theirs' (Bond, ed., *Chief of Staff*, p. 383). For Air Ministry views, see J. R. Colville, *Man of Valour. The Life of Field-Marshal the Viscount Gort* (London, 1972), p. 102, and Slessor, *The Central Blue*, pp. 154–5, 169–72, 214. The Admiralty shared the opinion that the crisis came at the worst possible time, given the number of major warships refitting or not yet delivered, and it was also sensitive to Dominion opposition (Roskill, *Naval Policy*, pp. 442–3). I am less clear as to its views on the long-term prospects of avoiding war.
30   *Britain, France and Germany*, p. 20; CAB 27/599/5887.
31   Howard, *The Continental Commitment*, p. 97.
32   ibid., p. 105.
33   ibid., p. 88. For Hankey's control over the drafting of the report, see Bond (ed.), *Chief of Staff*, pp. 34–7.
34   G. C. Peden, 'Sir Warren Fisher and British rearmament against Germany', *English Historical Review*, vol. 94 (1979), pp. 36, 38.
35   Roskill, *Naval Policy*, p. 297.
36   Howard, *The Continental Commitment*, p. 139.
37   Roskill, *Hankey*, Vol. III, pp. 155–64.
38   Five capital ships, one carrier, seven light cruisers, etc. (Roskill, *Naval Policy*, p. 292).
39   N. H. Gibbs, *Grand Strategy*, Vol. I: *Rearmament Policy* (London, 1976), p. 158.
40   Roskill, *Naval Policy*, p. 261.
41   R. A. C. Parker, 'Britain, France and the Ethiopian crisis 1935–1936', *English Historical Review*, vol. 89 (1974), p. 327.
42   *Staff Conversations with the Locarno Powers*, 1 April 1936 (CAB 94/24/5887), and *The Condition of Our Forces to Meet the Possibility of War with Germany*, 18 March 1936 (annexed to the above).
43   25 March 1936; see also 21 November and 16 December 1935.
44   15 June 1936.
45   Roskill, *Naval Policy*, p. 324.
46   ibid., pp. 377–8, 384. The following year, in response to a Cabinet inquiry, Gort dissociated the General Staff from his minister's view that France should be persuaded to intervene against Franco (Colville, *Man of Valour*, pp. 92–3).
47   Roskill, *Naval Policy*, pp. 354–5.
48   4 February 1938, quoted by Ian Colvin, *The Chamberlain Cabinet* (London, 1971), p. 94.
49   Earl of Avon (Anthony Eden), *Memoirs*, Vol. I, *Facing the Dictators* (London, 1962), pp. 500–1; Gibbs, *Grand Strategy*, Vol. I, pp. 628–9; Colvin, *The Chamberlain Cabinet* chs 5–7.
50   See Bond (ed.), *Chief of Staff*, p. 135.
51   *Military Implications of German Aggression against Czechoslovakia*, CAB 27/627/5887.
52   Alternatively, it was argued, France might intervene to defend Czechoslovakia and be

beaten for want of timely British aid. The Chiefs of Staff had been instructed to leave Russia out of the calculation; and they might have overestimated Germany and Japan. As for the future, there was no certainty that the *relative* strength of British air defences would improve. And, even if the small states of Eastern Europe were today a military liability, Germany might be able so to organise them as to enhance its capacity to fight a long war.

53 Conclusions of the Cabinet of 22 March 1938, CAB 23/93/6755.
54 Sir K. Feiling, *The Life of Neville Chamberlain* (London, 1970 edn), pp. 394, 401.
55 K. Middlemas, *Diplomacy of Illusion. The British Government and Germany, 1937–1939* (London, 1972), p. 447.
56 The strategy of assisting France only by sea and air power and with industrial production.
57 'It was clear', added the President of the Board of Trade, 'that some of the conditions under which we are now living could not last much longer – perhaps not for another year' (Conclusions of the Cabinet of 2 February 1939, CAB 23/97/6849).
58 Bond (ed.), *Chief of Staff*, pp. 34, 37; Gibbs, *Grand Strategy*, Vol. I, pp. 97–8.
59 Both the RAF and the navy could represent their own contribution as decisive to *deterring* (or fighting) a war; the army could not. Also from 1935 the government (aided by Liddell Hart) came to the comfortable conclusion that the superiority of the defence was such that France would not need help on land; nor could this help arrive in time if Germany opened with an *attaque brusquée* against France (instead of an aerial knock-out blow against Britain).
60 Liddell Hart, *Memoirs*, Vol. I, p. 382; Bond (ed.), *Chief of Staff*, p. 123.
61 Bond (ed.), *Chief of Staff*, pp. 170–1.
62 ibid., p. 197.
63 Roskill, *Naval Policy*, p. 460.
64 Colville, *Man of Valour*, pp. 119–21.
65 And perhaps also of bombing London.
66 Conclusions of the Cabinet of 24 May 1939, pp. 2, 15, CAB 23/99/6982.
67 R. J. Minney, *The Private Papers of Hore-Belisha* (London, 1960), pp. 145–6.
68 *German Aggression against Holland*, 25 January 1939, CAB 24/282/7041.
69 Among the contributory factors we may note the advice of Mason-Macfarlane, the military attaché in Berlin, who had been strongly dove-ish over Czechoslovakia in 1938 but was now as strongly hawkish.
70 The RAF doubted army estimates of the number of German troops that would be tied up in the East, and feared that the need to relieve German pressure on Poland would force it into a premature bombing campaign (Slessor, *The Central Blue*, pp. 230–1, 214). Also it did not rate Russian strength highly (Conclusions of the Cabinet of 24 May 1939, pp. 11–12).
71 S. K. Newman, *March 1939: The British Guarantee to Poland* (Oxford, 1976), pp. 118–19.
72 ibid., pp. 155–6; Gibbs, *Grand Strategy*, Vol. I, pp. 699–701; R. Manne, 'The British decision for alliance with Russia, May 1939', *Journal of Contemporary History*, vol. 9 (1974), pp. 13–15.
73 Liddell Hart, *Memoirs*, Vol. II, p. 221.
74 Chatfield's statements to the Cabinet on 10 May and to the Foreign Policy Committee on 16 May, and the Chiefs of Staff *aide-mémoire* circulated with the conclusions of the latter, CAB 23/99/6892 and 27/625/5887; Manne, 'British decision', pp. 22–6.
75 29 August 1939, Bond (ed.), *Chief of Staff*, p. 221.
76 27 August 1939, Colville, *Man of Valour*, p. 140.
77 Bond (ed.), *Chief of Staff*, p. 220; see also Slessor, *The Central Blue*, p. 234 for comparable Air Staff pressure a few days later on their minister.
78 As late as December 1938 the Chief of Air Staff was still arguing that this entailed a commitment to unlimited land warfare, which would be popularly unacceptable (Colville, *Man of Valour*, pp. 119–21); whereas the army always held that, whatever the current state of opinion, if war came it would change, the policy of 'limited liability' would be swept away, and troops would go to France whether they were prepared or not.
79 Gamelin's reluctance in the summer of 1939 to accept a comparable degree of ministerial oversight prevented the peacetime establishment of a joint Anglo-French Supreme War Council (Colville, *Man of Valour*, pp. 133–4).
80 Of course in some other contexts, notably submarines and German vulnerability to blockade, British military thinking was over-optimistic.
81 February 1938, quoted by Howard, *The Continental Commitment*, p. 118.

82   British participants in the 1939 staff talks noted the change in atmosphere since 1935, when the French had professed themselves unable to find any maps of their border with Italy (Colville, *Man of Valour*, p. 126).

83   Above, p. 198.

84   Slessor, *The Central Blue*, pp. 166–7. Personally I doubt whether the USSR was ever really available as a dependable component of a *status quo* alliance, though of course this cannot be definitely proved or disproved. Also the effectiveness of 'containment' must depend quite largely on the internal nature of the regime to be contained. And while I still think such a policy would have been helpful – especially if embarked on in 1934 rather than (as Slessor here suggests) 1937 – it would have been open to the charge of dividing Europe into hostile ideological camps. This most contemporaries were anxious to avoid (as R. A. C. Parker's paper in this volume shows); and Cold War revisionists have since been equally anxious to condemn it, albeit in another context.

13 The Continental Commitment in British Strategy in the 1930s

BRIAN BOND

From the cliffs of Dover on a clear day it is possible to see a grey rim of land shutting in the south-eastern horizon. It is not the coastline of Asia; nor of Japan; nor of Arabia, Africa or Asia Minor, but of Europe. England lies only twenty-two miles from the European shore. Simple, obvious, indeed well-known a fact as this was, the English were prone from time to time to forget all the implications which it bore for English policy and strategy.[1]

The isolationist attitude of mind here described by Corelli Barnett has probably never been more pronounced in Britain than in the interwar period. Several historians, notably Michael Howard in his survey *The Continental Commitment*, have analysed the dilemma confronting British strategy-makers regarding the priorities to be assigned to home security, imperial defence and military assistance to possible European allies. In this paper, based on my book *British Military Policy between the Two World Wars*,[2] I shall attempt to bring out the views of leading soldiers, the General Staff and the Chiefs of Staff, since these are often neglected in studies of diplomatic history and foreign policy.

Between 1919 and 1932 Britain's strategic planners were constricted by the political guidelines of the Ten Year Rule which assured them that the country would not be involved in a major war for at least ten years and, more specifically, that no Expeditionary Force need be provided for such a contingency. There was much to be said in favour of such a directive in the early 1920s on both financial and strategic grounds. The empire upon which the sun never set had reached its greatest extent and its preservation was to make increasing demands upon the army in a sphere where the Royal Navy had formerly been more important. In addition, burdensome mandates were accepted in the Middle East. It was easy – but unfair – to make jokes about the army's rapid return to pre-1914 'real soldiering' with India as its chief responsibility, but in reality a switch of strategic interest away from Europe to the empire was inevitable. Britain's continuing concern with European security was evident in her signature of the Versailles and Locarno Treaties, but as the 1920s wore on the Chiefs of Staff were at pains to stress repeatedly that no Expeditionary Force existed at home – nor could one be raised short of national mobilisation – to meet these possible commitments. By 1930, when the last British troops were withdrawn from the occupied zone of the Rhineland, a general attitude of disenchantment was prevalent regarding her unprecedented war effort between 1914 and 1918. 'Never again' seemed to be the watchword; even the services would have found it hard to believe that in less than a decade Britain would be involved in another great European war.

Nevertheless, it was generally agreed among defence experts that how-ever unpleasant – even horrific – its implications, the continental commit-ment remained valid in principle. Britain's traditional concern with the security of the Low Countries and the Channel ports remained of crucial importance; indeed it was widely accepted that the rapid development of air power *increased* rather than diminished the vital significance of having a friendly power on the other side of the narrow ditch. Stanley Baldwin epitomised this view in a House of Commons debate on air power in 1934 when he remarked that henceforth Britain's frontier lay on the Rhine. In the 1920s, with Germany disarmed and the Soviet Union in turmoil, the European threat to British security seemed to have disappeared, and it was possible for a CIGS (Sir George Milne) to state that Britain's involvement in an all-out European war was an aberration which was most unlikely ever to be repeated.[3] Some critics, such as Liddell Hart, went further in arguing that the dispatch of the BEF in 1914 had been a colossal mistake. But the advent to power of Adolf Hitler soon called this complacency into question.

In their early appraisals of the potential danger of a rearmed and aggressive Germany the Defence Requirements Committee and the Chiefs of Staff displayed remarkable unanimity in urging upon the government (still preoccupied with disarmament) the view that Britain had a *vital* strategic interest in the security of the Low Countries and that an Expeditionary Force was essential to meet it. In 1933 Japan still posed the most immediate threat, but the DRC (1933–4) successfully advocated that Germany would be a greater danger from 1939 onwards and that long-term rearmament should be directed primarily against the latter. The outcome of the DRC reports is too familiar to require elaboration, but it is worth stressing that its modest recommendations to remedy the worst deficiencies was the only substantial attempt to prepare all three services for war on an equal footing. Even then, and it is surely no cause for surprise, there was no agreed 'grand strategy' among the services for each had different priorities in various theatres and there was a recent history of bitter internecine rivalry. In private discussions the service representatives disagreed, sometimes heated-ly, on strategy, tactics and the nature of the next war, the Air Staff, for example, being sceptical, if not downright hostile, to the General Staff's notion that it would be feasible and worthwhile to send an Expeditionary Force across the Channel on the outbreak of hostilities. It is remarkable, however, that the COS usually managed to present at least a façade of unity when its reports were repeatedly challenged in the Cabinet, CID and ministerial committees. This was notably the case in regard to ministers' hostile reactions to the DRC proposals in favour of creating an Expedition-ary Force and reserves for a possible European campaign. There were two main grounds for opposition: the cost would be excessive; and public opinion was averse to involvement in another European war. The COS, aided and abetted by Hankey, resisted repeated challenges, particularly from Neville Chamberlain, to the effect that an Expeditionary Force was not necessary or could be substituted by an air contingent.[4]

The best defence of the army's continental role was formulated by Hankey in a memorandum for the Prime Minister dated 15 January 1936. Hankey's case was essentially political rather than military and it remained valid throughout the tergiversations of the next three years. War can only be averted, he argued, by a combination which includes at least France and Belgium. They and others are not satisfied that aircraft alone can defend them against invasion and still look on armies and fortifications as their mainstay. 'If we have no efficient army they will feel that we do not mean business.' Without some aid from us France will not help Belgium, Belgium will collapse; London will be exposed to the worst horrors of aerial bombardment; and we shall not have an effective base from which to retaliate on Germany. Hankey ended with an eloquent appeal: 'In a word an efficient army, if only a small one, is essential to reassure our potential allies, to put heart into them to make the necessary effort, and to deter war; and, on the day of battle, to cover our offensive air forces.[5]

The Chiefs of Staff's resistance prevailed to the extent that the government never explicitly rejected a possible continental commitment, but they were obliged to accept that when rearmament began in a modest way in 1935 the army would have the lowest priority. In particulr the General Staff reluctantly acquiesced in the fact that over the next few years only the five divisions of the Regular Army (at best) could be equipped for modern war so that no trained and organised reserve, in the shape of the Territorial Army, would be available.

In practice very little was done in the mid-1930s to prepare even the tiny Regular Army for war against a first-class opponent. On the contrary, for a variety of reasons the army at this time was losing what little momentum it had earlier enjoyed towards progressive doctrine, training and re-equipment. This was depressingly evident in the important sphere of mechanisation where Britain led the way in the first experimental armoured manoeuvres and the formation of a tank brigade. Scarcity of money, uncertainty over its role and a feeling that it was regarded as the 'Cinderella Service' all combined to demoralise the higher ranks in a naturally conservative institution.

In fairness to the army's leadership, however, it needs to be stressed that at precisely the time when its planning and preparations should have focused on Germany it became unavoidably preoccupied with the Middle East. As recently as 1934 Italy had been officially discounted as a possible future enemy, yet after the Abyssinian crisis of 1935 her unfriendly neutrality or outright hostility became increasingly likely.[6] Considerable reserves of men and new equipment, especially tanks, were dispatched to Egypt and never recalled. Worse still, in 1936 the Palestine rebellion entered an acute phase and by 1938 the army had been obliged to concentrate the equivalent of *two divisions* there. These two heavy commitments help to explain why the General Staff did not press more strongly for the creation of a continental Expeditionary Force. It is not too fanciful to suggest that some senior soldiers, such as Sir Edmund Ironside, were relieved to see this build-up of forces in the Middle East against a second-class power as *an alternative* to possible war on land against Germany.[7] In other words generals like Ironside believed that Britain was manifestly not in the European league as regards armies but could confidently take on Italy in North Africa if there were no other distractions.

There was, however, another important aspect of the continental commitment up to 1936 which has not yet been mentioned. Until that date the Chiefs of Staff did not view the continental commitment as purely (or in the case of the Air Staff even primarily) a matter for the army. A strategic concept which appealed to all three services was that of the RAF using Belgium as an advanced base from which bombers could threaten the Ruhr while the small Expeditionary Force protected its airfields and communications. Unfortunately at a time when Belgium appeared willing to enter into serious staff talks, the British (politicians and the service leaders alike) were distinctly cool towards any real commitment, and in 1936 Belgium's move towards a position of strict neutrality (partly as a consequence of Britain's unco-operative attitude) robbed the concept of much of its attraction.[8] Henceforth a continental commitment meant essentially direct support of France and this had little appeal for any of the services. Quite apart from France's assumed ability to take care of her own defence (and, if necessary, Belgium's too), technical developments after 1936 served to strengthen the belief that Britain's European interests could be safeguarded from the fortified home base. The longer range of bombers, the introduction of Hurricane and Spitfire fighters and the development of radar seemed to offer the attractive option of 'deterring' Germany without any physical commitment across the Channel. At the same time the government challenged the Air Staff's preoccupation with bombers and put more emphasis on both fighters and ground defence. Needless to say, this defensive air strategy accorded perfectly with the government's economic and financial priorities which played down the need for a large and expensively equipped army. Indeed the Territorial Army was increasingly committed to anti-aircraft defence duties, a policy which militated against preparedness for a possible European role. Thus in the later 1930s increased emphasis on home defence against a widely expected enemy attempt to deal a 'knock-out' blow from the air reduced the theoretical contribution to a European ally to a maximum of four under-equipped and ill-trained Regular divisions.

Senior soldiers, including Montgomery-Massingberd, Deverell and Hobart,[9] may be found arguing in general terms that the Regular Army and at least part of the TA must be prepared for war with Germany, but it is not to be wondered at that there was no equivalent of Sir Henry Wilson in the 1930s pressing single-mindedly and almost fanatically for a military undertaking to support France. To have done so would have confirmed the worst fears of critics like Liddell Hart who believed that the army was led by Colonel Blimps eager to repeat the blood-letting of the Somme and Passchendaele. But it must be noted that the army's case against sceptical politicians and rivals in the other services was not helped by the fact that some prominent generals frequently made public their opposition to a continental commitment. Foremost among them was General Sir John

Burnett-Stuart, who many considered should have been appointed CIGS in 1936. Burnett-Stuart's viewpoint was as follows:

> I knew that the dispatch of an Expeditionary Force to France on the outbreak of war with Germany was still an integral part of our Defence policy, and I was convinced that to send the British Army to a Continental War in its then condition would be to condemn it to disaster. That we should align ourselves unreservedly by the side of France was an obligation which we could not escape, but I could not make myself believe that the sacrifice at the commencement of hostilities of such an army as we had would help either of us . . .
>
> My one and only reason for thinking as I did, was the state of the army; whatever the political, strategical or ethical arguments for the dispatch of an Expeditionary Force, they must give way when faced with the fact that we had no Expeditionary Force fit to send.[10]

Many army officers, faced with this terrible dilemma, echoed these sentiments in private correspondence, in diaries, or in discussions at professional institutions.

There was thus a considerable amount of service support for the strategic concept which was increasingly emphasised in Cabinet discussions in the mid-1930s under the title of 'limited liability'. This meant that Britain was making her main rearmament effort in air and naval forces and had no intention of again becoming involved in a full-scale European war on land. If Britain decided to enter a European war, and that would depend on circumstances at the time, her aid to an ally would initially take the form of air and naval support. Land support was not entirely ruled out but it would take several weeks to assemble and would be limited to a token contingent of the Regular Army. Even this small and belated contribution would be dependent on the tranquillity of the empire. The TA would definitely not be made ready to serve as a reinforcement to the Expeditionary Force.

This trend in political thinking was immensely strengthened when Neville Chamberlain became Prime Minister in May 1937. Duff Cooper, who had stubbornly advocated preparing the army and part of the TA for a possible European role, was replaced at the War Office by Leslie Hore-Belisha who at that time shared the Prime Minister's views on limited liability. A drastic reappraisal of the services' programmes in the light of a fixed ceiling on expenditure laid down by the Chancellor of the Exchequer culminated in December 1937 in the government's reordering of strategic priorities. The continental role was now placed last among the army's roles and given an extremely low priority in rearmament. The most likely overseas role for the Expeditionary Force was henceforth to be the defence of Egypt. Its outdated equipment, including pre-1914 type field guns, would not be speedily replaced and its reserves, especially on ammunition, would be inadequate for a European war. As Michael Howard put it: 'What was generally termed a policy of "limited liability" in continental warfare had now shrunk to one of no liability at all.' Inskip, Minister for the Co-ordination of Defence, at least realised the risk that was being taken and warned his colleagues:

If France were again to be in danger of being overrun by land armies, a situation might arise when, as in the last war, we had to improvise an army to assist her. Should this happen, the Government of the day would most certainly be criticised for having neglected to provide against so obvious a contingency.[11]

The Chiefs of Staff acquiesced in this drastic revision of the army's priorities. The Air Staff view was that air power would dominate the early stages of a war in Western Europe, specifically in the form of a duel in long-range strategic bombing. The CAS did not believe that the Expeditionary Force could arrive in France in time to affect the decisive battle even assuming that the Luftwaffe allowed it to disembark at all. The Royal Navy was preoccupied with the Far East and the Mediterranean and understandably did not attach much importance to the army's continental role. The General Staff alone deplored the government's reordering of the army's priorities, not because it relished a European role or wanted to see conscription introduced, but because it thought a German attack in the west increasingly likely and did not see how Britain could remain aloof, whatever politicians might say beforehand. Major-General Henry Pownall, who became Director of Military Operations and Intelligence in January 1938, was a particularly caustic critic of limited liability:

There was a further and most dangerous heresy – the Chancellor's. That of 'limited liability' in a war. They cannot or will not realise that if war with Germany comes again (whether by Collective Security, Locarno or any other way) we shall again be *fighting for our lives*. Our effort *must* be the maximum, by land, sea and air. We cannot say our contribution is 'so and so' – and no more, because we cannot lose the war without extinction of the Empire. The idea of the 'half hearted' war is the most pernicious and dangerous in the world. It will be 100 per cent – and even then we may well lose it. We shall certainly lose it if we don't go 100 per cent. In God's name let us recognise that from the outset – and by that I mean *now*. The Chancellor's cold hard calculating semi-detached attitude was terrible to listen to.[12]

Pownall and other soldiers were worried that the ill-prepared Expeditionary Force would be dispatched in an emergency and that they would be unjustly held responsible for the resulting massacre. Ironside felt the army's unreadiness for war was so obvious that the government would not dare to send it overseas: 'Never again shall we even contemplate a Force for a foreign country', he gloomily noted in his diary on 29 May 1938. 'Our contribution is to be the Navy and the RAF.'[13] By this time the prevalent view at the War Office was that if the Expeditionary Force were to be sent to the Continent at all it would not be until *after* the French had stopped the initial German offensive. This led to the comforting assumption that there would be time to equip and organise the army *after* the outbreak of war with the aim of dispatching it in time to participate in the eventual Allied counter-attack. Hence there was thought to be no point in holding serious staff talks with the

French: the latter would only demand a larger and speedier contribution than Britain could contemplate.

The question of the continental commitment did not loom large in British foreign policy in 1938. On the contrary Chamberlain's aim in appeasing Germany was to remove the need for such a commitment and so avoid the horrifying prospect of having to raise a huge First World War type of army. The Chiefs of Staff believed that the overriding need was to gain time for further rearmament – especially in home defence – so they consistently presented 'worst case' appreciations over the possibility of supporting Czechoslovakia, in the process ignoring evidence that the latter would put up a formidable defence and cause the German forces considerable disorganisation before being overrun.[14]

After the Munich crisis, however, the military experts soon began to realise that the strategic balance had been sharply tilted in Germany's favour and against France. By the end of 1938 the General Staff (now aided by Hore-Belisha and with Halifax lending influential support in the Cabinet) was pressing for a revision of the army's priorities in order that the Regular Army might be equipped and trained for a European role and at least part of the TA organised as its reserve. When this matter was once again referred to the COS in January 1939 the CAS (Newall) remained sceptical about the value of a small Expeditionary Force in Europe, but the army's viewpoint received crucial support from the new CNS (Backhouse):

On 9 January 1939 Admiral Backhouse wrote to Ismay 'You soldiers . . . have got to tell us what minimum size Expeditionary Force could have any effect', and Ismay suggested four infantry divisions and two mobile divisions for a start. It seemed likely that Germany would again wheel through Belgium and the French were unlikely to intervene in that country unless we contributed a Field Force. Backhouse then sent Ismay a paper on the Role of the Army but significantly omitted to show it to the CAS. 'I cannot help feeling', Backhouse remarked in his covering letter, 'that it is not only a matter of letting down France, but, ultimately (unless Germany breaks up), of finding ourselves in a most dangerous position. It may be that too much is being undertaken in the way of Empire responsibilities by this Island, but the fact remains that it is our future security that we are primarily concerned with in this matter.[15]

Thus at the end of January 1939 the COS report was strongly in favour of accepting a military continental commitment though not, they stressed, on the scale of 1914–18. Waverers in the Cabinet were also influenced at this time by a false alarm that Germany was about to attack Holland. Halifax hinted darkly that Britain might not enjoy a monopoly of limited liability: if Germany used Holland as a springboard to attack Britain by air while reassuring France the latter might stand aside and see us overrun. In February the government belatedly informed the French that in the event of German aggression in the West (including Switzerland and the Low Countries) the Regular Expeditionary Force would definitely be dispatched to the Continent.

There followed an astonishing *volte face* in British foreign policy and strategy in late March and April 1939 as a consequence of the German occupation of Bohemia. The Territorial Army was doubled by a proverbial stroke of the pen, a form of conscription was introduced despite repeated government assurances to the contrary, and initially unilateral guarantees were given to Poland and Romania. So, where a few months previously Britain had been unwilling even to contemplate military support to far-off Czechoslovakia, she now voluntarily accepted a strategic frontier on the Vistula! The COS were quick to point out, however, that these guarantees could not be fulfilled and indeed made no strategic sense without an agreement with the Soviet Union. It seems likely that the Prime Minister regarded these steps as a deterrent to Hitler rather than as a final recognition that Britain would have to send troops to Europe.

The army at last had a clear mission and began to receive the up-to-date weapons and equipment of which it had been deprived for so long. A fair degree of understanding was achieved with the French in the summer of 1939, notably as regards the Allied command structure and the assembly area of the Expeditionary Force. At the time of Munich no detailed plans had existed for the dispatch of a British contingent to France, but these were hastily arranged just in time to be smoothly implemented in September 1939. In the short term, however, the combat value of Britain's land forces was considerably *weakened* by the unexpected doubling of the TA shortly followed by conscription. Despite the general agreement between soldiers and politicians that a repetition of the First World War experience must be avoided at almost any cost, the government now seemed bent on creating a large, immobile, predominantly infantry force suitable for static warfare. Regular units were deprived of experienced NCOs needed to train the Territorials and militiamen who remained desperately short of accommodation, clothing, equipment and transport in the remaining months of peace. As Pownall noted in his diary on 24 April:

> It is a proper Granny's knitting that has been handed out to us to unravel – on top of the new role of the Army and the doubling of the TA. What an unholy mess our politicians have made of the rebirth of the Army through shortsightedness, unwillingness to face facts and prejudice against the Army. There is but one alleviating feature. I have no doubt that these things, or something equivalent, would have been chucked at our heads to do immediately on the outbreak of war. It is better therefore that we should have them on us in advance, since every day, week and month is so much gained. We shall get some of the muddles off our chests before the war begins – for muddles there will be, that is inevitable under such conditions.[16]

In view of the lateness of the government's acceptance of the European role and the chaos that followed the emergency measures in March and April, the War Office did remarkably well to dispatch the first four Regular divisions to France so smoothly in the autumn. As some of the soldiers appreciated, it was very like a repetition of the '1914 show' except that this time the German offensive did not occur immediately. Had it done so the cruel costs of political indecision over the army's role would surely have been even more starkly exposed than in May 1940.

From a purely strategic viewpoint it was very hard to deny that Britain was a part of Western Europe and could not afford to see its interests there menaced without armed intervention. Most defence experts agreed that a land force was still essential to safeguard these interests (and to reassure potential allies), but the development of air power and its enormous impact on the public consciousness created uncertainty about the future relevance of the land battle. This uncertainty was fully exploited by the Air Staff which never shared the soldiers' view about the importance of an Expeditionary Force or displayed much interest in co-operation with ground forces.

Several other considerations also militated against a continental commitment:

(a) The electorate was thought to be utterly opposed to any undertaking to a European ally which might lead to a repetition of the First World War.

(b) There was a strong financial and industrial argument that Britain could not afford to rearm all three services. The RAF and Royal Navy were generally held to deserve priority over the army.

(c) The General Staff did not strengthen its inherently weak case by its preoccupation with imperial duties, vagueness about the actual role of an Expeditionary Force in Europe and hostility towards and mistrust of the French.

(d) The British government was understandably reluctant to accept the inevitability of war with Germany and hence to adopt military measures (including even staff talks) which would make appeasement more difficult.

Indeed the 'Appeasement' policy was in part designed to remove the issues which, if unresolved, might make a British military presence in Europe necessary. Only when this policy was clearly seen to have failed, in the spring of 1939, was a definite though still restricted continental commitment reluctantly accepted. The consequences of the delay were serious: Belgium and France lost confidence in Britain's support on land, while conversely Hitler was strengthened in his belief that she would remain aloof if he launched a quick, decisive attack in the West.

Whether an earlier and more substantial British military commitment to Europe would have made a significant difference in 1939 or 1940 can be argued endlessly. It is at least possible that Hitler might have been deterred from an attack in the West but, failing that, Allied morale and co-operation would surely have been better and resistance stronger.

As most students of the 1930s will agree, it is extremely difficult to achieve an objective and comprehensive view because so much depends on one's particular approach and interests. From a strategical standpoint, and particularly in the context of Britain's relationship with Europe in the present century, it is hard to escape the conclusion that the 'Continentalists' such as Duff Cooper, Hankey (most of the time), Montgomery-Massing-berd, Deverell, Hobart and Pownall were right, but at the same time it is easy to understand why the government was reluctant to accept so uncongenial a strategy until Germany's blatant drive towards European hegemony made it unavoidable.

Notes: Chapter 13

1   C. Barnett, *The Collapse of British Power* (London, 1972), p. 305.
2   B. Bond, *British Military Policy between the Two World Wars* (Oxford, 1980).
3   Public Record Office, London, CAB 53/1, COS 30th Meeting, 27 May 1926.
4   Bond, *British Military Policy*, pp. 191 ff.
5   CAB 21/422(A), DPR (DR).
6   L. A. Pratt, *East of Malta, West of Suez: Britain's Mediterranean Crisis 1936–1939* (Cambridge, 1975).
7   R. Macleod and D. Kelly (eds), *The Ironside Diaries, 1937–1940* (London, 1962).
8   D. O. Kieft, *Belgium's Return to Neutrality* (Oxford, 1972).
9   For example, Hobart's memorandum 'AFV and the field force', Hobart to Liddell Hart, 21 October 1937 (Liddell Hart Papers).
10 Bond, *British Military Policy*, p. 216.
11 N. H. Gibbs, *Grand Strategy*, Vol. 1 (London, 1976), p. 469.
12 B. Bond (ed.), *Chief of Staff: The Diaries of Lt. General Sir Henry Pownall*, Vol. 1 (London, 1972), p. 99.
13 Macleod and Kelly (eds), *The Ironside Diaries*, p. 58.
14 Bond, *British Military Policy*, pp. 280 ff.
15 ibid., pp. 296 ff.
16 Bond (ed.), *Chief of Staff*, p. 201.

Part Three

Appeasement and the European Powers

I

FRANCE'S PREDICAMENT

14 The Impact of the Economic Situation on the Foreign Policy of France, 1936–9

RENÉ GIRAULT

French foreign policy between 1936 and 1939 gives an impression of weakness, resignation and impotence; to describe it one can use Duroselle's word 'la décadence'.[1] Among the disturbing symptoms it is now traditional to stress French dependence on her British partner, the French government being usually content to follow 'the English governess'.[2] This dependence carried France on a course of appeasement towards Germany, for London maintained until March 1939 a conciliatory political line towards the Führer; thereafter France resigned herself to go to war – still sticking to British views. It was only towards Italy that France showed some signs of independence by opposing Chamberlain's aims. After the Second World War some of the French actors were strongly criticised for their passivity and their acquiescence, especially during the Munich crisis. They defended themselves by throwing responsibility for the choices made on their British ally; the alliance with London was indispensable, it was indeed necessary to follow Chamberlain's views.[3] This undeniable French subservience, accompanied by occasional starts, presents a problem for historians: why did French governments from Sarraut to Daladier, including Blum and Chautemps, agree to follow British diplomatic strategy, even though some of them in their hearts considered it extremely shortsighted?[4] Were they content to follow the advice of the leading officials who, aware of French isolation, had been won over to British friendship, officials such as the Secretary-General of the Quai d'Orsay, Alexis Léger, a reputed 'anglophile'? Were they, politicians and officials alike, weak men, incapable of taking courageous decisions, prisoners of ill-adapted institutions, who were relieved to follow the directives of the 'governess'?

In the foreign policy process of a state, the role of leading actors merits attention, including not only those belonging to the inner circle of administrators who in times of crisis act almost without parliamentary control, but also the politicians sensitive to internal political issues; it is necessary to analyse the career, the character of each, his background and environment and social life. However, it would seem that one yardstick has until now been relatively little used in the analysis of the decisions taken by French leaders between 1936 and 1939: how did they evaluate the economic situation of France when reaching diplomatic decisions? In other words, do the economic factors – understanding the term in its widest sense, including, for example, finance, currency and the state of industry and commerce – help to explain the conduct of French foreign policy? In particular, can one better understand certain 'dépendences françaises' by analysing France's external economic relations from 1936 to 1939?

A preliminary remark is necessary here. To investigate the economic component in political decision-making does not imply that an excessive importance is being attached to this criterion at the expense of other considerations. Rather, it is necessary to reconstruct as far as possible all of the factors involved in the choice of policy. Now even though the diplomats and politicians are not specialists in economic questions, it is practically impossible on the eve of war to forget the economic and financial conditions of a country and its neighbours. In all the major decisions the Prime Minister takes the advice of his leading colleagues, starting with the Minister of Finance, who is responsible for the planning of public resources and is a natural link with the banks and leading industrialists. The execution of rearmament programmes, the negotiation of loans, commercial agreements – all involve the participation of the Ministers of Finance and of Commerce in discussions; accordingly their advisers are closely concerned in the international field, particularly the *Direction du Mouvement des Fonds* which co-ordinates and directs all external aspects of the French economy.[5] The influence of the financial attachés, relatively few in number but present in all the main embassies (London, Berlin, Rome and Washington), is undeniable, especially since they were often *inspecteurs des finances*, members of an élite body with close connections with the heads of major enterprises. They were also young and preoccupied with France's future.[6] It is worth remembering that Georges Bonnet was several times Minister of Finance before taking the chair of Vergennes at the Quai d'Orsay at a critical period. In short, the economic conditions had to be taken into account along with the purely political and military factors when the leading decision-makers assessed the resources of French power on the eve of war.

At this period a power disposed of four economic arms for action abroad:

> the commercial arm
> the financial arm
> the industrial arm
> the technological arm.

She did not necessarily possess the four arms together; she might, for example, lack financial resources but possess a considerable industrial strength; such was Germany's position at the time. In theory, the recourse to one of these four arms assumed, on the one hand, the existence of unequal relations between the economies of states, on the other, the implicit or explicit recognition of the laws of the liberal capitalist economy, that is to say, the pursuit of the smallest cost for the largest return and the maximum profit. Thus, in world trade a primary producer depended on the purchasing capacity of the industrialised states (unless the exporters grouped themselves in a common front). A country's more advanced technology opened up possibilities of intervention overseas in the course of negotiations for licences and prototypes (military orders provide excellent examples). However, among the economic arms, two of them were especially effective in a liberal economy, the industrial arm and the financial arm. The capacity to sell industrial products at a low price and in large quantities meant a strong ability to exercise pressure, just as the capital holder 'holds' those who seek capital. However, in 1936–9 liberal capitalism was almost everywhere flouted. Commercial and industrial exchanges were often compromised by protectionist laws and by quota arrangements, financial transfers were often under exchange controls. Governmental interventions distorted the normal interplay of international economic relations. It is known that Germany skilfully managed to declare trade in Central Europe and the Balkans 'offside'.[7] Did other governments do the same by utilising their economic armoury? Let us see what France did.

Traditionally France made most use abroad of her financial arm. Before the First World War the action of French banks in certain parts of the world was famous.[8] French commerce entrenched itself in trade with neighbouring states, offering, with few exceptions, expensive products.[9] French technology cut a poor figure by comparison with foreign competitors, save in the automobile and aluminium industries. After the First World War things changed little, except when the weakness of the franc in 1924–6 made French exports more competitive and the exports of capital more speculative.[10] The recovery of the franc allowed Poincaré and the directors of the French banks to return to a foreign policy in which the financial weapon played a role which has already been described.[11] Then came the economic crisis which affected France after 1932. What from then onwards were France's resources in support of her foreign policy?

In 1934–5 'France had to be content with a vegetative economy stabilised at the depressed level to which the previous two years had reduced her after the great disappointment of 1933'.[12] This judgement of a contemporary economist, C. Rist, allows one to gauge the extent of the crisis in France. The main features of the crisis were clear: industrial firms, generally medium-sized, tried to escape the worst of the effects of the fall in prices by trade agreements, but it was much more a matter of surviving at a reduced level than of creating new possibilities of growth; the general decline in profits produced a fall in investments which limited technological development and modernisation. In such a context the possibilities of external action diminished further and besides, French industrialists, like so many others, who were interested in external markets, counted more on customs barriers and preferences (especially imperial) than on increased competitiveness. In a word, the industrial arm, already limited, disappeared almost completely.

French commerce soon felt the consequences. The index of commercial activity (at constant prices) is illuminating (see Table 14.1). As can be seen, France never managed before the war to recover a real exporting strength and her influence as a supplier of manufactured industrial products, modest before the crisis, fell still more. Although some signs of recovery appeared in 1936–8 – which explains the higher rate of imports – they were much more linked to the vicissitudes of the domestic market than to a return in strength to international competitiveness. French manufacturers were dominated by the national horizon. They barricaded themselves at home to the point of refusing the industrialisation of the colonies for fear of arousing in this way a new competition and the risk of not being able to sell sufficient manufactured goods.[13] In these conditions, the rate of cover of French imports remained weak: between 1931 and 1938 it oscillated from 77 per cent in 1934 (best year) to 56 per cent in 1937 (strong recovery of imports), for trade with all countries, colonies included; if the latter are deducted, the rate of cover is even lower: for the same period, it was between 71 per cent and 53 per cent. While the world indices showed a slight recovery from 1934–5 for exports, France remained prostrate. An analysis of trade between France and her main partners confirms, if needed, this mediocrity. Only Switzerland and Belgium bought more than they sold in France; Great Britain had an almost balanced trade account, while Germany constantly accumulated credits (especially in 1936–8), as also Spain, the Low Countries and above all the United States. Overall, France's place in world trade seriously fell to the point of making the period 1936–8 an exceptional moment in the secular evolution of the French economy, as Table 14.2 based on the works of P. Bairoch and J. C. Toutain demonstrates.[14] The table shows, on the one hand, that France's position among the industrialised nations declined appreciably during the 1930s and, on the other, that the French economy was never as indifferent to the external world as during these years. Thus the balance between national production and exports, usually over 20 per cent, fell well below, demonstrating an export capacity below the secular norm. Not only did France suffer from the crisis but she had a tendency to withdraw into herself.

Could financial resources compensate for this trading weakness? Until the crisis, French power overseas rested above all on financial strength. Did this survive? It is difficult to answer this question since we are venturing into territory little explored by historians and also complex in itself. First of all, our ignorance is still great as to the available amounts of exportable capital and on the size of the French portfolio of foreign investments. The situation in 1914 is well known: French investors then held about 42 milliards of gold francs in foreign assets.[15] The sales of assets during the First World War and the subsequent losses resulting from the Russian and Turkish revolutions reduced these riches by about 60 per cent; according to Moulton and Lewis

Table 14.1.   *French commercial activity 1931–8*

1928 = 100	Exports			Imports		
			Manufactured			Manufactured
	Total	Food	objects	Total	Food	objects
1931	76	77	73	122	153	158
1933	59	60	57	107	126	98
1935	55	66	49	89	98	80
1936	52	62	47	98	109	83
1937	57	65	49	104	101	103
1938	61	81	56	93	104	79

Source: A. Sauvy, *Histoire économique de la France entre les deux guerres, 1931–1939* (Paris, 1966–72), Vol. II, p. 564.

Table 14.2.   *French commercial and industrial position*

	1911–13 %	1926–9 %	1936–8 %	1970* %
France's share in:				
world exports of manufactured				
products	11·8	10·9	6·0	7·0
exports of 11 leading				
industrialised countries in	12·1	11·3	7·4	9·0
metals	5·4	11·0	7·2	
machines	3·5	5·7	2·7	
vehicles	16·1	8·1	3·8	
chemical products	11·5	11·2	9·1	
textiles	14·0	17·7	9·0	
Balance between imports and national				
production (%)	25·6	26·0	20·9	29·5
Balance between exports and national				
production (%) (at constant				
values)	22·2	21·2	13·6	26·0

*The figures for 1970 have been calculated on different bases and are therefore only approximate.

the balance remaining in 1923 would have been 18·9 milliards of gold francs.[16] Thereafter the bases of calculation become much more fragile, for the payment of war debts and the related issue of reparations obscured rather than clarified official statistics, which does not help the work of the historian; moreover, the new character of external investments, which made them speculative and short term, complicates retrospective accounting. Taking the information provided by the balance of payments, which was initiated in this period, it can be established that France had a capacity for capital exports of about 8·6 milliards of gold francs between 1922 and 1930 inclusive.[17] None the less, it is not possible to add this figure to the total for 1923 because short-term speculative capital movements must be taken into account, such as those which anticipated or accompanied the manipulations of the franc in the mid-1920s. As soon as the Poincaré franc was created account must also be taken of the part played by the Paris market in providing a haven for foreign capital. If it is agreed that the French portfolio of foreign investments was about 22 milliards of gold francs at the end of the 1920s, it should also be said that the strength of the Paris market was reinforced by the support of foreign capital holders, at least until 1933. French ambitions to play a determining role in the monetary reconstruction of Central Europe and the Balkans, exemplified in the Tardieu and Bonnet plans of 1932–3, demonstrated this recovery of power. The gold stock accumulated in the euphoric years reassured those who believed in French financial strength. At the London Conference of 1933, the last world conference aimed at reaching an international solution to world economic problems, such was the strength of France's position that she was criticised for being 'egoistic' when she vainly sought to conserve a system based on gold which she still held in large amounts.[18]

The years that followed seemed much more sombre. On the one hand, the normal capacity for exporting capital melted away like snow in the sun; on the other, the political jolts and the stupidity of a deflationist strategy incited French and foreign capital holders to avoid Paris. According to the balance of payments, which showed a large and constant trade deficit, but also a negative current balance since 1932, France had virtually lost the capacity to export new capital at the end of the 1930s. This picture of accounts does not mean that the flights of capital were no longer possible in face of political and economic vicissitudes; simply that they were by nature erratic movements, short-term and incapable of supporting a long-term strategy. In fact French governments expended much more energy in securing the return of exported capital than in encouraging the export of capital. When this private capital fled abroad there was no question of making use of it politically. How could an external strategy be based on these 'flights' of capital – often massive and rapid? Even if France was not intrinsically impoverished, she no longer possessed in the years preceding the war the financial weapon which had been so celebrated before 1914.

The overall picture of French economic activities abroad seems singularly limited for the period under consideration. Within a few years, a financially strong France, with a growing foreign trade, supported by a colonial empire on its way to playing an important economic role, became a country which, consciously or not, turned towards selfish or autarkic solutions. The overriding impression is that French illusions of being able to escape the world crisis or, at the very least, of having the means to resist it by a special policy based on the so-called 'spécificité' of the French economy, prevented French governments from seeing realities clearly. Today these seem self-evident: in herself, France was becoming a medium-sized power.

Of the illusions of the time, one of the most deeply rooted and fatal was the belief in monetarism or, to put it better, in the idea that the saving of the franc would be the remedy for the economic ills which afflicted France. Governments and economists, with few exceptions, were agreed that by the heavy devaluation of 1928 France had restored the value of her currency to a proper balance and that she could not endanger this value for social and political considerations. The rentiers had been flattened by the war and another devaluation would be a victimisation of the French middle classes. Any new devaluation would be a crime. Accordingly, when the experts noticed the serious gap between French prices and world prices (about 25 per cent) they tended to urge deflation as a solution to this weakness. By a severe curtailment of expenses, by strict budgetary equilibrium, the prices of competitors which had devalued (Great Britain and the United States in the first place) would naturally recover with the economic upswing, and little by little the difference between French prices and international prices would tend to narrow. Thus the conditions of trade would return to normal, an adjustment of the franc would be unnecessary and its stability towards other currencies would be a pledge of future strength. The key to success depended on the vigour and efficiency of the deflation. Moreover, the French position was not unique, at least in 1933–4. Other states on the gold standard had refused to follow the British precedent of 1931 (floating of the pound sterling) and along with France, they formed the 'Bloc-or' of wisdom (Belgium, the Low Countries, Italy, Poland, Czechoslovakia). In the French Press, especially the financial Press, there were condescending references to the fact that the British had been forced to allow their currency to float. In fact, until the spring of 1935 the evolution of international financial and monetary relations seemed to confirm the views of French experts. Thus, in March 1935 the pound was further weakened on the foreign exchange market; the French authorities were disposed to help the 'pauvre livre sterling', and were ready to provide 'munitions' for the British government.[19] The French government and the Bank of France seemed agreed on helping the Americans in order to provide joint assistance for the British.[20] However, the Americans took a line unacceptable to the French in asking France to accept a 15 to 20 per cent devaluation in order to create an enlarged Gold Bloc which would ensure the full stabilisation of the major currencies.[21] But for France the organisation of international solidarity did not mean modifying the value of the franc.

The situation changed radically during 1935. First of all, in March, Belgium changed methods and camp. Belgian exporters were being increasingly penalised by the overvalued Belgian franc, above all as a result of the new retreat of the pound sterling. Belgian devaluation became inevitable. In a lucid and pessimistic report the Quai d'Orsay's Assistant Political Director, Robert Coulondre, spelled out the consequences:

The situation is too serious for us to delude ourselves with appearances, even if we content ourselves with half-measures which would at once be overtaken by events. It would be best to recognise that the Gold Bloc does not have sufficient economic potential and complementary markets to be self-sufficient . . . If we are to maintain the stability of our currency, we must necessarily take indispensable measures for the protection of our economy: a further strengthening of quota arrangements, increased duties, increases in trading tax licences. Perhaps, thanks to a system of managed economy, we might be successful for a while in avoiding a worsening of our trade deficit. We cannot avoid the continuing reduction of the volume of trade. That is the danger. Little by little France will impose a closed economy on herself, as has happened in the case of agriculture . . . We will have . . . to close the still half-open doors and so lose our last external outlets without our anaemic market being able to absorb our production. How therefore do we check the crisis, unemployment and the budget deficit . . . What will be the fate of the capitalist system if it locks itself into this vice?[22]

Faced with the Belgian partners, who had just announced their inevitable devaluation and their departure from the Gold Bloc, this high French official explained clearly the fundamental choice which confronted France; either autarky, as a necessary defence of the currency, or else an approach to the outside world, that is to say, discussions with the other capitalist powers whose determination to restore international trade by lowering customs barriers and by realistic exchange rates was known. From the spring of 1935 the alternative was clear.

The political consequences of this choice are easy to identify. In 1935 Anglo-Saxon economic and financial strength, though weakened by the crisis, remained fundamental in the capitalist world. The idea of salvation by France's own efforts was clearly a myth. It was not an accident that the few politicians favourable to devaluation at the time were those who looked to the Anglo-Saxon world (Raymond Patenôtre, Paul Reynaud); on their side, bankers in touch with City colleagues began to suggest the alignment of the French currency with the pound and, in any case, urged the importance of not cutting oneself off from Anglo-Saxon markets.[23] In the summer of 1935 a trend became established among political and economic authorities which, without openly preaching devaluation, suggested at least the strengthening of links with London. It should be mentioned that this new orientation was the result, in the short-run, of the first violent storm to shake the franc in May 1935. By contrast to the situation in March when the French were ready to rescue the weakened pound sterling, in May the squall hit the franc. Suddenly from 21 May an offensive developed against the franc. The causes of this attack of fever were multiple, as in many cases of monetary crisis it is difficult to determine the principal cause of the trouble. Two internal political considerations may have played a part: on the one hand, municipal elections demonstrated the growth of the left with the Popular Front gaining in strength; on the other, certain leaders of the Bank of France, led by François de Wendel, decided to force Flandin, the Prime Minister, to follow a more traditional financial and monetary policy and were widely accused in the Press and in Parliament of having fired a warning shot by organising the flight of capital withholding confidence in the Flandin government (the latter resigned at the end of May).[24] Moreover, the devaluation of the Belgian franc in April 1935 and the uncertainties about the solidity of the Gold Bloc may have encouraged some speculators to gamble against the franc. Whatever the truth of the matter, the alert was serious: in ten days, 6·3 milliards of francs disappeared abroad. Even though capital returned afterwards, a pattern was established.

Such a shock convinced the advocates of devaluation of the wisdom of their views. Indeed, reading the internal records of the ministries concerned one had the impression of an evolution of opinion in the autumn of 1935. For example, in September the financial attaché in London, Mönick, sent a report to the Minister of Finance in which he discreetly suggested devaluation. His reasoning merits attention: it was illusory to wait for an early stabilisation of the pound and a foreign price rise to recover competitiveness; 'as long as we are determined in France not to loosen – however slightly – the link which binds us to gold and a too high parity, it must be recognised that our situation is particularly difficult, that our freedom of action is gravely impaired and that the recovery of our internal economy depends less on ourselves than on the foreigner'.[25] 'A wisely planned monetary adjustment' was needed. The Director of the *Mouvement des Fonds* annotated this document 'Important'. While the Laval government developed its deflation policy in full, the devaluationists were beginning to receive a hearing in political circles. Quite simply, confronted by a public opinion constantly warned against the mortal sin of devaluation, it was embarrassing to manoeuvre in this sense, especially on the eve of a general election.

Time was left to do its own work; or rather the results of the election were awaited. This neglect facilitated the activity of speculators who, by temporarily buying foreign currencies, were almost certain of winning when the inevitable devaluation took place. The flight of capital was resumed in the winter of 1935, doubtless encouraged by the fears of a Popular Front electoral victory, but also supported by those who sent their capital to the United States to benefit from an economic upturn. In short, between May 1935 and June 1936 11 to 13 milliards of francs were exported. This movement was on such a scale that it pushed French governments not only towards devaluation, but also towards dependence on the Anglo-Saxon powers.

A first manifestation of this financial dependence was noticeable in February 1936. Flandin, the Foreign Minister, wished to raise a short-term loan on the London market. For a total of 3 milliards of francs, this three-months loan, renewable for a year, was to help the French Treasury to combat foreign exchange losses.[26] On 17 February the Chancellor of the Exchequer, Chamberlain, agreed to this loan being raised by Lazard; but during the negotiations requests for commercial concessions (tax reductions, increase of quotas) were presented, and although finally nothing was imposed, the need for Franco-British solidarity was underlined. The fall of the Laval Cabinet a few days before, moreover, had facilitated the conclusion of an agreement. And reading the almost daily reports from the French financial attaché in London allows the change in the balance of economic strength during these crucial years to be measured: while the situation improved appreciably over the Channel, in France the difficulties increased. Certainly, the political and social shocks of the Popular Front played a part in this process, but it must be admitted that the decline in France's fortunes had started in 1935. Later, the policy of appealing for Anglo-Saxon financial aid was continued, especially to implement the inevitable devaluation of September 1936.

We will not trace here in detail the negotiations in the summer of 1936.[27] The tripartite Anglo-American–French Agreement of 25 September 1936, involving the 'guarantee' of the new value of the franc and the recognition by the French government of the utility of opening its frontiers to trade, constituted a kind of common front of these three countries in economic and financial matters. Yet there was no mistaking the strong and the weak in this trio.[28] Doubtless it was hoped on the French side that the Anglo-American duel – a fierce one concerning the parity between the dollar and the pound sterling – would enable France to extricate herself from an unfavourable settlement; but, in fact, on the American side, the question of unpaid and suspended war debts was immediately raised, while on the British side the granting of new short-term loans was accompanied by technical considerations calculated to impose certain political solutions. The negotiations regarding the loan raised in London by the Blum government in January–February 1937 illustrate this point.

The September 1936 devaluation, linked to the Tripartite Agreement, should have encouraged capital holders to repatriate their funds. It did nothing of the kind; from the end of October the slight movement towards repatriation which had followed devaluation dried up. Political mistrust of capital holders towards the Popular Front, calculations of self-interest in the belief that the new level of the franc had been fixed too high and that a new downward correction was inevitable – whatever the causes, from the autumn the franc was again in trouble.[29] Increased spending on defence, the unwillingness of the banks to prolong the Treasury bonds coming up for repayment, the public works policy – all meant recourse to advances from the Bank of France. While the economic context improved, the Treasury crisis deepened in December 1936 and January 1937. In November the loan raised in London by Flandin had been repaid, but from mid-January the Governor of the Bank of France asked for the help of his colleague at the Bank of England during a meeting at Basel.[30] According to a letter from Rueff to Mönick relating to this interview and asking the latter to discuss French needs with the British Treasury, it seems that a long-term loan of about 9 milliards of francs was envisaged.[31] The British reply was disappointing: London agreed only to a short-term loan and for a smaller amount. On 21 January Auriol, the Minister of Finance, informed Chamberlain that the sum requested was only 4·2 milliards of francs (as a result of a 'misunderstanding') while at the same time insisting that 'the loan should be for as long a period as possible'.[32] 'A refusal now would be vexatious, for it is known that negotiations have taken place in Basel and in London on this subject, and if we have to decide to borrow on another market, the refusal that we have received would be exploited at home for political reasons.'

The negotiations lasted until 26 January. They only ended in a new loan when the French agreed to renounce any request for customs concessions in future tariff talks (these were shortly to be held on French imports of English coal and French exports to Great Britain). In addition, the loan was a short-term one, on the usual loan conditions, 'according to the terms outlined by the Treasury and Bank of England'.[33] And, above all, this financial agreement was coupled with political talks held at the same time. On 20 January Blum met Anthony Eden who proposed to him a joint negotiation with the Germans. The British view was that the Western powers could bring economic and financial help to states in economic distress (such was then the case of Germany) provided that 'economic collaboration and political appeasement went hand in hand'.[34] In a speech at Lyons on 24 January Blum, who had agreed to modify his text on this point, accepted the British proposals, referring to 'the necessary liaison between economic co-operation on the one hand and peaceful organisation and a halt to the armaments race on the other'.[35] Some still considered that Schacht's influence might prevail over the Führer; the pursuit of appeasement with Germany still seemed possible. Although the connection between financial aid and diplomatic strategy is not clearly marked in the documents, one is struck by the concordance of dates between these facts; in any case, Blum wanted to tie French policy to Anglo-Saxon views. On 26 February Blum declared in the Chamber of Deputies:

The logical inclination of our internal policy would lead us to adopt coercive measures against the export of capital and currency speculation . . . But that would be to create a contradiction between our policy which seeks a community of action with the great Anglo-Saxon nations and the signing of a monetary agreement aimed at restoring activity and liberty to international trade.[36]

A few days earlier, the Blum government was able to measure the limits on its freedom of action in international financial policy. On 8 February Auriol requested an urgent and secret meeting with Chamberlain. Was it to obtain new financial aid or to prepare his neighbours for new measures? In any event, from 12 February the British government was careful to take precautions. In a message full of anxiety about the state of the French Treasury (the French exchange stabilisation fund was exhausted in spite of the recently concluded loan), the London authorities questioned the French government on the measures that it intended to take 'to restore promptly confidence in the franc'. Auriol's reply deserves analysis.[37] Recognising the extreme precariousness of the French situation, the French government presented a programme for future reform which responded perfectly to 'liberal' wishes: progressive re-establishment of budgetary equilibrium; reduction of public works; free circulation of gold, an agreed lowering of customs duties, restrictions on the making of quotas; above all, 'in full agreement with the Bank of France and despite inaccurate rumours spread for political ends about the action of its Governor, the French government refuses vehemently to establish exchange controls, which would in fact be contrary to the principles of the monetary agreement as well as the needs of close international collaboration'. The allusion to the Governor of the Bank of France, Labeyrie, only makes full sense if one knows that the latter had recommended exchange controls in August 1936 and that his ideas on the subject had hardly changed since then. But Blum chose the other path; in an interview with Rueff, on 6 February 1937, he declared to the Director of the *Mouvement des Fonds*: 'I will not bring in exchange controls. Not that I fear the domestic consequences – they do not frighten me – but because they will have the fatal effect of straining the ties which unite us to the Anglo-Saxon democracies, ties which are essential to the coherent development of our foreign policy.'[38] On the whole, foreign policy imperatives took precedence over ideological convictions, but these imperatives were the result of the disastrous situation of the French Treasury, incapable of meeting its numerous commitments arising from repayments of old loans, budget deficits, the needs of rearmament, and even indeed from help given to 'friendly' states (Poland, Romania, Czechoslovakia).[39] Having thus demonstrated its goodwill towards London, Paris in return asked the British government in its note of 17 February to sign a declaration of solidarity for the joint defence of Western currencies (this idea had already been put forward during the September 1936 negotiations). On 19 February London flatly refused such solidarity, although it expressed its interest in the programme presented for future recovery. To sum up, the British government had, in its way, contributed, with others, to the 'pause' in political and social reforms announced by Blum on 13 February 1937.

More generally, it seems that French governments henceforth needed Anglo-Saxon confidence or complaisance to satisfy their financial obligations. This has just been demonstrated with regard to the Blum government; the Chautemps government, in which Bonnet was at the Ministry of Finance, carried out a new devaluation with ease at the end of June 1937, thanks to the 'understanding' of London and New York where the exchange markets were temporarily closed. Solidarity with the Anglo-Saxons was again affirmed. They were equally reassured by the policy of strict budgetary equilibrium announced by Bonnet, well known in American financial circles (he had just spent several months as Ambassador in the United States). Bonnet had announced on his return to France that only severe restrictions on governmental spending could restore France's credit and the confidence needed for the return of exported capital! The minister even considered cutting defence expenditure, the defence of the franc having priority over all other considerations, as the Director of the *Mouvement des Fonds*, Rueff, suggested.[40] Preoccupied above all with restoring the confidence of capital holders, the Ministry of Finance tried to reduce the deficit to the minimum, even at the risk of bringing military strength into line with financial strength, though fully aware of its limitations at the time. But did not such a choice lead to a policy of appeasement?

In this perspective, there was perfect harmony with the British. Like them, France rearmed but at a slower tempo, more in keeping with financial resources. With them or thanks to them, the Treasury deficits could continue to be met while awaiting the recovery that would come with the return of capital. Some complained or showed themselves disillusioned with such a situation. Thus Pierre Laval, in February 1937, told the Financial Committee of the Chamber: 'It is fortunate that England is interested for two more years – that is until her rearmament is finished – in supporting France. But this help will not extend to a full financial sacrifice and England will not agree to take our place to cover our needs.'[41] Laval's anglophobia, understandable after his failures of 1935, perhaps renders him suspect, but his awareness of the precariousness of France's position is significant, as is also that of Admiral Darlan who, a few months later, displeased to see the credits of the navy sacrificed to satisfy the views of the defenders of the franc, concluded that, in these conditions, the French government would be forced 'to model' its foreign policy 'exactly' on that of the British government.[42]

France's financial destiny was now heavily dependent on the conditions of Anglo-Saxon markets. Witness the Daladier government's first financial measures in April 1938. The new devaluation carried out on 4 May 1938 no longer took as the franc's base its weight in gold but the rate of the pound sterling; this 'Franc-Sterling', to use the consecrated expression, had its fate tied to the vicissitudes of the British currency, which was itself affected by the hazards of international policy in 1938.[43] However, precautions were taken to preserve the position of the currency. Secret negotiations took place between the Finance Ministries of the three signatory states of the 1936 Agreement; a 'true experiment in financial collaboration' occurred in the words of Rueff, who represented the French government. In Washington the Secretary to the Treasury, Henry Morgenthau, had for a long time shown an anxious interest in the franc; he was as much aware as the French authorities were of the high level of French capital exports to the United States; some French exchange controls might even help in the common defence of currencies.[44] In any event, in the spring of 1938 the financial situation depended more than ever on Anglo-Saxon aid. Also, the French began to follow British methods of managing the Treasury, putting into effect, for example, a policy of 'open market' for the Bank of France (Decree-Law 17 June 1938). Should one therefore speak of French dependence on London?

It would seem that the very formulation of the question does not accurately reflect the situation. In fact the need for solid financial support from the Anglo-Saxons (and not only from London) was not seen at the time as a bond of dependence, quite simply because contemporaries were conscious of weaknesses as monetary, rather than as characteristic of a French decline. (France ahead of other European powers was caught up in the movement which reduced Europe to a more modest role in the world.) The reasoning of the leadership in 1937–9 can be outlined in the following manner: in the short run, we have the same interests as the British and we can follow their tactic of appeasement. We are suffering from serious financial troubles which are caused above all by the lack of confidence shown by French capitalists in the future of their own country. To restore their confidence, it is necessary, on the one hand, on the home front to return to a policy of budgetary and social rigour (thus turning one's back on the costly reforms of the Popular Front which are inopportune); on the other, on the international front, it is necessary to pursue a peaceful strategy, conciliatory towards aggressive states, since the financing of a real rearmament programme exceeds our present resources. It is necessary at least to gain some time in order to find some possibilities for compromise; perhaps one might even envisage avoiding a conflict with Germany by satisfying her purely national claims, since these relate to territories in Eastern Europe, Hitler having affirmed that he has no ambitions in Alsace-Lorraine. These calculations rested manifestly on a double postulate: first, Hitler's expansion would limit itself to Eastern Europe; secondly, the restoration of confidence in a 'well-governed' France would secure the return of capital.

One knows what happened. Hitler was not a gentleman, solely concerned with liberating Germans under foreign yoke, in Bohemia and Danzig. However, when the Daladier government by contrast finally ended all experiments savouring of the Popular Front, and especially once it vanquished trade union power during the great strike of November 1938, exported capital returned with remarkable rapidity.[45] The principal merit of Paul Reynaud was thus to symbolise this total return to financial and economic orthodoxy, even though some had difficulty in forgetting that the same Reynaud had seemed a heretic a few years earlier in urging devaluation. Following the May 1938 devaluation which created 'Franc-Sterling' and confirmed a 12 per cent fall in the value of the franc, about 18 milliards of francs returned;[46] between November 1938 and September 1939 an additional 25 milliards of francs was repatriated.[47] This phenomenon was on such a scale that it produced a double paradox: on the one hand, the value of the pound sterling was affected because a considerable amount of the capital which had sought refuge in Great Britain in the crisis years now flowed back to France reducing English revenues at a time when the cost of rearmament weighed heavily on the finances of that country; on the other, the franc was linked to the pound and felt the effects of British monetary weakness.[48] Nevertheless, on the eve of war the French Treasury and currency seemed to have recovered their health and with a confident pride Reynaud claimed to have prepared France effectively for an economic struggle. Anxiety now arose on account of her British ally whose uncertainties were known and who seemed to have difficulty in overcoming the post-Munich attack of uneasiness.[49] Yet, behind the two European democracies, could one rely on the material help of the formidable America? In any event, Franco-British solidarity could function in both directions.

From the summer of 1938, the analyses of the leadership, drawn up in terms of the economic and financial circumstances, differed not so much on the relevance of appeasement as on its future consequences. The majority of politicians, businessmen, civil servants, were agreed on the need to shape France's strategy to her resources, that is to say, by imitating British realism in Eastern Europe. Although it cannot be said that before Munich business and banking circles had already prepared a French retreat from Eastern Europe, they quickly adapted themselves to it.[50] However, beyond the acquiescence in Czechoslovakia ('It does not represent more than a kind of greater Luxembourg clinging to the flanks of the Reich and has no future except as a German protégé and vassal')[51] was it necessary to pursue a wider economic entente, including Italy and even Germany, as Bonnet seemed to hanker after in November 1938,[52] or was it necessary to envisage a kind of threshold beyond which any new retreat would be worse than the risk of war? At present, we lack sufficient historical studies to enable us to assess the numerical and political significance of the advocates of the first formula and of the defenders of the second. Doubtless, as in Great Britain, there were 'committed appeasers' who still believed the Germans might be interested in economic collaboration and who remained convinced that war would be financially and militarily unsupportable; but they were more and more criticised by the 'temporising appeasers' who were aware of the changing balance of financial strength and of the too obvious German encroachments. A single fact seemed certain in 1939: the French economic recovery modified the economic background of a future war and encouraged greater firmness in those who believed that any conflict would be long and essentially economic. But the 'pacifism' of the first group was able to feed on so many non-economic sources in France that it still seemed powerful on the very eve of war. It was a troubled, divided and therefore uncertain France which went to war.

At the close of this too rapid survey, despite the many shadowy areas which remain because of the lack of research in this field, a few conclusions can be presented. First, the weakness of the financial resources at the disposition of French governments, either for rearmament, or to provide economic arms for influence abroad, was caused by a combination of structural and conjunctural factors. The structures of French industry and commerce were obsolete, ill-adapted and, saving some exceptions, incapable of renewing themselves, totally insufficient to enable France to be more than a medium power. Nevertheless, a true economic policy, better adapted to the crisis, which could have taken into account neighbouring monetary experiments and which did not take the defence of the franc as a major, even exclusive, target, could have prevented the mediocre structures from getting worse. The permanent financial and budgetary crisis between 1935 and 1938 could have been avoided, especially when it began in 1935. In this respect the responsibilities can be plainly identified: the political leadership, badly advised by its public and private experts, aggravated the problem by the practice of deflation, then by a clumsy devaluation.

More serious was the responsibility of the financial leadership. The capital holders deprived France of the resources which were indispensable for her real political independence. It became necessary to ask for Anglo-Saxon aid at decisive periods, in 1936–7, at a time moreover when choices were still possible. Certainly, after all, at the end of 1938 the crisis was overcome and the financial resources needed for an effective rearmament policy reappeared, but was it not too late to make up for lost time? Above all, had France not been forced to resign herself, willingly or unwillingly, to the appeasement favoured by the British? When they had adopted the tactic of appeasement they had not been constrained to do so by financial decline and the flight of capital. In France it was not the same.

Appeasement, whether committed or temporising, has its economic justification in the crying insufficiency of financial resources, caused essentially by the flight of capital. Since many capital holders preferred to forget national priorities, and even national defence, for political reasons or out of self-interest, any government was condemned to a certain impotence or to a certain degree of dependence, given that coercion, that is to say, exchange controls, would have separated France from the liberal-democratic camp.[53] Fundamentally, politicians, in this matter, accepted the situation by seeking to adjust to it. In 1936 and 1937 Léon Blum chose to forget his doctrinal convictions; the very relative Western solidarity could not compensate for internal hostility. Appeasement was more acceptable to Chautemps and Bonnet for reasons of temperament, conviction and tactics. As for Daladier, he wanted above all to gain time 'while waiting for the Americans'. But, finally, was not the decisive gesture accomplished by those who obeyed the lure of profit? In December 1938 a capitalist who sold the dollars bought in May 1935 on the Paris Exchange made a profit of two-and-a-half times his outlay.[54] Was this a sufficient reason? Financial patriotism is also a form of national defence. In a cruel comment, the Secretary to the Treasury, Morgenthau, summed up the situation: 'La Belle France still has her virtue, but not much gold.'[55]

Notes: Chapter 14

1   J. B. Duroselle, *La Décadence, 1932–1939* (Paris, 1979).
2   F. Bédarida, 'La gouvernante anglaise', in R. Rémond and J. Bourdin (eds), *Edouard Daladier, Chef de Gouvernement* (Paris, 1977), p. 228.
3   The pejorative sense which the word Munich has acquired explains the zeal with which the political leaders of the time have sought an English 'cover' for their own choice of policy. It is true, however, that the reading of the official minutes of Franco-British meetings in 1938 reveals the extent to which the French were manipulated by their partners.
4   Daladier's interventions in September 1938 in Franco-British discussions show that he had a clear conception of what Hitler was and of what was to be expected from him. However, in the end Daladier followed Chamberlain.
5   The study of the archives of the *Direction du Mouvement des Fonds*, at the Ministry of Finance, series F 30, is illuminating in this respect.
6   cf. Duroselle, *La Décadence*, p. 282.
7   The normal 'game' of international trade relations passes through the observation of the movement of world prices and through the rules of competition in a liberal capitalist economy. But did such an economy survive still at the end of the 1930s?
8   For a work of synthesis, refer to my book, *Diplomatie européenne et impérialismes 1870–1914* (Paris, 1978). See also R. Poidevin, *Finances et relations internationales 1887–1914*, (Paris, 1970).
9   cf. *Histoire économique et sociale de la France*, Vol. IV/1: *1880–1914*, ed. F. Braudel and E. Labrousse (Paris, 1979), ch. IV, 'Place et rôle des echanges extérieurs'.
10 cf. *Histoire économique*, Vol. IV/2: *1914–1950*, ch. II, bk III (Paris, 1980).
11 See the memoirs of the Governor of the Bank of France, E. Moreau, published in Paris in 1954 (period 1926–8).
12 Cited in *Histoire économique*, Vol. IV/2, ch. II, bk II, p. 655.
13 French colonies remained relatively undeveloped, with few exceptions, in spite of the ambitious investment plans which had been proposed since the 1920s – for example, the Plan Sarraut. Many political leaders complained of this bitterly.
14 P. Bairoch, 'France's place in the international markets', and J. C. Toutain, 'The structures of France's foreign trade, 1789–1970', in M. Levy-Leboyer (ed.), *La Position internationale de la France, aspects économiques et financiers, XIX–XX siècles* (Paris, 1977).
15 The figures fluctuate between 38 and 45 milliards of francs according to the authorities. Our own research has confirmed this estimate.
16 L. Moulton and C. Lewis, *La Dette française* (Paris, 1926).
17 Calculations based on the book published by the Royal Institute of International Affairs, *The Problem of International Investment* (London, 1937).
18 In 1933 France possessed a gold stock of 3·022 millions of dollars (reserves of the central bank) against 4·012 in the United States and 928 millions in Great Britain, according to R. Nurkse, *L'Expérience monétaire internationale* (Geneva: SDN, 1944).
19 cf. Correspondence between the Ministry of Finance and the financial attaché in London, Archives des Finances (hereafter MDF), series F 30, no. 1419.
20 ibid., interview Lacour-Gayet (Bank of France) and Cochran (American financial attaché in Paris), 8 March 1935.
21 Soundings in this sense were made in March and April 1935, ibid.
22 Note of the Assistant Political Director, 11 March 1935, ibid.
23 Dossier Finaly, note submitted after a visit to London, June 1935, MDF, series F 30 no. 2354.
24 See J. N. Jeanneney, *François de Wendel en république, l'argent et le pouvoir 1914–1940* (Paris, 1976), p. 507.
25 Report of 1 September 1935, MDF, series F 30, no. 2354.
26 File on this loan in MDF, series B, no. 12619, second folio.
27 On the negotiation of the agreement of September 1936, cf. R. Girault, 'Léon Blum, la dévaluation de 1936 et la conduite de la politique extérieure de la France', *Relations Internationales*, no. 13 (1978), p. 91.

28 The French government was not able to impose its views which consisted in seeking a joint declaration of solidarity between the currencies. By contrast, the members of the Gold Bloc who had not yet devalued followed France's path.
29 This was the opinion of *The Times* of 14 April 1937.
30 The file relating to the loan of January 1937 is in MDF, series B, no. 12682.
31 Letter of Rueff of 15 January 1937. The amount of the loan would enable the French railways to pay off their deficit and cover the needs of the Treasury.
32 Personal letter from V. Auriol to the financial attaché in London, 21 January 1937, ibid.
33 The terms utilised by the financial attaché in a report of 27 January (note sur l'opération d'emprunt projeté à Londres), ibid.
34 Terms used in a speech to the House of Commons on 19 January by the Foreign Secretary, Anthony Eden.
35 Lyons speech, 24 January, R. Blum (ed.), *Oeuvres de L. Blum* (Paris, 1960), Vol. 3, p. 382.
36 Speech to the Chamber on 26 February, cited by G. Lefranc, *Histoire du Front Populaire* (Paris, 1965), p. 230.
37 Letter to the British government, 17 February 1937, MDF, series B, no. 12682.
38 Note for the Minister of Finance drawn up by Rueff after his interview with Blum on 6 February, reproduced by J. Rueff, *De l'Aube au crépuscule, autobiographie* (Paris, 1977), p. 130.
39 In his letter to the British government Auriol cited these three states as recipients of French aid. Poland had received help under the Rambouillet Agreement, which gave her a loan of 2 milliards of francs (September 1936).
40 The policy of G. Bonnet is well analysed by R. Frankenstein, *Le Financement du réarmement français, 1935–1939*, Thèse de 3è cycle (Paris, 1978); Frankenstein entitles the relevant chapter 'Bonnet extends the pause to rearmament'.
41 Cited by Frankenstein, p. 377.
42 Cited by Frankenstein, p. 444.
43 cf. F. Sedillot, *Histoire du Franc* (Paris, 1939), and L. Neurisse, *Histoire du franc* (Paris, 1963).
44 Rueff evokes this episode in his autobiography, *De l'Aube au crépuscule*, p. 156. See also MDF, series B, no. 12681.
45 On the role and the significance of this strike in French life, consult R. Rémond and J. Bourdin (eds), *La France et les français en 1938–1939* (Paris, 1978).
46 Figure given by Frankenstein, *Le Financement du réarmement*, p. 494.
47 cf. Frankenstein, 'Le financement français de la guerre et les accords avec les britanniques (1939–1940)', in *Français et Britanniques dans la drôle de guerre* (Paris, 1979).
48 cf. MDF, Correspondance de l'agence financière de Londres, series B, no. 12638.
49 The correspondence of the Ambassador Corbin reveals the financial and economic difficulties experienced at the time in Great Britain. Archives of the Ministry of Foreign Affairs, Grande Bretagne, no. 1089, série reconstituée.
50 One can cite the example of the Banque des Pays de l'Europe Centrale which always insisted on keeping a deposit equivalent to the share capital subscribed by French investors (say, 80 per cent of the latter) in a London bank, in order to be able to dispose of it freely. In May 1939 the bank was thus able to recover the relevant sum on the cession of its shares to the Dresdner Bank (MDF, series B, no. 12662).
51 Report of the French delegate to the International Commission in Berlin charged with the delimitation of the Czechoslovak frontiers in October 1938. Archives du Quai d'Orsay, carton Tchécoslovaquie, no. 1139 (SDN).
52 Minutes of the Franco-British Conference of 24 November 1938 in which Bonnet asked about the prospects of co-operation and development of commercial relations with central Europe. Archives Daladier, FNSP, 2 DA 4.
53 In March 1938 the Secretary of the Treasury, Morgenthau, informed Blum's government that he 'would understand' the necessity for France to establish exchange controls to defend its currency. Did this push Blum into considering exchange controls? cf. Morgenthau, letter to Cochran, 14 March 1938, J. Morton Blum, *From the Morgenthau Diaries* (Boston, Mass., 1959), p. 500.
54 Calculations based on monthly rate of exchange given in A. Sauvy, *Histoire économique de la France entre les deux guerres* (Paris, 1967), tome 2, p. 489. With 100 francs in May 1935

one could buy 6·58 dollars which, converted into francs in December 1938, returned 249·97 francs.

55   Letter to Roosevelt, mid-June 1937, Blum, *From the Morgenthau Diaries*, p. 474.

15 Against Appeasement: French Advocates of Firmness, 1933–8

MAURICE VAÏSSE

If the *antimunichois* are well known, it is not the same for the advocates of firmness in 1933.

At the time of Hitler's coming to power, as five years later during the Czechoslovak crisis, the advocates of firmness were a minority. Appeasement carried the day, but there were more than nuances between the two events. The Ethiopian affair, the remilitarisation of the Rhineland, the Spanish Civil War, the Popular Front, the *Anschluss* all profoundly shaped French opinion, which reacted much more strongly to the Munich Agreement. It is true that in the latter case war seemed imminent.

In 1933 French appeasement towards Hitler was of a special kind; it was based on temporisation.[1] Few Frenchmen saw in Nazism anything more than a passing phenomenon. The image of General Boulanger was symptomatic of this outlook. Like General Boulanger, Hitler would, it was believed, quickly cross Germany's political horizon. It was a difficult moment to get over and after all Hitler's advent did not confirm the pessimistic forecasts that had been made. The continuity in which the new Nazism dressed itself was reassuring. Daladier himself challenged uneasy senators: 'Gentlemen, I would like someone to tell me how Germany's policy has changed.'[2] In truth Hitler's advent to power was even reassuring in its Manichaean clarification of the diplomatic situation. François de Wendel was pleased with this event which would at last open the eyes of those who did not wish to see.[3] Daladier confided to deputies and senators that Hitler's policy had had a happy effect on France's diplomatic situation.

One can readily understand how temporisation led to inaction and ended in appeasement. It was a question of allowing Nazism to commit the mistakes that would isolate Germany and precipitate Hitler's fall – which was considered inevitable.

Opposing this passive appeasement, there were the advocates of firmness. Who were they? What policy did they have in mind? The replies to these questions are all the more interesting because it was undoubtedly during the first year of Hitler's rule that some action might have been possible. Who were they? We have distinguished four categories of persons: journalists, soldiers, diplomats, politicians. In the absence of adequate documentation, we have not considered business interests. For each of these categories we will take a specific example and analyse it.

First the journalists. If Pertinax's career is well known, less well known are the roles of Wladimir d'Ormesson and Pierre Lafue. Ormesson is extremely interesting for he was one of those who had advocated a Franco-German reconciliation and had participated in the attempts at reconciliation organised by the Mayrisch committee in 1932 and even at the beginning of 1933. Now, on 30 January 1933, Wladimir d'Ormesson took stock of the policy of *rapprochement* and conducted in the newspaper *Le Temps* a tenacious and lively campaign against the Hitler regime which was said to be playing a double game and wanted war.[4]

Pierre Lafue is above all known for having launched in 1933 Gaston Doumergue, by devoting to him a biography which appeared in the autumn of 1933, and by editing a periodical *1933* which numbered among its contributors several academicians, André Chaumeix, Abel Bonnard, Henry Bordeaux, and eminent writers, Jérôme and Jean Tharaud, Paul Géraldy, Pierre Mac Orlan, Robert Brasillach, Maurice Bardèche. This periodical openly spoke of the need for a revolution but a revolution of order, and one of the persons admired in the issues of *1933* and of its successor *1934* was the fascist dictator Mussolini. But in contrast to the admiration for Mussolini's Italy, one of the leitmotivs of this periodical was the threat of German rearmament. Thus, in one of the first issues, 25 October 1933, the fortnightly journal published a major article entitled 'The truth about Hitler's army', signed by 'one of the leaders of the Germany of yesterday'. It would be interesting to know who was supposed to be hiding behind this periphrasis.

Next the military leaders. Two cases have to be distinguished: the High Command and an individual officer. In the High Command, General Weygand and General Gamelin saw in Hitler's coming to power the opportunity to put an end to the policy of concessions; they vigorously rejected any reduction in French military power and opposed disarmament plans, particularly the MacDonald plan, and General Weygand resolutely refused any modification of the treaty limitations on German armaments. An individual case now: Lieutenant-Colonel de Gaulle. It was in fact in May 1933 that an article was published in the *Revue politique et parlementaire*, signed Charles de Gaulle, and entitled 'Towards a professional army'. This was the first version of the work which appeared a year later. The officer was then serving in the general secretariat of the SCDN and had the leisure to study the different components of French strategy. From these reflections came this article which de Gaulle said was based on a study of the necessities of *la couverture*, the exigencies of the profession of arms and on international developments.

As regards the diplomats, three examples may be cited: André François-Poncet, French Ambassador to Germany, the Ambassador to the Soviet Union, and the French Consul-General in Cologne, Dobler. François-Poncet clearly analysed the situation in numerous dispatches and he pointed out that the only way to prevent Hitler rearming was war. But François-Poncet knew that French governments either would not or could not resort to force. Consequently, he adopted a logical attitude which consisted in seeking to limit the pace of German rearmament by means of an agreement.[5] This was the very essence of the diplomat who is true to himself, and we will return to the theme.

The French Ambassador to the Soviet Union likewise favoured a policy of firmness.[6] Charles Alphand was indeed uneasy about the German attempt to divide France's allies and he counselled against any reduction of France's armed strength and against bilateral talks with Germany. He asked Paul-Boncour to uphold the Versailles Treaty and the League of Nations and to reinforce France's alliances.

Describing the atmosphere during the plebiscite of 12 November 1933, the French Consul-General at Cologne, Dobler, observed that there was no question of negotiating with Germany: 'The world can only save itself and Germany from a bloody fate by making this mass – which is already recklessly on the move – feel a sense of danger, because it has lost the idea of risk. There is just time to fling at this revived German Middle Age: So far and no further.'[7]

With the politicians, the nuances are numerous. For Paul-Boncour, Foreign Minister in 1933, the temptation to use force was latent. This can be perceived in a number of ways. On the issue of the Saar, Paul-Boncour was not only hostile to any arrangement with Germany – on the grounds that only the League could decide – but also he supported Weygand's proposals to win the plebiscite, that is to say by persuading the Saarlanders against reunion with Germany.[8] In the psychological war unleashed by Germany, Paul-Boncour scored a point when the *Petit Parisien* published German directives for propaganda abroad.[9] It was Paul-Boncour himself who, having received these documents, then had them published in a newspaper which had always shown sympathy for his ideas.[10]

Numerous politicians called for firmness towards Germany. Herriot and Tardieu were the most active, but they were not alone. Tardieu had already mounted an extra-parliamentary campaign by writing a weekly article for *L'Illustration* of which the themes were simple and clear: internal recovery through constitutional reform, external recovery by firmness towards Germany.

Other deputies were also active: for example Georges Mandel, whose speech during the great parliamentary debate of November 1933 painted a chilling picture of German rearmament; he invited the government to apply article 213 of the Versailles Treaty in order to initiate an investigation of the state of German armaments. Louis Marin, Pierre Taittinger, Colonel Fabry, were of the same opinion. And if the Chamber Foreign Affairs Committee did not take up a clear position on this matter, the Senate committee was clear in its rejection of German rearmament. Among its influential members were Henri Bérenger, Louis Barthou, General Bourgeois, Messimy, Charles-Dumont. The case of Pierre Viénot is a special one: as inspirer of the Franco-German dialogues and delegate of the Franco-German Committee to Berlin from 1926 to 1929, he had observed the 'decomposition of Germany'.[11] The author of *Incertitudes allemandes*, he was elected Deputy for the Ardennes in 1932, and was a member of the French delegation at Geneva and was thus in a position to analyse France's diplomatic situation. At the beginning of December 1933 he launched an appeal for a 'true recovery of our policy' and opposed bilateral talks with Germany. Thereafter he favoured an attitude of firmness.[12]

Having outlined the different categories of advocates of firmness, it is important to analyse clearly the policy that they envisaged. Let us look in turn at these different categories.

Among the journalists, Wladimir d'Ormesson argued for a policy which consisted of opposing demand by demand, and so preventing Germany from dominating the diplomatic bidding. But he warned French diplomacy not to allow itself to be isolated. Pierre Lafue preached a policy of firmness towards France's allies and especially towards Great Britain. In the periodical *1933*, André Chaumeix and Georges Mandel called for a common Franco-British front and for a policy which consisted in securing London's agreement to deliver a warning to Berlin. Pierre Lafue also hoped for a change of regime in Germany. On 27 December 1933 an article was published entitled 'The Reichswehr speaks'. This was an account of an interview Pierre Lafue was said to have had with General von Rundstedt, the former right-hand man of General von Schleicher; from this interview it emerged that the German army constituted the real strength of Germany, that it was organising itself into an internal opposition to Hitler, that although in agreement with Hitler's national aims it would oppose by all means the social revolution Hitler wanted, and as von Rundstedt said: 'It (the *army*) remained the last reserve of the Prussian order.' This interview however aroused a series of controversies. Pierre Lafue indicated that it had taken place in December 1933 in a Parisian café. The inquiry carried out by the *renseignements généraux* concluded that von Rundstedt had indeed visited France in the summer of 1933 but as part of a visit to the battlefields and that he had not gone to Paris and did not meet a French journalist. One sees what conclusion can be drawn. There must have been contacts between certain French emissaries and leading members of the *Reichswehr* opposed to Hitler; moreover, this idea of an opposition to Hitler certainly encouraged the firmness of a section of the French right towards Hitler in that this section of the right considered the *Reichswehr* to be the only true source of power and that Hitler could not survive against it.

As for the military chiefs, the High Command envisaged a strengthening of France's military defences. General Weygand urged that France should reoccupy the bridgeheads on the Rhine.[13] He considered that such an action would have the same pacifying effect on Germany as a couple of slaps on a mischievous urchin; it would completely stop all German rearmament. One would no longer hear talk of the revision of Versailles, for Germany would fear the creation of a buffer state, embracing the Saar and the Rhineland, which would dismember Germany. Weygand imposed one condition on this operation which would involve the mobilisation of the French army. This condition was the moral and eventually the naval support of Great Britain, on which he well knew he could not count given the state of British opinion.

Charles de Gaulle envisaged the transformation of the French military machine, incapable in 1933 of resisting a sudden German invasion.[14] According to him, fortification could not provide for defence. France needed a shock weapon, modern and of quality. This was a professional army of 100,000 men, well-equipped, motorised and progressively armoured. This army would have a double value – repressive and preventive. But his was a voice crying in the wilderness; the military establishment, bogged down in its internal quarrels and its conflict with the political leadership, reacted negatively to these proposals.

What did the diplomats envisage? We have seen what was involved for Paul-Boncour, for François-Poncet. As regards Alphand, Ambassador in Moscow, the policy that he contemplated was clear: an alliance had to be concluded with the Soviet Union, thus renewing the tradition of a counterbalance in the East, and Alphand urged the conclusion of a Franco-Soviet accord. Dobler was more enigmatic. It would seem, however, that he was prepared to consider a preventive war.

For the politicians, even for the advocates of firmness, preventive war was something to be rejected. Georges Mandel, in his speech of November 1933, took care to eliminate the hypothesis of a preventive war. As for Henry Lemery, after having denounced the secret armaments of Germany, he exclaimed: 'Preventive war, no one thinks of it and the very word fills us with horror.'

All that these men could agree on was to arraign Germany before international opinion and in particular the League of Nations, by establishing an inquiry into German armaments. Let us note in passing the irony of this situation in which the detractors of collective security and of the League in particular became the defenders and protagonists of the collective security which they did not want. Among certain advocates of firmness, extremism went even further. This was especially the case of André Tardieu and Gaston Doumergue who, it seems, counted on the fragility of the Hitler regime and on the early fall of Hitler. Numerous indications prove it: when François-Poncet went to Paris in April 1934 to convince the government of the necessity for a disarmament agreement with Germany, Tardieu engaged in a real diatribe against François-Poncet: 'You are wasting your time', he told him, 'the agreement which you propose will not be concluded. Never will we sign it. Hitler will not last long. His fate is sealed. An agreement with him would only strengthen him. If war comes, in less than a week he will be deposed and replaced by the Crown Prince.'[15] A few months later, André Tardieu's chief adviser, Louis Aubert, writing of the trumps of French policy against Hitler, revealed the assumption of this policy: 'Our policy is based on the idea that the essence of Hitlerism is not long-lived.'[16]

In conclusion, we can say that in the France of 1933 and 1934 firmness towards Germany was a snare. Its adherents almost all rejected the only means capable of stopping German rearmament and leading to the downfall of Hitler, that is to say, preventive war. These advocates of firmness urged only the strengthening of France's military defences, ultimately rearmament, but this was impossible in the financial, economic, social and psychological setting of 1933 and 1934. In the main, only two attitudes had the merit of coherence: the first was that of François-Poncet, which consisted in recognising the impossibility of resorting to preventive war and in the need to limit German rearmament while there was still time to do so. The other coherent attitude was that of Charles de Gaulle. He did not want a preventive war against Germany; what mattered for him was that France should have the military capability to intervene if she had the political will. What was lacking was not lucidity about events in Germany, but on the one hand political will and on the other, the means of intervention. France in fact at that time did not have a force capable of intervening quickly in Germany and in addition to the other factors, this reason explains the lack of realism of the advocates of firmness. These advocates of firmness, with the exception of Charles de Gaulle, envisaged British co-operation. Now Great Britain was not at all ready to take on new commitments in Europe and she evaded with a remarkable tenacity all French proposals for co-operation against German rearmament. So when Weygand recommended a preventive war against Germany while insisting on British moral or naval support, this was indeed proof that firmness was a snare.

Five years later, during the Sudeten crisis, attitudes were at once simpler and more complex. Confronted by a Hitler who had become a conqueror the French were very divided. There were the *demi-durs*, inclined towards strength and shocked by the concessions but hesitating because of the softness of public opinion. There were the *mous*, ready for concessions but seeking a certain respect for forms. There were the *realists* who accepted what seemed to them inevitable. The *durs*, who were not intimidated by Hitler's threats, were a minority. The options in foreign policy were the extension and echoes of internal policy. The new policy of the left aimed at limiting the expansion of the Third Reich was an extension of its struggle against internal fascism. The firmness of the men of the right can be explained in spite of the antipathy towards the Popular Front and the Soviet Union. This is why one finds advocates of firmness in all the political groupings, although when the Chambers voted only seventy-five Deputies (among them 73 communists and Henri de Kérillis) voted against.

The firmness of the Communist Party was part of a wider picture. In refusing 'to associate itself with the act of brigandage of Munich' it expressed a hostility which followed that of the Soviet Union, which had been excluded from Munich. 'The Czechs are dear to us for three reasons, because they were for a long time an oppressed people, because they are the last defenders of democracy in central Europe, because they are also the associates of the great Soviet people', wrote Maurice Thorez in *L'Humanité* on 3 June 1938. But the Communist Party also expressed its hostility to the Daladier Cabinet and to the decree laws. Moreover, the general strike that the section of the CGT closest to the Communist Party organised on 30 November 1938 was intended not only to protest against the financial and social policy of the government but also to say no to the Munich Agreement.

In the SFIO, the *bellicistes* experienced difficulties in calling in question the pacifist tradition.[17] Blum advocated close links with London and Moscow and the creation of a block of democratic powers opposed to Germany and Italy. He cherished the illusion that faced with this coalition Hitler would abandon his claims. Zyromski, however, 'preached a policy of force': he considered that every means should be used to stop international fascism. At the national congress of the SFIO on 24 and 25 December 1938, the *antimunichois* carried the day by 4,322 votes to 2,837.

For the Radicals, Jean Zay and César Campinchi were completely hostile to Munich, as also Pierre Cot.[18] Herriot, after a moment of discouragement, resumed the role of an energetic advocate of resistance: 'Force triumphs, right is dying . . . Let us be strong.'[19] As a convinced defender of collective security flouted at Munich, Paul-Boncour set up a group which he called 'Nation et liberté'.[20]

As for the right-wing parties, the reversal many times described took place: anti-communism contested the priority of germanophobia and succeeded in pushing the German danger into the background. A part of the right called for a reorientation of France's German policy and urged concessions to Germany. But there also existed on the right advocates of firmness: they were so 'through lucidity and attachment to the national interest'.[21]

Several members resigned from the *Alliance démocratique* to register their disapproval of Flandin's telegram to Hitler: Paul Reynaud, Joseph Laniel, Louis Jacquinot, Louis Rollin, Charles Reibel.[22] The majority of the *démocrates-populaires* were *antimunichois* behind Francisque Gay, Georges Bidault, Ernest Pezet, Edmond Michelet, Champetier de Ribes. In *Esprit* Emmanuel Mounier spoke of the 'ignominious peace'. At the Fédération Republicaine, François de Wendel chose gradually to accept the German danger.[23] 'At present there is an external German threat and an internal Bolshevik danger. For me, the second is greater than the first . . . the German threat is with us and we can do nothing about it.'[24]

Louis Marin expressed his disagreement in a vivid formula: 'France . . . has just announced to the entire world her abdication.' Jacques Bardoux, elected in October 1938 as senator for Puy de Dôme, at once adopted a firm tone in the foreign affairs committee.

In the government Georges Mandel, Paul Reynaud and Champetier de Ribes were with Jean Zay the strongest *résistants*. At the Cabinet of 25 September 1938 they opposed the German plan proposed to Chamberlain.

In Gamelin's case, the half-tint triumphed. When Chautemps greeted him at Le Bourget on Daladier's return: 'So, General, they are taking the bread from your mouth?' he replied: 'I have never wanted and will never want war. But there are times when honour and interest impose it.'[25] This verbal firmness came unexpectedly from a man who had censured General Faucher, head of the French military mission in Czechoslovakia, and who had delayed the Czech mobilisation. General Gamelin, who overestimated the existence in Germany of anti-war feelings and of opposition from the generals, cherished the illusion that a verbal firmness would be enough to deflate Hitler's bluff.

At the Quai d'Orsay, all the services did not follow the attitude of their minister who moreover did not consult them. The director of political affairs, René Massigli, who in 1933 followed a line closer to the British, considered that the consequences of the weakening of Czechoslovakia would be disastrous: 'Far from bringing Germany back to a policy of co-operation, the success of her method can only encourage her to persevere in it. The enormous sacrifice conceded by the Western powers will have no counterpart: once more we will be reduced to an act of faith in the peaceful evolution of the new Pangermanism.'[26] In the press, *L'Époque*, directed by Henri de Kérillis, Raymond Cartier, André Pironneau and *L'Ordre* of Emile Buré, resembled *Humanité* in their firmness.

How could firmness be expressed? The majority envisaged an action to counteract Hitler's expansionist policy and the formation of a large coalition of democratic states with the participation of the Soviet Union. For the left, the creation of an anti-fascist front was the only effective means of preventing aggression.

The communists called for the government's resignation. But the general strike of the CGT was an almost total failure. The advocates of firmness who were members of the government wondered whether to resign. Georges Mandel publicly registered his dissent by not going to Le Bourget to welcome the Prime Minister.[27] He arranged a meeting with Paul Reynaud and Champetier de Ribes to discuss their collective resignation. They decided to remain in the government to exercise more and more pressure on the Prime Minister: 'More than ever I am resolved not to remain associated with a policy of cowardice and desertion . . . Hitler feels encouraged to pursue his rapes since no one resists him.'[28]

Georges Mandel took it upon himself, without consulting anyone and scorning ministerial solidarity, to telephone Beneš and tell him forcefully why his country should reject what Britain and France suggested.

All envisaged the strengthening of national defence by intensive rearmament. They were also accused of 'bellicisme',[29] the worst insult in a country affected by the 'pacifist depression' and which rushed to forget Munich for *La belote* and *Tino Rossi*.[30]

On the whole what distinguished 1933 and 1938 was not the attitude of appeasement. In 1933 appeasement was confident. It was assumed that time would take care of the Nazi threat. In 1938 appeasement was a matter of fear. Concessions were made to gain time on a deadline which some considered inevitable. The advocates of firmness were distinguished in the first instance by their lucidity, while remaining rather unclear about the methods to use. In 1938 the advocates of firmness manifested a remarkable political courage since the men of the left seemed to deny their pacifism and those of the right scorned their anti-communism.

If in 1933 one does not find men of the left, with the exception of Paul-Boncour and Pierre Viénot, among advocates of firmness, at Munich moles of firmness appeared more on the left than on the right. In 1933 pacifism and nationalism seemed reliable criteria of political divisions between left and right. It was not the same in 1938. Everything happened as if these elements of 'cohesion' in French society no longer existed. Not only was national unanimity lacking but the social groups and political currents were divided between contradictory tendencies. The rare advocates of firmness in 1933, as in 1938, had no choice but to follow 'la gouvernante anglaise'.[31]

Notes: Chapter 15

1   The following discussion is based in part on my thèse de Doctorat-ès Lettres on 'La politique française en matière de désarmement entre les deux guerres', published in 1981 by Ledone (Paris) in connection with *Publications de la Sorbonne* (See Notes on Contributors).

2   Archives de la Commission de l'Armée, Sénat, 16 February 1933.
3   Jean-Noel Jeanneney, 'François de Wendel en république', thesis, Lille, p. 715.
4   In J. C. Delbreil, *Les Catholiques français et les tentatives de rapprochement franco-allemand (1920–1933)* (Centre de Recherche de Relations Internationales, Metz, 1972); *Le Temps*, 20 May 1933.
5   March 1933, François-Poncet/Paul-Boncour, *Documents diplomatiques français, 1932–39* (*DDF*), (Paris, 1964), Vol. III, no. 378.
6   Letter Alphand/Paul-Boncour, 5 December 1933,.*DDF*, Vol. V, no. 86.
7   D. no. 90, 9 November 1933, Dobler/Paul-Boncour, AD SDN 11884.
8   D. no. 606, 20 November 1933, Paul-Boncour/Sarraut, *DDF*, Vol. V, no. 34.
9   *Le Petit Parisien*, 16, 17, 19 and 22 November 1933.
10 J. Paul-Boncour, *Entre deux guerres* (Paris, 1945–7), Vol. II, pp. 393–7.
11 F. L'Huillier, *Dialogues franco-allemands, 1925–1933* (Strasburg, 1971), p. 99.
12 Letter Pierre Viénot/Massigli, 3 December 1933, *DDF*, Vol. V, no. 75.
13 D. no. 1352, 30 October 1933, Tyrrell/Simon, DBFP 2/V, no. 508.
14 'Vers l'armée de métier', *Revue politique et parlementaire*, May 1933.
15 A. François-Poncet, *Souvenirs d'une ambassade à Berlin* (Paris, 1946).
16 Note Aubert, 15 October 1934, AD, Papiers Tardieu, 643.
17 R. Gombin, 'Socialisme et pacifisme', in *La France et les Français (1938–1939)*, sous la direction de R. Rémond et J. Bourdin (Paris, 1978), pp. 245–60.
18 J. Zay, *Souvenirs et solitude* (Paris, 1946), p. 60.
19 M. Soulié, *La Vie politique d'Edouard Herriot* (Paris, 1962), p. 489.
20 Paul-Boncour, *Entre deux guerres*, Vol. III, pp. 106–8.
21 R. Rémond, *La Droite en France de 1815 à nos jours* (Paris, 1954), p. 229.
22 J. B. Duroselle, *La Décadence, 1932–1939* (Paris, 1979), p. 362.
23 Jeanneney, thesis, pp. 823–9.
24 Cited by Jeanneney, thesis, p. 827.
25 Cited by P. Le Goyet, *Le Mystère gamelin* (Paris, 1976), p. 163.
26 Note Massigli, DDF, Vol. 2/XI, no. 223.
27 G. Wormser, *Georges Mandel, l'homme politique* (Paris, 1967), p. 220.
28 ibid., p. 224.
29 A. de Monzie, *Ci-devant* (Paris, 1941), p. 60.
30 Here reference is made to a French game of cards and to a famous singer.
31 cf. F. Bédarida, 'La "gouvernante anglaise",' in *Edouard Daladier, chef de gouvernement (Avril 1938–Septembre 1939)*, sous la direction de R. Rémond et J. Bourdin (Paris, 1977), pp. 228–40.

16 The Decline of France and French Appeasement Policies, 1936–9[1]

ROBERT FRANKENSTEIN

It has often been said that French foreign policy on the eve of the Second World War towed the British line. Elsewhere in this volume, however, Adamthwaite argues shrewdly that the French statesmen had 'some freedom of action' and that their supposed dependence on Britain appeared sometimes as an alibi to justify their own appeasement action towards Germany. And as a matter of fact, more firmness against the Reich on the French side might have pushed Britain to adopt an attitude of resistance. If France with her continental interests and her first-line position in front of Germany lacked political will, how was it possible to imagine that Britain with different commitments and interests could have been more resolute? How could the British be more French than the French?

The two approaches are maybe not inconsistent. Girault shows in his paper that France was a declining economic power in the 1930s and that this decline was the cause of both true French dependence on Britain and genuine French appeasement policy.

I would add that the chronological factor and the domestic politics have to be taken into account: France discerned her own decline only in 1935–6, through the need to rearm which deprived the French leaders of their freedom of action; and this perception of decline set up not one but at least two French appeasement policies.

I

During the world economic crisis, France thought for a short time that she would be sheltered by her financial strength. In this context, France attempted twice, in 1934 and in 1935, a foreign policy independent of Britain.

In 1934 Louis Barthou had a lucid and firm position towards Germany. France would be protected from Nazi aggression by a great alliance not only with small powers (her traditional allies since the 1920s) but also with the USSR and Italy. In this continental system there was room of course for the British friend, but it was up to London, in Barthou's mind, to join the game or not. His colleague at the Foreign Office, Sir John Simon, was reluctant: he feared the influence which the Soviet Union could gain in Europe and wanted Britain to keep her Locarno-type arbitration power. But he finally accepted the plan. When France had the will, Britain had to follow. Admiral

Decoux wrote in July 1934 to his government: 'Les Anglais ne nous traitent plus en petits garçons depuis que nous sommes gouvernés.'[2]

On the other hand, by 17 April 1934 France understood that the disarmament negotiations had no chance of success and declared she would guard her security by her own means: a sort of 'Francia farà da sè' policy.

After the death of Barthou, on 9 October 1934, France gave up this double position of resistance against Germany and independence of Britain. It is difficult to say to what extent Barthou would have succeeded or failed if he had not been assassinated in Marseilles with King Alexander of Yugoslavia. But four contradictions would have appeared anyway, serious and difficult to overcome: the hostility between some of the Eastern allies and the USSR; the growing hostility to a Soviet alliance, in 1934–5, of many of Barthou's friends on the French right (in proportion with the left coalition's ascension); the complete lack of co-ordination between the proud proclamation of 17 April in matter of security and Germain-Martin's financial policy of deflation and reduction of the armament expenditure; and last but not least, the inconsistency between Barthou's dynamic diplomacy and the chilly defensive strategy of his colleague at the War Office, Marshall Pétain. President G. Doumergue did not sufficiently co-ordinate the actions of his different ministers.

After October 1934 Pierre Laval abandoned the resistance attitude for an appeasement policy towards Italy and even Germany: this was in a certain way more consistent with the French right's domestic fears and interests, with the reinforced deflation and with the defensive military strategy. None the less, there remained one common point with Barthou's action: the show of some independence of London. As everyone knows, the failure of Laval was complete: he did not prevent the *rapprochement* between Mussolini and Hitler, he provoked British irritation and his financial policy in 1935 broke the first impulse of French rearmament.[3] In spite of everything, capital outflow was at a peak, and French weakness could no longer be concealed. Decline and isolation combined their effects when in March 1936 France and the Sarraut government witnessed without any real reaction the German militarisation of the Rhineland.

II

After this time of illusion, the French realised in 1936 the extent of their dependence on Britain. Blum understood that while France would have to rearm to strengthen her position against Germany, French rearmament, as Mönick explained to him, could not be performed without British goodwill: indeed, an increase in military expenditure could not be covered without devaluation; and Britain had the power to ruin the good effects of this monetary operation by enacting a further sterling depreciation; for the sake of national defence, Paris could not act without negotiations and an 'entente cordiale' with London.[4]

The fact is that this decision to rearm, which was supposed to boost the country's military strength, also weakened it. It is well known that French arms were neither numerous nor efficient enough in 1939; but it must be clear that this rearmament effort was a great strain on France's limited budget and resources. In constant money, national defence from 1936 was more costly than on the eve of the First World War. In 1938 its financial burden was 2·5 times heavier than in 1913. The future war, because of the new and modern arms, was bound to be much more expensive than the previous one: France spent more in real terms during the year 1939 (with its four short months of 'phoney war') than in 1918 (with its ten-and-a-half months of total war). The weight of military expenditure on national income in 1938 was twice as much as in 1913 (8·6 per cent compared to 4·1 per cent); and in 1939 the percentage reached the peak of 23 per cent. Britain experienced the same figures but her economy had by this time recovered whereas that of France was still stuck in the Depression.

The burden of national defence was also very heavy on the French budget: between 25 per cent and 33 per cent from 1936 to 1938. At the same time the debt charges and the outlay for war pensions incurred since 1914–18 comprised half the total public expenditure. The result was that in 1936–9 France had not finished paying the costs of the First World War and already had to pay for the preparation of the following one. No other country was in this dramatic situation: Britain had financed a great deal of the 1914–18 expenses with taxes levied during the war itself; Germany, like France, borrowed a large amount, but the great inflation of 1919–23 had washed out the debt.

The burden of rearmament was particularly heavy on public resources which had declined quickly because of the economic crisis: military expenditure consumed half of the tax returns in 1938 (only 34 per cent in 1913). Furthermore, capital outflow between 1935 and 1938 rendered exceedingly difficult the financing of national defence. The consequences are easy to guess. First, France needed international help: in his paper Girault gave a very fine and subtle analysis of the French *financial* dependence on Britain. Secondly, the government could not afford to invest largely in the land, sea and air forces at one and the same time: from 1936 the French navy was in a way sacrificed to the army and air force; after the financial, therefore, came the *naval* dependence on Britain.

If French independence suffered from the strain of rearmament, so, too, did French unity. We said that national defence consumed one-third of the budget and that 'the charges of the past' accounted for half of it: not much was left in France during the 1930s (greatly different from Britain) for social investments such as public works,[5] housing, education, health, and so on.[6] One unknown fact deserves to be stressed: under the various Popular Front governments, because of the armament programmes decided in September 1936, military expenditure increased much more than the economic and social spending. The Popular Front did more for the 'guns' than for the 'butter' in France. In this respect, many legends should be reconsidered.[7]

French society and political groups had to bear the consequences of these requirements for national defence. Thus, although there was common consent for rearmament, many problems and dissensions arose. The French left was divided as to financial methods: should there be a liberal monetary policy or exchange control? In September 1936, when the rearmament decisions were taken, Blum and Auriol chose the liberal way of devaluation; in doing so, they assuaged American and British anxieties. Blum might then have been tempted and might actually have attempted to 'buy off peace' from Germany by economic and colonial concessions with Anglo-Saxon help.[8] In this first and temporary step to French appeasement, the French leader maybe hoped to be able to release the armament strain and save the Popular Front social programme. But in February 1937 he realised how hazardous these conciliatory approaches to the Reich were, with the result that the priority for rearmament was maintained.

Since French capital began to flow out again at this time (the effects of the devaluation did not last long) Blum understood that his new *resistance* policy towards Germany would have to involve appeasing capital at home. This was the main significance of the 'pause' decisions: the burden of military expenditure delayed further reforms. It was the price to pay for capital returning home. This situation brought division within the left coalition (between socialists and communists) and even within the Socialist Party.

If the increasing scale of military expenditure frustrated the domestic ambitions of the Popular Front, it also provided arguments for the opposition: in spite of the 'pause' policy, the more the government spent on national defence, the more important was the outflow of capital. The fall of Blum in June 1937 was closely connected with the financial crisis, and the 'guns' (more than the 'butter') took a prominent part in this failure. If the Popular Front did its best to rearm France, French rearmament indeed disarmed the Popular Front. And this situation weakened the national cohesion.

Moreover, a government of the left rearming and practising a firm policy *vis-à-vis* Germany could provoke fears on the French right: since the Russian example of 1917, the propertied classes saw in war risks of revolution. The Spanish Civil War was raging; the French Communist Party was urging the government to help the Republicans and to conclude a military alliance with the Soviet Union. The result was that a large part of conservative opinion (P. Reynaud, G. Mandel and H. de Kérillis excepted) was afraid to see France taking too harsh a position against Hitler and being involved in a European civil war on the same side as Moscow and the communists. 'Le communisme, c'est la guerre!' was a slogan one could read on French posters during the Spanish War. For many politicians, resistance to the Third Reich and negotiations with the USSR did not have the same sound and meaning in 1936–7 as in 1934: Barthou had the opportunity to act before the big events of 1936. This fear of the equation 'war = revolution' under the Popular Front government did not only affect French right but also the right wing of the Radical Party.[9] An informal opposition within the party, very critical of the financial and foreign policy of Blum, existed in the Chamber of Deputies around Malvy, Mistler, Bonnet and Lamoureux (who was re-elected in January 1937).[10] In the Senate the moderate radicals formed a group around Joseph Caillaux.

In their opinion, to avoid war, France had to deal with Italy in order to isolate Hitler: when Malvy came back from Rome in June 1936, he related to

Delbos, the new Foreign Minister, a conversation he had had with Mussolini. The Duce had told him that he was hoping for a French gesture: if not, Italy would have to seek a German guarantee of security; he had apparently added that he would accept this choice only as a last resort but it worried him because of Hitler's adventurous ambitions against Austria, Czechoslovakia and the colonies; he would wait for a hint of French sympathy before fixing his position. Delbos sent Malvy to Léon Blum who was, he said, 'as President of the Council . . . the master in the last resort of foreign policy'.[11] Blum replied to Malvy: 'I understand . . . But it is a policy I cannot take upon myself. I am the leader of the Popular Front . . . For this action, you need another Prime Minister and another majority.'

The *domestic* balance of political influence in France therefore forbade any further *rapprochement* with the Soviet Union (most of the Radicals refused) and with Italy (because of the left's opposition), whilst Britain was not openly rejected by anyone, and stood out as the only possible ally for France among the Great Powers.

Moreover, for the Radical Party, British friendship counterbalanced the *domestic* alliance with the communists. The French Radicals thought that the coalition including the communists had been essential to block the way of the Leagues and maybe of the fascists; but they believed, on the other hand, that the preferential entente with Britain was a good guard-rail against any 'risky' idea in foreign policy suggested by the Communist Party.

In the 1930s, Britain *and* the Radical Party appeared to many Frenchmen as the forces of the last resort able to regulate the Third Republic's unstable mechanisms. As the pernicious effects of rearmament and capital outflow on economic equilibrium and national unity proceeded, the Radicals and the British became more and more necessary for French stabilisation. One understands now how difficult it is to distinguish in French foreign policy after June 1937 between the efficiency of British pressure and the genuine political will of the Radicals. The latter were divided after the fall of Blum's first government: some would have been 'appeasers' anyway without British influence, but others were 'reluctant appeasers' and were waiting for better conditions in Paris and London in order one day to press for resistance.

III

Chautemps, Blum's successor at the Hotel Matignon, and Bonnet, the new Finance Minister, can certainly be considered the highest types of French appeasers. Men of the right wing of the Radical Party, they had, as far as Germany and the problem of national defence was concerned, nearly the same opinion as Flandin and many 'moderate' politicians of the French right. Their common idea was that France could not afford to sustain more rearmament expenses and should think of a full reappraisal of foreign strategy: less commitments in Eastern and Central Europe would be more consistent with real French capacities.

Moreover, not only did they fear, as already said, that *war* might produce revolution but also that even in *peace time* too heavy a burden of military expenditure could provoke social disruption: either by oppressive taxation, or by ruining the small French investors, or by galloping inflation.[12] Bonnet therefore heartily followed Rueff's three-year plan[13] and tried to slow down the growth in armaments expenditure which had resulted from the Blum government's military programmes: the national defence budget of 1938 had not to exceed the one of 1937. The Marine and the Air Ministry suffered more than the War Office from this policy.

At the same time Bonnet and Chautemps had separate private conversations in November with von Papen: their support for appeasement and concessions to Germany in Central Europe was obvious.[14] For the sake of social order in France, they seemed to accept a new balance of power on the Continent. Contrary to Blum who had wished in March 1937 to appease capital in order to finance the resistance policy against Germany, Chautemps and Bonnet preferred to appease Hitler in order to gain the confidence of French capital.

Edouard Daladier, the main leader of the Radical Party, did not have the same social dreads. He was precisely the man who had brought his party into the Popular Front coalition and who had initiated the great armament programme in Blum's Cabinet. Thereafter, in Chautemp's government, and still as War Minister, he had succeeded in resisting the drastic cuts wanted by Bonnet and had saved his four-year plan for land forces of September 1936. At the beginning of 1938 he had taken advantage of the new international tension and convinced Chautemps that the military budget for that year was quite inadequate, especially for the air force. The Premier himself had had to change his mind after his visit to London in November 1937: Chamberlain had shown himself worried about French aeronautical weakness.[15] Finally, in the matter of national defence, Daladier's position had prevailed over Bonnet's.

In Chautemps' new Cabinet of January 1938, Bonnet had to leave the 'Rue de Rivoli'; his successor Marchandeau, another Radical, quickly announced the additional estimates to the parliamentary commissions. These were laid down after the *Anschluss* in the Bill of 17 March by Blum's second government, and were definitively confirmed by the decrees published on 2 May by another government, headed by a Cabinet in which Daladier himself had become Premier.

This victory of Daladier over Bonnet did not mean that he rejected appeasement. After all, in Britain the chief appeaser, Neville Chamberlain, had also backed British rearmament first as Chancellor and then as Prime Minister. A better military preparedness would do no harm in appeasement negotiations: *si vis pacem, para bellum*. In April 1938 Daladier appointed Bonnet as Foreign Minister. As a matter of fact, there was a direct pressure on Daladier from the British Embassy: he had been cordially invited to move Joseph Paul-Boncour, who in the second Blum Cabinet had stood up firmly for Czechoslovakia, out of the Quai d'Orsay. The British had wanted Chautemps; they got Bonnet.[16] In this matter, Daladier proved semi-independent ('he did the semi-right thing', said Phipps, the British Ambassador in Paris),[17] but semi-independent only: Bonnet anyway seemed 'far less dangerous' than Paul-Boncour. Did Daladier need British pressure to appoint an appeaser at the Quai d'Orsay? Other domestic and political considerations, especially within the Radical Party, certainly played their part in this decision. And it did not facilitate the co-ordination of French foreign policy.

During the Sudeten crisis of the summer of 1938, Daladier and Bonnet agreed to say that France could not act without British support, but they did not quite feel the same about the French commitments towards Czechoslovakia. Is the note where Bonnet relates his conversation of 20 July with Osuski reliable or not? Did he really warn the Czech Ambassador that France, notwithstanding his own firm public declarations, would not go to war over the Sudetenland question? It is difficult to say;[18] but the important thing is that Daladier in the margin of this paper scribbled a few words which seem to imply that Bonnet in this affair had a personal policy which did not necessarily have his consent or that of the Cabinet. Of course, the weight of these sensitive differences between Bonnet and Daladier is weak indeed if one considers that the latter finally accepted the German annexation of the Sudetenland at Munich on 29 September. The Munich drama, however, had not exactly the same meaning for the two men. For Bonnet and for some businessmen and industrialists such as Marcel Boussac,[19] what had taken place was the inevitable recognition of a new balance of power in Europe.

For Daladier, Munich was a way to buy time for military preparations. As an 'ancien combattant' he remembered the war atrocities and would do everything to prevent the return of this cataclysm, but he knew also that it would be difficult; he was convinced that Hitler's ambitions would lead him further afield in Europe[20] and that the new balance of power was precarious. The problem was that France was not able in September 1938 to stop Hitler. Everyone knows how much Daladier had in mind the relative inferiority of the French air force, but it must be understood that his anxiety went far beyond this: his concern was that France not only lacked military preparedness but did not even meet the *conditions* which would enable the country to make the industrial preparation for war.

In 1936 the Popular Front had been the best government possible to provide a great boost to the national defence *effort*; moreover, it had been in view of the evident failure of private initiative that the Blum Cabinet had nationalised the armament plants and provided them with the means of modernisation. Daladier's own action had been important in this matter. However, by 1938, in Daladier's opinion, the social reforms enacted two years earlier by the same Popular Front had now become an obstacle to improving war production: the outflow of capital had not been stopped and employers felt reluctant to invest money to engage more workmen to pay for overtime work because of wage costs which they deemed too high.

From August 1938 to March 1939 Daladier engaged in a wage struggle with the workers' organisations: in November, he appointed Reynaud Finance Minister, and they both decided to diminish overtime rates. After the failure of the general strike on 30 November things became easier for the government, and new collective contracts were dictated to the working class: in particular, the wage costs in the aeronautical industry were reduced in the spring of 1939. Employers had their revenge and could now engage more and more workers without fears for their profit margin (47,000 men worked in the aeronautical industry in 1938, 81,000 in April 1939 and 100,000 in September).[21]

Daladier, who had been one of the chief architects of the left coalition in 1936, in 1938 assumed responsibility for dissolving the Popular Front: it was the price he had to pay for the French manufacturers' co-operation on national defence. The results came quickly indeed: capital returned home, and armaments production, especially aeronautical, experienced a real 'take off' in the first months of 1939. The gap between the great financial strain and the low industrial results disappeared.

This final defeat of the Popular Front did not occur in September 1938 but a few months later, and the restoration of the profit rate had not yet started when the Sudeten crisis blew up: Daladier was still involved in the wage battle. In this way one may understand the social and political background to Munich, as far as France is concerned.

If Bonnet dreaded the *social consequences* of rearmament strains, Daladier on the other hand attempted to find a solution to the *social causes* of rearmament delay. This great difference between the two men remained, and the distinction Girault makes between the 'full appeasers' and the 'temporising appeasers' applies very well to the two Radical leaders.

As economic recovery strengthened the French position in 1939, the Daladier line in foreign policy prevailed: Bonnet once more had to move back, as one year earlier over armaments. It was a slow retreat indeed (Bonnet remained an active appeaser at the Quai d'Orsay till September 1939) but it became all the more secure as Chamberlain and the British changed their opinion of Hitler's reliability.

One cannot analyse French foreign policy without having in mind the domestic problems of France. After 1936 the various attempts to appease were quite different from one another. Blum's first steps towards a policy of concessions to Germany were based on the hope that the democratic and wealthy powers could purchase peace under precise conditions: in France it would then be possible to save the Popular Front's reforms. After the spring of 1937, having realised how dangerous this action was, he intended to appease French capital in order to organise resistance to Germany. This 'pause', however, in his opinion, was to be a last concession to business and had not to ruin the social gains of 1936. Bonnet, first as Finance Minister then as Foreign Minister, pursued domestic and international policies designed to secure social stability in France and on the Continent. Daladier did not wish to go so far as Bonnet in the way of concessions to the Reich but he went far beyond Blum in his appeasement action towards French capital: when he achieved the social defeat of the Popular Front and gained the confidence of the manufacturers he returned to a policy of resistance.

The paradox was that the French leader who between 1937 and March 1939 suffered least from British pressure, was the man who most agreed with Chamberlain's strategy: Bonnet. His freedom of action was great because he did not need British advice to conceive his own appeasement policy, and this, at times, annoyed London. He could even play with British pressure to justify his own actions to the French. In this matter, I agree with Adamthwaite. The Daladier case was different: because he felt that war was bound to come and because he knew that France could not fight Germany without British support, he was much more dependent on Chamberlain's goodwill and personal friendship. From 1920 to 1935 France built several alliance systems while Britain, her old friend, was kept on the outskirts; but when in 1936 and afterwards the French leaders acknowledged the decline of France, they placed Britain in the centre of their diplomacy.

As for Britain, another movement may be discerned. After the victory of 1918 the British believed that France was now the first power on the Continent and had not to be helped too much any more. The Foreign Office held to its traditional policy of balance in Europe: that meant joint action in the 1920s in order to assuage both France's fears for security and Germany's feelings of humiliation after the 'Diktat' of Versailles. After 1933–4, in spite of the advent of Hitler, Britain did not immediately change attitude and until 1936 thought about European affairs in the same terms as in the 1920s: Germany was still the 'underdog' to be supported against France whose friendship had of course to be kept.

In 1936–7 the British realised that the French decline and what was regarded by Conservatives as the French 'disorder' upset the European equilibrium. The *triangle* was therefore broken: since France no longer counted for as much and carried the contagion of social disruption, it was easier for the British to take the lead in negotiations with Germany; it was also thought necessary for them to enter the lists on the Continent. There, the British government could no longer 'organise' a balance of power: it was forced into a very unusual and unpopular *bilateral* diplomacy, the *tête-à-tête* with *one* power, with Germany. Chamberlain inaugurated a new policy which was not in the British tradition. Till then, when Britain made concessions to one state it had been to gain advantage over a third. This was no longer the case in 1938: there was only a bet laid on Hitler's ability to moderate his ambitions in Europe.

French decline and French political divisions therefore not only contributed to French dependence on Britain, they partly contributed to Britain's appeasement policy itself.

Notes: Chapter 16

1   J. B. Duroselle entitled his masterly book on French policy during the 1930s *La Décadence 1932–1939* (Paris, 1979).
2   Quoted by Duroselle, *La Décadence*, p. 109.
3   R. Frankenstein, *Le Prix du réarmement français, 1935–1939* (Paris, 1982), ch. 2.
4   R. Girault, 'Léon Blum, la dévaluation de 1936 et la conduite de la politique extérieure de la France', *Relations internationales*, vol. 13 (1978).
5   P. Saly, *La Politique des grands travaux en France, 1929–1939* (New York, 1979).
6   A. Sauvy, *Histoire économique de la France entre les deux guerres*, Vol. 1 (Paris, 1965), p. 373.
7   Frankenstein, *Le Prix*, p. 33.
8   R. Girault, 'Léon Blum'.
9   A. Adamthwaite, *France and the Coming of the Second World War* (London, 1977), p. 108.

10   See the Lamoureux Papers, BDIC, Nanterre, p. 1676.
11   These conversations between Malvy and Mussolini on the one hand, and Delbos and Blum on the other, are indirectly reported by Lamoureux, ibid., pp. 1700–3.
12   A few years later, Y. Bouthillier, general secretary of the Finance Ministry, prophesied during the phoney war the 'proletarianisation' of the French bourgeoisie (no less!) if war had to last (P. de Villelume, *Journal d'une défaite, aôut 1939 – juin 1940*, Paris, 1976, pp. 56, 113).
13   J. Rueff, Director of the French Treasury, believed strongly in the virtues of balanced budgets. Whereas Sir Warren Fisher, the permanent secretary of the British Treasury, had been since 1933 'an advocate of greater armed preparedness' (G. C. Peden: see his contribution to this volume, Ch. 10), J. Rueff still did not wish in March 1938 (although after the *Anschluss*) the national defence expenditure to exceed that of 1937!
14   *Archives secrètes de la Wilhelmstrasse* (Paris, 1950), Vol. I, pp. 14–18.
15   Frankenstein, *Le Prix*, chs 8 and 9.
16   F. Bédarida, 'La gouvernante anglaise', in *Edouard Daladier, Chef de Gouvernement* (Paris, 1977), p. 237; R. J. Young, *In Command of France. French Foreign Policy and Military Planning, 1933–1940* (Harvard, 1978), p. 202.
17   ibid.
18   Duroselle, *La Décadence*, pp. 334–5; B. Michel, 'L'action de Stefan Osuski, ministre plénipotentiaire de Tchécoslovaquie à Paris', in 'Munich 1938, mythes et réalitiés', *Revue des études slaves*, vol. 52 (1979), p. 131.
19   In September 1938 and in August 1939 Boussac implored Lamoureux to come back to Paris and to help their common friend Bonnet against the 'parti de la guerre' who he says is 'inspired by the Jews': Lamoureux Papers, pp. 1779, 1854.
20   Duroselle, *La Décadence*, p. 336.
21   Archives of the Service Historique de l'Armée, Fonds 1919–1940, Dossier 'Conventions collectives'.

17 France and the Coming of War

ANTHONY ADAMTHWAITE

Until the 1970s French diplomacy on the eve of the Second World War was a neglected subject. Although the dearth of documents deterred researchers, it was widely assumed that there was very little French statesmen could do to influence events in the approach to war. Almost to a man French participants had blamed Britain for leading France to defeat. 'The Munich Agreement', declared André François-Poncet, Ambassador in Berlin in 1938, 'was the logical consequence of the policy practised by Britain and France, but principally inspired by Britain.'[1] Robert Coulondre, Ambassador in Moscow in 1938, claimed that after the *Anschluss* Neville Chamberlain 'took over the reins of the Franco-British team and guided it to war'.[2] British historians in hot pursuit of British appeasers readily accepted the French version. Thus Sir John Wheeler-Bennett considered that 'the key to French policy lay in the final analysis in London'.[3] Accordingly, France was treated as an also ran and in the 1950s and 1960s scholars concentrated on the study of British and German foreign policies.

The opening of the archives has stimulated new studies of French policy. By and large French historians have confirmed the stereotype of an 'English governess', bullying and cajoling French leaders along the road to war.[4] According to Duroselle, 'French statesmen practised appeasement because they needed British help and were subject to constant British pressure'. Appeasement was followed 'through fear and despondency, but without false illusions'.[5] By 1937–8, concluded Baumont, 'the French no longer played an important role in international politics . . . They avoided independent initiatives . . . They let England take action . . . They obeyed.'[6] Only Néré is more cautious. A propos the Rhineland he writes: 'It is always a temptation for a French historian of this period to put all the responsibilities on Britain. In the present case, this explanation would be inadequate.'[7]

This paper has three aims. First, to show that French leaders, far from being reluctant partners in a British-inspired enterprise, were convinced appeasers. French appeasement, like its British counterpart, was an amalgam of many influences. Fear of Germany did not exclude a genuine desire for Franco-German reconciliation. Secondly, I argue that by encouraging and exploiting British leadership France provided herself with a perfect pretext for disengagement from Central and Eastern Europe. While French ministers seemingly bowed to British initiatives, in practice they pursued a more active and independent line than supposed. Thirdly, I argue that although French statesmen were cabined and confined by circumstance they retained until the summer of 1938 some freedom of action. Much more might have been made of the diplomatic and military advantages that France still possessed. What was lacking was the political will to exploit these advantages. In short, London need not have been the capital of Paris. The paper is focused on France's last peacetime administration, Edouard Daladier's Cabinet of 1938–9.

The collection *Documents diplomatiques français* is now well into 1939 but the assessment of French policy remains greatly hampered by the paucity of material. The record is incomplete in two important respects. First, key discussions have left little or no trace in the archives. For example, we have only a brief summary of the Laval–Mussolini talks in Rome on 5–6 January 1935; there is no French record of the Munich Conference or of Georges Bonnet's second meeting with Ribbentrop on 7 December 1938. Second, there is nothing comparable to the private papers and correspondence of British statesmen and officials. Consequently, it is impossible to reconstruct in any detail the motives and ideas of French statesmen. Much remains obscure, especially Daladier's opinions. His personal papers offer few clues on his decision-making. One is forced to the conclusion that policy was made, not in Cabinet and committees, but in the Parisian salons, the lobby and at the dinner table.

The strongest motive which impelled French ministers was fear. Daladier told British ministers in April 1938:

We should be blind if we did not see the realities of the present situation. We were confronted by German policy . . . designed to tear up treaties and destroy the equilibrium of Europe. In his view, the ambitions of Napoleon were far inferior to the present aims of the German Reich . . . It was clear that if and when Germany had secured the petrol and wheat resources of Romania, she would then turn against the western powers.[8]

Moreover, France's survival as a Great Power was threatened not only by Germany but by her own internal convulsions. 'France', Daladier told a gathering of ex-servicemen on 12 November 1938, had to choose 'between a slow decline or a renaissance through effort'.[9]

Apprehensions of Germany and of decline were not the only motives at work. French ministers, like their British colleagues, detested war. Daladier defended his Munich policy on the grounds that France must 'not sacrifice another million or two million peasants'.[10] Daladier and his Foreign Minister, Georges Bonnet, also disliked the Versailles Treaties. 'Both are convinced', wired the American Ambassador, Bullitt, on 15 September 1938, 'that the treaty must be revised and at bottom regard an alteration in the Czechoslovak state as a necessary revision – the necessity for which they pointed out nearly twenty years ago.'[11]

Appeasement was also conditioned by domestic upheaval – social conflict and economic depression. The modest rearmament initiated by Léon Blum's Popular Front government in the autumn of 1936 provoked widespread gloom. Charles Spinasse, Minister for National Economy, asserted in April 1937 that Britain and France by their rearmament were 'incurring a serious danger of financial and economic collapse . . . France will find it difficult to continue for more than a year at the present pace.'[12] Above all, the Popular Front bitterly divided French society. For French conservatives Blum's government was an unmitigated disaster. Hence the slogan 'Better Hitler than Blum'. Blum's conciliatory approaches to Germany in 1936–7 were motivated by the desire to save his social legislation. International détente was needed for domestic détente. His radical-socialist successors, Camille Chautemps and Edouard Daladier, worked for détente but for different reasons. A settlement with Germany and Italy, it was hoped, would divide the left and assuage the anxieties of the propertied classes. Given peace abroad, Popular Front social legislation could be quietly dismantled. Resistance to Germany increased the risk of war and war, it was feared, would only strengthen the left and bring social revolution. Daladier did not conceal his fears: 'Germany would be defeated in the war . . . but the only gainers would be the Bolsheviks as there would be social revolution in every country of Europe . . . Cossacks will rule Europe.'[13] Bonnet was said to be 'resolved not to allow war because war would have meant the disappearance of the privileged class'.[14] Pierre Étienne Flandin warned Neville Chamberlain: 'It must not be forgotten that unpreparedness for war leads our people, so changeable in its opinions and reflexes, to cry treason and to rise in revolution. Already the Communist Party prepares this action in the red suburbs of Paris.'[15]

Was there an alternative to the Franco-German duel? Though the primary, motivating instinct of French policy was fear, French statesmen, like British leaders, nursed certain illusions about Germany. Before Neville Chamberlain became Prime Minister in May 1937, Blum and his Foreign Minister, Yvon Delbos, made strenuous efforts to reach agreement with Germany. On taking office Blum had at once declared his readiness for an entente provided Hitler accepted a new Western security pact in place of Locarno. The Prime Minister's friends assured the German Embassy that 'in spite of all doctrinal and domestic impediments' the socialist leader wanted a *rapprochement.*[16] Indeed, Popular Front ministers departed from the usual protocol and called on the newly appointed German Ambassador, Count Welczeck. One illusion common to French and British leaders was the idea that ideological differences were really secondary and should not get in the way of an agreement. 'I am a Marxist and a Jew', Blum told Dr Schacht, president of the Reichsbank and Minister of Economics, in August 1936, but 'we cannot achieve anything if we treat ideological barriers as insurmountable'.[17] Another illusion which French leaders shared with British ministers was the belief in economic and colonial appeasement aimed at the 'moderate' sections of the German government, represented by Schacht. It was assumed that if German colonial and economic demands could be satisfied then the moderates would prevail over party fanatics and Germany would be less likely to pursue an aggressive course. In August 1936 Schacht stressed Germany's need for colonies and markets. Without any pressure from London Blum and Delbos pursued this red herring assiduously over the following months. A settlement of the Spanish Civil War, Delbos informed Welczeck on 23 December 1936, would provide the basis for a Franco-German pact. Germany 'should have raw materials, colonies and loans, in return for which the only compensation was peace'.[18] On 20 February 1937

Delbos felt that 'Germany definitely had inaugurated a more moderate policy'. He wanted French participation in the Leith–Ross–Schacht negotiations. If all went well then he and Blum envisaged 'the creation of consortiums to develop sections of Africa . . . all the African colonies except French North Africa and British South Africa would . . . be put into a common pot'.[19] Germany, he continued, would not be able to put up much money but a large proportion of the development would be done by German equipment. The plan was so secret that Delbos and Blum had not discussed it with the Cabinet.

In 1938–9 Daladier and Bonnet still cherished hopes of a Franco-German settlement. A sharp contrast is often drawn between the two men – Bonnet the out-and-out appeaser, Daladier the realist, bowing to British pressure but deeply suspicious of Germany. In truth Daladier had much more faith in conciliation than has been realised. Despite or perhaps because of his recognition of the German danger he could not resist the lure of Franco-German reconciliation. His choice of Bonnet as Foreign Minister was a clear pointer to his outlook. The desire for a settlement with Germany was not a panic reaction to the Czech crisis but inspired by his war service in 1914–18. As Prime Minister in 1933 he had not only agreed to join Mussolini's Four Power Pact but had also used the journalist Count Fernand de Brinon, president of the Comité France-Allemagne, as an intermediary with Berlin. Plans for a secret Hitler–Daladier meeting and a Franco-German declaration seem to have been mooted. On his return from Munich he defended the agreement with the words: 'It's my policy, it's the Four Power Pact.'[20] Later in the day he told the Cabinet that contacts with Hitler and Goering might be fruitful.[21] Although Daladier recognised Munich as a diplomatic defeat, his faith in negotiations with Germany was unshaken. On 3 October 1938 the Prime Minister told Bullitt: 'If I had had a thousand bombers behind me . . . I would have been in a much stronger position at Munich to resist Hitler's demands.'[22] Significantly, Daladier assumed that a conference in Munich would still have met. At Marseilles at the end of the month he told the Radical Party Congress: 'When at Munich I heard the heart of the German people beating, I could not prevent myself thinking, as I had done at Verdun, that between the French and German peoples . . . there are strong ties of mutual respect which should lead to loyal collaboration.'[23] Hitler's 'export or die' Reichstag speech of 30 January 1939 revived the old illusion of economic accords changing the political climate. Daladier intervened personally in Franco-German economic talks. In February he 'thought he might invite Goering soon to make a visit to Paris'.[24] Again Brinon was sent as an unofficial emissary to Berlin. On the eve of Prague the French Prime Minister sent a message to Hitler assuring him that France was ready 'to pursue and develop with the Reich the policy of collaboration affirmed in the declaration of 6 December.'[25]

French policy-makers in the late 1930s are conventionally depicted as irresolute, harassed men, driven from pillar to post by a combination of Nazi might and British bullying. In reality appeasement was conducted with conviction and determination. A crucial period for the shaping of French policy was the winter of 1936–7 when Britain was distracted by the Abdication crisis and Germany took no major initiatives. After rather half-hearted attempts to strengthen the Eastern pacts and to establish staff talks with the Soviet Union Blum and Delbos finally accepted the logic of appeasement – conciliating Germany meant disengagement from Central and Eastern Europe. From the early summer of 1937 until March 1939 the twin themes of conciliation and retreat were pursued with consistency and determination. Publicly the Chautemps Cabinet of 1937 proclaimed its determination to fulfil alliance obligations, in practice it was ready to make substantial concessions. At the Radical Party Congress in Lille in October 1937 Delbos's reaffirmation of alliance pledges neither mentioned Czechoslovakia by name nor stated unequivocally what France would consider as a *casus foederis*. In early November, well before going to London, French ministers were reported to be willing to do their 'utmost to effect a general settlement with Germany' and would raise no objection 'to an evolutionary extension of German influence in Austria . . . or in Czechoslovakia'.[26]

Chautemps was inhibited from making overtures to Germany by the fear of breaking up the Popular Front majority. 'Chautemps', Bullitt cabled, 'will wish personally to enter into direct negotiations with Germany and perhaps make the necessary concessions: in other words, to abandon Austria and the Germans of Czechoslovakia to Hitler. But he will know that his Government will fall if he tried to put this policy into practice.'[27] However, where Britain led, France could safely follow. The government and its parliamentary majority were agreed on the vital importance of the British alliance. Acceptance of British leadership provided a shield for the government's foreign policy. At the London Conference on 29–30 November 1937 Chautemps and Delbos offered only token resistance to British designs. In February 1938 France called for a Franco-British declaration in defence of Austria but had no intention of resisting Germany by force.

The issue of military aid for Czechoslovakia was decided before British policy on Central Europe had been finalised. On 15 March 1938 the Comité permanent de la défense nationale concluded that France could not help her ally directly. In this discussion and in the exchanges which followed between London and Paris, it was, as Welczeck shrewdly saw, 'not so much a question of seeking possibilities of really giving help to Czechoslovakia as of seeking difficulties which would make help appear hopeless'.[28]

Assertions that France always obeyed her English governess are misleading because they ignore the fact that in practice French policy was much more assertive and independent than supposed. Acquiescence in British leadership in the Munich crisis had two purposes: first to ensure that Britain had the lion's share of responsibility for the abandonment of Czechoslovakia, secondly to secure additional British commitments. Thus French policy was not as passive as it seemed. Major modifications of British policy were secured, namely, the promise on 18 September of British participation in a guarantee for Czechoslovakia and on 26 September a British pledge of support for France in the event of war with Germany. When war appeared imminent on 27 September France not only seconded a British timetable for the transfer of the Sudetenland to Germany but tempted Hitler with a larger slice of the cake. During the summer Bonnet had skilfully played a double game – encouraging London to believe that he was exerting strong pressure on Prague while discreetly following a cautious and moderate line until early July. When in the night of 20–21 September a French ultimatum was sent to Prague to enforce acceptance of the Anglo-French plan of cession Britain was made to shoulder the main burden of responsibility. President Beneš was warned that by refusing the Anglo-French plan he would break 'Franco-British solidarity' and so 'deprive French assistance of any practical value'.[29]

After Munich the search for agreement with the fascist dictators quickened. Despite the acrimony which had soured Franco-Italian relations since the Ethiopian War the Daladier government strove to reach a *modus vivendi*. Only Italian cussedness prevented an agreement in October 1938. Overtures to Germany were more successful. Contrary to what was alleged at the time and afterwards the Franco-German Agreement of 6 December 1938 did not give Germany a free hand in the East. However, the withdrawal from Eastern Europe continued apace and Germany drew her own conclusions. For all practical purposes the Czech alliance was dissolved and France showed no interest in obtaining for her former ally the international guarantee promised in the Munich Agreement. The Franco-Soviet pact was said to have died a natural death and Moscow was kept at arm's length. Bonnet and his Ambassador in Warsaw, Léon Noël, talked of revising the Franco-Polish alliance of 1921. Criticism of the government's foreign policy was not strong enough to deflect Daladier and Bonnet from their central purpose. Behind a smokescreen of soothing reassurances of traditional interests French leaders redoubled their efforts to reach an economic accord with Germany.

The shock of Hitler's Prague coup revitalised French policy. Post-Prague events demonstrated that France could be firm not only with Germany and Italy but also with Britain. The revival of the economy in the winter of 1938–9 generated a new confidence. On four key issues – the Romanian guarantee, British conscription, contacts with Rome and negotiations with Moscow – France had her own way. Alas, the revival came too late to convince Hitler that Britain and France would implement their guarantees.

Could the defeats and capitulations that led to war have been avoided? Or was France, in Duroselle's words, trapped 'in a mechanism which seemed inexorable'?[30] The dilemma could only have been resolved in one of two ways. Either France had to accept a Hitler-dominated Europe or she had to oppose Germany. But acceptance of German domination was never practical politics. There was almost no public support for it. Replying in June 1939 to the question, 'Do you think that if the Germans try to seize Danzig, we should stop them by force?', 76 per cent said Yes, 17 per cent said No and 7 per cent had no opinion.[31] However, in the summer of 1938 there was some public support for resisting German claims. A variety of reasons – horror of war, fear of Germany, condemnation of the peace treaties, dread of social revolution, desire for Franco-German reconciliation – help to explain why appeasement was continued until March 1939. But this is not the whole explanation. The failure to envisage an alternative policy before 1939 reflected the timidity and over-cautiousness of the political and military leadership.

After a long, inconclusive meeting of service ministers and Chiefs of Staff on 4 April 1936 François Piétri, Navy Minister, commented: 'Certain people seem incapable of seeing that the only way to constrain a strong country is by war.'[32] At the critical moments – in March 1936, February and September 1938 – ministers and generals shrank from any suggestion of using force against Germany. 'There is a lack of courageous, vital, disinterested, resourceful and imaginative leadership', signalled the American Ambassador, Straus, in January 1936.[33] Two years later Bullitt reported a conversation with St Quentin, the newly appointed Ambassador to Washington: 'When I asked him whether he saw any possibility of preserving peace, he said that he saw none. He did not feel that there was anything France and England could do or should do except wait. I said to him that this seemed to me not the policy of a statesman but the policy of an undertaker.'[34]

One cause of this timidity was a sense of military inferiority *vis-à-vis* Germany. Yet the military advice given to the government was misleading and inconsistent. From 1933 onwards the general staff exaggerated German military preparations. General Maurice Gamelin, Chief of the General Staff, carried a heavy responsibility for misleading ministers on German strength. It is now known that after the Rhineland coup of 7 March 1936 Gamelin, although accurately informed of German strength, gave the government vastly inflated estimates of German strength.[35] His motives remain a mystery. Again in 1938 Gamelin constantly harped on the difficulties of a French offensive across the Rhine yet he was well informed of German weaknesses. On 12 May 1938 Guy la Chambre, Air Minister, claimed that 'Gamelin . . . believed that it was still possible to make a further attack on the Siegfried line . . . it was not yet impregnable'. La Chambre himself 'insisted that, even without an aviation force, the French army could still attack'.[36] In January 1939 Winston Churchill, after talking to the Ambassador, Sir Eric Phipps, and Léon Blum, wrote to his wife:

> They all confirm the fact that the Germans had hardly any soldiers at all on the French frontier during the crisis. And Blum told me (secret) that he had it from Daladier himself that both Generals Gamelin and Georges were confident that they could have broken through the weak unfinished German line, almost unguarded as it was, by the fifteenth day at the latest . . . I have no doubt that a firm attitude by England and France would have prevented war.[37]

Another reason for caution in 1937–8 was the conviction that France could not contemplate war against Germany without an assurance of British support. Yet an Anglo-French military alliance was an unconscionable time gestating. Nearly three years elapsed between Britain's renewal of the Locarno guarantee on 16 April 1936 and her offer of full staff talks in February 1939. French historians have stressed the character of the 'English governess' as the chief stumbling-block – warning Blum against intervention in the Spanish Civil War in July–August 1936, admonishing France against staff talks with the Soviet Union in 1936–7, refusing to guarantee support for France in the event of German aggression against Czechoslovakia. Yet

French leaders were strangely slow in seeking a full partnership. Not until the winter of 1938–9 did Paris make an energetic bid to win *un effort du sang*. At the Anglo-French conferences of November 1937 and April 1938 French ministers acquiesced all too readily in British views on Central Europe and Germany. A forceful defence of France's alliances at that stage might have modified British attitudes. In truth French leaders were their own worst enemies. British tutelage was deliberately fostered. Individual politicians and officials covertly sollicited British pressure – in August 1936 when the French Cabinet was divided on the issue of non-intervention,[38] and in 1939 on the question of Franco-Italian relations.[39] In London on the eve of the April conference it was 'Daladier's hope that Chamberlain and Halifax would themselves suggest that pressure should be put on Prague' so that the French 'could acquiesce without seeming to have taken the initiative'.[40] Bonnet wanted Britain 'to put as much pressure as possible' on Czechoslovakia 'to reach a settlement with the Sudetendeutschen in order to save France from the cruel dilemma of dishonouring her agreements or becoming involved in war'.[41] In short, French policies were as much a cause as a consequence of British leadership.

In their apologias French statesmen made great play of the passivity of French opinion in 1938. Only after 15 March 1939, it was argued, was it possible to consider resistance to Germany. However, the passivity of opinion has been overstated and a determined government might have mobilised opinion for a firmer line towards Germany. The quasi-unanimity of the Press and the delirious Parisian crowds of 30 September 1938 were not the only indicators of opinion. Two public opinion polls conducted shortly after Munich reveal the fluidity of opinion and the existence of a large minority opposed to Munich. Replying to the question, 'Do you approve of the Munich agreements?', 57 per cent said Yes and 37 per cent No. The second poll asked, 'Do you think that France and Britain should in future resist further demands by Hitler?' and the replies were: 'Yes 70 per cent, No 17 per cent.[42]

Marc Bloch, analysing the causes of the fall of France, stressed the failure of successive governments to inform opinion.[43] So much has been written about the influence of fascist propaganda on French opinion in the 1930s that it is easy to forget that the government was by far and away the most important single influence. The levers of influence were many – links with Havas, secret subsidies, informal contacts with proprietors, editors and journalists. In September 1938, faced with signs of stiffening resistance to concessions to Germany, the French Cabinet banned public meetings on international affairs and sought to guide public discussion of the issues. Witness Bonnet's attempt to suppress and discredit the British Foreign Office communiqué of 26 September. Pierre Comert, head of the Quai d'Orsay news department, claimed that the *fonds secrets* were exhausted by the end of September.[44] Analysing the second Blum government's foreign policy Welczeck wrote on 8 April 1938:

If a new government succeeds in bridging or suppressing the internal differences, it can, with better hope of success, exert its strong influence

on the press and its other means of propaganda for its foreign policy ideas
– a thing which in this question the present government has done only
hesitatingly, if at all. If the government knew how to inculcate in the
people the conviction that sooner or later hostilities between France and
Germany were inevitable, Czechoslovakia would assume an entirely
different significance in the minds of the people.[45]

Far from mobilising opinion in defence of Czechoslovakia Daladier tran-
quillised it. On 8 July 1938 the Cabinet was informed of a dispatch from
François-Poncet, warning of German mobilisation measures and the prob-.
ability of a war within six weeks. Paul Reynaud, Minister of Justice, wrote to
Daladier, calling for an acceleration of armaments and talks with the trade
unions:

> If you think that too frequent Cabinets might alarm opinion, the inner
> cabinet could meet regularly . . . It will be said that it is dangerous to alert
> opinion. The greater danger, however, is its present passivity. It is this
> passivity which encourages the dictators . . . It is necessary, in my
> opinion, to impress on our opinion and abroad that France is strong and
> will not allow herself to be taken by surprise. Let us beware of weakening
> opinion by giving it the impression that something is being withheld.[46]

The appeal went unheeded. Even Alexis Léger, secretary-general of the
foreign ministry, was a partner in this attempt to anaesthetise opinion. At
the beginning of September it was decided to implement a number of
military measures. Daladier at first thought of making them public but Léger
persuaded him not to do so, 'pointing out that a small and unimportant
section of French public opinion might criticise the French measures and
thereby convey a completely false impression to the German Government
. . . the smaller friends of France, including Czechoslovakia, will not be
informed, for fear of leakage and of undue encouragement to the latter to be
unyielding in the present negotiations'.[47] Léger and Daladier were not alone
in suppressing information. Evidence of the state of mind of German
military leaders never reached Paris. François-Poncet, who had earlier
warned of German plans against Czechoslovakia, 'received constant messages from emissaries of the Army . . . urging France to be firm and
unyielding and declaring that in case of war the Nazi regime would collapse'.
He 'never informed his government of these messages' since 'their origin
made them suspect and . . . they might unduly strengthen the hands of the
warmongers in France'.[48]

Analysts of French policy are generally agreed on two things: appeasement was disastrous for France; it was also unavoidable. The argument of
this paper is that France was not as weak as sometimes depicted. The focus in
many accounts on France's internal and external difficulties has obscured
her real and potential strengths. Although in urgent need of repair in 1937–8
the alliances with Czechoslovakia, Poland and the Soviet Union still stood.
The French army remained a formidable force with more trained reserves
than the German army, and the Maginot line was superior to the then

unfinished Siegfried line. In 1939 France produced more fighter aircraft than Germany and over twice as many tanks.[49] The emphasis on French short-comings has also had the effect of minimising the role of individual leaders. Different leaders could have given France the upsurge of energy needed to pursue firmer policies towards Germany and Britain. A vigorous effort to repair France's alliances and to establish a full partnership with Britain would have altered Hitler's perception of the international scene. French statesmen feared that resistance to Germany would only deepen internal divisions and weaken yet further France's international position. Daladier's discovery in March 1939 that firmness towards friends and foes alike brought personal popularity and a measure of national unity came too late to save France from war and defeat. Shortly after Munich the French Foreign Minister's wife wrote to an English friend: 'Georges has been admirable, so calm, so resolute. He never despaired. On the two final days, all the newspapers, ministers and even his assistants abandoned him . . . You see what a cool mind and willpower can do for the destinies of peoples.'[50] If Bonnet and his colleagues had concentrated their minds and wills on the defence of France's interests and allies the history of France and of Europe might have turned out very differently.

Notes: Chapter 17

1 *Souvenirs d'une ambassade à Berlin* (Paris, 1946), p. 314.
2 R. Coulondre, *De Staline à Hitler* (Paris, 1950), p. 134.
3 *Munich, Prologue to Tragedy* (London, 1963), p. 33.
4 F. Bédarida, 'La "gouvernante anglaise",' in *Edouard Daladier, chef de gouvernement (Avril 1938–Septembre 1939)*, sous la direction de R. Rémond and J. Bourdin (Paris, 1977), pp. 228–40.
5 *La Décadence, 1932–1939* (Paris, 1979), p. 368; 'Entente and mésentente', in D. Johnson, F. Crouzet and F. Bédarida (eds), *Britain and France: Ten Centuries* (London, 1980), p. 279.
6 *The Origins of the Second World War* (New Haven, Conn., and London, 1978), p. 212.
7 *The Foreign Policy of France from 1914 to 1945* (London, 1975), p. 190.
8 *Documents on British Foreign Policy, 1919–1939*, scries 3 (London, 1949) (hcrcaftcr *DBFP*), Vol. I, no. 164.
9 E. Daladier, *Défense du pays* (Paris, 1939), p. 94.
10 Quoted in G. Wright, *Rural Revolution in France* (Stanford, Calif., 1968), p. 28.
11 *Foreign Relations of the United States. Diplomatic Papers 1938* (hereafter *FRUS*), Vol. I (Washington, DC, 1954), p. 601.
12 *Franklin D. Roosevelt and Foreign Affairs*, 2nd series, January 1937 – August 1939, ed. D. B. Schewe (hereafter *FDR*), Vol. 5 (New York and Toronto, 1979), pp. 53–6.
13 *FRUS 1938*, Vol. I, p. 687,
14 Letter of Pierre Comert of 2 October 1938 published in *Politique aujourd'hui* (Paris, January 1969), pp. 109–13.
15 Bibliothèque Nationale, Don 31357, F75, letter of 14 September 1938.
16 *Documents on German Foreign Policy, 1918–1945* (hereafter *DGFP*), series C (London, 1950), Vol. V, no. 388.
17 *Documents diplomatiques français, 1932–1939* (hereafter *DDF*), 2nd series (1936–1939), Vol. III (Paris, 1965), no. 213.
18 *DGFP*, series D, Vol. III, no. 164. Delbos made the first approach in a conversation with the German chargé d'affaires, Forster, on 11 December 1936 (ibid., no. 97). There is no record of either talk in *DDF*, 2nd series, Vol. IV.
19 *FRUS 1937*, Vol. I, pp. 48–50. *DDF*, 2nd series, Vol. V, has no record of this conversation.

20   P. Reynaud, *Mémoires*, Vol. II: *Envers et contre tous* (Paris, 1963), p. 219.
21   J. Zay, *Carnet secrets de Jean Zay* (Paris, 1942), pp. 25–6.
22   *FRUS 1938*, Vol. I, p. 712.
23   Quoted in *L'Homme libre*, 28 October 1938.
24   O. H. Bullitt (ed.), *For the President. Personal and Secret* (London, 1973), pp. 308–10.
25   *French Foreign Ministry Archives*, Coulondre to Bonnet, 2 March 1939.
26   *DGFP*, series D, Vol. I, nos 22 and 63.
27   *FDR*, Vol. 7, p. 287, Bullitt to Roosevelt, 23 November 1937.
28   *DGFP*, series D, Vol. II, no. 120.
29   *DDF*, 2nd series, Vol. XI, no. 249.
30   *La Décadence*, p. 27.
31   *Gallup International Public Opinion Polls*, Vol. 2: *France* (London, 1977), p. 3.
32   *DDF*, 2nd series, Vol. II, no. 23.
33   *FDR*, Vol. 3, p. 168.
34   ibid., Vol. 8, p. 68.
35   Duroselle, *La Décadence*, pp. 167–8.
36   *FDR*, Vol. 10, pp. 93–4.
37   M. Gilbert, *Winston S. Churchill*, Vol. V (London, 1976), p. 1033.
38   *DBFP*, 2nd series, Vol. XVII, no. 81; J. Edwards, *The British Government and the Spanish Civil War* (London, 1979), pp. 25–6.
39   See A. Adamthwaite, *France and the Coming of the Second World War* (London, 1977), pp. 307–8.
40   *DGFP*, series D, Vol. II, nos 143, 147.
41   *DBFP*, 3rd series, Vol. I, no. 219, n. 2. *DDF*, 2nd series, Vol. IX, has no record of the Bonnet–Halifax conversations at Geneva in May 1938 nor does Bonnet refer to them in his memoirs.
42   C. Peyrefitte, 'Les premiers sondages d'opinion', in *Edouard Daladier, chef de gouvernement*, pp. 265–74.
43   *L'Étrange Défaite* (Paris, 1946), p. 162.
44   Letter of 2 October 1938 published in *Politique aujourd'hui* (Paris, January 1969), pp. 109–13.
45   *DGFP*, series D, Vol. II, no. 120.
46   *La France a sauvé l'Europe*, Vol. I (Paris, 1947), pp. 557–8. For the dispatch in question see *DDF*, 2nd series, Vol. X, no. 150.
47   Public Record Office, London, FO 371/21595, Phipps to Halifax, 4 September 1938.
48   FO 800/311, Phipps to Halifax, 31 October 1938. François-Poncet told Phipps 'under the seal of secrecy'. The letter is reproduced in *DBFP*, series III, Appendix II, pp. 619–20 but the section quoted above was deleted at the request of François-Poncet.
49   R. Frankenstein, 'Intervention étatique et réarmement en France 1935–1939', *Revue économique*, vol. 31, no. 4 (July 1980), p. 751.
50   G. Bonnet, *Dans la tourmente* (Paris, 1971), pp. 66–7.

II

ITALY AND THE WESTERN POWERS

18 Appeasement as a Factor in Mussolini's Foreign Policy

DENIS MACK SMITH

A wise foreign policy has to contain some element of appeasement, because diplomacy is the art of composing differences short of war and cannot operate without a readiness to make concessions. But Mussolini was accustomed to playing a different game with different rules. He saw his own foreign policy as concerned much more with creating new differences than composing existing ones; as he used to say, 'the more enemies the greater the honour'. Enemies were positively useful, because they could be blamed for the internal failures of fascism and the years of economic austerity; also by fostering discord he could give foreigners the impression that he was a dangerous person who had to be placated with minor victories of prestige.

It was therefore his practice at moments of difficulty to create artificial enmities, and this was well known to foreign ambassadors in Rome. In the single year 1934, according to the head of his press office, the orders to Italian newspapers included instructions for a propaganda offensive against thirty-four different countries, including Guatemala. It was a technique Mussolini learned in domestic politics: first manufacture a grievance; then, if you also managed to cultivate the reputation of being someone really dangerous as well as aggrieved, someone might decide to buy you off.

This was a very different attitude from that of the appeasers, and it was an essential ingredient of Mussolini's personal style, which was that of the bully rather than the negotiator. He always tried to avoid any situation where he would have to sit down and discuss: discussion was un-fascist, it implied a meeting between equals rather than between superior and inferior, and it would impugn the legend of omniscience and omnipotence that he tried so hard to cultivate. An all-powerful leader cannot easily afford to compromise without losing face. Or at least, if compromise is inescapable, better conceal the fact and pretend to be winning by the properly fascist methods of fear and force.

Within two months of winning power in 1922, Mussolini attended two international conferences, at Lausanne and London. On both occasions the Italian press called him the dominant figure in the discussions, which was far from true. At Lausanne, though he gave eleven press conferences in two days, so far as we know the only words he spoke in the conference meetings were 'I agree'. In London he managed to offend almost everyone by a calculated show of truculence: one Italian journalist reported that he had shown himself to be a wine that did not travel well and was better drunk in Italy. Certainly he never again relished attending international conferences except when he could stage-manage them as well as play the leading role.

The other fascist diplomats learned on these two occasions that he was a bad negotiator, because either he would stick fiercely and truculently to an entrenched position, or else he would throw away all the cards in his hand rather than give the appearance of negotiating and seeking compromise. His own ministers feared that he was ready to sign almost any international agreement so long as it would help to make him appear the strong man of quick decisions and decisive action. He himself used to boast that he signed more treaties and agreements than anyone else, and – again, according to his own colleagues – signing them was a propaganda exercise and the actual content of treaties meant little to him. Both the Locarno and Kellogg pacts he signed just so as not to be left out. Nor was he interested in negotiating what he called the petty details. He did not even bother to discuss the Pact of Steel, but simply let Hitler dictate its terms: terms, as Ciano confessed, that were real dynamite. The advantages of playing the bully were something else he had learnt in home affairs, because one essential ingredient of his conquest of power in Italy had been sheer terrorism, the 'punitive expeditions' of the fascist squads and the murder of the three most prominent leaders of the parliamentary opposition. Likewise in foreign policy he liked to talk of punitive expeditions and was anxious to make others so afraid of what the British used to call a mad dog act that they would prefer to appease him. In June 1935 Mr Eden came to Rome with the offer to surrender part of British Somaliland if that would prevent war. Later, in December 1935, the Hoare–Laval plan offered even more. And so he learned that the West was prepared to purchase peace at almost any price, while inside Italy he could exploit the fact as an example of fascism being feared abroad.

Here were some of the basic elements in what became Mussolini's foreign policy: first, to create the impression that he was someone with a legitimate grievance but who could be placated by appropriate gifts; secondly, to exploit, and if need be manufacture, international tensions so as to acquire a nuisance value that would make him worth appeasing. The argument was that the greater the friction, the greater the fear, the greater his prestige. He started by creating the legend of an Italy cheated of her due after the First World War, and this despite the fact that Italy had obtained perhaps more than any other country by the peace settlement. His first practical move was the badly mishandled attempt to annex Corfu, but throughout the 1920s he attempted to create trouble in a dozen other countries: encouraging anti-British forces in Egypt, and anti-French rebels in Corsica and Syria; stirring up secessionist movements inside Czechoslovakia and Yugoslavia; smuggling arms into Hungary and Austria; subsidising fascist movements in Malta, Switzerland and half a dozen other countries; backing the Macedonian liberation army and hiring assassination squads in Bulgaria; trying to start a revolution in Spain; negotiating with Abd el Krim for a submarine base in Morocco; sending arms to Afghanistan and the Yemen. In Ethiopia, too, he at once began thinking of how to establish an Italian protectorate, and as early as 1925 he ordered his army to plan the invasion of Ethiopia that took place ten years later.

None of these multiple destabilising activities was particularly successful in the 1920s. Only later did a strong Germany at last give him sufficient leverage. Italy, as an industrial and militarily weak country, had always gained from an equilibrium in Europe that would enable her to play off one Great Power against another. By the same token she was weakest whenever such a balance was lacking, as for example after 1871, or 1918, or 1945; whereas she was strongest with a balance of power that would let her act as a makeweight and so give an illusion of strength. From quite early on, Mussolini therefore worked to restore the German position in Europe, secretly helping to rearm Germany and training German airmen in Italy though this was in direct defiance of the Versailles Treaty that Italy had signed.

It is true that he knew in his more calculating moments that the process could go too far, and sometimes tried half-heartedly to insure against a German hegemony that would again leave Italy powerless. But the primary requirement was to rebuild German strength, because without that he would get nowhere. And Mussolini's tragedy was that he did not know when or how to stop the process; nor could he afford to let his colleagues imagine that he needed advice on this crucial point.

What gradually upset his judgement was the attractive argument that only by working in collusion with Germany could he become a major force in Europe, whereas in alliance with the Western democracies he could never be more than subsidiary. As one of his Ambassadors said, better be number two with Germany than a bad third after France and Britain; only with Germany could he challenge the dominant powers in the Mediterranean and break out of what he called Italy's 'imprisonment' in the inland sea. So in 1933 he put out tentative feelers to discover if Hitler would agree on a division of interest and admit that south-eastern Europe and the Mediterranean would be Italy's exclusive living-space.[1] The murder of Dollfuss put paid to this idea momentarily. But less than a year later, in May 1935, he again told Hitler that he was thinking of a basic reorientation of Italian policy, away from the Stresa front that he had just set up, and against the Western democracies.[2] Long before the Pact of Steel, and months before the Axis was born, Mussolini was talking of this common destiny, this *Schicksalsgemeinschaft* that was decreed by fate to unite Italy and Germany.[3]

One can simplify or oversimplify and say that Mussolini after 1935 had two separate foreign policies, which sometimes alternated and sometimes conflicted with each other. On the one hand he realised that, if he had to side with one or other power group, Germany was decreed by destiny to be his partner, simply because Germany and not the democracies offered him a chance to redraw the map in his own favour, and his chief territorial objectives were against the West – Corsica, Nice, Tunisia, Malta and Jibuti.

On the other hand it was still better to remain (at least in appearance and as long as possible) non-aligned or not completely aligned, because only by playing the old game of makeweight in the balance of power could he exact a higher price for his neutrality from the appeasers. That is why he still refused repeated requests from Berlin to turn the Axis of October 1936 into a formal alliance, and made half-serious gestures towards Britain in the Gentlemen's Agreement of 1937 and the Easter pact of 1938. This is also why he pretended that, after the conquest of Ethiopia, Italy was a satisfied power which had 'come over to the other side of the barricades' and joined the forces of conservatism and peace. Such statements were manifestly untrue and were rather intended to suggest that he was not finally committed to militant revisionism but was open to offers.

In dealing with the West he had one clear advantage not generally known at the time. Ever since 1933, if not earlier, he had been intercepting communications through the French and British Embassies in Rome, and must have known from this source that in London and Paris there was a determination to avoid war against Italy at almost any cost. This was the main reason why he did not take too seriously the movement into the Mediterranean of part of the British Home Fleet in September 1935. The public reason he gave for this defiant and contemptuous attitude was quite different, namely, that Italy had an absolute military superiority over the British; but this was entirely false and known to be false by both the British and his own Chiefs of Staff. The real reason was more likely his knowledge from intercepted messages that there was a clear commitment in London to giving priority to the Japanese threat in the Far East. Incidentally he must also have known from these intercepts some of the very wounding things said about him in the British diplomatic correspondence – for instance, that he could be relied on to be entirely opportunistic and to fight on whichever was going to be the winning side. Nothing can have been more calculated to annoy him than that.

This brings me to another important fact in Mussolini's expectations from appeasement: this fact was his growing contempt for the French and the British, a contempt that greatly increased when he saw the ineffectiveness of sanctions and their inability to prevent his conquest of Ethiopia. Propaganda now stressed that the Western democracies had sold out to the Jews. They were out-of-date liberals and pacifists who had forfeited their right to empire. He despised their dislike of wearing uniforms and their faltering steps towards decolonisation. He ridiculed the British for their lack of conscription, for their addiction to golf and their carrying of umbrellas – which to him was a real symbol of decadence – and for the fact, as he continued to believe, that they put on dinner jackets for afternoon tea. More seriously he derided their falling population, and convinced himself that by 1970 the population of the British Isles would be down to 30 million or less, and most of those would be too old to fight.

Fascist Italy believed that war was good for its own sake; war was the 'supreme court of appeal among the nations', 'as natural to men as maternity to women', and something that Mussolini positively looked forward to as a test of his own skill and the strength of the fascist revolution. Britain, on the other hand, was a declining power that had lost the will to defend her empire, and Ambassador Grandi told him from London that the British would give way if he remained firm. In part his confidence is attributable to the debate in the Oxford Union Society against fighting for king and country, and the half-serious vote of this one small undergraduate society was magnified by fascist propaganda into representing the unanimous opinion of all young men in Britain. Mussolini refused to listen to anyone who questioned this reasoning.

From the middle of 1935 he therefore began talking of fighting against the

British if they continued to stand in his way, and he reassured the Germans that the Italian armed services were quite equal to this on their own. In his capacity as minister in charge of the air force and the navy he convinced himself that he could attack the British fleet in Alexandria and sink it in a single day. He said he would not hesitate even if this should lead to a major European war, because his rearmament was so well advanced that he could now mobilise 10 million men in a single day (this was three times as many as he managed to mobilise in the whole of the Second World War). He was prepared if necessary to see Europe going up 'in a blaze'. Such irresponsible talk was probably intended to impress his underlings who did not know, as he himself knew, that the British would never fire the first shot against Italy so long as they believed that the major danger was from Germany and Japan.

It is hard to know how seriously to take Mussolini's warlike threats. Sometimes he must have been bluffing, because his armed forces were quite unequal to a major war, and perhaps he was just trying to make the appeasers yield even more by exaggerated threats. But it is also possible that, as well as trying to deceive others, he was also deceiving himself. When he told the Germans that he was strong enough to fight Britain or France single-handed, he must have expected to be believed, or else he would never have risked looking foolish by saying it. He must also have expected to be believed when he spoke of mobilising 10 million men in a single day, or blacking out the sun with his aircraft, or raising a coloured army of 2 million men to dominate the whole of Africa, or when he spoke as though he really possessed armoured divisions. All these statements were hopelessly unrealistic, but I think he would not have dared make them if he had not thought them sufficiently plausible to be believed by others. It may seem impossible that he believed them himself; yet one must also remember that he was in some ways a very gullible person and heavily protected from criticism; also that the colleagues he chose were almost all of them second-rate men and flatterers who kept their posts by telling him just what they knew he wanted to hear.

It is also possible that, because he knew so little of what was happening in other countries, he lacked any capacity for comparison and so deluded himself into thinking that he was strong enough to run the risk of war; at least he believed that the democracies were so irremediably behind the times, so terrorised by the mere thought of fighting, that they would constitute no danger to fascism backed by what he took to be his superior military strength. Reports about foreign countries from ambassadors abroad were ignored, just because he could not afford to let others think he needed advice, and some of his ambassadors followed Grandi's example and just tried to curry favour by reinforcing his own self-conceit. So did the Army Chief of Staff, General Pariani, who assured him that Italy was ahead of Germany in rearmament and quite equal to single combat against the British; and I guess Mussolini must have believed or half-believed this, otherwise Pariani would have been sacked much earlier. There was further foolish talk about a secret weapon and a surprise attack employing poison gas on a large scale. Mussolini was certainly prepared to use germ warfare if he thought it would be to his advantage, and perhaps hoped that a quick knock-out blow with such weapons might end the war in a matter of weeks.

At the Munich Conference in September 1938 he was confirmed in his thoughts about British cowardice and pacifism. He did not much enjoy having to engage in discussions with Daladier and Chamberlain; and while the other leaders talked at Munich, he preferred to walk about the room as though the details of the settlement did not interest him. But he hugely enjoyed being at the centre of world attention. On returning to Rome he told others that he had saved Europe. He subsequently remembered with pleasure how Chamberlain 'licked his boots', as Italy for what he called the first time played a preponderant role on the world stage; and he was only sorry that the immense enthusiasm that greeted him on his return home was not for victory in war as he would have preferred, but because Italians clearly wanted peace and were greeting him as a peacemaker. He was also worried that while appeasement had given the Germans both Austria and part of Czechoslovakia, Italy had got nothing. So he now formulated his own objectives, and ordered Grandi, to the latter's amazement, to tell the British that Italy wanted Corsica and Nice, as well as Canton Ticino from Switzerland, and perhaps Bizerta and Jibuti as well. Evidently he calculated that, as Germany had frightened the democracies into surrender, so could he.

In November 1938, a new twist was therefore given to fascist policy towards the appeasers as a virulent campaign of propaganda was begun against France. The climax came on 30 November when Deputies in the Rome Parliament interrupted Ciano's speech to shout for the annexation of Nice, Corsica and Tunis. This noisy demonstration was said by Mussolini to have been entirely spontaneous, but foreign journalists and ambassadors in Rome knew in advance and had already reported what was to happen. He gambled on the French giving way, whereas the main effect of his ill-considered gesture was to unify French conservatives and radicals into a common front against Italy. This came to him as a real surprise and taught him that the democracies had gone as far down the road of appeasement as he could push them on his own: so in December he finally agreed to go the whole hog and make a treaty with Hitler. As he had not been able to frighten the French into surrender, the next best thing was to persuade the German to underwrite his territorial ambitions.

Chamberlain's visit to Italy in January 1939 was asked for by Mussolini – though the Italians begged the British to put out the story that the request came from London so as to make it look more impressive. The object was to make one final effort to see if Britain could be separated from France, or could be persuaded to use her influence on the French to obtain more gestures of appeasement. It did not work, but meeting Chamberlain confirmed Mussolini in his conviction that the British would never fight and so could be provoked further with impunity.

He now told his ministers that there was no alternative but to ally with Germany, and he can have had little doubt that such an alliance, though he hoped it would encourage further appeasement, in the long run might mean war. He spoke with pleasurable anticipation of crushing France and demolishing some of her cities by razing them to the ground. Early in April he launched his long-prepared occupation of Albania; but he also toyed with the idea of attacking Greece and Turkey. Mention was also made of invading Switzerland, Tunisia and possibly Algeria, and the Chiefs of Staff were told to have plans ready for an attack on Yugoslavia. This was typical of Mussolini – to diffuse his attention among many gradiose-sounding projects but without planning any one of them seriously. He already knew that the Germans were building up the pressure against Poland, and was hoping to time his own 'parallel war' so as to coincide with theirs. He sent Hitler the incredible advice that in the first moments of fighting the Axis powers should at once occupy Romania, Bulgaria, Yugoslavia and Greece.

The commitment to Germany in the Pact of Steel marked Mussolini's realisation that his alternative policy – of holding the balance between rival power groups – no longer had much to offer, and the time was coming when his best hope would be to bank on a German military victory. On 24 July 1939 he told his new ally unambiguously that, if Hitler now thought the time was ripe to challenge the West in war, then he was ready to back this 'one hundred per cent' with all the forces at his disposal.[4] Nothing can have been better calculated to hasten the moment of catastrophe, and Hitler now told his generals that the help they could expect from Stalin and Mussolini was the decisive factor that made him choose to fight immediately and not later. Mussolini later claimed that he had done his utmost to save Europe from war, but this was either a lie or a delusion.

In the two weeks before war began there is no consistent policy to be found in Mussolini's sayings and actions. Certainly he now regretted his rash talk of 100 per cent support, but he funked a frank confession that he had been simply bluffing, and so missed his chance to influence and restrain his ally. He changed his mind almost every day in these two weeks, sometimes more than once each day, but eventually could not escape the realisation that his one real hope was another Munich-type settlement with himself in the role of mediator or honest broker. Clearly this best interest was to prevent a war, or at least to avoid Italy joining the war, and on 31 August, against Hitler's urgently expressed wishes, he secretly reassured the British that he would in no circumstances fight.[5] Hitler had been hoping that fear of Italy's intervention would at least tie down Western forces in southern France, but now learned about what he called his typical piece of Italian treachery, and convinced himself that the British had renewed their guarantee to Poland only because they knew about Italian neutrality; in other words, Hitler believed that Mussolini's betrayal was responsible for turning a local war into a world war where a German victory was far less certain.[6]

Italian historians have tried to refute such a terrible imputation by arguing that the British treaty with Poland was on 25 August, and only on 31 August did Mussolini act disloyally by making this admittedly treacherous statement to London.[7] But the truth is different, because already on 22 August, well before their guarantee to Poland, the British were able to rule out any possibility of Italian intervention.

This piece of vital information probably came through one of Ciano's girlfriends, and the fact that the information was accepted in London as entirely reliable and absolutely unattributable suggests that Ciano may possibly have sent it on purpose in a desperate attempt to avoid war; and the further fact that a week later Mussolini himself sent exactly the same message suggests that the Duce himself may just possibly have authorised the indiscretion. Not only was it prudent for him to propitiate both sides until he saw who was coming out on top, but on 21 August he spoke of rebelling against Hitler's 'treachery'. He only switched back again to supporting Germany when, later on the 22nd, he heard the astounding news that the Russians had been squared; but in this brief interval before hearing the news from Russia he may have wanted to encourage the British to stand firm. His actual intentions and actions are admittedly guesswork. What is not guess-work is that the British knew from what was regarded as a certain source in Rome that Italy would not fight, and they could adjust their policy accordingly.[8]

Appeasement as a policy sometimes works, and may indeed have helped on this occasion to keep Italy out of the war for the next nine months. It is equally true, however, that the alternative to appeasement – firmness and the threat of using force – can sometimes fail disastrously; as indeed it failed when sanctions were imposed against Italy in 1935 and resulted in a luke-warm Italian public becoming enthusiastic for the Ethiopian War; and it also failed when Mussolini himself tried to use the heavy hand and unwittingly solidified public opinion against him in France and Britain.

So there can be no easy answer to the question of whether it was right to appease the dictators. Perhaps it is a general rule that appeasement will almost always work if you are prepared to give in enough. And likewise the opposite policy will work provided you are strong enough. But clearly the democracies could not afford the first and were not strong enough for the second. Inevitably they had to try a mixture of the two, and to do so empirically, now yielding, now trying to assert themselves forcefully, and not always harmonising their policies to the point where they might jointly have had some chance of success. The result was bound to seem like dithering, but this was perhaps in the logic of the situation. Western politicians were almost bound to assume that Mussolini – like Franco, who was a better diplomat and had a far more accurate assessment of his own strength and weakness – was sensible enough not to push things as far as war. They could not know (even though they, like some of Mussolini's own colleagues, sometimes feared this was true) that he was a sick man and often unable to take a rational decision.

Looking back over Mussolini's foreign policy one can see that appease-ment had not won him a great deal, and perhaps could not have been expected to win more than minor territorial adjustments. But it had been sensible of him to play this card for all it was worth so long as the West was prepared to pay to keep him neutral. No doubt a better diplomat could have made more of such a fortunate position in the last months of peace, because at some moments, for instance in August 1939, and again in May 1940, the French and British were both ready to concede something fairly substantial; if he had concentrated his demands on Suez, Somalia, and an equal status with the belligerents at the peace conference, he would almost certainly have got what he asked for. Instead he decided to play for higher stakes, and though some people might have thought it a fair gamble, in fact he failed dismally and Italy suffered terribly from his mistake.

This final and fatal decision was, like earlier adventures from attacking Corfu onwards, conditioned by his own temperament, which made him prefer to act the bully rather than the diplomat. More than once he said that he would rather win Ethiopia or Albania by war than by negotiation, and the claim was entirely in keeping with fascist principles. Equally the logic of fascism placed him on a pedestal set apart from all his collaborators, and he hated discussing policy with them or taking their advice, because that would detract from the concept of *ducismo* on which fascism was built. Hence, with his limited sources of information, he was almost bound to make a major mistake sooner or later, and only his unusual political skills as a propagandist and myth-maker enabled him to get as far as he did. Having preached for so long that war was good in itself, it was torture to have to declare himself non-belligerent in September 1939; nor is it easy to think he could have endured remaining on the sidelines after 1940 like Franco. Fatally flattered by Hitler and fascinated by Hitler's offer of a share in world dominion, he could hardly have been satisfied with just the fruits of appeasement.

Notes: Chapter 18

The documentation for every statement in my text is given fully in Denis Mack Smith, *Mussolini* (London and New York, 1982).

1 *Documents on German Foreign Policy (DGFP)*, series C, Vol. 1, p. 30 (7 February 1933, Neurath); ibid., Vol. 4, p. 103, von Hassell, undated; P. Aloisi, *Journal: 25 Juillet 1932 – 14 Juin 1936* (Paris, 1957), p. 50.
2 *DGFP*, series C, Vol. 4, p. 154 (14 May 1935); ibid., p. 209 (26 May 1935).
3 R. H. Wheatley, 'Mussolini's ideological diplomacy. An unpublished document', *Journal of Modern History*, December 1967, p. 435; J. Peterson, *Hitler-Mussolini. Die Entstehung der Achse Berlin-Rom 1933–1936* (Tübingen, 1973), p. 470.
4 *Documenti Diplomatici Italiani (DDI)*, series 8, Vol. 12, pp. 497–8, Mussolini, 24 July 1939; *Nazi Conspiracy and Aggression*, Vol. 4 (Washington, DC, 1946), p. 463.
5 G. Ciano, *Diario 1939–1940* (Milan, 1946), p. 155; *I Documenti Diplomatici Italiani* (Rome, 1953), series 8, Vol. 13, p. 211.
6 F. Gilbert (ed.), *Hitler Directs His War* (New York, 1950), p. 32; F. Sierbert, *Italiens Weg in den Zweiten Weltkrieg* (Frankfurt, 1962), pp. 303–4; F. Halder, *Kriegstagebuch*, ed. H. A. Jacobsen (Stuttgart, 1962), Vol. 1, p. 34; *The Trial of the Major War Criminals before the International Military Tribunal* (Nuremberg, 1947), Vol. 9, p. 300 (Goering); ibid., Vol. 10, p. 183 (Ribbentrop).
7 A. Tamaro, *Venti anni di storia 1922–1943* (Rome, 1954), p. 390; G. B. Guerri, *Galeazzo Ciano: Una vita 1903–1944* (Milan, 1979); U. Alfassio Grimaldi and G. Bozzetti, *Dieci Guigno 1940: Il giorno della follia* (Bari, 1974); B. Milanesi, *In margine ad una storia della seconda guerra mondiale* (Naples, 1975), p. 81.
8 *Documents on British Foreign Policy 1919–1939*, ed. E. L. Woodward and others, series 3, Vol. 6, pp. 658–9, Loraine, 11 August 1939; ibid., Vol. 7, p. 139 (22 August 1939); ibid., Vol. 7, pp. 147–8 (23 August 1939); D. Susmel, *Vita sbagliata di Galeazzo Ciano* (Milan, 1962), pp. 86–7; *The Diaries of Sir Alexander Cadogan*, ed. D. Dilks (London, 1971), p. 196–7; G. Carboni, *Memorie segrete 1935–1948* (Florence, 1955), p. 75.

19 The Anglo-Italian Gentleman's Agreement of January 1937 and its Aftermath

CHRISTOPHER SETON-WATSON

On 5 May 1936 Italian troops entered Addis Ababa. That evening from the balcony of the Palazzo Venezia Mussolini announced the establishment of a Roman peace and declared Ethiopia to be irrevocably Italian. Four days later he presented the world with a *fait accompli* by proclaiming that King Victor Emmanuel III was assuming for himself and his successors the title of Emperor of Ethiopia. Never had Mussolini enjoyed such popularity and never had he felt so dangerously sure of himself.[1] Victory had been won, not over Abyssinia alone, but also over the League of Nations and the fifty 'sanctionist' nations led by Britain. In his first interview with the British Ambassador, Sir Eric Drummond, Count Galeazzo Ciano, Mussolini's son-in-law and newly appointed Foreign Minister, stated that 'Italy is now the military equal of any other nation in Europe', a view which Drummond observed 'is at present widely held in this country'.[2]

The British reacted to Italy's victory with feelings of dismay and humiliation. There was, at first, almost universal revulsion from the idea of allowing the aggressor to enjoy the rewards of his crimes. Anti-Italian feeling had been exacerbated by the Italian army's indiscriminate use of poison gas in the final stages of the campaign. When the Admiralty pressed for relaxation of the state of war readiness of the Mediterranean fleet, the Foreign Secretary, Anthony Eden, insisted that 'it was very inopportune to give the impression of weakening'.[3] Suggestions that sanctions might be lifted provoked an even greater number of letters of protest to MPs than after the publication of the Hoare–Laval pact in December.[4]

On 28 May Eden told the Italian Ambassador, Dino Grandi:

> We had acted as we had done because we considered that we were bound to do so by our signature of the Covenant of the League of Nations, which Covenant the League had pronounced that Italy had violated. There was neither in the Government's attitude nor in my own any vindictiveness towards Italy. We had done what we had felt it our duty to do. We do not pretend that the results had been what we had hoped for. Nevertheless we did not regret it.[5]

Such a statement seemed to Mussolini and his advisers just one more manifestation of the hypocrisy of 'Perfidious Albion'; nevertheless, it rep-

resented a large part of the truth. Ever since Italy's unification, friendship
with Britain had been a basic assumption of her foreign policy. Italy's attack
on Ethiopia was not perceived in Britain as a direct threat to vital British
interests. In January 1935 Laval had succeeded (albeit temporarily) in
terminating a long-standing antagonism with Italy. How much easier should
it have been for Britain to consolidate a long-standing friendship, had she
been prepared to abandon the League of Nations? But, as the Ethiopian
crisis, which had been ideological in origin, developed, it progressively
infected Anglo-Italian relations wherever the two countries' interests
touched, and magnified every minor and hitherto manageable disagreement. After the war ended, strong anti-fascist, as much as anti-Italian,
feeling persisted and exercised a continuous restraint on the British government's attempts to restore the traditional friendship.

Nevertheless during May 1936 the British government moved gradually
towards acceptance of the *fait accompli*. The French governments of Flandin
and his successor, Blum, pressed hard for an end to sanctions. There were
also economic arguments: unemployment was high in South Wales owing to
the loss of the coal trade with Italy. In a series of Cabinet meetings Eden
resisted the longest, but by 10 June he was 'rather veering towards the view'
that, rather than risk the petering out of sanctions 'owing to successive
defections or cupidities', Britain should take the initiative. In a memorandum for the Cabinet of 11 June he admitted that there was 'a strong body of
opinion in this country which now favours the abandonment of sanctions'.
On 16 June the Chiefs of Staff reiterated their desideratum of a 'liquidation
of the Mediterranean situation', which could be achieved only 'by returning
to a state of friendly relations with Italy'.[6]

On 18 June Eden announced in the House of Commons that he would
propose the ending of sanctions at the forthcoming League Assembly. There
followed a passionate debate; but on 23 June the opposition's vote of
censure was lost by 384 votes to 170, only two Conservatives, Harold
Macmillan and Vyvyan Adams, voting for it. On 30 June the League
Assembly met and received a relatively conciliatory note from Ciano. Eden
spoke on 1 July and on the 4th the Assembly voted to end sanctions with
effect from the 15th. Simultaneously the British Home Fleet returned to
England and the Mediterranean Fleet stood down from the state of readiness which it had assumed in August 1935. This, Ciano declared, was a great
step towards restoration of the old friendship between the two countries.[7]

But Mussolini was not satisfied. In December 1935 Britain had given
Greece, Turkey and Yugoslavia assurances of support should they be
attacked as the result of applying sanctions. In his speech of 18 June Eden
announced that for the time being those assurances remained in force. To
this Mussolini took strong exception. It seems to have been Drummond who
suggested a way out: that the Italian government should give the three
governments 'solemn assurances' of its pacific intentions. This was duly
done and on 27 July Eden was able to announce in the House of Commons
that the British assurances were no longer necessary.[8] Mussolini that day
hailed the raising of the white flag on the barricades of 'world sanctionism'.[9]

The British government now hoped that it would be possible to draw Italy back into what it perceived as the major task now confronting Europe: negotiation of a comprehensive settlement to replace the Locarno system which Hitler's occupation of the Rhineland had shattered. On 23 July an Anglo-Franco-Belgian conference met in London and issued an invitation to Germany and Italy to a five-power conference in the autumn. Ciano accepted in principle on 1 August, but the Germans dragged out the discussions into 1937, with the result that the conference never met. It was the importance which they attached to this project that made the British so anxious to keep Italy in a friendly mood. On 8 September Sir Robert Vansittart, Permanent Under-Secretary in the Foreign Office, expressed his hope to Grandi that the two governments 'could now sit round a table together and collaborate usefully and fruitfully'.[10]

From the Italian side there had been no lack of conciliatory statements. On 6 May the *Daily Mail* published an interview between Mussolini and Ward Price in which Mussolini declared that Italy had 'no more colonial ambitions'. On 27 May he declared in an interview in the *Daily Telegraph* that Italy was now to be numbered 'among the satisfied Powers'. On the 28th Grandi drew Eden's attention to the two statements, which he had personally discussed with Mussolini. He assured Eden that Mussolini was 'sincerely desirous of bringing about improved Anglo-Italian relations' and wished to let bygones be bygones. Grandi emphasised that 'Italy had no intention whatever of making difficulties for us in Egypt, in Palestine, in the Sudan or anywhere else'. In a memorandum of 11 June Eden wrote: 'I do not wish to imply that an ultimate friendly agreement with Italy is impossible. On the contrary, I do not propose that we should reject Mussolini's recent offers of goodwill and collaboration; we ought, indeed, to put them to the test in due course.'[11]

Eden's caution was justified by a series of minor incidents during the summer of 1936. Mussolini took umbrage at a visit of the Turkish fleet to Malta and at the suppression of the Italian language in Maltese schools. He also professed to be affronted by King Edward VIII's avoidance of Italy during his summer cruise (with Mrs Simpson) to Yugoslavia, Greece and Turkey. Ciano asked for a public message of thanks from king to king for the facilities afforded to the royal party, but had to remain content with an oral 'word of recognition' through the Embassy in Rome. When Grandi remarked to Vansittart on 8 September that 'so far from minor causes of friction being removed during the last month or so, they had rather tended to multiply', Vansittart retorted that the Italians 'were really far too susceptible for their own good', and expressed the hope that 'the era of the necessity of explanations on such innocuous matters would soon really be at an end'.[12]

On 7 October Drummond raised with Ciano the question of 'anti-British propaganda inspired from Italian sources in Egypt, in Palestine and in Arab countries', which he confidently expected would now cease. Ciano replied that he was completely ignorant of such activities, 'in fact did not believe that they were taking place. Such a policy would be entirely contrary to that of the Head of Government.'[13] More resentment arose from statements by Sir Samuel Hoare, now First Lord of the Admiralty, on his return from a

Mediterranean tour, that Britain was determined to consolidate and modernise her naval defences. There was also friction over Ethiopia. The Italians realised that recognition of the Empire was for the moment out of the question; but in a talk with Eden on 13 October, Grandi returned to the theme of letting bygones be bygones, and suggested that there might be 'some small gesture of good will that we [the British] could make which would have a psychological effect on Italian opinion quite out of all proportion to its real importance'. The only satisfaction given was Drummond's announcement to Ciano on 6 November that the military guard of the British Legation in Addis Ababa was about to be withdrawn.[14]

The greatest obstacle to the restoration of friendly relations was the Spanish Civil War, which broke out on 17 July, two days after sanctions came to an end. On 28 July Maurice Ingram, First Secretary in the British Embassy, reported that 'the Italian Government are clearly anxious lest they should be faced with governments in France and Spain in which Communist and anti-Fascist elements may predominate'.[15] On 7 August Ciano brazenly assured Ingram that Italy had observed, and would continue to observe, 100 per cent neutrality, and that 'if certain Italian aeroplanes had found their way to Spanish territory, that was purely a matter affecting a private firm'. On the 17th, when Ingram complained that the Italian government was now almost the only obstacle to international agreement on the banning of the export of arms to Spain, Ciano assured him that 'neither Italian government nor any Italian had had any dealings whatsoever with General Franco, nor was there any truth whatsoever in suspicions that Italy had done a deal or was contemplating dealing with Whites for the cession of Ceuta, Spanish Morocco or Balearic Island'.[16]

In the first weeks of the war the British government was more concerned with German and Russian violations of the non-intervention agreement than with Italian. But as firm evidence of Italian intervention emerged, it became increasingly apprehensive, first, that Italian support for Franco might change the territorial *status quo* and the Mediterranean balance of power to Britain's disadvantage; and second, that it might cause the spread of Spain's conflicts into Europe, which would then be divided into two hostile ideological blocs.

On 19 August Eden circulated to the Foreign Affairs Committee of the Cabinet a memorandum by O'Malley, head of the Southern Department of the Foreign Office, on 'Italian policy in the Spanish civil war'. O'Malley thought it likely that Italy 'will regard disturbances in Spain not only as a struggle between Fascism and Communism, but also and primarily as a field in which . . . she might find herself at once able to strengthen her own influence and to weaken British sea power in the Mediterranean'. Several recent Cabinet papers, he noted, 'make it clear that this is a supposition which should give rise to the deepest misgivings'. He recognised the need not to antagonise Italy unduly, in view of the prospect of the Five-Power meeting, but nevertheless felt it desirable to make some public declaration to the effect that 'any alteration of the *status quo* in the Western Mediterranean must be a matter of the closest concern to His Majesty's Government'. On 24 August a sub-committee of the Chiefs of Staff Committee set out their views. In the event of war, they stated, 'it would be essential to our interests that Spain should be friendly, or at worst, strictly neutral'. Although Italian occupation of the Balearic Isles would not be 'a vital menace', occupation of 'any territory in Spain itself' or of 'any part of Spanish Morocco, particularly of Ceuta', would be detrimental; and an Italo-Spanish alliance 'would constitute a most serious menace', not only to Gibraltar 'and to our control of the Straits, but also to our imperial communications'. The sub-committee endorsed the Foreign Office's suggestion of a public statement. At its meeting on 2 September the Cabinet took note of Ciano's assurances of 17 August to Ingram, and Eden was asked, when conveying his thanks to Ciano, to add a warning in the terms suggested by O'Malley. On 12 September Ingram was given a further assurance by Ciano 'that neither before the revolution in Spain nor since it broke out had the Italian Government engaged in, nor in future would the Italian Government engage in, any negotiation with General Franco which might alter the *status quo* in the Western Mediterranean'.[17]

Italian activities in the Balearic Islands caused particular concern to the French, who perceived a direct threat to their communications with North Africa. The chief troublemaker was a *squadrista* named Bonnacorsi, known as Count Rossi, who arrived in Majorca on 26 August in response to an appeal to Rome from the local Falangist leader, and played a leading part in the expulsion of the republican forces. Mussolini personally had dispatched him, but in an unofficial capacity so that he could be disowned.[18] On 13 October Grandi told Eden that he found it impossible to believe that Rossi's activities 'could be in any way anti-British', and remarked that 'if there was one thing about which England, France and Italy were all agreed, it was that the Balearic Islands should continue to belong to Spain'. On 30 October Ciano, in conversation with Drummond, dismissed Rossi's activities with a smile and gave an assurance that 'Italy had no designs whatever on the islands'.[19]

On 8 July Eden minuted: 'I am not convinced of this Italo-German rapprochement.' There was certainly a great deal of ambiguity in Italian statements during the summer. Overtures to Britain alternated with hints of movement towards Germany. This 'parallelism' was a reversion to Italy's traditional 'pendular' policy of oscillating between rival suitors. On 2 July Vansittart concluded from Grandi's evident anxiety about the slow pace of Anglo-Italian rapprochement that he feared it might 'be put out of court by an Italo-German rapprochement'. On the 11th Ciano told Drummond that though relations between Germany and Italy had considerably improved, and there was a good deal of understanding between them, which would be increased by the approaching agreement between Germany and Austria,[20] there was 'no definite political arrangement'.[21]

It was Ciano's much publicised visit to Germany in October that caused the first alarm. Drummond, who had seen Ciano just before his departure, suggested that:

Italy is playing up to Germany as hard as she can . . . If we show no visible signs of an advance on our present attitude, Italy may soon think that a choice is being forced on her between France and Germany, in which case she will certainly prefer to choose the latter . . . It may therefore be worth while considering what the Italians mean by being once more on really friendly terms with ourselves.

He thought that, as a minimum, it would be possible to achieve an exchange of declarations on British and Italian policies in the Mediterranean, which he regarded as 'far from being incompatible'.[22]

After talks with the German Foreign Minister, von Neurath, in Berlin, Ciano travelled to Berchtesgaden for his first meeting with Hitler. That day it was announced that 'the Führer has decided to recognise the Italian Empire of Ethiopia'. On the conclusion of his visit on 25 October, Ciano told the Press that the two governments had decided to recognise Franco's National Government, and added that they 'have no other wish than that Spain shall as soon as possible resume, with absolute national and colonial integrity, her due place in the community of nations'. On 30 October Ciano expressed his satisfaction to Drummond in Rome: good work had been done for European co-operation. The most important point, he said, had been 'the common policy of the two powers about Bolshevism'. Also on 30 October the French Ambassador in London told Eden that in the opinion of the French government Germany and Italy 'were already forming a bloc and gaining the consequent advantage'. To Eden it seemed 'plain that the results of Ciano's visit were in excess of those which had previously been reported to us from Berlin'.[23]

Meanwhile Mussolini had been touring Italy in celebration of the fourteenth anniversary of the march on Rome. At Bologna on 24 October he launched a 'message beyond the mountains and the seas . . . I raise a large olive branch sprouting from an immense forest of eight million bayonets well sharpened and wielded by young intrepid hearts.' Eden commented in a telegram to Drummond: 'Viewed from here it is difficult to see the branch for the forest.'[24] At Milan on 1 November Mussolini spoke of 'the vast amount of sympathy among the masses of the Italian people' which Germany had recently gathered, and stated that Ciano's visit had 'resulted in an understanding between our two countries over certain problems which had been particularly acute'. 'This Berlin–Rome vertical line', he continued, 'is not a diaphragm but rather an axis around which may revolve all those European states with a will to collaboration and peace.' Turning to the Mediterranean, he described it as 'just one road, one of many roads, or rather a shortcut' for Great Britain, 'but for us Italians it is life'. He concluded: 'Consequently, there is only one solution: a sincere, rapid and complete agreement based on the recognition of reciprocal interests.'

On 4 November the British Cabinet decided to respond to Mussolini's gesture and authorised Eden to make the first move in the House of Commons next day. Eden's speech was a direct reply to Mussolini's at Milan:

For us the Mediterranean is not a short cut but a main arterial road . . .

We do not challenge Signor Mussolini's words that for Italy 'the Mediterranean is her very life', but we affirm that freedom of communication in these waters is also a vital interest, in the full sense of the word, to the British Commonwealth of Nations . . . We take note of, and welcome, the assurance that Signor Mussolini gives us that Italy does not mean to threaten this route nor to interrupt it. Nor do we . . . In these conditions it should, in our view, be possible for each country to continue to maintain its vital interests in the Mediterranean not only without conflict with each other, but even with mutual advantage.

That day Eden minuted: 'Does anybody in the Foreign Office really believe that Italy's foreign policy will at any time be other than opportunist? . . . We must be on our guard against increasing the dictator's prestige by our own excessive submissiveness . . . We will have no more approaches to Italy, official or unofficial, until we know, and have studied, Italy's reaction to my speech.' Next day Grandi, in a very 'cast down' and 'spiritless' mood, warned Vansittart: 'Lose no more time, no more time.' Italian reactions, both public and private, were in fact favourable. On 10 November Drummond reported: 'I am inclined to believe that the first stage of a rapprochement is well under way.' On 9 November the Chiefs of Staff reaffirmed 'the importance, from a military point of view, of a resumption of our formerly friendly relations with Italy'.[25] Also on 9 November the *Daily Mail* published another interview of Ward Price with Mussolini, in which the latter spoke of the possibility of 'a gentleman's agreement', and denied all designs upon the Balearic Islands. On the 13th Grandi told Vansittart that Mussolini's interview had 'the force of official pronouncements'. Two further events contributed to the thaw: on 6 November a financial and commercial agreement removed the last damaging effects of sanctions; and on the 14th Eden thanked Grandi 'for some courtesies that Marshal Graziani [the butcher of the Senussi, now Viceroy of Ethiopia] had shown to our Chargé d'Affaires at Addis Ababa on the departure of our Legation Guard'.[26]

On 14 November Eden set out for Drummond his 'reservations and desiderata' for the conduct of any discussions: Italy was to be asked to accept the Mediterranean *status quo* without qualification, to end 'anti-British intrigue and propaganda in the Near East', to adhere to the Montreux Convention and the 1936 London Naval Treaty,[27] and to resume effectual participation in the League of Nations. Britain on her side was not prepared to take any course liable to disturb other Mediterranean countries; and there was to be no question of any limitation on British military or naval forces, nor of recognition of the Italian conquest of Ethiopia. Drummond pointed out on the 17th that Mussolini would regard a request to return to the League as an attempt to undermine his relationship with Germany: 'I therefore venture to urge with all the emphasis I can command that we should not make this an essential point for an understanding.' Eden concurred and replied on the 19th that he was inclined to work 'for an exchange of purely general declarations', hoping that this would lead to spontaneous acts by Italy 'calculated to produce confidence and good will all round'. On 25 November Grandi told Eden that though there was in Italy a public expectation of recognition, Mussolini and Ciano were willing to leave it out of the discussions. On 2 December Eden authorised Drummond to proceed.[28]

The discussions lasted almost exactly a month. The main difficulty arose from Mussolini's refusal to allow France to be associated with the agreement. 'If we insisted', Drummond reported, 'Signor Mussolini would prefer to let the whole negotiation drop.' Eden decided on 8 December not to press the matter, and instead to keep the French fully informed. On the 9th he conveyed his view to the French government that 'an improvement in Anglo-Italian relations is as much in the French interest as in our own, both because a politically dangerous situation in the Mediterranean would thereby be eased and because the probability of a firm German-Italian bloc would thereby be lessened'.[29] Mussolini also objected to any specific reference to 'the territories of Spain' in the clause dealing with the *status quo*. Eden got round this difficulty by suggesting that the Spanish problem should be dealt with in an exchange of notes separate from the agreement. In addition on 6 December Ciano again 'by a gesture expressed complete ignorance' about anti-British propaganda.[30]

On 10 December Eden gave vent to his exasperation in a long minute:

> The Italians are at their old game of getting something for nothing. They are apprehensive of our growing strength in the Mediterranean and would no doubt greatly like to be reassured. But what do we get in return? Anti-British propaganda in the Near East, a re-doubling of activity in Majorca, the most cavalier treatment of our representations or suggestions on any subject. This is not what we want . . . An agreement that only adds one more scrap of paper to the world, and changes nothing in fundamentals, is not worth so much effort.

On 16 December Eden submitted to the Cabinet a strongly worded memorandum on the Balearic problem, based on information from the French Embassy. He observed that there were the strongest indications that the Italians had forgotten, or chosen to overlook, British warnings, and argued that 'to permit the impairment of a vital interest' would be to abdicate the responsibilities of a Great Power. Furthermore, Germany's relations with Italy were now very close, and Britain could possibly conduct her relations with Germany 'with very much greater advantage' if she now stood up to Italy in the Mediterranean. But he got no support from his colleagues. On 22 December, however, Ciano informed Drummond that Rossi would be leaving Majorca next day.[31]

On 9 December the Non-Intervention Committee, at British and French prompting, adopted a resolution urging all member governments to extend the non-intervention agreement of August to cover volunteers. On the 24th the two governments circulated an urgent appeal for rapid action. When Drummond and his French colleague saw Ciano on the 26th, Ciano stalled and said he must refer the matter to Mussolini. But though it was well known in London that the Italians were the chief offenders, this knowledge was not allowed to affect the final stages of the negotiations.[32]

On 4 January 1937 the Press published the texts of a 'Mediterranean Declaration'[33] dated 2 January, and an 'Exchange of Notes' dated 31 December. In the Declaration Britain and Italy recognised that their vital interests in the Mediterranean 'are in no way incompatible with each other', and disclaimed 'any desire to modify . . . the *status quo* as regards national sovereignty of territories in the Mediterranean area'. Mussolini gave his assent to the exchange of notes only on 1 January over the telephone to Ciano in Drummond's presence.[34] In the British note Drummond recalled Ingram's warning of 12 September and Ciano's assurances on this and other occasions, in view of which 'His Majesty's Government assumes that, as far as Italy is concerned, the integrity of the present territories of Spain shall in all circumstances remain intact and unmodified'. In his reply Ciano confirmed the accuracy of 'His Majesty's Government's assumption'.

The conclusion of the negotiations inspired a series of hopeful minutes in the Foreign Office. Vansittart wrote:

> This is all most successful and gratifying. The Italians – in particular Mussolini – have behaved very well and accommodatingly . . . if we never *talk* of detaching them from Germany, but merely exploit this success . . . we shall automatically loosen the Italo-German tie, and so have a more reasonable, or anyhow tamer, Germany to deal with.

Eden wrote:

> It is particularly satisfactory that we should have obtained our formula regarding Spain, and I am glad that we were firm about this . . . Finally let us bear in mind during our new relations with Italy that the latter has at least as much to gain from this better state of affairs as we. We shall lose nothing in Italian eyes by continuing *nous faire valoir*.[35]

These feelings of satisfaction were short-lived. On the very day that the signature of the Agreement was announced, Eden learned that 3,000 Italian troops had landed at Cadiz, in clear violation of its spirit.[36] In February, while the Non-Intervention Committee debated a plan for controlling the dispatch of volunteers, Mussolini publicly praised the Italian troops which had taken part in the capture of Malaga. Though Ciano assured Drummond on 31 March that no more 'volunteers' would be sent, all proposals for phased withdrawal were systematically blocked by Grandi and his German colleague on the committee. Also in March, to the alarm of the British authorities in Egypt, Mussolini paid a much-publicised visit to Libya, where the Italian garrison now numbered 40,000, and was presented at a parade of Arab cavalrymen with a symbolic sword of Islam. The Italian Press, including unsigned articles by Mussolini himself, reverted to the anti-British diatribes of 1935, and Radio Bari stepped up its anti-British propaganda. Eden concluded from these events that Italian promises were worthless. Although he accepted the desirability of reducing tension in the Mediterranean, he advocated a cautious approach and a firm reaction to acts of provocation. In particular he insisted on evidence of Italian goodwill in

respect of propaganda, withdrawal of troops from Spain and Italian relations with France, before granting recognition of Italy's East African
Empire. On 15 June he told the Cabinet that 'Italy cannot be considered as a
reliable friend, and must for an indefinite period be regarded as a possible
enemy'.[37]

Neville Chamberlain, who succeeded Baldwin as Prime Minister on 28
May 1937, soon found himself out of sympathy with Eden's approach. He
was determined, unlike his predecessor, to conduct an active and personal
foreign policy and to break the diplomatic deadlock. Granted the imperative
need, reiterated by the Chiefs of Staff, to reduce the number of Britain's
potential enemies, he was ready to concede recognition as a necessary
condition for transforming the Gentleman's Agreement into a comprehensive and durable settlement. By July it had become clear that in pursuing this
aim, he was willing to bypass the Foreign Office and to listen instead to the
advice of men such as Sir Horace Wilson, chief industrial adviser, Sir
Maurice Hankey, secretary of the Cabinet, and Sir Joseph Ball, director of
the Conservative Party's Research Department. Ball enjoyed a private link
with Grandi through the Anglo-Maltese legal adviser to the Italian Embassy, Adrian Dingli. In mid-July Dingli saw Ciano in Rome, and on his
return he and Ball set out to arrange a meeting between Chamberlain and
Grandi and a message from Chamberlain to Mussolini, as first steps towards
opening negotiations.[38] They were successful: Chamberlain saw Grandi on
27 July and 2 August, on the second occasion in Eden's absence, and
personal messages with Mussolini were exchanged.[39]

This 'happy fortnight', as Grandi later described it, was rudely ended in
August by attacks by Italian submarines on British and other ships carrying
supplies to the Spanish Republicans. The attacks were directly authorised by
Mussolini in response to an appeal from Franco. Mussolini, never happy
in the role of peacemaker, had again, as in January, indulged his preference
for bellicose action over diplomatic conciliation. This pattern was to be
repeated regularly over the next three years. On 11 September Eden
achieved diplomatic success at a conference of Mediterranean powers at
Nyon, where Anglo-French proposals for naval measures to suppress
'piracy' were approved. The attacks had already ceased and some weeks
later the Italians were admitted to the international anti-piracy patrol. His
hand thus strengthened, and encouraged by a renewed assurance from
Ciano that no more 'volunteers' would be sent, Eden early in October
authorised a cautious start to negotiations. But on 6 November Italy joined
the German–Japanese anti-Comintern pact (which was primarily directed
against Britain), on 11 November Italy declined an invitation to a conference
on the Far Eastern crisis, and on 11 December Italy abandoned
the League of Nations. These actions intensified Eden's doubts, but to
Chamberlain they seemed arguments for making an even greater effort
for reconciliation. During January 1938 the breach between the two men
widened and on 20 February Eden resigned.[40]

Next day Chamberlain told Grandi that there were now no obstacles to
negotiation. Grandi confirmed the message from Mussolini, which he had
passed to Chamberlain through Dingli and Ball (before Eden's resignation

and without his knowledge) on the previous day, that Italy accepted the British formula for the progressive withdrawal of 'volunteers' from Spain.[41] Negotiations began on 8 March with the first of fifteen meetings between Ciano and Drummond, who on his brother's death in August had become Lord Perth. Three days later Hitler sent his troops into Austria. This eventuality had long been discounted by Mussolini: nevertheless he was affronted by Hitler's failure to warn him and apprehensive of the effect upon Italian opinion. The Austrian crisis, which had started with Schuschnigg's visit to Hitler on 12 February, thus created a favourable climate for an Anglo-Italian negotiation. Chamberlain was correct in surmising that Mussolini desired the prestige of an agreement, which would strengthen his hand in talking to Hitler during his forthcoming visit to Rome.

The Anglo-Italian Easter Agreement of 16 April 1938 reaffirmed the Gentleman's Agreement, and in addition covered in detail the whole range of Anglo-Italian conflict: propaganda, Arabia, British interests in Ethiopia, Libya, Spain and adhesion to the London Naval Treaty. It seemed that almost all Eden's desiderata of 14 November 1936 had been attained. On 16 March Ciano had assured Perth that Italy 'is not sending, nor will send, new contingents of volunteers to Spain'.[42] With regard to recognition, the British government undertook to raise the matter at the next meeting of the League Council.[43] In Italy the Agreement was popular, and Mussolini and Ciano rejoiced that parity between the two empires had at last been achieved. On 2 May Chamberlain, in presenting the Agreement to the House of Commons, spoke of the vigour, vision and efficiency of the new Italy 'under the stimulus of the personality of Signor Mussolini', and declared that already 'the clouds of mistrust and suspicion have been cleared away'. In the subsequent division fifty members of the majority abstained.

The date on which the Agreement was to come into force, however, was left to the two governments to determine, and on 2 May Chamberlain made it clear that 'a settlement of the Spanish question' was a prerequisite. On 26 July he told the House that when Spain had ceased to be a menace to the peace of Europe, 'I think we shall regard that as a settlement'. On 16 April it had seemed to both governments that Franco's current military success would shortly bring the war to an end. But this expectation proved false. Throughout the summer the ruthless actions of the Italian land and air forces, including the indiscriminate bombing of Barcelona and air attacks on British shipping, prolonged the tension. Six thousand additional Italian troops, together with more planes and warships, reached Franco during June and July. There were two further causes of tension: Italian violation of the undertaking to reduce the Libyan garrison, and Mussolini's rejection of French overtures to negotiate a parallel agreement to the Anglo-Italian. Chamberlain and Halifax therefore found themselves after 16 April 1938 in the same predicament as Eden after 2 January 1937.

The deadlock was resolved in September by the Czechoslovak crisis and the Munich settlement. Mussolini's quick and successful response to Chamberlain's appeal on 28 September to use his influence with Hitler for peace recreated a climate of hope and goodwill. Perth stated his conviction on 30 September that but for the Easter Agreement, Mussolini could not have acted as he did.[44] Chamberlain expressed the gratitude of 'Europe and the world' in the House of Commons on 3 October, and that day Ciano informed Perth that 10,000 'volunteers' were leaving Spain.[45] On 2 November Chamberlain asked the House of Commons to approve the government's intention to bring the Agreement into force. He argued that recent events had 'put the whole Spanish conflict into a new perspective': if peace could be saved over Czechoslovakia, war over Spain was unthinkable. In the subsequent debate Eden argued that the essential condition, a settlement of the Spanish question, had been waived, not fulfilled; but his, Churchill's and other abstentions did not rob Chamberlain of his victory. On 16 November the two governments announced that the Easter Agreement was in force, and Perth presented new credentials to 'the King of Italy and Emperor of Ethiopia'. 'All this is very important', Mussolini told Ciano that evening, 'but it does not change our policy. In Europe the Axis is fundamental. In the Mediterranean, collaboration with the English as long as it is possible. France remains outside.'[46]

A fortnight later Ciano addressed the Italian Parliament on foreign policy. When he mentioned 'the natural aspirations of the Italian people', a number of Deputies leapt to their feet and shouted 'Tunis, Jibuti, Corsica'. Once again Mussolini had felt it necessary to compensate for the image of peacemaker with an aggressive gesture.[47] The French reacted forcefully, and for the next nine months the 1935 roles of Britain and France were reversed: it was now the British who tried to placate Mussolini while the French remained intransigent. On 12 December Perth was instructed to warn Ciano that Italy's behaviour towards France might force Chamberlain and Eden's successor as Foreign Secretary, Lord Halifax, to cancel their visit to Rome, which they had hoped would contribute to 'the general appeasement' of Europe. The visit, when it took place on 11–13 January 1939, led to nothing. Chamberlain expressed anxiety about German ambitions in Eastern Europe, but Mussolini ignored hints that he might again use his influence to restrain Hitler.[48] During February he reinforced his troops in Libya, tension mounted on the Tunisian–Libyan frontier and the Italian Press speculated about war with France.

Hitler's occupation of Prague on 15 March seemed briefly to offer another opportunity. As in March 1938, Mussolini had not been warned, and there was evidence of public alarm in Italy. On 20 March Chamberlain appealed to him to take action to 'restore the confidence that has been shattered'. Mussolini replied that he could take no initiative until Italy's rights had been satisfied.[49] The meaning of this phrase became apparent when Italy invaded Albania on Good Friday, 7 April. This was a clear violation of the Mediterranean *status quo* and therefore of the Easter Agreement. On 13 April Britain announced her guarantee of Greece, and an Anglo-Turkish declaration of mutual support in the Mediterranean followed on 12 May. Britain was now committed to the defence of the Eastern Mediterranean, the very policy which the Chiefs of Staff had opposed since 1935, and Eden's 'assurances' of that year, cancelled on Mussolini's insistence in July 1936, had been renewed in a much stronger form.[50]

Mussolini was greatly angered by what he called the 'Anglo-Turkish alliance'. In a frigid interview with Perth's successor, Sir Percy Loraine, on 27 May he declared his unshakeable solidarity with Germany, upbraided the British government for adopting a policy of encirclement and asked whether it regarded the Easter Agreement as still valid. Five days earlier Ciano and Ribbentrop had signed a political and military Pact of Steel, based, in the words of the preamble, on 'the close relationships of friendship and affinity between National-Socialist Germany and Fascist Italy'. Loraine now regretfully concluded from Mussolini's aggressive stance that 'the die is cast'.[51]

This was not yet quite true. Chamberlain and Halifax persevered over the next two months in trying to keep the door open. As Loraine pointed out to Ciano on 2 June, the fact that Britain had not denounced the Easter Agreement after the invasion of Albania was clear proof of the value attached to it.[52] But all British attempts to reinforce it by diminishing the Franco-Italian antagonism failed. As the Polish crisis deepened during June and July, Halifax repeatedly warned Mussolini that Britain would honour her pledge to Poland, but otherwise took no initiative; in Loraine's words of 1 August: 'It is best for you to maintain your *silence menaçante* in London, and me my *silence souriante* in Rome.'[53] Chamberlain and Halifax hoped that Italy's unpreparedness for war, and popular animosity towards Germany, would induce Mussolini to use his new alliance with Hitler in the interests of peace.

Once again it was Hitler's cavalier treatment of his junior partner which opened the way for renewed Anglo-Italian collaboration. On 11–13 August Ciano met Hitler and Ribbentrop at Salzburg and learned for the first time that they intended to seize Danzig and smash Poland at the end of the month. Ciano returned to Rome disgusted and determined to persuade Mussolini to keep Italy out of war. Despite Mussolini's almost hourly vacillations, he finally succeeded. From Ciano himself and from other sources Loraine quickly learned what had happened. Over the next fortnight he, Halifax and Ciano worked in close harmony in the cause of peace, and Ciano was told more about the course of the crisis by Halifax than by Ribbentrop. On 23 August Loraine reported: 'I am now confident that Italy will not join with Germany if Herr Hitler makes war.' Next day he delivered a personal appeal from Chamberlain to Mussolini to intervene. Mussolini doubted whether he could do so effectively unless Poland could be brought to recognise Germany's claim to Danzig. But Chamberlain and Halifax made it clear that Poland was not to be treated as Czechoslovakia was treated in 1938: there could be no second Munich. Nevertheless, Ciano told Loraine on 28 August, Mussolini 'has already insisted in Berlin with all the power at his command that no irrevocable step be taken'. At 9.15 p.m. on 31 August Loraine telegraphed: 'The decision of the Italian Government is taken. Italy will not fight against either England or France.' Ciano, when giving him this news, was 'moved by the deepest emotion'. Next day at dawn Germany invaded Poland, and at 4.30 p.m. the public announcement of Italian neutrality was made.[54]

The nine months which followed were among the unhappiest of Mussolini's whole life. He had accepted neutrality only because his advisers had convinced him that Italy was unready to fight. Before the Salzburg meeting he and Ciano had believed that Hitler shared their wish for three years in which to prepare. After 1 September Ciano did his best to maintain Mussolini's resolve. But Hitler's victories, first in Poland, then in Norway, then in the West, were stronger than Ciano's counsels of prudence. By staying neutral Italy would forfeit her place at the peace conference. It was with feelings of enormous relief that on 10 June 1940 Mussolini went to war, to settle his long-standing quarrel with France, to build a Greater Roman Empire and to consummate the triumph of the fascist regimes over the democracies.

Notes: Chapter 19

This paper is based predominantly on the published *Documents on British Foreign Policy 1919–1939*, 2nd series, Volumes 16 and 17, here referred to as *DBFP*, Vol. XVI and Vol. XVII respectively. It has not been possible to make use of Vol. 18, covering the period January to June 1937, because it was published after this paper was written in June 1980.

1   On this point see Renzo de Felice, *Mussolini il duce* (Turin, 1974), pp. 798–804.
2   *DBFP*, Vol. XVI, no. 365.
3   Quoted in A. J. Marder, 'The British navy in the Italo-Ethiopian war 1935–36', *American Historical Review*, vol. 75 (June 1970), p. 1353.
4   D. Waley, *British Public Opinion and the Abyssinian War 1935–6* (London, 1975), pp. 81–5.
5   *DBFP*, Vol. XVI, no. 347.
6   *DBFP*, Vol. XVI, nos, 359–60; Marder, 'The British navy', p. 1354. From the FO documents it would seem that Neville Chamberlain's famous declaration of 10 June, that a continuation of sanctions would be 'the very midsummer of madness', was less decisive than was thought at the time; but it caused a sensation in both Britain and Italy.
7   *DBFP*, Vol. XVI, no. 428.
8   *DBFP*, Vol. XVI, nos. 439, 445, 471, 473; G. Ciano, *L'Europa verso la catastrofe* (Milan, 1948), pp. 37–8.
9   De Felice, *Mussolini il duce*, p. 757.
10 *DBFP*, Vol. XVII, no. 203. See also Cadogan's minute of 5 September, *DBFP*, Vol. XVII, no. 169.
11 *DBFP*, Vol. XVI, nos. 347, 361.
12 *DBFP*, Vol. XVII, nos. 169, 175, 203.
13 *DBFP*, Vol. XVII, no. 274; Ciano, *L'Europa*, pp. 35–6. For details of Italian relations with Arab nationalists, especially Shekib Arslan, which dated from 1933, see de Felice, *Mussolini il duce*, pp. 564–6.
14 *DBFP*, Vol. XVII, nos 226, 291, 358; Ciano, *L'Europa*, p. 100.
15 For evidence that the victories of the Spanish and French Popular Fronts had stimulated a modest revival of anti-fascist feeling in Italy, see de Felice, *Mussolini il duce*, pp. 777–8.
16 *DBFP*, Vol. XVII, nos 28, 69, 103; Ciano, *L'Europa*, pp. 51–3, 58–9. Italy adhered to the non-intervention agreement on 22 August.
17 *DBFP*, Vol. XVII, nos 115, 126, 151, 159, 188.
18 Full details of Bonnacorsi's activities may be found in J. F. Coverdale, *Italian Intervention in the Spanish Civil War* (Princeton, 1975), ch. 5.
19 *DBFP*, Vol. XVII, nos 291, 345.
20 Signed in fact on 11 July.
21 *DBFP*, Vol. XVI, nos 386, 436, 438.
22 DBFP, Vol. XVII, nos 312, 314.
23 *DBFP*, Vol. XVII, nos 343, 345. Eden's impression was correct. With both von Neurath and Hitler Ciano had discussed Britain's policy of 'encirclement' of Italy and the need for a joint counter-offensive under the guise of anti-Bolshevism against the 'democratic bloc'.

They also agreed on 'an immediate joint effort' in Spain to destroy the Republican government (Ciano, *L'Europa*, pp. 88–9, 93–5).

24 Lord Avon, *The Eden Memoirs: Facing the Dictators* (London, 1962), p. 356.

25 *DBFP*, Vol. XVII, nos 352, 353, 361, 363.

26 *DBFP*, Vol. XVII, pp. 377, 379; Avon, *Eden Memoirs*, p. 427. According to G. Pini and E. Susmel, *Mussolini, l'uomo e l'opera*, Vol. III (Florence, 1955), p. 366, it was the British decision to withdraw the Addis Ababa guard that inspired Mussolini's overture through Ward Price.

27 Italy declined an invitation to the Montreux Conference of June–July 1936 which revised the Straits Convention of 1923. Italy had been represented at the London Naval Conference of 1935–6 but declined to sign the resulting agreement in March 1936.

28 *DBFP*, Vol. XVII, nos 376, 380, 410, 426.

29 *DBFP*, Vol. XVII, pp. 440, 447, 451, 462.

30 On this occasion Drummond mentioned the names of Arslan and another Arab nationalist. On 1 January Ciano told Drummond that Arslan was in Rome, but that he had refused to see him and 'had taken care that he should receive no encouragement' (*DBFP*, Vol. XVII, nos 440, 526).

31 *DBFP*, Vol. XVII, no. 440, n. 6, nos 467, 471, 499.

32 *DBFP*, Vol. XVII, nos 449, 505, 507. For details of Italy's massive intervention, decided soon after the German–Italian recognition of Franco's government on 18 November, see Coverdale, *Italian Intervention*, ch. 6.

33 The title of 'Gentleman's Agreement' was officially dropped, presumably in response to Eden's suggestion of 4 December that 'exchange of assurances' would be better 'and less likely to raise a smile' (*DBFP*, Vol. XVII, no. 461).

34 *DBFP*, Vol. XVII, no. 526. 'Count Ciano was clearly delighted that we had reached agreement', Drummond reported.

35 *DBFP*, Vol. XVII, no. 527. Eden's anxiety to have Spain mentioned was due to his appreciation of the need to have 'most definite ground for replying to parliamentary questions satisfactorily' (*DBFP*, Vol. XVII, no. 508).

36 The 'volunteers' had sailed from Gaeta on 18 December when Drummond's talks with Ciano were in their critical stage. By the end of February 1937 the Italian forces in Spain numbered 48,000. Coverdale, *Italian Intervention*, pp. 170, 175.

37 D. T. Rotunda, 'The Rome embassy of Sir Eric Drummond, 16th Earl of Perth, 1933–1939', unpublished thesis, University of London, 1978, pp. 362–3; L. R. Pratt, *East of Malta, West of Suez* (Cambridge, 1975), pp. 75–6.

38 For Dingli's role as unofficial go-between in Anglo-Italian relations, see the appendix to R. Quartararo, 'Inghilterra e Italia. Dal Patto di Pasqua a Monaco', *Storia contemporanea*, vol. 7, no. 4 (December 1976), based on Dingli's diaries and memoirs.

39 The idea of a personal approach to Mussolini originated with Eden on 16 July, and he made a conciliatory speech in the House of Commons on the 19th; but he subsequently objected to the tone in which Chamberlain addressed Mussolini and resented not being consulted in the drafting. Pratt, *East of Malta, West of Suez*, pp. 80–4; Avon, *Eden Memoirs*, pp. 449–53.

40 Grandi's role in exploiting the breach between Chamberlain and Eden, notably at their meeting *à trois* on 18 February, is well documented: see Eden's account in Avon, *Eden Memoirs*, pp. 616–18, and Grandi's in Ciano, *L'Europa*, pp. 249–78. For the role of Ball and Dingli in January–February 1938, see Quartararo, 'Inghilterra e Italia', pp. 668–77. At this time Chamberlain also used his sister-in-law, Sir Austen's widow, then in Rome, as an intermediary.

41 Quartararo, 'Inghilterra e Italia', p. 677; Avon, *Eden Memoirs*, p. 623, quoting Iain Macleod's biography of Chamberlain.

42 Ciano, *L'Europa*, p. 295.

43 Halifax fulfilled this promise on 12 May when he secured a vote in the League Council which enabled each member of the League to take its own decision in the matter.

44 *DBFP*, 3rd series, Vol. II, no. 1231.

45 *DBFP*, 3rd series, Vol. III, no. 329. The troops arrived in Naples on 20 October and were welcomed by the king as heroes. But Italian troops continued to fight in Spain, and 10,000 reinforcements were dispatched between January and March 1939. After Franco's victory on 1 April and a victory parade on 20 May, Mussolini carried out his promise to evacuate all

his forces, not in order to please Britain but because Franco insisted that they should go. Coverdale, *Italian Intervention*, pp. 371–81.

46   G. Ciano, *Diario 1937–1938* (Bologna, 1948), p. 293. Italy adhered to the London Naval Treaty on 2 December.

47   'The Duce is very content, as always when he starts a battle', Ciano noted on 2 December. On the 3rd he told Perth that the demonstration was entirely spontaneous, and in his diary he recorded that 'nothing had been prepared'. His latest biographer, Guerri, states that this was one of the occasions when he lied in his diary. There was some doubt about what actually was shouted: Ciano in his diary of 30 November wrote 'Tunisi, Corsica, Nizza, Savoia', but next day the British press reported 'Tunis, Corsica, Nice', and the Italian 'Tunisi, Jibuti, Corsica'. Rodd, who was present, couldn't hear clearly but thought it had been 'Tunis, Tunis'. *DBFP*, 3rd series, Vol. III, nos 451, 462, 464, 473; Ciano, *Diario*, pp. 301–3; G. M. Guerri, *Galeazzo Ciano* (Milan, 1979), p. 339.

48   *DBFP*, 3rd series, Vol. III, nos 475, 500.

49   *DBFP*, 3rd series, Vol. IV, nos 448, 596.

50   As Pratt (*East of Malta, West of Suez*, pp. 170–80) points out, 'a revolution in British strategy', that is, the adoption by the Chiefs of Staff of an anti-Italian offensive strategy in the Mediterranean, had already taken place in February, and so 'cleared the way for the diplomatic revolution of late March–early April 1939'.

51   *DBFP*, 3rd series, Vol. V, nos 651, 653.

52   See also Halifax's *aide-mémoire*, describing the Easter Agreement as the 'keystone for many years to come', which Loraine gave to Ciano on 9 June. *DBFP*, 3rd series, Vol. V, nos 698, 708 and Vol. VI, no. 10.

53   *DBFP*, 3rd series, Vol. VI, no. 509.

54   *DBFP*, 3rd series, Vol. VII, nos 173, 220, 222, 422, 621, 665.

III

RUSSIA AS A FACTOR IN APPEASEMENT POLICIES

20 Was There a Soviet Appeasement Policy?

LORD BELOFF

It is striking that all the discussion about 'appeasement' in the 1930s deals with the alleged failures by Britain and France to understand the potential menace of Hitler and to take proper military precautions to prevent him from remoulding the map of Europe by force with the terrible consequences of which we are familiar. For one of the allegations most frequently made against the Western powers is their failure to conclude a 'grand alliance' with the Soviet Union which is the more understandable in the light of the major role played by Soviet forces in the eventual defeat of the Nazis. But this assumes that the Soviet Union was ready and willing to take part in such an alliance at any time before the German attack in June 1941 left its rulers with no option.

But this is to overlook the fact that Soviet policy was also influenced by the Soviet brand of appeasement which precluded such action. Soviet foreign policy in the interwar years can be seen as embodying two different strands. In the first place there was a long-term hope of the spread of world communism maintained during the period of the Soviet Union's own weakness largely through ideological combat and subversion which, after the consolidation of the situation in Europe from 1925 onwards, was primarily directed to the colonial world. Second was the desire to prevent an armed challenge against the Soviet homeland until it was in a military and economic state to repel it. The implications of this policy were that efforts should be made to have friendly relations at the state level, irrespective of ideology, with whatever government seemed to pose the major threat at the time. In the period of the civil war and 'intervention' and during the rest of the 1920s, this meant trying to come to terms with Britain and France. After the coming into power of Hitler and the rapid reconstitution of German military strength, Germany was clearly the power most feared. And through its earlier assistance in the clandestine rearmament of Germany, the Soviet Union was in a good position to know how massive a threat this could be.

It was thus the natural wish of the Soviet government in the 1930s to try to seek an accommodation with Nazi Germany (and in the Far East with Japan) irrespective of what appeared to be major ideological differences or the fate of communists outside the Soviet borders. The question between 1933 and 1941 was not whether or not the Soviet Union was ready to appease Nazi Germany but whether or not Hitler was prepared to accept the concessions that were on offer. Only when German policy seemed to be rigidly opposed to an accommodation did the Soviet Union embrace the alternative of 'collective security' and even then not in terms which would preclude a return to 'appeasement' if this should prove within reach.

The Ribbentrop–Molotov pact of August 1939 with its secret protocols was thus fully in line with Soviet policy at a time when the army purges of the past two years made it more than ever unthinkable for the Soviet Union willingly to accept the idea of war against a major power. Even after the signs grew from the autumn of 1940 onwards that Hitler was not content with what he was getting out of the arrangements and that he would go to war in order to establish a total domination of the East European land-mass, Stalin took very few measures to guard against an attack, probably believing that before it could be launched, Hitler would put up further demands which he would find negotiable.

Britain and France ended the period of appeasement when in March 1939 it appeared that the Nazi aims were incompatible with any conception of their own national interests and when they felt that the military disadvantages under which they had laboured at the time of Munich were at least beginning to disappear; Soviet appeasement ended when the German armies crossed the borders of the Soviet Union itself. In both cases, appeasement was motivated by a quite natural and understandable reluctance of governments to take still more reluctant peoples into war.

21 British Attitudes and Policies towards the Soviet Union and International Communism, 1933–9

GOTTFRIED NIEDHART

An attempt at evaluating the place of the USSR in British policy before the Second World War[1] needs to be set against the background of the general constraints which conditioned Britain's world policy during the 1930s. Any analysis of individual features of that policy – and thus of British policy towards the Soviet Union – has to take into account Britain's situation at the outset, for in each case this had its enduring effect on the decisions reached. That situation was itself determined by various factors resulting in a crisis and calling into question the traditional bases of British power. Without going into details, it will suffice to refer here to the crisis-laden trends and conditions in the economic and financial sphere, as well as in the military and strategic sphere, bound up with which was Britain's loss of power within an international system sliding into anarchy, and to changes in the structure of empire and commonwealth. These symptoms of crisis did not of course appear for the first time during the 1930s. But their noticeable intensification at that period aroused the British governing élite to an awareness of crisis in a form previously unknown. In essence their problem was how to preserve British interests which, despite Britain's relative loss of power within the international system, continued to be spread worldwide; and how to achieve, despite the elements of weakness which had started to be evident at the turn of the century and which had intensified after the First World War, the goal of maintaining Britain's political and economic status in international affairs.[2]

In what follows we shall relate British attitudes and policy towards the Soviet Union to certain fundamental aims of British policy-makers. Reaching these aims would have meant overcoming the crisis. In awareness of the crisis, the political leadership in Great Britain set its sights upon:

(1) stabilisation of the liberal system;
(2) keeping the peace in international affairs; and
(3) preparedness in defence and the containment of aggressors who might threaten to overturn the existing international system.

What, in the eyes of the British decision-makers, was the role of the Soviet Union in the pursuit of these goals, coincident as they were with Britain's national interest? Did the British see the Soviet Union as a member in the international community who might be reconciled with the goals Great Britain had in view? Was co-operation with the Soviet Union therefore a precondition for the stability and lack of conflict which people desired? Or was the Soviet Union regarded instead as yet another factor in the crisis, an obstacle to the attainment of British aims and an element making for further destabilisation of an already crisis-laden situation?

I

During the 1930s the liberal system was faced with challenges of a political and economic nature which in one or two countries had already made the system unworkable and which, even in Great Britain, had subjected it at the very least to severe strain. In Great Britain the appeal of alternatives to the familiar liberal conceptions of government undoubtedly increased following the shock of the world economic crisis and the formation of the National (Coalition) Government. The inspiration was provided not so much by the model of fascism or National Socialism but rather by the Soviet Union's idea of five-year plans. To the Labour movement in opposition it seemed obvious that there must be measures aimed at economic and social direction and more readiness on the part of the state to intervene. It was in this context that Attlee referred to the Soviet Union's 'great experiment in economic construction'.[3] To be sure, neither the leaders of the Labour Party nor indeed those of the trade unions had any thought of introducing Soviet methods into Britain. In contrast with their politically insignificant left wing, the leaders of the Labour movement did not share the marked infatuation with Soviet Russia of certain prominent intellectuals[4] and of the British Communist Party itself, an infatuation especially remarkable in university circles, where it was not without long-term political effects.[5] The decisive factor was the rejection of dictatorship of the Stalinist type which among Labour supporters led also to the eventual discrediting of the social and economic aspects of the Soviet regime. Labour's idea of aiming at gradual change tallied *in principle* with government policy, which was to achieve stabilisation and greater efficiency within the existing framework by means of reforms and adjustments in the economic and social sphere.

The Soviet Union and international communism, on the other hand, stood in principle for the exact opposite of this policy. Irrespective of the current aims of Soviet policy, which in the 1930s were scarcely occupied with world revolution, having veered round instead to the tactic of the Popular Front, Moscow continued to be regarded as the warehouse of revolutionary ideas and the USSR as the 'merchant of dangerous thoughts', as Vansittart put it in the context of the Spanish Civil War.[6] Soviet policy in regard to the Spanish Civil War posed again in acute form the question which had all along been central to evaluation of the USSR: how did the conventional elements in the government of the Soviet Union relate to the revolutionary pretensions of the Communist Party and the Comintern? Did Soviet intervention in Spain indicate a certain or even a distinct determination in favour of exporting the revolution?[7]

It can in general be said that no member of the British government regarded the activities of Soviet Russia or of the communists as a whole as a direct threat to the liberal order in Great Britain. All the same, the growing membership of the Communist Party of Great Britain, which in 1937 stood at 12,000 compared with 2,500 in 1931, and the rise to 70,000 copies in the circulation of the *Daily Worker*, which hinted that the number of fellow travellers, although it could not be precisely known, was certainly increasing, appeared 'distinctly disturbing'.[8] Recourse was even made to the well-tried propaganda device of raising the scare of communist infiltration of the trade unions,[9] admittedly not without a prompt reaction from the liberal press, which demanded concrete evidence.[10] Immunisation of the political and social system in Britain itself was not in fact the most pressing problem. It was otherwise with respect to communist propaganda and activity in regions where there was fear of encroachment on British interests along the empire's lines of communication or in the colonial territories themselves. It will be enough to cite as examples the Iberian peninsula following the outbreak of the Spanish Civil War,[11] and India. 'Communist propaganda, though probably ineffective in this country remains a considerable danger in other parts of the Empire, particularly India.'[12]

The problem of Comintern propaganda and activity remained in British eyes a standing source of disturbance to British-Soviet relations even when the Soviet Union became a member of the League of Nations.[13] The Comintern Congress in Moscow in 1935 was a sign that Stalin wanted the weapon of anti-Western propaganda to be kept in readiness, although for reasons of tactics its use was for the moment restricted, in order not to jeopardise at the outset the policy of the Popular Front.[14] There was still plenty of scope for provocation, aimed against Great Britain and the other Western nations. In 1935, for example, Dimitrov, the general secretary of the Comintern, described the British government as a pacemaker for fascism and speculated publicly about the progress towards a Soviet-type regime in Great Britain. The protest note this evoked from the British[15] was backed up by a warning from Hoare, the Foreign Secretary, to Litvinov, his Soviet opposite number: while Comintern propaganda continued, relations between the two powers could not be free of friction.[16] Party agitation, which to the British was inseparable from official Soviet policy, led again and again to the discounting of Litvinov's avowals to the League of Nations.[17]

The underlying antagonism which was thus present in the British-Soviet relationship – Neville Chamberlain spoke in April 1939 of ideological differences between London and Moscow[18] – should nevertheless not be exaggerated. It certainly did not lead to a consciously anti-Soviet policy. Anti-communism was not an important motive force in British policy, which had more pressing problems to deal with. Quantitative analysis of the speeches of leading British politicians would show that, compared with other problems, anxieties about communism and the Soviet Union were by no means uppermost.[19] All the same, the ideological difference engendered on the British side an emotional bias against communism to match the anti-capitalist sentiment of the other side, and this was an obstacle in the way of *rapprochement* between the two powers. Anti-communist feeling intensified in the mid-1930s when the image of the Soviet Union was determined by the Stalinist purges – proceedings scarcely explicable in Western terms[20] and responsible for the emergence of 'an increasingly unfriendly attitude towards the Soviet Union'[21] on a wide scale. The moderate majority in the Labour Party was equally affected. *Labour*, the organ of the National Council of Labour, noted a lessening of support for the Soviet Union within the international Labour movement, hitherto sympathetic.[22] The Soviet road to socialism was falling into disrepute.[23] The political tradition of Great Britain, in which the emphasis was on reform and gradual change, stood out in marked contrast with that of the USSR, characterised by violence and revolution. In his attempt to provide a rational justification for the trials and executions Churchill was hardly typical. He interpreted what had happened as a shift to the right. The Soviet Union of the Trotskyist type, with its plans for world revolution, had finally been superseded by Stalin's nationalistic military dictatorship. But because Stalin had renounced world revolution, the Soviet Union could now grow into an acceptable member of the international system.[24]

II

Stabilisation was the aim of external as well as of internal policy. Hand in hand with policies of reform and modernisation at home went the pursuit of a foreign policy intended to preserve peace and stability abroad. In the strategy of appeasement the two were inextricably linked. The preservation of peace, or more precisely the avoidance of war between the Great Powers, seemed a precondition as fundamental to the stabilisation of the liberal system as to that of Great Britain's status as a world power. How, in the eyes of the British government, did the Soviet Union fit into this scheme of things?

In the first place, the Soviet Union, too, was reckoned to be a power interested in keeping the peace. In view of its internal problems, it appeared that the USSR had no interest in military entanglements.[25] What was disputed, however, was whether the peace policy of the USSR signified a genuine desire to preserve peace or was instead the product of tactical calculation. The *Daily Herald* drew a clear distinction between 'internal' and 'external' policy. 'For whatever may be said about the internal policy of the Soviet Government, its external policy has been consistently based upon respect for the principles of peaceful organisation. It has neither committed nor advocated aggression. It has consistently used its great influence on the side of international justice.'[26] The Labour politician Herbert Morrison described the Soviet Union as a 'genuine power for peace'.[27] The Foreign Office and government circles tended towards a somewhat different interpretation. The view there was that the Soviet concern for peace was dictated much more by circumstances. Vansittart, for instance, held that at bottom the USSR was no more peacably inclined than Germany or Japan. It was merely that 'she feels it will take her longer to get fit'. Hence the Soviet decision to join the League of Nations.[28] To use an expression frequently employed at the time, the Soviet Union would always be ready 'to fish in troubled waters and will be a bad and faithless ally'.[29] Simon, the Foreign Secretary, regarded the Soviet application to join the League of Nations as sheer opportunism.[30]

These doubts about the aims of Soviet foreign policy need to be seen against the backcloth to the international strife of the 1930s depicted by the communist side: the present conflicts represented the preliminary stages of a second imperialist war which would not affect the Soviet Union. Thus the Soviet Union was paying homage to a conception of peace not in accord with that of the Western powers.[31] General distrust of Soviet motives[32] crystal-lised into suspicions that the Soviet leadership was only waiting for an outbreak of war in Central and Western Europe to step in triumphantly at the last as 'tertius gaudens'.[33] There was therefore in the British view another reason why a war in Europe should be avoided, the danger that it would hasten world revolution.[34]

The essential difference between British and Soviet foreign policy in the handling of conflict lay, as London saw it, in the fact that Britain was prepared to work for compromises and concessions, for the resolution of conflicts by peaceful means, whereas the Soviet Union was insistent that such a policy was unworkable in principle and described agreements reached with Germany, Italy, or Japan as sham agreements. To avoid conflict one should stick to the principle of collective security and stand firm, not make concessions to the dictators. It was precisely the latter, however, which was the cornerstone of the British policy of 'peaceful change' as opposed to a philosophy geared rigidly to the *status quo*. Only through adjustments to the international order could the multipolar structure of the latter, and with it the peace, be maintained. The upshot was that Britain's efforts at com-promise, whether in Europe or the Far East, met with obstruction from the Soviet Union. 'Russia has made trouble on whatever body she was sitting' was Eden's lament at the end of 1937.[35]

The Soviet demand to defend the *status quo* would have led, in the British opinion, to the establishment in international affairs of power blocs and entangling alliances, and hence to the exact opposite of what was wanted. For the sake of Britain's external trade and in view of her inability to pursue an interventionist balance-of-power policy of the old style, the aim must be to uphold an international system that was open, multipolar and unencum-bered by alliances. This idea, inspired not least by the desire to avoid alliances and an arms race which had preceded the First World War, still played an essential role even in 1939. At the talks which took place in Moscow that year with the aim of securing agreement between France, Great Britain and the USSR, the British delegation tried to prevent an alliance directed against Germany, which would have robbed Hitler of room to manoeuvre, and to promote instead a treaty whose terms were more flexible.[36]

This policy led inevitably to the isolation of the Soviet Union which only in

1939, under the pressure of events, began gradually to assume a greater role in British policy. Up to that time relations with Moscow had at best been 'correct'.[37] Promotion of British-Soviet relations took second place in comparison with the goal of a 'general settlement' which should include Great Britain, France, Germany and Italy but not the Soviet Union. This, moreover, was a line of policy that also commanded support in the dominions. All of them, New Zealand alone excepted, were opposed to closer co-operation with the Soviet Union. Hertzog, the Prime Minister of South Africa, was assuredly not alone when in May 1939 he voiced the opinion that an alliance with the Soviet Union would close the door to peace and make war virtually inevitable.[38] Lastly, there was in 1939 decided resistance in the threatened states of Eastern and Central Europe, and above all among the Polish leaders, to the idea of a treaty which would include the Soviet Union. This reason was itself enough to make the British government think twice about a direct alliance with the Soviet Union, all the more since the Soviet government desired to secure to itself a *de facto* right of intervention in the case of so-called indirect aggression.[39]

The Soviet Union – part European, part Asiatic[40] – occupied in British eyes a peripheral position: it did not properly count as a member of the 'family of European states'. For as long as the four-power diplomacy of a 'general settlement' in Europe continued to be given absolute priority, so long did the USSR continue to play a subordinate role in British foreign policy. All the same, the suspicion that the four-power diplomacy had a specifically anti-Soviet slant, as was asserted on the Soviet side[41] and has since been reiterated by Marxist historians,[42] does not conform with historical reality. Even Chamberlain's critics were not disposed to characterise his policy as being determined by a fundamentally anti-Soviet bias.[43] The isolation of the USSR was a secondary effect of British policy, which it is true looms the larger in retrospect because the intended primary effect, the pacification of Europe, was not achieved.

III

The British aim to preserve peace by means of worldwide détente, the policy of 'world appeasement' as Lord Halifax once called it,[44] was not without rational foundation: it cost little and at the same time represented the one hope for the continuation of Britain's global role despite a radical change for the worse in her basic position, and for the maintenance of Britain's status as a world power, even at a time of 'strategic over-commitment'.[45] But it must also be stressed that Britain's peace policy was by no means a policy of peace at any price. The *casus belli* was imminent whenever concessions to revisionist states would signify withdrawal from key positions in world politics. As a result the policy of appeasement, too, was always regarded as a policy at once of détente *and* of defence. It was as complements to the peacekeeping policy that rearmament and the resort, if need be, to war were drawn into the calculation. War as an instrument of policy was from one angle contrary to British interests, from another in keeping with them. While Britain's internal crisis made it advisable to remain at peace, the crisis of the international system eventually pushed Britain over the brink of war, in defence of external security.

Since the weight attached to the Soviet Union in British policy depended on the progress of détente, once those attempts seemed doomed to failure the Soviet Union moved more strongly into view as a factor in international politics, in the far East as much as in Europe. Yet it was not until the summer of 1939 – and then only hesitantly – that this failure was recognised to be the case,[46] although the possibility of a war on three fronts had been seen as far back as 1937 as a danger underlying all future strategies. The question that must be asked, as it was asked with increasing impatience by opponents from inside the Conservative Party as well as from the Labour and Liberal ranks,[47] is this: why did the Government hesitate for so long to consider co-operation with the Soviet Union as a deterrent to the aggressor states?

For one thing, a role was of course played by the political viewpoints to which reference has already been made. But, for another, there was the question whether anything was to be gained by setting aside political scruples. In other words, how high was the value to be placed on an alliance with the Soviet Union?

It has to be said in general that the evaluation of Soviet potential depended primarily on guesswork, since no precise information was available. The restrictive policy of the USSR in regard to news, which became tighter still with the start of the purges, meant that journalists and diplomats had to rely on information obtained by chance. It was as though the Soviet regime had erected a Wall of China between itself and the outside world.[48] Conceptions of the Soviet Union were thus based of necessity on preconceptions.

From such information as could nevertheless be gathered there emerged a picture of the economic and military potential of the USSR which was scarcely encouraging, and which served to reinforce the British government's already aloof attitude towards the Soviet Union. The argument that the Soviet Union had at its disposal a good stock of raw materials carried little weight in London, especially in view of warnings that the claim might be exaggerated.[49] What counted was the capacity of the Soviet Union to mobilise its economy in the event of war, and this, in the British view, was insufficient.[50] The verdict of the military experts was equally negative.[51] The progressive improvement the Red Army had undergone was not, indeed, ignored;[52] but the purges in the officer corps put an end to any positive evaluation of the military striking power of the Soviet Union. As late as July 1939 General Ironside still had his doubts about the efficacy of the Red Army leadership in the wake of the purges.[53] He thereby endorsed his previously expressed opinion that the value of an alliance with the Soviet Union would be minimal.[54] Defective leadership and lack of equipment combined to render the Red Army unfit to undertake an offensive war,[55] and the Soviet air force seemed to have the capacity only for a *short* campaign.[56]

On this assessment of the situation it was useless to bring the Soviet Union into play as a deterrent either in the Far East against Japan[57] or in Europe against Germany, even supposing that the British government could have overcome the repugnance it felt on political grounds. The plan for a Grand Alliance including the Soviet Union for which Churchill, despite his reservations about the value of the Soviet Union as an ally,[58] had long campaigned in public, was shelved by the government in March 1938 as impracticable.[59] During the Sudeten crisis of 1938 the Soviet Union remained excluded from the crucial consultation between the powers. In London it was gathered from British–Soviet exchanges in Geneva that no effective help for Czechoslovakia could be expected from the Soviet side.[60] In 1939, as doubts about the prospects of reaching a settlement with Germany increased and speculation about the aims of German foreign policy ran up against the problem of Hitler's striving for world domination,[61] the foundations of Britain's strategy against Germany began to take shape without serious recourse to the Soviet Union. It was true that the demands of the opposition for a more positive place for the Soviet Union in Britain's policy could not simply be ignored. But nor was the government in any way at the bidding of forces in Parliament and outside that were calling for more concrete indications of a British–Soviet *rapprochement*. In any case, there were signs early in July that people in the Labour Party were starting to cast a more critical eye on the way the Soviet Union was playing its part in the French-British-Soviet conversations.[62]

What London wished to avoid, and had been repeatedly warned against by the Foreign Office – if only in the most general terms – was a retreat by the Soviet Union into isolation or indeed into an alliance with Germany. All the same, when, to the complete surprise of the British authorities,[63] this development in fact occurred with the conclusion of the Hitler–Stalin pact, it had no influence on what had been all along, and not merely in 1939, the ultimate determinant of British policy, namely, that attempts at hegemony were to be resisted as soon as they became recognisable beyond doubt.

Notes: Chapter 21

1   On this in general see G. Niedhart, *Grossbritannien und die Sowjetunion 1934–1939. Studien zur britischen Politik der Friedenssicherung zwischen den beiden Weltkriegen* (Munich, 1972). In view of this I can here omit factual details of the historical events and concentrate on a few essential points. In the bibliographical references I confine myself chiefly to publications of more recent date.

2   For the connection between crisis factors and foreign conflict behaviour cf. G. Niedhart, 'Appeasement. Die britische Antwort auf die Krise des Weltreichs und des internationalen Systems vor dem Zweiten Weltkrieg', *Historische Zeitschrift*, vol. 226 (1978), pp. 67 ff.

3   Speaking in the House of Commons 23 November 1934, Parliamentary Debates (Parl. Deb.), House of Commons, vol. 295, col. 403.

4   For a survey see B. Jones, *The Russia Complex. The British Labour Party and the Soviet Union* (Manchester, 1977), pp. 15 ff. See in addition: B. Pimlott, *Labour and the Left in the 1930s* (Cambridge, 1977); J. Jupp, *The British Radical Left 1931–1941* (London, 1981); S. Macintyre, *Little Moscows. Communism and Working-Class Militancy in Inter-War Britain* (London, 1980).

5   A. Boyle, *The Climate of Treason* (London, 1979).

6   Memorandum of 31 December 1936, Public Record Office, London, FO 371/20354.

7   For British-Soviet differences 1936/7 see Niedhart, *Grossbritannien*, pp. 343 ff., and in W.

Schieder and C. Dipper (eds), *Der Spanische Bürgerkrieg in der internationalen Politik (1936–1939)* (Munich, 1976), pp. 275 ff. Soviet policy in this phase is discussed, without going into the effects of its ambivalence on the British and European public, by H. Geiss, 'Das "Internationale Komitee für die Anwendung des Abkommens über die Nichteinmischung in Spanien" als Instrument sowjetischer Aussenpolitik 1936–1938' (dissertation, Frankfurt/M., 1977).

8　Eden, on a report from the Commissioner of Police, August 1937, FO 371/21105. On the Communist Party: J. Klugmann, *History of the Communist Party of Great Britain*, 2 vols (London, 1968–9).

9　By Inskip (Minister for the Co-ordination of Defence 1936–9), for example, in a speech to the Bute Unionist Association, *Glasgow Herald*, 7 September 1936.

10　*Manchester Guardian*, 7 September 1936.

11　J. Edwards, *The British Government and the Spanish Civil War 1936–1939* (London, 1979), pp. 23, 111.

12　Eden's memorandum of 7 February 1936, CAB 24/259. See also Cabinet meetings of 12 and 19 February 1936, CAB 23/83. In India itself the resonance of Soviet ideas was throughout very muted in character, notwithstanding a generally well-disposed attitude towards Soviet foreign policy, for example on the part of Nehru. On this see N. Joshi, *Foundations of Indo-Soviet Relations: A Study of Non-Official Attitudes and Contacts 1917–1947* (New Delhi, 1975); C. Singh Samra, *India and Anglo-Soviet Relations 1917–1947* (Bombay, 1959).

13　Memorandum of the North Department of the Foreign Office, 6 December 1934, FO 371/18306.

14　See Kermit E. McKenzie, *Comintern and World Revolution 1928–1943* (London/New York, 1964), pp. 144, 151 ff. Bullitt, the US Ambassador to the USSR, was forthright in his conclusion, writing on 19 July 1935 as follows: 'The aim of the Soviet Union is and will remain to produce a world revolution': *Foreign Relations of the United States (FRUS)*, *The Soviet Union 1933–1939* (Washington, 1952), p. 227.

15　Protest note, 15 August 1935, FO 371/19451.

16　Hoare in conversation with Litvinov at Geneva, 12 September 1935, FO 371/19452.

17　See, for example, *The Times*, 9 July 1936; *Observer*, 3 October 1937; *The Times*, 3 May 1938: 'Comintern. Design for world revolution'.

18　Parl. Deb., House of Commons, vol. 345, col. 2492 (3 April 1939).

19　In the published papers of a leading Conservative politician one finds, to take an extreme example, no reference at all to communism and the Soviet Union, let alone any talk of disagreement with them: R. Rhodes James, *Memoirs of a Conservative. J. C. C. Davidson's Memoirs and Papers 1910–1937* (London, 1969).

20　Eden to Litvinov, 11 May 1937, FO 371/21102.

21　Collier, Head of the Northern Department in the Foreign Office, to Woermann, 12 January 1938, Pol. Archiv des AA Bonn, Pol. II, Bez. zwischen England und Russland 1936–9.

22　*Labour*, vol. 4 (1936/7), p. 2; and cf. ibid., p. 272 (July 1937).

23　*Daily Herald*, 10 June 1937. See also W. Citrine, *I Search for Truth in Russia* (rev. edn, London, 1938), pp. 353 ff.

24　W. S. Churchill, *Step by Step 1936–1939* (London, 1939), p. 61 (4 September 1936) and p. 71 (16 October 1936).

25　Thus and repeatedly the British Embassy in Moscow in its situation analyses; see for example the Annual Report for 1935 dated 31 January 1936, FO 371/20352. Also cf. Chamberlain to Morgenthau, 26 March 1937, *FRUS* 1937, vol. 1, p. 99. A good analysis of the factors determining Soviet policy is provided by H. Hecker, 'Sowjetunion – Stalins innenpolitische Konzeption und die aussenpolitischen Gegebenheiten als Basis der sowjetischen Reaktion auf die nationalsozialistische Aussenpolitik', in E. Forndran *et al.* (eds), *Innen- und Aussenpolitik unter nationalsozialistischer Bedrohung* (Opladen, 1977), pp. 58 ff.

26　*Daily Herald*, 17 November 1937.

27　Parl. Deb., House of Commons, vol. 332, col. 308 (22 February 1938).

28　Vansittart's note dated 27 March 1934, FO 371/18298.

29　J. T. Henderson (Far Eastern Department, Foreign Office), 23 December 1937, FO 371/20961.

30 *Documents on British Foreign Policy 1919–1939 (DBFP)*, 2nd series, Vol. 7, no. 669 (29 March 1934).
31 Thus for example the British Ambassador in Moscow, 19 April 1938, *DBFP*, 3rd series, Vol. 1, no. 162.
32 See, for example, K. Feiling, *The Life of Neville Chamberlain* (London, 1947), pp. 325, 403, 408; Lord Templewood, *Nine Troubled Years* (London, 1954), pp. 342, 370; Earl of Avon, 'Forty years on', *Foreign Affairs*, vol. 41 (1962/3), p. 114.
33 To give just a few instances: Eden, 1 June 1937, *FRUS* 1937, vol. 1, p. 318; Neville Chamberlain, 21 September 1938, *FRUS* 1938, vol. 1, p. 632; Memorandum of the General Chief of Staff on the occasion of the Imperial Conference 1937: Review of Imperial Defence, 22 February 1937, CAB 53/30.
34 Thus Baldwin, for example, 9 November 1936, reported *Daily Telegraph*, 10 November 1936.
35 *The Moffat Papers. Selections from the Diplomatic Journals of Jay Pierrepont Moffat 1919–1943*, ed. N. H. Hooker (Cambridge, Mass., 1956), p. 174.
36 Neville Chamberlain, 19 May 1939: his was 'not a policy of lining up opposing blocs of Powers in Europe animated by hostile intentions towards one another and accepting the view that war is inevitable'. His policy was, on the contrary, 'a policy of precaution'. 'We are trying to build up, not an alliance between ourselves and other countries, but a peace front against aggression'. Parl. Deb., House of Commons, vol. 347, cols 1843, 1849.
37 Especially in consideration of Germany relations with the Soviet Union should not be too close – 'correct is all that they should be' (Eden, 21 May 1936, PRO 371/20338).
38 CAB 21/551.
39 For details see Niedhart, *Grossbritannien*, pp. 267 ff., 418 ff.
40 Chamberlain, 21 February 1938: 'After all, Russia is partly European but partly Asiatic', Parl. Deb., House of Commons, vol. 332, col. 154. Victor Cazalet, a Conservative MP, described the Soviet Union as a 'semi-oriental country'. 'Impressions of a trip to Russia', *The Nineteenth Century and After*, vol. 121 (1937), pp. 174 ff.
41 This was how it appeared to the ex-diplomat Sir Horace Rumbold, writing to his son in June 1939 – the manner of expression is doubtless quite typical: 'The Russians having been cold-shouldered for so long and being semi-Orientals are very suspicious.' M. Gilbert, *Sir Horace Rumbold. Portrait of a Diplomat 1869–1941* (London, 1973), p. 444.
42 See for example the memoirs of the Soviet diplomat and historian I. M. Maiski, *Memoiren eines sowjetischen Botschafters* (Berlin, 1967). The charge that the Western powers aimed to divert Germany's aggressiveness on to the Soviet Union, for which there is no evidence whatsoever, has recently been remounted on a massive scale by O. Rsheschewski, 'Gegen Verfälschung der Geschichte. Zu einigen Konzeptionen der bürgerlichen Literatur über den Zweiten Weltkrieg', *Probleme des Friedens und des Sozialismus*, vol. 23 (1980), pp. 696 ff.
43 Gilbert Murray, 18 May 1938, after a meeting with Eden: 'He was as severe on His Majesty's Government as anybody could wish, but said he had never seen any particular sign of anti-Russian bias in Neville [Chamberlain].' Bodleian Library, Oxford, Gilbert Murray Papers.
44 Parl. Deb., House of Lords, vol. 107, col. 790 (17 February 1938).
45 R. Meyers, *Britische Sicherheitspolitik 1934–1938* (Düsseldorf, 1976), p. 79.
46 On this see: R. Manne, 'The British decision for alliance with Russia: May 1939', *Journal of Contemporary History*, vol. 9 (1974), no. 3, pp. 3 ff.; R. Wheatley, 'Britain and the Anglo-Franco-Russian negotiations in 1939', in *Les Relations Franco-Britanniques de 1935 à 1939* (Paris, 1975), pp. 201 ff.
47 See on this, for example, L. Kettenacker, 'Die Diplomatie der Ohnmacht. Die gescheiterte Friedensstrategie der britischen Regierung vor Ausbruch des Zweiten Weltkriegs im Sommer 1939', in W. Benz and H. Graml (eds), *Die Grossmächte und der europäische Krieg* (Stuttgart, 1979), pp. 258 ff.
48 Thus Collier, 28 June 1938, FO 371/21908.
49 British Embassy, Moscow, 20 February 1939: 'It would be a mistake to regard the Soviet Union, as is so often done, as an unending source of raw materials': *DBFP*, 3rd series, Vol. 4, no. 614.
50 British Embassy, Moscow, 6 March 1939, ibid., pp. 197 ff.
51 See the more detailed study by J. S. Herndon elsewhere in this volume.

52   War Office memorandum of 20 January 1936 on the 'Reliability, efficiency and value for war of the Russian army', FO 371/20348.
53   Ironside to Chamberlain, 10 July 1939, *The Ironside Diaries*, ed. R. Macleod and D. Kelly (London, 1963), p. 78.
54   Memoranda of the General Chief of Staff, 9 February 1937 and 12 November 1937, CAB 24/268; FO 371/20702.
55   Summing up in March 1939, Neville Chamberlain said of the USSR: 'I have no belief whatever in her ability to maintain an effective offensive, even if she wanted to': Feiling, *Neville Chamberlain*, p. 403.
56   Air Ministry, December 1937, FO 371/22292; British Embassy, Moscow, 6 March 1939, *DBFP*, 3rd series, Vol. 4, p. 197.
57   Eden during the Franco-British conversations on 29 November 1937 regarding the Brussels Conference: 'The weakness of Russia was one of the underlying causes of events in the Far East': CAB 27/626. This was still the standpoint when on 28 June 1939 Prime Minister Chamberlain declared, in face of pressure from Labour Party spokesmen for closer co-operation with the USSR, that he attached very little value to Soviet military potential against Japan: Premier 1/325. It is these judgements of the political leadership, quite apart from the opinions of the various experts cited by Herndon in this present volume, that have to be regarded as decisive.
58   M. Gilbert, *Winston S. Churchill*, Vol. 5 (London, 1976), p. 724.
59   Halifax's memorandum of 18 March 1938, CAB 27/623. See also Feiling, *Neville Chamberlain*, p. 347. In a diary entry for 19 February 1938 in which Chamberlain reflects, with reference to Britain's difficulties over rearmament and finance, on the exposure of Britain in Europe to the double threat from Germany and Italy, the Prime Minister sees himself as in practice without allies. France was 'in a terribly weak condition', in the United States isolationism still had the upper hand. The Soviet Union is not even considered. ibid., p. 322. Also cf. J. Ramsden, *The Age of Balfour and Baldwin 1902–1940* (London/New York, 1978), p. 365.
60   The British partner in the conversations with the Soviet Foreign Secretary, Litvinov, who was staying in Geneva, was R. A. Butler, then Under-Secretary of State for Foreign Affairs. See Lord Butler, *The Art of the Possible. Memoirs* (London, 1971), pp. 69 ff. For a more positive judgement of Soviet policy, which maintains that in 1938 priority was still accorded to co-operation with Great Britain and France and that, in conformity with treaty obligations, intervention was envisaged on the Czechoslovak side, see J. Haslam, 'The Soviet Union and the Czechoslovakian crisis of 1938', *Journal of Contemporary History*, vol. 14 (1979), pp. 441 ff. Also cf. B. Mendel Cohen, 'Moscow at Munich: did the Soviet Union offer unilateral aid to Czechoslovakia?', *East European Quarterly*, vol. 12 (1978), pp. 341 ff.
61   Thus Chamberlain in Cabinet, 20 March 1939, and in the Committee on Foreign Policy, 27 March 1939, CAB 23/98; CAB 27/624. See in addition a private letter from J. C. C. Davidson to von Ribbentrop early July 1939. The two had become acquainted through talks on various matters during von Ribbentrop's time as Ambassador in London. These sentences sum up very precisely the elements of which British policy in the summer of 1939 was compounded, willingness to reach agreement balanced by threat of war. 'Of the result of a war the British people have no doubt whatever. Of the necessity for a war, they are completely unconvinced; and war must surely be the last thing which your people can desire . . . If Germany wants world domination, or even European domination, then we stand to bar the way . . . but that does not mean that Great Britain would not be willing to hold out the hand of friendship to Germany, were she willing to agree upon rules that would be binding on both sides' (James, *Memoirs of a Conservative*, p. 424).
62   For this see the entries dated 4 and 10 July 1939 in the diaries of Hugh Dalton, the Labour Party's expert on foreign affairs. Dalton Diaries, British Library of Political and Economic Science, London.
63   On this most recently F. H. Hinsley *et al.*, *British Intelligence in the Second World War*, Vol. 1 (London, 1979), p. 46.

22 British Perceptions of Soviet Military Capability, 1935–9

JAMES S. HERNDON

In 1935 the Soviet Union apparently entered the ranks of those nations which opposed any revision of the *status quo* by Germany, Italy, or Japan. This event was marked by the signature of the Franco-Soviet Mutual Assistance pact and by the promulgation of the 'United Front' (or 'Popular Front') doctrine by the Seventh Congress of the Communist Third International (Comintern).[1] In addition to these diplomatic developments, the expansion and reorganisation of the Soviet military establishment,[2] the introduction of ranks for officers and men (abolished in late 1917) and the public demonstration by the Red Army at its Autumn Manoeuvres all seemed designed to signify Soviet determination and military ability to implement the Kremlin's new policy.

Many factors shaped the British policy towards the USSR during the years 1935–9. Among these was a distrust of Soviet intentions, reliability and capability.[3] It is upon the third element – specifically, British perceptions of Soviet military capabilities – that this paper will concentrate.

Just as the fear of German and Japanese aggrandisement played a role in the Soviet diplomatic *volte-face*, it similarly influenced British perceptions of the USSR. The Permanent Under-Secretary of State for Foreign Affairs, Sir Robert Vansittart, had no love for the Soviet Union but he early recognised Germany and, to a lesser extent, Japan as the primary threats to British interests. In 1933 he wrote to the Foreign Secretary, Sir John Simon, and rejected the argument that the Nazi regime in Germany was no more dangerous than the Soviet regime in Russia: 'Russia has been too incompetent a country to be really dangerous, even under Bolshevism. But Germany is an exceedingly competent country.'[4] In a similar vein he spoke to John Reith whose diary entry of 28 March 1934 recorded that Vansittart 'thought Germany was the real menace'. While Vansittart had conceded great antagonism between Japan and the USSR, Reith noted that Vansittart did not expect a Soviet–Japanese war because neither country was prepared for it.[5] On 8 May 1934 the US Ambassador to England, Robert Bingham, informed President Roosevelt that Vansittart was preoccupied with the danger posed by Germany in Europe and hoped for a Sino-Soviet–American coalition to restrain Japan in the Far East.[6] On the other hand, Vansittart did not expect the USSR to adopt an active stance against Japan. He was not surprised when the Soviets sought to appease Japan by the sale of the Chinese Eastern Railway: in a memorandum to Simon dated 28 August 1934 he described this action as 'the natural human instinct to get rid of a bone of contention between a weaker and stronger power by a settlement in favour of the latter'.[7]

Vansittart's concern over Germany was shared by Simon[8] and by Neville Chamberlain, at that time the Chancellor of the Exchequer. Chamberlain particularly worried about the British ability to meet the dual threat posed by Germany and Japan. Like Vansittart, he considered Germany to be the primary danger and, therefore, he sought to neutralise Japan so that British resources could be concentrated against Germany. In a memorandum which evaluated the British strategic dilemma, he proposed an Anglo-Japanese pact as a means to this end despite the obstacles created by the recent Japanese aggression in Manchuria and by Japanese defiance of the League of Nations. Chamberlain discounted the possibility that Japan, in the interest of retaining complete freedom of action, would reject a British approach and pointed to Japanese 'anxieties' over the USSR, 'the only Power which really threatens their present acquisitions or their future ambitions. With Russia on their flank it seems to me that Japan would gladly see any accession of security in other directions.'[9]

The Foreign Office (FO) saw little merit in Chamberlain's proposal. The head of the Far Eastern Department, C. W. Orde, immediately pointed to the impact of such an alliance upon the interests of other powers in the area. A defection by Britain from the ranks of its possible enemies might encourage Japan to move against China, Holland, the USA, or the USSR. Not only would such an arrangement alienate the USSR and prejudice Anglo-Soviet relations but the Soviet position was especially critical since the USSR was a valuable counterweight to both Germany and Japan. Orde emphasised that an Anglo-Japanese pact would weaken the USSR in Europe (as 'a potential check on Germany') thereby increasing the German danger for Britain. Such a pact might encourage Japan to attack the USSR in order to eliminate the threat of Soviet 'air power based at Vladivostok' and, if the USSR fought, Soviet resources would be strained so that 'Germany will find herself in a stronger position'. Moreover, '*after* [sic] a successful settling of accounts with Russia and a pause for recovery . . . Japan may become a real danger to our possessions in the Far East'. Orde contended that so long as the Soviet threat to Japan remained intact, Japan was unlikely to attack British territory. Thus, an Anglo-Japanese pact might bring about the very eventuality it was designed to prevent. Orde discounted the likelihood of a Soviet–Japanese pact which would permit Japan to move south.[10]

This FO perception of the USSR was not universally shared. B. H. Liddell Hart later recounted a conversation with the Director of Military Operations and Intelligence (DMOI), General John Dill, in March 1935. Dill disliked the prospect of an Anglo-Soviet alliance or even of an Anglo-Soviet wartime coalition against Germany. He suggested the possibility of Britain allowing Germany to 'expand eastwards at Russia's expense' which Liddell Hart rejected as a possibly beneficial short-term tactic but sure to be disastrous in the long term. Dill questioned the military value of the USSR as an ally and Liddell Hart responded that 'Russia is the only effective counterpoise to a Japanese threat to our position in the Far East'. Dill demurred that 'Russia's inefficiency made her a poor ally' but Liddell Hart emphasised the improvement of the Red Army (with which Dill agreed) and added that the Soviet air force could bomb Japanese cities from Vladivostok, a potential threat which surely would deter Japan from military adventures.[11]

The French government also looked to the East in search of a counterweight to the growing German power. From 1933 to 1935 Franco-Soviet negotiations proceeded intermittently[12] and the FO sought to ascertain what military benefits would accrue to France from such an agreement. In June 1934 the British Ambassador to France, Sir George Clerk, noted 'what had clearly become the French policy of utilizing Russia as a counterpoise to Germany' and expressed the opinion that 'the French do not anticipate that in the event of a German aggression on France the Russian Army, even if it were possible for it to leave its own frontiers, would be of any great practical assistance'. Soviet involvement in the Franco-Soviet (or Eastern Locarno-type) pact, therefore, was expected to exert diplomatic pressure on Hitler and to act as a restraint upon him.[13] A week later, Clerk reported a conversation with the *Chef du Cabinet* of the French Foreign Ministry, Alexis Léger, in which they discussed the French efforts to form an 'Eastern Locarno' regional pact involving both Germany and the USSR in a guarantee of borders. If Germany refused, Léger indicated that France would consider a full Franco-Soviet alliance although 'its value in terms of military assistance in the field might be little or nothing'. The important elements, according to Léger, were for France to be able to 'draw on Russia's vast industrial resources' and to prevent the Kremlin from negotiating a pact with Germany.[14] The French military was even less enamoured by the military benefits of the pact for France. According to one French officer, while the Soviet air force was numerically strong and the Red Army possessed a large number of modern tanks, the Soviet military could not operate effectively outside Soviet borders because of the inadequate communications-transport system which would impair supply and mobilisation and because of a weak High Command.[15]

The obvious geopolitical obstacles to an 'Eastern Locarno' pact were quickly articulated by British military and foreign service officials stationed in Central Europe. Almost without exception, each one emphatically predicted that Poland would oppose the arrangement out of a disinclination to permit Soviet military passage across Polish soil.[16] It is interesting that, during the years between 1934–5 and 1939, no policy was formulated to deal with the aversion of the border states for the USSR and Soviet military aid. In many ways, the French experience of 1934–5 provided a preview of things to come in 1939 but the lesson appears to have been lost.

Even after the signature of the Franco-Soviet pact (2 May 1935), the FO remained dubious about the military benefit for France. On 16 May, for example, a First Secretary of the FO, James L. Dodds, in a lecture to the Imperial Defence College, suggested that the French had been motivated by the desire to prevent a Nazi–Soviet *rapprochement* as well as by a respect for Soviet military potential. From a strictly military perspective, said Dodds, the pact was a negative precaution since the USSR could not assist France against Germany without transit across Poland and/or the Baltic States and these countries were unlikely to permit Soviet passage. Since, however, influential military-industrial circles in Germany were known to favour a Nazi–Soviet *rapprochement*, the precaution was worthwhile. Although there was no sign of such a *rapprochement*, Dodds told the assembled officers 'it is to our interests that there should not be'.[17]

In an effort to relieve European tension, Chamberlain wrote to his sister, the Cabinet persuaded the reluctant Prime Minister, Stanley Baldwin, that Simon and Eden should visit Hitler in Berlin after which Eden would proceed on to Warsaw and then to visit Stalin in Moscow.[18] The decision seemed justified by the dangerous situation which the recent growth in German armed strength occasioned. According to the British Ambassador in Berlin, Germany was 'fast becoming the most powerful military nation in Europe'. The decision of the German government to expand its army to thirty-six divisions (500,000 men) sobered British officials but the rationale advanced by Berlin that the expansion was necessitated by increases in Franco-Soviet military power was considered 'pretty flimsy'.[19] Chamberlain was not particularly receptive to this line of reasoning (he wrote to his sister that 'Hitler's Germany is the bully of Europe') nor did he share the pessimism of his colleagues, particularly Simon and Eden, over the prospects of dealing with Hitler. He had told Eden that Hitler must be made to understand that there were two ways of guaranteeing European security – 'a system of Locarno pacts or a system of alliances. We very much preferred the first but if he would not play he would force us into the second.' While Chamberlain was optimistic, he was also convinced that 'it will be necessary for Simon to speak plainly in Berlin'.[20]

Indeed, when Eden saw Hitler, he deprecated the German fear of the USSR and denied that the Soviets would 'be a military menace for many years'. Yet he later recalled that, after visiting Moscow, he came away 'impressed' by the 'signs of growing Soviet military power' which he hoped would be 'a helpful restraint' on Hitler.[21] Simon was disappointed with the results of the Berlin conversations; on 27 March he noted Hitler's refusal to enter into a pact with the USSR and reflected in his diary upon Hitler's ambitions: 'All of this is pretty hopeless; for if Germany will not co-operate in confirming the solidarity of Europe, the rest of Europe will co-operate to preserve it in spite of Germany . . . We may see the curious spectacle of British Tories collaborating with Russian Communists.'[22]

The British generally were not sympathetic to German claims that their military expansion was the result of and justified by Soviet military increases. On 11 February 1935 the British Ambassador to Moscow, Lord Chilston, forwarded reports by his air and military attachés (Wing Commander A. C. Collier and Col. E. O. Skaife, respectively) on the 30 January speech by the Soviet Deputy Commissar for Defence, Mikhael Tukhachevsky, in which the figures for Soviet military expansion were published. In his summary, Chilston remarked: 'the *Reichswehr* authorities are probably in as good a position as anyone to know the real strength of the Red Army, and M. Tukhachevsky's statement is unlikely to alarm them particularly; on the other hand, it will provide them with an admirable pretext for increasing their claims to rearmament'.[23]

On 22 May Lord Lloyd questioned the need for German rearmament during a debate in the House of Lords on imperial defence. He asked whom Germany feared and, when he was reminded of the German claim that the USSR was a threat, replied: 'I do not think that Germany has any real fears of the Russian Army today, or of its mobility, or of her Air Force . . . I do not think the mobility of the Russian Army is a thing which has caused Germany the smallest anxiety so far.'[24]

Similarly, in a War Office (WO) memorandum dated 9 July, Col. H. L. Ismay discussed German contentions and probable Soviet policy. In his view, the Soviets posed no threat to Germany and, in fact, feared a two-front war against Germany and Japan. The Soviets, he said, were in the midst of a massive industrial and agricultural transformation which required peace, the Red Army – although much modernised – was in no fit state for war, and the transportation system was in a 'parlous' condition.[25]

On 9 March 1936 Wing Commander Collier reported a conversation with the very knowledgeable German military attaché, General Ernst Köstring. As they discussed the state of the Soviet air force, Köstring discounted Soviet figures (on the size of their air force) as exaggerated and characterised most of the Soviet aircraft as 'old and inefficient'. He doubted if Soviet aircraft production could be increased in wartime due to the shortage of skilled personnel in industry and noted a parallel weakness in the air force itself where the competence of the service personnel was dubious. With only one reservation, Collier agreed 'substantially' with Köstring. Back in the FO, Daniel Labouchere and Laurence Collier (this Collier was head of the Northern Department and Labouchere was a member of his staff) agreed that Köstring's assessments were accurate, that they probably represented the real German view and that Goering's expressions of apprehension over the Soviet air threat were propaganda attempts to justify German rearmament.[26] Laurence Collier later minuted that the German fear of the Soviet air threat was 'much exaggerated if not wholly insincere'.[27]

In the autumn of 1935 and again in 1936, the Red Army staged manoeuvres to which representatives of the international military community were invited. In these exercises, aircraft, cavalry, armour, artillery and infantry were employed in mobile operations; for the first time, airborne operations were utilised: paratroopers were introduced and tanks were transported by aircraft. These manoeuvres captured foreign attention and stimulated the development of paratrooper units in other armies.[28] However spectacular these paratroopers drops were, Köstring was not over-impressed – he dismissed the exhibition as a 'game for the people' but conceded that the Soviet plan to drop paratroopers ahead of a mechanised advance was a 'good' idea – and his views were reported to the FO.[29]

The Soviets produced a film of the manoeuvres which was shown in Britain. On 12 March 1936 the Secretary of State for War, Duff Cooper, during an address to the House of Commons on the subject of the Army Estimates for 1936, referred to the film. He spoke of the 'very interesting experiment' in which men were parachuted from aircraft and tanks were air-lifted and observed: 'I do not pretend that we are as up-to-date as that.' In the exchanges which ensued, Leo Amery, Sir Henry Croft and J. T. C.

Moore-Brabazon emphasised the military significance of the development while Josiah Wedgwood and Sir Alfred Knox deprecated it as 'propaganda'.[30] Later that month, the Under-Secretary of State for Air, Sir Phillip Sassoon, was questioned by Geoffrey Mander and Duncan Sandys in the Commons on the subject of whether or not the RAF had the capability of air-lifting tanks and replied in the negative. Similarly, the Financial Secretary to the War Office, Sir Victor Warrender, was questioned by Sandys about parachute troops and replied that the only paratroopers of which he knew were in the Red Army but that the British army was investigating the possibility of developing such a unit.[31]

The 1936 Soviet autumn manoeuvres were attended by a British mission which included General Archibald Wavell, Wing Commander H. E. P. Wigglesworth, Major Gifford Martel and the service attachés. Wavell's report was mixed. Although he found the paratroopers impressive, they were too slow in forming up after their jump; he considered the parachute drop of 'doubtful' tactical value. The Soviets used much cavalry, mechanised infantry and armour, which was technically good: 'There is nothing new or original about their tanks, which are all copied from foreign designs; but their performance is well ahead of similar types in our service. Their reliability is remarkable.' Apart from the armoured and mechanised units, most transport was horsedrawn and there was less anti-tank and anti-aircraft artillery than in Western armies. The officers were young and enthusiastic (Wavell declined to assess their competence on such brief acquaintance) while the rank and file were 'magnificent' physically, with high morale. Although 'lavishly' equipped, the Soviets had 'comparatively little to show in the way of tactical progress' and Wavell was critical of the absence of any independent action by the mechanised columns which were limited to supporting cavalry and infantry operations. The Soviet infantry was as clumsy as its Tsarist predecessor; it was deployed in long lines with no fire plan and poor use of terrain. The cavalry were capable of fighting dismounted but appeared to prefer mounted action in tandem with armour, a practice which would result in heavy casualties in combat. Wavell saw little artillery but doubted whether any effective fire control existed. The air tactics were clumsy and inept, limited to ground support with no attempt to strike rear areas and with poor reconnaissance. No attention was paid to aerial combat – Soviet air supremacy was apparently assumed – and the air formations were expected to suffer heavy casualties in combat. The fighters and medium bombers were 'well-armed, fast, and manoeuvrable' but the light bomber and reconnaissance aircraft were slow, cumbersome and frequently employed at odds with their design and capability. Generally, Wavell saw great improvement in material and armament, especially in armour and mechanised forces but emphasised the poor tactical use of these arms. Apart from its armament, the Red Army was not much different from the Tsarist army: it still possessed the traditional qualities of hardiness and endurance and the traditional weakness of clumsiness. In Wavell's view, the Red Army would be 'formidable' in defence, but 'clumsy and less formidable' in offensive operations.[32]

Wigglesworth's report on the performance of the Soviet air force contained many of the same criticisms. The tactics were clumsy, unimaginative and sure to cause great loss. Even the best planes had serious design and structural defects and the pilots were 'safe' but not particularly inspiring in ability or performance.[33]

According to Liddell Hart, Wavell and Martel 'were greatly impressed' by the Soviet BT tank (the light medium tank derived from the American Christie prototype and from which the famous T34 tank later evolved) which Martel described as 'at least twice as good' as the latest British experimental model. Martel had recommended to the WO that the British army purchase the third Christie prototype (the US army had purchased the first, the Soviet the second) remaining in the possession of the inventor-designer. While Martel was critical of the way the Soviets had altered the original design (the 'fighting qualities' had been reduced to 'produce a spectacular perform-ance'), he pressed his proposal with such vigour that the Christie prototype was in the possession of the British army on 17 November – he had returned from the USSR on 26 September. Liddell Hart spoke approvingly of the decision to the Editor of *The Times*, Geoffrey Dawson, because the British experimental model was inferior to continental models (including the Soviet) and the tank currently in use by the British army had been developed in 1923 and was obsolete.[34] Similarly, Lord Lloyd complained to the House of Lords on November 19 that 'We have no modern medium tanks at all. All we have . . . are tanks of the 1923 model, and only about 100 of them. The 1923 model is quite unfit for war and barely fit for use in practice . . . It is estimated that Russia has probably five to six thousand tanks, but our equipment is as I have told you.'[35]

On 17 November Lord Strabolgi described the film he had seen of the 1936 Soviet manoeuvres where tanks and men had been air-lifted in large numbers. He told the assembled peers: 'This impressed me very seriously indeed. The fact that this system is being copied in the German and French Armies makes it worthy of attention by those responsible for the efficiency of His Majesty's Army.'[36]

Apart, however, from the new tanks and the spectacular airborne opera-tions which so captivated civilian imaginations, the consequences of the Soviet military weaknesses, as enumerated by Wavell, were apparent to military and diplomatic analysts. In November the Counsellor of the French Embassy, Roland de Margerie, told Liddell Hart that while glowing reports had been received from the French military mission in 1935, the reports on the 1936 manoeuvres were more critical. Margerie showed Liddell Hart a copy of the French report which he found similar to the British report: 'The men were good, the equipment good, but the higher handling defective, and the manoeuvres were too staged to form a judgement. It then leapt to the judgement that the Russian Army could not exert an effective influence in the West.'[37]

The perceptions of both the FO and the WO from 1935 to June 1937 (the beginning of the military purge) conformed closely to the assessments of Wavell, Wigglesworth and Liddell Hart. One is impressed by the consist-ency of the evaluations for these years: military attaché and other reports were almost repetitive, informed foreign opinion agreed and strategic appreciations and policy proposals reflected the influence of these data. The Red Army was seen as powerful in manpower (with enormous reserves) and equipment, particularly in armour, aircraft and mechanised units. The soldiery was impressive, discipline and morale good, but the officers were less impressive, and there was too heavy a reliance upon set-piece exercises and solutions – little initiative or imagination was displayed. Often equipment was faulty – even the tanks and aircraft. Reconnaissance was almost always inadequate and co-ordination between the different branches consistently poor. Industry was powerful but beset with the same lack of skilled personnel. The transportation system was woefully inadequate – a major weakness. On the other hand, Soviet accomplishments in the military, transportation and industrial sectors were considered prodigious, the improvements in these areas were emphasised and the admonition against underestimating the Soviets repeatedly appeared in reports and minutes. Since, however, peace was a necessary prerequisite to the successful completion of these modernisation programmes, British observers assumed that the Kremlin would seek to avoid involvement in war under any circumstances unless the USSR itself were attacked. Nor was the Soviet *rapprochement* with the West considered more than a temporary expedient founded upon fear of Germany and Japan and the need for peace; Soviet hostility to Britain was expected to re-emerge sooner or later, probably later. The overall assessment was that the Soviet war machine was a dangerous defensive weapon but ineffectual offensively.[38] Members of Parliament (Commons and Lords) tended to be more impressed by the Soviet industrial production and military expansion; the large number of tanks, aircraft and men under arms seemed to stimulate frequent commentary.[39]

With the outbreak of the Spanish Civil War and the Soviet intervention,[40] British officials were able to observe the performance of Soviet equipment in action against German and Italian material. The intelligence reports compiled by the WO generally confirmed the picture which had earlier emerged, at least so far as aircraft were concerned. Soviet aircraft performed respectably but flaws in tactics and design were apparent.[41] Accordingly, the secretary of the Committee of Imperial Defence (CID), Sir Maurice Hankey, wrote to his son, Robin, on 31 January 1937 about Soviet war material in Spain: 'Their air forces have proved less successful than they had hoped.'[42] Eden later recalled that, in early 1937, 'we were given reassuring reports about the quality of our aeroplanes as compared with those of Germany, Italy, and Russia . . . The Russian fighters, although good, were said to be inferior to our own Gauntler and Fury types.'[43] The British observer in Spain, Major-General A. C. Temperley, later rated the Italian armour as almost worthless and the Soviet light and medium tanks as generally better than the German while Soviet fighters and bombers were 'of very high quality'. He considered the Soviet pilots better than their German and Italian counterparts.[44] Parliamentary reaction to the performance of the Soviet tanks and planes was generally favourable.[45]

In its assessments, the military were preoccupied with the threat posed by Germany and Japan – and, to a lesser extent, by Italy. The USSR was an unknown element, potentially dangerous. On 29 April 1935 the Chiefs of

Staff Sub-Committee (COS) perceived three potential threats to British interests: Germany in Europe, Japan in the Far East and the USSR in Central Asia. Concerning the Soviet threat, the COS pointed to the recent expansion of Soviet industry, the Red Army and the Soviet air force. Soviet air power was considered especially dangerous in India, given the paucity of Indian air defences. On the other hand, the USSR was considered to be temporarily non-aggressive because of its extensive internal reorganisation in progress and because of Soviet fears of Germany and Japan. Thus, Japan (in Asia) and Germany (in Europe) were considered more pressing threats.[46] Accordingly, the fear of a Soviet attack on India faded although it never vanished altogether; the USSR was never eliminated as a potential enemy.[47]

Those very factors, however, which rendered the USSR less dangerous than Germany and Japan in British perceptions also created doubts that the Soviet Union could be relied upon as an effective ally against Germany and Japan. This was certainly the case in 1935 when British planners were very conservative in their expectations, apparently preferring to err on the side of caution, and assumed Soviet neutrality in their contingency scenarios.[48] By 1936, however, they became a little more optimistic; during this year, the assumption was that the USSR probably would not intervene immediately (British planners did not feel it was safe to assume immediate Soviet intervention) but *might* intervene later in limited fashion with aircraft operating from Czechoslovakia and possibly even a few troops via Romania and Czechoslovakia. In the event of a Far Eastern war, the USSR was expected to intervene 'sooner or later'.[49]

Indeed, the Far Eastern situation differed significantly from the European one. Apart from the obviously simpler geopolitical configuration (no border states separating the USSR from Japanese territory), the balance of power was thought to have shifted from 1933–4, when the moment seemed propitious for a successful Japanese invasion, to the point where the Soviet position appeared much stronger. Certainly, by 1935 British military analysts recognised that the massive Soviet effort to reinforce the Siberian military establishment, the accumulation of supply stockpiles in the Far East considered sufficient to permit independent action by the Red Banner Army for six months (thereby eliminating the logistical restrictions of the deficient Soviet transport system) and the relative superiority of Soviet armour and aircraft as compared to those of the Japanese seemed to place the advantage on the Soviet side.[50] By December 1936 this apparent Soviet military preponderance worried Vansittart, who feared that the Japanese government might be so intimidated by the prospect of war with the USSR that it would seek a Soviet-Japanese non-aggression pact and direct its expansionist activities southwards, thereby threatening British interests. This assessment, however, was not universally shared and the debate over relative Soviet–Japanese strength and the likelihood of a *rapprochement* continued.[51]

During the first six months of 1937 (before the purge), British military planners were no less uncertain of Soviet intervention in either a European or an Asian war. In the former instance, they thought that while a fear of

Soviet intervention *might* deter the Germans from attacking the West, they considered the deterrence value limited: if the German High Command were sure enough of a swift victory in the West, the fear of Soviet intervention would not deter them. In any case, given the state of German eastern defences, the state of the Red Army and the possibility of Polish neutrality, the Soviet impact on the course of the war would be minimal. Conversely, in the Far East the possibility of Soviet intervention was expected to have a profound deterrent effect upon Japan and, in the event of war, a Soviet intervention would significantly influence the course of military operations.[52]

The entire situation was apocalyptically altered by the Stalinist military purge. The purge had begun with the arrests of Kamenev and Zinoviev in August 1936 but was not directed against the Red Army until the following June. On 18 May 1937 the new British military attaché to Moscow, Lt Col. Roy Firebrace, noted and reported the first disturbing signs. In subsequent reports, the Moscow Embassy informed London of the arrest and trial of Tukhachevsky and others. While the Embassy was convinced that the charges were fabricated as a rationale to justify the elimination of the officers, Laurence Collier vacillated, at first accepting the Embassy's analysis, but later leaning toward the official Moscow line that they were traitors.[53] Collier continued to accept this interpretation for some time, later contending that Tukhachevsky was at least pro-German.[54]

The purge effectively gutted the Red Army, especially the higher ranks of the officer corps (from colonel upwards).[55] Attaché and Embassy reports on visits to individual units during the summer and autumn retained the general character of earlier assessments.[56] However, it soon became obvious that the consequences of the purge were not, as one British general staff officer (Major E. C. Hayes) expressed it, purely domestic but were of the gravest international import. He referred to the elimination of the best Soviet generals which meant that 'the further development of the Army must be retarded even if it is not stopped altogether'. From the international perspective, said Hayes, 'If the value for war of the Red Army has declined as a result of recent events then the value of the Soviet Union as an ally to France has decreased to a corresponding extent; and, conversely, her danger to Germany as an enemy has also declined. In these circumstances it is not surprising that Germany, Japan and Italy are jubilant over this affair.'[57]

Indeed, many in the West were demoralised by implications of the purge; doubts as to Soviet military capability assailed British leaders and persisted, in some cases, right up to 1941. While Eden later spoke of these doubts as 'exaggerated',[58] he was as despondent as others at the time. For example, Liddell Hart recalled a conversation with Eden on 3 November in which 'he talked of Russia's lost value to France, and to us, through recent internal symptoms'.[59] On 9 March 1938 Harold Nicolson wrote to his wife of a meeting with Sir Edward Spears and Vansittart in which 'we came to the unhappy conclusion that now that Russia has dropped out, we are simply not strong enough to resist Germany'.[60] These doubts were also aired in Parliament.[61]

Nor can there be any doubt that Hayes was correct in his assessment of the response of Germany, Italy and Japan. Indications were abundantly available that the leaders of these countries considered the Red Army effectively neutralised.[62] Indeed, on 20 May 1938 Firebrace reported from Moscow that Köstring had told him that the purge had so damaged the Red Army that it was 'no longer of international importance' nor was it a factor in German military planning. Prior to 1937, said Köstring, the Red Army had been strong and improving steadily but the purges had emasculated it: 'If there had been no purge and it had gone on improving we would not now be in Austria.'[63]

Moreover, there were indications that, by January 1938, the Kremlin was aware of the consequences of Stalin's ill-advised action. The FO and WO were much concerned that the USSR would adopt an isolationist position, thereby ceasing to act as a restraint upon either Germany or Japan.[64] Several officials, both in higher and lower echelons, at the FO began to despair of Soviet ability to perform effectively as a military ally – the feeling was that Britain could not afford to rely upon the USSR.[65] Eden, very early on, had predicted that the USSR was unlikely to intervene in any war unless directly attacked (or until the issue was close to resolution and the danger past), not only because of the purge damage to the army, but because of the internal situation which had previously rendered Soviet participation unlikely.[66] Indeed, the military assessments of late 1937 and 1938 reflected the view that all problems which had rendered the USSR a dubious ally before had been exacerbated by the purge and the USSR was less reliable than ever.[67]

These reservations were apparently confirmed in the summer (on the eve of the Munich crisis) when a Soviet–Japanese battle erupted on the Siberia–Manchukuo border. Soviet troops occupied a string of hills along the ill-defined border and the Battle of Changkufeng ensued. On 31 July, after a 'severe engagement' which lasted three days, the Japanese evicted the Soviets and seized the hills. All Soviet efforts to dislodge them and regain their position failed until 9–10 August, when a Soviet attack was 'partially successful and a foot-hold was gained in the Changkufeng hills'. Thereafter, a truce was negotiated and a border commission was established to delineate the frontier.[68] British criticisms of Soviet tactics seemed vindicated: reconnaissance was poor, infantry was brave but poorly deployed and failed to press the attack, armour was clumsily and ineffectively employed, aerial attacks were ineffectual and the clumsy Soviet frontal assaults were bloodily repulsed. Only the artillery, which performed poorly initially, recovered to show any effectiveness. The British Ambassador to Japan, Sir Robert Craigie, pointed to the significance of Changkufeng: 'The impression of military invincibility which the Russians have been seeking to build up in the Far East . . . has been to a great extent dissipated.' In response to a later report, a FO commentator minuted: 'This confirms previous reports about the inefficiency of the Soviet troops.' Another noted: 'The Russians certainly put up a very poor show; and this is all the more significant when it is remembered that the Far Eastern Red Army is regarded as a cut above the Red Army as a whole.' Subsequent reports and minutes reflected this general pattern of response.[69]

It would seem unfair, therefore, to fault the British government for not considering the USSR a viable military ally during the Munich crisis: before the purge, the USSR was a dubious element (but at least the Red Army showed signs of improving its potential for effective offensive action); after the purge, there was every reason to assume that whatever limited value it had previously possessed as an ally had been severely reduced; and, after Changkufeng, these doubts certainly appeared substantiated. Quite apart from the condition of the Red Army (and, for that matter, of Soviet transport and industry), there remained the geographical obstacles to effective Soviet intervention. Poland was expected to resist Soviet transit and the Romanian communications system was incapable of transporting sufficient troops to have any real impact at all. There were other problems as well with using Romania as a corridor for a Soviet advance.[70] From a purely military perspective, therefore, at least on the basis of all empirical evidence available, it would seem that the British government had no alternative but to discount the USSR as a military factor in its policy formulation at the time of Munich. Moreover, the Soviets made no military moves to alter this attitude. After Munich, one FO commentator (R. L. Speaight) reflected that the only specific information on Soviet military preparations received by the FO from official Soviet sources was that received by R. A. Butler from Litvinov at Geneva on 23 September: 'Litvinov said that he could not state to what extent the Russian Army was mobilised or the Air Force ready to help Czechoslovakia . . . Actually we have no information to show that there was even a move of reinforcements towards the Western frontiers. There are believed to have been certain troop movements in the Ukraine, but only amongst the troops already stationed there.'[71]

In the aftermath of Munich, and especially after the German absorption of the truncated Czechoslovak state, political pressure mounted for the British government to take effective action against further German expansion and, as a corollary, to reach an accommodation with the USSR. Throughout the winter, spring and summer of 1939 the need for an Anglo-Soviet accord was advocated increasingly in parliamentary debates. Frequent favourable reference was made to the size of the Red Army and the Soviet air force and conclusions advanced as to the proper role to be assigned to the USSR in the European arena.[72]

Indeed, many in the FO and WO were awake to the benefits of such a coalition. On 3 January 1939 for example, the assistant private secretary to the Foreign Secretary, Harold Caccia, wrote a long memorandum eloquently espousing the need for an Anglo-Soviet understanding and urging a fresh approach to the problem. In the discussion which ensued, the commentators did not so much disagree with Caccia in theory but expressed reservations from a practical perspective: they were all too aware of the difficulties. But no one questioned the importance of the USSR; as one minute expressed it, 'Russia is no friend of ours, though in certain circumstances she might be an ally . . . she remains a very important makeweight in the uncertain balance of Europe.'[73] At the end of the month, an officer on the staff of the DMI, Lt Col. N. C. D. Brownjohn, told Laurence Collier that, even though the USSR were militarily weak, unable to fight an offensive war, due to its internal difficulties and, therefore, only a 'bogey', it was 'better to have a bogey up your sleeve than nothing at all!' In any case, Brownjohn thought that the USSR had a very 'definite bogey value' in the Far East and Britain should 'collaborate with the Soviets and . . . do everything possible to strengthen them as a Far Eastern bogey'.[74]

Nevertheless, the Soviet military condition was not reassuring. In January both the COS and the FO thought it unlikely that the USSR would intervene actively in any war unless directly attacked by Germany; it was possible though that the Kremlin would assume a more firm position if Germany attacked one of the border states. The FO thought that 'the USSR is in no condition to wage offensive war effectively' and would go to great lengths to avoid becoming involved in a war. The most that could be hoped for, it was thought, was that the Soviets would restrain Japan in the event of a Western European war.[75]

Chamberlain was very much influenced by these assessments and, throughout the spring and summer, expressed his scepticism of Soviet reliability and military capability in letters to his sisters; he repeatedly wrote of his doubts concerning the Soviet ability to effectually aid the Western Allies against Germany due to the reputed inability of the Red Army to fight an offensive war.[76] Nor was he alone in his doubts. In the Cabinet Committee on Foreign Policy meeting of 27 March, for example, only Sir Samuel Hoare and Oliver Stanley pressed for more favourable consideration of the military value of the USSR as an ally. Halifax and Chatfield considered Poland the better ally.[77]

The Chiefs of Staff were in a dilemma over Soviet military value as an ally. On 18 March they were emphatically in favour of immediate 'diplomatic action' to bring the USSR into an Anglo-French coalition to preserve Romanian independence because an ultimatum from Britain, France and the USSR might deter Germany whereas, without Soviet assistance, Britain and France could do little to assist Romania and an Anglo-French ultimatum would carry less weight. Conversely, the USSR could do little to assist Western Allies against Germany if Poland were neutral nor was it thought likely that the USSR would enter a war unless attacked. Reports from Moscow continued to cast great doubt on Soviet offensive capability. Again, in the Cabinet Committee on Foreign Policy meeting of 19 April only Hoare favoured dealing with the Soviets but he was overruled because the adverse political consequences outweighed the military benefits of an alliance with the USSR.[78]

On the other hand, on the 24th the COS were considerably less enthusiastic about Soviet military capability and, in a lengthy analysis of the Soviet military condition, concluded that the Soviet ability to influence military operations in Europe was limited. This was not the case in the Far East, however, where the USSR could play a significant role against Japan. Still, the COS were gravely concerned over the possibility of a Nazi–Soviet alliance. The Cabinet Committee on Foreign Policy was not more optimistic than the COS over the value of the USSR as a military ally.[79]

From a strictly military perspective, as the First Lord of the Admiralty, Earl Stanhope, told Halifax on 25 May, it was only reasonable to include the

USSR in any anti-German coalition, but he enumerated the political disadvantages and concluded:

> I feel that the only circumstances in which the military advantages . . . would outweigh these political objections would be if the help we might expect to receive from Russia in war with the Axis powers was so great that it would make the difference between success and defeat. The Chiefs of Staff have reported on the value of Russia as an ally and have stated that this value is not nearly so great as is commonly supposed. I cannot feel therefore that it can be said that Russia's help would really be the deciding factor . . . The military advantages only arise if we eventually come to war. If we assume that somehow or other we are going to avoid this, I feel that more than ever the political disadvantages outweigh the possible military advantages.[80]

The COS were of the view that Soviet aid against Germany would be so limited that Spanish enmity (with the consequent threat to British Mediterranean communications) would be more dangerous militarily than the loss of the USSR as an ally, although the Soviet threat would contain significant German forces in the East after the collapse of Poland and Romania. Moreover, there was the issue of Soviet reliability: 'We are not in a position to assess the degree of reliance that could be placed on any Russian undertaking. But we would point out the dangerous military consequences if, when we have accepted an alliance with Russia with all its disadvantages, the latter were to withdraw from her obligations once a major war had become inevitable.' Succinctly, the problem was summarised at the conclusion of the assessment: 'We can place no reliance on the military value of an alliance with Russia.'[81]

But the COS, although uncertain of Soviet reliability and capability, wanted more than 'the bare neutrality of Russia' since the Soviets could supply arms to Poland and Romania. Moreover, a pact with the USSR would have the political advantage of presenting a 'solid front of formidable proportions against aggression' and might deter Hitler from war. Finally, 'if Russia remained neutral she would be left in a dominating position at the end of hostilities'.[82] By 16 May the COS came out unequivocally in favour of a tripartite Anglo-Franco-Soviet alliance. In the Cabinet Committee on Foreign Policy meeting that day, Chatfield pressed for the alliance (he was supported by Stanley and Hoare) on the grounds that the 'active and whole-hearted assistance of Russia' would be of 'appreciable value' as a supplier of war material to Poland and Romania and also by containing enemy forces after the collapse of Poland and Romania. Chatfield emphasised Polish military weakness and Polish inability to hold out long against a German attack without Soviet aid. Halifax conceded that the 'Triple Alliance' advocated by the COS was 'sound' militarily but added that it was politically problematical given Polish and Romanian objections. Chamberlain opposed the idea and accused the COS of reversing its earlier position.[83]

In any case, the COS were not particularly optimistic over the prospects for a successful Polish defence against a German attack and thought that the

Poles had both underestimated German military power and overestimated their own ability to resist. The hope was forlornly expressed from time to time that the Poles might adopt a more realistic attitude towards Soviet aid before it was too late.[84] By August the British military had lost patience with Polish intransigence and, on the 16th, the Deputy Chiefs of Staff emphatically urged that strong pressure be applied to Poland and Romania to permit Soviet troops on to their soil. Failure to obtain this concession, warned the Deputy Chiefs, would endanger, perhaps wreck, the Moscow talks, and possibly lead to a Nazi–Soviet pact.[85]

The British effort to secure Soviet adherence to an anti-German coalition during the spring and summer of 1939 failed. The progress was impeded by unresolved political and diplomatic obstacles, most notably the opposition of the Polish government, and it was upon these obstacles that it foundered.[86] Once Poland had been guaranteed, Soviet participation assumed a new importance, at least as a negative precaution: (1) to prevent a Nazi–Soviet accommodation; and (2) to obtain Soviet support for Poland, at least as a supplier of armaments, and perhaps to contain German forces after the collapse of Polish resistance. The heartbreaking pilgrimage to Moscow was almost tantamount to a desperate gesture of despair; the decision to guarantee Poland had been essentially a response to political and diplomatic factors, with little regard for the military realities, and predictably placed Britain in a very difficult military position. Having guaranteed Poland (and, for that matter, Romania), the British government, in effect, also guaranteed the western frontier of the Soviet Union and forfeited whatever diplomatic leverage it might otherwise have exerted in both Moscow and Warsaw to construct a strong eastern bastion. Moreover, the overall strategic situation might not have been significantly improved even if the USSR had entered into the so-called 'Peace Front': it seemed that Soviet participation could only prove beneficial if Germany attacked Poland instead of the West, and even then, given the political, diplomatic and military realities, it remained highly problematical.[87] The caution with which Chamberlain moved in deciding to approach Stalin was clearly a function of his scepticism of Soviet reliability and capability which was based upon all the information at his disposal: even after the Polish guarantee, the British government never had any evidence to substantiate its hopes that the USSR would prove a reliable or capable ally.

One could argue that, perhaps, the British government might have sought an agreement with Moscow sooner, *before* the situation had deteriorated to the extent that it had in 1939. Certainly, nobody would contend that the Baldwin and Chamberlain governments pursued an accommodation with Moscow vigorously in the years 1935–9. On the other hand, there was very little intelligence to indicate that it was worthy of pursuit. In considering the positive and negative consequences of such an entanglement, British officials had little reassurance that, in a 'worst-case scenario' (a German attack in the West, followed by an Italian and Japanese entry into the war on the German side, which might, they feared, be precipitated by a British entry into the Franco-Soviet alliance), Soviet assistance would be of any great value without Polish co-operation. The French experience of 1934–5 seemed to preclude much hope relative to Polish co-operation – and the Anglo-French experience in 1939 would appear to confirm the validity of this argument. The fear that the USSR would exploit such a conflict, possibly in violation of treaty pledges, to the detriment of British interests (in, for example, the Middle East) was never far from the minds of those responsible for formulating policy. Essentially, the military benefits accruing from an Anglo-Soviet pact were not perceived to balance the negative political-diplomatic (and possibly even military) consequences, especially after 1937. Accordingly, the British governments of this period were not inclined to approach Moscow and this reticence was based upon all the empirical data at their disposal rather than upon wishful thinking or ideological predisposition: the problem was one of Soviet credibility. As Halifax observed in early 1939: 'We must found our policy on concrete realities and vital interests.'[88] Only with the increased domestic political pressure which developed in the wake of Munich and the transformed political and diplomatic situation which followed the German absorption of the truncated Czechoslovak state were the 'vital interests' redefined in March 1939 in such a manner as to alter the 'concrete realities'.

Finally, one question remains: how sound were British perceptions of Soviet military potential? The British assessments of Soviet military capability advanced during the years 1935–9 were generally consistent. Succinctly expressed, the Red Army was expected to prove a dangerous opponent to an invader, but less formidable offensively. At least within the European context, this analysis proved reasonably accurate: the performance of the Red Army in Poland, Romania, the Baltic States and Finland in 1939–40 would seem to confirm the second part of the prediction, while the Red Army demonstrated its defensive prowess convincingly against the *Wehrmacht* in 1941–5.

Notes: Chapter 22

1   The process had begun in 1933 when the first tentative Soviet approaches were made to France. The United States, of course, recognised the USSR in that same year and the Soviets entered the League of Nations in 1934.
2   The peak strength of the Red Army had been established in 1924 at 562,000 men where it remained until 1934 when the expansion began. In that year its strength was increased to 940,000 men and in 1935–6 a further increase raised the number to 1,300,000. See J. Erickson, *The Soviet High Command. A Military-Political History, 1918–1941* (London, 1962), p. 763.
3   The British government considered its distrust of Soviet intentions and reliability fully justified by the record of Comintern propaganda and intrigue, both at home (in the British Isles) and abroad, against British interests. Many British statesmen later freely conceded as much. See, for example, A. Eden (1st Earl of Avon), *The Eden Memoirs: Facing the Dictators* (London, 1962), p. 520; S. Hoare (Viscount Templewood), *Nine Troubled Years* (London, 1954), p. 350; H. Macmillan, *Winds of Change, 1914–1939* (London, 1966), p. 594; E. Percy (1st Baron), *Some Memoirs* (London, 1958), p. 350; and R. Vansittart, *The Mist Procession* (London, 1958), p. 456. See also, for example, the Home Office comments on Communist activities in Britain contained in Public Record Office, London, CAB 53/25 – COS 382, Scott to Hankey, 5 June 1935, pp. 3–4.

4   I. Colvin, *Vansittart in Office: An Historical Survey of the Origins of the Second World War Based on the Papers of Sir Robert Vansittart* (London, 1965), p. 26.

5   C. H. Stuart (ed.), *The Reith Diaries* (London, 1975), p. 117.

6   D. C. Watt, *Personalities and Policies. Studies in the Formulation of British Foreign Policy in the 20th Century* (London, 1965), p. 90. Indeed, Vansittart hoped for a stalemate between the USSR and Japan in which both nations would act as a deterrent upon the other, thereby preserving the *status quo* (Mounsey to Cadogan, 31 May 1934, FO 800/293). Vansittart had a very clear and simple perception of the problem. He later told the Defence Requirements Sub-Committee that all totalitarian states were aggressive: 'Italy, Germany and Japan fell within this category. Democracies as a rule were not aggressive and Russia, at the moment, was incapable of aggression.' CAB 16/112: Committee of Imperial Defence, Defence Requirements Sub-Committee (15th meeting), 3 October 1935, p. 9.

7   Colvin, *Vansittart in Office*, p. 28. On the Soviet sale of the CER, see G. A. Lensen, *The Damned Inheritance. The Soviet Union and the Manchurian Crises, 1924–1935* (Tallahassee, Fla, 1974), chs 7–10, pp. 212–334.

8   On 20 November 1934 Simon reflected somberly in his diary: 'Germany is rapidly rearming, and while Hitler reiterates his peaceful intentions the day is fast approaching when she will be strong enough to repudiate openly the Versailles limitations which she is secretly disregarding' (Simon Papers: 11 – Diaries, 1934–8).

9   *Documents on British Foreign Policy*, 2nd series, Vol. XIII, *Naval Policy and Defence Requirements, 20 July 1934–25 March 1936* (London, 1973), p. 27, Memorandum by N. Chamberlain on the Naval Conference and Relations with Japan, 1 September 1934.

10 ibid., pp. 32–3, Memorandum by Mr C. W. Orde on Mr N. Chamberlain's Proposals, 4 September 1934. For indications of Japanese fears of the USSR, see ibid., pp. 35, 44. Report from HM Military Attaché at Tokyo, 5 September 1934, and Clive to Simon, 3 October 1934.

11 B. H. Liddell Hart, *The Memoirs of Captain Liddell Hart* (London, 1965), Vol. I, pp. 291–2. There were some signs that Germany sought to expand eastwards and was not, therefore, some contended, an immediate threat to British interests. MI3 argued that rather than a return to the 1914 *status quo*, German revisionist aims, at least for the moment, were limited to Central and Eastern Europe. See WO 190/303: MI3 Memorandum of 28 February 1935 in which MI3 took issue with paragraph 12 of JP/105 (21 February 1935). Later (11 August 1936), Simon considered the comfort the British might derive from the possibility that Hitler would move east rather than west and remarked, 'The Cyclops paid Odysseus the compliment of promising to eat him *last* [*sic*]' (Simon Papers: 11 – Diaries, 1934–9).

12 See L. Radice, 'The eastern pact, 1933–1935. A last chance at European co-operation', *Slavonic and East European Review*, vol. LV (January 1977), pp. 45–64.

13 *DBFP*, 2nd series, Vol. VI, *1933–1934*, pp. 753, 756. Clerk to Simon, 21 June 1934.

14 ibid., p. 770: Clerk to Simon, 21 June 1934. The same general opinion was later advanced to the British Ambassador to Switzerland, Sir George Warner, by his new French colleague, Charles Alphand, who had just come from the USSR. See FO 371/20346/N6375: Warner to Eden, 18 December 1936. For arguments that a failure to conclude either a Locarno-type Eastern pact or a Franco-Soviet pact would result in a Nazi-Soviet pact, see *DBFP*, Vol. VI, pp. 875–7: Campbell to Simon, 26 July 1934.

15 FO 371/18833/C2819: Clerk to Simon, 2 April 1935. See also CAB 64/14: Beaumont-Nesbitt to Clerk, 6 April 1939.

16 *DBFP*, 2nd series, Vol. VI, pp. 836, 839, 860: Phipps to Simon, 12 July 1934, Erskine to Simon, 14 July 1934, and Memorandum Regarding the Attitude of the Polish Government towards the Disarmament Conference, and Regarding Polish Military Policy in its Bearing on the Proposed Eastern Guarantee Pact, 21 July 1934. The last memorandum was written by the British military attaché to Poland, Lt Col. G. F. Connal Rowan. The Polish Foreign Minister, Josef Beck, also provided information on the fears of the Baltic States that the USSR would exploit such a pact for purposes of aggression (ibid., pp. 885–6: Erskine to Simon, 31 July 1934).

17 FO 371/19470/N2504: Address on the USSR to the Imperial Defence College on 16 May 1935 by James L. Dodds. For a cogent analysis of the risk of Nazi–Soviet *rapprochement* and the possible means of preventing this eventuality, see Phipps Papers: Phpp 5/6, 'Britain, France and Germany' by Sir Robert Vansittart, 3 February 1936, p. 12. Many

British officials, both civilian and military, but especially the latter, feared that the Franco-Soviet link might increase the danger of Britain becoming involved in a war for which it was not militarily prepared. See, for example, ADM 116/4053: MO5495/36, Minute by E. A. Seal, 30 November 1936, and CAB 4/25 – Paper 1305-B: Review of Imperial Defence by the Chiefs of Staff Sub-Committee, 22 February 1937. This last report was produced for the 1937 Imperial Conference.

18   Chamberlain Papers: NC18/1/908, Neville Chamberlain to Hilda Chamberlain, 18 March 1935. See also Pownal Diaries: HRPO DIARY 3, 1935, diary entry of 18 February 1935.

19   Phipps Papers: Phpp 1/16, Annual Report, 6 January 1935, p. 4; Simon Papers: 11 – Diaries, 1934–8, diary entry of 13 March 1935; and Pownal Diaries: HRPO Diary 3, 1935, diary entries of 28 January and 18 March 1935.

20   Chamberlain Papers: NC 18/1/909, Neville Chamberlain to Ida Chamberlain, 16 March 1935, and NC 18/1/910, Neville Chamberlain to Hilda Chamberlain, 18 March 1935.

21   Eden, *Facing the Dictators*, pp. 135, 160.

22   Simon Papers: 11 – Diaries, 1934–8.

23   FO 371/19454/N753, Chilston to Simon, 11 February 1935.

24   Parliamentary Debates (Lords), 5th series, vol. XCVI (London, 1935), col. 1001. Hereafter the citation will take the following form: 96 HL Deb. 5s., 1001.

25   FO 371/19460/N3489, Ismay to Collier, 9 July 1935. At this time, Ismay was on the staff of DMOI. The addressee was not the air attaché in Moscow, but Laurence Collier, head of the Northern Department (FO). The Soviet transport system in general and Soviet railroads in particular were considered inadequate and a major weakness in the Soviet military support infrastructure for many years. See FO 371, N311/52/38, Chilston to Simon, 12 January 1935. See also Phipps Papers: Phpp 1/14, Phipps to Simon, 15 May 1935; WO 190/330: First Draft of War Office Paper for the Foreign Office, 15 May 1935, pp. 7–8; and WO 190/361: Note on the Possibilities of Future German-Russian Co-operation, 24 October 1935. For analyses, reports, etc. by the Director of Military Intelligence (DMI) on Soviet communications and transport for the years 1937–46, see WO 208/1753. On the Soviet railway system, see J. N. Westwood, 'Soviet railway development', *Soviet Studies*, vol. XI (July 1959), pp. 22–48. See also Michael S. Mirski, 'The Soviet railway system. Policy and operation', *The Russian Review*, vol. XIII (January 1954), pp. 18–32.

26   FO 371/20353/N1477: Chilston to Eden, 9 March 1936.

27   ibid., N5631: Committee of Imperial Defence. The USSR Air Force: Memorandum by the Secretary of State for Air, 10 November 1936.

28   In 1929 Tukhachevsky began to experiment with paratroopers and, after the 1935 demonstration, attended by General Henri Loiseau, French troops received training in the USSR before returning to France as instructors. In December 1936 the German army held its first paratrooper exercises and the British and Italian armies began to experiment with the concept. See Erickson, *Soviet High Command*, p. 327; and Col. O. L. Spaulding, 'Air infantry landing', *Command and General Staff School Quarterly*, vol. XVIII (June 1937), pp. 85–7.

29   FO 371/19455/N5533: Charles to Hoare, 22 October 1935. Köstring probably did not consider the military use of paratroopers *per se* to be unworthy of attention but more likely thought their use on a large-scale strategic basis to be unsound. This seemed to be the view of the German army which subsequently began to train paratrooper units for small-scale operations. See WO 190/489: Memorandum by Col. B. C. T. Paget, 12 October 1936.

30   Parliamentary Debates (Commons), 5th series, vol. CCCIX (London, 1937), cols 2349–72 *passim*. The quotation from Cooper's speech is to be found at col. 2350. Henceforth, this citation will appear as 309 HC Deb. 5s., 2349–72.

31   310 HC Deb. 5s., 290, 1215, 1236.

32   FO 371/20352/N5048: Wavell to Dill, 10 September 1936. Wavell had considerable experience with the Tsarist army. He spoke Russian, visited Imperial Russia several times, attended the Imperial Army manoeuvres for three consecutive years (1911–13), served in the Russian section of Military Operations and Intelligence from 1912 to 1914, and was the British liaison officer with the Russian army in the Caucasus under the command of the Grand Duke Nicholas in 1916–17. J. Connell [John Henry Robertson], *Wavell: Scholar and Soldier. To June 1941* (London, 1964), pp. 71–2, 78.

33   FO 371/20353/N5401: Medhurst to Collier, 30 October 1936. For general RAF opinion of

the Soviet air force, see AIR 40/1210: Lecture on Foreign (European) Air Forces for Headquarters, Fighter Command, 6 November 1936, by Wing Commander R. V. Goddard. These views remained generally unchanged until June 1937. See, for example, ibid.: A Lecture on the Air Forces of France, Germany, Italy and Russia by Wing Commander R. V. Goddard at HQ, No. 22 Group, RAF, 29 June 1937.

34   Liddell Hart, *Memoirs*, Vol. I, p. 378; and Sir Gifford Le Quesne Martel, *An Outspoken Soldier. His Views and Memoirs* (London, 1949), pp. 127–8. Generally, Martel agreed with Wavell's assessment of the Red Army: see pp. 135–48.

35   103 HL Deb. 5s., 288.

36   ibid., 151.

37   Liddell Hart, *Memoirs*, Vol. I, p. 384. Vansittart had earlier observed: 'Russia seeks safety in armaments which outstrip her technical efficiency.' See Phipps Papers: Phpp 5/6, 'Britain, France and Germany' by Sir Robert Vansittart, 3 February 1936, p. 11.

38   For attaché and Embassy reports as well as FO commentary, 1935 – June 1937, see the following sources from FO 371/19450/N2379; 19454: N753/N1597; 19455: N4116/N5533; 19466: N1318/N4371/N5293; 19469: N1308/N1524/N2643/N3654; 19470: N2504; 19910: C5356; 20341: N5005; 20344: N1138/N4119/N6018; 20348: N751; 20349: N2609/N4796; 20351: N5255; 20352: N871; 20353: N5631; 20377: R4609; 21104: N2361; 21105: N506/ N1720/N2197; 21106: N2199/N2694; and 21107: N2466. For WO policy papers, strategic planning, etc., see the sources enumerated in notes 46–52. See also B. H. Liddell Hart. 'The armies of Europe', *Foreign Affairs*, vol. XV (January 1937), pp. 246–50.

39   See, for example, 297 HC Deb. 5s., 1567; 96 HL Deb. 5s., 63, 70–1, 96–7, 522; 97 HL Deb. 5s., 865; 304 HC Deb. 5s., 1471; 308 HC Deb. 5s., 722–3; 100 HL Deb. 5s., 132, 134–5, 185, 204; 321 HC Deb. 5s., 201–2.

40   See D. C. Watt, 'Soviet military aid to the Spanish republic in the civil war, 1936–1939', *Slavonic and East European Review*, vol. XXXVIII (June 1960), pp. 536–43.

41   See, for example, CAB 53/33 – COS 622 (JIC): CID/COS. Spain: Intelligence Regarding Air Warfare. Report by the Joint Intelligence Sub-Committee. Report No. 1. Anti-Aircraft (Artillery) Defence, 6 October 1937; and ibid., COS 624 (JIC): Report No. 4. Low Flying Attack on Land Forces, 6 October 1937. By 1939 Soviet, Italian and German aircraft in Spain were considered obsolescent. The same reaction is apparent in reports of Soviet aircraft operating in China against the Japanese. Still, the general reaction seemed to be that Soviet aircraft had performed respectably, both in Spain and in China. See CAB 54/6 – DCOS 100 (JIC): COS/Deputy Chiefs of Staff (DCOS). Spain and China: Intelligence Regarding Air Warfare, 10 June 1939. See also ibid., DCOS 101 (JIC), DCOS 103 (JIC) and DCOS 104 (JIC).

42   S. W. Roskill, *Hankey. Man of Secrets*, Vol. III, *1931–1963* (London, 1974), p. 243.

43   Eden, *Facing the Dictators*, p. 484. See also Knatchbull-Hugessen Papers: Knat 2/50, Wigram to Knatchbull-Hugessen, 2 March 1937, p. 2.

44   Major-General A. C. Temperley, 'Military lessons of the Spanish civil war', *Foreign Affairs*, vol. XVI (October 1937), pp. 37, 41. On the performance of Soviet armour in Spain see WO 106/1581: MI3 Interview with Wing Commander A. James, 8 October 1937; WO 106/1583: Some Impressions of the Nationalist Army in Spain, [undated] May 1938 by Lt Col. A. F. G. Renton; and WO 106/1585: Fuller to Gort, 27 April 1938, p. 4. For MI3 report on Spain, see WO 106/1582.

45   See, for example, 319 HC Deb. 5s., 129; 328 HC Deb. 5s., 587–8; and 333 HC Deb. 5s., 348.

46   CAB 4/23 – Paper 1181-B (also COS 372): CID. Annual Review by the Chiefs of Staff Sub-Committee, 29 April 1935. On the Soviet need to avoid war, see CAB 55/7 – JP 111: CID/Joint Planning Sub-Committee (JP): Strategical Review of Europe, 1 August 1935. See also CAB 53/24 – COS 372: CID/COS. Imperial Defence Policy: Annual Review by the Chiefs of Staff, 1935 (Prepared in conjunction with discussions with Dominion Prime Ministers), 29 April 1935. See also ibid., COS 368: The Situation in the Far East. Memorandum prepared in the Foreign Office, 16 March 1935; and COS 370: Naval Staff Memorandum on the Memorandum Prepared by the Foreign Office on the Situation in the Far East, 5 April 1935. See also CAB 4/23 – Paper 1183-B: CID. Imperial Defence Policy, 1 June 1935. The bulk of this report was concerned with Germany and Japan. See also ibid., Papers 1182-B through 1187-B (2 July–23 September 1935) and Paper 1189-B (19 September 1935) for the British preoccupation with the German threat. See also

CAB 4/24, Papers 1198-B and 1905-B (13 November and 17 December 1935). See also AIR 9/24: Germany as the Potential Aggressor, 12 February 1937, pp. 1–4.

47 See, for example, Knatchbull-Hugessen Papers: Knat 2/30, Knatchbull-Hugessen to the King, 27 December 1935, p. 5; and Baldwin Papers, vol. 107: Linlithgow to Baldwin, 10 September 1936, pp. 158–9. See also CAB 53/27 – COS 377: CID/COS. Memorandum Prepared by the India Office for the Use of the Chief of Staff in their Annual Review, 9 May 1935. See also CAB 53/7 – COS 196th Meeting (8 February 1937); CAB 4/25 – Paper 1305-B (22 February 1937); CAB 53/39 – COS 736: Creedy to Hankey, 13 June 1938. Annex II: The Defence of India and the Composition and Organisation of the Army and Royal Air Force in India. Report by the Sub-Committee, 12 May 1938; CAB 27/654 – COS 737: CID/COS. Defence of India, 2 July 1938; CAB 53/48 – COS 895; CID/COS. Plan of Operations (India), 1938; and CAB 27/654 – Report of the Expert Committee on the Defence of India, 1938–1939, 30 January 1939. For the COS reaction to the 'Expert Committee' report, see CAB 53/47 – COS 874. For the reaction of the Cabinet Committee on the Defence of India, see CAB 54/45 – COS 848. See also AIR 8/529: Note on a Meeting on Indian Defence Problems, 28 April 1938 and Newall to Zetland, 28 March 1938, p. 2. See also AIR 8/256, AIR 8/255, and AIR 8/1199. The question of Indian defence against a Soviet attack arose occasionally in Parliament. See, for example, 97 HL Deb. 5s., 453–4, 520.

48 See, for example, CAB 4/23 – Paper 1175-B: CID. Advisory Committee on Trade Questions in Time of War – Sub-Committee on Economic Pressure: Economic Pressure on Germany Without there being a State of War, 3 June 1935; and CAB 53/25 – COS 401: CID/COS. Defence Plans for the Event of War Against Germany, 2 October 1935.

49 See, for example, CAB 53/6 – COS/174th Meeting (13 May 1936), p. 8; CAB 64/14 – Possibility of German Aggression in the Immediate Future and the British Army's Action in this eventuality: Note by the Chief of the Imperial General Staff, 16 June 1936, p. 6; CAB 53/28 – COS 491 (JP): CID/COS. Strategical Review by the Joint Planning Sub-Committee, 3 July 1936, p. 3. CAB 55/2 – JP/121st Meeting (21 October 1936), p. 2; CAB 53/29 – COS 513 (JP): CID/COS. Appreciation of the Situation in the Event of War Against Germany in 1939 by the Joint Planning Sub-Committee: Provisional Report, 26 October 1936, p. 3; CAB 54/1 – DCOS/8th Meeting (12 November 1936), p. 2; and CAB 54/3 – DCOS 34: CID/COS. Appreciation of the Situation in the Event of War with Germany, 14 December 1936, p. 2.

50 WO 106/5631: Enclosure to Tokyo dispatch No. 283, Clive to Simon, 24 May 1935; WO 106/5499: Ismay to Steward, 7 October 1935; and ibid., Appreciation of the Probable Plans of Operations and Initial Deployment in a Russo-Japanese War, October 1935.

51 Vansittart Papers: Vnst 1/19, 'The world situation and British rearmament' by Sir Robert Vansittart, 31 December 1936, p. 2. See also WO 106/5631: 'Appreciation of the probable plans of operations and initial deployment in a Russo-Japanese war', 6 March 1936, by Lt. Col. G. E. Grimsdale, and 'Appreciation of the probable plans of operations and initial deployment in a Russo-Japanese war', 6 May 1936, by Col. E. A. H. James.

52 CAB 4/26 – Paper 1311-B (COS 551): CID/COS. Comparison of the Strength of Great Britain with that of certain other Nations as at May 1937, 9 February 1937; CAB 53/30 – COS 549: CID/COS. Planning for War with Germany, 14 February 1937. Annex: Extracts from a Report by the Joint Planning Sub-Committee on the Situation in the Event of War with Germany. Part III – Courses of Action, p. 8; CAB 4/25 – Paper 1305-B: CID. Review of Imperial Defence by the Chiefs of Staff Sub-Committee, 22 February 1937, p. 11; and CAB 59/9 – JP 202: CID/COS/JP. Far East Appreciation, 1937, 7 May 1937, pp. 75–7. See also WO 106/5499: Appreciation of the Probable Plans of Operations and Initial Deployment in a Russo-Japanese War, 23 April 1937.

53 FO 371/21104: N2700: Chilston to Eden, 18 May 1935. See also ibid., N2921/N3010/N3075/N3076/N3177.

54 ibid., N4936: Hayes to Collier, 1 October 1937. See Collier's minute.

55 See Erickson, *Soviet High Command*, pp. 449–509.

56 See, for example, FO 371/21094/N5456/N5955/N5969 and 21104: N3907/N4130/N4367.

57 ibid., 21104: N3447. Hayes had been consulted by Collier.

58 See, for example, Chamberlain Papers: NC 18/1/1091, Neville Chamberlain to Ida Chamberlain, 26 March 1938; W. Churchill, *The Second World War*, Vol. I: *The Gathering Storm* (London, 1948), p. 226; Eden, *Facing the Dictators*, p. 162; The Earl of Halifax,

Fullness of Days (London, 1957), p. 206; Hoare, *Nine Troubled Years*, pp. 342–3; and Sir H. L. Ismay, *The Memoirs of General the Lord Ismay* (London, 1960), p. 224. The French certainly shared British doubts over the efficacy of Soviet aid. See, for example, Phipps Papers: Phpp 1/20, Phipps to Halifax, 28 October 1938, and Phpp 1/21, Phipps to Halifax, 3 November 1938.

59   Liddell Hart, *Memoirs*, Vol. II, p. 137.

60   Nigel Nicolson (ed.), *Harold Nicolson. Diaries and Letters, 1930–1939* (London, 1966), p. 329. Indeed, French reliability and capability were also dubious so that the British government found itself facing the crisis with two very shaky potential allies. See, for example, Pownall Diaries: HRPO Diary 5, 1938, diary entry of 23 May 1938, pp. 45–6; Phipps Papers: Phpp 1/20, Phipps to Halifax, 10, 16 and 24 September 1938, and Halifax to Phipps, 12 September 1938; and Phpp 1/21, Halifax to Phipps, 25 and 28 October 1938, and Phipps to Halifax, 25 October 1938.

61   See, for example, 105 HL Deb. 5s., 944.

62   See, for example, Colvin, *Vansittart in Office*, p. 152; R. J. Minney (ed.), *The Private Papers of Hore-Belisha* (London, 1960), p. 118; and General Sir K. Strong, *Intelligence at the Top. The Recollections of an Intelligence Officer* (London, 1967), p. 31.

63   *DBFP*, 3rd series, Vol. I, *1938*, pp. 172–3: Firebrace to Vereker, 20 May 1938.

64   See, for example, FO 371/22288: N97/N488/N524/N748/N750/N1482; 22289: N3374/N5164 and N129/N549. Despite the reassessments of Soviet military power, British military analysts continued to consider the vulnerability of Japanese cities to Soviet air attack from Vladivostok to be a deterrent on Japanese action against the USSR. See, for example, AIR 9/23: 'Japan's reaction to the threat of bombing by Soviet aircraft', 4 November 1937, by Squadron Leader C. B. R. Pelly.

65   See, for example, FO 371/21674: C1866/C3314; 22286: N1758/N1984; 22294: N220; and 22299: N1735.

66   CAB 4/27 – Paper 1373-B: CID. Strength of Great Britain and of certain other Nations as at January 1938: Memorandum by the Secretary of State for Foreign Affairs, 26 November 1937.

67   CAB 4/26 – Paper 1366-B: CID. Comparison of the Strength of Great Britain with that of certain other Nations as at January 1938. Report by the Chiefs of Staff Sub-Committee, 12 November 1937. See also CAB 4/27 – Paper 1386-B: The Air Forces of the USSR. Memorandum by the Secretary of State for Air, 23 December 1937. See also CAB 53/40 – COS 747 (JP): CID/COS. Draft Appreciation of the Situation in the Event of War Against Germany in April 1939, 15 July 1938. See also AIR 9/76: COS/216th Meeting: Item 3, 'The Estimated Preparedness for War of Great Britain and Certain Other Powers on November 1, 1937', 18 September 1937; AIR 9/86: Annex II: Foreign Office Comments on Joint-Planning Sub-Committee Papers Regarding War with Germany, Italy and Japan; and WO 106/1594B: JIC Forecast of Situation for JPC: Conclusions – USSR, October (undated) 1938.

68   WO 106/5624: Soviet–Japanese Border Incident – Changkufeng. For views on Soviet–Japanese strength, see WO 106/5536: Russo-Japanese Relations, 2 December 1937; and WO 106/1009: Major–Ismay–Hankey Correspondence, January 1938. See also WO 208/847 – Memorandum 072044: Views of the French Ambassador on the Soviet–Manchukuo Border Incident, (undated), Comments on 072044 by Major D. Stansby, 24 August 1938, and FO minute on 072044 by N. B. Ronald, 23 August 1938. Stansby was on the staff of DMOI and Ronald was the First Secretary, Far Eastern Department.

69   FO 371/22145: F7688 ff., and 22146: F9863/F10253/F10759/F11060.

70   See, for example, *DBFP*, 3rd series, Vol. I, pp. 162–5, 172–3 and 420–4, Firebrace to Chilston, 18 April 1938 (two separate reports), and Firebrace to Vereker, 30 May 1938. See also ibid., vol. II, p. 355, UK Delegation at Geneva to Halifax, 15 September 1938. See also FO 371/21720: C706/C5394. See also Liddell Hart, *Memoirs*, Vol. II, p. 162, and K. Young (ed.), *The Diaries of Sir Robert Bruce Lockhart*, Vol. I: *1915–1938* (London, 1973), p. 367. See also FO 800/296: Memorandum by Lord Cranborne, 8 February 1937. For parliamentary debates on the subject of Soviet capability and the role which the USSR should have played, see 340 HC Deb. 5s., 65–164 *passim*, 238–40; 341 HC Deb. 5s., 427–9, 648–52; 342 HC Deb. 5s., 2537, 2548. See also Chamberlain Papers: NC 18/1/1042, Neville Chamberlain to Ida Chamberlain, 30 March 1938.

71   FO 371/21908/C13407.

72   See, for example, 343 HC Deb. 5s., 125, 144; 112 HL Deb. 5s., 260; 345 HC Deb. 5s., 2480–2574 *passim*; 346 HC Deb. 5s., 19–138 *passim*; 347 HC Deb. 5s., 46–7, 69–73, 110–47 *passim*; 113 HL Deb. 5s., 403–29; and 349 HC Deb. 5s., 1790–1.

73   FO 371/23677/N57: Foreign Office Minute by Harold Caccia, 3 January 1939.

74   FO 371/23684/N559: Brownjohn to Collier, 30 January 1939.

75   CAB 53/44 – COS 831 (JP): CID/COS. European Appreciation 1939–1940, 26 January 1939, pp. 6–7, 28, 48 and 69.

76   Chamberlain Papers: NC 18/1/1091/1096/1099/1101–2/1103/1107–8, Neville Chamberlain to Hilda and Ida Chamberlain, 9 April – 23 July 1939. Many shared Chamberlain's doubts. See, for example, FO 800/311: Loraine to Phipps, 6 April 1939. See also FO 800/310: Meeting with Dominions High Commissioners, 17 May 1939, pp. 3–4.

77   CAB 27/624 – FP (36) 38th Meeting (27 March 1939). Many of the reasons against an alliance with the USSR were political rather than military and, therefore, outside the scope of this paper. It may have been political rather than military considerations which prompted Halifax and Chatfield to prefer Poland as an ally. One political problem, for example, was the Canadian and South African opposition to a British alliance with the USSR. See CAB 21/551. See also FO 800/310: Telegram from High Commissioner in Canada, 24 March 1939, and Minute by R. H. Hadow, 24 May 1939. The Australians, apprehensive over Japanese policy, were more inclined to favour an Anglo-Soviet accord. See ibid., Burgin to Halifax, 18 May 1939. On the general question of dominions' attitudes towards British policy, see DO 121/5. For other political obstacles to an Anglo-Soviet pact which may have influenced Halifax, see FO 800/321: Halifax to Hardinge, 27 March 1939.

78   CAB 53/10 – COS/283rd Meeting (18 March 1939); and CAB 27/624 – FP(36) 43rd Meeting (19 April 1939). See also *DBFP*, 3rd series, Vol. IV, pp. 188–99, Seeds to Halifax, 6 March 1939 for one report on Soviet military capability from the Moscow Embassy.

79   CAB 27/627 – COS 887: Military Value of Russia, 24 April 1939; and CAB 27/624 – FP (36) 44th Meeting (25 April 1939). On British perceptions on the Soviet role in the Far East, see CAB 21/1010: Major to Ismay, 27 March 1939; CAB 27/627 – COS 928: The Situation in the Far East, 19 June 1939; and WO 208/207: Firebrace to Pownal, 5 July 1939.

80   CAB 21/551: Stanhope to Halifax, 25 May 1939, pp. 1–2, 5.

81   CAB 54/39 – COS 904(JP): CID/COS. Balance of Strategical Value in War Between Spain as an Enemy and Russia as an Ally, 8 May 1939.

82   CAB 53/11 – COS/295th Meeting (16 May 1939).

83   CAB 27/625 – FP (36) 47th Meeting (16 May 1939). Note especially Appendix II. Negotiations with Soviet Russia. Aide-Mémoire by the Chiefs of Staff. See also CAB 53/11 – COS/296th Meeting (16 May 1939). Despite his awareness of the political problems which beset the proposed Anglo-Soviet association, Halifax hoped for the success of the negotiations and defended the policy of seeking agreement with Moscow. See, for example, FO 800/322: Halifax's Correspondence with Various Ecclesiastical Personalities, April – May 1939; and FO 800/270: Halifax to Henderson, 14 and 30 June 1939.

84   See, for instance, CAB 29/159 – COS 872: CID/COS. Military Implications of an Anglo-French Guarantee of Poland and Romania, 3 April 1939; CAB 35/49 – COS 903(JP): CID/COS. Staff Conversations with Poland. Report by the Joint Planning Sub-Committee, 15 May 1939; CAB 53/50 – COS 927: CID/COS. Anglo-Polish Staff Conversations, 1939. Report by the United Kingdom Delegation, 12 June 1939; CAB 54/8 – DCOS 126(JP): CID/DCOS. Staff Conversations with Poland. Commentary by the Joint Planning Sub-Committee, 13 July 1939.

85   CAB 54/11 – DCOS 179: CID/DCOS. Russian Conversations: Use of Polish and Romanian Territory by Russian Forces, 16 August 1939.

86   FO 800/294: Henderson to Cadogan, 31 May 1939; and Pownal Diaries: HRPO Diary 6, 1939, diary entry of 14 August 1939, pp. 74–5. Of course, there were other problems – political and diplomatic – which hampered the progress. Soviet intentions and reliability remained suspect, not only to British officials but to those of other nations as well. See, for example, FO 800/315: Henderson to Halifax, 11 May 1939. Indeed, after several years of Soviet propaganda to the effect that the USSR would support any British initiative to contain German, Italian and Japanese aggression, some British officials were surprised that the Soviets used the negotiations as an occasion to extract concessions. See, for example, CAB 55/18: JP485 – also DCOS 144(JP) – CID/JP, 'Anglo-Franco-Russian Staff

Conversations Report', 27 July 1939, p. 1. For other problems, see CAB 27/624 – FP(36) 45th Meeting (5 May 1939); and CAB 27/625 – FP(36) 56th Meeting (4 July 1939).

87   For British assessments of the capability of the Red Army and what the British hoped to obtain from Soviet co-operation, see CAB 55/8: JP488 – also DCOS 150(JP) – 'Anglo-Franco-Russian Staff Conversations: A Memorandum for the Guidance of the United Kingdom Delegation to Russia', 28 July 1939.

88   Halifax Papers: Speech at the Grotius Luncheon, 15 February 1939.

Part Four

Appeasement in Global Perspective

I

THE BRITISH COMMONWEALTH AND THE JAPANESE THREAT

23 Britain, the Dominions and the Coming of the Second World War, 1933–9

RITCHIE OVENDALE

Until the early 1960s the European orientation of scholars meant that little attention was given to the dominions as a factor influencing British foreign policy.[1] An examination of internal movements in the dominions could lead to the conclusion that the so called united front of the commonwealth in September 1939 was more as a result of attitudes within the dominions, and the actions of certain dominion statesmen, than a deliberate and successful policy of the British government. Looking at the issue from the British angle, however, it is possible to see it as an interaction of constructive British policy and a natural, even guided evolution of dominion opinion.

On 22 March 1934 the British Cabinet discussed the direction of foreign affairs. It was thought that a policy designed to keep Britain out of all war in Europe and the Far East would mean adopting too narrow a view. Britain could not restore international peace and confidence by 'backing out of Europe and leaving others to take the consequences'. But the Cabinet was reminded of the attitude of the dominions at the time of the Locarno Treaty in 1925 which guaranteed Germany's western frontier and the demilitarised zone. The dominions and India were not bound by the treaty. As Foreign Secretary, Sir Austen Chamberlain had told the House of Commons, Britain needed to act on its own and could not wait for a common policy for the empire.[2] The dominions approved, and after that most of them had taken a strong line against becoming involved in any commitments.[3] Indeed the contention of the Canadian Prime Minister, W. L. Mackenzie King – following Lloyd George's appeal in September 1922 for dominion support over the Chanak crisis – that only the Parliament of a dominion could decide whether that country was at peace or war,[4] was accepted by the British government with the passing of the Statute of Westminster in 1931. It was not, however, until May 1939 that British War Book plans acknowledged the likelihood of a dominion's neutrality in the event of Britain being at war. With the rise of Hitler and Mussolini in Europe successive British governments, conscious of their imperial and world responsibilities, had to weigh carefully the opinion of the dominions. Britain was more than just a European power. The issues of information for or consultation with the dominions was an important one. Bilateral exchange of information was supplemented by meetings of the dominion High Commissioners in London with British officials, and an imperial conference in 1937. By the end of 1934 it was as if the British government were anxious to avoid a repetition of its action over Locarno, and care was taken to inform the dominions of the conversations with the Japanese and United States delegations to the Naval Conference. The British stand was endorsed by the dominion High Commissioners in London.[5]

With rearmament under way the British government thought it necessary to encourage the dominions to accelerate their defence programmes and to sound out the possibility of defence co-operation. In this regard each dominion had to be considered individually. South Africa, with its policy towards blacks, presented a particularly difficult case. Oswald Pirow, the South African Minister of Defence, envisaged his country playing a crucial role in the defence of the whole continent and hoped to discuss this with the Secretary of State for Air, the Marquess of Londonderry, in Cairo towards the end of 1934.[6] The view of the Colonial Office was that while Britain would not want to turn down an offer of co-operation from South Africa in time of war, it would be 'greatly embarrassed' by such co-operation in time of peace. The defence forces in East Africa, Northern Rhodesia and Nyasaland were 'native regiments' staffed by British officers. South African officers or contingents could not be introduced into these.[7] Sir Maurice Hankey, the secretary to the Cabinet and to the Committee of Imperial Defence, visited South Africa, New Zealand and Australia in the second half of 1934 to sound out these countries on defence matters. He saw the South African Prime Minister, J. B. M. Hertzog, on 6 September. Warned in advance of Hertzog's German sympathies Hankey emphasised Hitler's unpleasant activities, and Germany's intention to rearm. Britain was not contemplating any new commitment, but needed to be sure that it could intervene to preserve its own security. Hertzog did not dissent from this policy: even South Africa, far away from the danger zone, was taking steps to rearm. But he was critical of British policy towards France which 'had not always been sufficiently firm'; France, after all, had been responsible for the repression of Germany which lay at the root of the existing difficulties. Hertzog hoped that Britain would never allow itself to be drawn into a war in Europe unless that were 'absolutely essential to its own security'. In the interests of co-operation within the commonwealth Britain should not 'get involved on the continent'. The Deputy Prime Minister, J. C. Smuts, was, however, more enthusiastic about Britain's programme of rearmament. Smuts was concerned about Japanese ambitions in Mozambique and Abyssinia; should Singapore fall South Africa would be in the front line. For him the British navy was the shield of the whole empire, and its strength should be maintained.[8] Hankey's visit to Australia in October and November was marked by two changes in the commonwealth's government. He was, however, welcomed as a 'brother in arms' by the Chiefs of Staff: co-operation between Australia and Britain on defence seemed promising but Australia's defence arrangements all hinged on the maintenance of a naval position in the Far East.[9] Similarly in New Zealand the new British policy was received warmly and even the attempt to improve relations with Japan endorsed.[10]

On the occasion of King George V's Silver Jubilee the dominion Prime Ministers met in London and were briefed on the deteriorating international situation by Ramsay MacDonald. The British Prime Minister emphasised, however, that Britain 'must not allow itself to be pushed into a position of entering into a system of military alliances for the defence of Europe'.[11] R. B. Bennett of Canada concentrated on the extent to which British foreign policy had affected the dominions, and whether it met with general approval there; the British example of disarmament and the desire for peace probably did just this.[12] But Bennett felt that Britain was unprepared to meet the prevailing situation in Europe; the dominions overseas would be a prize to a hostile power. In reply Ramsay MacDonald pointed out that Britain kept faithfully to the 1930 agreement on the conduct of foreign policy by the members of the British commonwealth: unless a dominion objected to British policy its agreement would be assumed. R. G. Menzies of Australia was especially concerned about the dispute between Italy and Abyssinia and the difficulties that this would create for the League of Nations.[13] Indeed the methods of consultation established between Britain and the dominions during the Abyssinian crisis created the precedent for the remaining years leading up to the outbreak of the Second World War.

An important aspect of this consultation was the meetings between the dominion High Commissioners in London and British officials. This was so effective that on 2 December 1935 the Cabinet was reminded of the 'remarkable unanimity' between the dominions and the mother country on the question of sanctions against Italy. So intimate was this consultation that soundings were even taken on occasion from the High Commissioners as to the likely reaction of their governments to proposals even before these went to the British Cabinet.[14] At an early discussion with the dominion High Commissioners, Howard Ferguson of Canada, in July 1935, warned that the use of collective sanctions would find no advocates within the empire, and that the attitude of dominion governments was uncertain. Sir Samuel Hoare, the British Foreign Secretary, gave the assurance that if war were to come it should be limited and that everything possible should be done to preserve the League of Nations.[15] In a note prepared by the Foreign Office on the dispute it was acknowledged that if Britain were to go to war in defence of international order the 'practically unanimous' assent of the British people would be essential. Dominion concern over the racial aspects of the war, portrayed by Mussolini as being one between blacks and whites, was noted. Repercussions were expected not only from 'native opinion' in Africa but also from the 'other races' in the Far East.[16]

The dominion High Commissioners in London also headed their countries' delegations to Geneva and similar consultation took place there. Some were even anxious to take the initiative. Before leaving for Geneva Stanley Bruce of Australia, personally convinced that economic sanctions against Italy should not be enforced unless they could be made effective, suggested a 'deliberately dramatic' declaration by Britain and the dominions to the effect that they had 'decided upon a large increase in their armed forces to serve as a factor towards the stability of the world'.[17] At a meeting with dominion representatives at Geneva the South African Charles te Water, supported by Bruce, outlined a scheme of 'tutelage' for Abyssinia on the grounds that this could pre-empt German claims for colonies in Africa.[18] The dominion governments, however, seemed anxious for close co-operation with Britain: on 3 September the Canadian government indicated its willingness to help to secure a peaceful settlement;[19] the Australian government, though it felt that sanctions were impracticable and could lead to a general war, indicated its willingness to co-operate with Britain and the dominions 'in any action that will be conducive to upholding the principles of the League but most of all of their desire to ensure the unity and safety of the Empire';[20] South Africa opposed any compromise by the League.[21] At Geneva Hoare found the co-operation of the dominion delegates 'whole-hearted'.[22]

The High Commissioners were informed on 5 December that the British Cabinet had decided to support the proposal that the export of oil to Italy be prohibited. Both Bruce and te Water favoured a postponement of the decision to fix a date for this action, though the latter emphasised the need to avoid any appearance of weakening. Vincent Massey, speaking for the newly elected liberal administration in Canada under W. L. Mackenzie King, said it would loyally observe any sanctions but emphasised that there should be no repetition of an earlier incident which had given the impression that Canada was taking the lead in this matter.[23] A socialist government had been returned in New Zealand. Sir James Parr, the High Commissioner, thought however that it would be equally forthcoming in its support of the League.[24]

This endorsement of British policy by the dominions was challenged by the apparent concessions to Italy in the negotiations leading up to the Hoare–Laval pact. On 10 December the Secretary of State for the dominions, Malcolm MacDonald, was warned of te Water's fears that the League could find itself in the position of condoning the original aggressor. Parr felt that the proposals went further than anything the League had in mind. Massey was worried about the effect on public opinion in Canada.[25] The following day the Cabinet learned from MacDonald that the High Commissioners, apart from Bruce, were alarmed at the probable effect on public opinion in their respective dominions of the peace proposals. Te Water in particular was worried about the prospect that blacks might be armed. MacDonald hoped for modification in the details to meet these dominion fears. Consequently Anthony Eden just before he left for Geneva was instructed to bear in mind the criticism that the High Commissioners had directed against the proposals for an Italian zone of economic expansion and colonisation in Abyssinia: Eden should be 'on his guard against acquiescing in any modification of the proposals in favour of Italy such as M. Laval might be expected to suggest'. In line with the suggestion of the High Commissioners there should be no date fixed for oil sanctions.[26] The South African government let Britain know in rather 'violent' language that it disapproved of the Hoare–Laval peace proposals that emerged from Paris. New Zealand couched its censure in more friendly terms, but the Irish Free State and Canada said nothing. At a meeting on 20 December 1935 te Water suggested that if Britain were attacked it could not be assumed that the dominions would be involved automatically.[27] The British War Book arrangements were based on the assumption that the dominions were prepared fully to co-operate with Britain in warlike measures.[28]

Following Hoare's resignation the High Commissioners endorsed Eden's policy of taking stock rather than proceeding immediately to consideration of the oil sanction. But New Zealand was prepared to support any country that was attacked for applying sanctions. Massey advised that with the memories of the Chanak incident in Canada any such appeal for assistance should come from the League rather than Britain. Australia with its cruisers in the Mediterranean was likely to be involved anyway, and te Water thought the time had come for League members to face up to the implication of sanctions.[29] When, at the end of February 1936, the British Cabinet decided to impose the oil sanction the High Commissioners did not demur.[30] Indeed early in March, despite reservations over the complications of any South African participation, the British government, prompted by Bruce and a sudden New Zealand interest in air defences, raised once again the possibility of dominion co-operation over defence.[31]

The common front achieved with the dominions over Abyssinia was, however, seriously challenged by Hitler's reoccupation of the Rhineland. On 12 March the Cabinet was exercised by the difficulties of conducting conversations under the Locarno Treaty on the question. As Malcolm MacDonald pointed out the dominions were not a party to this treaty, but te Water had asked whether representatives of the dominions could listen to the Locarno conversations. The difficulty was that the governments of the Irish Free State and Canada were likely to reject any such invitation. It was decided to turn down the request on the grounds that that might lead to anyone being able to attend.[32] In any case Hertzog warned immediately that the South African government felt the European atmosphere was poisoned by the unequal terms imposed on Germany by the Treaty of Versailles, together with the French preoccupation with security and the consequent fear and distrust of Germany: European appeasement could only be secured by the negotiation of a new settlement. South Africa considered the proposal to purchase the co-operation of Italy against Germany by abandoning the League's policy of sanctions as subversive of the whole League system and a 'sufficient condemnation of French policy'. Furthermore, Germany's offer of a twenty-five-year non-aggression pact presented a sounder basis for peace than Locarno.[33] Two days later Hertzog was even more explicit: there was a danger that the commowealth could be shaken to its foundations. Not only might South Africa have to withold its support but also condemn Britain's participation in a war. After the German offer any country imposing sanctions against Germany or invading its territory would be the real aggressor: should France declare war against Germany on the grounds that Germany had taken military occupation of territory otherwise in its full possession, South Africa would consider France's act 'one of inexcusable aggression'.[34] The Australian government, though it could not agree that Britain was supporting France unduly, did advise that war would find little support in Australia. Australia supported wholeheartedly the British attempt to find a formula acceptable to Germany, pending negotiations for a general settlement with the German proposals as a basis for discussion.[35]

Malcolm MacDonald impressed on the British Cabinet that 'it was extremely important as negotiations proceeded to bear the position of the

Dominions in mind'. Their representatives in London did not agree with the French attitude and MacDonald therefore hoped that under any new arrangement Britain would not be committed to action unless an actual invasion of French or Belgian territory took place. Eden assured the Cabinet that this would be the case.[36]

In April it was evident that Mussolini's army was rapidly defeating the Abyssinians. Eden learned of the differing attitudes of the dominion representatives on sanctions: most favoured continuing them in some form.[37] But on 6 May Bruce's arguments for discontinuation swayed Massey and Parr.[38] Hertzog remained opposed to the lifting of sanctions and this view was passed to Eden on 8 May at a time when the Foreign Secretary was explaining Mussolini's desire for détente with Britain to the dominion High Commissioners.[39] Indeed at a dinner party at Massey's house on 22 May te Water insisted that sanctions should be continued indefinitely, or at least until Mussolini agreed to a scheme which acknowledged that Abyssinia, as a barbarous country, should never have been admitted to the League, and hence should be administered by Italy as a mandate with the specific provision that the natives should not be armed.[40] MacDonald told the Cabinet of South Africa's attitude on 27 May, explaining at the same time that while the High Commissioners of Canada, Australia and New Zealand favoured the lifting of sanctions they did not know their countries' attitudes. The line taken by the Irish Free State was likely to be similar to that of South Africa.[41] Pirow repeated the South African mandatory scheme to Mac-Donald and Eden.[42] This South African position made unity among the commonwealth delegations to the League impossible.[43] Pirow, however, was not particularly concerned over the British suggestion that sanctions be lifted: he explained that Hertzog and Smuts felt strongly on the subject, as did the South African Press which was inclined to be more liberal than public opinion, but that South Africans as a whole were not really interested.[44]

Following the isolationist and even pro-German views offered by some of the dominions during the Abyssinian crisis the preparations by the British government for the Imperial Conference of 1937 were of considerable importance. At the end of February 1937 the British Chiefs of Staff drew up a review of imperial defence outlining schemes to facilitate co-operation amongst members of the commonwealth. Dominion assistance, at least in the form of munitions, was anticipated in the event of a war against Germany. The ability of a dominion to help, however, did not constitute any commitment for that dominion.[45]

Foreign policy was a more complex issue. W. L. MacKenzie King, the Prime Minister of Canada, was as ardent an isolationist as some of his United States friends; General J. M. B. Hertzog in South Africa favoured his country's neutrality and had debated for seven years on this issue with General J. C. Smuts, the Deputy Prime Minister; J. A. Lyons in Australia was faced by a vociferous and influential Labour opposition pledged to fight any commitments outside Australia; only New Zealand was happy to come to Britain's assistance in time of war, but that dominion still clung to the ideal of the League of Nations and openly criticised any British deviation from the

Covenant. It was no longer possible to generalise about the commonwealth as a whole. Each dominion had to be considered individually.

The Imperial Conference chaired by the new British Prime Minister, Neville Chamberlain, met in London in May 1937 amidst the patriotic fervour of King George VI's coronation. Eden's persuasions did not win around the delegates.[46] Except for New Zealand the dominions remained opposed to European commitments. Efforts to secure a joint defence scheme for the commonwealth were similarly not successful. The dominions were willing to increase their defence expenditure in their own interests, but there were obstacles in the way of any imperial defence scheme.[47]

MacDonald was rather optimistic when he reported to the Cabinet that the policies of the members of the commonwealth were closer than they had been before the conference.[48] When the Prime Ministers returned to their various dominions it seemed that little had changed. Direct influence of dominion opinion on British policy at this time is difficult to discern. The Imperial Conference convinced Chamberlain that his policy of preserving peace in Europe was the right one, but to say that it caused him to embark upon it is probably an exaggeration.

Chamberlain, in his renewed attempts to reach an agreement with Germany and Italy, at the beginning of 1938, was partially limited by dominion opinion on the colonial issue. The Prime Minister, in drawing up his scheme of colonial development, had to consider South Africa's refusal to hand over South West Africa, and that country's sensitivity about Tanganyika.[49] The dominions were not informed of the scheme, and, in any case, the matter was dropped as Hitler said that the colonial settlement would have to wait. The *Anschluss* evoked little response from the dominions and, with the exception of New Zealand, they approved the Anglo-Italian Agreement of April 1938.

After the *Anschluss* the British government considered how to prevent 'an occurrence of similar events in Czechoslovakia'. On 18 March MacDonald warned the Cabinet Committee on Foreign Policy:

He had never favoured our adopting a particular foreign policy merely in order to please the Dominions. In view of our geographical position and our many connections and interests with the Continent of Europe, he had always thought that if we came to the conclusion that a particular policy in regard to foreign affairs was a right and proper one for us to follow we ought to adopt it irrespective of the views of the Dominions. In the present case, however, we might, if we accepted the . . . alternative of the new commitment to Europe in effect guaranteeing Czechoslovakia, find ourselves engaged in a European war to prevent Germans living in the Sudeten districts of Czechoslovakia from being united with Germany. On this issue the British Commonwealth might well break in pieces. Australia and New Zealand would almost certainly follow our lead. Eire would no doubt take the same line partly because she would feel that on an issue of this kind she could not take a line different from our own, but South Africa and Canada would see no reason whatever why they should join in a war to prevent certain Germans from rejoining their fatherland.

MacDonald said that he realised that this factor would have to be considered alongside other considerations, and might in the end be outweighed.[50] Two principal obstacles emerged in the Cabinet and the Cabinet Committee on Foreign Policy to a guarantee of Czechoslovakia: such a move might mean the end of the commonwealth; and, in any case, it would be logistically impossible to save Czechoslovakia.[51] The attitude of the dominions was considered, and was a factor militating against any British guarantee to Czechoslovakia.

On 30 August British policy was discussed at a meeting of ministers. Halifax pointed out that the only effective deterrent against Hitler would be to declare that if Germany invaded Czechoslovakia Britain would declare war: such a move would only divide opinion in Britain and the commonwealth. Chamberlain was particularly concerned about South Africa's reaction: 'The policy of an immediate declaration or threat might well result in disunity, in this country, and in the Empire.' Lord Maugham, the Lord Chancellor, thought 'that the other members of the Commonwealth would be placed in a very difficult position and the position might lead to the break-up of the Empire'. MacDonald considered the question of whether Britain should go to war if Czechoslovakia were invaded by Germany:

> The result of consultation with the Dominions would probably be that we should not be in a position to utter the threat. If, nevertheless, we made the threat, we should put a great strain on the loyalty of the Dominions and might break up the Commonwealth. The British Commonwealth of Nations and the United States of America together were the only force which could eventually check the progress of dictatorship; one day this combination might have to fight to defeat the growing evil. His Majesty's Government should not take a step now which would break the Commonwealth.

In the end the arguments of Chamberlain, Halifax and MacDonald were conceded;[52] it would have been unwise for the British government to guarantee Czechoslovakia at that time, as such a step might have broken up the commonwealth. From 12 September to 1 October care was taken to keep the dominions informed of British policy. MacDonald even said that the dominions had more information at their disposal than members of the Cabinet.[53] It could be said that during these weeks the High Commissioners in London formulated what was closest to a common commonwealth foreign policy, and were more effective in influencing British policy than the individual dominion leaders.

From 22 September the dominion High Commissioners became particularly active. Only Bruce of Australia supported a stand on the basis of principle. Te Water doubted whether the occupation of the Sudeten areas by German troops should be regarded as a question of principle, and suggested a compromise on methods. Chamberlain took special note of te Water's view. Dulanty and Massey agreed with te Water.[54] At a meeting of the Inner Cabinet of Halifax, Simon and Hoare – which for the previous week had discussed policy though not necessarily decided it – MacDonald explained the High Commissioners' views. Commonwealth support would be less likely over Czechoslovakia than if the issue were French security.[55] These opinions seemed to influence Chamberlain. On 25 September he told the Cabinet:

> It was clear that a position had arisen in which we might before long be involved in war. If that happened, it was essential that we should enter war united, both as a country and as an Empire. It was of the utmost importance, therefore, that whatever steps we took, we should try to bring the whole country and Empire along with us, and should allow public opinion to realise that all possible steps had been taken to avoid a conflict.[56]

Chamberlain planned to send Sir Horace Wilson to see Hitler with a message suggesting an international commission to put into effect proposals already accepted by the Czechoslovak government. This move might 'also help to rally the Dominions to our side'.[57] That day Massey was horrified that there might be war over the method of transfer of the Sudeten territory which was already ceded. He effectively banded the High Commissioners together with the view that failure to improve on the terms of the German memorandum should on no account involve the commonwealth in war.[58] Bruce, representing the High Commissioners, put this view to the Inner Cabinet on 27 September.[59] Chamberlain spoke to the Cabinet at 9.30 p.m. that day. He had reports that the Czechoslovaks would offer a feeble resistance. But 'more disturbing than this was the fact that the Dominions were far from happy about the situation'. Chamberlain read messages from Lyons and Hertzog to this effect. The High Commissioners also all had visited Downing Street that afternoon and made representations that pressure should be put upon the Czechoslovak government to accept Hitler's terms. 'The situation *vis-à-vis* the Dominions was thus very delicate'. MacDonald elaborated the position: in his view 'all the Dominions would sooner or later come in with us, but it was clear that they would come in only after making a number of reservations half-heartedly and with mental reservations about our policy'. MacDonald ceded that it was difficult to be certain about public opinion in the dominions, and mentioned the telegram from the acting High Commissioner in Australia which had contradicted Lyon's message. There was no doubt, however, about the unanimity of the High Commissioners.[60]

MacDonald met the High Commissioners immediately after the Cabinet meeting. Massey, te Water and Bruce stressed the dangerous reaction in the commonwealth if Britain went to war over the issue of how Hitler was to take possession of territory already ceded to him in principle. Chamberlain's fears were confirmed. Bruce and te Water urged these views on behalf of their governments and warned that the effect of war in such circumstances 'must be most seriously to endanger the future unity and cohesion of the Commonwealth'. Massey feared that 'the minority of Canadians who were not favourably disposed towards the British connexion would, long after the war was over, continue to use the fact that Canada had become involved in it to reinforce their view'. Te Water similarly agreed that 'South Africa would be most unwilling to fight on this issue and that the result of becoming involved in war would be to strengthen enormously the position of those hostile to the British connexion'. Dulanty took the same view.[61]

When the Prime Minister left for Munich he knew of dominion opposition to war over Czechoslovakia. Chamberlain disliked war, and feared the suffering that air raids would bring to Britain. But it was the attitude of the dominions which weighed most heavily in the account that Chamberlain had given of the situation to the Cabinet on 27 September. Chamberlain and most of the Cabinet still believed in the commonwealth. It seemed clear that a war over Czechoslovakia would endanger the continued existence of that body. The commonwealth still counted.

After Munich British policy was, in Chamberlain's words, 'to drive two horses abreast: conciliation and rearmament'. Australia, New Zealand and Canada helped Britain to increase production capacity. On the whole the dominions favoured the British policy of conciliation and rearmament and assisted the British government where they could, but were careful to maintain freedom of choice in their hands. The attitude of South African ministers forced Britain to reconsider the colonial question, and unfavourable United States opinion brought the refugee issue to the fore. Pirow, on a visit to Britain to obtain assistance for South African defence, acted as a messenger of the British government on both these issues. But Pirow's visit to Hitler showed that no further steps in the direction of the appeasement of Europe could be expected from Germany. Britain had to prepare itself for the likelihood of war, and it was necessary to secure the support of the dominions for co-operation in defence.

From January to April 1939 the views of the dominions were considered, but they did not decisively influence policy. Possibly the dominions would not have wished that: they were informed rather than consulted, and thus Canada and South Africa could feel that they were not committed by British policy. Inskip, the new Secretary of State for the Dominions, told the High Commissioners on 30 March of the Polish guarantee: in the time available it had only been possible to inform the dominion governments. Inskip felt sure that the dominions 'would not have wished that the United Kingdom should invite them to share responsibility for the decision'. Massey and te Water agreed. The other High Commissioners did not comment.[62] It was the views of the dominion High Commissioners in London that probably had most influence on the Cabinet.

The dominions did not always receive full information, and that which was circulated deliberately presented a serious picture of the situation in Europe.[63] The dominions were neither consulted nor informed about the changed defence plans which affected their interests directly. The Committee of Imperial Defence even controlled some Cabinet information that went to the dominions,[64] such as the conclusion that Japan could embarrass Britain 'by making a strategic disposition of her forces which would constitute a severe threat to Australia and New Zealand'.[65]

By the time of Hitler's occupation of Prague education of opinion in the dominions had progressed considerably. Hitler, with his anti-Semitic purges and broken promises, probably played as large a part in this as any efforts by

Chamberlain or the dominion leaders. The euphoria of Munich did not last, and from December 1938 the dominions made decisive moves towards rearmament, military preparedness and even conscriptions.

After Hitler's occupation of Prague, Australia and New Zealand were, in reality, committed to British policy. In South Africa Hertzog would not be drawn, and Smuts offered no lead. Mackenzie King, from internal considerations, and possibly personal convictions, tried to stand outside European affairs till the last moment. The commonwealth was not united after Prague.

With the Russian negotiations in progress attention shifted to the Far East in June. Japanese intransigence and maltreatment of British subjects in the Tientsin concession meant that for a time it seemed as if war would start in the Far East and not in Europe. This meant a serious rethinking of British contingency planning. If war did start in the East, it was unlikely that Germany and Italy would be able to resist the temptation to move in Europe. Britain might have to fight on three fronts simultaneously. The dispatch of a fleet to the Far East had to be questioned seriously, with obvious ramifications for Australia and New Zealand. Australia was especially concerned. On 24 June Menzies, the new Prime Minister, asked for confirmation that Australia be entitled to assume 'that in the event of war with Japan the United Kingdom government would send a fleet to Singapore within appropriate time capable of containing Japanese fleet to a degree sufficient to prevent a major act of aggression against Australia'.[66] The British could not give satisfactory assurances, and the Australians were able to infer that the sending of a fleet to Singapore might not be a top priority in the new situation.[67]

Throughout the negotiations with Russia the dominions were kept fully informed. Initially opposed to an agreement with Russia the dominions were brought around to recognising its advisability. The decisions on the policy towards Russia were Cabinet decisions: Chamberlain had to give way under pressure from his colleagues. The Cabinet and the Foreign Policy Committee did consider the views of the dominions although they were not a crucial factor.[68]

In assessing the influence of the dominions during these months it is important to consider the role of the High Commissioners in London. Their suggestions again came close to a collective commonwealth foreign policy. At times their influence was more decisive than that of the official telegrams from the various dominion governments. Te Water, Massey and Bruce were particularly active and they all, in various degrees, continued to favour the appeasement of Europe to the end. In this they did reflect the attitudes of their respective governments to some extent. Even Australia, though prepared to fight at the end of August, urged restraint on Poland. During this period some dominions even offered advice as to what British policy should be. This was the first time that this had happened.

Until May 1939 British contingency planning for possible war was based on the assumption that the dominions would fight. It was not until then that the Committee of Imperial Defence tailored its plans to fit the possible contingency of a dominion opting for neutrality.[69] The Irish Free State, however, was virtually not considered a dominion, and precautions were taken to prevent security leakage through that country.[70]

When war came Britain did have the support of four dominions. The months between Hitler's occupation of Prague and the march into Poland were crucial in bringing this about.

In South Africa the position was uncertain until the day war was declared. It depended on the stand taken by Smuts. By a narrow majority of thirteen votes South Africa went to war a divided country. The Governor-General, Patrick Duncan, and the British High Commissioner, W. H. Clark, both played their part in this. Clark confirmed Duncan in his decision to refuse Hertzog a dissolution of Parliament, and at a crucial stage in the debate leaked this information to a member who had come to see him on behalf of Smuts. Hertzog's supporters were spreading the rumour that if Hertzog were defeated, Duncan would grant him a dissolution and a general election. It was thought that some of Smuts's would-be supporters were hesitating because of this.[71] English-speaking South Africa, for reasons of sentiment and ties of kin, probably was always willing to fight for Britain. But it was in the minority. The vote was carried by those Afrikaners who still believed in the Smuts/Botha ideal of conciliation. Smuts's position is enigmatic. He might have seen his chance to become Prime Minister. South Africa declared war, but as R. H. Hadow minuted, it was 'torn asunder on social lines'.

Chamberlain's tactics of exploring every avenue of peace probably helped to convince Australians. Certainly the Australian Press was sceptical of the campaign to include Churchill in the government in July. Even Menzies, so impressed by Germany during his visit in 1938, had tempered his praise by August 1939. Menzies did insist that he favoured the British policy of keeping the door of the international conference open till the last moment.[72] The threats of the Labour opposition did not disturb Menzies as they had his predecessor. Curtin, the Labour spokesman, said that it would be a bold man who 'committed the lives of Australians as pawns in the fate of Poland. The safety of the Australian people impelled us to recognise our inability to send Australians overseas to take part in a European war.'[73] A few minutes after Chamberlain announced that Britain was at war with Germany, Menzies broadcast: 'Britain is at war therefore Australia is at war.' The Federal Parliament was not summoned on this issue as the government felt that no separate declaration of war by Australia was required. Australia fought for king and country. Menzies, despite his insecure position, ignored Labour criticism, and did not even concede that Australia had the constitutional right to make a separate declaration of war.

Although there had never been any question of New Zealand's loyalty, that country had proved awkward with its insistent belief in the ideals of the League of Nations, and because of the pacifist convictions of its Prime Minister. During this period both these obstacles fell away. The Pacific Defence Conference in Wellington in April convinced Savage of the need for an efficient army.[74] On 28 June Viscount Galway, the Governor-General, in his speech from the throne said: 'But in the circumstances of today my Advisers have most reluctantly been forced to recognise the fact that a full and effective application of the Covenant is for the time being, impracticable.'[75] New Zealand took the decision to go to war as a unified country. On 23 August Mr Hamilton, the leader of the opposition, assured the government of its unanimous backing.[76] New Zealand expressly approved the British decision to stand by the Polish guarantee on 28 August and just before midnight on 3 September the Cabinet decided to go to war.[77] In this dominion sentiment and ties of kinship were paramount. Defence considerations were only a factor. A united country was prepared to stand and fight by Britain's side.

In Canada the key figure was Mackenzie King, and he is difficult to evaluate. His confidence in Chamberlain, and the conviction that the British Prime Minister had done all that was possible to preserve peace, probably helped to convince Mackenzie King that he should lead his country into war. What cannot be assessed is the influence of spiritualism. Mackenzie King spoke in terms of the forces of good and evil.[78] Canada did participate in closer defence co-ordination with Britain.[79] Canada did not declare war until 10 September, as the declaration had to go through Parliament, but in effect Canada was at war as soon as Britain as all war measures were in full operation. Canada did not fight for a vague concept of collective security, but for the values of the commonwealth. As the High Commissioner, Campbell, wrote:

> While it would be untrue to suggest that Canada guards her independence one whit less jealously today than she did a year ago the visit of Their Majesties earlier this year and the ordeal which now faces the democracies of the world have served to show, if the lesson were needed as I think it was, in some quarters here, that equality of status is not incompatible with co-operation in common aims, loyalty to a common allegiance, and the defence of common principles.[80]

Chamberlain was particularly conscious of the need to educate the dominions to the realities of the European situation. Far away from the European theatre the dominions could not always understand Britain's concern with the dictators. But Britain was still, in a sense, an imperial power, and the dominions had to be carried along somehow. The dominions were not bound by British policy decisions: they were informed rather than consulted. That – with the exception of the Irish Free State which was hardly a dominion anyway – they fought, was little short of a miracle. Apart from New Zealand the dominions favoured the policy of the appeasement of Europe. They were not responsible for it: dominion opinion only confirmed Chamberlain on a course of action on which he had already decided. Over Czechoslovakia Chamberlain saw the reluctance of the dominions to fight, and the consequent break-up of the commonwealth, as decisive. This was the view he put to the Cabinet. As the European situation became more serious with Hitler's occupation of Prague, dominion influence was not so great. Their opinions were considered, and weighed against other factors. But care was taken to sift information on the European situation going to the dominions. In January 1937 Chamberlain was worried lest too gloomy a picture be painted for the dominions. In March 1939 the worry was that the dominions would have too optimistic an impression. Information was selected accordingly. The personal trust that some dominion leaders placed in Chamberlain after the Imperial Conference probably helped to secure dominion participation in the war. Another important factor was that Chamberlain did show the dominions that every means to preserve peace had been tried. This was essential as some dominions continued to favour the appeasement of Europe until the day war was declared.

Notes: Chapter 23

1   See R. Ovendale, *'Appeasement' and the English Speaking World. Britain, The United States, the Dominions, and the Policy of 'Appeasement', 1937–1939* (Cardiff, 1975), pp. 4–8.
2   See UK Parl. Deb., H. of C., 188, cols 520–1, 18 November 1925.
3   Public Record Office, London: CAB 23, 78, fos 330–7, CAB 12(34)1, Secret, 22 March 1934.
4   See W. K. Hancock, *Survey of British Commonwealth Affairs. Problems of Nationality* (London, 1937), pp. 251–319.
5   CAB 23, 80, fo. 185, CAB 40(34)3, Secret, 14 November 1934.
6   Prem 1, 174, Londonderry to Ramsay MacDonald, 18 June 1934.
7   ibid., P. Cuncliffe-Lister to Londonderry, Secret, 18 June 1934; J. H. Thomas (Dominions Office) to Londonderry, 21 June 1934.
8   ibid., Hankey to Ramsay MacDonald, 7 September 1934.
9   ibid., Hankey to Ramsay MacDonald, Telegram No. 212, Most Secret, 26 October 1934; Telegram No. 225, Secret, 14 November 1934; Personal, 15 November 1934.
10   ibid., Hankey to Ramsay MacDonald, December 1934.
11   *Documents on Canadian External Relations*, vol. 5, pp. 107–10, First Meeting of Prime Ministers, Secret, 30 April 1935.
12   ibid., pp. 110–13, Second Meeting of Prime Ministers, Secret, 7 May 1935.
13   ibid., pp. 113–16, Third Meeting of Prime Ministers, 9 May 1935.
14   CAB 23, 82, fo. 350, CAB 50(35)2, Secret, 2 December 1935.
15   Do 114, 66, fo. 3, 6109/A/111A, Meeting with Dominion High Commissioners, 29 July 1935.
16   ibid., fos 5–9, 6109A/111S, Note prepared by the Foreign Office on the Italo-Abyssinian Dispute and its Effect on British Foreign Policy, undated.
17   ibid., fos 9–12, 6109A/11S, Meeting with Dominion High Commissioners, 21 August 1935.
18   ibid., fos 12–13, 6109A/334S, Meeting with Dominion Representatives at Geneva, 9 September 1935.
19   ibid., 67, fos 6–7, A/270, Canadian Government to Dominions Office, Telegram No. 62, 3 September 1935 r. 4 September 1935.
20   ibid., fo. 16, 6109A/314, Office of High Commissioner of Australia to Foreign Office, 2 September 1935.
21   ibid., fo. 25, H. T. Andrews to Private Secretary of Ramsay MacDonald, 2 August 1933.
22   ibid., 66, fos 40–2, 6109A/17/528, Meeting with Dominion Representatives at Geneva, 1 November 1935.
23   See J. Eayrs, *In Defence of Canada. Appeasement and Rearmament* (Toronto, 1965), pp. 16–29 for an account of the 'Riddell incident'.
24   DO 114, 66, fos 42–5, 6109/A322/1, Meeting with Dominion High Commissioners, 5 December 1935.
25   ibid., fos 45–8, 6109A322/2, Meeting with High Commissioners, 10 December 1935.
26   CAB 23, 82, fos 415–16 CAB 54(35)3, Secret, 11 December 1935; fo. 420, Communicated as Draft to Eden just before Departure for Geneva on 11 December at 2 p.m.
27   DO 114, 66, fos 48–9, 6109/A/22/3, Meeting with Dominion High Commissioners, 20 December 1935.

28 Prem 1, 197, 6109.J/4, E. J. Harding to Sir Francis Floud, Most Secret, 15 November 1935; Memorandum by Hankey, undated.
29 DO 114, 66, fos 50–1, 6109A/22/4, Meeting with Dominion High Commissioners, 24 December 1935.
30 ibid., 68, fos 12–14, 6109A/22/7, Meeting with Dominion High Commissioners, 29 February 1936.
31 ibid., 72, fo. 129, 6454C/1, Sir Henry Batterbee to Sir William Clark, Most Secret, 12 March 1936; fo. 130, enclosing Meeting between Hankey and High Commissioners, 5 March 1936.
32 CAB 23, 83, fos 298–300, CAB 19(36)1, Secret, 12 March 1936.
33 Prem 1, 194, te Water to Malcolm MacDonald, Secret, 12 March 1936, enclosing Hertzog to te Water, Telegram No. 321, Secret, 12 March 1936.
34 ibid., Hertzog to te Water, Telegram No. 323, Most Immediate, 14 March 1936; apparently circulated to Cabinet on 18 March 1936.
35 Prem 1, 194, S. M. Bruce to Malcolm MacDonald, 17 March 1936 and Enclosure.
36 CAB 23, 83, fo. 313, CAB 20(36)3, Secret, 16 March 1936.
37 DO 114, 68, fos 15–18, 6109A/22/8, Meeting with Dominion High Commissioners, 6 May 1936.
38 ibid., fos 19–23, 6109A/3/9, Meeting with Dominion High Commissioners, 6 May 1936.
39 ibid., fos 23–6, 6109A/22/10, Meeting with Dominion High Commissioners, 8 May 1936; 67, fo. 25, 6109A/6/76, High Commissioner in South Africa to Dominions Office, Telegram No. 45, Secret, 6 May 1936.
40 ibid., fos 26–7, 6109A/22/10A, Note by MacDonald, 23 May 1936.
41 CAB 23, 84, fo. 216, CAB 39(36)8, Secret, 27 May 1936.
42 DO 114, 67, fos 26–7, 6109A/6/94, Note by MacDonald, 8 June 1936; fo. 27, 6109A/6/95, Note by Eden, 9 June 1936.
43 ibid., 68, fos 27–8, 6109A/22/11, Meeting with High Commissioners on 8 June 1936, 9 June 1936; fos 29–30, 6109A/22/12, Meeting with High Commissioners on 16 June 1936, 17 June 1936; fos 30–1, 6109A/22/13, Meeting with High Commissioners, 30 June 1936.
44 ibid., fos 27–8, 6109A/6/106, Note by MacDonald, 19 June 1936.
45 CAB 24, 268, C P 73 (37); Memorandum by Inskip, Secret, 26 February 1937; 1305-B, Review of Imperial Defence by the Chiefs of Staff Sub-Committee as amended by the Committee of Imperial Defence at their 289th Meeting on 25 February 1937, Secret, 22 February 1937; CAB 23, 87, fo. 25, CAB 10(37)11, CAB 2, 6(2), Committee of Imperial Defence Minutes of 288th Meeting, Secret, 11 February 1937 (copy), No Dominion Representatives present.
46 CAB 32, 128, fos 3–11, E (PD) 37 4th Meeting Lock and Key, 22 May 1937; pp. 5–12, E (PD) 37 12th Meeting, Secret Lock and Key, 3 June 1937.
47 CAB 32, 130 E (D) 37 1st Meeting Secret Lock and Key, 10 June 1937; E (D) 37 2nd Meeting, Secret Lock and Key, 11 June 1937.
48 CAB 23, 88, fos 278–80, CAB 24(37)5, Secret, 17 June 1937.
49 CAB 27, 623(2), fos 1–26, F P (36) 21, Lock and Key, 24 January 1938.
50 ibid., fos 1–27, F P (36) 26, Lock and Key, 18 March 1938.
51 CAB 23, 93, fos 1–10, CAB 15(38), Secret, 22 March 1938.
52 CAB 23, 94, fos 1–33, Notes of a Meeting of Ministers, Secret, 30 August 1938.
53 DO 114, 94, fos 3–4, Memoranda General.
54 ibid., fos 30–1, Appendix I, No. 16, F82/208, Note of a Discussion between MacDonald and Dominion Representatives, Most Secret, 23 September 1938; Premier 1, 242, fo. 47; the relevant paragraph is marked.
55 CAB 27, 646, fos 81–2, C S (38) 11, Meeting of Ministers, Secret Lock and Key, 23 September 1938.
56 CAB 23, 95, fo. 227, CAB 43(38), Secret, 25 September 1938.
57 ibid., fos 240–5, CAB 44(38), Secret, 25 September 1938.
58 DO 114, 94, fos 33–4, Appendix I, No. 19, F82/252, Note of a Discussion between MacDonald and Dominion Representatives, Most Secret, 26 September 1938.
59 CAB 27, 646, fos 102–3, C S (38) 15, Meeting of Ministers, Secret Lock and Key, 27 September 1938; *Documents on Australian Foreign Policy 1937–49*, vol. I, pp. 484–97, Bruce to Lyons, Personal and Secret, 7 October 1938.
60 CAB 23, 95, fos 261–76, CAB 46(38)1, Secret, 27 September 1938.

61   DO 114, 94, fos 36–7, Appendix I, No. 22, F82/288, Note by the Duke of Devonshire of a Talk between MacDonald and the Dominion High Commissioners on 27 September 1938, 28 September 1938.
62   FO 371, 22969, fos 13–15, C5265/15/18, Hankinson to Harvey, 6 April 1939; transmitting Notes of Meeting between Inskip and Dominion High Commissioners, 30 March 1939.
63   ibid., 23053, fos 293–5, C2298/691/18, Hadow to Sir O. Sargent, 22 February 1939 r. in r. 24 February 1939; Foreign Office Minute by O. E. Sargent, 22 February 1939; CAB 23, 97, fo. 293, CAB 8(39)2, Secret, 22 February 1939.
64   FO 372, 3316, fos 184–7, T2301/436/384, Foreign Office Minute by Hadow, 18 February 1939.
65   CAB 23, 97, fo. 211, CAB 6(39), Secret, 8 February 1939.
66   CAB 2, 9, fo. 32 Annex I to Appendix I, Menzies to Chamberlain, Telegram, Secret Personal, 24 June 1939 (copy).
67   ibid., fos 33–9, 14/13/72, Record of Meeting between Chamberlain, Inskip, Nash and Bruce, Secret, 28 June 1939; fos 40–5, Record of Meeting with Bruce, Secret, 11 July 1939.
68   CAB 23, 99, fos 275–80, CAB 30(39)1, Secret, 24 May 1939; DO 800, 310, fos 67–74, H/IX/129, Inskip to Halifax, 26 May 1939; enclosing Memorandum by Bruce.
69   CAB 15, 183A, DPP (P) 54, Enclosure, Memorandum by Inskip on the Position of the Dominions in the Event of War, Lock and Key, 5 May 1939, printed for the Committee of Imperial Defence, June 1939.
70   CAB 2, 8, fos 201–4, Committee of Imperial Defence Minutes of 354th Meeting DPR, Secret Lock and Key, 27 April 1939.
71   DO 114, 98, fo. 47, No. 66, C6/49, High Commissioner in South Africa to Dominions Office, No. 267, Confidential, 13 September 1939 r. 9 October 1939.
72   *Sydney Morning Herald*, 14 August 1939.
73   *The Times*, 25 August 1939.
74   F. L. W. Wood, *The New Zealand People at War. Political and External Affairs*, Official History of New Zealand in the Second World War 1939–45 (Wellington, 1958), pp. 72–83.
75   *NZ Parl. Deb.*, 254, Leg. Co, p. 4, 28 June 1939.
76   ibid., 255, H of R, p. 492, 23 August 1939.
77   Wood, p. 97.
78   Do 114, 98, fo. 39, No. 65, WG 3/1/2, High Commissioner in Canada to Dominions Office, No. 283, Very Confidential, 20 September 1939 r. 23 September 1939.
79   V. Massey, *What's Past is Prologue* (London, 1963), pp. 272–3, 278; FO 371, 23960, fo. 183, High Commissioner in Canada to Dominions Office, Telegram No. 286, Important, 28 August 1939 r. 29 August 1939.
80   DO 114, 98, fo. 43, No. 65, WG 3/1/2, High Commissioner in Canada to Dominions Office, No. 283, Very Confidential, 20 September 1939, r. 23 September 1939.

24 British Imperial Interests and the Policy of Appeasement

REINHARD MEYERS

Discussion of the empire's role in the formulation of British foreign policy in the interwar years is essentially a product of historical revisionism. Whether the dominions had influenced or even urged Britain to pursue a policy of appeasement[1] was of no concern to historians in the 1950s and in the early 1960s. Writers like Namier, Celovsky, Wheeler-Bennett, Gilbert and Gott, Eubank or Rock hardly spared them a line. When used at all, the argument exhibited certain distortions: the dominions not only supported appeasement as a logical consequence of their refusal to be bound by Britain's commitments in the 1920s, but even more so, we may presume, because they had 'little chance to do otherwise . . . Uninstructed as to the course of a personal and secretive diplomacy, soothed by urbane pronouncements by British leaders, they naturally opposed involvement in war and rejoiced that appeasement was keeping the threat of war at a distance.'[2] Yet, there are also contrasting points of opinion: after 1918 'every major decision of British policy had to be preceded by an inquiry into the likely attitude of the British Dominions'.[3] Fear 'of the commonwealth breaking up if there were war over certain issues was predominant in the minds of those deciding British policy'.[4]

I have argued repeatedly elsewhere that, in the context of British foreign policy-making in the 1930s, the dominions' role was a subsidiary and supportive one rather than one of taking the initiative.[5] British decision-makers employed references to the empire as 'a rationalisation for a policy already decided upon on other grounds'.[6] The argument about 'the need to keep the Dominions in step' came in handy 'to answer critics at home'.[7] It served to stabilise a political course embarked upon by British decision-makers mainly for metropolitan economic, military, or domestic reasons. Dominion influence hardly actively caused the selection of a specific course of action from a given set of alternatives. At most, one might attribute to it a retarding, at times an even more pronouncedly negative effect.[8] The dominions, as in the case of the 1937 Imperial Conference, 'set certain limits on British policy'.[9] If, however, Cabinet ministers 'came to the conclusion that a particular policy in regard to foreign affairs was a right and proper one for us to follow we ought to adopt it irrespective of the views of the Dominions'.[10]

Instead of reopening the debate on the dominions' role in British foreign policy-making, I would like to address myself to a related subject: the connection between the definition of British imperial interests and appeasement. One may claim that imperial interests on the one hand, and British attitudes towards Europe on the other, represent two poles between which overall concepts guiding foreign policy-makers oscillated according to the configuration of main actors in the international system at respective given points in time. More recently, one of those poles – the 'Continental Commitment' – has received substantial attention from historians;[11] in contrast, the other has been somewhat neglected so far.[12] Apart from Correlli Barnett's passionate indictment of Britain's road from 'the Workshop of the World' to 'an ill-defended, ill-organised, ill-developed and immensely vulnerable empire' having to rely on 'an inadequate industrial machine and insufficient national wealth',[13] only Britain's Far Eastern quandaries are adequately documented.[14] Therefore, the following arguments and conclusions can claim only very provisional validity. Their main objective is to stimulate discussion rather than to furnish hard-and-fast answers to as yet unsolved questions.

Some basic tenets upon which this paper is based should be stressed at the outset:

(1)   The definition of British imperial interest can hardly proceed along monocausal lines. Exclusive reference to financial, commercial and industrial needs and expectations, following the classic economic interpretation as set out by Hobson, Lenin and others,[15] would be as far off the mark as the exclusive reduction of empire-building to political and strategic considerations.[16] Even if a case could be argued for interpreting the acquisition of empire in terms of the material requirements of a nation the ongoing economic development of which seemed to ask for the continuous geographic expansion of the new industrial system into overseas territories, the argument would be lopsided if it did not take account of a quasi-ideological element. It was, as Lord John Russell's Colonial Secretary, the third Earl Grey, once explained, part of Britain's responsibility 'by the acquisition of its Colonial dominions' to maintain 'peace and order in many extensive regions of the earth and thereby' to assist 'in diffusing amongst millions of the human race, the blessings of Christianity and civilisation'.[17]

(2)   The sense in which the term 'appeasement' is used in this paper relates to a particular mode of international behaviour: that is, to a policy of recognising and settling international disputes by means of rational negotiation, diplomatic bargaining and balanced compromise, avoiding recourse to armed conflict. Rooted in classic political and economic liberalism, that approach stresses the need for peaceful conflict resolution in an international society pervaded by reason, harmony of interests and historical optimism.[18] Belonging to the 'Anglo-American tradition of thought',[19] it is diametrically opposed to the continental mode of thinking about international relations centring on the idea of necessity or reason of state. It represents a philosophy of choice bound to be ethical, searching for the best way of applying accepted moral principles to the regulation of international society's business. Against a Machiavellian philosophy of necessity, faced by the insoluble dilemma of reconciling morality with the pursuit of one's own

national interest in an international arena equalling the principles of actors' behaviour with the rules of a zero-sum game, this approach to foreign politics is characterised by Harold Nicolson as the 'mercantile or shop-keeper', as opposed to the warrior, concept of diplomacy.[20] Regarded as an aid to peaceful commerce, it assumed that a compromise between rivals is generally more profitable than the rival's complete destruction, that negotiation should be comprehended as an attempt to reach some durable understanding by mutual concession, that conflicting interests can be reconciled upon discovery of some middle point between the parties involved, and 'that to find this middle point, all that is required is a frank discussion, the placing of cards upon the table, and the usual processes of human reason, confidence and fair-dealing'.[21]

This 'particularly British form of diplomacy',[22] based on the claim 'that "Peace as National Interest" is a valid description of Britain's overall strategy',[23] cannot, in my opinion, be confined to the 1930s, as much as it may then have gained a new quality, given the effects of the Depression and Nazism's challenge to the *status quo* powers based on a qualitatively different approach to international affairs.[24] Rather, divested of its negative connotations,[25] the origins of appeasement might at least be traced back to the mid-nineteenth century[26] – if not to the period after the Napoleonic Wars and that period's concomitant broadening of the framework of international politics towards a global political system.[27] Formulated provocatively, appeasement's ancestors would comprise Castlereagh,[28] Gladstone,[29] Lansdowne[30] – to name but a few practitioners of the elimination of international grievances, the settlement of overseas disputes by peaceful means, the uniting together of the powers to further 'the common good of them all'.[31]

(3) Thus, analysis of the connection between imperial interests and appeasement too has to reach back into the nineteenth-century history of British imperialism. That history itself has recently become subjected to changing interpretations. Instead of seeing in the empire a source of 'power, wealth, fame, influence',[32] Britain's imperial expansion is now regarded by some as 'a symptom and an effect of her decline in the world'.[33] This argument is primarily based on economic considerations: while Britain's initial success in the international economy relied heavily on exporting, besides investment capital,[34] traditional staple goods,[35] failure to modernise and innovate – in particular to redress a distorted industrial structure in favour of newer, notably electrical engineering and chemical, industries – led to a decline of her position *vis-à-vis* her industrial competitors.[36] While her staple industries found 'an economic advantage in persisting with old, well-tried methods',[37] they became increasingly dependent upon 'traditional-style markets in India, the Far East and the Empire',[38] where steady profits could still be realised for their old unimproved products.[39] Thus, in this view, the empire played a prominent part in 'obscuring but at the same time aggravating a deep-seated malaise in the British national economy which set in around 1870'.[40]

In this context, not only could one tend to regard Britain, from the mid-nineteenth century onwards, as a satisfied power, but in terms of her standing in the international economy also as an imperial power in decline. The 'scramble for Africa', the transmogrification of 'informal' into 'formal' empire, could in this way be interpreted as primarily *defensive* moves, destined to protect imperial interests and markets against other powers' encroachments.[41] British interests in this situation had to be defined in a twofold manner: the preservation of the imperial *status quo – including* the securing of lines of communication by the acquisition of bases, harbours, coaling stations, territorial corridors, and the like – *and* the preservation of the open market principle, being based on equal access to and non-discrimination in those parts of the world where the British writ did not run.[42] Finally, it could be argued that those cartographic bargains with European rivals, by which Britain consolidated her position in Africa in 1890 and 1904, and in Asia in 1907, represented instances of that mercantile approach to diplomacy outlined above. The settling of colonial differences was arguably the only viable alternative open to an overextended, hard-pressed imperial power, which allowed her to concentrate her attention elsewhere – a diplomatic strategy comparable in style, if not in content, to that of a later period. Admittedly, the argument hinges upon formal similarities. Yet, one wonders whether further investigation would not conclude that appeasement is a typical response of imperial powers in decline to an inimical international situation.

The empire's position after the Great War was characterised by a paradox: in the moment of its largest geographic expansion its security began to wane. *Prima facie* still secure from outside attack,[43] it was, perhaps more than ever before, vulnerable to threats from within: local nationalisms stimulated by the experience of war, concessions to the principle of self-determination exacted as a heavy price for the collaboration of some of Britain's depen-dencies, damage to her prestige and authority given the fact that the Great War had turned into a struggle 'which Britain only just won, and with many defeats along the way'.[44] A not unfamiliar theme[45] reasserted itself: that the empire provided a classical example of strategic overextension, to use Liddell Hart's term: the possession by a state of numerous defence burdens and obligations without the corresponding resources and capabili-ties to meet them. Derived from racial kinship, common history, common political culture, literary, scientific, artistic and religious traditions, the empire hardly incorporated the logic of political and strategic con-venience: '[the] haphazard operation of history had produced what was, in the twentieth century, a strategical absurdity pregnant with difficulties and dangers'.[46]

Any analysis of imperial interests in the interwar period would first and foremost have to take account of the context of Britain's overall politico-strategic situation, governed by two groups of principal aims: (*a*) the maintenance of the strategic unity of the British Isles, dominance over the Channel and the North Sea, and the independence of the Netherlands; (*b*) the defence of the freedom of the seas, the keeping open of the maritime trade routes on which Britain's exchange of goods with the outside world and thereby her chance of survival depended, and the safeguarding of intra-imperial lines of communication, enabling all members of the common-wealth to support each other in case of danger.[47] The empire's geographic dispersal, not easily overcome by the communications technology of the 1920s and 1930s, implied three mutually interlocking complexes of prob-lems: home defence, the defence of imperial communications in the Mediterranean and the Middle East, the defence of India and Far Eastern interests – constants dating from the nineteenth century.[48] Given the consequences of substantial disarmament in the 1920s as well as a grave diminution of economic resources, Britain's strategic position in the 1930s was of such vulnerability that any threat to her originating within any one of the areas mentioned automatically endangered the security of the other two. She was faced with an insoluble security dilemma: the situation in Europe forbade her active intervention in the Far East as much as the situation in the Far East forbade her military involvement in European matters.

While all this constituted a serious but manageable obligation in relatively peaceful times, it turned into 'an impossible burden if the potential enemies could not be kept apart'.[49] In the last run, appeasement, the confinement of Britain's role to that of an honest broker mediating between European revisionist and *status quo* powers, evolved out of the necessity of matching the demands of home defence and of Europe with those made by the defence of the empire. A policy of conciliation and conflict resolution seemed to be the only means to avoid large-scale military entanglements on the Conti-nent, which Britain could only ill afford, and in which dominion support would not necessarily be forthcoming.[50]

What distinguished Britain's imperial position in the interwar period from her nineteenth-century one was a change in the configuration of potential enemy powers in Asia which made the inadequacy of her overall defence resources even more critical. While much of prewar strategic planning concerning the defence of India as a regional system[51] centred upon the Russian threat to British security in India itself and to British commercial expansion in the rest of Asia,[52] that danger receded *de facto* at least in the 1930s, even if it still formed part of military appreciations.[53] Russia's role as villain in the Asiatic theatre – and this was clear from the Manchurian crisis onwards – was taken over by Japan which menaced Britain's position in a double respect: militarily, by posing a naval threat to imperial communica-tions in the Indian Ocean, the China seas and the Southern Pacific, economi-cally, by drawing into the orbit of its intended Asian Co-Prosperity Sphere China and Korea, and by competing with British industry in the Indian market proper.[54] The history of British preparations against this danger is one of parsimony – witness the chequered fate of the Singapore base[55] – as well as of strategic fumbling. Each of the services had its own particular area of concern in those years. And while the Indian regional defence system might have continued to be regarded 'as the hub of imperial defence', in fact 'most attention was paid to the spokes . . . there was no integrated strategic doctrine'.[56]

The predicaments of British defence planning are fully documented elsewhere.[57] Should one provide primarily against Germany or Japan?[58] What was to be expected from Italy?[59] Could one send a strong enough fleet to the Far East to provide cover against Japan and yet retain enough forces in home waters to prevent the strongest European navy from gaining control of Britain's terminal areas?[60] Was the RAF to deter a likely enemy by bombing his territory, or was it to pit its fighters against the 'knock-out blow from the air'?[61] Ought the army to prepare for a continental commitment, or for imperial policing given otherwise limited liabilities?[62]

Throughout the mid-1930s, a common theme can be detected weaving its way, with an ever-increasing sense of urgency, through military appreciations of the various configurations of powers: that Britain, given her military weakness and deficiencies, ran the danger, first, of being embroiled in a two-front war in widely separated theatres;[63] and secondly, in a three-front war once Italy's role as a potential enemy had been established. Chances that a future war would be limited to any one of the three enemy powers were regarded as negligible.[64] In consequence, so long as that quandary remained 'unresolved diplomatically, only very great military and financial strength'[65] could, in the opinion of the Chiefs of Staff, give the empire security.

Keeping in mind that warnings like these could be multiplied nearly at will – why then did decision-makers not cut their responsibilities according to their cloth? Why did they not concentrate exclusively on the menace emanating from Nazi Germany, which, after all, had been declared Britain's 'ultimate potential enemy'[66] in 1934?

One of the answers to this question would certainly have to reflect the central position of the imperial idea 'at the heart of Great Britain's political culture' in the interwar period, its unquestioned acceptance as 'part of the existing order of things rather like the monarchy and the weather'.[67] Given this popular conception of the empire's place in British politics, it could be argued that politicians operating in a democratic mass society were well advised to give priority to the empire over Europe. This at least reinforced the case for appeasement made on other grounds. Indeed, with Conservative supporters of appeasement, imperial interests were a prime motive behind an approach to international affairs which could, by a British and 'above all an imperial'[68] government, be seen as the only realistic mode of survival in the inimical circumstances of the 1930s. Yet, against this it could also be stressed that the English 'in their romantic idealism about the Empire had failed to see it and deal with it in terms of English power', the white commonwealth above all 'representing the triumph of sentiment over strategy'.[69]

A second answer, closely related to the first, would dwell upon the governing élite's general perception of the situation: its members 'appeared more pre-occupied with the stresses within the Empire than with any threat from outside'.[70] Though it remains a debatable point whether 'British policy was becoming more dominated by Dominion attitudes than the other way around', there may be a fair degree of truth in the contention that, in her continued faith in empire, 'Britain had become imprisoned by it', though, amongst her ruling circles, 'the emphasis was now on maintaining what existed rather than engaging in any serious attempt to change the *status quo*'.[71]

Weighty as these socio-psychological considerations may be, the relative importance of the imperial connection was, in the final run, dependent upon the kind of war one expected to fight. A new theme began to be developed in strategic appreciations during 1937: that, over and against German attempts to settle matters by *Blitzkrieg*, Britain could only hope to survive by fighting a war of attrition.[72] In this context, the dominions might prove 'a decisive factor in the later phases of any European war',[73] placing Germany, in comparison with the British Empire, at a great disadvantage. Yet, we are back to our old quandary: if Britain's only hope lay in a long-drawn-out war of attrition, and if the empire was vital in that exercise, the problem still presented itself in simple terms:

> . . . an island lying off the shores of Europe, deficient in all the main minerals except coal, unable to grow more than about half its food and with a population of rather more than 40 million, was supposed to defend territories in every continent except Europe, covering in total about a quarter of the habitable surface of the globe and including about a quarter of its population . . .[74]

In such a situation, he would be a wise man who heeded the counsels repeatedly offered by the Chiefs of Staff: that the only way out of a situation in which European commitments reduced 'our ability to secure our Empire and its communications'[75] lay in 'any political or international action that can be taken to reduce the numbers of our potential enemies and to gain the support of potential allies'.[76] This, in a nutshell, represented, in the 1930s, the interlocking of imperial interests and appeasement.

> The maintenance of credit facilities and our general balance of trade are of vital importance, not merely from the point of view of our strength in peace time, but equally for purposes of war . . . If we are to emerge victoriously from such a war, it is essential that we should enter it with sufficient economic strength to enable us to make the fullest use of our resources overseas, and to withstand the strain.[77]

These assumptions, upon which Sir Thomas Inskip based his 1937 report on defence expenditure in future years, not only determined much of Britain's rearmament from there on,[78] but also the complex process of strategic reappreciation, military hardware procurement, distribution of forces and development of tactical employment doctrine, which in turn established the frames of reference for imperial defence. In their emphasis on maintaining economic stability as a precondition of national survival they also reflected the basic characteristics of a situation which had come about as a reaction to adverse world economic problems[79] – but a reaction heightened by the failure of the British economy 'to adapt quickly to changing world requirements and competitive standards'.[80] To describe, in this context, Britain's position in the interwar international economy in terms of crisis, to hold responsible for it a succession of certain historical phenomena and events – be it the Great War itself,[81] the 'economic consequences of the peace' (Keynes), the maladjustment of international finance contingent upon the reparations problem,[82] the return to gold in 1925,[83] the Great Slump and the Depression in the early 1930s,[84] the reduction of primary producers' purchasing power and adverse movement of the terms of trade,[85] unemployment and domestic welfare problems,[86] unimaginative governmental responses and failings of traditional economic theory,[87] or whatever – would not reach far enough, though, of course, all these factors exerted contributory pressures on Britain's international standing. Rather, what is occasionally – and perhaps somewhat unkindly – termed 'l'anémie britannique'[88] must, in the end, be judged in structural, longer-lasting terms: not as a succession of crises, but 'une sorte de maladie chronique',[89] the roots of which extend, as we have stressed, far back into the nineteenth century.

Again, the main theme is one of a fundamental contradiction between Britain's great power status and her peculiar economic structure, one of a widening gap between her commitments and her capacities to meet them. Economically speaking, she required peace, stability and ongoing international commerce in order not to fall back further in the international power hierarchy; politically and strategically speaking, concrete threats to her international position in the 1930s required a diversion of economic, financial and manpower resources to rearmament to such an extent that she ran a real danger of undermining that very position of modest economic prosperity upon which her international standing was predicated. In the late 1930s

> ... Britain was swiftly becoming bankrupt, and the harder Britain increased its armaments production, and the more determinedly it waged war, the quicker the financial collapse would be. Britain could either have a balanced economy and vulnerable defences, or adequate armed forces and national bankruptcy, but not both.[90]

Britain's economic plight, however, could supply us with another answer to our earlier question as to the importance of the imperial connection. Given her continued reliance on those older export industries which were, by now, 'becoming increasingly the dinosaurs of the economy',[91] she also came to be dependent more and more on imperial markets relative to third country ones for exports, investment facilities and returns, and invisible earnings to undershore her economic and financial stability.[92] At the same time her dominions and colonies, most of them overdependent on a few primary products, were increasingly anxious for an assured customer in Britain. Whereas international trade contracted in the interwar period, trade flows also shifted in geographical emphasis: imperial countries were gaining on others, both as markets and suppliers for Britain;[93] likewise, the proportion of inter-imperial trade in comparison to that with third countries increased.

While this statement has to be qualified in a number of aspects,[94] it allows one conclusion: that the empire, and Britain with it, was tentatively disengaging itself from the world economy, in an effort to sit it out until the advent of better times. Assuming a quasi-mercantilist natural division of labour within the empire – with Britain supplying manufactures, capital and immigrants, while the empire furnished primary products and food[95] – British supremacy could perhaps be re-established 'on the narrower basis of formal empire'.[96] If Great Britain could no longer be the workshop of the world, she might at least remain the workshop of the empire, and conceivably, the dominions would be grateful for it.[97]

What concerns us here is the fact that discussion of a sheltered economic system concept adds to the triumph of sentiment over strategy mentioned earlier, the triumph over strategy of the benefits of trade – or, more realistically, of what parts of the governing élite *believed* were the benefits of trade. Considering that the imperial protectionists' position was reinforced by a 'siege mentality' contingent upon the economic dislocations wrought by the Great War and the Depression,[98] one wonders whether it materially contributed to solving the basic problem outlined in the preceding paragraphs. The more the empire decoupled itself from the world economy and turned inward, the more vital became the need to secure its lines of communication – and the more imminent became the danger that imperial protectionism 'fostered economic nationalism, envy, hostility and discrimination from outside',[99] thereby putting the beneficial effects of the whole scheme into jeopardy. There was no escape from the vicious circle besetting a Great Power in decline – and appeasement could only halt the downward trend for a few elusive, illusory years.

Notes: Chapter 24

1 D. C. Watt, *Personalities and Policies. Studies in the Formulation of British Foreign Policy in the Twentieth Century* (London, 1965), p. 159 ff.
2 C. L. Mowat, *Britain between the Wars 1918–1940* (London, repr. 1972), p. 591.
3 F. S. Northedge, *The Troubled Giant. Britain among the Great Powers 1916–1939* (London, 1966), p. 627.
4 R. Ovendale, *'Appeasement' and the English Speaking World. Britain, the United States, the Dominions, and the Policy of 'Appeasement', 1937–1939* (Cardiff, 1975), p. 5.
5 R. Meyers, 'Die Dominions und die britische Europapolitik der dreissiger Jahre', in J. Hütter *et al.* (eds), *Tradition und Neubeginn. Internationale Forschungen zur deutschen Geschichte im 20. Jahrhundert* (Cologne, 1975), pp. 173–201; idem, 'Britain, Europe and the Dominions in the 1930s. Some aspects of British, European and Commonwealth policies', *Australian Journal of Politics and History*, vol. 22 (1976), pp. 36–50.
6 E. M. Andrews, *Isolationism and Appeasement in Australia. Reactions to the European Crisis* (Canberra, 1970), p. 213.
7 M. Beloff, 'The imperial factor in appeasement', in *Culture, science et développement. Contribution à une histoire de l'homme. Mélanges en l'honneur de Charles Morazé* (Toulouse, 1979), pp. 419–32; cf. in this context pp. 421 ff.
8 I am most grateful to Lord Beloff for having drawn my attention to this point in the course of discussion following my lecture on 'The Younger Children. On the role of the dominions in British foreign policy-making in the interwar years', St Anthony's College, Oxford, 16 November 1979. The situation is even more confounded by the fact that dominion opinion offered to the Cabinet quite often was that of the respective High Commissioner in London who in turn tended to be influenced by British supporters of appeasement, 'so that what was being invoked as though it were an independent source of information or criticism was only a deliberately induced echo'; cf. Beloff, 'Imperial factor', p. 422.
9 J. Garner, *The Commonwealth Office 1925–1968* (London, 1978), p. 87; revealingly, Garner continues that 'Chamberlain kept within those limits for as long as possible (though not necessarily for Commonwealth reasons)'; cf. also R. Tamchina, 'In search of common

causes: the Imperial Conference of 1937', *Journal of Imperial and Commonwealth History*, vol. 1 (1972), pp. 79–105, who argues that, by withholding essential information, Chamberlain 'relegated the dominion governments to a position of passive acceptance of, rather than active participation in, British policies' (ibid., p. 100).

10   Malcolm MacDonald, Cabinet Committee on Foreign Policy, 18 March 1938; FP (36) 26th, CAB 27/623, p. 159.
11   cf. notably M. Howard, *The Continental Commitment. The Dilemma of British Defence Policy in the Era of the Two World Wars* (London, 1972); also Brian Bond, *British Military Policy between the Two World Wars* (Oxford, 1980).
12   Unfortunately, due to the vagaries of the German international library loans system, I have not been able to use R. F. Holland, *Britain and the Commonwealth Alliance 1918–1939* (London, 1981).
13   Correlli Barnett, *The Collapse of British Power* (London, 1972), p. 15.
14   cf. in this context R. Louis, *British Strategy in the Far East 1919–1939* (Oxford, 1971); C. Thorne, *The Limits of Foreign Policy. The West, the League and the Far Eastern Crisis of 1931–1933* (London, 1972); B. A. Lee, *Britain and the Sino-Japanese War 1937–1939. A Study in the Dilemmas of British Decline* (Stanford, Calif., 1973); Ann Trotter, *Britain and East Asia 1933–1937* (London, 1975); P. Lowe, *Great Britain and the Origins of the Pacific War. A Study of British Policy in East Asia 1937–1941* (Oxford, 1977); W. D. McIntyre, *The Rise and Fall of the Singapore Naval Base, 1919–1942* (London, 1979).
15   cf. on this W. G. Hynes, *The Economics of Empire. Britain, Africa and the New Imperialism 1870–95* (London, 1979), p. 4; M. E. Chamberlain, *The Scramble for Africa* (4th edn, London, 1979), pp. 94 ff.; W. J. Mommsen, *Imperialismustheorien* (Göttingen, 1977), pp. 11 ff.; P. Hampe, *Die ökonomische Imperialismustheorie. Kritische Untersuchungen* (Munich, 1976).
16   cf., for example, D. K. Fieldhouse, 'Imperialism. An historiographical revision', *Economic History Review*, vol. 14 (1961), pp. 187–209, who suggests that imperialism may best be seen as the extension into the periphery of the political struggle in Europe after the Franco-Russian War.
17   Quoted in B. Porter, *The Lion's Share. A Short History of British Imperialism 1850–1970* (2nd edn, London, 1977), p. 14.
18   Reasons of space forbid to expound this view in fuller detail here; cf., however, R. Meyers, *Weltpolitik in Grundbegriffen*, Vol. I: *Ein lehr- und ideengeschichtlicher Grundriss* (Düsseldorf, 1979), pp. 38 ff.; the same argument is advanced by Iring Fetscher, *Modelle der Friedenssicherung* (2nd edn, Munich, 1973), pp. 38 ff.
19   cf. A. Wolfers, *Discord and Collaboration. Essays on International Politics* (3rd edn, Baltimore, Md, 1971), pp. 243 ff.
20   Harold Nicolson, *Diplomacy* (3rd edn, London, 1969), p. 25.
21   ibid., p. 26.
22   Paul M. Kennedy, 'The tradition of appeasement in British foreign policy 1865–1939', *British Journal of International Studies*, vol. 2 (1976), p. 196.
23   ibid., p. 198; cf. also G. Niedhart, 'Friede als nationales Interesse. Grossbritannien in der Vorgeschichte des Zweiten Weltkriegs', *Neue Politische Literatur*, vol. 17 (1972), pp. 451–70.
24   On this, cf. Bernd-Jürgen Wendt's paper in this volume.
25   On these, cf. R. Meyers, *Britische Sicherheitspolitik 1934–1938. Studien zum aussen- und sicherheitspolitischen Entscheidungsprozess* (Düsseldorf, 1976), pp. 19 ff., for a review of pertinent works.
26   So at least Kennedy's argument: cf. idem, 'Tradition of appeasement', p. 195.
27   This argument is developed by W. D. Gruner, '"British Interest" in der Zwischenkriegszeit. Aspekte britischer Europapolitik 1918–1938', in K. Bosl (ed.), *Gleichgewicht-Revision-Restauration. Die Aussenpolitik der Ersten Tschechoslowakischen Republik im Europasystem der Pariser Vorortverträge* (Munich, 1976), pp. 85–151.
28   cf. C. Bartlett, 'Britain and the European balance, 1815–1848', in A. Sked (ed.), *Europe's Balance of Power 1815–1848* (London, 1979), pp. 145–63.
29   cf. his Third Midlothian Campaign Speech, quoted in K. Bourne, *The Foreign Policy of Victorian England 1830–1902* (Oxford, 1970), pp. 420 ff.
30   cf. D. Gillard, *The Struggle for Asia 1828–1914. A Study in British and Russian Imperialism* (London, 1980), p. 170.

31 Gladstone, Third Midlothian Campaign Speech, quoted in Bourne, *Foreign Policy*, p. 421. I am of course conscious of some slight flaws in this argument: (1) actor's *motives* and specific configurations of the international system in their respective times may not easily be comparable: (2) by stretching the concept of appeasement as far back as Castlereagh it would merge into what I have described elsewhere (Meyers, *Sicherheitspolitik*, p. 57) as the non-interventionist variety of balance-of-power politics; (3) appeasement as a set concept originating from the debate of British policies in the 1930s could be denuded of its material meaning. Against this, I would suggest that we might distinguish between two general appeasement concepts: a *formal* one, which deals with a *specific mode of international behaviour* and a *material* one, which refers to British policies *vis-à-vis* Hitler in the 1930s. G. Niedhart, 'Appeasement: Die britische Antwort auf die Krise des Weltreiches und des internationales Systems vor dem Zweiten Weltkrieg', *Historische Zeitschrift*, vol. 226 (1978), pp. 67–88 offers (p. 71) another example for the use of 'appeasement' in a formal sense.

32 C. C. Eldridge, *England's Mission. The Imperial Idea in the Age of Gladstone and Disraeli 1868–1880* (London, 1973), p. 247; cf. also W. D. McIntyre, *Colonies into Commonwealth* (rev. edn, London, 1974), pp. 35 ff.

33 Porter, *The Lion's Share*, p. xi.

34 On the paramount importance of overseas investments for adjusting Britain's overall balance of trade cf. W. J. Mommsen, *Der europäische Imperialismus* (Göttingen, 1979), pp. 12–57 *passim*; on Britain's role as the 'underwriter' of the nineteenth-century international financial system cf. R. J. A. Skidelsky, 'Retreat from leadership. The evolution of British economic foreign policy, 1870–1939', in B. M. Rowland (ed.), *Balance of Power or Hegemony. The Interwar Monetary System* (New York, 1976), pp. 149–89.

35 Notably cotton manufactures, engineering products, pig iron, steel and coal; cf. W. W. Rostow, *The World Economy. History and Prospect* (London, 1978), pp. 373 ff.; also P. Mathias, *The First Industrial Nation. An Economic History of Britain 1700–1914* (repr., London, 1978), pp. 407 ff.

36 cf. in this context W. Ashworth, *An Economic History of England 1870–1939* (repr., London, 1978), pp. 103 ff.

37 ibid.

38 Mathias, *First Industrial Nation*, pp. 413 ff.

39 Porter, *The Lion's Share*, p. 141; Ashworth, *Economic History*, pp. 39, 153.

40 Porter, *The Lion's Share*, p. xi.

41 cf. Lord Salisbury's dictum: 'We only desire territory because we desire commercial freedom', quoted in Porter, *The Lion's Share*, p. 145.

42 cf. on this A. Hodgart, *The Economics of European Imperialism* (London, 1977), p. 7.

43 Though the first indications of strategic weakness had already arisen in the latter half of the nineteenth century; cf. P. M. Kennedy, 'British defence policy Part II. An historian's view', *Journal of the Royal United Services Institute for Defence Studies*, vol. 122 (1977), pp. 14–20.

44 cf. in detail Porter, *The Lion's Share*, pp. 250 ff.

45 cf. Lord George Hamilton, Indian Secretary, on the effects of the Boer War in 1899: it had made 'self-evident that our Empire is in excess of our armaments, or even of our power to defend it in all parts of the world'; quoted in D. Dilks, *Curzon in India*, Vol. I (London, 1969), p. 126.

46 Barnett, *Collapse of British Power*, p. 167.

47 For a more extensive review, cf. Meyers, *Sicherheitspolitik*, pp. 74 ff.

48 Howard, *The Continental Commitment*, p. 13.

49 D. Dilks, '"The unnecessary war"? Military advice and foreign policy in Great Britain, 1931–1939', in A. Preston (ed.), *General Staffs and Diplomacy before the Second World War* (London, 1978), pp. 98–132.

50 For a more detailed substantiation of that statement, cf. Meyers, 'Die Dominions', pp. 192–201.

51 On the main factors in brief P. Darby, *British Defence Policy East of Suez 1947–1968* (London, 1973), pp. 2 ff.

52 Fully documented in Gillard, *The Struggle for Asia*; cf. ibid., p. 26 for an analysis of the historical roots of British threat perceptions.

53   cf. N. H. Gibbs, *Grand Strategy*, Vol. I, *Rearmament Policy* (London, 1976), pp. 824 ff.; Bond, *British Military Policy*, pp. 98 ff.
54   cf. above, note 15, for references to pertinent works.
55   On this now in full detail McIntyre, *Rise and Fall*.
56   Darby, *British Defence Policy*, p. 5.
57   cf. Meyers, *Sicherheitspolitik*, p. 80; Gibbs, *Rearmament Policy*, II, passim; Bond, *British Military Policy*, chs 7 and 8 passim; also Public Record Office, London: CP 64(34), CAB 24/247; CP 205(34), CAB 24/250; CP 183(37), CAB 24/270; Cabinet of 14 July 1937, CAB 23/89, pp. 1 ff., for relevant overall strategic appreciations.
58   On this, *inter alia*, Gibbs, *Rearmament Policy*, pp. 393 ff.; Trotter, *Britain and East Asia*, pp. 34 ff.; Meyers, *Sicherheitspolitik*, pp. 90 ff.
59   L. R. Pratt, *East of Malta, West of Suez. Britain's Mediterranean Crisis 1936–1939* (London, 1975).
60   S. Roskill, *Naval Policy between the Wars*, Vol. II, *The Period of Reluctant Rearmament 1930–1939* (London, 1976), pp. 326 ff.
61   H. Montgomery Hyde, *British Air Policy between the Wars 1918–1939* (London, 1976), pp. 318 ff.
62   Bond, *British Military Policy*, chs 7 ff.
63   cf. for example CP 205(34), CAB 24/250, pp. 4 ff.
64   cf. CP 73(37), CAB 24/268, p. 13; Halifax, Cabinet of 22 March 1938, CAB 23/93, pp. 33 ff.; Hailsham, Cabinet of 30 August 1938, CAB 23/94, pp. 298 ff.
65   CP 73(37), p. 5.
66   CP 64(34), CAB 24/247.
67   G. Peele, 'Revolt over India', in G. Peele and C. Cook (eds), *The Politics of Reappraisal 1918–1939* (London, 1975), pp. 114–45.
68   M. Beloff, 'Appeasement – for and against', *Government and Opposition*, vol. 7 (1971/2), pp. 112–19.
69   Barnett, *Collapse of British Power*, p. 232.
70   N. Branson and M. Heinemann, *Britain in the Nineteen-Thirties* (London, 1971), p. 296.
71   R. R. James, *The British Revolution. British Politics, 1880–1939*, Vol. II, *From Asquith to Chamberlain 1914–1939* (London, 1977), p. 335.
72   cf. CP 73(37), CAB 24/268.
73   ibid.; cf. also Inskip's similar argument, CP 316(37), CAB 24/273, p. 2.
74   Dilks, *The Unnecessary War*, p. 101.
75   CP 218(36), CAB 24/263, p. 1.
76   CP 296(37), CAB 24/273, p. 11.
77   CP 316(37), CAB 24/273, p. 2.
78   cf. in fuller detail Meyers, *Sicherheitspolitik*. pp. 333–424; Robert Paul Shay, Jr, *British Rearmament in the Thirties, Politics and Profits* (Princeton, NJ, 1977); G. C. Peden, *British Rearmament and the Treasury 1932–1939* (Edinburgh, 1979).
79   On these, cf. in brief W. Fischer, *Weltwirtschaftliche Rahmenbedingungen für die ökonomische und politische Entwicklung Europas 1919–1939* (Wiesbaden, 1980); also D. H. Aldcroft, *The European Economy 1914–1970* (London, 1978).
80   Mathias, *First Industrial Nation*, p. 436; that this judgement was particularly valid in the case of Britain's older staple industries, but has to be qualified with regard to newer industries and the development of the domestic market, is shown by the contributions in N. K. Buxton and D. H. Aldcroft (eds), *British Industry between the Wars. Instability and Industrial Development 1919–1939* (London, 1979).
81   cf. Ashworth, *Economic History*, p. 285; Aldcroft, *European Economy*, ch. 1.
82   Summary in H. van B. Cleveland, 'The international monetary system in the interwar period', in Rowland (ed.), *Balance of Power or Hegemony*, pp. 1–60.
83   D. E. Moggridge, *British Monetary Policy 1924–1931. The Norman Conquest of $4·86* (Cambridge, 1972); S. Pollard (ed.), *The Gold Standard and Employment Policies between the Wars* (London, 1970).
84   J. K. Galbraith, *The Great Crash 1929* (repr., Harmondsworth, 1975); C. P. Kindleberger, *Die Weltwirtschaftskrise 1929–1939* (Munich, 1973).
85   C. P. Kindleberger, *The Terms of Trade. A European Case Study* (Boston, Mass., 1956); for a recent critical review of the traditional concept W. Fischer, *Die Weltwirtschaft im 20.Jahrhundert* (Göttingen, 1979), pp. 23 ff.

86　S. Constantine, *Unemployment in Britain between the Wars* (London, 1980); J. R. Hay, *The Development of the British Welfare State, 1880–1975* (London, 1978).

87　Ashworth, *Economic History*, p. 382; R. Skidelski, 'The reception of the Keynesian Revolution', in Milo Keynes (ed.), *Essays on John Maynard Keynes* (London, 1975), pp. 89–107.

88　G. Dupeux and B. Michel, 'Modalités européennes', in Georges Dupeux (ed.), *Guerres et Crises 1914–1947* (Paris, 1977), pp. 207–46.

89　A. Siegfried, *La Crise britannique au vingtième siècle*, quoted in Dupeux and Michel, 'Modalités européennes', p. 219.

90　Kennedy, 'Defence policy', p. 17.

91　Mathias, *First Industrial Nation*, p. 432.

92　I. M. Drummond, *British Economic Policy and the Empire 1919–1939* (London, 1972), pp. 19 ff.; idem, 'The British empire economies in the great depression', in H. van der Wee (ed.), *The Great Depression Revisited. Essays on the Economics of the Thirties* (The Hague, 1972), pp. 212–35.

93　cf. Mowat, *Britain between the Wars*, p. 436; in particular table 6; Porter, *The Lions Share*, pp. 259 ff.

94　cf. Drummond, *Economic Policy*, pp. 18 ff., and D. H. Aldcroft, *The Inter-War Economy, Britain 1919–1939* (London, 1970), pp. 289 ff.

95　W. D. McIntyre, *The Commonwealth of Nations. Origins and Impact, 1869–1971* (Minneapolis, Minn., 1977), ch. 20 *passim*; I. M. Drummond, *Imperial Economic Policy 1917–1939. Studies in Expansion and Protection* (London, 1974), pp. 31 ff.

96　Skidelski, 'Retreat from leadership', p. 179.

97　A. J. P. Taylor, *English History 1914–1945* (Oxford, 1965), p. 333.

98　McIntyre, *Commonwealth*, p. 318.

99　T. B. Millar, *Australia in Peace and War. External Relations 1788–1977* (London, 1978), p. 82.

25 The Road to Singapore: British Imperialism in the Far East, 1932–42

Wm ROGER LOUIS

Reflecting on the consequences of the Manchurian crisis, the British Ambassador in Japan, Sir Francis Lindley, in late 1932 drew an analogy based on Britain's experience in the Boer War. At the turn of the century Britain had stood in isolation, vilified by the European powers and generally denounced throughout the world for a war fought to aggrandise the British Empire. The absorption of the two Afrikaner republics into the empire marked a turning-point in British imperialism just as the creation of Manchukuo represented a landmark in the history of Japanese expansion. Britain had not altered her policy in South Africa because of international pressure, nor could Japan be expected to change course in similar circumstances.[1] Lindley had a sense of the historic drift in Anglo-Japanese relations. He implied that things probably would be worse and definitely not better unless Britain adopted a sympathetic attitude towards an expansive Japan whose problems were, after all, not dissimilar to those of the British Empire only a few decades earlier.

This historical perspective is not especially profound, but it was common in circles of a 'good solid Englishman' (as one contemporary described Sir Francis Lindley) who lamented the decline of Anglo-Japanese friendship. And it is useful in illuminating the salient aspects of the relations between the two island empires. In the same year that Britain concluded peace in South Africa, the long era of 'splendid isolation' closed with the conclusion of the Anglo-Japanese Alliance of 1902. During the First World War the British fleet was able to concentrate in the Atlantic because of Japanese support in the Pacific. The Alliance ceased at the time of the Washington Conference of 1921–2, for reasons that remained controversial in the 1930s. For those Englishmen who tended to be pro-Japanese, the appeasement of the United States and misguided views about the League of Nations had brought about the alienation of Japan. At the end of the Manchurian crisis relations between Japan and Britain nevertheless remained better perhaps than between Japan and any other major power.[2] During the 1930s a powerful group of British statesmen, including Neville Chamberlain (Chancellor of the Exchequer 1931–7, Prime Minister 1937–40) attempted to improve Anglo-Japanese relations and to resuscitate the spirit of the Alliance. This effort ended in failure. Far from managing to conciliate Japan, the British in only a matter of years found themselves faced with the disastrous possibility of a war in Asia fought against a former ally now in concert with their arch-enemy in Europe. The history of Anglo-Japanese relations in the 1930s is thus the history of one important part in the origins of the Pacific War; moreover, it is a cardinal theme in the story of the decline and fall of the British Empire. The British failed to check the erosion of British military and economic power, and, not least, that incalculable basis upon which the British Empire in Asia ultimately rested, prestige. With the fall of Singapore on 15 February 1942, the Japanese dealt the British Empire a blow from which it never recovered.

The perspective is no less illuminating from the angle of the British Minister in China, Sir Miles Lampson (later Lord Killearn). Lampson, also reflecting in the aftermath of the Manchurian crisis, emphasised, as had his predecessors, that the entire problem of the Far East could be summed up as one of Japan's position in China. He held strong views about the recent history of China and the interaction of Japanese and British aims on the Asian mainland. He believed that individuals as well as nations possessed the capacity to make decisions at certain 'turning-points' in their national history. These decisions had far-reaching consequences. This tenet held true for Lampson's own career in China. He was the key figure in the British revision of the 'unequal treaties' and indeed in the general Western accommodation of Chinese nationalism. He represented the nineteenth-century pro-consular tradition of assuming unquestioned British authority. He possessed a sense of self-confidence associated with such Victorian heroes as General 'Chinese' Gordon. Lampson later became a paramount figure in Egypt and the Sudan before and during the Second World War and afterwards in South-East Asia, in other words, two of the most sensitive and important assignments in all of the British Empire. His views are of particular importance here because he left what might be called the 'Lampson legacy' in China. He believed that Britain should not yield an inch to nationalist or anti-British forces. British policy would adjust and accommodate in kind, but the strength and prestige of the British Empire would be maintained against all comers, whether they be Chinese nationalists or Japanese imperialists.

Lampson defined the object of British policy in China as 'our determination not to permit ourselves to be deprived by forceful action of our treaty rights, and, on the other hand, our readiness at any moment to negotiate the revision of the old treaties in a peaceful spirit'.[3] He believed in firmness combined with a sense of British justice and he brought to bear an absolute determination not to capitulate to anti-British influences in commerce or diplomacy. He drove a hard bargain. By mid-1931 he could look back with considerable satisfaction on the negotiations with the Chinese by which Britain yielded nineteenth-century privileges *in return for* twentieth-century safeguards for British trade and commerce. Japan's intervention in Manchuria in September 1931 and the attack on Shanghai in February 1932 brought his work of treaty revision to a standstill. In one of his moments of contemplation on what the British Empire represented in Asia and other parts of the world, he philosophically asked himself whether there might be historical explanations for Japan's actions. He identified four momentous 'decisions' on the part of the Japanese leaders. He presented a distinctly British interpretation which is all the more interesting for the purposes of this essay. Obliquely his analysis serves as a commentary on adverse developments for British imperialism and the origins of the Pacific War.

Lampson thought that the first turning-point was the Sino-Japanese War of 1894, from which Japan emerged as an Asiatic power. Japan had the opportunity of 'playing the role of the champion of the yellow race in the fight for freedom against the Imperialist powers of the west'. Instead Japan chose the opposite course and joined the imperialist powers, herself imposing treaty rights on the 'decadent' government in Peking. This choice was a deliberate decision on the part of Japanese leaders, and one to which British statesmen at the time did not object. 'In those days, before and after 1900', Lampson continued, 'Russian penetration was the principal menace to British interests in the Far East, and we looked to the co-operation of Japan in preserving the integrity of China.'[4]

The second turning-point occurred during the First World War, when Japan, with the twenty-one demands of 1915, obtained special concessions in China that exceeded those of the Western powers. Again, this was essentially a decision to pursue an imperialist course, but now the British had cause for alarm. 'It was at this time', Lampson wrote, 'that we were first led to suspect that Japan's ambitions might be nothing less than to dominate China and become the leader of Asia against the White races.' This period was brought to a close by the end of the First World War. Here Lampson made a surprising omission in his historical survey. At the Paris Peace Conference the Americans together with the British deprived Japan of formal assurance of 'racial equality'. He certainly was not oblivious to the explosive nature of the racial issue. Indeed he suspected that the Japanese might exploit it to anti-British advantage. 'There is reason to believe', he wrote, 'that they, the Japanese, have in fact already [by 1933] made approaches to certain quarters in China, and that these approaches have been along the lines of pan-Asian doctrines and the alliance of the Yellow races under the leadership of Japan.'[5]

The third juncture was the era of the Washington Conference of 1921–2, when Japan reluctantly agreed to preserve the integrity of China and the doctrine of the 'Open Door'. In Lampson's view Japan's conciliatory attitude was deceptive. The Japanese remained adamant about maintaining special rights in Manchuria; and, despite a seemingly complaisant attitude towards treaty revision, their attitude towards China continued to harden. Japan, according to Lampson, remained 'unaffected by this post-war mentality' of anti-imperialism. Japan, in contrast to Britain and the United States, 'saw no reasons to give up her treaty rights and privileges except in so far as they could be used as bargaining factors to obtain her political objectives. In these circumstances a head-on collision between Japanese policy and Chinese nationalism was hardly to be avoided.' The result was the fourth turning-point, the Manchurian crisis of 1931–2, which Lampson could only describe as an incalculable setback for Britain. He wrote in June 1933:

Japan's great military adventure has, it seems, met with a full measure of success. She has seized, and to all intents and purposes secured, a

protectorate over Manchuria, rounded off her conquests by the occupation of Jehol, defied the behests of the League of Nations, and . . . forced
the Chinese to admit military defeat and to accept, at least tacitly and for
the time being, the loss of Manchuria and the *de facto* position created by
the Japanese army.[6]

Lampson speculated that it might be best for the British to reconcile
themselves to the Japanese take-over in Manchuria because it was preferable for Japan to expand there rather than in the Pacific towards the white
dominions. But this line of thought did not appeal to him. The greater the
Japanese successes on the mainland, the greater would be the Japanese
appetite for more aggrandisement. Lampson's attitude is important in
understanding British policy during the rest of the 1930s. Though British
officials continued to emphasise their generosity in treaty revision and
assistance to China, in fact British policy became less flexible because of
suspicion of Japan. On this point the explanation of the origins of the Pacific
War as one of a clash of empire certainly holds true for Anglo-Japanese
relations in China. The British were determined to hold their own, and Sir
Miles Lampson personified this determination.

It would do Lampson an injustice to suggest that he always painted the
picture of the situation in China in such black and white (or rather, perhaps,
yellow and white) colours, but there was a consistency to his views and they
were representative of certain British attitudes. Many of Britain's difficulties
in Asia could be traced to Japanese economic, political and military aggression. Rather than 'turning-points' it might be more accurate to describe
Lampson's junctures as representing stages of growth of virulent Japanese
imperialism. Though it might assume different guises, and sometimes
appear more conciliatory than at other times, Japanese imperialism was a
constant ingredient in the power politics of the Far East. In short, Japanese
imperialism might lead to the subjugation of all of China. Should this prove
to be the case, then, in Lampson's judgement, there would be no future 'for
British political influence in Asia, east of Singapore'. To prevent this
catastrophe, Britain would have to throw her weight behind China. 'A
united China, master in her own house, could hardly be dominated by Japan
or any other power', Lampson concluded. China would respond to moral
support against Japan and specific acts of British friendship such as technical
and financial aid by developing into a nation, if not exactly a nation along
Western lines, at least a pro-British nation. Throughout the 1930s, despite
setbacks, Lampson and Foreign Office officials of the 1930s in general
persistently held out hope for a united, prosperous and friendly China.

The Foreign Office was of course only one governmental department. The
Colonial Office had its own empire in the Far East and it would be no less
interesting to trace the turning-point of the 1930s as seen for example
through the eyes of officials in Hong Kong – officials who were in daily
contact with the traders and missionaries who formed just as much a real a
part of the British Empire as did the officials themselves. Of the military
branches of the government, the Admiralty had the most pronounced views
about the strategic situation in the Far East. The policy of the Treasury at

times rivalled the Foreign Office's, in part because of the severe problems resulting from the Depression. The India Office and the Board of Trade were also concerned with Asian commercial issues. The Dominions Office attempted to co-ordinate and represent the views of Australia and New Zealand. Various Cabinet committees (notably the Committee of Imperial Defence) and the Cabinet itself intervened in the affairs of the Far East from time to time. In short, it is possible to regard the British Empire in Asia as composed of several constituent parts rivalling among themselves for ascendancy.

Of those various bodies the Foreign Office possessed the longest official memory and greatest continuity of policy in Asia. Like the British government itself, the Foreign Office was a complex institution. Of the various internal branches the Far Eastern Department probably ranked behind its American and European rivals in prestige and influence. Nevertheless the Far Eastern Department had acquired a tradition and an intellectual distinction associated with the half-dozen of its members who had had careers in Asia or had long experience in the department itself. For example, Sir John Pratt (who retired in 1938) and Sir John Brenan (1937–43) had served with distinction in the consular service in China. Their expertise commanded the respect of their principals. Though the interests of the Permanent Under-Secretary, Sir Robert Vansittart, lay primarily in Europe, the Far Eastern experience of the supervising Deputy Under-Secretary, Sir Victor Welles-ley, stretched back to the days of the First World War and he continued to follow Asian affairs with an incisive eye until his retirement in 1936. The head of the Far Eastern Department was Charles W. Orde, who, like Lindley and Lampson, holds a particular place in the history of Britain and the origins of the Pacific War. He was an official of balanced and moderate inclination who saw the complexity of Britain's situation in the Far East probably as acutely as any of his contemporaries. His minutes reflect an agony of careful choices, and his reluctance to take a firm stand either pro-Chinese or anti-Japanese (or vice-versa) characterises another important strand of Foreign Office policy of the 1930s.

Orde was a person of supreme rationality, a virtue which, along with a certain aridity of character and style, perhaps explains why his reasoned views were sometimes misinterpreted as lacking in decisiveness. He was not popular among his peers and climbed the ladder of the Foreign Office only to arrive at the less than lofty pinnacles of Riga and Santiago. He was willing to grant the Japanese a rationality denied by many of his colleagues. 'Proud and excitable as the Japanese may be', he wrote in December 1933, 'they have shown caution and self-control in the major crises of their history.' He thought it understandable why the Japanese, with a population growth of one million a year, felt a need for space to emigrate – but he ranked the necessity for emigration below the need for trade and the control of raw materials. On the point of emigration he wrote: 'It is the stigma of racial differentiation, with its implication of inferiority, that they resent rather than the need of [immigration] facilities in practice'. This was a shrewd psychological insight that eluded many of his contemporaries. At the same time Orde argued that it was equally important to recognise Japan's real necessity for raw material and trade outlets. But, rather than a possible cause of war, these economic needs might help to keep the peace, at least with the United States and Britain. In the early 1930s, for example, the United States took 80 per cent of Japan's raw silk export, her most valuable exported commodity. In return Japan depended largely on the United States for raw cotton. Her trade with India was less important but nevertheless a similar deterrent to war with Britain. In other words Japan had powerful economic reasons for remaining on peaceful terms. How realistic, then, were common British fears that Japan intended to dominate China and extinguish British trade? Was there no hope that British and Japanese economic aims in China could be reconciled?

Britain's economic stake in China can be stated briefly. Though the old myth of the China market lingered on, by 1933 only 2 per cent of the world's trade went there, and Chinese purchases from Britain were less than half of India's. In the same year, 1933, China absorbed 2·5 per cent of Britain's total export, ranked sixteenth in the list of British customers, and held only 5·9 per cent of Britain's total foreign holdings. Almost 77 per cent of British investment in China was in Shanghai. By contrast Japan was China's best customer. Beyond any doubt Japan's interest in China was infinitely greater than Britain's.

Britain's needs in China, according to Orde, could be summed up in a single word, *prosperity*. A prosperous China need not necessarily be a *strong* China. Britain would continue to pursue the policy of conciliation initiated by that landmark in British diplomacy in the Far East, the December memorandum of 1926, or in other words the basis of peaceful treaty reform. Chinese friendship would be the best protection against 'the aggressive instincts of Japan'. Only over a period of many years, however, would there be the possibility of a strong and independent China. In the meantime China might 'muddle along much as she has been doing in the last few years without much "reconstruction" and without relapsing into chaos'.[7] This was not a cause for undue alarm. Japan, on the other hand, during the foreseeable future would have her hands full in Manchuria. This also should not cause any particular worry for Britain, provided Japan was not unduly provoked. 'There is no need to go out of our way', Orde wrote, 'to obstruct her plans in Manchukuo, and it will be a mistake to oppose her trade expansion, except where it comes into serious conflict with our own trade.'[8]

Orde's reasoned opinion may be taken as representative of British foreign policy in the early 1930s, at least in the sense that it reflected the consensus of the experts in the Far Eastern Department. It could be described as mildly anti-Japanese, yet it was not without sympathy. It looked out for British interests. 'We should recognise the real needs of [the] Japanese economy', Orde wrote, 'avoid any appearance of deliberate antagonism and confirm our action within essential defensive limits.' On the other hand this balanced view was not stalwartly pro-Chinese, and it held that the Chinese themselves were quite capable of adversely changing the situation in the Far East just as much as any of the other powers. There was the danger that too much aid and comfort to China would arouse Japan. 'Our policy should be to work for China's *prosperity*, but *not*, except with great caution, for China's political and military strength, the prospect of which must always be abhorrent to Japan.' Orde's outlook may be summed up in his own balanced words, which appeared to some to be indecisive but in fact were resolute: 'We should continue our policy of avoiding antagonising either country'.[9]

The Foreign Office generally tried to pursue the course of moderation, but that policy won neither unanimous respect nor consensus in the decade before the Second World War. Laurence Collier, the head of the Northern Department, for example, upheld the extreme view that power politics consisted of the perpetual clash between rival imperialisms. He espoused a view of British *Realpolitik* in the tradition of Lord Palmerston. Britain had no eternal friends or enemies but only eternal interests. He believed that Japan as well as Germany by nature was an aggressive power. 'I use the word [aggressive] not in the moral sense, but in the sense of wanting to expand at the expense of others.' Collier wrote those words shortly after the proclamation of the 'Amau doctrine' of April 1934, which the British interpreted as a Japanese Monroe Doctrine for Asia or, in Collier's words, Tokyo's declaration 'warning other powers off China'. He believed that Britain should respond by vigilantly maintaining the *status quo* throughout the world. Accommodation with either Japan or Germany would be an impossibility. 'A Power vitally interested in the maintenance of the *status quo*, as we are, can keep on tolerable day-to-day terms with Japan, as with Germany, but cannot hope to do more than that, in the long run, and ought not to want to do so.'[10] He thought that any suggestion of bargaining for security in China should be condemned. If Britain acquiesced in Japanese control of China, or a Japanese attack on Russia, any hope of Britain thereby improving her own position should be regarded as a dangerous fallacy comparable to the illusion that German attention would be diverted from Britain by encouraging the Germans to swallow Austria. 'In either case the "aggressive" Power, having increased its strength, would in the long run become an even greater danger than it is now.'[11]

Collier represented an important element in the Foreign Office's intellectual make-up. Japanese expansion should be resisted, just as the imperialist ambitions of Germany should be checked. Unstinting efforts should be made in Asia as in Europe to protect the British Empire:

> Japan is the determined enemy of all European interests in China, including our own, and . . . an understanding with her to safeguard those interests is therefore impossible . . . unless we are prepared to sacrifice our whole position in the Far East, with effects which would not be confined to those regions – unless, indeed, we are prepared to contemplate losing most of our trade with Asia as a whole, and holding all our Asiatic possessions on sufferance from Japan, we must take every possible step to keep Japan in check – build up the Singapore base, cultivate good relations with the Americans, the Dutch, the French and all others whose interests are threatened with a view to concerted measures against further Japanese aggression, and . . . see to it, as far as we can, that Russia is kept where she now is, in the Franco-British orbit, and not allowed to drift into the German-Japanese orbit.[12]

The chronology of this clear warning about a possible Japanese–German link is significant. During 1934 British attitudes hardened. Analogies began to appear in the minutes of the Foreign Office officials about the possibility of a 'Hitlerite revolution' in Japan. Again in Collier's words, Japanese policy 'is directed by nationalist-military elements preaching a philosophy of expansion by force even more openly than Herr Hitler preaches it in Germany'.[13] He penned those thoughts linking the philosophy of Hitler with the ideology of the militarists of Japan at a key time in the history of British rearmament, February 1934.

February 1934 is a convenient landmark because at that time Sir Robert Vansittart, the Permanent Under-Secretary at the Foreign Office, signed his name to a report on defence deficiencies by the Defence Requirements Committee (a sub-committee of the Committee of Imperial Defence).[14] He did so along with Sir Warren Fisher, the Permanent Secretary at the Treasury. Vansittart and Fisher together constituted two of the most powerful voices in the civil service. The report identified Germany as the long-range potential enemy of the British Empire. The corollary of that proposition was the necessity to remain on good terms with Japan, though it is important to note that the report also urged the completion of the Singapore base. Both Vansittart and Fisher were obsessed with Germany. They differed in their attitude towards Japan. Vansittart, wishing to devote all energies towards Germany, was less assertive in his views about the Far East. In general he followed the line of the Far Eastern Department and the Deputy Under-Secretary, Sir Victor Wellesley. For example, Vansittart concurred in the following minute by Wellesley:

> The Anglo-Japanese Alliance was abrogated for several very good reasons. In the first place it had outlived its usefulness and had degenerated into a sort of umbrella under which the Japanese considered themselves safe to perpetrate every kind of iniquity in China which was bringing us into bad odour with the Chinese. Secondly the renewal of the Alliance would have gravely endangered our relations not only with America, which were at the time considered, and I think still are, of paramount importance, but with Canada also. But for the disappearance of the Alliance there would have been no Washington Naval Agreement in 1922.[15]

Vansittart agreed with Wellesley and Orde that, while nothing should be done to antagonise either Japan or China, nothing also should be done to try to realign Britain's policy to Japan's advantage. Vansittart was more flexible in his attitude towards Japan than towards Germany; but he disfavoured concessions that might appear to the Japanese to be a sign of weakness. He believed that the Japanese had their hands full in Manchuria and could be restrained from further aggression by a stiff attitude on the part of the other great powers concerned with China. 'Vansittartism' in the Far East was thus a moderate but firm force, and it was rather vague in its application. Often as not it carried a philosophical or moral message. For example: 'If we show that we are really about to rehabilitate ourselves as a nation – until others cease to impose the crude test – we shall be able to look after ourselves and our interests without serious challenge.' 'If we don't', he concluded, in the Far East as elsewhere, the British would have to admit that they were 'impotent'. More concretely Vansittart wished simply to avoid a collision with Japan. In a remark that sums up his general ideas in the mid-1930s, he wrote that 'we are in no condition to have trouble with Japan. The state of Europe is far too delicate and dangers are perhaps far too near.'[16]

By contrast Sir Warren Fisher believed that Britain should take active and specific steps to reverse the drift into Anglo-Japanese antagonism.[17] To Fisher's restive and creative mind there was one self-obvious and imperative truth about the defence of the British Empire. It surpassed all others. It recurred in his writings. '*We cannot simultaneously fight Japan and the strongest European naval Power.*'[18] Though he agreed with Vansittart and the Foreign Office that the British should not negotiate with the Japanese from a position of weakness, he saw no reason whatsoever to prepare for a war in the Far East. The danger lay nearer to home. It could be summed up in the phrase 'the German menace'. That danger would be considerably lessened if the British fleet were free to strike in European waters. With that object in view Fisher was prepared to go to almost any length to win Japanese friendship. '[W]e not merely cannot afford further to alienate Japan, but it is an imperative and pressing need for us to effect a genuine and lasting reconciliation with her.'[19] Thus to Fisher the stakes could not be higher or the issues clearer. Britain's survival against Germany depended on a benevolent or at least a neutral Japan. With an insight that proved to be historically accurate, he saw that the British Empire could not survive an onslaught in Asia while fighting for survival in Europe and the Middle East.

Fisher knew of course that an Anglo-Japanese *rapprochement* would create an adverse reaction in the United States. He was entirely willing to run this risk. Indeed a distinctly anti-American sentiment runs through his minutes. Not since the days of Lord Curzon did any British official articulate such exasperation at the unpredictability and fickleness of the Americans. Expressing his ideas about the United States in relation to Japan and Germany, he wrote:

It is common ground that we cannot successfully fight both Japan and Germany at the same time. The first essential, therefore, to our own safety is that we must be free to concentrate our strength where it is most needed . . . What, then is the prime condition for attaining this essential object of definitely relieving ourselves of any danger of being involved in a war with Japan? I suggest that the first and, indeed, cardinal requirement for this end is the disentanglement of ourselves from the United States of America.[20]

To Fisher's dismay as well as the Admiralty's, the battlecry 'Rule Britannia!' had been replaced by the degrading slogan 'Rule Columbia!' at the Washington Conference. The Americans had actively promoted Anglo-Japanese discord. They wanted to possess 'an unlimited luxury armada' for reasons that ultimately could only be described as arrogance and vanity. Such rhetorical excesses did not blind Fisher to an important point: it seemed quite improbable that the United States would attack the British Empire. The Americans could not be depended on to come to Britain's aid and in any case probably would do nothing; but they would not become a belligerent in the event of war. Thus it seemed clear to Fisher that Britain should take whatever risks might be necessary in Anglo-American relations in order to bring about 'a thorough and lasting accommodation with the Japanese'.

Neville Chamberlain's ideas were in line with Fisher's and were only slightly more cautious. Since 1931 Chamberlain had been Chancellor of the Exchequer. He conceived of his office as one responsible for the resources of the British Empire at large rather than limited to purely financial questions. He did not hesitate in attempting to find solutions for difficult general problems such as rearmament. Like Fisher he recognised that rearmament could proceed at only a slow pace and that Britain could never be adequately prepared to wage war simultaneously in Asia and Europe. He also shared with Fisher a scepticism about the United States. '[D]on't let us be browbeaten by her', he wrote in September 1934. 'She will never repay us for sacrificing our interests in order to conciliate her and if we maintain at once a bold and a frank attitude towards her I am not afraid of the result.'[21]

Chamberlain hoped that the Naval Conference of 1935 could be used as an opportunity to bring about a closer understanding with the Japanese. Specifically he thought it possible and desirable to build into the Naval Conference not only an agreement about rearmament and technical naval issues but also 'a gentleman's understanding' between Britain and Japan (and the United States) 'not to fight one another for the next ten years'. In short, Chamberlain argued for a non-aggression pact with Japan. 'The main point to be kept in mind', he wrote to the Foreign Secretary, 'is that the *fons et origo* of all our European troubles is Germany.' Whether it be a matter of two, five, or ten years, Chamberlain believed that trouble with Germany would come, and that Japanese friendship might determine not only the future of Great Britain but the whole of the British Empire.

Chamberlain together with Sir John Simon explored the possibilities of drawing closer to Japan. 'I can't help reflecting', the Chancellor wrote to the Foreign Secretary, 'that if you could bring off an agreement with Japan . . . it would stamp your tenure of office with the special distinction that is attached to memorable historical events, and, incidentally would add greatly to the prestige of the National Government in the most difficult of all fields.'[22] Simon was receptive to these ideas. The experience of the Manchurian crisis had driven home to him the difficulties of co-operating with the United States and supporting the League. For his efforts to steer a balanced course he had been reproached for working behind the back of the Americans and undermining the principles of the League. Though he had no personal high regard for the yellow men of the 'anthill' (his phrase), he grasped the complexity of the Manchurian problem and refused to heap all the blame on Japan. He wanted to be *pro*-League without being *anti*-Japan. He wished to protect British trading interests without antagonising China. He hoped to patch up minor quarrels with Japan without offending the United States. He recognised the Japanese sense of national pride as a legitimate force in international affairs. He thought it undesirable to try to impose a naval quota on the Japanese that they would regard as unfair. As with racial equality, so with naval parity, which he believed the Japanese regarded as a matter of national prestige. 'I do not believe that Japan will accept an inferior ratio imposed by Treaty', Simon wrote to Vansittart. 'Japan feels the impulses of "equality of status" as much as Germany.' Along with Chamberlain, Simon hoped that a revival of the 'atmosphere' of the Anglo-Japanese Alliance might alleviate some of Japan's anti-Western sentiment and help to stabilise the situation in the Far East. 'As regards [a] non-aggression pact', he wrote, '*why not?*'[23]

Simon and Chamberlain emerged as the two leaders of the pro-Japanese movement within the Cabinet. From their respective vantage-points of the Exchequer and the Foreign Office the two of them could argue a vigorous case on grounds of economy as well as on the need to lessen tension in the Far East. The attitude of the Cabinet as a whole was characterised by a concern for the cost of armaments, as reflected in the decision to accept only one-third of the Defence Requirements Committee's projected expenditures.[24] The British public and Parliament would not tolerate an extensive programme of rearmament. The Cabinet's priority lay with the development of the air force for protection against Germany which meant that only inadequate defence measures could be taken against Japan. In Chamberlain's writings as in Fisher's there ran the dominant proposition 'that we cannot provide simultaneously for hostilities with Japan and Germany and that the latter is the problem to which we must now address ourselves'.[25] To Chamberlain as to Fisher this conclusion led to the clearcut necessity for *rapprochement* with Japan. Simon accepted the logic of the pro-Japanese stand but he was less resolute. Characteristically he weighed both sides of the question. A non-aggression pact with Japan would be misunderstood by the Americans; and he saw that British security in the Pacific in the long run would rest with the United States. In this sense history proved Simon to be just as right as Chamberlain. Chamberlain perceived that a hostile Japan would destroy the British Empire in Asia, but Simon saw that its ultimate protector and means of resurrection would be the United States.

Simon and Chamberlain hoped to achieve a quasi-recognition of Manchukuo, phrased so that it would not blatantly appear to contradict the non-recognition policy of the United States and the League. Japan would guarantee the integrity of China proper, which would signify the end of Japanese ambitions for expansion. On the naval side of the equation, the British hoped that a non-aggression pact might discourage both the Japanese and the Americans from a programme of unlimited building.[26] The project eventually foundered because of Japanese scepticism and the stalemate in the naval discussions of late 1934; but long before then it had encountered heavy attacks within British circles.

These assaults influenced Simon more than Chamberlain. Simon perceived the pro-American sentiment of the Prime Minister, Ramsay MacDonald. He listened sympathetically to Sir Maurice Hankey (secretary to the Cabinet and the Committee of Imperial Defence), who argued that dependence on Japan would mean the end of the sea power of the British Empire. And he faced strong criticism within the Foreign Office itself. Though he tried to keep his permanent officials at arm's length, he recognised the strength of their arguments, especially those of Charles Orde. These varied influences help to explain why Simon responded to the idea of Anglo-Japanese *rapprochement* at one moment as 'a flash in the pan', at another with mild enthusiasm, and most often with that indecisiveness that critics have identified as a fault in his character.

Though by no means an 'Imperial' statesman by interest or temperament, Simon clearly saw the issues at stake in the Far East for the empire-commonwealth as a whole. His broader vision is apparent in a document written in November 1934 when General J. C. Smuts of South Africa was in London. Smuts attended a meeting at the Dominions Office on an occasion when Simon candidly expounded the dilemmas facing the British. Smuts brought to bear on the discussion his wide knowledge of the First World War and its legacies as well as his views on the commonwealth and the League of Nations. There was a vigorous exchange of ideas.

After explaining the complex and detailed issues of the naval conversations, Simon stated that the Japanese believed that they had nothing to lose by having no naval agreement at all. They demanded equality with the other Great powers and, failing to reach it through international agreement, would attempt to achieve it on their own. There would be increasing antagonism between the Japanese and the Americans. Simon predicted a bleak picture of the Pacific basin – in short, one of anarchy that would exacerbate the European situation because France and Italy also belonged to the Washington treaty system. Smuts responded to Simon's reasoned exposition with questions that indicate his reluctance to believe in the severity of the crisis. He asked whether Japan might be bluffing. He inquired whether there might be a way of enabling her to 'save her face'. He stated that in any event the British Empire should keep company with the United States. At this stage of the discussion Simon did not necessarily agree. 'The British Empire did not want to stand in with the United States of America', he said, 'if by doing so she made a certain enemy of Japan'.[27]

Smuts then made it pointedly clear that if there was ultimately going to be a war in the Pacific, then the British Empire should unite with the United States. Far from being a danger to the British fleet, the size of the American navy should be a comfort. If Japan were truly an aggressor, then the British Empire would have to stand up and fight. There could be no appeasement.[28] Smuts drew a parallel with the Roman Empire. The frontiers of the Roman Empire had been land frontiers, while those of the British were sea frontiers.

Naval defence went to the roots of her Imperial defence system. If Japan was now out to establish a mastery in the East, and to this end intended to build nearer to the British [naval] strength, it became a very serious matter for the Empire. There was then a threat to the whole Imperial system. If the British Empire made concessions to Japan which went too far, then she would become a second rate Power and go the way that the Roman Empire had gone.[29]

Smuts argued forcefully that the British must keep their position in the race and at the same time maintain good relations with the United States. Simon now yielded to Smuts's line of argument, saying that friendship with the Americans was a *sine qua non*. He lamented American unpredictability, but there was no question that he and most other Englishmen of the mid-1930s, when pressed to their ultimate position, hoped that over the longhaul the British Empire would stand side by side with the United States.

An Anglo-Japanese reconciliation might rupture the tenuous Anglo-American friendship, and it would also affect the entire network of international relations not only in the Far East but also in Europe. Within the Foreign Office the most weighty analysis of the far-reaching consequences of a *rapprochement* came from the pen of Charles Orde. Orde pointed out that at the other end of the ideological spectrum Russia was the key. Despite the ideological antipathy shared by most British (as well as American) officials towards the Soviet regime, they regarded Russia as a valuable counter-weight against both Japan and Germany. Anything that Britain might do to weaken Russia in the Far East would increase the danger of Germany. 'An Anglo-Japanese pact', Orde wrote, '. . . can hardly have any other effect.' It might also encourage Japanese designs for an attack on Russia, which, if successful, might lead to further Japanese aggression in South-East Asia: 'A pact will surely bring nearer the day when she will attack Russia and then, after a pause for recovery from the effort, proceed against the East Indies'.[30]

Not least, in Orde's view, an Anglo-Japanese combination would lead to a revival of anti-British sentiment in China. 'A pact pure and simple could hardly fail to arouse consternation and violent resentment in China', he wrote; 'which could only be removed by explanations which would show the Chinese that we were afraid of Japan.' Such an indication of British anxiety would result in an increase of Japanese influence and, at the same time, an encouragement to the Chinese to attack British interests. There were still further considerations. A non-aggression pact would represent to the world at large no less than a repudiation of the principles of the League of Nations. These were powerful thoughts. They were summed up in Orde's conclusion that an Anglo-Japanese pact would 'increase the chances of a Russo-Japanese war and of a weakening of Russia'. Moreover it would entail 'violent Chinese resentment against us, a diminution in the authority of the League, and most likely a worsening of our relations with the United States'.[31] Thus the long-range results of an Anglo-Japanese pact would be almost entirely undesirable.

The pessimistic assessment of the Far Eastern Department was shared by Sir George Sansom, Commercial Counsellor to the Embassy in Tokyo. Sansom is of particular interest in the debate of the 1930s because he was, in Simon's words, 'generally acknowledged to be the greatest living authority' on Japan with over thirty years' experience with that country.[32] Sansom believed that the only conditions on which the British could gain relief from trade competition in Asia would be to give political support to Japan. Thus the question arose whether Japan had any economic advantages 'sufficient to justify our mortaging – for good or for evil – our political future in the Far East'. Sansom doubted it. 'Even assuming a genuine intention on the part of the Japanese Government to moderate Japanese competition in foreign markets', he wrote, 'it would [not] be possible for them in practice to enforce upon their industry any trade restrictions which would satisfy us.' In Sansom's opinion the recent history of Anglo-Japanese relations provided no ground for optimism: 'Since 1931 Japan has been a very difficult country to deal with, in matters both of diplomacy and commerce. The attitude, now aggressive, now intractable, of the officials with whom we have to do business has made negotiations on large and small matters extremely trying.'[33]

Putting the issues in their most exaggerated form, Sansom on another occasion wrote that a mission of visiting Englishmen representing the Federation of British Industries in 1935 had given rise to wild speculations. These rumours included the hope on the part of the Japanese that Britain might be prepared to recognise Manchukuo in return for trade concessions, that she might be eager to renew the Anglo-Japanese Alliance, and, moreover, that Britain might be ready to 'tell the USA to go to the devil, split up China, desert the League of Nations, and (I suppose) ensure the peace of the Far East by encouraging Japan to have a whack at Russia and thus precipitate another world war'.[34] These ideas went beyond those entertained even by Chamberlain and Fisher, though they were not entirely incompatible. Sansom thought they were alarming. Intelligent Japanese officials might not place any credence in them, but such rumours nevertheless encouraged lesser and still dangerous hopes. Sansom summarised the Japanese mood in late 1934: 'In their present frame of mind the Japanese conception of friendship is give-and-take; we give and they take.' On Anglo-Japanese *rapprochement* he wrote: 'I am all for friendship. I am all against wantonly offending Japan or scoring points for the sake of scoring them. But . . . it would be folly on our part in the name of this abstraction [of friendship] to surrender to Japan all that she wants in order to make her position such that our friendship is not necessary to her.'[35]

Sir Warren Fisher resented such remarks as a caricature of his position. But there can be no question that his views were diametrically opposed to Sansom's and the Far Eastern Department's. In January 1935 Fisher erupted with anger when Simon circulated a memorandum to the Cabinet enclosing critiques of the situation by Sansom and Orde. Orde not only challenged the Treasury's assumption that trade relations with Japan could be improved but he also questioned the *moral validity* of drawing closer to the power responsible for the twenty-one demands and 'the rape of Manchuria'. 'We cannot morally afford in the present-day world to put ourselves in the same camp with an exponent of such policies', Orde concluded.[36] To Fisher these words were misguided as well as offensive. They conveyed a lack of realism about power politics and represented a weak effort to justify a policy of drift. He referred to Orde's recent writings as 'a revised version of the Book of Lamentations'. Fisher's reaction indicates the pitch of emotion on the subject of Japan. He wrote to Chamberlain: 'Orde can, I think best be described as a pedantic ass, admirably suited to join the eclectic brotherhood of Oxford or Cambridge.' He denounced the head of the Far Eastern Department's condemnation of Japan with biting words: Orde's pedantry was 'only equalled by his quite obvious ignorance of human nature, and at the same time he is obsessed with the fixed idea that original sin is monopolised by Japan, and our only proper attitude is, therefore, never to soil ourselves by contact with such impiety'.[37] To Sir Warren Fisher the original sin of his generation was the failure to recognise the transcendent danger of Germany.

Fisher and Chamberlain persevered in the quest for security with Japan. With a rich political inventiveness coupled with a faith that economic expertise could solve the problems of the Great Depression in Asia as well as in Europe, they embarked on a project to put China on a sound financial footing through Anglo-Japanese co-operation. They acted in response to the Chinese currency crisis of late 1934 and, in Fisher's words, 'the wholly selfish silver policy of the US government'.[38] The Chinese requested a loan of £20 million. So complex and serious was the economic situation in China that the Treasury urged the appointment of an economic adviser to be sent to the Far East to give expert advice. The Foreign Office agreed that the appointment of an expert was desirable. Then to the astonishment of the Foreign Office the Treasury designated none other than the Chief Economic Adviser to the British government, Sir Frederick Leith-Ross. His status rivalled that of a Minister of State. The effect of his appointment created the impression that Britain would in effect have two Ambassadors in China. This was the beginning of the 'dual diplomacy' conducted by the Treasury, on the one hand, and the Foreign Office on the other. The Foreign Office continued to try to balance friendship with both China and Japan, to protect economic interests and at the same time to take account of Britain's strategic vulnerability. The Treasury pursued a 'forward' policy of active friendship with Japan and at the same time the stabilisation of China by means of a currency loan.

With a confidence not shared by the Foreign Office, the Treasury believed that British economic genius, as personified by Leith Ross, could resuscitate China and provide a basis for co-operation between Britain and Japan. China in financial straits might accept economic aid, upon which Britain and Japan could mutually agree. China might be persuaded to recognise Manchukuo. Britain and Japan might reach agreement about naval disarmament, and Japan might even return to the League of Nations. With such hopes in mind Leith Ross sailed for the Far East in August 1935. He discovered that the Japanese were even more profoundly suspicious of his mission than the Far Eastern Department had warned, and that the Chinese would not willingly submit to foreign financial control. Nor would the Chinese listen to the concrete suggestion that might have helped to reconcile Japan and Britain, the recognition of Manchukuo. Leith Ross therefore began to work on the technical part of his mission first. He devised a complicated scheme for currency reform that won the admiration of his fellow economists. But it had the opposite of the intended political effect. The greater his involvement in China the more sceptical he became about the good faith of the Japanese. The longer he stayed in China the more he became intrigued with the potential of the China trade for Britain. Political friction with Japan rather than accommodation was the result. Sir John Pratt wrote in November 1935: 'We set out to win the good will and the co-operation of Japan but in Japanese eyes the Leith-Ross mission must appear as an attempt to assert and strengthen Great Britain's influence in China, and as a challenge to the position claimed by Japan.'[39]

The 'forward' policy of Leith Ross and the Treasury consisted of economically bolstering the Chinese government to prevent its collapse. The leading British firms in China hailed this 'stronger' stand as an indication that the British government did not intend to abandon them. On the other hand the Ambassador in Tokyo warned that the Japanese would regard a British loan as an attempt to subjugate China to British economic control. They would respond by tightening their grip on northern China, which might result in political as well as economic separation. Rather than strengthening China, Leith Ross was pursuing a course that might bring about disintegration and Japanese hostility. In late 1935 this danger materialised with dramatic swiftness. The Japanese responded to anti-Japanese sentiment in China which was not unconnected with the prospects of the loan. They began to mass troops in Manchuria. The Chinese attitude stiffened. The British found themselves likely to be caught between Japanese imperialism and Chinese national resistance. Leith Ross continued to press forward with the loan. The Foreign Office judged that the Treasury had landed British policy in 'a rare mess'. Vansittart wrote that he could not understand 'the working of Sir Warren Fisher's mind'.[40] The Treasury had constantly urged reconciliation with Japan, but no move could be more calculated to stir up Japanese hostility than British intervention in China. The Japanese would never be convinced that the purpose of an economic loan was not to make the Chinese government the puppet of Britain. Sir Victor Wellesley wrote in a remark that summarises the attitude of the Far Eastern Department: 'All this is the result of allowing our Far Eastern policy to drift into the hands of the Treasury. It is very dangerous. I have always sympathised with Sir F. Leith Ross for being sent out on a wild goose chase. It is high time he came home for as long as this bull remains in the China shop there is no knowing how much political crockery may be broken.'[41]

The British retreated. Neville Chamberlain instructed the Treasury that no action should be taken that might antagonise the Japanese. The failure of the Leith Ross mission helps to explain why a policy of appeasement did not work in the Far East. Though the pro-Japanese faction in the British government was willing to recognise Manchukuo (and indeed believed that recognition would create more prosperous opportunities for British trade), recognition would undermine Britain's position in China. At best the British would substitute some measure of Japanese friendship with unmitigating Chinese hostility. In China proper the British believed that they had little to give. The situation was not analogous to the Ethiopian case or that of the former German colonies. In Africa the British were prepared to yield, though at the expense of others – the Ethiopians, the Belgians, or the Portuguese. In China they stood by their treaty rights. They paid lip-service to the ideology of the open door and the dismantling of the unequal treaties, but neither the Treasury nor the Foreign Office intended to give the Japanese an economic advantage. And there was more than commercial interest at stake. What might be the effect, Wellesley asked, 'of abandoning our interests to the Japanese'? What would be the effect on 'the whole Oriental world'?[42] For that matter how would a collapse in China affect Britain's status as a great power?

Though more remote geographically from England than Central Europe or Ethiopia, China impinged more directly on the British Empire. Part of the question of Britain's position involved prestige, as Wellesley's minute suggests. Part of it can be traced to anxiety about British economic competitiveness, or lack of it. In profits British companies in China continued on the whole to prosper, but in expansion and innovation the Japanese were gaining the upper hand. The British were determined to hold their own, but their economic drive appeared to be failing. Perhaps this says something about the decline of the British Empire. In any case the Japanese noted that the British seemed to be more enthusiastic about making trade concessions to the Germans or Italians than to them. Though the Japanese protested new restrictive tariffs in the wake of the Ottawa Conference of 1932, the British did not undertake any serious study of tariff revision in, for example, Nigeria and the Gold Coast. In short, political appeasement sounded appealing in principle, especially because it seemed like a reasonable price to pay for strategic security; but it became more and more elusive when examined in the light of concrete steps to achieve it. The British did not yield easily when the issues boiled down to specific economic concessions. The great act of appeasement did not occur in the Far East, but eventually in Central Europe, where the British Empire had no direct involvement.

By the time of the publication of the German–Japanese anti-Comintern pact in November 1936, the Leith Ross mission had died a natural death. Leith Ross claimed credit for alleviating the Chinese currency crisis;[43] but the 'forward' policy of the Treasury certainly had not succeeded in bringing about a reconciliation with Japan. Instead Japan had moved towards the German orbit, though the significance of the anti-Comintern pact for the British Empire was not clearcut. Laurence Collier believed that it should be regarded definitely as 'inimical to British interests'.[44] But Anthony Eden, now Foreign Secretary, did not take the matter too 'tragically' and refused to take an alarmist view. Nor did Charles Orde, who gave the matter sustained thought. Like Eden he attached little importance to ideology. Orde believed that the pact amounted to little more than anti-communist propaganda, though he did grant that it might have 'psychological' effects that could eventually lead to a military alliance.

Orde's views are again of interest at this particular time – in other words at the time of the anti-Comintern pact and less than a year before the resumption of Japanese–Chinese hostilities in 1937 – because they represented the triumph of the Foreign Office's traditional policy. That policy can be described as essentially passive and opportunistic, as a policy carefully attempting to maintain friendship with China rather than to rupture Chinese relations in a gamble with Japan. He believed that Japan would remain preoccupied with Russia, essentially for strategic reasons, and that the anti-Comintern agreement had not altered the balance of power in the Far East. On the other hand a *military* as opposed to an ideological pact between

Germany and Japan would truly be a cause for alarm to both Russia and Britain. No one could predict what Japan might do if both those countries were simultaneously engaged in a war against Germany. But Orde had no doubt at all about Japan's action if either Russia *or* Britain were to go to war against Germany: 'If one [i.e. Russia or Britain] were engaged there could be little doubt that Japan would attack that one.' Since circumstances might change quickly and unpredictably, Britain's only safeguard, Orde concluded, 'will come from the completion of the Singapore Base and the possession of a really strong fleet based upon it'.[45]

The phrase 'Singapore Base' conveys the great illusion of British Asian security in the 1930s. Since 1923 British defence in the Far East was based on the proposition that the fortress – Churchill once used the word 'citadel' – at the tip of the Malayan peninsula would form the lynchpin of protection for Australia and New Zealand as well as the Far Eastern empire. The slogan 'Main Fleet to Singapore' became an almost unquestioned writ, despite anxiety about Germany in the Atlantic and Italy in the Mediterranean. According to the Singapore strategy a British fleet could arrive at Singapore within a period of forty-eight to seventy-two days to handle a defensive emergency against Japan and still retain control of European waters. Misguided though this scheme might seem in retrospect, in the 1930s it could be defended as a rational strategy. The French could be expected to help neutralise Italy and to deny Japan air and sea bases in Indochina. After the fall of France in 1940 the British were left alone to deal with Japan, Italy and Germany. Long before then, however, the grand design for the defence of the Far Eastern empire had been called into question not only by sceptics in London but also by those most vitally concerned, the Australians and New Zealanders.

At the Imperial Conference of 1937 the First Lord of the Admiralty, Sir Samuel Hoare, discussed the Singapore issue with a candour that at once assured and alarmed the antipodean delegates. He took full measure of the responsibilities of the imperial government for the defence of the empire, yet at the same time he surveyed the dangers of an aggressive Japan in a way that surpassed British alarm even at the time of the Manchurian crisis. Hoare's blunt assessment of the issues of imperial security and the response of the participants of the Imperial Conference in May–June 1937 well indicate the temper of the British Empire on the eve of the war between China and Japan.

Hoare took an extreme position. He represented the view (also shared by Sir Maurice Hankey and Sir Ernle Chatfield, the First Sea Lord) that the defence of the Eastern empire as a priority ranked second only to the defence of the British isles. He believed that the loss of a British colony such as Hong King would be disastrous to British prestige. Failure to stand up to the Japanese might lead to the break-up of the empire. Hoare emphasised the dangers of Japanese imperialism as well as the necessity for the dominions to stand together with the imperial government. He requested the conference to ponder the worst possible circumstances. What might happen, he asked, if Japan were left free to exercise her sea power in the Far East unopposed by the British fleet? 'Let me assume', he continued, 'that, in these circumstances, Japan decides to invade Australia and launches an expedition covered by the full strength of her naval forces and her naval air forces.' The very existence of the Pacific dominions would be imperilled.

> I am convinced that, if this act of aggression took place, no measures of local defence, no Army and no Air Force which the Commonwealth of Australia could conceivably maintain could save her from invasion and defeat at the hands of the Japanese. The Dominion of New Zealand would be exposed to exactly the same danger, and every word I have said about Australia is equally applicable to New Zealand.[46]

Nor was the Japanese menace restricted to Australia and New Zealand. Hoare also tried to place the fear of Japan in the hearts of the South African, Indian and Canadian delegates:

> With Australia and New Zealand dominated by the Japanese and the Indian Ocean under the control of Japanese sea power, where would be the security of the Union of South Africa and of the India Empire? Or let me suppose that Japan casts her eyes eastward across the Pacific, what is to deter her from action against the Dominion of Canada?[47]

He now came to the main point. In the event of a Far Eastern emergency, Britain unequivocally would dispatch the fleet to the Far East. *'[W]e believe that the very existence of the British Commonwealth of Nations as now constituted rests on our ability to send our fleet to the Far East, should the need arise.'*[48]

If Hoare had been more candid he might have added that the empire was so overextended that only an optimistic assessment would hold that it *could* be defended – even with the wholehearted support of all of the dominions. One set of risks had to be balanced against another. The defence of Singapore and the antipodean dominions rested on the mobility of the fleet. For obvious economic reasons an effective fighting force could not be maintained simultaneously in both the Western and Eastern hemispheres (though at the Imperial Conference the New Zealand Prime Minister had irreverently asked, if the fleet could be sent to Singapore in time of emergency, why could it not from time to time be stationed there in time of peace?) Singapore consequently suffered in priority despite the view of ranking strategists such as Hankey and Chatfield that it was second only to home defence. At the time of the Imperial Conference of 1937 there were prevalent doubts on the part of the dominion representatives whether the imperial government could or would support the Singapore strategy. Hoare's powerful speech was calculated to reassure; but everyone present knew that British involvement in a Far Eastern war would be influenced if not determined by European circumstances.

In fact the key to imperial defence in the Far East lay in the Mediterranean.[49] Insecurity in the Middle East could paralyse British policy in China and Japan. By 1939, as a result of the Abyssinian crisis, Britain's

Far Eastern strategy had to be carefully calculated in relation to Italy. The principal British naval base in the Mediterranean, Malta, appeared to be increasingly vulnerable to Italian air power. Hence the view of Hankey that the British 'should grasp the hand held out by Signor Mussolini, however repugant it may be'. The courting of Italy, 'Europe's most expensive whore', thus lay at the bottom of Britain's defence in Asia.[50]

The 'Eastern' outlook that characterised the 1937 Conference stands in contrast to the view of Churchill about the paramount importance of the Mediterranean and the balance of power in Europe. When Churchill later altered British priorities from Singapore and the Far East to Egypt and the Mediterranean, he endorsed a political as well as a strategic principle. The empire meant different things to different men. What counted most? The unity of the dominions? The empire as opposed to the dominions? The Far Eastern as opposed to the Middle Eastern and African empires? Evolution of the colonies into self-governing dominions such as Australia and New Zealand? Or, as Churchill would have had it, the continuing power and prestige of the empire itself? Could the empire live compatibly with the Chinese and Japanese (as Chamberlain hoped)? Or should the empire respond to the Chinese with contempt and the Japanese with suspicion (as was in fact Churchill's private attitude)? These sorts of general questions were seldom given direct answers. But they have a direct bearing on the question of 'appeasement'. If the Japanese were unscrupulous and imperialistic, should they nevertheless be accommodated because of the pre-eminent danger of Germany? Or should the empire-commonwealth be prepared to wage war in both hemispheres?

According to the Chiefs of Staff in June 1937, the British should hold their own in the Far East, even at great risk in Europe and elsewhere. The commitment to Australia and New Zealand was absolute. Even the defence of Hong Kong, a controversial point, was held to be in the vital interest of imperial security. In the event of war with Germany, the British had two choices in Hong Kong: to evacuate, cut losses and avoid commitments in China; or defend a strategically indefensible outpost knowing full well that the Japanese would eventually conquer the colony. The argument for defence prevailed: 'the evacuation of an important fortress on the outbreak of war would itself entail a very serious loss of prestige, not only in the Far East, but throughout the world; and might influence other potentially hostile Powers to form an exaggerated idea of the weakness of our position, and to throw in their lot against us'.[51] Hong Kong would be held as long as humanly possible. Not only would Britain's pledge to Australia and New Zealand be upheld but the circumference of the Far Eastern empire would also be defended. These sorts of arguments worked in favour of those who wanted to preserve the empire and avoid commitment in Europe. As Michael Howard has pointed out, the burden of the empire's worldwide defence was so great that it lessened Britain's ability to intervene in Europe.[52]

Yet commitment to home defence and the Eastern Mediterranean made it increasingly improbable that the Singapore strategy would actually work – especially with an Arab revolt in Palestine occurring at the same time as the

Abyssinian crisis. Should the dominions be candidly told about Britain's dilemmas? Chamberlain feared that frank discussion would cause political rupture within the Commonwealth. South Africa and Canada, for different reasons, were isolationist. Australia was alarmed at Japan and pressed for greater defence measures. New Zealand remained loyal to the ideals of the League and collective security. How could the dominions be convinced of the need for a common front on the issue of imperial security, especially when there was no agreement within the imperial government? Though the plight of the statesmen and strategists in London might seem understandable in retrospect, the dominion leaders later believed that the discussions about imperial security had been less than honest.[53]

From the vantage-point of the Foreign Office the most important conclusion of the Chiefs of Staff's assessment was the decision to defend Hong Kong. 'Decisive weight', Charles Orde wrote on 2 July 1937, 'is given to considerations of prestige and our ultimate position in China.'[54] When the Defence Plans Committee (a sub-committee of the Committee of Imperial Defence) discussed the issue of Far Eastern security, Eden stated that he was 'very glad, for political reasons, that the Chiefs of Staff had decided that Hong Kong should not be evacuated'.[55] Chamberlain, now Prime Minister, agreed. But between Eden and Chamberlain there existed an important difference about the political future of the Far East. Eden believed that one of the large issues would be the importance of gaining American co-operation. Only by asserting a sort of combined Anglo-American 'white race authority' (his phrase) could the British preserve their influence. Chamberlain continued to distrust the United States and to hope for an accommodation with Japan even at the risk of disorder or 'chaos' in China. The resumption of hostilities between the Japanese and Chinese in July 1937 eventually made Chamberlain's position untenable. The 'moderate' forces in Japan did not inspire confidence. But the clash of outlook within the government in London persisted. Estimates of American reliability continued to be a divisive issue.

In September 1937 Eden requested Sir Alexander Cadogan to assess the possibility of Anglo-American co-operation in the Far East. Cadogan had served as Ambassador in China in 1933–6. On Victor Wellesley's retirement he became Deputy Under-Secretary and in January 1938 he succeeded Vansittart as Permanent Under-Secretary. Though Vansittart now held the position of 'Chief Diplomatic Adviser', a revolution had occurred at the Foreign Office. In contrast with Vansittart, who obsessively dwelt on the need for stalwart resistance to Hitler, Cadogan believed that all of the 'gangster belligerents' should be treated with an attitude that would neither provoke nor give an impression of impotence. 'If you are too bellicose', Cadogan once wrote about Mussolini, 'you provoke Dictators into doing something irrevocable. If you are too passive, you encourage them to think they can do anything.'[56] In this vein he reflected in September 1937 about the danger of provoking Japan with sanctions: 'If we *and the US* cut off all trade with Japan, the latter would be faced with the most serious consequences. So serious, that she might "see red" and, in that event, *we*, and not the US would bear the first brunt, at any rate, of her attack.'[57] With such realistic points in mind, Cadogan continued to analyse the dangers as well as the benefits of concerted action with the United States.

Cadogan believed that the Americans would 'recoil in horror' at the idea of joint action with Britain. 'US public opinion', he wrote, 'is a very unpredictable element.' The sentiment for non-intervention appeared to be waxing rather than waning. And without American support the British in the Far East were powerless:

> I think it really all comes back to this, that if the US won't play, there is nothing really effective to be done. If they really come in with both feet, the situation might be very different, but we must be frightfully careful not to scare them: they must be allowed (if they will) to come round to it themselves – and probably take all the credit if they do![58]

Cadogan went on to note the incongruity of American indecisiveness. 'Here indeed is a case where, I should have thought, with no risk to themselves, and with comparatively little material loss, the Americans would have a golden opportunity of putting into practice all their preaching about collaboration for the prevention of the horrors of war!'[59] But he concluded that there was little hope for American action. Cadogan had an open mind as well as experience in the Far East. At this stage his judgement tended to confirm Chamberlain's pessimism about the United States rather than Eden's guarded optimism that the two powers might work together to restrain Japan.

Roosevelt's 'quarantine' speech of October 1937 encouraged even Chamberlain to hope that the United States might at last be moving away from isolation. Chamberlain doubted whether the Americans would invoke effective sanctions against Japan (as he interpreted the implicit threat of Roosevelt's speech), but he said to the Cabinet that he did not underrate the importance of the President's statement, 'especially as a warning to the Dictator Powers that there was a point beyond which the United States of America would not permit them to go'.[60] Nevertheless Chamberlain's scepticism predominated in his overall judgement of the situation in late 1937. Privately he wrote: 'It is always best and safest to count on nothing from the Americans but words'.[61] Eden, again in contrast, emphasised the necessity of working together with the Americans and avoiding the accusation that Britain would remain passive in the Far East in order to preserve the British Empire. The ghost of the Manchurian crisis visited both Chamberlain and Eden in different incarnations. Chamberlain remained wary of the Americans and was determined not to give the Japanese the impression that they would again be put 'in the dock' by the League of Nations; Eden feared another American reproach that 'England has let us down'.

At the time of the Manchurian crisis the British had thrown their support behind the League and had earned the enmity of Japan. They had attempted to co-operate with the United States but had won American moral disapproval for failure to adopt a policy of non-recognition of Japanese claims. They had placed themselves in a position of seeming not to sympathise with

China. Eden now resolved not to repeat those mistakes. At the Brussels Conference of November 1937 (attended by most of the major and minor powers concerned with China, but boycotted by Japan), he took the line that the British would follow American initiatives. The Americans produced none. Roosevelt's speech about quarantining Japan had misfired. The American representatives could not commit themselves to anything that might lead to foreign difficulties, or even to a domestic debate about isolationism. The Conference produced little other than a few platitudes deploring the use of force. Eden nevertheless created a spirit of co-operation between the American and British delegations. He had an intuition about the President's purpose. He sensed that Roosevelt was 'deeply perturbed at the prospects in the Far East' and perhaps even more alarmed at the possibility of the United States having to bear the brunt of an Asian war.

The attack by Japanese aircraft on the British gunboat *Ladybird* and the sinking of the American *Panay* in December 1937 acutely raised the question whether the British fleet should be mobilised in protest and, again, whether joint action with the Americans was possible. With mild astonishment the British learned of Roosevelt's response. He did not wish to precipitate a crisis leading to a war for which the American public was not prepared. Softening the public protest (against the advice of some of his advisers), he wished to step up the naval armament programme and secretly to move closer to the British. He talked vaguely of an economic and naval blockade against Japan and, more specifically, about secret staff talks between the two navies. The British Ambassador in Washington reported to London: 'You may think that these are the utterances of a hair-brained statesman or of an amateur strategist, but I assure you that the chief impression left on my own mind was that I had been talking to a man who had done his best in the Great War to bring America in speedily on the side of the Allies and who now was equally anxious to bring America in on the same side before it might be too late'.[62] Plans for the staff talks were made immediately. On New Year's day 1938 Eden greeted Captain Royal E. Ingersoll of the United States navy in London. The Ingersoll mission represented a landmark in Anglo-American relations in the Far East. With Roosevelt's own emissary the British discussed the state of readiness and possible movements of the fleet as well as general strategic policies. Though the talks were technical rather than in the nature of political planning, they marked, as Eden noted in his memoirs, the beginning of the alignment of power of the United States and Britain against that of the dictator states.[63]

In the midst of the controversy between Chamberlain and Eden, Cadogan noted in his diary that both of them exaggerated in opposite directions.[64] Both of them had accurate perceptions of the dangers to the British Empire. 'We are a very rich and a very vulnerable Empire', Chamberlain wrote in January 1938, 'and there are plenty of poor adventurers not very far away who look on us with hungry eyes.'[65] Chamberlain of course had in mind the Italians as well as the Germans. By recognising Italy's claims in Ethiopia, perhaps as part of a comprehensive settlement, he hoped not only to detach Italy from Germany but also to make the position in the Far East more secure by neutralising the Italian threat in the Mediterranean and Red Sea.

After the Italian intervention in the Spanish Civil War, Chamberlain and the Admiralty became increasingly preoccupied with the western as well as the eastern Mediterranean. Italy was a delicate problem. For this reason, in part, Chamberlain did not respond enthusiastically to Roosevelt's intrusion in January 1938, when the President put forward his good offices to co-operate with the British in establishing a general basis for peace in Europe.

Eden believed that it would be no less than a calamity for the British Empire not to work together with the United States, with whom, he thought, Britain should properly share the hegemony of the western Pacific. He was away from the Foreign Office briefly in January 1938 and was not consulted by Chamberlain. He regarded the Prime Minister's attitude towards Roosevelt's initiative as a setback in satisfactory progress in Anglo-American relations as well as an affront to his conduct of foreign relations. The Americans were bound to react to a settlement with Mussolini with suspicion. If Britain recognised Italian claims in Ethiopia, the United States might regard this step as a prelude to British accommodation with Japan. Chamberlain and Eden thus were indeed pulling in different directions, though both of them had a firm grasp of the essential issues. Eden's resignation in February 1938 in part represented a protest over the persistent inclination on the part of the Prime Minister to accommodate Japan – despite Chamberlain's own recognition that 'the Japs are growing more and more insolent and brutal'[66] – as well as the question of appeasement in Europe and the issue of the control of foreign policy.

If Japan could not be appeased at least she ought not to be provoked. This was Chamberlain's premiss, and it provided continuity in British policy when Lord Halifax succeeded Eden as Foreign Secretary. To the Admiralty this outlook appeared to be more realistic and less dangerous than Eden's estimation of the Far Eastern situation. Eden had believed that, after the *Ladybird* and *Panay* incidents, part of the fleet should be sent to Singapore. Like Churchill he believed that the Japanese would be daunted by a show of force. Since the First Lord of the Admiralty only a few months earlier at the Imperial Conference had given a firm assurance that the 'Singapore strategy' was designed to meet any emergency created by Japan, Eden's response was not unreasonable. The Admiralty however now had grave reservations. Chatfield informed Cadogan in November 1937 that the dispatch of capital ships to the Far East would 'denude' the Mediterranean.[67] Moreover, unless the Americans could be depended upon to mobilise their fleet also, then British ships at Singapore could undertake only a defensive strategy. Indeed such a movement of the fleet might provoke rather than deter further Japanese action. Again the British faced the recurring dilemma: the more their difficulties in Europe, the less their ability to defend the empire. The failures to reach an accord with the United States exacerbated the dilemma: the greater the danger in the Far East, the smaller the latitude for man-oeuvre in Europe. In other words, there were powerful Asian reasons for an appeasement policy in Europe.

In a sense Halifax unimaginatively pursued the objectives of both his Prime Ministers, Chamberlain and Churchill (the latter from May to December 1940); but there was also an internal consistency to his own views. It can perhaps be best described in the phrase associated with British imperial history in India, where Halifax had served as Viceroy from 1926 to 1931 – 'masterly inactivity'. Events would determine themselves with discreet and sometimes decisive British influence in the background. To the problems of the late 1930s Halifax brought to bear certain suppositions that had served him well in India: with proper guidance, non-Western nations, Japan as well as India, eventually might develop along the same lines as the Western democracies; the Japanese, like the Indians, must be kept 'in play' until they could be convinced of Britain's goodwill and desire for peace. Keeping the Japanese 'in play' became one of Halifax's paramount goals. In the eyes of some of his critics he had 'sipped tea with treason' with Gandhi. He demonstrated similar patience, if not obliquity (again according to his critics), with the Japanese. Halifax was a great believer in conciliation, a virtue that afforded him distinction in his career as wartime Ambassador to the United States. The value he placed on conciliation also explains his relative failure with the dictators of the 1930s.

The permanent staff at the Foreign Office needed no persuasion about the desirability of a policy of 'masterly inactivity'. 'I trust we shall not get involved in negotiations between the two parties', Charles Orde had written shortly after the outbreak of war between China and Japan. If Britain were to intervene and help to bring about peace, any settlement that had any chance of stability would be regarded as a 'betrayal of China' by the world at large as well as by the Chinese. There were also dangers in trying to tilt the balance in favour of China: again in Orde's words, 'the Chinese are such inveterate wrigglers and self-deceivers that they are really best helped by leaving them to face hard facts by themselves'.[68] Despite such reservations about the ethical defects of the Chinese people, the sentiment of the Foreign Office was pro-Chinese. Apart from expressing moral sympathy, Orde and others, including Halifax, believed that the staying power of the Chinese should not be underestimated. 'The kind of spontaneous, passive, elastic resistance of which the Chinese are perhaps the world's greatest masters will continue.'[69] In the end Chinese resistance would perhaps defeat Japanese imperialism. The Japanese would become bogged down in China. In the long run China, as a diversion to Japan, would be of incalculable importance. 'It is not to our disadvantage', Orde wrote, should Japan find herself 'unable to cope' with the situation in China. He expressed the consensus of the Foreign Office when he wrote the following words in late 1937: 'The best effect on Japan would I believe be produced by a failure in China without assistance to China from other countries.'[70]

The Far Eastern Department of the Foreign Office did not, on the whole, sympathise with the policy of 'appeasement' indelibly associated with Halifax's name. The general attitude of the department remained the same as it had during the mid-1930s – 'generosity towards China, firmness towards Japan' – despite a change in personnel. In the spring of 1938 Orde was relegated to the Baltic (perhaps through the influence of Sir Warren Fisher?) and Sir John Pratt retired. Sir John Brenan emerged as the leading authority on China. Brenan was a former Consul-General of long experience at

Shanghai. Like Pratt, he was respected for his independent and vigorous ideas as well as his knowledge of Asia. His views generally found support in Orde's successor, Robert Howe (head of the department, 1938–40), who had served at the Embassy at Peking. During part of this period Sir George Sansom was in London and acted as adviser in the Far Eastern Department. Sansom's knowledge of Japan's economic affairs was unsurpassed, and he also held strong ideas about political trends. These three officials believed in common that Japan could not be appeased by Britain's giving way in China. They held that it was a false hope to think that moderate opinion in Japan might predominate over that of the extremists. There was no way for Britain – or any other foreign power – to bolster the moderates. The extremists would have to be defeated by outside forces. Later, after war had broken out in Europe, Brenan expressed a thought that represented the sentiment of the Far Eastern Department in the 1938–42 period: 'China is fighting our battle and is doing us great service by exhausting a dangerous potential enemy. It is obviously in our interest to give her all the help we can spare from our own war effort.'[71]

The project of economic assistance to China (the initial proposal was a loan of £20 million) first met with failure, despite its support by Halifax. 'China is fighting the battle of all the law-abiding States', he wrote to the Chancellor of the Exchequer in May 1938.[72] This line of argument did not appeal to the Treasury. Nor was the Cabinet persuaded. Chamberlain feared the dangers of a clash with Japan at the especially inauspicious time of the impending crisis in Czechoslovakia. Cadogan noted that it was 'all very well' for Brenan and others in the Far Eastern Department to press for aid to China, but that they did not have a sufficient grasp of the 'awful situation in Europe'.[73] The Far Eastern Department, though disappointed, was not surprised. 'We did our best for the Chinese over the question of a loan', Ronald Howe wrote to the British Ambassador in China, 'but . . . the Powers-that-Be felt that in the existing critical situation in Europe they would not be justified in taking any risk, however slight, of provoking the Japanese to take further, and possible more direct, action against us in the Far East.'[74] Halifax had followed the lead of the Far Eastern Department but had then wavered in the face of such arguments as the hostility of Japan and the futility of intervention on the Chinese side. One critic pointed out that the only predictable aspect of the situation was the certainty that the Chinese would ask for more. Halifax clearly sympathised with the Chinese, but, in weighing the various considerations, he chose to act with caution. He also chose not to make clear-cut decisions, and, perhaps unconsciously, adopted an attitude of what one historian has aptly described as an air of 'puzzled rectitude'.[75]

At roughly the same time as the Chinese loan question, the Cabinet decided to acquiesce in Japan's insistence that the customs revenues at Shanghai and Tientsin be placed in a Japanese bank. The amount of money involved only enough to pay the interest on Chinese foreign loans and thus was relatively trivial. But there was more at stake than might be apparent. The British and Americans feared further take-overs. What began with the usurpation of customs revenues might end with the appropriation of the international concessions. British and other Western traders might be ousted from the China coast. The British and American governments protested accordingly, but they did not match their protests with threats of retaliation. The British in particular were more inclined to accept Japan's assurances that the customs revenues would be dealt with equitably by the Japanese bank. To the Chinese it seemed clear that the British were more interested in protecting their finances than in defending the Chinese administration. To the Foreign Office it was a disagreeable but not intolerable concession. It could in fact be defended as a test to see whether the Japanese would keep their word and as an attempt to curb more extreme Japanese action. In May 1938 the Foreign Office thus announced that the customs revenues would be administered by the Hokohama Specie Bank.[76] The agreement hardly compared with bargains being contemplated with the European dictators. But it is instructive in judging the impact in the Far East of Britain's appeasement policy in Europe. It helps to reveal Halifax's general handling of Far Eastern problems. A minor point had been conceded to Japan without much loss of British honour or prestige. The Japanese were being kept 'in play'.

On Far Eastern questions Halifax was temperamentally inclined to follow the guidance of the experts in the Far Eastern Department, some of whom held just as strong feelings about Germany as about Japan. On the other hand Halifax loyally attempted to pursue Chamberlain's line of appeasement. The goal of maintaining a balance of power in Europe was not always compatible with that of preserving the British Empire in Asia and other parts of the world. Just as Halifax was sometimes torn between the Prime Minister and the Foreign Office, so also on a broader scale did he feel the conflicting pressures in the commonwealth. Both Chamberlain and Halifax knew that war with Germany in 1938 would split the dominions. Australia and New Zealand would enter reluctantly, but South Africa and Canada probably would refuse to enter at all. Halifax was also sensitive, in a way that Chamberlain was not, to the sentiment of the dependent empire. There was an important moral element involved. The British, not least Halifax and his advisers, believed that the British Empire in Asia and Africa rested on a moral foundation. If Britain were to conclude a dishonourable agreement in the name of appeasement, the repercussions would be felt throughout the empire. 'I'd rather be beat than dishonoured', Cadogan wrote on 24 September 1938. Contemplating the terms of Hitler's demands on Czechoslovakia, he continued: 'How can we look any foreigner in the face after this? How can we hold Egypt, India and the rest?'[77]

It is clear from Cadogan's diary, among other sources, that such ethical questions weighed heavily on Halifax's mind during the great Czechoslovakian crisis of September 1938, and that Cadogan himself persuaded the Foreign Secretary to take a firmer stand against Hitler than Chamberlain liked or anticipated. Cadogan acted as a check on Halifax's conciliatory impulses in Asia as well. As the Foreign Secretary's principal adviser he could sometimes exert decisive influence. Since he had served as Ambassador in China, his minutes reflected a greater knowledge of China than Japan, but they did not reflect any particular bias in favour of the British trading community in China. Indeed he wrote in the aftermath of the Munich crisis – when he attempted a general review of the major issues facing Britain at that time – that the China trade was probably important as much for the 'prestige' of the empire as for its economic significance – and thus trading interests intrinsically were probably not worth the risk of war with Japan. His ideas coincided with Halifax's in the hope that China would continue to divert Japan and prevent her from turning southwards towards the vital part of Britain's eastern empire, Malaya, and beyond Singapore, to Australia and New Zealand. Most important of all, the Permanent Under-Secretary and the Foreign Secretary were at one in the view of the United States as the ultimate protector of Britain's position. '[T]he shadow of possible trouble with America', Cadogan wrote in October 1938, 'has undoubtedly re-strained Japan in recent times from doing as much damage as she would like to do to our interests in the Far East.'[78] Perhaps more than anything else, anxiety about future American action acted as a brake on appeasement in the Far East. Cadogan wrote on another occasion that 'making up to Japan' would not only be morally offensive to the British themselves but would also alienate the Americans: 'We have America to consider, and we should lose the last shreds of respect and sympathy that we may enjoy in that country if we did so'.[79]

The fall of Hankow and Canton in October 1938 and Prince Konoye's subsequent proclamation of a 'New Order in Asia' caused Sir John Brenan to remark that events in the Far East had now taken a truly ominous course. According to the Japanese, the Chinese nationalist government now no longer existed except as a mere local regime. The 'New Order' would be founded on a tripartite bloc of Japan–Manchuria–China, a bloc from which Britain would be more and more excluded unless she proved to be more co-operative. Brenan, for one, did not believe that the Japanese were offering any real choice. His analysis of the situation is of particular interest for the immediate prewar period because he disliked the policy of appease-ment in Europe and believed that it would be even less effective with Japan. The Japanese would regard British willingness to negotiate as a sign of weakness, not strength. Their demands would increase and not diminish. In Brenan's view the best response would be to maintain British rights and give way only under protest – to keep Japan in play short of provoking war. This firm line towards the Japanese stands in contrast to British appeasement in Europe, but it carried Halifax's endorsement.[80] As with all oriental peoples, the Japanese would have to be dealt with firmly.

The word 'prestige' occurred frequently in the deliberations about Japan. When the Tientsin crisis erupted in 1939 one of the paramount concerns was the stripping and searching of British subjects as they entered and left the British concession. Stripping was a dramatic affront to imperial prestige. There is nothing so undignified as a naked Englishman, or so at least the Japanese appeared to think. And they had other motivations. They were incensed at Chinese guerrillas using the settlement as a haven as well as angered at long-standing British economic policies supporting Chinese currency. Tientsin was a symbol of resistance to the 'new order'. The Japanese blockaded the concession in mid-June. Emotions rose quickly.

British subjects were slapped and kicked as well as forced to submit to the indignity of stripping. Halifax informed the Japanese Ambassador that such measures were 'unworthy' of a civilised people. Even Chamberlain spoke of the Japanese insults as being 'almost' intolerable. Nevertheless he was prepared to be humble in order to avoid war, in Asia as well as Europe. Halifax and his advisers were only slightly less willing to accept a loss of prestige. In Brenan's words, 'it is desirable to secure a local *détente* if it can be done without too great a sacrifice of principles'.[81] If they would not suffer too great a loss of face, the British were prepared to negotiate on the concessions, which the Far Eastern Department regarded more in the nature of liabilities than assets. In time of war they could not be defended; in time of peace they provided provocation to both Japan and China. They were remnants of nineteenth-century British imperialism. The British would act firmly, but they would also act prudently, again in Brenan's words, on these questions concerning the 'excrescences' of a bygone era.

The Englishman responsible for trying to bring the Japanese to reason was Sir Robert Craigie, Ambassador in Tokyo since August 1937. Craigie recognised the logic of appeasement towards Japan and came close to endorsing it. He stood apart, in virtual isolation, from the consensus of Foreign Office opinion. He thought that the moderates in Japan were sympathetic to Britain and that their position against the extremists would be strengthened if the British adopted a more conciliatory attitude towards Japanese aims in China. Craigie was a friend of Sir Warren Fisher, and he agreed with Fisher's views on the necessity of Anglo-Japanese friendship. Though he had no previous experience in Asia, part of his career had been devoted to naval disarmament and thus he had definite ideas about the strategic situation in the western Pacific. He shared Neville Chamberlain's distrust of the United States. Chamberlain in turn regarded Craigie's efforts as a valuable corrective to the anti-Japanese bias of the Foreign Office. During the Tientsin crisis the Prime Minister wrote in praise of the Ambassador's calm attitude and his disposition 'never to get rattled'. Craigie's critics on the other hand detected a lamentable inclination to accept Japanese assurances at their face value and a refusal to recognise that the Japanese intended to dominate Asia at the expense of the British Empire. With a certain pomposity of character, Craigie worked to revive the spirit of the Anglo-Japanese Alliance.

Sir Archibald Clark Kerr, Craigie's counterpart in China, expressed almost the opposite sentiments about the general situation in the Far East. Clark Kerr was sympathetic to the ideas of the political left. He was optimistic about Chiang Kai-shek's ability to prolong the struggle against the Japanese and he had faith in the vitality and greatness of the Chinese people. He attached great importance to Britain's moral responsibility. In the Far East as elsewhere, British honour and decency counted as a force for good in world affairs. 'I am in a difficulty and I need your fearless guidance', he wrote to Halifax in May 1939 about the four Chinese nationalists at the British concession at Tientsin. The Japanese demanded that they be handed over for punishment as terrorists. Clark Kerr wrote that if the British acquiesced in this demand they would forever reflect upon it with shame.

Here was a clear-cut case of appeasement versus resistance to Japanese imperialism.

Or so it seemed to Clark Kerr. From Craigie's vantage-point it appeared, on the basis of Japanese evidence, that the four Chinese were guerrillas guilty of blowing up railroads and other acts of sabotage. To Clark Kerr this crime appeared to be that of fighting for their country. To Craigie they were terrorists, and refusal to hand them over to the Japanese would further strain Anglo-Japanese relations. In sombre tone he warned that the incident might even lead to war. The blockade demonstrated that the Japanese were prepared to take extreme measures. To those in London some of the measures were little short of intolerable. The stripping of British subjects provoked indignation in the Press as well as in the government. When word reached London that even an English*woman* had been subjected to this indignity, Chamberlain and Halifax recognised the extent of the crisis. There was a point beyond which even the appeasers would not go. Seeking to avoid 'a very humiliating position', in Halifax's phrase, the Cabinet devised a formula: the Japanese had a right to maintain order in the areas under their occupation, but the British government refused to acknowledge any general change in the policy of taking a firm line towards Japanese aggression. The British thus were able to avoid the semblance of a Far Eastern Munich.[82]

The outbreak of the European war in September 1939 did not seem at the time necessarily to mean a turn for the worse in Far Eastern affairs. The Nazi–Soviet non-aggression pact of 23 August, though a setback for Britain, had far worse implications for Japan. Russian aims would now preoccupy the Japanese and might divert them from such conflicts as the Tientsin controversy. The Japanese were also certainly not unaware of growing American support for the British war effort in Europe and its consequences for Asia. In the words of the British Ambassador in Washington: 'If the United States is to rely upon Great Britain to prevent totalitarian Europe from entering the Atlantic through the Straits of Gibraltar and the exits from the North Sea, the United States must themselves underwrite the security of the British Empire in the Pacific because they cannot afford the weakening of Great Britain itself which would follow the collapse of her dominions in the Pacific.'[83] Another element of hope in the Far Eastern crisis was the resilience of the Chinese. According to Sir Robert Craigie, 'Japan has her hands far too full in China and is too apprehensive of the United States in its present mood to think seriously of any move involving danger to Australia and New Zealand, or to territories in which those Dominions are interested.'[84] These were the sort of optimistic comments used to buck up the dominions. But they are indicative of genuine hopes held by the British in the 1939–40 period. The Japanese might decide, in the words of a Foreign Office appreciation of the situation, that the best course would be 'to sit on the fence'; or rather, they might be forced to do so, not only because of the United States and Russia but also because of China. In these various possibilities, one certainty appeared to be the tenacity of the Chinese. The greater Japan's involvement in China, the less likely would be the chances of a general Far Eastern war. Hence Britain's interest in a prolonged Chinese–

Japanese conflict. Sir John Brenan wrote in December 1939: 'It seems to me obvious that the longer Japan is embroiled in China the less likely is she to take the opportunity of fishing in the troubled waters of the world war, and that our policy, far from bringing about a patched-up peace, should still be to encourage Chinese resistance until we can again enter the Far Eastern theatre with something of our former influence.'[85]

The British stance can also be regarded as a calculated gamble that Japan would remain neutral. To win the gamble some officials such as Sir Robert Craigie and R. A. Butler, at this time parliamentary under-secretary, believed that little as possible should be done to antagonise Japan and that economic concessions should be made in order to improve relations. In the spirit of reconciliation of Chamberlain and Fisher, Butler wrote in September 1939: 'I have never been happy since the Japanese Treaty was allowed to lapse . . . I believe there is in the Japanese a desire to improve their relations with us. I believe that they are a nation who keep their words when given.'[86] Butler hoped that Japan's economic situation might be eased by agreements about raw materials, possibly in exchange for war supplies. Rather than standing by and letting Japan 'explode' into South-East Asia, he wanted to administer certain 'therapeutic' measures that would enable the Japanese to resolve their economic and political problems by peaceful means – notably by Britain facilitating a negotiated peace between Japan and China. Peace in China would help to put Japan on a more moderate course, and Butler believed this might be accomplished without sacrifice of principle on Britain's part.

Thus there were two strategies to survival. The one, urged by Butler and to some extent by Sir Robert Craigie, held out hope for a neutral Japan where the moderates might prevent the extreme militarists from waging war against Britain. The other, expressed most articulately by Sir George Sansom and Sir John Brenan, was based on the premiss that the extremists in Japan held the upper hand and that they would be turned back only because of military failure in China. Sansom wrote in December 1939: 'The so-called moderate elements in Japan are unimportant. The only thing that can conceivably give them importance or increase their numbers is a manifest failure of extremist policies. No concessions to Japan, by us or by anybody else, can help the moderates, whatever they may tell us.'[87] Sansom had observed earlier, in lines of persistent analysis: 'All Japanese want a "new order" in Asia, and a "new order" involves the ultimate displacement of Great Britain in the Far East. The difference between the extremists and the moderates is not one of destination, but of the road by which that destination is to be reached and the speed at which it is to be travelled.'[88] That is the interpretation which eventually predominated in London, even among latter-day appeasers such as Butler. As for the idea of a negotiated peace in China, Brenan expressed a growing sentiment in the Foreign Office when he wrote at the time of the fall of France: 'Japan is a potential enemy and it is not in our interest to get her out of the Chinese morass in order that she may be better able to take advantage of our difficulties in the European war.'[89]

When Churchill became Prime Minister in May 1940, he faced an upheaval in Europe that simultaneously had undermined Britain's position in the Far East. The Singapore strategy rested on the axiom that France would help to hold the Mediterranean if the British fleet were engaged in Eastern waters. After the occupation of the low countries and the collapse of France, there now existed the danger of a Japanese take-over of the Dutch East Indies and Indochina. Control of the latter territory would give the Japanese a land approach to Singapore. Churchill nevertheless minimised the possibility of an attack on Malaya either by land or by sea. He had long-held preconceptions about the Japanese, and he greatly underrated their ability to wage war on the British Empire. In 1925 he had written: 'Japan is at the other end of the world. She cannot menace our vital security in any way . . . The only war it would be worth our while to fight with Japan would be to prevent an invasion of Australia.'[90] He continued to entertain such ideas. In short he held that, if worse came to worse, the British could cut their losses in the Far East and settle with the Japanese after the war. He respected Japan as a minor military power that would not be so unwise as to go to war against Britain.

His respect was mixed with a contempt for oriental peoples. The fact of his racial bias helps to explain his blindspot in the Far East. Churchill miscalculated the forces of Asian nationalism while he maintained an almost nineteenth-century notion of the prestige, if not the power, of the British Empire. He once wrote when contemplating the broader dangers of war in Asia: 'As for India, if the Japs were to invade it would make the Indians loyal to the King Emperor for a hundred years.'[91] As for China, 'Japan has done for the Chinese people what they could, perhaps, never have done for themselves. It has unified them once more.'[92] As for the Far East in general, he recounted in his memoirs that 'nothing we could have spared at the time . . . would have changed the march of fate' in Malaya, the Netherlands East Indies and other territories overrun by the Japanese.[93] Though many of his critics have challenged that view as entirely misguided, it stands as an accurate reflection of his attitude in 1940–1.

Churchill's sense of inevitability hinged on the distinct possibility of inaction on the part of the United States. His Far Eastern policy aimed at aligning Britain and America and at avoiding war with Japan as long as possible. He also wished to strengthen China, but, just as he put the Far East generally low on his list of priorities, so also he regarded assistance to China as a relatively unimportant or futile matter. On the other hand he saw great value in prolonging the war between China and Japan as an inexpensive means of keeping the Japanese occupied. The Chinese were succoured, both materially and morally, by supplies reaching them from Burma. In June 1940, shortly after the collapse of France, Churchill learned that the Japanese threatened war with Britain unless the supplies ceased. The Chiefs of Staff reported that it was 'doubly important' to avoid war with Japan now that Britain had lost her principal ally. The Foreign Office was under no illusion that Japanese demands would increase in proportion to the intensity of the crisis in Europe. 'The severity of the actual pressure applied to us', Brenan noted, 'would fluctuate with British fortunes in Europe.'[94] The Foreign Office invented an ingenious solution, which the Japanese accepted. Britain closed the Burma road for a period of three months, with the face-saving provision that there would be a genuine search for peace. Once again the Japanese were being kept in play, with only a little sacrifice of principle on Britain's part. Chamberlain wrote in July 1940: 'I was relieved and gratified to find that Winston, with the responsibilities of a P.M. on his shoulders, was firmly against the bold line.'[95] If war were to come, Churchill wanted the United States to bear the brunt of it. In the meantime he hoped for a continuation of hostilities between China and Japan. 'I have never liked the idea of our trying to make peace between Japan and China', he wrote in July 1940. He noted that he had yielded to the formula of a search for peace in exchange for the temporary closing of the Burma road, 'but it is certainly not in our interests that China and Japan should end their quarrel'.[96]

Hoping for the best in the conflict between the Japanese and Chinese, Churchill adopted a passive role for Britain. He reversed the Singapore strategy of the mid-1930s. After the defence of the British isles came the Middle East and the Mediterranean, not the Far East, which in Churchill's estimate ranked at the bottom of strategic priorities. He was consistent in outlook. In September 1939, as First Lord of the Admiralty, he had written, for the guidance of the Australians, an appreciation of the situation at Singapore. He believed that there was no need to fear an attack from Japan because the Japanese were 'a prudent people' who would not embark on such a 'mad enterprise'. He assured the Australians that a battlefleet would be sent to Eastern waters to act as a deterrent to Japan if the need arose, and in the meantime he thanked the Australian government for the 'loyal and clairvoyant strategy' whereby Australian forces were deployed where needed most, in other words, in the Middle East. Singapore as a consequence had been left, in his own phrase, 'denuded', but Australian troops were serving in 'decisive' battlefields.[97] Churchill continued to believe that the Japanese could be deterred by a show of force. When he insisted on sending the two great ships to Singapore in order to restrain Japan, he overrode the advice of the Admiralty and those less contemptuous than he about the fighting prowess of the Japanese. The loss of *Prince of Wales* and *Repulse* in December 1941 represented more than a failure to assess Japanese air power, just as the fall of Singapore reflected more than a deficiency in defence preparations. Churchill persistently underestimated the fighting capability of the Japanese.

In the 1940–1 period the Far East remained at the end of the list of strategic imperatives. The Prime Minister adopted a cavalier attitude towards the Singapore strategy, yet he gave repeated assurances to the Australians that the Middle East would be sacrificed 'for sake of kith and kin' if Australia were threatened by Japanese invasion. If Churchill was able to keep a clear conscience about the commitment to Australia and New Zealand, the Far Eastern Department of the Foreign Office was not. M. E. Dening (who during the war was political adviser at the South East Asia Command and later Ambassador to Japan) wrote in July 1940:

I think we have been a little dishonest . . . because before September 1939 the potential menace of Germany and Italy made it necessary to retain all our main forces in the Atlantic and Mediterranean. On the outbreak of war and the subsequent entry of Italy, it must have been apparent even in Australia that we had no fleet to spare. Australia may well feel that she has been induced to send troops to the Near East and to England on false pretences.[98]

Churchill was not disposed to ponder the niceties of past commitments. In his persistent view Japan would be restrained if necessary by the dispatch of capital ships – a disastrous miscalculation. On the other hand his political and strategic instinct served him well by placing all bets on the Americans. He foresaw that only the United States could make a decisive stand in the struggle against Japan and at the same time tilt the balance in Europe. His transcendent purpose was to bring America into the war on the side of Britain. He wrote shortly after Japan joined the Axis powers in September 1940: 'The entry of the United States into the war either with Germany and Italy or with Japan is fully conformable with British interests . . . if Japan attacked the United States without declaring war on us we should at once range ourselves at the side of the United States and declare war on Japan.'[99] To the time of the Japanese attack on Pearl Harbor, British policy aimed at tightening economic restrictions on Japan without provoking her into a war that would involve only Britain. Though the Japanese onslaught proved to be calamitous for the British Empire in the Far East, it was a godsend for the British cause. In Churchill's famous phrase: 'So we had won after all.'

The collapse of British power in the Far East ended an era in which the political influence of the British had outlived their military strength. 'We lived on bluff from 1920–1939', Sir Alexander Cadogan wrote in July 1940, 'but it was eventually called.'[100] Though a few perceptive observers had been uneasily unaware of the discrepancy between British power and British pretention, most Englishmen, not least Churchill, believed that the prestige of the British Empire still counted as an intangible and powerful force in Asia. The word 'prestige', as Sir John Brenan once pointed out, is an abused word. In its contemporary usage it meant, in his phrase, 'respect inspired by military strength'. The sinking of *Prince of Wales* and *Repulse* together with the fall of Singapore brought an end to the illusion of both the power and prestige of the British Empire in the Far East.

Notes: Chapter 25

1   Lindley to Simon, 1 January 1933, enclosing his annual report for 1932, Public Record Office, London: FO 371/17158/F694. For a work sympathetic with Lindley's point of view, see M. D. Kennedy, *The Estrangement of Great Britain and Japan, 1917–35* (Manchester, 1969). Recent scholarly accounts of Britain and the Far East in the 1930s include: C. Thorne, *The Limits of Foreign Policy. The West, the League and the Far Eastern Crisis of 1931–1933* (London, 1972); A. Trotter, *Britain and East Asia, 1933– 1937* (Cambridge, 1975); S. L. Endicott, *Diplomacy and Enterprise. British China Policy, 1933–1937* (University of Columbia Press, 1975); B. A. Lee, *Britain and the Sino-Japanese War, 1937–1939. A Study in the Dilemmas of British Decline* (Stanford, Calif., 1973); A. Shai, *Origins of the War in the East: Britain, China and Japan 1937–39*

(London, 1976); and P. Lowe, *Great Britain and the Origins of the Pacific War: A Study of British Policy in East Asia 1937–1941* (Oxford, 1977).

2   'It is not much comfort to the Americans that in spite of everything [i.e. Manchuria] we still stand better with the Japanese than any other nation.' Minute by Richard Allen of the Far Eastern Department of the Foreign Office, 25 March 1933, FO 371/17158/F1967.

3   Lampson to Simon, 24 August 1933, FO 371/17064/F6991.

4   ibid.

5   ibid.

6   ibid.

7   Minute by Orde, 13 July 1933, FO 371/17158/F4284.

8   Minute by Orde, 16 September 1933, FO 371/17081/F5709.

9   ibid.

10   Minute by Collier, 20 April 1934, FO 371/18184/F2101.

11   ibid.

12   Minute by Collier, 30 October 1934, FO 371/18169/F5943.

13   Minute by Collier, 16 February 1934, FO 371/18176/F639.

14   The other members of the Committee were the three Chiefs of Staff and Sir Maurice Hankey, secretary to the Cabinet and the Committee of Imperial Defence. For the Defence Requirements Committee and the problem of rearmament at this time, see especially N. H. Gibbs, *Grand Strategy. Rearmament Policy* (London, 1976), ch. IV.

15   Minute by Wellesley, 9 February 1934, FO 371/18184/F677.

16   Minute by Vansittart, 28 July 1935, FO 371/19287/F4811.

17   For an essay central to this theme see D. C. Watt, 'Britain, the United States and Japan in 1934', *Personalities and Policies* (London, 1965).

18   See for example his memorandum of 19 April 1934, *Documents on British Foreign Policy* [hereafter *DBFP*], 2nd series, Vol. VIII, appendix I.

19   ibid.

20   ibid.

21   Chamberlain to Simon, 1 September 1934, *DBFP*, Vol. VIII, no. 14.

22   ibid.

23   Simon to Vansittart, 20 August 1934, *DBFP*, Vol. VIII, no. 8.

24   For the DRC report see Gibbs, *Rearmament Policy*, ch. IV.

25   K. Feiling, *The Life of Neville Chamberlain* (London, 1946), p. 258.

26   Memorandum by Chamberlain and Simon, 16 October 1934, *DBFP*, Vol. VIII, no. 29.

27   Notes of a meeting of 13 November 1934, *DBFP*, Vol. VIII, no. 55.

28   Smuts did not use the word 'appeasement' during this particular discussion, but for his ideas in this regard see W. K. Hancock, *Smuts. The Fields of Force* (Cambridge, 1968), p. 272.

29   Meeting of 13 November 1934.

30   Memorandum by Orde, 4 September 1934, *DBFP*, Vol. VIII, no. 15.

31   ibid.

32   Memorandum by Simon, 11 January 1935, CP 8 (35), CAB 27/596.

33   Memorandum by Sansom, 29 October 1934, enclosed in ibid.

34   Sansom to Crowe, 12 October 1934, copy in T. 172/1831.

35   ibid.

36   Memorandum by Orde, 7 January 1935, enclosed in Simon's memorandum cited in note 32.

37   Memorandum by Fisher, 21 January 1935, T. 172/1831.

38   Memorandum by Fisher, 28 March 1935, FO 371/19240/F2384.

39   Memorandum by Pratt, 25 November 1935, FO 371/19247/F7505. For the Leith Ross mission, see Endicott, *Diplomacy and Enterprise*, chs 6 and 6; and Trotter, *Britain and East Asia*, chs 8 and 9.

40   Minute by Vansittart, 29 October 1935, FO 371/19245/F6729.

41   Minute by Wellesley, 22 January 1936, FO 371/20215/F320.

42   Minute by Wellesley, 25 September 1935, FO 371/19287/F4811.

43   For example, his memorandum of 4 September 1936, PEJ 251 (36), CAB 27/296.

44   Minute by Collier, 26 November 1936, FO 371/20285/F7223.

45   Memorandum by Orde, 19 November 1936, FO 371/20287/F7146.

46   Imperial Conference minutes, 5th meeting, 24 May 1937, CAB 132/28. For the Confer-

ence see R. Tamchina, 'In search of common causes: The Imperial Conference of 1937', *Journal of Imperial and Commonwealth History*, vol. I, no. 1 (October 1972).
47 ibid.
48 ibid., italics added. For Hoare's autobiographical account, see Viscount Templewood, *Nine Troubled Years* (London, 1954), which refers occasionally to matters of Far Eastern interest.
49 This is the theme of L. R. Pratt, *East of Malta, West of Suez. Britain's Mediterranean Crisis, 1936–1939* (Cambridge, 1975).
50 For Hankey and problems of imperial defence at this time see S. W. Roskill, *Hankey: Man of Secrets, 1931–1963*, Vol. III (London, 1974).
51 'Appreciation of the situation in the Far East, 1937, by the Chiefs of Staff Sub-Committee', FO 371/20952.
52 M. Howard, *The Continental Commitment* (London, 1972), p. 138.
53 Roskill, *Hankey*, Vol. III, p. 395; on this general theme see R. Ovendale, *'Appeasement' and the English Speaking World. Britain, the United States, the Dominions, and the Policy of 'Appeasement', 1937–1939* (Cardiff, 1975).
54 Minute by Orde, 2 July 1937, FO 371/20952.
55 Minutes of the DPC, 13 July 1937, ibid.
56 D. Dilks (ed.), *The Diaries of Sir Alexander Cadogan* (New York, 1972), p. 171.
57 Minute by Cadogan, 23 September 1937, FO 371/20956.
58 Minute by Cadogan, ibid.
59 ibid.
60 See Cabinet minutes of 6 and 13 October 1937, CAB 23/89.
61 Feiling, *Chamberlain*, p. 325.
62 L. Pratt, 'The Anglo-American naval conversations of the Far East of January 1938', *International Affairs*, vol. 47, no. 4 (October 1971), p. 752; for Roosevelt's ideas see also especially J. M. Haight, 'Franklin D. Roosevelt and a naval quarantine of Japan', *Pacific Historical Review*, vol. XL, no. 2 (May 1972).
63 Anthony Eden, Earl of Avon, *Facing the Dictators* (Boston, Mass., 1962), p. 620.
64 *Diaries of Sir Alexander Cadogan*, p. 37.
65 Feiling, *Chamberlain*, p. 323.
66 ibid., p. 336.
67 Memorandum by Cadogan, 29 November 1937, FO 371/20960.
68 Minute by Orde, 29 July 1937, FO 371/50951.
69 Minute by Orde, 22 November 1938, FO 371/20559.
70 Minute by Orde, 20 October 1937, FO 371/20951. Orde went on to note that in dealing with China there was, as usual, a paradox: if China were to defeat Japan without foreign assistance, Chinese xenophobia could be expected to increase.
71 Minute by Brenan, 21 May 1940, FO 371/24661.
72 Lowe, *Origins of the Pacific War*, p. 41; for the question of later assistance see appendix D. As Lowe notes, the aid was more in the realm of moral support than supplies and money.
73 *Diaries of Sir Alexander Cadogan*, p. 86.
74 Howe to Clark Kerr, 19 July 1938, Halifax Papers, FO 800/299.
75 A. J. P. Taylor, *English History, 1914–1945* (Oxford, 1965), p. 372.
76 On this issue see especially Lee, *Britain and the Sino-Japanese War*, pp. 116–19.
77 *Diaries of Sir Alexander Cadogan*, p. 104.
78 ibid., p. 119.
79 Minute by Cadogan, 23 December 1938, FO 371/22110.
80 See Halifax's memorandum of 29 November 1938, FO 371/22110.
81 Lowe, *Origins of the Pacific War*, p. 73.
82 For a discussion of this general subject see Shai, *Origins of the War in the East*.
83 Lothian to Halifax, no. 747, 10 November 1939, FO 371/23562.
84 Foreign Office, 'Appreciation of probable Japanese policy in the Far East', 15 November 1939, FO 371/23562.
85 Minute by Brenan, 13 December 1939, FO 371/23551.
86 Lowe, *Origins of the Pacific War*, pp. 106–7.
87 Minute by Sansom, 12 December 1939, FO 371/23551.
88 Minute by Sansom, 3 August 1939, FO 371/23529.

89   Minute by Brenan, 17 May 1940, Fo 371/24661.
90   M. Gilbert, *Winston S. Churchill*, Vol. V (London, 1976), p. 26.
91   S. Roskill, *Churchill and the Admirals* (London, 1977), p. 126.
92   Gilbert, *Churchill*, p. 938.
93   Churchill, *The Second World War*.
94   Minute by Brenan, 8 July 1940, FO 371/24725.
95   Lowe, *Origins of the Pacific War*, p. 149.
96   Minute by Churchill, 17 July 1940, FO 371/24661.
97   Memorandum by Churchill, 17 November 1939, DMV (39), 3, CAB 99/1.
98   Minute by Dening, 10 July 1940, FO 371/24725; for discussion about Australia, see especially J. McCarthy, *Australia and Imperial Defence 1918–39: A Study in Air and Sea Power* (University of Queensland Press, 1976); G. St J. Barclay, 'Australia looks to America: The wartime relationship, 1939–1942', *Pacific Historical Review*, vol. 46 (May 1977); and Ovendale, *'Appeasement' and the English Speaking World*.
99   Minute by Churchill, 4 October 1940, FO 371/24729.
100 Minute by Cadogan, 27 July 1940, FO 371/24708.

II

THE UNITED STATES AND THE
FASCIST POWERS

26 The Ambiguities of Appeasement: Great Britain, the United States and Germany, 1937–9

HANS-JÜRGEN SCHRÖDER

From the late nineteenth century the rise of the United States to world power status was reflected in Washington's challenge to Great Britain's position as a Great Power.[1] Although the 'special relationship' of the two Great Powers of the English-speaking world was on occasion emphasised, rivalry with Britain nevertheless remained an important element of US foreign policy in the twentieth century. The First World War prompted the American government to develop systematic aspirations towards the inheritance of the British Empire. Recent research on Wilson's war aims policy has brought impressive evidence of this to light.[2] This American strategy, directed against British imperial policy, then clearly found concrete expression in plans for the amputation of the British Empire evolved during the Second World War. By 'outlining a general "pax Americana" for the future in the form of the Atlantic Charter', US President Franklin D. Roosevelt revealed that even before its entry into the Second World War the USA did not really consider Britain as a Great Power on an equal footing, but merely as a junior partner upon which American ideas on world order were to be imposed.[3]

In view of the fact that Roosevelt was aiming at 'indirect US world leadership'[4] as early as the 1930s, it is surprising that the 'American factor' has so far been underestimated by historical research in its analysis of British foreign policy, in particular as regards relations with Germany, before the Second World War. The existence of the common Anglo-American front against the totalitarian states has certainly helped conceal the conflict of interests between Britain and America. How else can it be explained why an 'Anglo-American' appeasement policy is so often referred to? Such a homogeneous concept reinforces analyses of prewar British foreign policy which underrate the role of the United States in London's calculations. The lack of diplomatic activity in Washington's relations with Hitler's Germany up to the end of 1938 has always given historical research occasion to define US policy *vis-à-vis* Germany – parallel to that of Britain – as a policy of appeasement. The American historian Arnold Offner gave his work on American foreign policy and Germany in the years 1933–8 the title *American Appeasement* (published 1969).[5] And more recently he has repeatedly maintained that the overriding aim of Washington's policy in Europe was 'to appease Germany during 1933–1940'.[6] In his survey, *The Origins of the*

Second World War, Offner, referring to the similarities in British and American policy, speaks in general terms of 'an era of appeasement'.[7] For 1938 he still comes to the conclusion that 'American diplomacy floundered in the sea of appeasement'.[8] The British historian Ritchie Ovendale – to quote another example – comes to similar conclusions in his book *Appeasement and the English Speaking World*, published in 1975.[9]

Although it has often been assumed that Britain and America were following a uniform line *vis-à-vis* Germany, this will not withstand closer analysis. It is essential to include the domestic driving forces behind both London and Washington's policy as an integral part of our interpretation, and at the time of the World Depression this means first and foremost domestic economic forces. As regards British policy, particular reference must be made to Bernd-Jürgen Wendt's innovative work.[10] In a major work, published in 1971, Wendt demonstrated in detail the overriding importance of economic considerations in Britain's policy towards the Third Reich. London wanted to keep the German market at least partially open for products of the 'old and declining industries'. The policy of an economic balance with National Socialist Germany, already reflected in the Trade and Payment Agreement of 1 October 1934, was consistently pursued throughout the following years. This policy of *economic appeasement* was not only aimed at reducing economic tension in bilateral relations but was also seen in London as a means of pacifying Europe politically and therefore regarded as an integral part of overall foreign policy. Economic agreements with Germany 'would obviously have great possibilities as a stepping stone to political appeasement', as Hudson, under-secretary in the Department of Overseas Trade, stated in July 1938.[11]

The interdependence of economic and political aims is clearly evident from Foreign Office records. Particular emphasis was often given to the fact that 'economic and political appeasement must go hand in hand'.[12] Above all Chamberlain (as shown by C. A. MacDonald)[13] assumed that concessions in the economic field would help to strengthen the position of the so-called 'moderates' within the Reich government. Reinforcement of the moderate elements within the Reich leadership in this way would make it easier to convince Berlin that *legitimate* German demands in the political and economic fields could be fulfilled without a massive armament programme and warmongering. Chamberlain's foreign policy calculations accorded closely with his assessment of the economic basis of Britain's position; he was influenced less by the prospect of possible British trade advantages than by the conviction that Britain could not bear the economic strain of an arms race with the Third Reich.

As will be seen later, the political stratagem inherent in the British concept of *economic appeasement* on foreign affairs – was soon to be vitiated by Chamberlain himself by his intensification of economic co-operation with the USA.

Like Britain's relations with Germany, Washington's policy towards the Third Reich must also be seen within the context of domestic and, in particular, internal economic developments. The conclusion drawn by Offner and other historians that enormous internal economic difficulties caused the Roosevelt administration to be so preoccupied with solving domestic problems that it was prevented from pursuing an active foreign policy, can only be considered valid on the basis of an artificial division between the economic and political spheres. Such an approach is in any case untenable if it is considered exactly *how* the US administration tried to overcome the Depression. Here it should be noted that the regaining of foreign markets was an essential part of measures taken to combat the internal crisis. Since so many American products were dependent on export, internal economic expansion alone was not regarded as a viable alternative. The growth of agricultural and industrial exports was to play a decisive role in the revival of the economy.

This line of thinking largely reflects William A. Williams's approach. Williams defines the overseas economic expansion of the USA from the late nineteenth century as an integral part of American domestic stabilisation policy and interprets expansive foreign trade policy, not only as one element of internal economic consolidation, but also as a crucial means of preserving the liberal-capitalist system.[14] With regard to the implementation of expansive foreign trade policy, which President Roosevelt also considered necessary, the US administration was faced with the following alternative in its relations with Germany: given the sales prospects on the traditionally important German market, should Washington agree to trade concessions – similar to those made by London – thus recognising the bilateral German foreign trade system *de facto*, or should she concentrate on the re-establishment of multilateral world trade, even at the expense of losses on the German market?

Regardless of the forfeits on the German market, bound to be considerable in the immediate term, the second alternative policy, directed by Secretary of State Cordell Hull, was to prevail in the Roosevelt administration from 1934 onwards: by setting up a comprehensive trade agreement network on the basis of the most-favoured-nation clause, US economic interests were to be enforced worldwide and American hegemony established. The White House and the State Department propagated the new American trade agreement policy on the one hand as an active contribution towards the revival of the liberal world trading system which would automatically imply the reduction of economic tension. This development would more than compensate for losses on the German market. On the other hand, this strategy of *economic appeasement* was also defined as the prelude to the reduction of political tension, 'the promotion of peace through the finding of means for economic appeasement', according to a White House press release. 'There will not be military disarmament without economic appeasement', emphasised Secretary of State Hull.[15]

Similarly to Britain, the US administration also based its policy on a realisation of the close interdependence of economic and political problems, in particular questions of security. However, the American concept of *economic appeasement* begins to diverge *fundamentally* from the above-mentioned British interpretation when forces gained ground within the State Department advocating an uncompromising line towards the Third Reich and the enforcement of *economic appeasement* on American conditions alone, that is, on the basis of the new foreign trade programme. As this trade agreement system was expanded, Germany would increasingly be subject to economic pressure in the field of foreign trade. This would be a basis for finally exerting political pressure on the Third Reich: Moffat, head of the Division of European Affairs noted at the beginning of 1938: 'The development of our trade agreement program will automatically put economic pressure on Germany and in this we have a ready forged weapon in hand to induce Germany to meet general world trade and political sentiment.'[16] According to the hard-liners in the State Department, trade concessions, similar to those granted by London, would in the long term only make it easier for the National Socialist regime to gain hegemony in Europe and to carry out its plans of world domination.

Assistant Secretary of State George S. Messersmith, who as a former Consul-General in Berlin and Minister to Vienna was particularly well informed about National Socialist policy, stressed again and again that a hard line in the economic field would offer the opportunity of weakening National Socialist Germany both economically and politically to such an extent that the Reich would ultimately be forced to accept compromises in both the economic sphere and in foreign affairs. Heinrich Brüning incidentally put forward similar arguments at the beginning of 1938 when he implored the US administration to stick to trade agreement policy for political reasons. If, as a result of economic pressure, the National Socialist regime were forced to reform its economic system fundamentally, there would be people in Germany ready to introduce the necessary political reforms also.[17]

This forceful American policy had already been developed at a time when there was no question of a German threat to US security from the military and strategic point of view. It was a strategy formulated in response to the National Socialist economic offensive, above all in South America and south-east Europe. Whereas until 1939 British policy was aimed at finding a *modus vivendi* with German methods of conducting foreign trade, with the hope that this would result in their gradual liberalisation, American diplomacy, by exerting economic pressure, tried to force the Reich to return to a liberal multilateral trade system. Whereas the British conception of *economic appeasement* aimed at political détente by granting economic concessions, American diplomacy, by actively pursuing a contrary economic policy, was designed to deprive the National Socialist regime of its economic basis for military action; ideally economic pressure would even bring about a change of system inside Germany.

For Washington *economic appeasement* admittedly also implied the reduction of political tension by economic means. However, this was to be achieved by *pressure, not* by granting concessions. The fact that the term 'economic appeasement' is used to describe both Washington and London's essentially divergent outlooks, that is, the fact that the same term is applied in contemporary usages, doubtless helps to explain why the theory that the USA was also following a policy of appeasement *vis-à-vis* the Reich has so stubbornly persisted.

If we assume that British and American concepts of *economic appease-*

ment can be interpreted as *divergent* strategies of foreign policy and further that the two powers were not following a homogeneous policy as regards Germany, then we must also reassess the Anglo-American *rapprochement* from 1937/8, reflected above all in the Anglo-American Trade Agreement.

For the American government the Trade Agreement with Britain was not only the logical follow-up to its foreign trade policy; it was regarded as the climax of Washington's foreign policy, in particular as far as relations with Germany were concerned. In March 1937 US Under-Secretary of State William Phillips had already described a trade agreement of this kind as the most important step the State Department could at that time take in foreign affairs. Assistant Secretary of State Sayre also interpreted the Agreement as an outstanding American contribution towards economic *and* political stabilisation, upon which the well-being of the whole of humanity was dependent.[18]

Secretary of State Hull in particular repeatedly stressed that a trade agreement with London was indispensable and warned the British Ambassador of the consequence of a break-down in bilateral negotiations:

> If a *great trading* country like Great Britain and another great trading country like the United States became inert and undertook further self-containment alone, such countries as Japan, Germany, and Italy with their armies and navies would in two or three years dominate nearly every square foot of trade territory other than that under immediate control of Great Britain and the United States. That would leave our two countries in an amazingly disadvantageous situation.[19]

The combined political/economic function of the Anglo-American Trade Agreement was again and again emphasised by the State Department in particular and has also been recognised by historical analysis, with the political aspects standing out even more prominently. In view of the isolationist trends in American public opinion and Congressional neutrality legislation, the only instrument open to the Roosevelt administration in foreign affairs up to 1939 was trade policy. Even if we reject the theory of the great influence of economic driving forces behind US foreign policy, focusing instead on the political and ideological aspects of Roosevelt's prewar diplomacy, the *instrumental* use of trade policy for the achievement of the Roosevelt administration's aims in foreign policy nevertheless remains unaffected.

The importance of American trade policy in foreign affairs was clearly diagnosed by the British government for whom the political aspects of the trade negotiations with Washington were in fact of central importance. It was, for example, purely for political reasons that in October 1937, even before the opening of official trade agreement negotiations, the British Cabinet agreed to accept a number of the 'essentials' put forward by the USA, although some members of the Cabinet were to protest against this unusual procedure. After the Board of Trade had drawn up its instructions for the British negotiating delegation in Washington, the Foreign Office put through a number of amendments, pinpointing the political priorities:[20]

Your general instructions are to use your best endeavours to obtain from the Government of the United States an agreement which represents a reasonable balance of mutual commercial advantages and is, therefore, fair and commercially valuable to both sides. At the same time it must always be borne in mind that the commercial advantages of the agreement may be relatively inferior to its political importance. It is recognised that the fact of an agreement being reached between the two countries . . . is likely to have a very great effect on the international situation, and may be of special importance in view of the present position both in Europe and in the Far East. The Prime Minister in his address to the principal delegates to the Imperial Conference on the 27th May last year said that the moral and psychological effect of such an agreement throughout the world would be tremendous, that it was through economic co-operation that American sympathy was to be won and that that sympathy would be of incalculable value if we were once again involved in a great struggle. You are so fully aware of the political background of these negotiations that there is no need to elaborate further this aspect of your task. It is desirable, however, to emphasise this in the forefront of your instructions, since the following paragraphs necessarily deal with the purely commercial aspect.

In July 1938, following American demands for further economic concessions, the British Cabinet again reviewed the trade agreement negotiations in great depth. Members of the Cabinet agreed to 'place on record the importance that they attached, from a political and international point of view, to the conclusion of a Trade Agreement with the United States of America'.[21] With reference to this central political aspect, the President of the Board of Trade was asked to inform the Premier at once of any difficulties which might arise during the negotiations; failure was to be avoided at all costs. Chamberlain emphasised his personal interest in a trade agreement with the United States. A conversation with the US Ambassador had convinced him 'that the practical results of the agreement might not be very great, but that the psychological effect on the world was of great importance. The more the impression could be created in Europe that the United Kingdom and the United States were getting together, the less would have to be spent on armaments.'[22]

The extent to which London was prepared to pay for political *rapprochement* with the USA in economic concessions can be seen for example in the so-called 'cotton–rubber barter deal' in the spring of 1939. The Foreign Office, above all, was 'certainly anxious for major political reasons that everything should be done that might prove to be materially possible to meet the American suggestion . . . Our sole interest in the matter is the effect on Anglo-American relations.' London obviously wanted to avoid everything that might undermine the success of the Trade Agreement of November 1938.[23]

In Berlin, especially in the Wilhelmstrasse and the Ministry of Propaganda, the Trade Agreement was also interpreted as a political step – levelled at Germany. For the government of the Reich, however, it was of the utmost importance that these aspects of foreign policy should not be discussed in public. Before the Agreement was concluded the Ministry of Propaganda had confidentially let journalists be given an indication of its political significance, but at the same time instructions had been given that the Trade Agreement 'should not give rise to speculation about a close political alliance of the western democracies'. When the Agreement was signed, the Press, following a Foreign Office proposal, was once again expressly forbidden from 'indulging in polemics about the Agreement so as not to create the impression that we consider this as a victory of the democracies'.[24]

The fact that the Anglo-American Trade Agreement was seen in Berlin as proof that the two powers were pursuing an anti-German policy leaves no doubt that Chamberlain, if only because of the internal contradictions in his policy, had miscalculated that *economic appeasement* would also lead to the establishment of a political balance with the Third Reich. For in his considerations Chamberlain was banking on the so-called 'moderates' whose moderate influence on Hitler's policy was to be backed up by economic concessions from Britain. However, with his policy towards America Chamberlain had himself knocked the very bottom out of his policy towards Germany from 1937/8. As for Wendt's hypothesis that with his *economic appeasement* policy Chamberlain had a 'type of European economic block clearly directed against the United States in mind', such a generalising statement is hardly tenable.[25] If Chamberlain's policy *vis-à-vis* America from 1937/8 is interpreted as an attempt to find an alternative to a policy of appeasing Germany – at least in the medium and long term – then British foreign policy on the eve of the Second World War, as far as the Third Reich is concerned, must appear much less of a 'Diplomacy of Illusion' than is generally assumed.[26]

Despite the fact that British policy began to be orientated towards Washington in the years 1937–8, London nevertheless maintained its efforts to strike an economic balance with the Third Reich into 1939. In view of the rising unemployment figures (over 2 million in January 1939) and a £70 million trade deficit, Chamberlain had no alternative to this policy of *economic appeasement*, as MacDonald for example points out.[27] Indeed, for economic reasons – especially in the immediate term – due to the recession in the USA, too close economic ties with Washington did not appear a viable alternative. In Britain's relations with the United States, interest was centred on political and strategical considerations while economic questions were primarily of functional importance.[28]

The economic containment strategy manifested in the Anglo-American Trade Agreement against the economic and politico-military expansion of National Socialist Germany was doubtless at the centre of Washington's calculations. At the same time the US concept of *economic appeasement*, based on 'Open Door' policy, was directed against British imperial preference and in essence against Britain's position as an empire. Thus in American criticism of London's imperial policy it was pointed out that it was inappropriate to demand that 'have-nots' should lift foreign trade controls and to press for the bilateralisation of foreign trade 'while the "have" countries maintain their empires and zones of interest . . . A German closed area and a British Empire closed area are different simply in degree, and the instruments used to effect the German and British purposes are of secondary importance.'[29]

The chief reasons why these divergent aims – the British imperial preference on the one hand and US free trade imperialism on the other, incompatible at least from the American point of view – did not lead to open conflict between Washington and London lay in the joint front formed by Britain and America against the totalitarian states. The internal policy considerations of members of the American government and the course of Anglo-American Trade Agreement negotiations leave no doubt about the fact that the US offensive in foreign trade from 1934 was aimed at undermining Britain's status as a world power. The demand for tariff concessions therefore fulfilled a dual function for Washington: the opening up of markets and the fundamental erosion of the British preference system. The economic expansion of the United States at international level, dictated by internal economic reasons, and Washington's claims to overall hegemony complemented each other perfectly.

Britain's dependence on the USA in the political and strategical fields, a result of increasing tension on the critical international scene, was consistently exploited by the Roosevelt administration to achieve both these ends. Since 1938 the State Department in particular greatly increased diplomatic pressure on Great Britain and its means of doing so was not always altogether gentlemanly. Growing criticism of Hull's foreign trade programme within America may have been partly responsible for this. In August 1938, for example, the US Secretary of State told Lindsay, British Ambassador in Washington, that

> I must admit my great and growing concern in regard to the failure of the British Government thus far to make a single utterance in support of the broad program of reciprocal trade and peace based on mutually profitable commerce and equality of treatment; that I had been wondering whether there is not a real connection between this lack of support by the British Government, in Europe as well as elsewhere, of the philosophy and the spirit and the letter of this wholesome peace-making program of trade restoration and their apparent indisposition to grant what is to that country the paltry concession of these commodities (lumber, lard, tobacco, and hams) as requested by this Government . . . When I emphasized the lard proposition, the Ambassador said there was a terriffic controversy in the British Cabinet about reducing the 10% Empire preferential rate to 5%. I replied that that must explain the British indisposition to grant the four final concessions we are asking; that if the great British Cabinet would have a serious controversy about reducing the duty of 10% on lard to 5% . . . I could begin to understand how on some other theory the British Cabinet has been indifferent to our strong claims for concessions on these four commodities mentioned by me.[30]

Hull declared on a number of occasions that there was no alternative to the conclusion of a trade agreement between London and Washington and in negotiations with the British he was not afraid – against his better judgement – of conjuring up images of American isolation:

> We hope that the British seek this agreement, not primarily for the dollars and the cents immediately involved . . . We seek it primarily as a powerful initiative to help rectify the present unstable political and economic situation everywhere . . . Should this opportunity be lost, I am convinced . . . it would result in the American people turning this country in the other direction and moving definitely toward political and economic isolation.[31]

In the dispute on trade policy with the USA, the British government had originally hoped to avoid any discussions in principle of the world economic order and on imperial preference in particular. 'It may well be unpleasant to have extent of Imperial preference turned into a subject of discussion with a foreign Power but the alternative is to have the whole principle of it attacked at its very root by the most powerful economic unit in the world', argued Ambassador Lindsay.[32]

The conclusion of the Trade Agreement with the USA did not, however, mean the long-term recognition by the USA of British imperial preference. The initial undermining of imperial preference, manifested in the Anglo-American Trade Agreement of November 1938 (and the US–Canadian Trade Agreement concluded at the same time), was merely the first step in Washington's endeavours ultimately to apply its 'Open Door' policy to Britain as well. The Lend–Lease Programme of January 1941 gave the Roosevelt administration an excellent means of challenging imperial preference even more effectively.[33]

Not only did the 'synchronisation of Japanese, Italian and German attacks on central, vital British positions and interests' call 'secure rule in the Empire' into question;[34] London's imperial policy was also being increasingly undermined by the Roosevelt administration's indirect economic influence from 1937/8. This multiple threat to British interests can doubtless partly explain the contradictions in Chamberlain's policy *vis-à-vis* the Reich.

Notes: Chapter 26

1   cf., for example, H.-U. Wehler, *Der Aufstieg des amerikanischen Imperialismus. Studien zur Entwicklung des Imperium Americanum 1865–1900* (Göttingen, 1974).
    The following notes essentially give references for quotations made. The following abbreviations are used: BA (Bundesarchiv Koblenz), FRUS (Papers Relating to the Foreign Relations of the United States), NA (National Archives, Washington, DC), PRO (Public Record Office, London), RG (Record Group).

2   cf. in particular C. P. Parrini, *Heir to Empire. United States Economic Diplomacy, 1916–1923* (Pittsburgh, Pa, 1969).

3   A. Hillgruber, *Der Zenit des Zweiten Weltkrieges, Juli 1941* (Wiesbaden, 1977), pp. 32–3.

4   ibid., p. 31.

5   A. A. Offner, *American Appeasement. United States Foreign Policy and Germany, 1933–1938* (Cambridge, Mass., 1969).

6   A. A. Offner, 'Appeasement revisited: the United States, Great Britain, and Germany, 1933–1940', *Journal of American History*, vol. 64 (1977/8), p. 373.

7   A. A. Offner, *The Origins of the Second World War. American Foreign Policy and World Politics, 1917–1941* (New York, 1975), pp. 104 ff.
8   ibid., p. 124; cf. also Offner's contribution in this collection.
9   R. Ovendale, *'Appeasement' and the English Speaking World. Britain, the United States, the Dominions, and the Policy of 'Appeasement', 1937–1939* (Cardiff, 1975).
10 B.-J. Wendt, *Economic Appeasement. Handel und Finanz in der britischen Deutschland-politik 1933–1939* (Düsseldorf, 1971); cf. also Wendt's contribution in this volume.
11 Hudson minute, 8 July 1938, FO 37/21647; cf. also quoted from C. A. MacDonald, 'Economic appeasement and the German "moderates" 1937–1939. An introductory essay', *Past and Present*, no. 56 (1972), p. 117.
12 Ashton-Gwatkin minute, 14 November 1938, FO 371/21704.
13 cf. in particular MacDonald's and Wendt's publications quoted in notes 10 and 11.
14 W. A. Williams, *The Tragedy of American Diplomacy* (New York, 1972).
15 *The Public Papers and Addresses of Franklin D. Roosevelt*, Vol. *1938* (New York, 1941), p. 248; C. Hull, *Foreign Trade, Farm Prosperity and Peace* (Washington, DC, 1938), p. 16.
16 Moffat memorandum, 31 January 1938, NA, RG 59, 611.6231/1002 1/2.
17 Messersmith memorandum, 31 January 1938, Messersmith Papers, Newark/Delaware.
18 Phillips to Sayre, 24 March 1937 and Sayre to Harold Hartley, 27 May 1937, Sayre Papers, Library of Congress, Washington, DC.
19 C. Hull, *The Memoirs of Cordell Hull* (New York, 1948), p. 522.
20 Balfour to Stirling, 24 January 1938, FO 371/21490.
21 Cabinet 36 (38), PRO, CAB 23/94.
22 As above.
23 Perowne minute, 23 May 1939, FO 371/22797.
24 Instructions to the Press, 19 November 1937 and 18 November 1938, BA Koblenz, Brammer collection, vol. 10, Traub collection, vol. 10.
25 Wendt, *Economic Appeasement*, p. 526.
26 See K. Middlemas, *Diplomacy of Illusion. The British Government and Germany 1937–39* (London, 1972).
27 MacDonald, 'Economic appeasement', especially pp. 125–30.
28 This is in contrast to R. N. Kottman, *Reciprocity and the North Atlantic Triangle 1932–1938* (Ithaca, NY, 1968). However, the unpublished British documents were at that time not available to Kottman.
29 Grady to Hull, 3 April 1937, FRUS 1937 I, p. 814.
30 Hull memorandum, 19 August 1938, FRUS 1938 II, p. 52.
31 Hull to Kennedy, 25 July 1938, ibid., p. 41.
32 Lindsay to Foreign Office, 9 June 1937, FO 371/20660.
33 cf., for example, W. F. Kimball, 'Lend–lease and the open door: the temptation of British opulence, 1937–1942', *Political Science Quarterly*, vol. 86 (1971), pp. 232–59.
34 G. Niedhart, 'Appeasement. Die britische Antwort auf die Krise des Weltreichs und des internationalen Systems vor dem Zweiten Weltkrieg', *Historische Zeitschrift*, vol. 226 (1978), p. 82; cf. also A. Hillgruber, 'Forschungsstand und Literatur zum Ausbruch des Zweiten Weltkrieges', in W. Benz and H. Graml (eds), *Sommer 1939. Die Grossmächte und der Europäische Krieg* (Stuttgart, 1979), especially pp. 344–5.

27 The United States, Appeasement and the Open Door

CALLUM A. MACDONALD

American attitudes towards British appeasement between 1937 and 1939 can only be understood in relation to the overall aims of US policy in the period. As revisionist historians such as William Appleman Williams and Lloyd C. Gardner had demonstrated, the dominant US goal after 1933 was to restore the Open Door economic order which had promoted American trade expansion in the previous decade.[1] The introduction of protection and trade diversification by the major powers in response to the Depression hit the United States particularly hard. As Hull later remarked: 'Trade was being readjusted and we were losing out at every turn.'[2] It was an article of faith at the State Department that there could be no recovery from the Depression until world trade had been restored. In its approach to the world economy, therefore, the United States was a revisionist power, determined to reverse the developments of the 1930s and to abolish closed economic blocs such as German autarky and the British Ottawa system. Indeed economic revisionism was to be the fundamental element in US policy, not only in this period, but also throughout the war. Britain was viewed as the key to the attainment of US aims. It was believed in Washington that an Anglo-American trade agreement might 'stampede' the world towards economic liberalism and encourage those in Germany who argued that autarky should be abandoned. At the very least it would align the two leading commercial nations against the Nazi system of state-controlled and subsidised trade. It was within this framework that US policy-makers viewed Chamberlain's efforts to reach a settlement with Hitler. The subject of this paper is the growth of suspicion in Washington that, instead of collaborating with the US in restoring the Open Door, Chamberlain might prefer to seek a 'selfish deal' at American expense between the imperial economic bloc and a Nazi-dominated *Mitteleuropa*.

The main issue in Anglo-American relations during this period was the system of imperial preference created by Britain at the Ottawa Conference in 1932. The State Department complained in 1934 that recent British commercial policy seemed to have 'injury to American trade' as one of its 'principal purposes'.[3] The United States objected, not only to imperial preference, but also to the bilateral trade and payments agreements concluded between Britain and countries outside the empire, such as Argentina. It was felt that such treaties artificially promoted British exports at the expense of American. In Argentina, for example, the US market share dropped from 22·1 per cent in 1930 to 14·4 per cent in 1936, a decrease for which the Roca–Runciman Agreement was blamed.[4] Moreover, Britain had signed a trade and payments agreement with Germany in 1934, a step which the United States refused to take and which was regarded in Washington as an unsavoury compromise with Nazi trade policy.[5] American suspicion that London might widen this arrangement into a broader economic understanding with Berlin was to become acute between 1937 and 1939. Hostility towards British trade policy, therefore, permeated the highest levels of US policy-making. Hull denounced the Ottawa system as 'the greatest injury in a commercial way, that has been inflicted on this country since I have been in public life'.[6] According to Welles, the Under-Secretary of State, the 'whole history of British Empire Preferences' was a 'history of economic aggression' against the United States.[7] It was the 'passionate concern' with the impact of British trade and tariff policy which helped shape the US response to appeasement under Chamberlain.

The United States hoped to conclude a reciprocal trade agreement with the United Kingdom which would break open the 'oyster' of imperial preference and signal a move by London away from strict bilateralism in its dealings with countries outside the empire. As Hull argued, the two powers should co-operate in promoting multilateral trade and 'the abandonment of conflicting trade practices of a purely bilateral nature'.[8] An Anglo-American trade agreement would benefit US exporters, particularly in the agricultural sector, and consolidate support for Hull's trade policy amongst powerful interest groups. It would also be a major step towards the goal of an open world economy since it would create a liberal trading bloc, capable of resisting the extension of the Closed Door system promoted by Berlin. Germany would find it difficult to pursue its policies of state-directed commerce and strict bilateralism when faced by a combination of the world's two leading trading powers against such methods. According to Hull, the very announcement of Anglo-American trade negotiations might 'stampede' the world towards economic liberalism.[9] A trade treaty, therefore, was seen by Washington as a major step towards recovery from the Depression and as a powerful lever in US relations with Nazi Germany.

The manner in which such a lever would be used was a matter of debate in Washington. Until late 1938 the Roosevelt administration was divided on the issue of Nazi Germany into 'appeasers' and 'anti-appeasers'. Common to both groups was the belief that autarky and rearmament in Germany were producing severe internal strains which would ultimately create a situation in which Hitler would be faced with the choice of total economic collapse or military expansion to seize new markets and sources of raw materials. The 'appeasers', represented by officials such as Welles and Berle, argued that the Führer must be offered some escape from this position short of war. A negotiated solution must be sought which would meet legitimate German grievances in return for the abandonment of armaments and the reintegration of Germany into a liberal world trading system.[10] As a State Department memorandum noted in February 1937: 'Can a compromise be found or a price paid which will satisfy the economic necessities of the German people without war or without making Germany paramount on the Continent?'[11]

'Anti-appeasers', such as George Messersmith, believed on the contrary that a German economic collapse should be encouraged. A joint front of the Western powers should leave Hitler to 'stew in his own juice', in the hope that internal strains would bring down the regime and replace it by a government with which the United States could 'do business'. As Messersmith argued in September 1936: 'For the present the only steps which can be taken in the direction of peace in Europe are to . . . keep the balance of armaments against Germany, and to maintain the economic pressure against her, for it is this latter which is the only means . . . of bringing about reason in Germany.'[12] Both groups agreed on the importance of an Anglo-American trade treaty to their German policies. Messersmith believed that the treaty, by creating a liberal economic blow, would preclude the possibility of a 'deal' between London and Berlin which would prop up the system of autarky and place Hitler in a better position to arm and threaten, a development which he had feared since 1933.[13] The 'appeasers' believed that the treaty would strengthen 'moderate' elements in Germany which opposed autarky and favoured the reintegration of the Reich into a liberal-capitalist trading system. It would provide the basis on which Britain and the United States could work out a comprehensive agreement with Berlin. As Norman Davis informed Eden in April 1937, the United States was 'vitally interested in economic rehabilitation and disarmament and desirous of collaborating [with Britain] to that end'. It was, however, 'absurd' to expect any progress towards world peace and stability while the two major trading powers, Britain and the United States, pursued 'diametrically opposite' commercial policies.[14]

US moves towards a comprehensive trade agreement and a common approach to the problem of Nazi Germany coincided with Chamberlain's rise to the premiership in London. He was already an object of suspicion in the United States because of his association with the creation of the Ottawa system and his supposed commitment to his father's dream of an imperial economic bloc.[15] As Prime Minister, Chamberlain expressed interest in an Anglo-US trade agreement, but emphasised the difficulties involved in negotiations and clearly envisaged a more limited pact than Hull.[16] As Kennedy noted in July 1938, Chamberlain promised to do everything possible to facilitate a trade treaty, but what 'he thinks possible and what we think possible, is of course liable to be very different'.[17] The speedy conclusion of the talks sought by Washington proved impossible and negotiations dragged on until November 1938 when a much narrower agreement emerged than the treaty originally envisaged by Hull. Not only did it prove difficult to conclude a commercial treaty, but Chamberlain also seemed uninterested in co-ordinating a common approach to Berlin with the United States. In July 1937 he rejected an invitation to the White House for a general discussion of world problems with Roosevelt.[18] In January 1938 he turned down a US proposal for parallel approaches to Berlin and Rome. The American plan, drawn up by Welles, envisaged a meeting of the smaller powers under US auspices in Washington to establish new rules of international law, discuss arms limitation and consider the questions of tariff reduction and equal access to raw materials. Britain, meanwhile, was to begin negotiations on political issues with Germany and Italy and the United

States was to act as 'a channel of information' between both sets of discussions.[19] Chamberlain rejected the plan on the grounds that it would 'cut across' his own approaches to the dictators.[20] As Kennedy reported in March 1938, the Prime Minister was 'convinced concrete concessions must be made to Germany and Italy and is prepared to make them to avert a war. He really does not expect America to do anything.'[21]

Chamberlain's reluctance to co-operate unreservedly with the United States raised doubts in Washington about his commitment to the US goal of a liberal world economy. His insistence on bilateral relations with Germany, which excluded the US, raised the spectre of an Anglo-German agreement based on an exclusive economic deal. London and Berlin would work out arrangements between their own blocs, perhaps on the basis of British access to the markets of *Mitteleuropa* in return for German access to the empire. This suspicion had been growing in the United States since the summer of 1937. Indeed one of the aims of the Welles plan of January 1938 was to ensure that the US had a voice in any Anglo-German agreement which might emerge as a result of Lord Halifax's visit to Berlin in November 1937.[22] By assuming the main responsibility for reshaping the world economy, Washington could ensure that US interests were safeguarded, something which was by no means guaranteed if economic negotiations were left in the hands of Chamberlain.

United States suspicion of Chamberlain's policy became acute with the resignation of Eden as British Foreign Secretary and the *Anschluss* in February–March 1938. Eden had been identified as the member of the Chamberlain Cabinet most committed to co-operation with the United States and a collective approach to the problem of Nazi Germany. His resignation was believed to represent the triumph of a 'pro-German' group with 'heavy support from the City and financial interests', whose leading members were 'Chamberlain, Simon, Hoare, the Astors, Lothian, Geoffrey Dawson and Lord Halifax'. These 'City' men were prepared to collude in German expansion eastwards in order to preserve the empire and contain communism. They argued:

From a purely materialistic point of view, England would stand to gain financially and commercially by coming to terms with Berlin . . . England could, by sacrifices today, for the most part at the expense of other countries in Central and Eastern Europe, win for herself security for an appreciable time to come . . . Such a policy would necessarily be at the expense of general principles, but the group is more interested in material advantages than in moral abstractions.

Thus, with Eden gone, Chamberlain would 'play ball' with Hitler, allowing German expansion east and south to create a new *Mitteleuropa*.[23]

This process of German expansion began with the *Anschluss* and it was clear that Prague would be the next object of Nazi pressure. It was assumed in Washington throughout the Czech crisis that Chamberlain would be prepared to sacrifice Beneš in pursuit of a deal with Hitler. As Kennedy reported in July 1938: 'He hopes that the Czech matter will be adjusted without difficulty and that in the fall . . . they will start negotiations with Germany.'[24] British collusion in the creation of *Mitteleuropa* was symbolised by the refusal to undertake any new security commitments in the wake of the *Anschluss* and by the extension of the Anglo-German payments agreement to cover the new situation created by the annexation of Austria in July 1938. Both governments committed themselves to 'improve trade relations' and seemed to envisage the conclusion of a broader commercial agreement in the future. London seemed more concerned to guarantee its position in the new German Empire than to halt aggression or to join the United States in constructing an open world economy.[25] As Roosevelt remarked, Chamberlain was a 'City man', anxious to strike a 'business deal' with the dictators.[26]

US policy-makers often equated the sources of Chamberlain's support with the 'reactionary' interests which opposed the New Deal in the United States. As Bowers remarked, the Prime Minister 'gets his ideology from the City – England's Wall St . . . Where he an American would elbow Du Pont and Raskob from their thrones in the Liberty League.'[27] Reports from London confirmed the sympathies which existed between the City and 'selfish' US business groups opposed to Roosevelt. According to the US Embassy in a report of March 1938, leading London bankers felt it imperative that 'an effort should be made to ameliorate America's internal strife and restore confidence'. The President should 'take the lead and refrain from provocative speeches criticising businessmen as a class'.[28] Moreover, there were disturbing hints throughout the period that US business interests were co-operating with their City counterparts in the search for a deal which would prop up the Nazi regime for short-term commercial advantage. Companies with investments in Germany, such as General Motors, were known to be anxious to deal with Berlin on Nazi terms in order to safeguard their holdings in the Reich and argued in favour of an accommodation with Hitler.[29] It was believed that these 'Wall Street' groups, blocked from a direct approach to Germany by official US trade policy, were co-operating with the 'City' in Britain, promising to contribute to some form of credit to Hitler in return for an improvement in the position of foreign companies in the Reich.[30]

An Anglo-German deal over *Mitteleuropa* was viewed in Washington as a threat to US interests. Despite the *Anschluss*, the administration remained divided between 'appeasers' and 'anti-appeasers', but both groups shared a common fear that Chamberlain's policy might not ultimately benefit the United States. 'Anti-appeasers', such as Messersmith, argued that an Anglo-German economic agreement would strengthen autarky and prevent the collapse of the regime. By underwriting the German economy, Chamberlain would increase Hitler's capacity to accumulate armaments, thus making war inevitable in the long term. In the short term, an alignment of the British and German economic blocs would undermine the reciprocal trade agreements programme and leave the United States with the 'crumbs' of world trade. Once he had consolidated his position in *Mitteleuropa*, Hitler would be better able to challenge the United States in the Western hemisphere where German trade penetration was already causing concern.[31] 'Appeasers', such as Welles and Berle, were similarly concerned about the possibility of an Anglo-German agreement. By itself, they did not regard German expansion along the Danube basin as necessarily threatening or unnatural. As Berle noted, the reconstruction of the Austrian Empire unit under Germany was probably inevitable, as was revision of the treaty system which had created composite states such as Czechoslovakia. If Germany established a presence in the area it might not only defuse Nazi radicalism, but would also contain Soviet Russia, which this group saw as a more serious threat to world order and US interests than the Nazi Reich. As Berle admitted, if placed in the same position as Chamberlain, he would probably follow the same line and sacrifice Czechoslovakia.[32] The 'appeasers', however, believed that the establishment of a German presence in Central and south-eastern Europe should take place within the context of the Open Door. In other words, what they objected to was not the *political* aspect of Chamberlain's policy but the inherent possibilities within it of a bilateral economic arrangement which would align the British imperial system and a German *Mitteleuropa* against US trade expansion.

Thus, throughout the Munich crisis the 'appeasers' were determined that while Chamberlain might be allowed to work out the political aspects of a deal with Germany, the United States must have a leading voice in the economic aspects of a European settlement. As Berle noted, once the Prime Minister had 'sold' the Czechs, the United States must sponsor a conference on economic appeasement to set the seal on any bilateral agreements worked out between London and Berlin.[33] In the period of euphoria which followed the Munich Conference, the 'appeasers' prepared to launch such an initiative – a new Congress of Berlin which would definitively settle European problems.[34] While the European powers concentrated on political issues, Washington was to have a major voice in the economic deliberations of the conference. The goal of the Open Door would be thus achieved and a narrow Anglo-German economic deal, which might be expanded into a four-power bloc including France and Italy, prevented.

The development of events after Munich denied both Chamberlain and the American 'appeasers' the opportunity to work out new relationships with Germany. Hitler's Saarbrücken speech seemed to show that the Führer was uninterested in negotiations and the *Kristallnacht* pogrom confirmed the impression of a radical regime, committed to repression at home and expansion abroad. These events crystallised opinion in Washington into a common hostility to Nazi Germany. 'Appeasers', such as Welles, could join Messersmith in arguing that negotiations with Hitler would prove fruitless and that the kind of arrangements which could be worked out with a Brüning or a Stresemann could not be made with the Nazis. The United States must join Britain and France in containing further German expansion which, if unchecked, must ultimately threaten the Western hemisphere. Specifically, the United States should build up its arms industry and repeal the Neutrality Act as a signal to Berlin that Washington stood behind London and Paris. Anglo-US trade negotiations should also be concluded, creating a liberal economic bloc to combat Nazi trade methods and threaten Germany with the combined resources of the world's leading trading nations.[35] After October 1938, therefore, US policy had shifted towards containment of

Germany, the line favoured by the 'anti-appeasers' before Munich. The question remained, however, whether Chamberlain would be prepared to join the United States in this approach, any more than he had welcomed the efforts of American 'appeasers' in January 1938 to co-ordinate policy with London.

At first the prospects seemed favourable. In November 1938 an Anglo-US trade agreement was signed which, while not the wide-ranging pact for which Hull had hoped, represented some concession of imperial preference and a step towards the US goal of multilateralism. In Washington it was assumed that with this treaty, the threat of an Anglo-German economic agreement had been averted. It symbolised a move by London away from collusion with the Nazi system towards the kind of world economic structure favoured by the United States. As Messersmith remarked in November 1938, the trade agreement meant that Chamberlain and his friends would be unable to go ahead with any plans for an economic deal with Berlin.[36] The break between London and the Nazi trade system seemed to be confirmed in December 1938, when following complaints about German dumping, the government passed the Export Credit Guarantees Act, designed to subsidise British trade against unfair Nazi competition. In December 1938 the US Embassy in London noted 'indications of a stiffening in Chamberlain's attitude against gratuitous concessions . . . to Germany. This reinforced attitude has been indicated in various ways, particularly in the economic field, and the recent drive by the Department of Trade to protect British markets against German competition in third countries.'[37] By the beginning of 1939, therefore, an Anglo-US containment system seemed to be emerging. Germany was to be economically contained by the threat of trade retaliation by the United States and Britain. Politically, Hitler was to be deterred by rearmament in Britain, France and the USA, coupled with the repeal of the American Neutrality Act which would show that US industrial resources stood behind London and Paris and raise the threat of ultimate US involvement in the event of war. Prevented from breaking out of this encirclement by the balance of forces against him, Hitler would be forced to watch the deterioration of the German economy to a point where the Western powers could dictate their terms, terms which he would have to accept or face the threat of a coup against the regime stimulated by internal discontent.

American confidence in the development of Anglo-US co-operation, however, proved premature and in the spring of 1939 Washington again believed that it was faced with the threat of a bilateral Anglo-German deal. In February 1939, following a statement by Hitler in his Reichstag speech that Germany 'must trade or die', Chamberlain pursued serious economic talks with the Reich, designed both to broaden the scope of the Anglo-German payments agreement and to reach marketing and pricing arrangements between British and German industry.[38] The United States regarded the negotiations extremely seriously and viewed them as a violation of the spirit, if not the letter, of the Anglo-American Trade Agreement. As one US official noted: 'This development has potential, far-reaching significance for the policies of the Department and for American interests in foreign trade.'

The creation of international cartels envisaged in the Anglo-German industrial talks was 'the direct antithesis of the free competition and the free flow of trade' desired by the United States. There could be 'no question but that it will have very extensive repercussions both upon our own policy and upon the interests of our exporters.'[39] The whole episode was regarded in Washington as an attempt to create an economic bloc against the United States, an impression which was confirmed by the Düsseldorf Agreements between the Federation of British Industry and the *Reichsgruppe Industrie* in March 1939. The Americans objected particularly to clause 8 of that agreement which suggested that in the event of a third country refusing to become party to the pricing and marketing arrangements concluded at Düsseldorf, 'it may be necessary for the organisations to obtain the help of their governments and the two organisations agree to collaborate in seeking that help'.[40] The clause raised the possibility of the Export Credit Guarantees system being used, not to combat German trade methods, but to collaborate with the Reich in the Nazi drive against the Open Door in world markets. Hull complained to Roosevelt that although Britain 'was doing lip service to freer trade and a breakdown of barriers, yet in practice she was encouraging clearing agreements, exchange controls, preferential tariffs and international cartels'.[41] Welles protested against the Düsseldorf Agreements in London, complaining that 'from the beginning' the US had 'been disturbed lest the outcome [of Anglo-German talks] should serve to strengthen the present German system of trading and handicap the type of commercial policy which this government has sought to advance'. The cartel arrangements envisaged at Düsseldorf 'did not make a happy impression' in Washington.[42]

The United States was particularly concerned that an Anglo-German economic agreement, perhaps accompanied by a British credit to Berlin, would be coupled with acquiescence in German expansion. London would agree to the further extension of the closed economy in Europe in return for short-term peace and immediate profits. It was believed in Washington that the German plan was to organise the Balkan area, as far as Turkey, into a gigantic autarkic bloc, a scheme to which Chamberlain's 'City' supporters, such as Montague Norman, did not object, provided Hitler guaranteed the empire and allowed Britain favoured access to the markets of *Mitteleuropa*.[43] It had already been decided in Washington that such an outcome would endanger the peace and security of the United States. As Roosevelt argued in January 1939, the small countries of Europe were America's first line of defence. If Hitler could dominate them, and then used 'the economic weapon' which would be his, he could threaten the US 'without even a thought of trying to land a soldier on our shores'. By the manipulation of state-controlled trade and the strength which would come from possessing the largest market in Europe, Hitler could undermine the US position in Latin America, suggesting to the South American republics that unless they accepted Nazi economic methods and fascist governments, their trade with the Continent would be cut off. The United States would be powerless in the face of such a development and would have no alternative but to retreat within its own borders, there to 'get along' as best it could.[44]

Washington believed it already had enough evidence of Nazi intrigues in countries such as Argentina and Brazil to confirm the existence of such a long-term German plan. It could not, therefore, view calmly the further extension of the Nazi closed economy in Europe. Thus in February/March 1939 the United States feared that it faced the situation predicted by Messersmith in the wake of the Munich Conference. Chamberlain was 'giving away something precious' that belonged to the United States, namely, the political and economic security of the Americas.[45]

Despite the failure to follow up the Düsseldorf Agreements because of the Prague coup and the British guarantee to Poland, Washington remained suspicious of Chamberlain's ultimate intentions. In May 1939 the President of the Board of Trade, Stanley, informed the Commons that he would be 'only too glad' to see trade discussion resumed with Germany once tension had abated. The same month, City gossip reaching the United States reported Chamberlain's intention to build 'a golden bridge' to Berlin in the near future.[46] Such rumours seemed to be confirmed in July by the press revelations of the Hudson–Wohltat talks. Hudson had already been defined by the State Department as being

> unfriendly to American interests, or at least . . . unwilling to subordinate immediate British interests with a view to obtaining a broader agreement with us in world trade. Not only was he on the side of the negotiators of the British Trade Agreement last year, but he has certainly encouraged the FBI to try to work out cartel agreements with Germany. He is ready to sacrifice principle for the sake of pounds sterling.[47]

According to information reaching Washington from 'a reliable source' in Warsaw, Hudson was acting on behalf of the City group in his talk with Wohltat. Chamberlain, Simon and Wilson were still anxious to buy off Hitler and to 'conciliate rather than to stand up to aggressors'.[48] The type of deal supposedly envisaged in the talks, a British credit, economic co-operation and mutual non-interference in *Mitteleuropa* and the empire, represented much the kind of terms which Washington had always suspected the Prime Minister favoured. Accordingly, during the Polish crisis in September, the United States was by no means convinced that it would not be faced with a second Munich.

In the final days before the outbreak of war, Washington kept a careful watch on the diplomatic exchanges between London and Berlin. In particular, American attention focused on the response to Hitler's offer of 25 August to guarantee the British Empire once the Polish question had been settled. The British reply to the Führer on 28 August, while emphasising that London would not allow the partition of Poland, expressed interest in a Polish-German settlement and raised the possibility of an economic conference if a 'fair deal' could be worked out between Warsaw and Berlin. The hand of the 'City' group was immediately detected in this offer. It was thought that a struggle was raging in London between 'appeasers' and those who argued that the time had come to stand up to Hitler. As Berle noted, Chamberlain, Simon and Wilson were 'all for appeasement' and had only been prevented from concluding a deal on the basis of the German offer by Halifax's threat to resign and bring down the government. The final version of the British reply to Hitler represented a compromise between the two factions. It was a 'goulash', which 'began with some firm talk and wound up by offering to discuss a lot of things which really, under [the British] alliance with Poland, are not open for discussion'.[49] According to Moffat, the British note 'struck us all as a mere play for time and completely unrealistic . . . the most charitable explanation was that Britain and Germany were playing to throw the actual blame for a breach on each other. The less charitable explanation was that the British were not above a dicker leaving Poland to pay the price.[50] When it was learned on 30 August that Hitler had agreed to direct German-Polish negotiations, provided a Polish emissary was sent at once to Berlin, it was feared that the 'City' group might seize this opportunity to sacrifice Poland in the cause of an Anglo-German settlement. On 31 August, in an interview with Lord Lothian, the British Ambassador, Roosevelt made plain US opposition to such a development. The President

> expressed the view that the most serious danger from the standpoint of American public opinion would be if it formed the conclusion that Herr Hitler was entangling the British Government in negotiations leading to pressure on Poland . . . to abandon vital interests. What right had Germany to demand that a Polish representative should go to Berlin to be treated like Dr. Schuschnigg or Hacha and not to some neutral capital or with proper security against such treatment.[51]

Thus suspicions about Chamberlain's intentions lingered in Washington until the end. As Roosevelt remarked when he received the news of the British declaration of war, 'up to the last, Cordell Hull had said that personally he was from Missouri. He had no faith that Chamberlain would not again turn his hand from the plow.'[52]

American distrust of Chamberlain and the desire to preclude an Anglo-German deal at US expense did not vanish with the outbreak of war. From the beginning, Washington was determined to have a voice in the economic aspects of any compromise peace in Europe. In January 1940 investigations began into the possibility of a US-mediated settlement, which would contain the threat of Nazi expansion and reintegrate London and Berlin into an Open Door world economy.[53] The German spring offensive, however, destroyed any hopes of such a compromise peace and forced the United States to take a more active role in the war. Despite the Anglo-American alliance which emerged after the fall of France, Washington never lost its suspicion of British commercial policy or its feeling that the Open Door economic system sought by the United States did not enjoy the full support of London. Throughout the war, by mechanisms such as article VII of the Lend–Lease Agreement, the United States attempted to commit the United Kingdom to the dismantling of imperial preference and the restoration of multilateralism as the pattern for postwar trade. As Berle remarked in July 1941, there would be no point in the US assuming the burdens of the war merely to move the centre of the closed economy from Berlin to London.[54]

In the years after 1939, it became evident that the Anglo-American trade treaty of November 1938 was merely the beginning and not the end of the US assault on the Ottawa system. Moreover, the relative power relationships after 1940, granted British economic exhaustion, meant that the United States had greater leverage to force compliance with its aims. As Harry Dexter White noted after one round of financial talks with the British in December 1940: 'The atmosphere was all "Hands across the sea" but one of them had a brass knuckle.'[55] His words make clear that in the period after 1940, unlike before, there could be no doubt as to where real power lay in the Anglo-US relationship.

Notes: Chapter 27

1   W. Appleman Williams, *The Tragedy of American Diplomacy* (New York, 1972); L. G. Gardner, *Economic Origins of New Deal Diplomacy* (Madison, Wis., 1974).
2   C. Hull, *The Memoirs of Cordell Hull* (London, 1947), p. 354.
3   Memorandum by the Division of Western European Affairs, 20 February 1934, State Department Records, State Decimal File A/B 641.11/3, National Archives of the United States, Washington, DC.
4   D. Rock (ed.), *Argentina in the Twentieth Century* (London, 1975), p. 115.
5   M. N. Rothbard, 'The new deal monetary system', in L. P. Liggio and J. J. Martin (eds), *Watershed of Empire. Essays on New Deal Foreign Policy* (Colorado Springs, Col., 1976).
6   R. N. Gardner, *Sterling-Dollar Diplomacy* (New York, 1969), p. 19.
7   R. S. Russell, *Imperial Preference* (London, 1949), p. 11.
8   R. N. Kottman, *Reciprocity and the North Atlantic Triangle* (Ithaca, NY, 1968), p. 128.
9   ibid., pp. 164–5, 118.
10 Memorandum by Welles, 26 October 1937, *Foreign Relations of the United States, 1937* (Washington, DC, 1954), Vol. 1, pp. 667–78; Berle diary, 17 September 1937, 7 October 1937, Box 210, Adolf A. Berle Papers, Franklin D. Roosevelt Library, Hyde Park, New York.
11 Memorandum by the Division of Western European Affairs, 16 February 1937, Norman H. Davis Papers, Box 24, Library of Congress, Manuscripts Division, Washington, DC.
12 Messersmith to Dunn, 18 September 1936, Messersmith Papers, File 921, University of Delaware Library, Newark, Delaware.
13 Messersmith to Phillips, 20 June 1935, Messersmith Papers, File 510; Messersmith to Hull, 2 March 1937, ibid., File 867; Messersmith to Heineman, 28 November 1938, ibid., File 1083.
14 Davis to Hull, 10 April 1937, 740.00/143.
15 Bingham to Hull, 24 May 1937, *FRUS 1937*, Vol. 2, pp. 32–3.
16 Davis to Hull, 29 April 1937, 740.00/154.
17 Kennedy to Hull, *FRUS 1938*, Vol. 2, pp. 44–5.
18 D. Borg, *The United States and the Far Eastern Crisis, 1933–1938* (Cambridge, Mass., 1964), pp. 377–8.
19 Memorandum by Welles, 10 January 1938, *FRUS 1938*, Vol. 1, pp. 115–17.
20 Chamberlain to FDR, 14 January 1938, ibid., pp. 118–20.
21 Kennedy to Hull, 4 March 1938, 711.41/389.
22 B. B. Berle and T. B. Jacobs (eds), *Navigating the Rapids 1918–1971. From the Papers of Adolf A. Berle* (New York, 1973), p. 150.
23 Moffat to Hull, 1 February 1938, 741.62/228; N. H. Hooker (ed.), *The Moffat Papers. Selections from the Diplomatic Journals of Jay Pierrepont Moffat* (Cambridge, Mass., 1956), p. 190.
24 Kennedy to Hull, 26 July 1938, 741.65/620.
25 C. A. MacDonald, *The United States, Britain and Appeasement* (London, 1981), pp. 85–6.
26 St Quentin to Bonnet, 11 March 1938, *Documents diplomatiques français*, 2nd series (Paris, 1973), Vol. 8, p. 729.

27 Bowers to Roosevelt, 24 October 1938, President's Confidential File, Spain, Franklin D. Roosevelt Library, Hyde Park, New York.
28 Butterworth to Morgenthau, 30 March 1938, 841.5151/848.
29 Messersmith to Geist, 8 December 1938, Messersmith Papers, File 1093; E. Roosevelt and J. Brough (eds), *A Rendezvous with Destiny* (New York, 1975), pp. 193–4.
30 Biddle to Roosevelt, 27 July 1939, President's Safe File, Poland, Franklin D. Roosevelt Library.
31 Memorandum by Messersmith, 18 February 1938, *FRUS 1938*, Vol. 1, pp. 17–24.
32 Berle diary, 18 February 1938, 19 March 1938; Berle and Jacobs (eds), *Navigating the Rapids*, pp. 183–5.
33 Berle and Jacobs (eds), ibid.
34 Berle diary, 30 September 1938.
35 MacDonald, *The US, Britain and Appeasement*, pp. 106–24.
36 Messersmith to Heineman, 28 November 1938, Messersmith Papers, File 1083.
37 Johnson to Moffat, 29 December 1938, Jay Pierrepont Moffat Papers, Houghton Library, Harvard.
38 Callum A. MacDonald, 'Economic appeasement and the German "moderates" 1937–1939. An introductory essay', *Past and Present*, no. 56 (August 1972), pp. 124–6.
39 Davies to Hull, 2 February 1939, Joseph E. Davies Papers, File 9, Library of Congress, Manuscripts Division, Washington, DC.
40 *House of Commons Debates*, vol. 345, cols 1107–9.
41 Moffat diary, 26 March 1939; Berle diary, 20 February 1939.
42 Welles to Kennedy, 7 March 1939, 641.6231/167; Welles to Kennedy, 20 March 1939, 641.6231/178.
43 Gilbert to Hull, 4 February 1939, 762.00/240; Morgenthau diary, 3 January 1939, vol. 159, Morgenthau Papers, Franklin D. Roosevelt Library; Kennedy to Hull, 27 February 1939, PSF Confidential, Great Britain.
44 H. L. Ickes, *The Secret Diary of Harold L. Ickes*, Vol. 2 (London, 1955), pp. 569–70.
45 Memorandum by Messersmith, 29 September 1938, *FRUS 1938*, Vol. 1, pp. 704–7.
46 Johnson to Hull, 11 May 1939, 641.6231/193; Morgenthau diary, 24 May 1939, vol. 191.
47 Moffat diary, 10 May 1939.
48 Biddle to Roosevelt, 27 July 1939, PSF Poland.
49 Berle diary, 28 August 1939.
50 Hooker, *Moffat Papers*, p. 256.
51 Lothian to Halifax, 31 August 1939, *Documents on British Foreign Policy*, series 3, Vol. 7, pp. 428–9.
52 Ickes, *Secret Diary*, Vol. 2, p. 713.
53 Berle and Jacobs (eds), *Navigating the Rapids*, pp. 283–4.
54 ibid., p. 373.
55 Morgenthau diary, 9 December 1940, vol. 337.

Bibliography: Chapter 27

Barclay, Glenn, *Struggle for a Continent* (London, 1971).
Berle, Beatrice B. and Jacobs, Travis B. (eds), *Navigating the Rapids, 1918–1971. From the Papers of Adolf A. Berle* (New York, 1973).
Blum, John M. (ed.), *From the Morgenthau Diaries*, 3 vols (Cambridge, Mass., 1959–67).
Borg, Dorothy, *The United States and the Far Eastern Crisis* (Cambridge, Mass., 1964).
Dallek, Robert, *Franklin D. Roosevelt and American Foreign Policy, 1932–1945* (New York, 1979).
Gardner, Lloyd C., *Economic Aspects of New Deal Diplomacy* (Madison, Wis., 1974).
Gardner, Richard N., *Sterling-Dollar Diplomacy* (New York, 1969).
Hooker, Nancy H., *The Moffat Papers. Selections from the Diplomatic Journals of Jay Pierrepont Moffat* (Cambridge, Mass., 1956).
Hull, Cordell, *The Memoirs of Cordell Hull*, 2 vols (London, 1947).
Kolko, Gabriel, *The Politics of War* (New York, 1970).
Kottman, Richard N., *Reciprocity and the North Atlantic Triangle* (Ithaca, NY, 1968).

Langer, William and Gleason, S. Everett, *The Challenge to Isolation*, 2 vols (New York, 1962).

Liggio, Leonard P. and Martin, James J., *Watershed of Empire. Essays on New Deal Foreign Policy* (Colorado Springs, Colo, 1976).

MacDonald, Callum A., *The United States, Britain and Appeasement* (London, 1981).

Offner, Arnold A., *American Appeasement. United States Foreign Policy and Germany 1933–1938* (Cambridge, Mass., 1969).

Roosevelt, Elliott and Brough, James, *A Rendezvous with Destiny* (New York, 1975).

Rowland, Benjamin J., *Balance of Power or Hegemony. The Interwar Monetary System* (New York, 1976).

Schröder, Hans-Jürgen, 'Das Dritte Reich, die USA und Latin Amerika', in Manfred Funke (ed.), *Hitler, Deutschland und die Mächte* (Düsseldorf, 1976).

Watt, Donald, *Personalities and Policies* (London, 1965).

Welles, Sumner, *The Time for Decision* (London, 1944).

Williams, William A., *The Tragedy of American Diplomacy* (New York, 1972).

28 The United States and National Socialist Germany

ARNOLD A. OFFNER

Between January 1933 and spring 1940 Adolf Hitler's diplomacy, sabre-rattling and *Blitzkrieg* tactics established National Socialist Germany's dominance over Western and Central Europe. This essay explains the reasons which underlay American efforts first to appease Germany and then to contain or to destroy what Americans perceived to be a Nazi, or fascist, design to impose a dictatorial new order upon the globe. The policy of the United States is best understood by reference to the American attitude towards the European order created at the Paris Peace Conference in 1919; the way in which American diplomats viewed the major nations, or actors, upon the European stage; and the role which Americans believed most appropriate for the United States to play in resolving Europe's problems.

Throughout the 1930s American diplomats believed that European instability stemmed chiefly from Germany's effort to throw off the Treaty of Versailles and from the acute nationalistic political and economic rivalries and dislocations that sprang from the national states created out of the sundered Austro-Hungarian Empire. As Roosevelt's friend and closest diplomatic adviser, Under-Secretary of State Sumner Welles, said in July 1937, the world's current ills derived from the injustices and maladjustments resulting from the Great War, and 'these obviously are political as well as economic and financial. A vicious circle has been created and no one set of these problems can be solved without simultaneous adjustment of others.'[1] More pointedly, Assistant Secretary of State Adolf A. Berle reminded Roosevelt in September 1938 that at the Paris Peace Conference 'one branch of the American Delegation felt that it was a mistake to break up the Austro-Hungarian Empire', but that French military considerations prevailed over 'trained political men', while in the 1920s French support for the Little Entente prevailed over liberal policy which favoured reconstituting the empire in the form of a customs union or other federal arrangement. Now, even as Germany poised to absorb 'some, if not all' of Czechoslovakia, 'emotion is obscuring the fact that were the actor anyone other than Hitler, with his cruelty and anti-Semitic feeling, we should regard this as merely reconstituting the old system, undoing the unsound work of Versailles and generally following the line of historical logic'. Finally, despite current sentiment that 'fascism must be destroyed', not even a 'successful great Germany will forever be the hideous picture it is today', whereas American intervention in a European war would achieve no more than the last intervention.[2]

American diplomats also had serious reservations about the chief architects or underwriters of the post-1919 European order. Typically,

Roosevelt denigrated the 'Bank of England crowd' and Neville Chamberlain, and believed that 'the trouble is when you sit around the table with a Britisher he usually gets 80 percent of the deal and you get what is left'.[3] He saw Anglo-American co-operation as problematic because 'the British conception of mutuality differs from mine'; in good times they showed a 'national selfishness', and in bad times sought to push the Americans out front or make them 'a tail to the British kite'. He characterised the June 1935 Anglo-German Naval Agreement as a long-run British mistake, suspected secret British–German agreement on other issues, viewed the December 1935 Hoare–Laval effort over Ethiopia as outrageous, and longed for the day the British Foreign Office showed 'a little more unselfish spine' and abandoned its 'muddle-through' attitude. In February 1939 he said the British needed 'a good stiff grog' to induce the proper belief that they – not America – could 'save civilization' by resisting Hitler.[4]

Americans believed that the French could not distinguish between their security needs and their desire for political–military hegemony in Europe. Their government – 'or what goes by that name', one diplomat said in 1934 – could not rule at home or abroad and had upset the balance of power in Europe.[5] Two years later Ambassador Jesse Straus reported that 'Business here is rotten. Prices are high; the franc is overvalued', and French politicians displayed little moral or intellectual honesty. Members of the Chamber of Deputies 'behave like a lot of naughty children in a nursery', while 'the same old political hacks revolve in different jobs in successive cabinets, many of them not knowing what it is all about'. Even the most outspoken critic of Germany's regime, Ambassador William E. Dodd, blamed French intransigence over armaments for helping Hitler to consolidate his power, while Roosevelt's roving emissary, Norman Davis, wrote that 'the French want the British to commit themselves so definitely with France for the *status quo* in Europe as to close the door to any possible appeasement with Germany', and that the British felt they had to rearm to exercise moral influence over Germany – all of which led Europe's leaders to thinking 'how best to prepare for the war which they think Germany is going to force upon them', rather than 'how to avert such a war'.[6]

There was considerable American sympathy for Italy's economic plight and recognition of its conquest of Ethiopia.[7] Ambassador Breckinridge Long's early letters praised the fascist order for its alleged efficiencies, but Long was suspect as being 'hypnotized' by Mussolini, and he soon branded the fascists as 'obdurate, ruthless, and almost vicious' and expected them to be little more than international 'troublemakers'.[8] Roosevelt politely ignored Mussolini's overture in 1936 for a meeting, and used Italy only as a conduit for messages to Hitler in 1938 and 1939, evidently with some slight hope that Mussolini might be a restraining influence.[9]

The Third Reich's domestic and foreign policies often horrified Americans, but they retained basic respect for German (as distinct from Nazi) culture and productive capacities. Roosevelt wrote in 1933 that he hoped to see a return to 'that German sanity of the old type that existed in the Bismarck days', and even after war began in 1939 he sought to allay British – and Ambassador Joseph P. Kennedy's – fear about the structure of a defeated Germany: 'They might blow up and have chaos for a while', FDR wrote, but German 'upbringing', 'independence of family life' and property-holding traditions would 'not . . . permit the Russian form of brutality for any length of time'.[10] Ambassador Long insisted in 1935 that while the Anglo-French-Italian Stresa front had 'put a military ring around Germany', it would yield to German pressure in the east and south, and Europe would have to 'accept something of German leadership rather than French leadership'. Europe would have to choose between German and Soviet domination, and whereas 'I shudder to think of Russian domination', German domination – albeit 'hard and cruel' at first – would be an 'intensification of a culture which is more akin to ours' and a bulwark against Soviet expansion. In 1936 Ambassador John Cudahy in Poland lamented that the 'proud, capable, ambitious and warlike' Germans were denied opportunity and resources for a prosperous life, while the 'crude and uncouth' Russians, three hundred years behind civilisation, possessed an empire – and the 'day of reckoning' was coming on this issue.[11] Similarly, Hugh R. Wilson, Ambassador to Germany during 1938–9, consistently argued that Germany had to be integrated into the Western orbit and made 'prosperous and reasonably contented'. In December 1939 he wished that the current war would end so that Germany could take care of 'the Russian encroachment' and further the ends of Western civilisation.[12]

Conviction ran deep that the Treaty of Versailles was the primary cause of German discontent. In 1933 Roosevelt expressed to the (much surprised) British that he favoured returning the Polish Corridor to Germany, and Ambassador Dodd opined that the French, 'standing too stubbornly against all concessions to Germany', had precipitated its withdrawal from the Geneva Disarmament Conference and the League of Nations.[13] During the crises over Germany's announced rearmament in 1935 and reoccupation of the Rhineland in 1936 Americans maintained a studied 'hands off' policy, and Roosevelt took diplomatically convenient fishing trips off the Florida coast. The American military attaché in Berlin expressed the prevailing underlying sentiment: Hitler sought to end France's political domination – not threaten its security – and at last the World War was ending. 'Versailles is dead. There may possibly be a German catastrophe and a new Versailles, but it will not be the Versailles which has hung like a dark cloud over Europe since 1920.'[14]

These views did not mean that Americans did not object strenuously to German diplomacy in the 1930s. Nor do they confirm the contention that ultimately it was not German political and military expansionism but rather the clash, especially in Latin America and the Balkans, between the American conception of a world political economy based on multilateral or Open Door economic policies and Nazi autarkic economic and bilateral trade programmes that determined the American–German confrontation in the Second World War. This thesis, put forward most comprehensively by Hans-Jürgen Schröder, has led numerous historians to cite frequently Secretary of State Cordell Hull's opinion about the alleged impact of reciprocal trade agreements, namely, that during the Second World War 'the political line-up followed the economic line-up'.[15]

The economic argument has been exaggerated. For example, the primary decline of 65 per cent to 71 per cent in German-American trade occurred during the worldwide collapse of 1929–32, and while German–American trade recovery lagged behind world trade recovery in the 1930s, the United States still ranked first in the value of exports to Germany in 1933, 1934 and 1938. The Germans had constant access in America to critical materials (petroleum, copper, iron, scrap steel, uranium) and grains through 1938. Further, while the State Department always protested against Germany's subsidising exports through currency manipulation and 'Aski' or 'blocked' marks, it usually compromised its liberal trade principles to allow American importers and exporters to use clever book-keeping devices to 'barter' American goods (cotton, copper, petroleum) for German products. By 1939 barter accounted for 50 per cent of American–German trade. As Graeme K. Howard, vice president for exports of General Motors, declared in 1939, 'clearing, barter, and quota arrangements must be encouraged within the most-favoured-nation principle'.[16]

American direct investment in manufactures in Germany rose by over 33 per cent between 1936 and 1940, firms that could not repatriate their profits from subsidiaries bought materials and built globally useful transportation and storage facilities in Germany, and Standard Oil of New Jersey, General Motors and DuPont maintained secret agreements (some through 1941) with German firms which restricted production of rubber, chemicals and aviation fuel. GM also facilitated German stockpiling of strategic materials.[17]

American diplomats were prepared to hedge their liberal trade principles to achieve political goals through economic appeasement. In 1935 State Department Counsellor R. Walton Moore proposed to the British that they satisfy German 'land hunger' by offering colonies in Africa. Ambassador Davis thought Germany might sign an arms agreement and rejoin the League of Nations in 1936 if given 'a special economic position in South-Eastern Europe'. Ambassador William Bullitt thought that an arms agreement and a revived feeling of 'European unity' could be achieved when in 1936 he implored Roosevelt to recognise that it was 'perfectly obvious' that Germany had to dominate trade – including through barter – in Central Europe, the Balkans and even Turkey, and that economic domination did not have to mean political domination, nor revival of the 'old Berlin to Bagdad bloc'.[18] From June until October 1938 Ambassador Kennedy sought to visit Hitler to propose a free economic hand in the Balkans. Even a firm liberal trader like Under-Secretary Welles was willing to be expedient about the use of barter agreements (with Italy in 1935, for example), and in March 1940 he suggested to the British that prevailing trade patterns might justify conceding Germany a preferential position in neighbouring countries.[19]

Clearly it was the worsening world political and military situation, from the German occupation in March 1939 of Bohemia and Moravia through the spring offensives of 1940, that led the United States to confront Germany, first by imposing permanent countervailing duties on German exports to the United States, then by freezing European assets in America, and finally by using licences and subsidies to force American firms to cut their ties with

German firms in the Balkans and Latin America and to gain control over critical resources and communications and transportation channels where German interests were deemed a threat to American security. As Assistant Secretary Berle summarised matters in autumn 1939, reorganising three or four major geopolitical areas based on economics (including perhaps a 'German–Dutch–Scandinavian and Baltic region') 'so that everyone could live' was merely 'technical work'. 'The real question', he said, 'is the moral, philosophical concept within any of these areas'.[20]

The United States took the major threat of National Socialist Germany to be its political and military thrust. Hence, when in 1934 Consul General George Messersmith and commercial attaché Douglas Miller in Berlin campaigned successfully against renewal of the commercial treaty with Germany because the latter would not include a non-discriminatory most-favoured-nation clause, both men emphasised political considerations – namely, that the Germans wanted a trade agreement, credits and raw materials primarily for rearmament and political propaganda. As Miller said, 'the Nazis are not satisfied with the existing map of Europe', they desire peace only to gain time to 'rearm and discipline their people', and the more they succeeded in their experiments, 'the more certain is a large-scale war in Europe'. Ambassador Dodd told the Germans that American reluctance to open trade talks 'was more attributable to *political* than to economic reasons', especially fears (including Roosevelt's) about German rearmament and war preparations.[21]

From spring 1933 onwards Roosevelt received a steady stream of reports from business and diplomatic observers (many favourably disposed toward Germany) that Hitler had so extinguished personal liberty and brought to a frenzy nationalistic and militaristic passions that Germany, 'a nation which loves to be led, is again marching', and that the likelihood of war was at least 50 per cent.[22] Ambassador Dodd's reports in 1934–5 on the 'extensive military preparation' in Germany led him to conclude that German annexations and predominance over 'the whole of Europe' was virtually inevitable, and that Germany's 'fixed purpose' was war within two or three years. By early 1935 Ambassador Long reported that he and every European leader (including Mussolini) expected war with Germany shortly, and that there was no escape from 'a real cataclysm'. Likewise Bullitt reported that he now agreed with Roosevelt's hunch that war would come first in Europe – not Asia – and that Hitler would advance down the Danube, or perhaps into the Ukraine, and that nothing could stop the 'horrible' march of events.[23] Ambassador Cudahy stressed repeatedly that war was inevitable unless the Hitler government was 'overthrown and this war preparation brought to a stop'. By November 1936 Ambassador Davis concluded that it was impossible to achieve any arms agreement because no national leader believed that Germany, Italy, or Japan would honour it, and that 'it is not possible to reason with Dictators like Hitler and Mussolini, who have a Frankenstein that forces them to keep on the move'.[24]

Within this context the American response – frequently ambiguous and ambivalent – to the challenge of National Socialist Germany emerges. The Americans believed that post-1919 Europe needed political and economic reordering, including redress of German political and economic grievances. But the Americans' jaundiced view of the British and French meant pursuit of any diplomatic initiative at arm's length – and occasionally at cross purposes – while fear and loathing of National Socialism meant uncertainty as to whether Germany ought to be appeased faster or resisted sooner. Without choosing between alternatives, the Roosevelt administration in 1936 set out to preserve peace in Europe, which it believed to be in the same state as in 1914: 'at the mercy of an incident'.[25] Thus Ambassador Bingham wrote from London that whereas Germany's unilateral revision of the Treaty of Versailles had brought political equality, Europe was dividing into two armed camps and that inevitably the United States would again be drawn into a European war. 'Therefore, the question arises as to what we can do in our own interest to aid an appeasement in Europe.'[26] Moral leadership was ineffective, direct involvement in political settlements domestically unacceptable. Consequently, recourse had to be to traditional American faith in the peaceful effect of arms limitation, increased equality of access to markets and materials, and reduced trade barriers. Political appeasement in Europe would be achieved through economic appeasement, which served as a diplomatic tactic and a legitimate, publicly acceptable end.

Roosevelt first inquired in mid-1936 through Ambassador Dodd whether Hitler would outline German foreign objectives over the next decade, or attend a heads-of-state meeting to draft disarmament and other peace procedures. Dodd unearthed no interest on Hitler's part in a conference.[27] Early in 1937 the State Department sent Norman Davis to London for secret talks with a memorandum, 'Contribution to a Peace Settlement', that sought a 'comprehensive' political and economic settlement that would preclude the need for a 'restless, dynamic, dissatisfied' Germany from having to 'explode' down the Danube. The State Department was convinced that arms limitation, 'which hinges upon political adjustment', and 'economic stabil-ization' were all of one piece, and that the 'problem of European peace' would be determined by whether a compromise could be achieved, 'or a price paid', that would satisfy German economic demands 'without making Germany paramount on the Continent'.[28] Roosevelt explored similar pro-posals with Canadian and other officials over the next months, but nothing materialised. The British often denigrated Roosevelt's ideas as 'drivel, and dangerous drivel', while the new Prime Minister, Neville Chamberlain, turned aside the President's invitation to the United States.[29]

Under-Secretary Welles in October 1937 prevailed upon Roosevelt to summon a world conference on Armistice Day to establish codes governing international relations, equal access to raw materials, peaceful revision of treaties and neutral rights. Welles insisted that the proposal would 'almost inevitably create a favorable reaction' in Germany, and he advised Roosevelt to declare that it would be necessary 'to remove those inequities which exist by reason of the nature of certain of the settlements reached at the termination of the Great War'. The United States would not participate in the political revision but the codes would facilitate them. Assistant Secretary Messersmith, convinced that Germany was the 'most important factor' in the current scene of international conflict and that the 'United

States are the ultimate object of attack of the powers grouped in a new system of force and lawlessness', believed that the State Department had to make this appeasement effort if only to educate the public to the present danger. Hull acceded, but at the last minute, fearful that the United States was assuming too much responsibility, and resentful of Welles's influence, the Secretary caused Roosevelt to shelve the plan.[30]

When shortly Bullitt reported that Reich Air Marshal Hermann Goering affirmed German interest in an offensive and defensive pact with France provided that Austria and the Sudeten Germans were incorporated into the Reich, and that the French would consider returning Germany's former colonies, Welles got Hull and Roosevelt to revive the conference proposal. Welles insisted that it would help the British reach agreement with Germany over colonies and security, appeal to Hitler's interest in an arms agreement and limit German and Italian aid to Japan, which would have to make peace with China. British consent would be secured in advance, but Germany, Italy and France would be notified to preclude charges of an Anglo-American deal.[31]

The Welles–Roosevelt plan, communicated to London on 12 January 1938, gained grudging Foreign Office support, but Chamberlain dismissed the project as 'preposterous', and 'likely to excite the derision of Germany and Italy', and asked Roosevelt 'to consider holding his hand' while the British negotiated with Germany and Italy.[32] Roosevelt and Welles were offended, and lectured the British about not recognising Italy's conquest of Ethiopia except as 'an integral part of measures for world appeasement' nor making a 'corrupt bargain' in Europe at American expense in the Far East.[33] Foreign Secretary Anthony Eden, hastily returned from a vacation, finally got Chamberlain to wire approval on 21 January and Roosevelt indicated he would proceed. But the collapse of Sino-Japanese talks, Hitler's purge of his military, the appointment of Joachim von Ribbentrop as Foreign Minister and recognition of Manchukuo, followed by the *Anschluss* of 11–12 March, led Roosevelt to abandon his proposal.[34]

Throughout the ensuing German–Czech crisis American policy remained of two minds. Roosevelt worried that negotiations would only postpone the 'inevitable conflict' and that the British and French would abandon Czechoslovakia and 'wash the blood from their Judas Iscariot hands'. He also told the British that if Hitler got his way now he would press further territorial demands until war came. Yet the President said he did not want to encourage the Czechs to 'vain resistance', and he was prepared to attend a conference to reorganise 'all unsatisfactory frontiers on rational lines'.[35] Roosevelt's cables to the heads of state on 26 September 'originally contained a definite hint of treaty revision' to induce Germany to request the President's good offices, but Hull watered it down. The Welles–Berle draft of Roosevelt's appeal to Hitler the next day suggested parallel political and economic conferences, but was then made less explicit.[36] After the Munich Conference Welles said that there was now more opportunity than at any time in the last twenty years to establish an international order based upon law and justice, and Roosevelt wrote that he rejoiced that war had been averted. But soon he said that 'peace by fear has no higher or more enduring quality than peace by the sword'; or as Berle put it: 'A German government which was not heavily armed would be less of a threat to the outside world.'[37]

By January 1939 Roosevelt was telling the Senate Military Affairs Committee in private that Germany, Italy and Japan sought 'world domination' and that America's first line of defence in the Atlantic included the 'continued, independent existence' of eighteen nations stretching from the Baltic through the Balkans to Turkey and Persia. The German occupation of Bohemia and Moravia in March 1939 and Italy's invasion of Albania in April led Berle to record that 'no one here has any illusions that the German Napoleonic machine will not extend itself indefinitely; and I suppose this is the year', while the State Department divided narrowly against breaking relations with Germany. Secretary of Agriculture Henry Wallace opposed an appeal to Hitler or Mussolini because 'the two madmen respect force and force alone', and it would only be 'delivering a sermon to a mad dog'. Even Hull warned a group of Congressmen that the coming struggle was not going to be 'another goddamn piddling dispute over a boundary line' but a global contest against nations 'practicing a philosophy of barbarism'.[38] None the less, on 14 April Roosevelt proposed to Hitler and Mussolini ten-year non-aggression pacts in return for parallel political and economic appeasement conferences. The notes the President scrawled for use in conversation with the Italian Ambassador revealed FDR's mixed motives, or impulses: 'Muss. holds key to peace', Hitler was in 'bad shape' and needed war (and Italy, although he would 'cast her aside') as a 'way out'. Italy, he thought, should serve its best interests and 'sit around the table and work it out' and thereby 'save peace – save dom. of Europe by Germany'.[39]

As the crisis over Poland developed, Americans believed that the Germans were 'beginning to beat the tom-toms for a final work up to a war psychology', and while 'readjustments in Central Europe are necessary', the Germans could not be allowed to dominate the Atlantic, and an unchecked German–Italian combination would leave the United States to confront 'imperialist schemes in South and Central America, not on a paper basis, as we do now, but backed up by an extremely strong naval and military force'. The Nazi–Soviet pact of 22 August created a 'bloc running from the Pacific clear to the Rhine', the 'combined Soviet–Nazi allies now have all Europe' and would partition Poland. The British, Welles felt, 'will sell out the Chinese completely . . . in return for an Anglo-Japanese understanding'. Roosevelt appealed to Berlin and Warsaw on 24 August for negotiations, but this was to do what had not been done in 1914: 'put the bee on Germany'.[40]

The start of war produced many mediation calls, but Roosevelt turned these aside primarily because, as Hull said, the United States would not act to consolidate a regime of 'force and aggression'. The Soviet attack on Poland gave dark reality to Berle's 'nightmare': Hitler and Stalin 'able to rule from Manchuria to the Rhine . . . and nothing to stop the combined Russian–German force at any point . . . Europe is gone'. Roosevelt worried that the Germans intended to 'keep on going while the going was good', including 'into Persia or towards India'. Then there would be 'a drive at the west. The real objective would be to get into the Atlantic.'[41] The ensuing

Soviet 'dreadful rape of Finland', to use Roosevelt's words, left the Americans wondering what horrors would come next.[42]

Despite the dark prospect – or perhaps because of it – Roosevelt inclined towards a negotiated settlement. The State Department believed that it might propose the principles of peace, and soon organised committees to consider postwar political, arms limitation and economic problems.[43] Columnist Walter Lippmann expressed a public hope that the British and French, unencumbered as in the First World War by secret deals or territorial ambitions, could offer Germany 'a revision of the Versailles system', including colonies.[44] Then in November and December the young, independent German emissary, Adam von Trott zu Solz, pressed State Department officials to urge the Allies to offer a 'peace of reconciliation'. Finally there persisted hope, as Assistant Secretary Long summarised it, that the Germans might be tempted to 'retire' Hitler in favour of Goering: 'He is a practical man and not a psychopath like Hitler. The western Powers could deal with him.'[45]

By December 1939 Roosevelt was hinting that he would make peace in the spring. He said he did not have the 1918 notion to make a century of peace, but he also feared a 'patched up temporizing peace which would blow up in our faces in a year or two'. Some observers, he said, felt the Russians and Germans would war, others felt that they would divide Europe and reach to Asia and Africa, and imperil the Americas.[46] In January 1940 Roosevelt decided to send Welles to Europe on a mission that reflected the full ambiguity of American appeasement in the 1930s: at best Welles would achieve a negotiated settlement; perhaps he might divide Italy from Germany and postpone the spring offensives; at worst, the American people would start to think about the 'ultimate results in Europe and the Far East' and develop that needed 'deep sense of world crisis'.[47]

Welles doubtless inspired his mission. He had authored the aborted conferences of 1937–8, was appropriately antagonistic to the British, hostile towards the Russians while aware of their historical and security concerns, favoured mollifying Mussolini by recognising his conquest of Ethiopia and rejected the Versailles system as 'a series of conditions imposed upon a conquered foe'. He blamed the Allies for failure to encourage Germany's few liberal leaders, and looked to Goering as the one German who understood the outside world and American public response to a German war.[48]

Welles's intentions are perhaps best revealed by his talks in Rome during 26–8 February 1940. He, Mussolini and Foreign Minister Galeazzo Ciano agreed that Germany needed colonies, and had to retain Austria, Danzig, the Polish Corridor and ethnically German portions of western Poland (with Russia regaining territory in the East); that Russia had to be restrained in the Balkans; and that recognition of Italy's conquest of Ethiopia could come in a general settlement.[49]

In Berlin, where Hitler had issued a directive forbidding serious talks, when Welles asked if German aims – spheres of influence and room for nations that had shown 'historical proof' of independent national life – could be negotiated, Ribbentrop replied that only a German victory would 'attain the peace we want'. (Welles concluded that Ribbentrop had a 'completely closed' and 'very stupid' mind.) Welles reiterated American interest in a 'just' peace and parallel arms, economic and political conferences, and Mussolini's interest in negotiations. Hitler only assailed the Versailles system and enumerated his accomplishments of the last seven years, and Germany's determination to achieve colonies, economic hegemony in Eastern and south-eastern Europe, and security. Goering was more cordial but no more encouraging.[50]

Welles seemed most impressed in Paris by Prime Minister Edouard Daladier and Minister of Finance Paul Reynaud, who thought that the 'political and territorial issues now at stake' between Germany and the Allies were negotiable. Welles also offended the French by stressing their need to seek a compromise peace and the 'singularly strategic' role he expected Mussolini would play.[51]

The British vehemently opposed negotiations. Chamberlain spoke with 'white-hot' anger about German deceitfulness and desire to dominate Europe; the need to teach the Germans that 'force did not pay'; and the need to secure German troop withdrawals and absolute guarantees for independent Polish, Czech and other small nations before talks could be considered. Anthony Eden and others insisted that peace was not possible 'until Hitlerism has been overthrown', while Welles tended to admonish his hosts that no nation could be taught a lesson or have peace imposed.[52]

In his final talk on 13 March Welles pressed Chamberlain and Foreign Secretary Lord Halifax to agree to negotiate if *first* satisfactory terms were reached for restoring Poland and Bohemia-Moravia and disarmament-security proposals were marked out. Halifax enlarged the basis for negotiations to include restoration and reparation of Poland and Bohemia-Moravia; freedom of decision for Austria; relative British and French strength *vis-à-vis* Germany; and liberty and knowledge of the outside world for Germans. Chamberlain agreed, provided this 'miracle' occurred, and Welles told Washington that Chamberlain would negotiate if Hitler gave an 'earnest', such as troop withdrawal from Poland and Bohemia-Moravia, and that the British would not be inflexible over ultimate boundaries.[53]

Welles returned to Rome to encourage Mussolini that peace could be established along the political lines discussed if the British and French, who were not obdurate, were given 'security'. But Mussolini – invited by Hitler to meet at the Brenner Pass because of the Welles mission – warned that it was 'one minute before midnight' and that only an American political guarantee could help. By telephone Welles and Roosevelt decided against a commitment.[54]

After Mussolini returned from his meeting, Welles concluded that the Italian leader's 'obsession' was to recreate the Roman Empire, that he admired 'force and power' and would lead Italy to war if Germany attacked Belgium and Holland. Yet Welles encouraged improved relations with the Italians through commercial ties and avoiding use of the term 'fascism' when attacking their government. The Germans, he said, were living on 'another planet' where 'lies have become truth; evil, good; and aggression, self-defense', and they were united behind Hitler because they feared the British and French. Security and disarmament, however, remained the primary barriers to peace – although the task should not be underestimated 'so long as Hitler and his regime remain in control' – and an American initiative would get Italian and Vatican support.[55] Less sanguine was the unread appraisal from the young diplomat – George F. Kennan – who now wrote that Hitler's sense of 'mission' was uncomplicated by any responsibility to European culture, that the German 'colossus is genuine', armed with the greatest power ever seen, and 'determined to dominate Europe or to carry the entire continent to a common destruction'. Peace could only be temporary because 'the Nazi system is built on the assumption that war, not peace, represents the normal condition of mankind'.[56]

The Welles mission, like American appeasement, probably succeeded only in angering the British and French, rousing Soviet suspicions and causing Hitler to strengthen his ties with Mussolini. Roosevelt declared on 29 March that there was 'scant immediate prospect' for peace in Europe, though privately he pressed the British to state that they sought only security, disarmament and access to markets and materials, and would not break up Germany.[57]

The German assault on Western Europe beginning in April 1940, however, led the Roosevelt administration henceforth to abandon mention of Germany and to speak only about a 'totalitarian', unappeasable Nazi state bent on global conquest. 'Old dreams of universal empire are again rampant', Roosevelt said on 15 April, and Old World developments threatened the New World. On 10 June, castigating Italy's attack on France, he pledged America's material resources to the Allies who battled the 'gods of force and hate'. Following signature in September 1940 of the Tripartite Pact, Roosevelt on 12 October denounced the 'totalitarian powers' and warned that 'no combination of dictator countries of Europe and Asia' would stop American aid to those 'who now hold the aggressors from our shores', and that the American people 'reject the doctrine of appeasement'. Then on 29 December Roosevelt proclaimed that the 'new order' of Axis powers was an 'unholy alliance of power and pelf', and that the 'Nazi masters' intended 'to enslave the whole of Europe and then . . . the rest of the world'. The past two years had proved that 'no nation can appease the Nazis', that there could be 'no appeasement with ruthlessness', no negotiated settlement with 'a gang of outlaws', and that America had to become 'the great arsenal of democracy'.[58]

The themes remained the same – only more so – throughout 1941. In January 1941 Roosevelt wrote that 'the hostilities in Europe, in Africa, and in Asia are all parts of a single world conflict'. In declaring a national emergency in May 1941, he insisted that the Nazis had escalated the war in Europe into one for 'world domination' and would treat Latin America the same as the Balkans.[59] Following the *Greer* episode in September, Roosevelt assailed the 'Nazi design to abolish freedom of the seas' as another step towards building a 'permanent world system based on force, on terror, and on murder', and shortly issued his 'shoot on sight' orders. Then in his Navy Day address in late October Roosevelt made his most dramatic (and perhaps unnecessary) depiction of the struggle when he professed to have a 'secret' map and documents purporting to show Nazi intentions to transform Central and South America into vassal states, to substitute an 'International Nazi Church' for all others and to have the 'God of Blood and Iron' take the place of the 'God of Love and Mercy'. But we Americans, he declared, 'have cleared our decks and taken our battle stations' and are prepared 'to do what God has given us the power to see as our full duty'.[60]

Rhetorically as well as literally the Roosevelt administration had gone as far as it could to wage undeclared war against Nazi Germany and its Axis allies. Resolution of the dilemma of how to achieve a formal state of war, of course, awaited Japan's attack upon Pearl Harbor on 7 December and the German and Italian declarations of war on 11 December.

But the shape of events was long since clear. From 1933 to 1940 the United States had done all it believed it could to appease Germany politically and economically, to take account of Germany's national political and economic aspirations and its relations to its European neighbours. Not until the spring of 1940, when events left no other conclusion but that the Nazi state rested on the assumption that 'war, not peace, represents the normal condition of mankind', did the Americans determine to muster their political and economic power to defeat the new – or Nazi – Germany and its Axis allies. What remained unresolved were the perplexing questions of how to reconstruct a defeated Germany, what its position would be within the new international order of the Grand Alliance and whether appeasement would ever be useful. These issues underlay the diplomacy of the Second World War and the incipient cold war.

Notes: Chapter 28

1 *New York Times*, 8 July 1937; F. W. Graff, 'The strategy of involvement. A diplomatic biography of Sumner Welles', Ph.D dissertation, 2 vols (University of Michigan, 1971), Vol. I, p. 168.
2 Berle to Roosevelt, 1 September 1938, in B. Berle Bishop and T. Beal Jacobs (eds), *Navigating the Rapids, 1918–1971. From the Papers of Adolf A. Berle* (New York, 1973), pp. 183–4.
3 Roosevelt to Edward M. House, 21 November 1933, in E. Roosevelt (ed.), *F.D.R.: His Personal Letters, 1928–1945*, 2 vols (New York, 1950), Vol. I, pp. 371–3 (hereinafter *FDRL*); quoted in J. M. Blum, *From the Morgenthau Diaries. Years of Crisis, 1928–1938* (Boston, Mass., 1959), p. 141.
4 Roosevelt to Robert Bingham, 11 July 1935, in E. B. Nixon (ed.), *Franklin D. Roosevelt and Foreign Affairs, 1933–1937*, 3 vols (Cambridge, Mass., 1969), Vol. II, p. 554 (hereinafter *FDRFA*); Memorandum from the Files of President Roosevelt's Secretary [19 October 1937], in *US Department of State, Foreign Relations of the United States, Diplomatic Papers, 1937*, 5 vols (Washington, DC, 1954), Vol. IV, pp. 85–6 (hereinafter *FR*); entry for 15 December 1935, in *The Secret Diary of Harold L. Ickes. The First Thousand Days, 1933–1936*, ed. Jane D. Ickes, 3 vols (New York, 1953–5), Vol. I, p. 484; Roosevelt to Arthur P. Murray, 7 October 1937, and Roosevelt to Kennedy, 30 October 1939, in: *FDRL*, Vol. I, pp. 715–16 and *FDRL*, Vol. II, pp. 949–50; Roosevelt to Roger Merriam, 14 February 1939, in D. B. Schewe (ed.), *Franklin D. Roosevelt and Foreign Affairs*, 2nd series, January 1937 – August 1939, 14 vols (New York, 1979), Vol. 13, p. 324 (hereinafter *FDRFA*).
5 Owen Johnson to Roosevelt, 12 May 1933, and Roosevelt to Johnson, 24 June 1933, and Breckinridge Long to Roosevelt, 7 February 1934, *FDRFA*, Vol. I, pp. 120–3, 632–6.

6 Strauss to Roosevelt, 20 January 1936, Davis to Roosevelt, 18 February 1936, and Dodd to Roosevelt, 3 March 1936, *FDRFA*, Vol. III, pp. 166–70, 201–2, 229–30.
7 Hull to Ronald Lindsay, 29 January 1936, *FR 1936*, Vol. I, pp. 629–34, and A. W. Schatz, 'The Anglo-American trade agreement and Cordell Hull's search for peace, 1936–1938, *Journal of American History*, vol. LVII (1970), pp. 89, 91; William Phillips to Roosevelt, 30 July 1937, Franklin D. Roosevelt Papers, President's Secretary's Files, Italy, Franklin D. Roosevelt Library, Hyde Park, NY, and Alexander Cadogan Memorandum, 24 September 1937, Records of the British Foreign Office, File Number 371, Piece 20675, Public Record Office, London (hereinafter cited by file no./piece). The latter cites Welles's views in favour of recognition.
8 Long to Roosevelt, 27 June and 16 November 1933, *FDRFA*, Vol. I, pp. 255–8 and 488–92; Long to Roosevelt, 6 September 1935, and Louis Howe to Roosevelt, 18 October 1935, *FDRFA*, Vol. III, pp. 3–6, 28.
9 A. A. Offner, *American Appeasement. United States Foreign Policy and Germany, 1933–1938* (Cambridge, Mass., 1969), pp. 182–96, 271.
10 Roosevelt to George Earle, 22 December 1933, and Roosevelt to Kennedy, 30 October 1939, *FDRL*, Vol. I, pp. 379–80 and *FDRL*, Vol. II, pp. 942–4.
11 Long to Roosevelt, 19 April 1935, Breckinridge Long Papers, Box 114, Library of Congress, Washington, DC; Cudahy to Roosevelt, 26 December 1936, *FR 1937*, Vol. II, pp. 24–6.
12 Wilson to Hull, 9 October 1936, Cordell Hull Papers, Box 39, Library of Congress; Wilson to Alexander Kirk, December 1939, in H. R. Wilson, *A Career Diplomat. The Third Chapter: The Third Reich* (New York, 1960), pp. 80–1.
13 F. Freidal, *Franklin D. Roosevelt. Launching the New Deal* (Boston, Mass., 1973), p. 104; Dodd to Roosevelt, 23 December 1933, *FDRFA*, Vol. I, pp. 547–8.
14 Offner, *American Appeasement*, pp. 112–15, 141–3; Report by Truman Smith, 20 March 1936, *FR 1936*, Vol. I, p. 260.
15 H.-J. Schröder, *Deutschland und die Vereinigten Staaten 1933–1939: Wirtschaft und Politik in der Entwicklung des deutsch-amerikanischen Gegensatzes* (Wiesbaden, 1970), and 'Das Dritte Reich und die USA', in M. Knapp *et al.* (eds), *Die USA und Deutschland 1918–1975: Deutsch-amerikanische Beziehungen zwischen Rivalität und Partnerschaft* (Munich, 1978), pp. 107–52; C. Hull, *The Memoirs of Cordell Hull*, 2 vols (New York, 1948), Vol. I, p. 365. See also W. Appleman Williams, *The Tragedy of American Diplomacy* (New York, 1962), pp. 166–98, and L. C. Gardner, *Economic Aspects of New Deal Diplomacy* (Madison, Wis., 1964), pp. 59–60, 98–109, 170, 328. For 'post-revisionist' assessments, see S. E. Hilton, *Brazil and the Great Powers, 1930–1939. The Politics of Trade Rivalry* (Austin, Texas, 1975); D. Steward, *Trade and Hemisphere. The Good Neighbour Policy and Reciprocal Trade* (Columbia, Mo., 1975); and A. F. Repko, 'The failure of reciprocal trade. United States–Germany commercial rivalry in Brazil, 1934–1940', *Mid-America. An Historial Review*, vol. 60 (1978), pp. 3–20.
16 *US Tariff Commission, Foreign-Trade and Exchange Controls in Germany* (Washington, DC, 1942), pp. 153–5; Offner, *American Appeasement*, pp. 146–53; Henry Morgenthau, Jr, to Roosevelt, 17 January 1939, *PSF*, Henry Morgenthau Jr, 1933–9, Box 31, Roosevelt Papers; Howard, quoted in E. Tenenbaum, *National Socialism vs. International Capitalism* (New Haven, Conn., 1942), pp. 106–7.
17 A. A. Offner, 'Appeasement revisited. The United States, Great Britain, and Germany, 1933–1940', *Journal of American History*, vol. LXIV (1977), pp. 375–6.
18 Moore to Roosevelt, 29 November 1935, *FDRFA*, Vol. III, pp. 396–7; Davis's opinion in Anthony Eden to Ronald Lindsay, 7 February 1936, FO 414/273; Bullitt to Roosevelt, 8 November 1936, *FDRFA*, Vol. III, pp. 471–7. See also Paul Claudel to Roosevelt, 9 January 1937, *FDRFA* (second series), Vol. 4, pp. 13–28.
19 Offner, *American Appeasement*, pp. 251–3; Welles to Roosevelt, 22 May 1935, *FDRFA*, Vol. II, pp. 510–13; Lord Halifax to Lord Lothian, 13 March 1940, FO 371/24406.
20 M. Wilkins, *The Maturing of Multinational Enterprise: American Business Abroad from 1914 to 1970* (Cambridge, Mass., 1974), pp. 258–60; diary entries for 15 November and 13 December 1939, Berle and Jacobs (eds), *Navigating the Rapids*, pp. 270, 276–7.
21 George Messersmith to William Phillips, 24 March, 29 March, 13 April and 3 May 1934, General Records of the Department of State, Record Group 59, File Numbers 862.00/3418, 862.00/3419, 862.00/3420, 862.00/3423 (hereinafter *DS*, file number); D. Millier, *Via*

Diplomatic Pouch (New York, 1944), pp. 133–62, 171–88, 207–21; Dieckhoff Memorandum, 12 December 1934, US Department of State, *Documents on German Foreign Policy, 1918–1945*, Series C (1933–7), *The Third Reich: First Phase*, 5 vols (Washington, DC, 1957–66), Vol. III, pp. 736–7.

22   Samuel R. Fuller to Roosevelt, 11 May 1933, and George Earle to Roosevelt, 27 November 1933, *FDRFA*, Vol. I, pp. 172–6, 504–7; J. V. A. MacMurray to Roosevelt, 27 March 1934, and John Montgomery to Roosevelt, 13 July 1934, *FDRFA*, Vol. II, pp. 41–6, 165–7.

23   Dodd to Roosevelt, 5 November 1934, *FDRFA*, Vol. II, pp. 275–7, and Dodd to Hull, 17 November 1934, *FR 1934*, Vol. II, p. 252; Dodd to Phillips, 29 May 1935, in William E. Dodd Papers, Box 44, Library of Congress; Dodd to Roosevelt, 29 June and 31 October 1935, DS 862.00/35181/2 and DS 862.00/35581/2; Long to Roosevelt, 8 February and 12 February 1935, and Bullitt to Roosevelt, 1 May 1935, *FDRFA*, Vol. II, pp. 401–4, 426–9 and 493–5.

24   Cudahy to Roosevelt, 11 October 1935 and 20 March 1936, *FDRFA*, Vol. III, pp. 21–3, 267–8; Davis to Hull, 17 November 1936, Hull Papers, Box 40.

25   Bullitt to Roosevelt, 4 March 1936, *FDRFA*, Vol. III, pp. 233–6.

26   Bingham to Roosevelt, 26 March 1935, *FDRFA*, Vol. II, pp. 453–4.

27   Roosevelt to Dodd, 5 August 1936, *FDRL*, Vol. I, p. 606; Dodd's activities are detailed in Offner, *American Appeasement*, pp. 171–4.

28   Department of State, Division of Western European Affairs, Memorandum for the Honourable Norman H. Davis, 16 February 1937, Norman H. Davis Papers, Box 24, Library of Congress.

29   MacKenzie King to Roosevelt, 6 March 1937, *FDRL*, Vol. I, pp. 664–8; Lord Tweedsmuir to Roosevelt, 8 April 1937, *FDRFA* (second series), Vol. 5, pp. 29–34; Lindsay to Robert Vansittart, 8 March 1937, and Vansittart minute, 31 March 1937, FO 371/20670; Chamberlain to Roosevelt, 28 September 1937, *FR 1937*, Vol. I, pp. 131–2.

30   Welles to Roosevelt, 26 October 1937, *FR 1937*, Vol. I, pp. 667–70; Messersmith to Hull, 11 October 1937, ibid., pp. 140–5; Hull, *Memoirs*, Vol. I, pp. 547–8.

31   Bullitt to Hull, 23 November 1937, and Welles to Bullitt, 1 December 1937, in O. H. Bullitt (ed.), *For the President. Personal and Secret: Correspondence Between Franklin D. Roosevelt and William C. Bullitt* (Boston, Mass., 1972), pp. 237–40; Welles memorandum for Roosevelt, 10 January 1938, *FR 1938*, Vol. I, pp. 115–17.

32   Lindsay to Foreign Office, 11 January and 12 January 1938 (6 cables), FO 371/21526; Cadogan to Anthony Eden, 13 January 1938, FO 371/21526; diary entries for 1–13 January and 14 January 1938, in J. Harvey (ed.), *The Diplomatic Diaries of Oliver Harvey, 1937–1940* (London, 1970), pp. 67–70; Conclusions of a meeting of the Cabinet, 24 January 1938, CAB 23/92; I. Macleod, *Neville Chamberlain* (New York, 1962), p. 212; Chamberlain to Roosevelt, 14 January 1938, *FR 1938*, Vol. I, pp. 118–20.

33   Welles to Roosevelt and Roosevelt to Chamberlain, 17 January 1938, *FR 1938*, Vol. I, pp. 120–2; Lindsay to Foreign Office, 17 January 1938, FO 371/21526.

34   Chamberlain to Roosevelt, 21 January 1938, FO 371/21526, and Lindsay to Foreign Office, 12 March 1938, FO 371/21526.

35   Diary entry for 18 September 1938, in *The Secret Diary of Harold Ickes. The Inside Struggle 1936–1939*, ed. Jane D. Ickes, 3 vols (New York, 1953–5), Vol. II, pp. 467–9; Lindsay to Halifax, 20 September 1938, in E. L. Woodward and R. Butler (eds), *Documents on British Foreign Policy, 1919–1939*, 3rd series, 10 vols (London, 1949–61), Vol. VII, pp. 627–9.

36   Entry for 24 September and 25 September 1938, Jay Pierrepont Moffat diary, Vol. 31, Jay Pierrepont Moffat Papers, Houghton Library, Harvard University; J. Alsop and R. Kintner, *American White Paper: The Story of American Diplomacy and the Second World War* (New York, 1940), p. 10; Roosevelt to Hitler, 27 September 1938, *FR 1938*, Vol. I, pp. 684–5.

37   *New York Times*, 4 October 1938; Roosevelt remarks to *Herald Tribune Forum*, 26 October 1938, *FDRL*, Vol. I, p. 820; Berle to Hull, 30 September 1938, in Berle and Jacobs (eds), *Navigating the Rapids*, pp. 189–90.

38   Roosevelt Conference with Senate Military Affairs Committee, 31 January 1939, *FDRFA*, 2nd series, Vol. 13, pp. 197–223; diary entry for 17 March 1939 in Berle and Jacobs (eds),

Navigating the Rapids, p. 201; Wallace and Hull quoted in R. Dallek, *Franklin D. Roosevelt and American Foreign Policy, 1932–1945* (New York, 1979), pp. 186–7.

39 Roosevelt to Hitler and Roosevelt to Mussolini, 14 April 1939, *FR 1939*, Vol. I, pp. 130–3; Roosevelt memorandum, 3 April 1939, *FDRL*, Vol. II, pp. 875–6. See also Welles memorandum of Roosevelt–Ambassador Prince Ascanio Colonna conversation, 22 March 1939, and FDR to Welles, 4 April 1939, *FDRFA*, 2nd series, Vol. 14, pp. 124–30, 254.

40 Diary entries for 26 June, 24 August and 26 August 1939, in Berle and Jacobs (eds), *Navigating the Rapids*, pp. 229, 242–5.

41 Hull to Kennedy, 11 September 1939, *FR 1939*, Vol. I, p. 424; diary entries for 13 September and 21 September 1939, in Berle and Jacobs (eds), *Navigating the Rapids*, pp. 254, 258.

42 Roosevelt to Lincoln MacVeagh, 1 December 1939, *FDRL*, Vol. II, p. 961.

43 Graff, 'Strategy of involvement', Vol. I, pp. 383–6.

44 *New York Herald Tribune*, 10 October 1939.

45 H. Rothfels, 'Adam von Trott und das State Department', *Vierteljahrshefte für Zeitgeschichte*, vol. 7 (1959), pp. 319–22; diary entry for 11 October 1939 in F. L. Israel (ed.), *The War Diary of Breckinridge Long. Selections from the Years 1939–1944* (Lincoln, Neb., 1966), pp. 26–8.

46 Roosevelt to William Allen White, 14 December 1939, *FDRL*, Vol. II, pp. 967–8.

47 Roosevelt to Frank Knox, 29 December 1939, ibid., pp. 975–6; diary entries for 5 December and 29 December 1939, in Berle and Jacobs (eds), *Navigating the Rapids*, pp. 275, 280–1.

48 S. Welles, *The Time for Decision* (New York, 1944), pp. 6–7, 115–16, 330–4, 339–40.

49 Welles memoranda, 26 February 1940, *FR 1940*, Vol. I, pp. 21–33; Ciano memorandum, 26 February 1940, in M. Muggeridge (ed.), *Ciano's Diplomatic Papers* (London, 1948), pp. 337–9.

50 Directive for conversations with Mr Sumner Welles, 29 February 1940, in US Department of State, *Documents on German Foreign Policy (DGFP) 1918–45*, series D (1937–1945), 13 vols (Washington, DC, 1949–64), Vol. VIII, pp. 817–19; Welles memoranda, 1 March, 2 March and 3 March 1940, *FR 1940*, Vol. I, pp. 33–41, 43–9, 51–6; Memoranda Hitler–Ribbentrop–Meissner–Welles–Kirk conversation, 2 March 1940, and Welles–Goering conversation, 3 March 1940, *DGFP*, D, Vol. III, pp. 838–45, 850–62.

51 Welles memoranda, 7 March and 9 March 1940, *FR 1940*, Vol. I, pp. 60–7, 70–2; Bullitt to Roosevelt, 18 April 1940, in Bullitt (ed.), *For the President*, pp. 409–10, and Ronald Campbell to Foreign Office, 8 March 1940, FO 371/24406.

52 Welles memoranda, 11 March and 12 March 1940, *FR 1940*, Vol. I, pp. 75–83; The Memoirs of Anthony Eden (Earl of Avon), *The Reckoning* (Boston, Mass., 1965), pp. 105–6.

53 Welles memorandum, 13 March 1940, *FR 1940*, Vol. I, pp. 87–90; Halifax to Lothian, 13 March 1940, FO 371/24406.

54 Welles memoranda, 16 March 1940, *FR 1940*, Vol. I, pp. 96–105; Welles, p. 139.

55 Welles memorandum, 19 March 1940, *FR 1940*, Vol. I, pp. 110–17.

56 G. F. Kennan, *Memoirs, 1925–1950* (Boston, Mass., 1967), pp. 115–19.

57 *New York Times*, 30 March 1940; Sir L. Woodward, *British Foreign Policy in the Second World War*, 5 vols (London, 1970–1), Vol. I, pp. 171–2.

58 Roosevelt's speeches are in S. I. Rosenmann (comp.), *The Public Papers and Addresses of Franklin D. Roosevelt*, 13 vols (New York, 1938–50), Vol. IX, pp. 158–64, 259–64, 460–7, 633–44 (hereinafter *PPFDR*).

59 Roosevelt to Joseph C. Grew, 21 January 1941, in J. C. Grew, *Ten Years in Japan* (New York, 1944), pp. 361–3; *PPFDR*, Vol. X, pp. 194–6.

60 *PPFDR*, Vol. X, pp. 384–92, 438–45.

Notes on Contributors

Donald Cameron Watt is Stevenson Professor of International History at the University of London. His publications include *Personalities and Policies*, *Too Serious a Business*, an edition of Hitler's *Mein Kampf* and upwards of a hundred articles on the history of international relations in the 20th century.

R. A. C. Parker is a Fellow of Queen's College, Oxford. He has written studies of British foreign policy and of British rearmament in the 1930s. His other publications deal with English agriculture in the 18th century.

Ronald Smelser is an Associate Professor of History at the University of Utah in Salt Lake City. He is the author of *The Sudeten Problem: 1933–1938* and numerous articles on the Czech-German problem and German foreign policy between the wars. He is currently researching a book on the problem of national integration in Germany.

Wolfgang Michalka is a Hochschulassistent at the Institut für Geschichte der Technicschen Hochschule Darmstadt and editor of the periodical *Neue politische Literatur*. His published works include *Ribbentrop und die deutsche Weltpolitik 1933–1940*.

Klaus-Jürgen Müller is Professor of Modern and Contemporary History at the Armed Forces University Hamburg and at the University of Hamburg. His publications include *Das Heer und Hitler*, *General Ludwig Beck*, *Armee, Politik und Gesellschaft in Deutschland* and *Das Ende de Entente Cordiale*. His other publications deal with French modern history.

Roy Douglas is a Reader in the University of Surrey. He is author of *The History of the Liberal Party 1895–1970*; *Land, People and Politics*; *In the Year of Munich*; *The Advent of War 1939–40*; *New Alliances 1940–41*; *From War to Cold War 1942–48*, and a number of articles on historical subjects.

Robert P. Shay, Jr. received his Doctorate in History from Columbia University. Author of *British Rearmament in the Thirties: Politics and Profits*, he is currently a specialist in the field of videotex working for a major New England financial institution.

Gustav F. Schmidt is Professor of Political Science/International Politics at the Ruhr University Bochum. He is author of *England in der Krise: Grundzüge und Grundlagen der britischen Appeasement-Politik (1930–1937)* and has also published *Deutscher Historismus und der Übergang zur parlamentarischen Demokratie*. He has written on various aspects of German and British history and politics on a comparative level.

Sabine Wichert is a lecturer in Modern History at the Queen's University of Belfast, where she teaches 19th and 20th century British and European history. Her special interests are Britain, Germany and Greece in the 1930s.

G. C. Peden is a lecturer in Economic and Social History at the University of Bristol. His publications include *British Rearmament and the Treasury 1932–1939* and articles on economic aspects of policy.

Bernd-Jürgen Wendt is Professor of Modern and Contemporary History at the University of Hamburg. He has written inter alia *Economic Appeasement. Handel und Finanz in der britischen Deutschlandpolitik, 1933–1939*, and specialises in comparative studies on British and German history and in Anglo-German relations in the 19th and 20th centuries.

John Dunbabin is a Fellow of St Edmund Hall, Oxford. His published writing is on British social and political history and includes *Rural Discontent in Nineteenth Century Britain*. He is currently engaged on a history of international relations since 1945.

Brian Bond is a Reader in War Studies at King's College, London. He is author of *France and Belgium 1939–40, Liddell Hart: A Study of His Military Thought, British Military Policy between the Two World Wars* and other books and articles on military history. His latest book, *War and Society in Europe, 1870–1970*, will be published later this year.

Professor René Girault is Director of the Centre d'Histoire de la France Contemporaine at the Université de Paris X Nanterre. He is the author of *Emprunts russes et investissements français en Russie, 1887–1914*, (1972); *L'Impérialisme française d'avant 1914*, (1976); *Diplomatie européenne et impérialisme, I, Histoire des relations internationales contemporaines, 1871–1914*, (1979).

Maurice Vaisse is Professor of Contemporary History at the University of Reims. He is author of *Sécurité d'abord: la politique française en matière de désarmament 1930–1934*, and numerous articles on the French army and diplomacy.

Robert Frankenstein is Maitre-Assistant at the University of Paris X – Nanterre. He has published several articles on the economic problems of the French rearmament in the 1930s. He is author of *Le prix du réarmament français 1935–1939*.

Anthony Adamthwaite is Professor of History at the University of Loughborough. He is the author of *France and the Coming of the Second World War*; *The Making of the Second World War*; *The Lost Peace: International Relations in Europe, 1918–1939*.

Danis Mack Smith is a Senior Research Fellow at All Souls College, Oxford. He has published a dozen books on modern Italian history, of which the most recent are *Mussolini*, and *Mussolini's Roman Empire*.

Christopher Seton-Watson is Lecturer in Politics and Fellow of Oriel College, Oxford. He is author of *Italy from Liberalism to Fascism* and is currently engaged in research on the history of contemporary Italy since 1943.

Lord Beloff is a former Gladstone Professor of Government and Public Administration in the University of Oxford and the author of, inter alia, *The Foreign Policy of Soviet Russia, 1929–1941*.

Gottfried Niedhardt is Professor of Modern History at Mannheim University and has published a number of books and articles on modern British history and the history of international relations.

James S. Herndon studied for four years at St John's College, Oxford under the supervision of Professor Michael Howard (Oriel College, Oxford), while on leave from his administrative post at Georgia State University. Recently, he returned home to resume his position and hopes to complete his doctoral dissertation on British Soviet Policy (1935–41) this year.

Ritchie Ovendale is a lecturer in the Department of International Politics at the University College of Wales, Aberystwyth. He has published *'Appeasement' and the English Speaking World. Britain, the United States, the Dominions, and the Policy of 'Appeasement', 1937–1939*, articles on British imperial policy in South Africa and the foreign policy of the British Labour Government, 1945–1951.

Reinhard Meyers is a lecturer in the Department of Politics, University of Bonn. He is the author of *Britische Sicherheitspolitik 1934–1938* and has published numerous articles on international relations in the inter-war period. Further books and papers deal mainly with the history, epistemology and theory of international relations.

Wm. Roger Louis is Professor of History (and Curator of Historical Collections, Humanities Research Center) at the University of Texas. His books include *British Strategy in the Far East, 1919–1939; Imperialism at Bay;* and, edited with Prosser Gifford, *The Transfer of Power in Africa.* His forthcoming book, *The British Empire in the Middle East, 1945–1951* will be published this year.

Hans-Jürgen Schröder is Professor of Contemporary History at the University of Giessen. He has published *Deutschland und die Vereinigten Staaten 1933–1939* and various articles on German and American foreign policies in the 20th century.

Callum A. MacDonald is lecturer in Comparative American Studies, University of Warwick, and author of *The United States, Britain and Appeasement,* as well as of various articles on the appeasement period. He is currently engaged in research on the history of the Cold War.

Arnold A. Offner is Professor of History at Boston University. He is author of *American Appeasement: United States Foreign Policy and Germany, 1933–1938; The Origins of the Second World War: American Foreign Policy and World Politics,* and articles on American-European relations. He is writing a book on President Harry S. Truman and the Transformation of American Foreign Policy.

Index